Readings in Industrial Organization

Blackwell Readings for Contemporary Economics
This series presents collections of writings by some of the worlds's foremost economists on core issues in the discipline. Each volume dovetails with a variety of existing economics courses at the advanced undergraduate, graduate, and MBA levels. The readings, gleaned from a wide variety of classic and contemporary sources, are placed in context by a comprehensive introduction from the editor. In addition, a thorough index facilitates research.

Published
Wassmer: *Readings in Urban Economics: Issues and Public Policy*
Cabral: *Readings in Industrial Organization*

In preparation
Kuenne: *Readings in Applied Microeconomic Theory: Market Forces and Solutions*
Kuenne: *Readings in Social Welfare: Theory and Policy*
Rasmusen: *Readings in Games and Information*
Mookherjee/Ray: *Readings in the Theory of Economic Development*

Readings in Industrial Organization

Edited by

Luís M. B. Cabral
London Business School

First published 2000

2 4 6 8 10 9 7 5 3 1

Blackwell Publishers Inc.
350 Main Street
Malden, Massachusetts 02148
USA

Blackwell Publishers Ltd
108 Cowley Road
Oxford OX4 1JF
UK

Library of Congress Cataloging-in-Publication Data

Readings in industrial organization / edited by Luís M. B. Cabral.
     p.   cm. — (Blackwell readings for contemporary economics)
    A collection of journal articles previously published 1977–1995.
    Includes bibliographical references and index.
    ISBN 0–631–21616–2 (hardbound: alk. paper). — ISBN 0–631–21617–0
(pbk. : alk. paper)
    1. Industrial organization (Economic theory)   2. Industrial concentration.
3. Competition.   4. Industrial policy.   I. Cabral, Luís M. B. II. Series
HD2326.R4 2000
338.8—dc21   99–41198
                                                   CIP

British Library Cataloguing in Publication Data

A CIP catalogue record for this book is available from the British Library.

Typeset in 10/11½ pt Ehrhardt
by Kolam Information Services, Pondicherry, India
Printed in Great Britain by MPG Books, Bodmin, Cornwall

This book is printed on acid-free paper.

Contents

Authors

Philippe Aghion
Harvard University
University College, London

B. Douglas Bernheim
Stanford University

Steven Berry
Yale University

Patrick Bolton
Princeton University

Timothy F. Bresnahan
Stanford University

Luís M. B. Cabral
London Business School

Claude d'Aspremont
Université Catholique de Louvain, Center for Operations Research and Econometrics (CORE)

Avinash K. Dixit
Princeton University

Drew Fudenberg
Harvard University

J. Jaskold Gabszewicz
Université Catholique de Louvain, Center for Operations Research and Econometrics (CORE)

Richard J. Gilbert
University of California–Berkeley

Edward J. Green
University of Minnesota

Boyan Jovanovic
New York University

David M. Kreps
Stanford University

James Levinsohn
University of Michigan

N. Gregory Mankiw
Harvard University

Paul Milgrom
Stanford University

David M. G. Newbery
Cambridge University

Ariel Pakes
Harvard University

Robert H. Porter
Northwestern University

Jennifer F. Reinganum
Vanderbilt University

Michael H. Riordan
Columbia University

John Roberts
Stanford University

Julio J. Rotemberg
Massachusetts Institute of Technology

Garth Saloner
Stanford University

José A. Scheinkman
University of Chicago

Avner Shaked
University of Bonn

Joseph E. Stiglitz
Stanford University
World Bank

John Sutton
London School of Economics

Jacques-François Thisse
Université Catholique de Louvain, Center for Operations Research and Econometrics (CORE)

Jean Tirole
University of Toulouse
Massachusetts Institute of Technology

Michael D. Whinston
Northwestern University

Robert Wilson
Stanford University

Preface

Industrial organization (IO) has been a field of very intense and successful research over the past 25 years or so.[1] Assembling a reader with a page constraint of a few hundred pages is therefore a difficult task.

Some choices needed to be made. My first choice was to restrict the reader to the core areas of IO. This excludes regulation and competition policy, auction theory, contracts and the theory of the firm, experiments, and other areas which, important as they are, would make the task of assembling this reader nearly impossible.

A second important choice pertains to the balance between theory and empirical analysis. A quick glance through the contents list reveals a predominance of theory over empirical work. In addition to a possible bias resulting from the author's preferences, the mix of theory and empirical work reflects the fact that IO work, in the past twenty-five years, has been mostly of a theoretical nature.[2] I thus chose to include only one section on empirical work, containing three papers. I also make reference to a number of other empirical papers throughout the notes that preceed each section.

Reader's Intended Readers

Several people may find this reader useful. Students of graduate IO may prefer the reader to a photocopy pack with the main papers discussed in the course. In fact, the reader covers most of the papers "starred" in most of the course syllabus I had a chance to look at (by "starred," I mean papers that are studied in greater detail).

For the IO researcher, the reader may be a useful reference point. Although I would expect IO researchers to be familiar with most of the papers included, the possibility of quick, direct access to the original sources may prove useful in a variety of circumstances.

Finally, for the economist to whom IO is not the main field of research, I hope this reader may serve as a useful point of entry to the IO literature. Having this in mind, I have started each section with a series of notes that place the papers within the context of the IO literature: which papers were written before and which papers were written after; what the important questions are and why the paper selected was an important step in answering those questions; and so forth.

Notes

1   A recent ranking of field journals ranks IO as the third most important field of Economics research, Macro and Micro being the two first ones. Rankings are based on number and impact of papers listing the JEL IO code (L). See Barrett et al. (forthcoming).
2   Moreover, there seems to be less agreement over what the relevant empirical papers are than what the important theoretical papers are. This is based on a non-scientific survey of reading lists of various graduate courses in IO. The list of "usual suspects" in IO theory is much longer than that of empirical IO.

References

Barrett, Christopher, Aliakbar Olia and Dee Von Bailey (forthcoming): "Subdiscipline-Specific Journal Rankings: Whither Applied Economics," *Applied Economics*.

Acknowledgments

Thanks are due to the many publishers who allowed works to be reproduced within this reader.

1   Kreps, David M. and José A. Sheinkman (1983): "Quantity Precommitment and Bertrand Competition Yield Cournot Outcomes," *Bell Journal of Economics*, 14, 326–37.
2   Fudenberg, Drew and Jean Tirole (1984): "The Fat-cat Effect, the Puppy-dog Ploy and the Lean and Hungry Look," *American Economic Review*, 74, 361–8.
3   Green, Edward J. and Robert H. Porter (1984): "Noncooperative Collusion Under Imperfect Price Information," *Econometrica*, 52, 87–100.
4   Rotemberg, Julio, J. and Garth Saloner (1986): "A Supergame-Theoretic Model of Price Wars During Booms," *American Economic Review*, 76, 390–407.
5   Bernhein, B. Douglas and Michael D. Whinston (1990): "Multimarket Contact and Collusive Behavior," *Rand Journal of Economics*, 21, 1–26.
6   D'Aspremont, Claude, J. Jaskold Gabszewicz, and Jacques-François Thisse (1979): "On Hotelling's 'Stability of Competition'," *Econometrica*, 47, 1145–50.
7   Shaked, Avner and John Sutton (1982): "Relaxing Price Competition Through Product Differentiation," *Review of Economic Studies*, 49, 3–13.
8   Dixit, Avinash K. and Joseph E. Stiglitz (1977): "Monopolistic Competition and Optimum Product Diversity," *American Economic Review*, 67, 297–308.
9   Bresnahan, Timothy F. (1982): "The Oligopoly Solution Concept is Identified," *Economics Letters*, 10, 87–92.
10 Porter, Robert H. (1983): "A Study of Cartel Stability: The Joint Executive Committee, 1880–1886," *Bell Journal of Economics*, 14, 301–14.
11 Berry, Steven, James Levinsohn and Ariel Pakes (1995): "Automobile Prices in Market Equilibrium," *Econometrica*, 63, 841–90.
12 Dixit, Avinash K. (1980): "The Role of Investment in Entry Deterrence," *Economic Journal*, 90, 95–106.
13 Aghion, Philippe and Patrick Bolton (1987): "Contracts as a Barrier to Entry," *American Economic Review*, 77, 338–401.

14 Mankiw, N. Gregory and Michael D. Whinston (1986): "Free Entry and Social Inefficiency," *Rand Journal of Economics*, 17, 48–58.

15 Jovanovic, Boyan (1982): "Selection and Evolution of Industry," *Econometrica*, 50, 649–70.

16 Gilbert, Richard J. and David M. G. Newbery (1982): "Preemptive Patenting and the Persistence of Monopoly," *American Economic Review*, 72, 514–26.

17 Reinganum, Jennifer F. (1982): "Uncertain Innovation and the Persistence of Monopoly," *American Economic Review*, 73, 741–8.

18 Cabral, Luís M. B. and Michael H. Riordan (1994): "The Learning Curve, Market Dominance, and Predatory Pricing," *Econometrica*, 62, 1115–40.

19 Fudenberg, Drew and Jean Tirole (1985): "Preemption and Rent Equalization in the Adoption of New Technology," *Review of Economic Studies*, 52, 383–401.

20 Kreps, David M. and Robert Wilson (1982): "Reputation and Imperfect Information," *Journal of Economic Theory*, 27, 253–79.

21 Milgrom, Paul and John Roberts (1982): "Limit Pricing and Entry under Incomplete Information," *Econometrica*, 50, 443–60.

22 Milgrom, Paul and John Roberts (1986): "Price and Advertising Signals of Product Quality," *Journal of Political Economy*, 94, 796–821.

PART I
Static Oligopoly Theory

Introduction

The beginning of oligopoly theory – and, in fact, the beginning of industrial organization – can be traced back to the seminal book by Cournot (1838). Cournot considered a duopoly model where each firm chooses its output, the market price resulting from the aggregate output chosen by the duopolists. Cournot derived the equilibrium of this model, whereby each firm chooses an optimal output level given the rival's output level (a concept which Nash (1951) later generalized). In this equilibrium, price is greater than marginal cost but lower than monopoly price.

Although output is the primary strategic variable in some oligopoly situations (e.g., the oil market), it is more common for firms to choose prices than to choose output levels. This observation formed the basis of Bertrand's (1883) criticism of the Cournot model. Bertrand further showed that, were firms to set prices, then the outcome would be quite different from the output-setting case: even if there are only two competitors (with equal, constant marginal cost), equilibrium price is equal to marginal cost.

Comparison of the Cournot and Bertrand models gives rise to a sort of "paradox:" although the Bertrand model is more realistic in assuming prices as the strategic variable, it gives rise to a result that seems a bit extreme: even if there are only two competitors, equilibrium price is the same as under perfect competition. The Cournot model, in turn, predicts that duopoly prices are between the monopoly and perfect competition prices, which seems more realistic; but it assumes that firms are output setters, not price setters.

Several approaches have been attempted to solve this "paradox." One approach is given by the first paper in this reader. Kreps and Sheinkman (1983) consider a two-stage model where firms set production capacities in the first period and prices in the second period. This game structure is consistent with the idea that capacity is a long-run variable, whereas price is a short-run variable. Kreps and Sheinkman obtain a remarkable result: In equilibrium, firms set the same price, the price that exactly clears the market (that is, the price such that total demand is equal to total capacity). Moreover, firms choose capacity level as the output they would choose if they were competing à la Cournot. In summary, the equilibrium of the two-period capacity and pricing game is isomorphic to that of Cournot competition.[1]

The idea of modeling price competition with capacity constraints dates back to Edgeworth (1897). Another important contribution prior to Kreps and Sheinkman (1983) is given by Levitan and Shubik (1972), who examine the case when both firms have the same capacity level. Two important papers have appeared since the 1983 paper was published. Davidson and Deneckere (1986) show that Kreps and Sheinkman's result depends critically on their assumption of how demand is rationed when capacity is not sufficient to satisfy all demand. Herk (1993), however, shows that Kreps and Sheinkman's assumption (namely that demand is efficiently rationed) is correct in a model with consumer switching costs.

The model introduced by Kreps and Sheinkman (1983) is a particular example of a more general framework where firms choose a long-run variable (first period) as well as a short-run variable (second period). In this context, first-period decisions have both a direct effect on payoff and an indirect effect (also known as *strategic effect*) through changes in short-run (second-period) variables. A general analysis of this two-period framework was proposed by Fudenberg and Tirole (1984). Their series of zoologic metaphors pertains to the nature of the strategic variables chosen by firms. A similar analysis was proposed by Bulow, Geanakoplos and Klemperer (1985), to whom the terminology *strategic complements* and *strategic substitutes* is due.

Notes

1 An interesting coincidence: Kreps and Sheinkman's paper was published exactly one hundred years after Bertrand's.

References

Bertrand, Joseph (1883): "Book review of *Théorie Mathématique de la Richesse Social* and of *Recherches sur les Principes Mathématiques de la Théorie des Richesses*," *Journal de Savants*, 67, 499–508.

Bulow, Jeremy, John Geanakoplos and Paul Klemperer (1985): "Holding Idle Capacity to Deter Entry," *Economic Journal*, 95, 178–82.

Cournot, A. A. (1838): *Recherches sur les Principes Mathématiques de la Théorie des Richesses*, Paris.

Davidson, Carl and Raymond Deneckere (1986): "Long-run Competition in Capacity, Short-run Competition in Price, and the Cournot Model," *Rand Journal of Economics*, 17, 404–15.

Edgeworth, F. (1897): "La Teoria Pura del Monopolio," *Giornale degli Economisti*, 40, 13–31.

Fudenberg, Drew and Jean Tirole (1984): "The Fat-Cat Effect, the Puppy Dog Ploy and the Lean and Hungry Look," *American Economic Review*, 74, 361–8.

Herk, Leonard F. (1993): "Consumer Choice and Cournot Behavior in Capacity-constrained Duopoly Competition," *Rand Journal of Economics*, 24, 399–417.

Kreps, David M. and José A. Sheinkman (1983): "Capacity Precommitment and Bertrand Competition Yield Cournot Outcomes," *Bell Journal of Economics*, 14, 326–37.

Levitan, R. and M. Shubik (1972): "Price Duopoly and Capacity Constraints," *International Economic Review*, 13, 111–22.

Nash, John (1951): "Non-Cooperative Games," *Annals of Mathematics*, 54, 286–95.

CHAPTER ONE

Quantity Precommitment and Bertrand Competition Yield Cournot Outcomes

DAVID M. KREPS AND JOSÉ A. SCHEINKMAN

Source: *Bell Journal of Economics*, 1983, 14, 326–37.

Bertrand's model of oligopoly, which gives perfectly competitive outcomes, assumes that: (1) there is competition over prices and (2) production follows the realization of demand. We show that both of these assumptions are required. More precisely, consider a two-stage oligopoly game where, first, there is simultaneous production, and, second, after production levels are made public, there is simultaneous production, and, second, after production levels are made public, there is price competition. Under mild assumptions about demand, the unique equilibrium outcome is the Cournot outcome. This illustrates that solutions to oligopoly games depend on both the strategic variables employed and the context (game form) in which those variables are employed.

1. Introduction

Since Bertrand's (1883) criticism of Cournot's (1838) work, economists have come to realize that solutions to oligopoly games depend critically on the strategic variables that firms are assumed to use. Consider, for example, the simple case of a duopoly where each firm produces at a constant cost b per unit and where the demand curve is linear, $p = a - q$. Cournot (quantity) competition yields equilibrium price $p = (a + 2b)/3$, while Bertrand (price) competition yields $p = b$.

In this article, we show by example that there is more to Bertrand competition than simply "competition over prices." It is easiest to explain what we mean by reviewing the stories associated with Cournot and Bertrand. The Cournot story concerns producers who simultaneously and independently make production quantity decisions, and who *then* bring what they have produced to the market, with the market price being the price that equates the total supply with demand. The Bertrand story, on the other hand, concerns producers who simultaneously and independently name prices. Demand is allocated to the low-price producer(s), who *then* produce (up to) the demand they encounter. Any unsatisfied demand goes to the second lowest price producer(s), and so on.

There are two differences in these stories: how price is determined (by an auctioneer in Cournot and by price "competition" in Bertrand), and when production is supposed to take place. We demonstrate here that the Bertrand outcome requires both price competition and production after demand determination. Specifically, consider the following game between expected profit maximizing producers: In a first stage, producers decide independently and simultaneously how much they will produce, and this production takes place. They then bring these quantities to market, each learns how much the other produced, and they engage in Bertrand-like price competition: They simultaneously and independently name prices and demand is allocated in Bertrand fashion, with the proviso that one cannot satisfy more demand than one produced for in the first stage.

In this two-stage game, it is easy to produce one equilibrium. Let each firm choose the Cournot quantity. If each firm does so, each subsequently names the Cournot price. If, on the other hand, either chooses some quantity other than the Cournot quantity, its rival names price zero in the second stage. Since any defection in the first stage will result in one facing the demand residual from the Cournot quantity, and since the Cournot quantity is the best response to this residual demand function, this is clearly an equilibrium. What is somewhat more surprising is that (for the very special parameterization above and for a large class of other symmetric parameterizations) the Cournot outcome is the unique equilibrium outcome. Moreover, there is a perfect equilibrium that yields this outcome. (The strategies above constitute an imperfect equilibrium.) This note is devoted to the establishment of these facts.

One way to interpret this result is to see our two-stage game as a mechanism to generate Cournot-like outcomes that dispenses with the mythical auctioneer. In fact, an equivalent way of thinking about our game is as follows: *Capacities* are set in the first stage by the two producers. Demand is then determined by Bertrand-like price competition, and production takes place at zero cost, subject to capacity constraints generated by the first-stage decisions. It is easy to see that given capacities for the two producers, equilibrium behavior in the second, Bertrand-like, stage will not always lead to a price that exhausts capacity. But when those given capacities correspond to the Cournot output levels, in the second stage each firm names the Cournot price. And for the entire game, fixing capacities at the Cournot output levels is the unique equilibrium outcome. This yields a more satisfactory description of a game that generates Cournot outcomes. It is this language that we shall use subsequently.

This reinterpretation in terms of capacities suggests a variant of the game, in which both capacity creation (before price competition and realization of demand) and production (to demand) are costly. Our analysis easily generalizes to this case, and we state results for it at the end of this article.

Our intention in putting forward this example is not to give a model that accurately portrays any important duopoly. (We are both on record as contending that "reality" has more than one, and quite probably more than two, stages, and that multiperiod effects greatly change the outcomes of duopoly games.) Our intention instead is to emphasize that solutions to oligopoly games depend on both the strategic variables that firms are assumed to employ and on the context (game form) in which those variables are employed. The timing of decisions and information reception are as important as the nature of the decisions. It is witless to argue in the abstract whether Cournot or Bertrand was correct; this is an empirical question or one that is resolved only by looking at the details of the context within which the competitive interaction takes place.

2. Model Formulation

We consider two identical firms facing a two-stage competitive situation. These firms produce perfectly substitutable commodities for which the market demand function is given by $P(x)$ (price as a function of quantity x) and $D(p) = P^{-1}(p)$ (demand as a function of price p).

The two-stage competition runs as follows. At the first stage, the firms simultaneously and independently *build capacity* for subsequent production. Capacity level x means that up to x units can be produced subsequently at zero cost. The cost to firm i of (initially) installing capacity level x_i is $b(x_i)$.

After this first stage, each firm learns how much capacity its opponent installed. Then the firms simultaneously and independently name prices p_i chosen from the interval $[0, P(0)]$. If $p_1 < p_2$, then firm 1 sells

$$z_1 = \min(x_1, D(p_1)) \tag{1}$$

units of the good at price p_1 (and at zero additional cost), for a net profit of $p_1 z_1 - b(x_1)$. And if $p_1 < p_2$, firm 2 sells

$$z_2 = \min(x_2, \max(0, D(p_2) - x_1)) \tag{2}$$

units at price p_2 for a net profit of $p_2 z_2 - b(x_2)$. If $p_2 < p_1$, symmetric formulas apply. Finally, if $p_2 = p_1$, then firm i sells

$$z_i = \min\left(x_i, \frac{D(p_i)}{2} + \max\left(0, \frac{D(p_i)}{2} - x_j\right)\right) = \min\left(x_i, \max\left(\frac{D(p_i)}{2}, D(p_i) - x_j\right)\right) \tag{3}$$

at price p_i, for net profits equal to $p_i z_i - b(x_i)$. (In (3), and for the remainder of the article, subscript j means *not* i. Note the use of the *capacity* and *subsequent production* terminology.)

Each firm seeks to maximize the expectation of its profits, and the above structure is common knowledge between the firms. At this point the reader will notice the particular rationing rule we chose. Customers buy first from the cheapest supplier, and income effects are absent. (Alternatively, this is the rationing rule that maximizes consumer surplus. Its use is not innocuous – see Beckmann (1965) and Levitan and Shubik (1972).)

The following assumptions are made:

ASSUMPTION 1.   The function $P(x)$ is strictly positive on some bounded interval $(0, X)$, on which it is twice-continuously differentiable, strictly decreasing, and concave. For $x \geq X, P(x) = 0$.

ASSUMPTION 2. The cost function b, with domain $[0, \infty)$ and range $[0, \infty)$, is twice-continuously differentiable, convex, and satisfies $b(0) = 0$ and $b'(0) > 0$. To avoid trivialities, $b'(0) < P(0)$ – production at some level is profitable.

3. Preliminaries: Cournot Competition

Before analyzing the two-stage competition formulated above, it will be helpful to have on hand some implications of the assumptions and some facts about Cournot competition between the two firms. Imagine that the firms engage in Cournot competition with (identical) cost function c. Assume that c is (as b), twice-continuously differentiable, convex, and nondecreasing on $[0, \infty)$. Note that from Assumption 1, for every $y < D(0)$ the function $x \to xP(x + y) - c(x)$ is strictly concave on $[0, y - x)$. Define

$$r_c(y) = \underset{0 \le x \le X - y}{\operatorname{argmax}} \ xP(x + y) - c(x)$$

That is, $r_c(y)$ is the *optimal response function* in Cournot competition if one's rival puts y on the market. It is the solution in x of

$$P(x + y) + xP'(x + y) - c'(x) = 0 \tag{4}$$

LEMMA 1.

(a) For every c as above, r_c is nonincreasing in y, and r_c is continuously differentiable and strictly decreasing over the range where it is strictly positive.

(b) $r'_c \ge -1$, with strict inequality for y such that $r_c(y) > 0$, so that $x + r_c(x)$ is nondecreasing in x.

(c) If c and d are two cost functions such that $c' > d'$, then $r_c < r_d$.

(d) If $y > r_c(y)$, then $r_c(r_c(y)) < y$.

PROOF. (a) For any y, we have

$$P(r_c(y) + y) + r_c(y)P'(r_c(y) + y) - c'(r_c(y)) = 0$$

Increase y in the above equation while leaving $r_c(y)$ fixed. This decreases the (positive) first term and decreases the second (it becomes more negative). Thus the concavity of $xP(x + y) - c(x)$ in x implies that, to restore equality, we must decrease $r_c(y)$. Where P is strictly positive, the decrease in $r_c(y)$ must also be strict. And the differentiability of r_c follows in the usual fashion from the smoothness of P and c.

For (b), increase y by h and decrease $r_c(y)$ by h in the equation displayed above. The first (positive) term stays the same, the second increases (becomes less negative), and the third increases. Thus the left-hand side, at $y + h$ and $r_c(y) - h$, is positive. The strict concavity of the profit function ensures, therefore, that $r_c(y + h) > r_c(y) - h$ (with the obvious qualifications about values y for which $r_c(y) = 0$).

For (c) and (d), arguments similar to (b) are easily constructed.

Because of (d), the picture of duopoly Cournot competition is as in Figure 1. For every cost function c, there is a unique Cournot equilibrium, with each firm bringing forward some quantity $x^*(c)$. Moreover, for c and d as in part (c) of the lemma, it is clear that $x^*(c) < x^*(d)$. In the next section, the case where c is identically zero plays an important role. To save on subscripts and arguments, we shall write $r(y)$ for $r_0(y)$ and x^* for $x^*(0)$. Also, we shall write $R(y)$ for $r(y)P(r(y) + y)$, the revenue associated with the best response to y when costs are identically zero.

(The astute reader will notice that the analysis to follow does not require the full power of Assumptions 1 and 2. All that is really required is that, for each $y < D(0)$, the functions $x \to xP(x + y) - b(x)$ and $x \to xP(x + y)$ are strictly quasi-concave (on $(0, X - y)$), and that r_b and r appear as in Figure 1. The former does require that $p \to pD(p)$ is strictly concave where it is positive, but this is not quite sufficient. In any event, we shall continue to proceed on the basis of the assumptions given, as they do simplify the arguments that follow.)

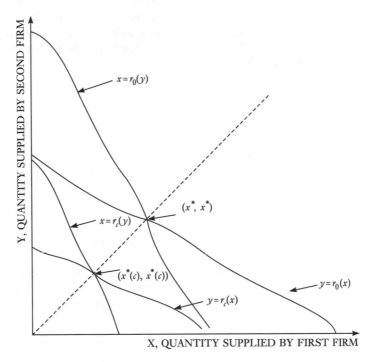

Figure 1   The picture of Cournot competition under the assumptions of the model

4. The Capacity-Constrained Subgames

Suppose that in the first stage the firms install capacities x_1 and x_2, respectively. Beginning from the point where (x_1, x_2) becomes common knowledge, we have a *proper subgame* (using the terminology of Selten (1965)). We call this the (x_1, x_2) capacity-constrained subgame – it is simply the Edgeworth (1897) "constrained-capacity" variation on Bertrand competition. It is not *a priori* obvious that each capacity-constrained subgame has an equilibrium, as payoffs are discontinuous in actions. But it can be shown that the discontinuities are of the "right" kind. For subgames where $x_1 = x_2$, the existence of a subgame equilibrium is established by Levitan and Shubik (1972) in cases where demand is linear and marginal costs are constant. Also for the case of linear demand and constant marginal costs, Dasgupta and Maskin (1982) establish the existence of subgame equilibria for all pairs of x_1 and x_2, and their methodology applies to all the cases that we consider. (We shall show how to "compute" the subgame equilibria below.)

The basic fact that we wish to establish is that for each (x_1, x_2), the associated subgame has unique expected revenues in equilibrium. (It is very probably true that each subgame has a unique equilibrium, but we do not need this and shall not attempt to show it.) Moreover, we shall give formulas for these expected revenues.

For the remainder of this section, fix a pair of capacities (x_1, x_2) and an equilibrium for the (x_1, x_2) subgame. Let $\bar{p}_i$ be the supremum of the support of the prices named by firm i; that is, $\bar{p}_i = \inf\{p : \text{firm } i \text{ names less than } p \text{ with probability one}\}$. And let $\underline{p}_i$ be the infimum of the support. Note that if $\min_i x_i \geq D(0)$, then, as in the usual Bertrand game with no capacity constraints, $\bar{p}_i = \underline{p}_i = 0$. And if $\min_i x_i = 0$, we have the monopoly case. Thus we are left with the case where $0 < \min_i x_i < D(0)$.

LEMMA 2.   For each $i, \underline{p}_i \geq P(x_1 + x_2)$.

PROOF.   By naming a price p less than $P(x_1 + x_2)$, firm i nets at most px_i. By naming $P(x_1 + x_2)$, firm i nets at worst $P(x_1 + x_2)(x_1 + x_2 - x_j) = P(x_1 + x_2)x_i$.

LEMMA 3.   If $\bar{p}_1 = \bar{p}_2$ and each is named with positive probability, then

$$\underline{p}_i = \bar{p}_i = P(x_1 + x_2) \quad \text{and} \quad x_i \leq r(x_j) \quad \text{for both} \quad i = 1 \quad \text{and} \quad i = 2$$

PROOF.   Suppose that $\bar{p}_1 = \bar{p}_2$ and each is charged with positive probability. Without loss of generality, assume $x_1 \geq x_2$, and suppose that $\bar{p}_1 = \bar{p}_2 > P(x_1 + x_2)$. By naming a price slightly less than $\bar{p}_1$, firm 1 strictly improves its revenues over what it gets by naming $\bar{p}_1$. (With positive probability, it sells strictly more, while the loss due to the lower price is small.) Thus $\bar{p}_1 = \bar{p}_2 \leq P(x_1 + x_2)$. By Lemma 2, we know that $\bar{p}_i = \underline{p}_i = P(x_1 + x_2)$ for $i = 1, 2$.

By naming a higher price p, firm i would obtain revenue $(D(p) - x_j)p$, or, letting $x = D(p) - x_j, xP(x + x_j)$. This is maximized at $x = r(x_j)$, so that were $r(x_j) < x_i$, we would not have an equilibrium.

LEMMA 4.   If $x_i \leq r(x_j)$ for $i = 1, 2$, then a (subgame) equilibrium is for each firm to name $P(x_1 + x_2)$ with probability one.

PROOF.   The proof of Lemma 3 shows that naming a price greater than $P(x_1 + x_2)$ will not profit either firm in this case. (Recall that $xP(x + x_j)$ is strictly concave.) And there is no incentive to name a lower price, as each firm is selling its full capacity at the equilibrium price.

LEMMA 5. Suppose that either $\bar{p}_1 > \bar{p}_2$, or that $\bar{p}_1 = \bar{p}_2$ and $\bar{p}_2$ is not named with positive probability. Then:

(a) $\bar{p}_1 = P(r(x_2) + x_2)$ and the equilibrium revenue of firm 1 is $R(x_2)$;
(b) $x_1 > r(x_2)$;
(c) $\underline{p}_1 = \underline{p}_2$, and neither isnamed with positive probability;
(d) $x_1 \geq x_2$; and
(e) the equilibrium revenue of firm 2 is uniquely determined by (x_1, x_2) and is at least $(x_2/x_1) R(x_2)$ and at most $R(x_2)$.

PROOF. For (a) and (b): Consider the function

$$\Xi(p) = p \cdot [\min(x_1, \max(0, D(p) - x_2))]$$

In words, $\Xi(p)$ is the revenue accrued by firm 1 if it names p and it is undersold by its rival. Under the hypothesis of this lemma, firm 1, by naming $\bar{p}_1$, nets precisely $\Xi(\bar{p}_1)$, as it is certain to be undersold. By naming any price $p > \bar{p}_1$, firm 1 will net precisely $\Xi(p)$. If firm 1 names a price $p < \bar{p}_1$, it will net at least $\Xi(p)$. Thus, if we have an equilibrium, $\Xi(p)$ must be maximized at $\bar{p}_1$.

We must dispose of the case $x_2 \geq D(0)$. Since (by assumption) $D(0) > \min_i x_i$, $x_2 \geq D(0)$ would imply $D(0) > x_1$. Thus, in equilibrium, firm 2 will certainly obtain strictly positive expected revenue. And, therefore, in equilibrium, $\bar{p}_2 > 0$. But then firm 1 must obtain strictly positive expected revenue. And if $x_2 \geq D(0)$, then $\Xi(\bar{p}_1) = 0$. That is, $x_2 \geq D(0)$ is incompatible with the hypothesis of this lemma.

In maximizing $\Xi(p)$, one would never choose p such that $D(p) - x_2 > x_1$ or such that $D(p) < x_2$. Thus, the relevant value of p lies in the interval $[P(x_1 + x_2), P(x_2)]$. For each p in this interval, there is a corresponding level of x, namely $x(p) = D(p) - x_2$, such that $\Xi(p) = x(p)P(x(p) + x_2)$. Note that $x(p)$ runs in the interval $[0, x_1]$. But we know that

$$\underset{x(p) \in [0, x_1]}{\text{argmax}} \, x(p)P(x(p) + x_2) = r(x_2) \wedge x_1$$

by the strict concavity of $xP(x + x_2)$. If the capacity constraint x_1 is binding (even weakly), then $\bar{p}_1 = P(x_1 + x_2)$, and Lemma 2 implies that we are in the case of Lemma 3, thus contradicting the hypothesis of this lemma. Hence it must be the case that the constraint does not bind, or $r(x_2) < x_1$ (which is (b)), $\bar{p}_1 = P(r(x_2) + x_2)$, and the equilibrium revenue of firm 1 is $R(x_2)$ (which is (a)).

For (c): Suppose that $\underline{p}_i < \underline{p}_j$. By naming $\underline{p}_i$, firm i nets $\underline{p}_i(D(\underline{p}_i) \wedge x_i)$. Increasing this to any level $p \in (\underline{p}_i, \underline{p}_j)$ nets $p(D(p) \wedge x_i)$. Thus, we have an equilibrium only if $D(p_i) < x_i$ and $\underline{p}_i$ is the monopoly price. (By the strict concavity of $xP(x)$, moving from $\underline{p}_i$ in the direction of the monopoly price will increase revenue on the margin.) That is, $\underline{p}_i = P(r(0))$. But $\underline{p}_i < \bar{p}_1 = P(r(x_2) + x_2) < P(r(0))$, which would be a contradiction. Thus $\underline{p}_1 = \underline{p}_2$. We denote this common value by $\underline{p}$ in the sequel. This is the first part of (c).

For the second part of (c), note first that $\underline{p} > P(x_1 + x_2)$. For if $\underline{p} = P(x_1 + x_2)$, then by naming (close to) $\underline{p}$, firm 1 would make at most $P(x_1 + x_2)x_1$. Since $x_1 > r(x_2)$ and the equilibrium revenue of firm 1 is $R(x_2)$, this is impossible.

Suppose that the firm with (weakly) less capacity named $\underline{p}$ with positive probability. Then the firm with higher capacity could, by naming a price slightly less than $\underline{p}$, strictly increase its expected revenue. (It sells strictly more with positive probability, at a slightly lower price.) Thus, the firm with weakly less capacity names $\underline{p}$ with zero probability. Since $\underline{p}$ is the infimum of the support of the prices named by the lower capacity firm, this firm must therefore name prices arbitrarily close to *and above* $\underline{p}$. But if its rival named $\underline{p}$ with positive probability, the smaller capacity firm would do better (since $\underline{p} > P(x_1 + \bar{x}_2)$) to name a price just below $\underline{p}$ than it would to name a price just above $\underline{p}$. Hence, neither firm can name $\underline{p}$ with positive probability.

For (d) and (e): By (c), the equilibrium revenue of firm i must be $\underline{p}(D(\underline{p}) \wedge x_i)$. We know that $\underline{p} < \bar{p}_1 = P(x_2 + r(x_2))$, so that $D(\underline{p}) > D(P(x_2 + r(x_2))) = x_2 + r(x_2)$, and thus $D(\underline{p}) > x_2$. Hence, firm 2 certainly gets $\underline{p}x_2$ in equilibrium. Firm 1 gets no more than $\underline{p}x_1$, so that the bounds in part (e) are established as soon as (d) is shown.

Suppose that $x_2 > x_1$. Then $D(\underline{p}) > x_1$, and firm 1's equilibrium revenue is $\underline{p}x_1$. We already know that it is also $R(x_2)$, so that we would have $\underline{p} = R(x_2)/x_1$, and firm 2 nets $R(x_2)x_2/x_1$. By naming price $P(r(x_1) + x_1)(> \underline{p}_1 = P(r(\bar{x}_2) + x_2))$, firm 2 will net $R(x_1)$. We shall have a contradiction, therefore, if we show that $x_1 > r(x_2)$ implies $x_1 R(x_i) > X_2 R(X_2)$.

Let $\Theta(x) = xR(x) = xr(x)P(r(x) + x)$.

We have

$$\Theta'(x) = r(x)P(r(x) + x) + xr'(x)P(r(x) + x) + xr(x)P'(r(x) + x)(r'(x) + 1)$$
$$= (r(x) - x)P(r(x) + x) + x(r'(x) + 1)(P(r(x) + x) + r(x)P'(r(x) + x))$$

The last term is zero by the definition of $r(x)$, so that we have

$$\Theta'(x) = (r(x) - x)P(r(x) + x)$$

Thus $x_2 R(x_2) - x_1 R(x_1) = \Theta(x_2) - \Theta(x_1) = \int_{x_1}^{x_2}(r(x) - x)P(r(x) + x)dx$. The integrand is positive for $x < x^*$ and strictly negative for $x > x^*$. We would like to show that the integral is negative, so that the worst case (in terms of our objective) is that in which $x_1 < x^*$ and x_2 is as small as possible. Since $x_1 > r(x_2)$, for every $x_1 < x^*$ the worst case is where x_2 is just a bit larger than $r^{-1}(x_1)$. We shall thus have achieved our objective (of contradicting $x_2 > x_1$, by showing that the integral above is strictly negative) if we show that for all $x < x^*, \Theta(x) - \Theta(r^{-1}(x)) \geq 0$.

But $\Theta(x) - \Theta(r^{-1}(x)) = xr(x)P(x + r(x)) - r^{-1}(x)xP(r^{-1}(x) + x)$. This is nonnegative if and only if $r(x)P(x + r(x)) - r^{-1}(x)P(r^{-1}(x) + x) \geq 0$, which is certainly true, since $r(x)$ is the best response to x.

LEMMA 6. If $x_1 \geq x_2$ and $x_1 > r(x_2)$, there is a (mixed strategy) equilibrium for the subgame in which all the conditions and conclusions of Lemma 5 hold. Moreover, this equilibrium has the following properties. Each firm names prices according to continuous and strictly increasing distribution functions over an (coincident) interval, except that firm 1 names the uppermost price with positive probability whenever $x_1 > x_2$. And if we let $\Psi_i(p)$ be the probability distribution function for the strategy of firm i, then $\Psi_1(p) \leq \Psi_2(p)$: firm 1's strategy stochastically dominates the strategy of firm 2, with strict inequality if $x_1 > x_2$.

REMARKS. The astute reader will note that the first sentence is actually a corollary to the previous lemmas and to the (as yet unproven) assertion that every subgame has an equilibrium. The actual construction of an equilibrium is unnecessary for our later analysis, and the casual reader may wish to omit it on first reading. It is, however, of sufficient independent interest to warrant presentation. In the course of this construction, we obtain the second part of the lemma, which is also noteworthy. At first glance, it might be thought that firm 1, having the larger capacity, would profit more by underselling its rival, and therefore it would name the (stochastically) lower prices. But (as is usual with equilibrium logic) this is backwards: Each firm randomizes in a way that keeps the other firm indifferent among its strategies. Because firm 1 has the larger capacity, firm 2 is more "at risk" in terms of being undersold, and thus firm 1 must be "less aggressive."

PROOF. Refer to Figure 2. There are five functions depicted there: $pD(p), p(D(p) - x_2)$, $p(D(p) - x_1), px_1$, and px_2. Note that:

(i) $px_1 = p(D(p) - x_2)$ and $px_2 = p(D(p) - x_1)$ at the same point, namely $P(x_1 + x_2)$.
(ii) $px_1 = pD(p)$ at the point where $p(D(p) - x_1)$ vanishes, and similarly for 2.
(iii) The first three functions are maximized at $P(r(0)), P(r(x_2) + x_2)$, and $P(r(x_1) + x_1)$, respectively.
(iv) Because P is concave, the first three functions are strictly concave on the range where they are positive. And every ray from the origin of the form px crosses each of these three functions at most once. (The latter is a simple consequence of the fact that $D(p)$ is decreasing.)

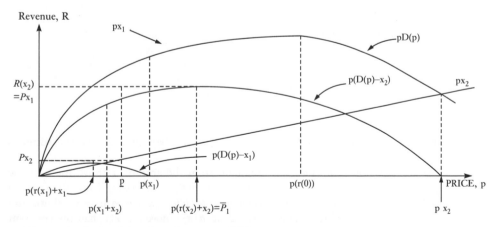

Figure 2 Determining the subgame equilibrium

Now find the value $p = P(r(x_2) + x_2)$. This is $\bar{p}_1$. Follow the horizontal dashed line back to the function $p(D(p) \wedge x_1)$. We have drawn this intersection at a point p where $D(p) > x_1$, but we have no guarantee that this will happen. In any event, the level of p at this intersection is p. Follow the vertical dashed line down to the ray px_2. The height px_2 will be the equilibrium revenue of firm 2. Note that even if the first intersection occurred at a point where $x_1 > D(p)$, this second intersection would be at a level p where $D(p) > x_2$, since $x_2 = D(p)$ at $P(x_2)$, which is to the right of $P(r(x_2) + x_2)$. Also, note that these intersections occur to the right of $P(x_1 + x_2)$, since $R(x_2) > x_1 P(x_1 + x_2)$.

Suppose that firm 1 charges a price $p \in [\underline{p}, \bar{p}_1]$. If we assume that firm 2 does not charge this price p with positive probability, then the expected revenue to firm 1 is

$$E_1(p) = \Phi_2(p)p(D(p) - x_2) + (1 - \Phi_2(p))p(D(p) \wedge x_1)$$

where Φ_2 is the distribution function of firm 2's strategy. A similar calculation for firm 2 yields

$$E_2(p) = \Phi_1(p)p[\max(D(p) - x_1, 0)] + (1 - \Phi_1(p))px_2$$

(Note that for $p \in [\underline{p}, \bar{p}_1]$, we know that $D(p) - x_2 > 0$.)

Solve the equations $E_1(p) = R(x_2)(= \underline{p}(D(p) \wedge x_1))$ and $E_2(p) = \underline{p}x_2$ in $\Phi_2(p)$ and $\Phi_1(p)$, calling the solutions $\Psi_2(p)$ and $\Psi_1(p)$, respectively. Note that:

(v) Both functions are continuous and begin at level zero.

(vi) The function $\Psi_2(p)$ is strictly increasing and has value one at $\bar{p}_1$. To see this note that $p(D(p) - x_2)$ is getting closer to, and $p(D(p) \wedge x_1)$ is getting further from, $R(x_2)$ as p increases. And $R(x_2) = \bar{p}_1(D(\bar{p}_1) - x_2)$.

(vii) The function $\Psi_1(p)$ is strictly increasing, everywhere less than or equal to one, and strictly less than one if $x_1 > x_2$. (If $x_1 = x_2$, then it is identical to $\Psi_2(p)$.) To see this, note first that for $p \geq P(x_1)$, $\Psi_1(p) = 1 - \underline{p}/p$. And for values of p in the range $\underline{p} \leq p < P(x_1)$, we have $R(x_2) = \underline{p}x_1$, and, thus,

$$\Psi_1(p) = \frac{(p - \underline{p})x_2}{p(D(p) - x_1 - x_2)}$$

and

$$\Psi_2(p) = \frac{(p - \underline{p})x_2}{p(D(p) - x_1 - x_2)}$$

That is, for p between $\underline{p}$ and $P(x_1)$, $\Psi_1 = x_2 \Psi_2 / x_1$. Noting step (vi), the result is obvious.

(viii) $\Psi_1(p) \leq \Psi_2(p)$ for all p. This is immediate from the argument above for p in the range $\underline{p} \leq p < P(x_1)$. For $p \geq P(x_1)$, note that $pD(p)$ is receding from $R(x_2)$ more quickly than px_2 is receding from $\underline{p}x_2$ [since $p(D(p) - x_2)$ is still increasing], and $p(D(p) - x_2)$ is increasing, hence approaching $R(x_2)$ more quickly than the constant function zero is approaching $\underline{p}x_2$.

(ix) $\underline{p}x_2 \geq R(x_1)$. To see this, note first that $\underline{p}x_1 \geq R(x_2)$. Thus $\underline{p}x_2 \geq x_2R(x_2)/x_1$. To get the desired result, then, it suffices to show that $R(x_1) \leq x_2R(x_2)/x_1$, or $x_1R(x_1) \leq x_2R(x_2)$ (with strict inequality if $x_1 > x_2$.) Recall that $x_1 > x_2$. If $x_2 \geq x^*$, then the result follows easily from the formula $x_1R(x_1) - x_2R(x_2) = \int_{x_2}^{x_1}(r(x) - x)P(r(x) + x)dx$. If $x_2 < x^*$, then $x_2 > r(x_1)$ (since $(x_1 > r(x_2))$), and the argument from the previous lemma applies.

Putting all these points together, we see that we have an equilibrium of the desired type if firm 1 names prices according to the distribution Ψ_1, and firm 2 names them according to Ψ_2. Each firm is (by construction) indifferent among those strategies that are in the support of their (respective) distribution functions. The levels of $\bar{p}_1$ and $\underline{p}$ are selected so that firm 1 has no incentive to name a price above the first or below the second. Since firm 2 gets no more than $R(x_1)$, it has no incentive to go above $\bar{p}_1$; neither (by construction) will it gain by naming a price below $\underline{p}$.

Since the construction of the equilibrium took us rather far afield of our main objective, we end this section by compiling the results established above that are important to subsequent analysis:

PROPOSITION 1.   (Refer to Figure 3). In terms of the subgame equilibria, there are three regions of interest.

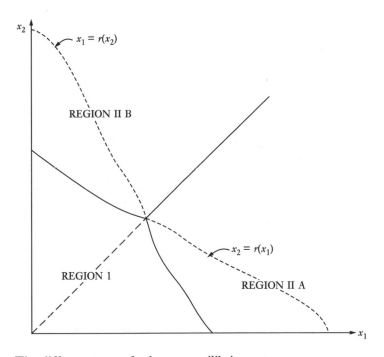

Figure 3   The different types of subgame equilibria

(a) If $x_i \leq r(x_j)$ for both $i = 1$ and $i = 2$ (which is labelled as region I in Figure 3), the unique equilibrium has both firms naming price $P(x_1 + x_2)$ with certainty. The equilibrium revenues are, therefore, $x_i P(x_1 + x_2)$ for firm i.

(b) If $x_1 \geq x_2$ and $x_1 > r(x_2)$ (labelled region IIA in Figure 3), then, in equilibrium, firm 1 has expected revenue $R(x_2)$, and firm 2 has expected revenue determined by (x_1, x_2) and somewhere between $R(x_2)$ and $x_2 R(x_2)/x_1$. If $x_2 < D(0)$, the equilibrium is the randomized one constructed in Lemma 6; if $x_2 \gneqq D(0)$, both firms net zero and name price zero with certainty.

(c) If $x_2 \geq x_1$ and $x_2 > r(x_1)$ (labelled region IIB in Figure 3), then, in equilibrium, firm 2 has expected revenue $R(x_1)$, and firm 1 has expected revenue determined by (x_1, x_2) and somewhere between $R(x_1)$ and $x_1 R(x_1)/x_2$. Similar remarks apply concerning $x_1 \lesseqgtr D(0)$ as appear in (b).

(d) The expected revenue functions are continuous functions of x_1 and x_2.

5. Equilibria in the Full Game

We can now show that in the full game there is a unique equilibrium outcome. We state this formally:

PROPOSITION 2. In the two-stage game, there is a unique equilibrium outcome, namely the Cournot outcome: $x_1 = x_2 = x^*(b)$, and $p_1 = p_2 = P(2x^*(b))$.

PROOF. The proposition is established in four steps.

STEP 1: PRELIMINARIES. Consider any equilibrium. As part of this equilibrium firm i chooses capacity according to some probability measure μ_i with support $S_i \subseteq R$. Let us denote by $\Phi_i(x_1, x_2)$ the (possibly mixed) strategy used by firm i in the (x_1, x_2) subgame. Except for a $\mu_1 \times \mu_2$ null subset of $S_1 \times S_2$, $\Phi_i(x_1, x_2)$ must be an optimal response to $\Phi_j(x_1, x_2)$. That is, $\Omega_i = \{(x_1, x_2) : \Phi_i(x_1, x_2) \text{ is an optimal response to } \Phi_j(x_1, x_2)\}$ is such that $(\mu_1 \times \mu_2)(\Omega_1 \cap \Omega_2) = 1$. (For subgame perfect equilibria $\Omega_1 \cap \Omega_2 = R^2$, but we do not wish to restrict attention to such equilibria.) In particular, if $E(x_i) = \{x_j : (x_1, x_2) \in \Omega_1 \cap \Omega_2\}$ and $\hat{X}_i = \{x_i \in S_i : \mu_j(E(x_i)) = 1\}$, then $\mu_i(\hat{X}_i) = 1$. Let π_i denote the expected profit of firm i in this equilibrium and $\pi_i(x_i)$ the expected profit when capacity x_i is built. If $X_i = \{x_i \in \hat{X}_i : \pi_i(x_i) = \pi_i\}$, then again $\mu_i(X_i) = 1$. Let $\bar{x}_i$ and $\underline{x}_i$ denote the supremum and infimum of X_i. Because the subgame equilibrium revenue functions are continuous in x_1 and x_2, and because revenues are bounded in any event, $\bar{x}_1$ and $\underline{x}_1$ must yield expected profit π_i if firm j uses its equilibrium quantity strategy μ_j and firms subsequently use subgame equilibrium price strategies.

Assume (without loss of generality) that $\bar{x}_1 \geq \bar{x}_2$.

STEP 2: $\bar{x}_1 \geq r_b(\underline{x}_2)$. Suppose contrariwise that $\bar{x}_1 < r_b(\underline{x}_2)$. For every $x_1 < \bar{x}_1$, the subgame equilibrium revenue of firm 2, if it installs capacity $\underline{x}_2$, is $\underline{x}_2 P(x_1 + \underline{x}_2)$. That is,

$$\pi_2 = \int_{\underline{x}_1}^{\bar{x}_1} (\underline{x}_2 P(x_1 + \underline{x}_2) - b(\underline{x}_2)) \mu_1(dx_1)$$

If firm 2 increases its capacity slightly, to say, $x_2 + \epsilon$, where it remains true that $\bar{x}_1 < r_b(x_2 + \epsilon)$, then the worst that can happen to firm 2 (for each level of x_1) is that firm 2 will net $(\underline{x}_2 + \epsilon)P(x_1 + \underline{x}_2 + \epsilon) - b(\underline{x}_2 + \epsilon)$. Since for all $x_1 < \bar{x}_1, \underline{x}_2 + \epsilon < < r_b(x_1)$ it follows that $(\underline{x}_2 + \epsilon)P(x_1 + \underline{x}_2 + \epsilon) - b(\underline{x}_2 + \epsilon) > \underline{x}_2 P(x_1 + \underline{x}_2) - b(\underline{x}_2)$, and this variation will raise firm 2's profits above π_2. This is a contradiction.

STEP 3: $\bar{x}_1 \leq r_b(\bar{x}_2)$. Suppose contrariwise that $\bar{x}_1 > r_b(\bar{x}_2)$. By building $\bar{x}_1$, firm 1 nets revenue (as a function of x_2)$R(x_2)$ if $\bar{x}_1 > r(x_2)$ and $\bar{x}_1 P(\bar{x}_1 + x_2)$ if $\bar{x}_1 \leq r(x_2)$, assuming that a subgame equilibrium ensues. That is,

$$\pi_1 = \int_{(r^{-1}(\bar{x}_1), \bar{x}_2)]} (R(x_2) - b(\bar{x}_1))\mu_2(dx_2) + \int_{[\underline{x}_2, r^{-1}(\bar{x}_1)]} (\bar{x}_1 P(\bar{x}_1 + x_2) - b(\bar{x}_1))\mu_2(dx_2)$$

$$(5)$$

Consider what happens to firm 1's expected profits if it lowers its capacity from $\bar{x}_1$ to just a bit less – say, to $\bar{x}_1 - \epsilon$, where $\bar{x}_1 - \epsilon > r_b(\bar{x}_2)$. Then the worst that can happen to firm 1 is that firm 2 (after installing capacity according to μ_2) names price zero. This would leave firm 1 with residual demand $D(p) - x_2$ (where $x_2 \leq \bar{x}_2$). Firm 1 can still accrue revenue $R(x_2)$ if $\bar{x}_1 - \epsilon > r(x_2)$ and $(\bar{x}_1 - \epsilon)P(x_2 + \bar{x}_1 - \epsilon)$ otherwise. Thus, the expected profits of firm 1 in this variation are at least

$$\int_{[r^{-1}(\bar{x}_1 - \epsilon), \bar{x}_2]} (R(x_2) - b(\bar{x}_1 - \epsilon))\mu_2(dx_2)$$

$$+ \int_{[\underline{x}_2, r^{-1}(\bar{x}_1 - \epsilon))} ((\bar{x}_1 - \epsilon)P(x_2 + \bar{x}_1 - \epsilon) - b(\bar{x}_1 - \epsilon))\mu_2(dx_2) \tag{6}$$

We shall complete this step by showing that for small enough ϵ, (6) exceeds (5), thereby contradicting the assumption.

The difference (6) minus (5) can be analyzed by breaking the integrals into three intervals: $[r^{-1}(\bar{x}_1 - \epsilon), \bar{x}_2]$, $[\underline{x}_2, r^{-1}(\bar{x}_1)]$, and $(r^{-1}(\bar{x}_1), r^{-1}(\bar{x}_1 - \epsilon))$. Over the first interval, the difference in integrands is

$$(R(x_2) - b(\bar{x}_1)) - (R(x_2) - b(\bar{x}_1 - \epsilon)) = \epsilon b'(\bar{x}_1) + O(\epsilon)$$

Note well that $b'(\bar{x}_1)$ is strictly positive. Over the second interval, the difference in integrands is

$$((\bar{x}_1 - \epsilon)P(\bar{x}_1 - \epsilon + x_2) - b(\bar{x}_1 - \epsilon)) - (\bar{x}_1 P(\bar{x}_1 + x_2) - b(\bar{x}_1))$$
$$= \epsilon(b'(\bar{x}_1) - \bar{x}_1 P'(\bar{x}_1) - P(\bar{x}_1 + x_2)) + O(\epsilon)$$

Here the term premultiplied by ϵ is strictly positive except possibly at the lower boundary (where it is nonnegative), since by step 2, $\bar{x}_1 \geq r_b(\underline{x}_2) \geq r_b(x_2)$. Over the third interval, the difference in the integrands is no more than $O(\epsilon)$, because of the continuity of $xP(x + x_2) - b(x)$. Thus as ϵ goes to zero, the integral over the first interval will be strictly positive $O(\epsilon)$ if μ_2 puts any mass on $(r^{-1}(\bar{x}_1), \bar{x}_2)]$. The integral over the second interval will be strictly positive $O(\epsilon)$ if μ_2 puts any mass on $(r_b^{-1}(\bar{x}_1), r^{-1}(\bar{x}_1))]$. The integral over the third interval must be $O(\epsilon)$, since it is the integral of a term $O(\epsilon)$ integrated over a vanishing interval. The hypothesis $\bar{x}_1 > r_b(\bar{x}_2)$ implies that μ_2 puts positive mass on either $(r_b^{-1}(\bar{x}_1), r^{-1}(\bar{x}_1))]$ or on $(r^{-1}(\bar{x}_1), \bar{x}_2]$ (or both). Hence for small enough ϵ, the difference between (6) and (5) will be strictly positive. This is the desired contradiction.

STEP 4. The rest is easy. Steps 2 and 3 imply that $\bar{x}_1 = r_b(\bar{x}_2) = r_b(\underline{x}_2)$, and hence that firm 2 uses a pure strategy in the first round. But then firm 1's best response in the first round is the pure strategy $r_b(x_2)$. And firm 2's strategy, which must be a best response to this, must satisfy $x_2 = r_b(x_1) = r_b(r_b(x_2))$. This implies that $x_2 = x^*(b)$, and, therefore, $x_1 = r_b(x^*(b)) = x^*(b)$. Finally, the two firms will each name price $P(2x^*(b))$ in the second round (as long as both firms produce $x^*(b)$ in the first round, which they will do with probability one); this follows immediately from Step 1 and Proposition 1.

6. The Case $b \equiv 0$

When $b \equiv 0$ it is easy to check that the Cournot outcome is an equilibrium. In this case, however, there are other equilibria as well. If imperfect equilibria are counted, then one equilibrium has $x_1 = x_2 = D(0)$ (or anything larger) and $p_1 \equiv p_2 \equiv 0$. Note well that each firm names price zero regardless of what capacities are installed. This is clearly an equilibrium, but it is imperfect, because if, say, firm 1 installed a small capacity and the subgame equilibrium ensued, each would make positive profits.

There are also other perfect equilibria, although it takes a bit more work to establish them. Let $x_1 \geq D(0)$. If firm 2 installs capacity greater than $D(0)$, it will net zero profits (assuming a subgame equilibrium follows). If it installs $x_2 < D(0)$, then its profits (in a perfect equilibrium) are $\underline{p}(x_2)x_2$, where $\underline{p}(x_2) \leq \underline{p}(0)$ solves the equation $\underline{p}(x_2)D(\underline{p}(x_2)) = R(x_2)$. Hence, in any perfect equilibrium where $x_1 \geq D(0)$, x_2 must be selected to maximize $\underline{p}(x_2)x_2 = R(x_2)x_2/D(\underline{p}(x_2))$. The numerator in the last expression is increasing for $x_2 \leq x^*$ and is decreasing thereafter. (See the proof of Lemma 5.) And as $\underline{p}(x_2)$ decreases in x_2, the denominator increases in x_2. Thus, the maximizing x_2 is less than x^*. But as long as firm 2 chooses capacity less than x^*, the best revenue (in any subgame equilibrium) that firm 1 can hope to achieve is $R(x_2)$, which it achieves with any $x_1 \geq D(0)$. Thus, we have a perfect subgame equilibrium in which firm 1 chooses $x_1 \geq D(0)$ and firm 2 chooses x_2 to maximize $\underline{p}(x_2)x_2$.

7. When both Capacity and Production are Costly

In a slightly more complicated version of this game, both capacity (which is installed before prices are named and demand is realized) and production (which takes place after demand is realized) would be costly. Assuming that each of these activities has a convex cost structure and that our assumptions on demand are met, it is easy to modify our analysis to show that the unique equilibrium outcome is the Cournot outcome computed by using the sum of the two cost functions. (This requires that capacity is costly on the margin. Otherwise, imperfect equilibria of all sorts and perfect equilibria of the sort given above will also appear.) It is notable that the cost of capacity need not be very high relative to production cost: the only requirement is that it be nonzero on the margin. Thus, situations where "most" of the cost is incurred subsequent to the realization of demand (situations that will "look" very Bertrand-like) will still give the Cournot outcome. (A reasonable conjecture, suggested to us by many colleagues, is that "noise" in the demand function will change this dramatically. Confirmation or rejection of this conjecture must await another paper.)

References

Beckmann, M. (1965): "Edgeworth-Bertrand Duopoly Revisited" in R. Henn, ed., *Operations Research-Verfahren, III*. Meisenheim: Verlag Anton Hein, 55–68.

Bertrand, J. (1883): "Théorie Mathématique de la Richesse Sociale." *Journal des Savants*, 499–508.

Cournot, A. (1838) (1897): *Recherches sur les Principes Mathématiques de la Théorie des Richesses*. Paris: English translation: (N. Bacon, trans.), *Researches into the Mathematical Principles of the Theory of Wealth*, New York: Macmillan & Company.

Dasgupta, P. and Maskin, E. (1982): "The Existence of Equilibrium in Discontinuous Economic Games, 2: Applications." Draft, London School of Economics.

Edgeworth, F. (1897) (1925): "La Teoria Pura del Monopolio." *Giornale degli Economisti*, 40, 13–31. Reprinted in English as "The Pure Theory of Monopoly," in F. Edgeworth, *Papers Relating to Political Economy*, Vol. 1, London: Macmillan & Co., Ltd., 111–42.

Levitan, R. and Shubik, M. (1972): "Price Duopoly and Capacity Constraints." *International Economic Review*, 13, 111–22.

Selten, R. (1965): "Spieltheoretische Behandlung eines Oligopolmodells mit Nachfragetragheit." *Zeitschrift für die gesamte Staatswissenschaft*, 121, 301–24.

CHAPTER TWO

The Fat-Cat Effect, the Puppy-Dog Ploy, and the Lean and Hungry Look

DREW FUDENBERG AND JEAN TIROLE

Source: *American Economic Review*, 1984, 74, 361–8.

Let me have about me men that are fat....

Julius Caesar, Act 1, Sc. 2

The idea that strategic considerations may provide firms with an incentive to "overinvest" in "capital" to deter the entry or expansion of rivals is by now well understood. However, in some circumstances, increased investment may be a strategic handicap, because it may reduce the incentive to respond aggressively to competitors. In such cases, firms may instead choose to maintain a "lean and hungry look," thus avoiding the "fat-cat effect." We illustrate these effects with models of investment in advertising and in $R\&D$. We also provide a taxonomy of the factors which tend to favor over- and underinvestment, both to deter entry and to accommodate it. Such a classification, of course, requires a notion of what it means to overinvest; that is, we must provide a benchmark for comparison. If entry is deterred, we use a monopolist's investment as the basis for comparison. For the case of entry accommodation, we compare the incumbent's investment to that in a "precommitment" or "open-loop" equilibrium, in which the incumbent takes the entrant's actions as given and does not try to influence them through its choice of preentry investment. We flesh out the taxonomy with several additional examples.

Our advertising model was inspired by Richard Schmalensee's (1982) paper, whose results foreshadow ours. We provide an example in which an established firm will underinvest in advertising if it chooses to deter entry, because by lowering its stock of "goodwill" it establishes a credible threat to cut prices in the event of entry. Conversely, if the established firm chooses to allow entry, it will advertise heavily and become a fat cat in order to soften the entrant's pricing behavior. Thus the strategic incentives for investment depend on whether the incumbent chooses to deter entry. This contrasts with the previous work on strategic investment in cost-reducing machinery (Michael Spence,

1977, 1979; Avinash Dixit, 1979, our 1983a article) and in "learning by doing" (Spence, 1981; our 1983c article) in which the strategic incentives always encourage the incumbent to overaccumulate. Our *R&D* model builds on Jennifer Reinganum's (1983) observation that the "Arrow effect" (Kenneth Arrow, 1962) of an incumbent monopolist's reduced incentive to do *R&D* is robust to the threat of entry so long as the *R&D* technology is stochastic.

Our examples show that the key factors in strategic investment are whether investment makes the incumbent more or less "tough" in the post-entry game, and how the entrant reacts to tougher play by the incumbent. These two factors are the basis of our taxonomy. Jeremy Bulow et al. (1983) have independently noted the importance of the entrant's reaction. Their paper overlaps a good deal with ours.

1. Advertising and Goodwill

In our goodwill model, a customer can buy from a firm only if he is aware of its existence. To inform consumers, firms place ads in newspapers. An ad that is read informs the customer of the existence of the firm and also gives the firm's price. In the first period, only the incumbent is in the market; in the second period the entrant may enter. The crucial assumption is that some of the customers who received an ad in the first period do not bother to read the ads in the second period, and therefore buy only from the incumbent. This captive market for the incumbent represents the incumbent's accumulation of goodwill. One could derive such captivity from a model in which rational consumers possess imperfect information about product quality, as in Schmalensee (1982), or from a model in which customers must sink firm-specific costs in learning how to consume the product.

There are two firms, an incumbent and an entrant, and a unit population of *ex ante* identical consumers. If a consumer is aware of both firms, and the incumbent charges x_1, and the entrant charges x_2, the consumer's demands for the two goods are $D^1(x_1, x_2)$ and $D^2(x_1, x_2)$, respectively. If a consumer is only aware of the incumbent (entrant), his demand is $D^1(x_1, \infty)$ and $(D^2(\infty, x_2))$. The (net of variable costs) revenue an informed consumer brings the incumbent is $R^1(x_1, x_2)$ or $R^1(x_1, \infty)$ depending on whether the consumer also knows about the entrant or not, and similarly for the entrant. We'll assume that the revenues are differentiable, quasi concave in own-prices, and they, as well as the marginal revenue, increase with the competitor's price (these are standard assumptions for price competition with differentiated goods).

To inform consumers, the firms put ads in the newspapers. An ad that is read makes the customer aware of the product and gives the price. The cost of reaching a fraction K of the population in the first period is $A(K)$, where $A(K)$ is convex for strictly positive levels of advertising, and $A(1) = \infty$.[1] There are two periods, $t = 1, 2$. In the first period, only the incumbent is in the market. It advertises K_1, charges the monopoly price, and makes profits $K^1 \dot{R}^m$. In the second period the entrant may enter.

To further simplify, we assume that all active firms will choose to cover the remaining market in the second period at cost A_2. Then assuming entry, the profits of the two firms, Π^1 and Π^2, can be written

$$\Pi^1 = [-A(K_1) + K_1 R^m] + \delta[K_1 R^1(x_1, \infty) + (1 - K_1)R^1(x_1, x_2) - A_2]$$
$$\Pi^2 = \delta[(1 - K_1)R^2(x_1, x_2) - A_2] \tag{1}$$

where δ is the common discount factor.

In the second period, the firms simultaneously choose prices. Assuming that a Nash equilibrium for this second-stage game exists and is characterized by the first-order conditions, we have

$$K_1 R_1^1(x_1^*, \infty) + (1 - K_1)R_1^1(x_1^*, x_2^*) = 0 \tag{2}$$
$$R_2^2(x_1^*, x_2^*) = 0 \tag{3}$$

where $R_j^i \equiv \partial R^i(x_1, x_2)/\partial x_j$, and x_i^* is the equilibrium value of x_i as a function of K_1.

From equation (2), and the assumption that $R_{ij}^i > 0$, we see that

$$R_1^1(x_1^*, \infty) > 0 > R_1^1(x_1^*, x_2^*)$$

The incumbent would like to increase its price for its captive customers, and reduce it where there is competition; but price discrimination has been assumed impossible.

Differentiating the first-order conditions, and using $R_{ij}^i > 0$, we have

$$\partial x_1^*/\partial K_1 > 0 \qquad \partial x_1^*/\partial x_2^* > 0$$
$$\partial x_2^*/\partial K_1 = 0 \qquad \partial x_2^*/\partial x_1^* > 0 \tag{4}$$

The heart of the fat-cat effect is that $\partial x_1^*/\partial K_1 > 0$. As the incumbent's goodwill increases, it becomes more reluctant to match the entrant's price. The large captive market makes the incumbent a pacifistic "fat cat." This suggests that if entry is going to occur, the incumbent has an incentive to increase K_1 to "soften" the second-period equilibrium.

To formalize this intuition we first must sign the *total* derivative dx_1^*/dK_1. While one would expect increasing K_1 to increase the incumbent's equilibrium price, this is only true if firm 1's second-period reaction curve is steeper than firm 2's. This will be true if $R_{11}^1 R_{22}^2 > R_{12}^1 R_{21}^2$. If dx_1^*/dK_1 were negative the model would not exhibit the fat-cat effect.

Now we compare the incumbent's choice of K_1 in the open-loop and perfect equilibria. In the former, the incumbent takes x_2^* as given, and thus ignores the possibility of strategic investment. Setting $\partial \pi^1/\partial K_1 = 0$ in (1), we have

$$R^m + \delta(R^1(x_1^*, \infty) - R^1(x_1^*, x_2^*)) = A'(K_1) \tag{5}$$

In a perfect equilibrium, the incumbent realizes that x_2^* depends on K_1, giving first-order conditions

$$R^m + \delta(R^1(x_1^*, \infty) - R^1(x_1^*, x_2^*) + (1 - K_1)R_2^1(dx_2^*/dK_1)) = A'(K_1) \tag{6}$$

As R_2^1 and dx_2^*/dK_1 are positive, for a fixed K_1 the left-hand side of (6) exceeds that of (5), so if the second-order condition corresponding to (6) is satisfied, its solution exceeds that of (5).

The fat-cat effect suggests a corollary, that the incumbent should underinvest and maintain a "lean and hungry look" to deter entry. However, while the "price effect" of increasing K_1 encourages entry, the "direct effect" of reducing the entrant's market goes the other way. To see this, note that

$$\Pi_k^2 = \delta[(1 - K_1)R_1^2(dx_1^*/dK_1) - R^2] \tag{7}$$

The first term in the right-hand side of (7) is the strategic effect of K_1 on the second-period price, the second is the direct effect. One can find plausible examples of demand and advertising functions such that the indirect effect dominates. This is the case, for example, for goods which are differentiated by their location on the unit interval with linear "transportation" costs, if first-period advertising is sufficiently expensive that the incumbent's equilibrium share of the informed consumers is positive. In this case, entry deterrence requires underinvestment.

2. Technological Competition

We now develop a simple model of investment in $R\&D$ to illustrate the lean and hungry look, building on the work of Arrow and Reinganum. In the first period, the incumbent, firm 1, spends K_1 on capital, and then has constant average cost $\bar{c}(K_1)$. The incumbent receives the monopoly profit $V^m(\bar{c}(K_1))$ in period 1. In the second period, both the incumbent and firm 2 may do $R\&D$ on a new technology which allows constant average cost c. If one firm develops the innovation, it receives the monopoly value $V^m(c)$. Thus the innovation is "large" or "drastic" in Arrow's sense. If both firms develop the innovation, their profit is zero. If neither firm succeeds, then the incumbent again receives $V^m(\bar{c})$. The second-period $R\&D$ technology is stochastic. If firm i spends x_i on $R\&D$, it obtains the new technology with probability $\mu_i(x_i)$. We assume $\mu_i'(0) = \infty, \mu_i' > 0$, $\mu_i'' < 0$. The total payoffs from period 2 on are

$$\Pi^1 = \mu_1(1 - \mu_2)V^m(c) + (1 - \mu_1)(1 - \mu_2)V^m(\bar{c}) - x_1 \tag{9}$$
$$\Pi^2 = \mu_2(1 - \mu_1)V^m(c) - x_2$$

The first-order conditions for a Nash equilibrium are

$$\mu_1'[V^m(c) - V^m(\bar{c})](1 - \mu_2) = 1 \tag{10}$$
$$\mu_2'V^m(c)(1 - \mu_1) = 1$$

We see that since the incumbent's gain is only the difference in the monopoly profits, it has less incentive to innovate than the entrant. This is the Arrow effect.[2] We have derived it here in a model with each firm's chance of succeeding independent of the other's, so that we have had to allow a nonzero probability of a tie. Reinganum's model avoids ties, because the possibilities of "success" (obtaining the patent) are not independent.

Because $\mu_i' > 0$ and $\mu_i'' < 0$, the reaction curves in (10) slope downward – the more one firm spends, the less the other wishes to. Since increasing K_1 decreases the incumbent's gain from the innovator's we expect that the strategic incentive is to reduce K_1 to play more aggressively in period 2. As in our last example, this is only true if the reaction curves are "stable," which in this case requires $\mu_1'' \mu_2'' (1 - \mu_1)(1 - \mu_2) > (\mu_1' \mu_2')^2$. This is true for example for $\mu_i(x) = \max(1, bx^{1/2})$, with b small. We conclude that to accommodate entry the incumbent has a strategic incentive to underinvest. Because K_1 has no direct effect on Π^2, we can also say that to deter entry the incumbent has an incentive to underinvest.[3]

3. Taxonomy and Conclusion

In the goodwill model the incumbent could underinvest to deter entry, while in the *R&D* model the strategic incentives always favored underinvestment. To relate these results to previous work, we next present an informal taxonomy of pre-entry strategic investment by an incumbent. In many cases, one might expect both "investment" and "production" decisions to be made post-entry. We have restricted attention to a single post-entry variable for simplicity. We should point out that this involves some loss of generality. Strategic underinvestment requires that the incumbent not be able to invest after entry, or more generally that pre- and post-entry investments are imperfectly substitutable. This was the case in both of our examples. However, if investment is in productive machinery and capital costs are linear and constant over time, then underinvestment would be ineffective, as the incumbent's post-entry investment would make up any previous restraint.

Before presenting the taxonomy, it should be acknowledged that since Schmalensee's (1983) article, several authors have independently noticed the possibility of underinvestment. J. Baldani (1983) studies the conditions leading to underinvestment in advertising. Bulow et al. (1983) present a careful treatment of two-stage games in which either production or investment takes place in the first period, with production in the second, and costs need not be separable across periods. They focus on cost minimization as the benchmark for over- and underinvestment. The starting point for the Bulow et al. (1983) paper was the observation that a firm might choose not to enter an apparently profitable market due to strategic spillovers on other product lines. This point is developed in more detail in K. Judd (1983).

Our taxonomy classifies market according to the signs of the incentives for strategic investments. Because only the incumbent has a strategic incentive, given concavity, we can unambiguously say whether the incumbent will over- or underinvest to accommodate entry (compared to the open-loop equilibrium).[4] We continue to denote the incumbent's first-period choice K_1, the post-entry decisions x_1 and x_2, and the payoffs Π^1 and Π^2. For entry deterrence there are two effects, as we noted before: the "direct effect" $\partial \Pi^2 / \partial K_1$, and the "strategic effect" $\partial \Pi^2 / \partial x_1^* \cdot \dot{\partial} x_1^* / \partial K_1$. We saw in the goodwill case that these two effects had opposite signs, and so the overall incentives were ambiguous. In all the rest of our examples, these two effects have the same sign.

In Table 1, first the entry-accommodating strategy and then the entry-deterring one is given. The fat-cat strategy is overinvestment that accommodates entry by committing the incumbent to play less aggressively post-entry. The lean and hungry strategy is underinvestment to be tougher. The top dog strategy is overinvestment to be tough; this is the familiar result of Spence and Dixit.

Table 1

| Slope of Reaction Curves | Investment Makes Incumbent: | |
	Tough	Soft
Upward	Case IV	Case I
	A: Puppy Dog D: Top Dog	A: Fat Cat D: Lean and Hungry
Downward	Case III	Case II
	A: Top Dog A: Top Dog	A: Lean and Hungry A: Lean and Hungry

Note: $A =$ Accommodate entry; $D =$ Deter entry.

Last, the puppy-dog strategy is *underinvestment* that accommodates entry by turning the incumbent into a small, friendly, nonaggressive puppy dog. This strategy is desirable if investment makes the incumbent tougher, and the second-period reaction curves slope up.

One final caveat: the classification in Table 1 depends as previously on the second-period Nash equilibria being "stable," so that changing K_1 has the intuitive effect on x_2^*.

Our goodwill model is an example of Case I: goodwill makes the incumbent soft, and the second-period reaction curves slope up. The *R&D* model illustrates Case II. Case III is the "classic" case for investing in productive machinery and "learning by doing" (Spence, 1981; our paper, 1983c) with quantity competition. Case IV results from either of these models with price competition (Bulow et al. (1983), our paper, 1983b; Judith Gelman and Steven Salop, 1983). A more novel example of the puppy-dog ploy arises in the P. Milgrom and J. Roberts (1982) model of limit pricing under incomplete information, if we remove their assumption that the established firm's cost is revealed once the entrant decides to enter, and replace quantity with price as the strategic variable. To accommodate entry, the incumbent then prefers the entrant to believe that the incumbent's costs are relatively high.

We conclude with two warnings. First, one key ingredient of our taxonomy is the slope of the second-period reaction curves. In many of our examples, downward slopes correspond to quantity competition and upward slopes to competition in prices.[5] These examples are potentially misleading. We do not intend to revive the Cournot vs. Bertrand argument. As David Kreps and José Scheinkman (1983) have shown, "Quantity Precommitment and Bertrand Competition Yield Cournot Outcomes." Thus, "price competition" and "quantity competition" should not be interpreted as referring to the variable chosen by firms in the second stage, but rather as two different reduced forms for the determination of both prices and outputs. Second, our restriction to a single post-entry stage eliminates many important strategic interactions. As our 1983a paper shows, such interactions may reverse the over- or under-investment results of two-stage models.

Notes

1 See Gerard Butters (1977), and Gene Grossman and Carl Shapiro (1984) for examples of advertising technologies.

2 For large innovations, the monopoly price with the new technology is less than the average cost of the old one. Richard Gilbert and David Newbery (1982) showed that for "small" innovations, because the sum of the duopoly profits is (typically) less than $\Pi^m(c)$, the incumbent loses more than the entrant gains if the entrant obtains the patent. With a deterministic R&D technology, the incumbent's incentive to innovate thus exceeds the entrant's, because the incumbent's current patent is certain to be superceded and thus the current profits are not "sacrificed" by the incumbent's R&D. Reinganum showed that with stochastic R&D and a small innovation, either effect can dominate. In her R&D model the reaction curves slope up.

3 For small innovations the direct effect goes the other way.

4 This does not generalize to the case in which both firms make strategic decisions. In our paper on learning by doing (1983c), we give an example in which one firm's first-period output declined in moving from the precommitment to the perfect equilibrium. The problem is that if, as expected, firm 1's output increases when it plays strategically, firm 2's strategic incentive to increase output can be outweighted by its response to firm 1's change.

5 Bulow et al. (1983) point out that while these are the "normal" cases, it is possible, for example, for reaction curves to slope up in quantity competition.

References

Arrow, K. (1962): "Economic Welfare and the Allocation of Resources to Innovation," in R. Nelson (ed.), *The Rate and Direction of Economic Activity*, New York: National Bureau of Economic Research.

Baldani, J. (1983): "Strategic Advertising and Credible Entry Deterrence Policies," mimeo., Colgate University.

Bulow, J., Geanakoplos, J. and Klemperer, P. (1983): "Multimarket Oligopoly," Stanford Business School, R. P. 696.

Butters, G. (1977): "Equilibrium Distributions of Sales and Advertising Prices," *Review of Economic Studies*, October, 44, 465–96.

Dixit, A. (1979): "A Model of Duopoly Suggesting a Theory of Entry Barriers," *Bell Journal of Economics*, Spring, 10, 20–32.

Fudenberg, D. and Tirole, J. (1983a): "Capital as a Commitment: Strategic Investment to Deter Mobility," *Journal of Economic Theory*, December, 31, 227–50.

—— and ——, (1983b): "Dynamic Models of Oligopoly," IMSSS T. R. 428, Stanford University.

—— and ——, (1983c): "Learning by Doing and Market Performance," *Bell Journal of Economics*, Autumn, 14, 522–30.

Gelman, J. and Salop, S. (1983): "Judo Economics," mimeo., George Washington University.

Gilbert, R. and Newbery, D. (1982): "Preemptive Patenting and the Persistence of Monopoly," *American Economic Review*, June, 72, 514–26.

Grossman, G. and Shapiro, C. (1984): "Informative Advertising with Differentiated Goods," *Review of Economic Studies*, January, 51, 63–82.

Judd, K. (1983): "Credible Spatial Preemption," MEDS D. P. 577, Northwestern University.

Kreps, D. and Scheinkman, J. (1983): "Quantity Precommitment and Bertrand Competition Yield Cournot Outcomes," mimeo., University of Chicago.

Milgrom, P. and Roberts, J. (1982): "Limit Pricing and Entry under Incomplete Information," *Econometrica*, 50, 443–60.

Reinganum, J. (1983): "Uncertain Innovation and the Persistence of Monopoly," *American Economic Review*, September, 73, 741–8.

Schmalensee, R. (1982): "Product Differentiation Advantages of Pioneering Brands," *American Economic Review*, June, 72, 349–65.

——(1983): "Advertising and Entry Deterrence: An Exploratory Model," *Journal of Political Economy*, August, 90, 636–53.

Spence, A. M. (1977): "Entry, Capacity, Investment, and Oligopolistic Pricing," *Bell Journal of Economics*, Autumn, 8, 534–44.

——(1979): "Investment Strategy and Growth in a New Market," *Bell Journal of Economics*, Spring, 10, 1–19.

——(1981): "The Learning Curve and Competition," *Bell Journal of Economics*, Spring, 12, 49–70.

Introduction

Most real–world oligopoly interaction takes place over a number of periods. In this sense, static oligopoly models are of limited use: they either assume that decisions are taken once and for all, or that the same strategic choice is made in each period.

From a game theoretic point of view, the best way to analyze ongoing oligopoly interaction is to make use of repeated games. A repeated game, as the name suggests, is a game that is repeated – indefinitely, in the case of an infinitely repeated game, or for a fixed number of periods, in the case of a finitely repeated game.

It has long been known that there may exist equilibria in repeated games that do not correspond to equilibria in the respective static game.[1] For example, in the static Bertrand game, the only equilibrium is for firms to set price equal to marginal cost. However, in the repeated Bertrand game, there may be equilibria where firms set prices above marginal cost. In fact, dynamic interaction is one of the solutions for the "paradox" alluded to in part I (namely, that in a price-setting context prices equal marginal cost even with only two competitors). The first formal application of the principles of repeated games to oligopoly theory is due to Friedman (1971), who examined a repeated Cournot game and confirmed the above results.

Repeated games provide a very reasonable explanation for cartels and collusion, one that static models cannot offer. In these repeated-game equilibria, notwithstanding the absence of explicit binding contracts, firms refrain from setting prices that would increase their short-run profits. The reason is that a short-run deviation from the equilibrium price is followed by a price war that creates greater harm for the deviant firm than the profits from deviation. However, in doing so, models like that of Friedman (1971) go a little too far in the opposite direction: they predict that, if firms interact frequently enough, then monopoly prices are set in every period (if firms pick the profit maximizing equilibrium). Moreover, although price wars are the deterrent of deviations from a collusive agreement, price wars do not actually take place along the equilibrium path. Such prediction fails to match the empirical observation that price wars do occur.

Inspired by Stigler's (1964) pioneering ideas, Green and Porter (1984) provide a formal, consistent repeated game where price wars take place along the equilibrium path. The key ingredient in the Green–Porter model is that firms cannot observe each other's actions (output level), only a public signal (price) which is a function of every players' actions and of exogenous noise. A firm that deviates by setting a high output will induce a lower price (stochastically speaking). To prevent this happening, when price is sufficiently low, firms revert into a (finite) price war, upon which they revert back to the cooperative phase of setting monopoly output levels.

Rotemberg and Saloner (1986) propose an alternative explanation for price wars. As in Green and Porter, they assume that demand fluctuates over time. However, they assume that both current demand and past prices are observable. In this context, "price wars" (specifically, periods of lower prices) result from the need to balance the benefits and costs of short-run deviations in prices. Specifically, the models predicts (under some assumptions) that prices are lower in periods of high demand, that is, periods when short-run deviations would be more profitable.

Both the Green-Porter and the Rotemberg-Saloner papers have spawn a series of theoretical works that extend and generalize the original ideas. To mention a few, Porter (1983b) extends Green and Porter (1984) to optimal cartel equilibria.[2] Abreu, Pearce and Stacchetti (1990) propose a more general theory of collusion with imperfect observability. Haltiwanger and Harrington (1991) and Kandori (1992) extend Rotemberg and Saloner (1986) to more complex demand fluctuation patterns. On the empirical front, Porter (1983a) (cf part IV) and Ellison (1994) propose empirical specifications based on the theoretical models.

As mentioned above, collusive equilibria must balance the short-run benefits from deviation against the long-run costs from entering into a price war. When firms interact with each other in more than one market, the list of possible arrangements for stable collusive pricing increases. Or does it? Anecdotal evidence suggests that multi-market contact makes collusion easier to sustain. Bernheim and Whinston (1990) provide formal conditions such that collusion is indeed easier to sustain under multi-market contact. They also provide conditions under which multi-market contact is irrelevant from the perspective of collusion.

The idea that multi-market contact may facilitate collusion is not new: Scherer (1970) lists a series of examples and Telser (1980) briefly mentions the theoretical possibility. However, Bernheim and Whinston (1990) provided the first systematic analysis of the problem. Since then, a number of empirical papers have confirmed the theory's prediction, including Evans and Kessides (1994), Parker and Röller (1997), Fernández and Marín (1998). An interesting area for theoretical extension is the inclusion of incomplete observability of firms' actions, a possibility not considered by Bernheim and Whinston (1990).

Notes

1   Specifically, the *Folk theorem* (thus called on account of its uncertain origin) states that if players interact frequently enough then any payoff profile that is feasible and individually rational can be attained from an equilibrium of the repeated game.
2   Other important references on optimal cartel equilibria, though not in an imperfect observability context, include Abreu (1986, 1988).

References

Abreu, Dilip (1986): "Extremal Equilibria of Oligopolistic Supergames," *Journal of Economic Theory*, 39, 191–228.

Abreu, Dilip (1988): "On the Theory of Infinitely Repeated Games with Discounting," *Econometrica*, 56, 383–96.

Abreu, Dilip, David Pearce and Ennio Stacchetti (1990): "Toward a Theory of Discounted Repeated Games with Imperfect Monitoring," *Econometrica*, 58, 1041–64.

Bernheim, B. Douglas and Michael D. Whinston (1990): "Multimarket Contact and Collusive Behavior," *Rand Journal of Economics*, 21, 1–26.

Ellison, Glenn (1994): "Theories of Cartel Stability and the Joint Executive Committee," *Rand Journal of Economics*, 25, 37–57.

Evans, W. N. and I. N. Kessides (1994): "Living by the 'Golden Rule': Multimarket Contact in the US Airline Industry," *Quarterly Journal of Economics*, 109, 341–66.

Fernández, Nerea and Pedro L. Marín (1998): "Market Power and Multimarket Contact: Some Evidence from the Spanish Hotel Industry," *Journal of Industrial Economics*, 46, 301–15.

Friedman, James (1971): "A Noncooperative Equilibrium for Supergames," *Review of Economic Studies*, 28, 1–12.

Green, Ed and Robert Porter (1984): "Noncooperative Collusion Under Imperfect Price Information," *Econometrica*, 52, 87–100.

Haltiwanger, J. and J. E. Harrington, Jr. (1991): "The Impact of Cyclical Demand Movements on Collusive Behavior," *Rand Journal of Economics*, 22, 89–106.

Kandori, Michihiro (1992): "The Use of Information in Repeated Games with Imperfect Monitoring," *Review of Economic Studies*, 59, 581–93.

Parker, Philip M. and Lars-Hendrick Röller (1997): "Collusive Conduct in Duopolies: Multimarket Contact and Cross-Ownership in the Mobile Telephone Industry," *Rand Journal of Economics*, 28, 304–22.

Porter, Robert H. (1983a) "A Study of Cartel Stability: the Joint Executive Committee, 1880–1886," *Bell Journal of Economics*, 14, 301–14.

Porter, Robert H. (1983b): "Optimal Cartel Trigger Price Strategies," *Journal of Economic Theory*, 29, 313–38.

Rotemberg, Julio and Garth Saloner (1986): "A Supergame-Theoretic Model of Price Wars During Booms," *American Economic Review*, 76, 390–407.

Scherer, F. M. (1970): *Industrial Market Structure and Economic Performance*, Boston: Houghton Mifflin Co.

Stigler, George (1964): "A Theory of Oligopoly," *Journal of Political Economy*, 72, 44–61.

Telser, L. G. (1980): "A Theory of Self-enforcing Agreements," *Journal of Business*, 53, 27–44.

CHAPTER THREE

Noncooperative Collusion under Imperfect Price Information

EDWARD J. GREEN AND ROBERT H. PORTER

Source: *Econometrica*, 1984, 52, 87–100.

Recent work in game theory has shown that, in principle, it may be possible for firms in an industry to form a self-policing cartel to maximize their joint profits. This paper examines the nature of cartel self-enforcement in the presence of demand uncertainty. A model of a noncooperatively supported cartel is presented, and the aspects of industry structure which would make such a cartel viable are discussed.

1. Introduction

Long-standing questions about how widespread is the occurrence of collusion in industries having several firms, and about the extent to which the performance of industries experiencing such collusion departs from the competitive norm, continue to provoke spirited debate. In this paper we offer a theory of collusive industry equilibrium which will provide a means of clarifying these questions.

In his classic paper "A Theory of Oligopoly" [15], George Stigler appealed to dynamic considerations to explain how apparently cooperative industry performance might result from noncooperative motives. According to this theory, the firms of an industry form a cartel, which is designed to enforce monopolistic conduct in a self-policing way. "Self-policing" means precisely that the agreed-upon conduct is noncooperatively viable and that it remains so over time.

Stigler's theory differs markedly from traditional oligopoly theories based on static equilibrium concepts (e.g., Cournot and Stackelberg). This difference is particularly striking in the case of an industry structure which is essentially immune from entry. The traditional theories would suggest that the performance of such an industry should be largely determined by its degree of concentration – the number of firms in the industry and their relative sizes – and by the extent to which substitute goods are available. In contrast, Stigler suggested that the greatest obstacle to collusion in the absence of entry would be what he characterized as "secret price cutting." By informally relating concentration and various other features of industry structure to the immunity of a cartel from entry and to its ability to deter inimical firm behavior, and by assuming that industry profitability reflects successful operation of a cartel, he justified the use of cross-industry regressions to test his theory.

The obvious interpretation of Stigler is that he made explicit a theory of oligopoly which implicitly conceived of a cartel as a "policeman" which with some frequency is required to punish destabilizing "offenses" of individual cartel members. The somewhat different interpretation of this paper is that Stigler had a view of cartel organization as an instance of an optimization problem: to design an institution which achieves an efficient equilibrium outcome subject to the constraint that agents in the institution behave noncooperatively. On this interpretation, the optimal cartel structure may be one which provides member firms with strong positive incentives which make collusive behavior attractive, rather than one which provides insufficient incentives and which severely punishes defecting firms after the fact.

In fact, two formulations of the cartel problem exist already which treat noncooperative collusion in a rigorous way. Osborne [8] proposes a reaction function equilibrium in which firms respond to changes in output by other firms in order to maintain their proportionate share of industry output. (See also the extensions of Spence [13, 14].) Knowing that other firms will respond in this manner, each firm will realize that it does not pay to deviate from the collusive output level.

Friedman [3], on the other hand, outlines a strategy in which firms respond to suspected cheating, which they infer from a drop in the market price below the price that obtains when all firms produce at agreed-upon levels, by producing at Cournot levels thereafter. If future profit streams are discounted sufficiently slowly, then a firm would reduce the discounted value of its returns by failing to collude. Therefore, for all firms to adopt the collusive strategy would be a noncooperative equilibrium.

The trouble with these formulations, from an applied industrial organization viewpoint, is that incentives in these equilibria are so perfect that the deterrent mechanisms are never observed. Then it may be difficult to infer from econometric time-series evidence whether the observed market data is the outcome of a quasicompetitive or collusive equilibrium (cf. T. Bresnahan [2]). The substance of the present contribution is that this perfection is an artifact of the certainty world in which these models are formulated. When the considerations of imperfect information, which played a decisive role in Stigler's theory, are reintroduced, optimal incentive structures may involve episodic recourse to the kind of short-run unprofitable conduct which would have been characterized as "price wars" or "punishment" previously.

Our argument has three parts. First, we frame a precise definition of collusion in terms of industry conduct. Second, we show that collusive conduct may, in a particular industry structure, result in a pattern of industry performance marked by recurrent episodes in which price and profit levels sharply decrease. Thus we reject the received view that performance of this type necessarily indicates an industry where firms are engaging in a sequence of abortive attempts to form a cartel. Since this opinion is often used as a basis to deny the need for intervention to promote competition in such industries (because the market purportedly is already withstanding the collusive assaults), our argument suggests the need to re-examine a widely held assumption about policy.

Third, we point out that the distinctive character of the phenomenon just discussed and the necessary appearance of this phenomenon if collusion is to take place (given the particular industry structure in question) make it possible to draw clear-cut conclusions about the presence or absence of collusion in some specific industries on the basis of market data. This is a singular opportunity to learn about whether collusion does indeed exist in situations where it might plausibly occur, without having to face the many problems of interpretation surrounding the usual cross-industry tests of its extent.[1]

2. Collusion under Uncertainty

Collusive equilibria exhibiting stable performance may possibly characterize some industries. For instance, a market might be segmented geographically because firms have divided it. As long as this agreement was adhered to, each firm would be a monopolist within its area. Moreover, poaching by one firm in another's territory would be quickly and surely detected, and would invite retaliation. In that situation, no one would poach. All that would ever be "observed" is monopolistic conduct.[2]

Similarly, in an industry in which contracts are awarded by competitive bidding, a scheme to rotate winning bids might be perfectly enforceable. Each firm would act as a monopolist when its turn came, and would clearly see that bidding low out of turn would jeopardize a profitable arrangement. Again, only monopolistic conduct would ever be "observed."[3]

We will study a model in which demand fluctuations not directly observed by firms lead to unstable industry performance. Intuitively firms will act monopolistically while prices remain high, but they will revert for a while to Cournot behavior when prices fall. Specifically, it will be assumed that firms agree on a "trigger price" to which they compare the market price when they set their production.[4] Whenever the market price dips below the trigger price while they have been acting monopolistically, they will revert to Cournot behavior for some fixed amount of time before resuming monopolistic conduct.

Suppose that, at a given time, firms are supposed to be colluding (i.e., they expect one another to collude). If a firm produces more than its share of the monopoly output, its net return at that time will increase. However, by increasing the probability that the market price will fall below the trigger price, the firm incurs a greater risk that the industry will enter a reversionary episode during which profits will be low for everyone. For producing its monopolistic share to be the firms' noncooperatively optimal action, the marginal expected loss in future profits from possibly triggering a Cournot reversion must exactly balance (in terms of present discounted value) the marginal gain from over-producing. For appropriate distributions of the demand disturbance, reversionary episodes will sometimes occur without any firm defecting, simply because of low demand. Thus, over a long period, both Cournot behavior and collusive behavior will be observed at various times. In this respect, collusion under uncertainty differs markedly from the collusive equilibria under certainty discussed earlier. The fact that both monopolistic and Cournot performance are observed will make it possible to identify statistically the collusive equilibrium under uncertainty.

We now address the question of exactly what sort of industry our model might appropriately describe. Such an industry would have a structure possessing four features.

First, the industry is presumed to be stable over time. Temporal stability is required if the assumption that firms have rational expectations – an assumption which underlies the use of Nash equilibrium – is to be credible. On a more technical level, it justifies the use of stationary dynamic programming to characterize equilibrium.[5]

Second, output quantity is assumed to be the only decision variable which firms can manipulate. In particular, firms should not be able to engage in product differentiation or have ability to divide their market regionally. With firm decisions so restricted, asymmetric cartel incentive schemes are ruled out. In particular, even if one firm were suspected of violating a cartel agreement, other firms would have no way of isolating it and punishing it differentially.

Third, except for each firm's private knowledge about its present and past production, information about the industry and its environment is public. The Nash equilibrium assumption presupposes that firms have an accurate idea of their competitor's cost functions, for example. Also, for firms to coordinate effectively in keeping track of whether the industry is in a collusive or a reversionary state, they must all observe the realization of a common variable.

Fourth, the information which firms use to monitor whether the cartel is in a collusive or reversionary state must be imperfectly correlated with firms' conduct. Otherwise, if compliance were optimal for firms in collusive periods, reversion would never occur. Price is not the only information variable which could be used for monitoring – price data with correction for a systematic demand component, or market-share information, would also be subject to error. However, this assumption of imperfect information is incompatible with transactions in the industry being few and publicly announced (e.g., with individual contracts being awarded on the basis of sealed-bid auctions) or with completely accurate and current market-share information being available to firms.

In our model firms monitor market price, which imperfectly reflects the output levels of other firms. We assume that the products of the firms are of homogeneous quality, and so they face a common market price. This structure is adopted for expositional ease. An environment in which firms monitored their own market share, which imperfectly reflected the price choices of other firms, would be more in the spirit of Stigler's paradigm.

We now give a formal description of collusion under uncertainty as a Nash equilibrium in contingent strategies. Consider an oligopoly of n firms which produce an undifferentiated product in a stationary and time separable environment. This environment is like that described in Friedman [3], except that demand is subject to multiplicative uncertainty. Specifically, i, j range over *firms* $1, \cdots, n . \pi_i : R_+^2 \to R$ is the *return function* of $i.\pi_i(x_i, p)$ is i's net return from producing x_i units and selling at price p. β is the discount rate. Firms are risk neutral and maximize $E[\sum_{t=0}^{\infty} \beta^t \pi_i(x_{it}, p_t)]$. Observed price $p_t = \theta_t p(\sum_{i=1}^{n} x_{it})$, where $p : R_+ \to R_+$. The random variables θ_t are i.i.d. with c.d.f. F having continuous density f. $E(\theta) = 1$. Each θ_t is a demand shock which firms cannot observe directly.[6]

A *contingent strategy* for firm i is an infinite sequence $s_i = (s_{i0}, s_{i1}, \ldots)$, where S_{iO} is a determinate initial output level x_{i0}, and $S_{it+1} : R_+^{t+1} \to R_+$ determines i's output level at time $t+1$ as a function of past prices by $S_{it+1}(p_0, \ldots, p_t) = x_{it+1}$. The choice of domain reflects the assumption that firms do not observe rivals' production levels directly.

A strategy profile $(S_1, \ldots, S_n)$ determines recursively a stochastic process of prices, which in turn induces a probability distribution on the space of infinite sequences of prices. Expectation with respect to this distribution will be denoted by $E_{s_1} \ldots s_n$.

A *Nash equilibrium* is a strategy profile $(S_1^*, \ldots, S_n^*)$ which satisfies

$$E_{S_1^* \ldots S_i \ldots S_n^*} \left[\sum_{t=0}^{\infty} \beta^t \pi_i (S_{it}(p_0, \ldots, p_{t-1}), p_t) \right]$$

$$\leq E_{S_1^* \ldots S_i^* \ldots S_n^*} \left[\sum_{t=0}^{\infty} \beta^t \pi_i (S_{it}^*(p_0, \ldots, p_{t-1}), p_t) \right]$$

(1)

for all firms i and feasible strategies S_i.

Now consider how the industry might produce at a monopolistic level most of the time (i.e., except during reversionary episodes) in a Nash equilibrium in trigger price strategies. Firms will initially produce their respective shares of this restricted industry output, and will continue to do so until the market price falls below a trigger price $\bar{p}$. Then they will produce Cournot outputs for the duration (we will specify this to be $T - 1$ periods) of a reversionary episode, regardless of what happens to prices during this time. At the conclusion of the episode, T periods after the price drop, they will resume monopolistic production. This will continue until the next time that $p_t < \bar{p}$, and so forth.[7]

Formally, let $y = (y_1, \ldots, y_n)$ be a profile of restricted outputs, and let $z = (z_1, \ldots, z_n)$ be a Cournot output profile. Choose a price level $\bar{p}$ and a length of time T. Define time t to be *normal* if (a) $t = 0$, or (b) $t - 1$ was normal and $\bar{p} \leq P_{t-1}$, or (c) $t - T$ was normal and $p_{t-T} < \bar{p}$. Define t to be *reversionary* otherwise. Define strategies for firms by

$$x_{it} = \begin{cases} y_i & \text{if } t \text{ is normal} \\ z_i & \text{if } t \text{ is reversionary} \end{cases}$$

These are well-defined policy strategies.

Each firm faces a stationary two-state (normal and reversionary) T-stage Markov dynamic programming problem. Its optimal policy is to produce z_i in reversionary periods, and to produce some fixed quantity r in normal periods. Let $V_i(r)$ be the expected discounted present value of firm i if it sets $x_{it} = r$ in normal periods. Define

$$w_i = \sum_{j \neq i} y_j, \gamma_i(r) = E_\theta \pi_i(r, \theta p(r + w_i)) \qquad \delta_i = E_\theta \pi_i \left[z_i, \theta_p \left[\sum_{j \leq n} z_j \right] \right]$$

In normal periods, i anticipates that the aggregate output of the other firms will be w_i, and so $\gamma_i(r)$ is the expected profit of then producing r. The expected profit in reversionary periods is δ_i. Let $Pr(\cdot)$ denote probability with respect to the distribution of θ. We assume that $\gamma_i(y_i) > \delta_i$ for each firm i. Then V_i satisfies the functional equation

$$V_i(r) = \gamma_i(r) + \beta Pr(\bar{p} \leq \theta p(r + w_i)) V_i(r) + Pr(\theta p(r + w_i) < \bar{p}) \left[\sum_{t=1}^{T-1} \beta^t \delta_i + \beta^T V_i(r) \right]$$

(2)

$Pr(\theta p(r + w_i) < \bar{p}) = F(\bar{p}/p(r + w_i))$, so (2) is equivalent to

$$V_i(r) = \frac{\gamma_i(r) + F(\bar{p}/p(r + w_i))((\beta - \beta^T)/(1 - \beta))\delta_i}{1 - \beta + (\beta - \beta^T)F(\bar{p}/p(r + w_i))} \tag{3}$$

$$= \frac{\gamma_i(r) - \delta_i}{1 - \beta + (\beta - \beta^T)F(\bar{p}/p(r + w_i))} + \frac{\delta_i}{1 - \beta}$$

Thus the expected discounted present value of firm i equals what it would be in a Cournot environment, plus the single-period gain in returns to colluding, appropriately discounted. Inequality (1), the defining condition for Nash equilibrium, can now be rewritten

$$V_i(r) \leq V_i(y_i) \qquad \text{for all } r \text{ and } i \tag{4}$$

The first-order condition for (4) is

$$V_i'(y_i) = \qquad 0 \text{ for all } i \tag{5}$$

Using the fact that $(f/g)' = 0$ if and only if $f'g - fg' = 0$, (5) is equivalent to

$$0 = \left[1 - \beta + (\beta - \beta^T)F\left(\bar{p}/p\left(\sum_{j \leq n} y_j\right)\right)\right]\gamma_i'(y_i) \tag{6}$$

$$+ (\beta - \beta^T)f\left(\bar{p}/p\left(\sum_{j \leq n} y_j\right)\right)\left[\bar{p}p'\left(\sum_{j \leq n} y_j\right)\Big/\left(p\left(\sum_{j \leq n} y_j\right)\right)^2\right] \times (\gamma_i(y_i) - \delta_i)$$

for all i.

Equation (6) states that the marginal return to a firm from increasing its production in normal periods ($\gamma_i'(y_i)$) must be offset exactly by the marginal increase in risk of suffering a loss in returns ($\gamma_i(y_i) - \delta_i$) by triggering a reversionary episode. When this condition holds for all firms, n differential constraints are placed on the n-dimensional vector y of restricted outputs in equilibrium. Thus, the assertion that an equilibrium which satisfies an additional constraint exists will require careful justification. In particular, the output profile which maximizes total returns to the industry may not be supportable in equilibrium.[8]

There are two related final observations about the formal model of collusion under uncertainty. First, no firm ever defects from the cartel. More precisely, no firm i has any private information that would lead it to assess its return function π_i more accurately than its competitors do. Thus, every competitor is able to figure out what i will do to maximize profits. The market price reveals information about demand only, and never leads i's competitors to revise their beliefs about how much i has produced. In equilibrium, the frequency of reversion from normal states will be given by $F(\bar{p}/p(\sum y_j))$.

Second, despite the fact that firms know that low prices reflect demand conditions rather than overproduction by competitors, it is rational for them to participate in reversionary episodes.[9] Basically, a reversionary episode is just a temporary switch to a Nash equilibrium in noncontingent strategies. It does not pay any firm to deviate unilaterally from its Nash strategy in this temporary situation, any more than it would if the industry were permanently a Cournot industry. It might be asked why Cournot equilibrium is appropriate at all. If firms know at a particular time that a low price has been observed in the past, and that the cartel has had a perfect record of monopolistic conduct, why do firms not disregard the price and continue to act monopolistically? The answer is that everyone understands the incentive properties of equilibrium. If firms did not revert to Cournot behavior in response to low prices, equation (5) would not hold the rest of the time, so monopolistic behavior would cease to be individually optimal for firms.

We realize that the assumptions about industry structure are quite restrictive. We emphasize that the particular Nash equilibrium we are studying is not the only sort of Nash equilibrium which would be collusive according to the definition offered in this section, and that evidence that this particular Nash equilibrium occurs in a specific industry is not the only evidence relevant to forming an opinion about the extent of collusion in various sectors of the economy. However, even though the direct applicability of our model is severely limited, it would be valuable to examine an industry for which it would be appropriate. We believe that the American rail freight industry in the 1880s was one example of an industry which satisfies our structural conditions quite well. Studies of that industry by Paul MacAvoy [7] and Thomas Ulen [16, 17] have produced qualitative conclusions which are consistent with our model. Recent econometric work by Porter [10] (based on the extensive time series data collected by Ulen) strengthens these conclusions.

3. Price Processes Generated by Collusion

The equilibrium discussed in the preceding section is noteworthy because it reverses the traditional interpretations of a certain kind of industry price pattern. According to these traditional interpretations, an episode in which price drops sharply, remains low for some time, and then sharply rises again without there being an apparent cost or demand shock would indicate one of two possible events. The episode might be a symptom of the predatory reaction of incumbent firms to a threatened entry. Alternatively, it might signal (as in Stigler's theory) a breakdown of a cartel agreement followed by the reestablishment of the agreement. In either case, such evidence would indicate the fragility of collusion among the incumbents. Thus, in the formulation of policy, it has sometimes been argued that intervention to promote competition would likely be redundant in markets where these episodes are already occurring.

In marked contrast, such episodes play an essential role in the maintenance of an ongoing scheme of collusive incentives in the model presented here. While the traditional views would predict the transience of collusion in a market marked by these episodes of price depression, and with the demise of collusion also the cessation of the price instability which it engendered, our model suggests that industries having certain structural characteristics (i.e., the four characteristics enumerated in the previous section) will exhibit price instability as a feature of a stable, time-stationary pattern of prices if its member firms are colluding. This observation raises the question of whether it is possible to estimate consistently, from the stochastic process of prices generated by a collusive equilibrium of the form described in section 2, the trigger price $\bar{p}$ and the reversionary length T which determine that equilibrium. The answer to this question is affirmative. Moreover, there also exists an estimator which is computationally attractive and which has only a small asymptotic bias if the interval between price observations is short relative to both the length of reversionary episodes and the expected length of normal episodes – the situation which one would expect to encounter in an industry where collusion actually did confer significant market power on firms.

While a discussion of estimation *per se* lies beyond the scope of this paper, we characterize in the Appendix the stochastic process of prices which arises in the equilibrium of the model presented in section 2. It can be shown that any data series of prices may be treated as a sample path of a stationary ergodic process. This result provides a foundation for the study of asymptotic properties of estimation of the model, because it justifies the use of the ergodic theorem [1, Theorem 6.28] to generalize the role which the law of large numbers plays in the estimation theory of independent processes.[10] (In particular, the existence of consistent estimators of $\bar{p}$ and T is a consequence of the ergodic theorem.) In the Appendix, the price process will be compared to an alternative process which is a Markov version of the well-known Bernoulli switching process (cf. [6]). It can be shown that a data series of prices may be regarded as a "contaminated sample path" of the alternative process, and the degree of contamination will be computed as a function of the true parameters of the equilibrium.

Appendix

To begin, consider a very general definition of the class of stochastic processes which will be under consideration. The observed price process $\{X_t\}_{t \in \mathbb{N}}$ will be determined by two processes $\{Y_t\}_{t \in \mathbb{N}}$, the price process which would ensue if all periods were normal (i.e., if the industry were to produce the restricted output vector y at all times), and $\{Z_t\}_{t \in \mathbb{N}}$, the price process which would ensue if all periods were reversionary (i.e., if the industry were to operate in Cournot equilibrium at all times, producing the output vector z). Whether the observed price is drawn from the normal or the reversionary distribution is determined by a process $\{W_t\}_{t \in \mathbb{N}}$, which specifies whether the industry is in a normal or a reversionary state. Note that $\{X_t\}_{t \in \mathbb{N}}$ is the only component of the joint process $\{(W_t, X_t, Y_t, Z_t)\}_{t \in \mathbb{N}}$ which is observed.

Formally, define a *switching process* to be determined by a probability space (Ω, β, m), a state space S, a subset $N \subseteq S$, and four sequences of random variables $\{W\} = \{W_t : \Omega \to S\}_{t \in \mathbb{N}}$, $\{X\} = \{X_t : \Omega \to \mathbb{R}\}_{t \in \mathbb{N}}$, $\{Y\} = \{Y_t : \Omega \to \mathbb{R}\}_{t \in \mathbb{N}}$, and $\{Z\} = \{Z_t : \Omega \to \mathbb{R}\}_{t \in \mathbb{N}}$ which satisfy

$\{Y\} \cup \{Z\}$ is a set of independent r.v.s $\hfill$ (A1)

$\{Y\}$ is identically distributed with c.d.f. G $\hfill$ (A2)

$\{Z\}$ is identically distributed with c.d.f. H $\hfill$ (A3)

$\{W\}$ is a Markov process with stationary transition probabilities $\hfill$ (A4)

$\forall t \, S_t \in N \Rightarrow X_t = Y_t$ w.p.1 $\hfill$ (A5)

$\forall t \, S_t \notin N \Rightarrow X_t = Z_t$ w.p.1 $\hfill$ (A6)

Note that the special case of a switching process usually studied occurs when $S = \{0, 1\}, N = \{0\}$, and $\{W\}$ is a Bernoulli process which is independent of $\{Y\} \cup \{Z\}$.

In the case of a collusive price process, G and H are the c.d.f.s of the normal and reversionary price distributions, respectively. $S = \{0, \ldots, T - 1\}$ and $N = \{0\}$ (that is, $W_t = 0$ signifies that the industry is in a normal period at time t.) The Markov process $\{W\}$ is defined recursively by starting with an arbitrary $W_0 : \Omega \to S$, and then imposing

if $W_t(\omega) = 0$ and $Y_t(\omega) \geq \bar{p}$, then $W_{t+1}(\omega) = 0$ (A7)

if $W_t(\omega) = 0$ and $Y_t(\omega) < \bar{p}$, then $W_{t+1}(\omega) = 1$ (A8)

if $W_t(\omega) = k$, $1 \leq k < T - 1$, then $W_{t+1}(\omega) = k + 1$ (A9)

if $W_t(\omega) = T - 1$, then $W_{t+1}(\omega) = 0$ (A10)

The process $\{W\}$ defined by (A7)–(A10) is Markov with stationary transition probabilities because, by (A1) and (A2), $\{Y\}$ is i.i.d. The transition graph of $\{W\}$ is shown in Figure 1, in which each arrow is labeled with its transition probability.

The aim is to show that W_0 can be chosen in such a way that $\{X\}$ will be a stationary ergodic process. Conditions (A5) and (A6) show that $X_t(\omega)$ is a function of $(W_t(\omega), Y_t(\omega), Z_t(\omega))$, so by [1, Proposition 6.32] it is sufficient to show that the joint process $\{W, Y, Z\}$ is ergodic. By [1, Theorem 7.16], this process is ergodic if it is a stationary Markov process having a unique invariant distribution (i.e., a unique distribution such that, if W_1 is defined by (A7)–(A10), then $\{W_0, Y_0, Z_0\}$ and $\{W_1, Y_1, Z_1\}$ have identical joint distributions). This follows from [1, Theorem 7.18], completing the proof that $\{X\}$ is ergodic.

In [10], a maximum likelihood estimator for a switching process somewhat different from (A1)–(A10) is used to study the pre-ICC rail freight cartel in the U.S. That process is obtained by replacing (A1), (A2), and (A7)–(A10) with

$\{Y\}$ is identically distributed with c.d.f.

$$\mathcal{J}(p) = \max\left[(1 - G(\bar{p}))^{-1}(G(p) - G(\bar{p})), 0\right] \qquad \text{(A11)}$$

(that is, $\mathcal{J}$ is the distribution of p according to G, conditional on $p \geq \bar{p}$.)

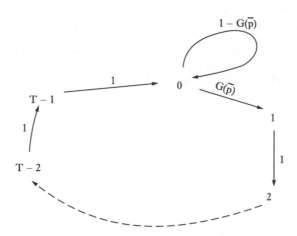

Figure 1.

$\{W\} \cup \{Y\} \cup \{Z\}$ is a set of independent random variables   (A12)

and

$\{W\}$ is a stationary Markov process having the transition probabilities specified by Figure 2.[11]

(A13)

That is, this process is defined by relaxing the usual assumption that the switching process is Bernoulli, while retaining the assumption that it is independent of the underlying variables which determine the observed prices. Call the process defined by (A1)–(A10) the *price process*, and that defined by (A3)–(A5), (A11)–(A13) the *approximating process*.

The advantage of the approximating process over the price process is that it permits adaptation of much of the work which has been done on maximum-likelihood estimation of the Bernoulli switching process. In particular, it is possible both to compute the ML estimator economically and to appeal to theoretical results asserting its consistency and asymptotic normality. The crucial question raised by use of the approximating process is of how seriously misspecified it is as a model for data actually generated by the price process. We now address this question.

The basis for comparing the two processes is that, given a stationary price process $\{W, X, Y, Z\}$ with parameters $(\bar{p}, T, G, H)$, a stationary approximating process $\{W', X', Y', Z'\}$ with the same parameters can be obtained by a kind of censoring. Looking at the matter from the opposite perspective, the sample paths of Z can be viewed as a contaminated (by reinsertion of the censored observations) version of the approximating process. The extent of the contamination is easily computable from the parameters of the process. If it is slight, and if the ML estimator is regarded as robust, then the ML estimator of the approximating process should also be considered to have small asymptotic bias as an estimator of the price process.

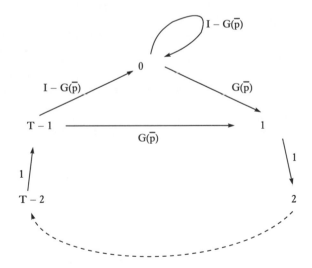

Figure 2.

The approximating process $\{W', X', Y', Z'\}$ is defined from $\{W, X, Y, Z\}$ simply by censoring the triggering events (i.e., the events in which $W_t = 0$) and $Y_t < \bar{p}$). Formally, this is done by means of a sequence of stopping times $\{\tau_t : \Omega \to \mathbb{N}\}_{t \in \mathbb{N}}$. Define

$$\tau_0(\omega) = \begin{cases} 1 & \text{if W0 } (\omega) = 0 \text{ and } Y_0(\omega) < \bar{p} \\ 0 & \text{otherwise} \end{cases} \tag{A14}$$

and

$$\tau_{t+1}(\omega) = \begin{cases} \tau_t(\omega) + 2 & \text{if } W_{\tau_t(\omega)+1}(\omega) = 0 \text{ and } Y_{\tau_t(\omega)+1}(\omega) < \bar{p} \\ \tau_t(\omega) + 1 & \text{otherwise} \end{cases} \tag{A15}$$

Then define

$$W_t'(\omega) = W_{\tau_t(\omega)}(\omega) \qquad X_t'(\omega) = X_{\tau_t(\omega)}(\omega) \qquad \text{and} \qquad Z_t'(\omega) = Z_{\tau_t(\omega)}(\omega) \tag{A16}$$

Finally, take a set $\{Y_t''\}_{t \in \mathbb{N}}$ which are identically distributed with c.d.f. $\mathcal{J}$ and such that $\{Y\} \cup \{Z\} \cup \{Y''\}$ is independent, and define

$$Y_t'(\omega) = \begin{cases} Y_{\tau_t(\omega)}(\omega) & \text{if } W_t'(\omega) = 0 \\ Y_t''(\omega) & \text{if } W_t'(\omega) > 0 \end{cases} \tag{A17}$$

(N.B. The definition of the observed component $\{X'\}$ of the approximating process is the same whether $\{Y'\}$ is defined by (A17) or by $Y_t'(\omega) = Y_{\tau_t(\omega)}(\omega)$ for all ω. The reason for using (A17) is both to satisfy (A11) and to keep $\{W'\}$ and $\{Y'\}$ independent so that (A12) is satisfied. Under the simpler definition, (A15) would have introduced dependency between them.)

The effect of (A15) and (A16) is to continue to let a low realization of Y_t be the event which causes the state to change from zero to one, but to censor this event if it occurs. Thus the dependence of W_{t+1} on $\{W_t, Y_t\}$ in the price process is removed, and (A12) holds. By the strong Markov property [1, Proposition 7.8], the censored process is a stationary Markov process, so (A13) holds, that is, $\{W', X', Y', Z'\}$ is an approximating process with parameters $(\bar{p}, T, \mathcal{J}, H)$.

It remains to calculate how much censoring of the price series $X(\omega)$ is required to construct the approximating series $X'(\omega)$. (Alternatively, how much contamination of $X'(\omega)$ is required to reconstruct $X(\omega)$?) Formally, what is $\lim_{t \to \infty} (\tau_t(\omega) - t)/\tau_t(\omega)$? If this quotient is close to zero for almost every ω, then the asymptotic bias of the approximating-process ML estimator applied to date generated by the price process should be small.

To calculate the quotient, first define $\sigma(W, Y) = 1$ if $W = 0$ and $Y < \bar{p}$, and $\sigma(W, Y) = 0$ otherwise. By (A14) and (A15), $\tau_t(\omega) = t + \sum_{u=0}^{\tau_t(\omega)} \sigma(W_u(\omega), Y_u(\omega))$, or

$$\frac{\tau_t(\omega) - t}{\tau_t(\omega)} = \frac{1}{\tau_t(\omega)} \sum_{u=0}^{\tau_t(\omega)} \sigma(W_u(\omega), Y_u(\omega)) \tag{A18}$$

By the ergodic theorem,

$$\lim_{t \to \infty} \frac{1}{\tau_t(\omega)} \sum_{u=0}^{\tau_t(\omega)} \sigma(W_u(\omega), Y_u(\omega)) = m(\{W_0 = 0, Y_0 < \bar{p}\}) G(\bar{p}) \text{ a.s.} \tag{A19}$$

(Recall that m is the stationary measure on Ω.) Combining (A18) and (A19), and appealing to the fact that the stationarity of the price process forces W_0 and Y_0 to be independent yields

$$\lim_{t \to \infty} \frac{\tau_t(\omega) - t}{\tau_t(\omega)} = m(\{W_0 = 0\})G(\bar{p}) \text{ a.s.} \tag{A20}$$

The calculation of $m(\{W_0 = 0\})$ is an easy matter. For $1 \le k < T - 1$, by (A9) and stationarity, we have

$$m(\{W_0 = k\}) = m(\{W_1 = k + 1\}) = m(\{W_0 = k + 1\}) \tag{A21}$$

Also, by (A7) and stationarity, we have

$$m(\{W_0 = 1\}) = m(\{W_1 = 1\}) = m(\{W_0 = 0\})G(\bar{p}) \tag{A22}$$

Since the probabilities of the states sum to unity, (A21) and (A22) yield

$$m(\{W_0 = 0\}) = [1 + (T - 1)G(\bar{p})]^{-1} \tag{A23}$$

Thus, by (A22) and (A23),

$$\lim_{t \to \infty} \frac{\tau_t(\omega) - t}{\tau_t(\omega)} = G(\bar{p})[1 + (T - 1)G(\bar{p})]^{-1} \tag{A24}$$

For example, consider a hypothetical industry in which a trade association disseminates weekly price data to its members, that is, the appropriate interpretation of a period in the discrete-time model is one week. Suppose that the parameters of this industry were estimated using the ML estimator for the approximating process, with the results that $\hat{G}(\hat{p}) = 0.025$ and $\hat{T} = 11$. Since the expected duration of an episode of normal conduct is $(G(\bar{p}))^{-1}$, these estimates indicate that a reversionary episode occurs once a year on average, and lasts ten weeks. Thus there is (on average) one price observation a year (that being the observation of the price which triggers the reversionary episode), which would not be included if the approximating process were really generating the data. This is a contamination ratio of one in fifty, or $(0.025)[1 + 0.25]^{-1}$ which is the expression obtained from (A24).

The ML estimator is computed by dividing the data into two subsamples, one of which is presumed to have been drawn from distribution G and the other from H, and then estimating these distributions from the respective subsamples. If the "contaminating" observations were to comprise equal proportions of the two subsamples, then each subsample is being estimated with 2 percent contamination, and one might reasonably suppose the discrepancy between the price process and the approximating process to be rather small. If all of the "contaminating" observations were assigned to the subsample presumed to be generated by normal conduct, then this subsample would have $2\frac{1}{2}$ percent contamination, which still might reasonably be ignored. However, if the "contaminating" observations were all included in the subsample presumed to reflect reversionary conduct, then that subsample would have a 10 percent contamination level. In this worst case, it is easy to imagine that the observations actually drawn from the lower tail of G would seriously bias the estimation of H.

The parameter estimates for the example just given are approximately the same as those reported by Porter [10] for the rail freight industry. Thus, while the foregoing analysis is insufficiently precise to rule out the worst-case assumption concerning bias of his estimator relative to the price process, it has shown that under more optimistic assumptions the bias would plausibly be slight. While acknowledging that there is an inevitable element of subjective judgment in a situation such as this, we suggest that Porter's study provides presumptive evidence that the rail freight industry may have exemplified the kind of equilibrium which has been studied here.

Notes

1   These problems, involving both the nature of the cross-industry data and also the logical difficulties of using it as a basis for inference are described in the essays by J. McGee, H. Demsetz, and L. Weiss in [4].

2   A referee has suggested that the U.S. steel industry employed such an enforcement device during the first half of this century.

3   For example, a "phases of the moon" system has been used to allocate low-bidding privileges in the high voltage switchgear industry. (See Scherer [12, Chapter 6].)

4   It is logically possible for this agreement to be a tacit one which arises spontaneously. Nevertheless, in view of the relative complexity of the conduct to be specified by this particular equilibrium and of the need for close coordination among its participants, it seems natural to assume here that the equilibrium arises from an explicit agreement.

5   Radner [11] considers the case of time-average utilities. His work relies essentially on the measurability of utility in the tail sigma-field of payoffs, which asymptotic-average utility satisfies. In contrast, discounted utility is not measurable with respect to the tail sigma-field, so that our work is not directly comparable to [11].

6   James Friedman has suggested to us that the variables θ_t might alternatively be specified to be a martingale, so that the prices p_t would also be a martingale. This property ought to be satisfied if the good is a durable, or if consumption is perfectly substitutable across times. We retain the i.i.d. specification which makes the analysis simpler, but acknowledge that it is restrictive.

7   For simplicity, we are considering only the simplest variant of a trigger price strategy. For example, firms might condition T on the amount by which $\bar{p}$ exceeds the observed market price.

8   In [9] it is shown that, for symmetric firms under imperfect price information, the output profile for normal periods which will maximize discounted industry profits in a noncooperative equilibrium in trigger price strategies is different from the profile which would be chosen if the industry were a monopoly. In other words firms forgo some profits in normal periods in order to reduce the frequency and duration of reversion needed to provide appropriate incentives, if $\bar{p}$ and T are chosen to maximize expected discounted profits subject to the incentive compatibility constraint (5).

9   To be precise, we argue here that the equilibrium is perfect or sequentially rational. A formal statement and proof of this assertion are given in [5].

10 A stochastic process is ergodic if every event definable in terms of the tails of sample paths (e.g., the set of sample points having convergent paths) has probability zero or one. The ergodic theorem extends the strong law of large numbers to such processes.

11 Using extensive information including industry prices, macroeconomic variables, and firm-specific quantity data, Porter estimates the structural equations of a detailed industry model. His method may be viewed as an imposition of prior constraints on the reduced-form estimation described here.

References

1   Breiman, L. (1968): *Probability*. Reading: Addison-Wesley.

2   Bresnahan, T. (1982): "The Oligopoly Solution Concept is Identified," *Economics Letters*, 10, 87–92.

3   Friedman, J. W. (1971): "A Non-cooperative Equilibrium for Supergames," *Review of Economic Studies*, 28, 1–12.

4   Goldschmid, H. J., H. M. Mann, and J. F. Weston (eds) (1974): *Industrial Concentration: The New Learning*. Boston: Little, Brown and Co.

5   Green, E. J. (1980): "Non-cooperative Price Taking in Large Dynamic Markets," *Journal of Economic Theory*, 22, 155–82.

6   Kiefer, N. M. (1980): "A Note on Switching Regressions and Logistic Discrimination," *Econometrica*, 48, 1065–9.

7   MacAvoy, P. W. (1965): *The Economic Effects of Regulation*. Cambridge: MIT Press.

8   Osborne, D. K. (1976): "Cartel Problems," *American Economic Review*, 66, 835–44.

9   Porter, R. H. (1983): "Optimal Cartel Trigger-Price Strategies," *Journal of Economic Theory*, 29, 313–38.

10 ——: "A Study of Cartel Stability: The Joint Executive Committee 1880–1886," *Bell Journal of Economics*, 14 (1983), 301–14.

11 Radner, R. (1980): "Collusive Behavior in Noncooperative Epsilon-Equilibria With Long But Finite Lives," *Journal of Economic Theory*, 22, 136–54.

12 Scherer, F. M. (1980): *Industrial Market Structure and Economic Performance*, 2nd edn. Chicago: Rand McNally.

13 Spence, M. (1978): "Tacit Coordination and Imperfect Information," *Canadian Journal of Economics*, 11, 490–505.

14 —— (1978): "Efficient Collusion and Reaction Functions," *Canadian Journal of Economics*, 11, 527–33.

15 Stigler, G. J. (1964): "A Theory of Oligopoly," *Journal of Political Economy*, 72, 44–61.

16 Ulen, T. S. (1978): "Cartels and Regulation," unpublished Ph.D. dissertation, Stanford University.

17 —— (1980): "The Market for Regulation: The ICC from 1887 to 1920," *American Economic Review, Papers and Proceedings*, 70, 306–10.

CHAPTER FOUR

A Supergame-Theoretic Model of Price Wars During Booms

JULIO J. ROTEMBERG AND GARTH SALONER

Source: American Economic Review, 1986, 76, 390–407.

This paper explores the response of oligopolies to fluctuations in the demand for their products. In particular, we argue on theoretical grounds that implicitly colluding oligopolies are likely to behave more competitively in periods of high demand. We then show that, in practice, during those periods, various oligopolistic industries tend to have relatively low prices. The few price wars which have been documented also seem to have taken place during periods of high demand. Finally, we study the possibility that this oligopolistic behavior has macroeconomic consequences. We show that it is possible that the increase in competitiveness that results from a shift in demand towards goods produced by oligopolies may be sufficient to raise the output of all sectors.

We examine implicitly colluding oligopolies of the type introduced by James Friedman (1971). These obtain above competitive profits by the threat of reverting to competitive behavior whenever a single firm does not cooperate. This threat is sufficient to induce cooperation by all firms. It must be pointed out that there are usually a multitude of equilibria in such settings. Following Robert Porter (1983a), we concentrate on the best equilibrium of this type the oligopoly can achieve.

The basic point of this paper is that oligopolies find implicit collusion of this type more difficult when their demand is relatively high. The reason for this is simple. When demand is relatively high and price is the strategic variable, the benefit to a single firm from undercutting the price that maximizes joint profits is larger. A firm that lowers its price slightly gets to capture a larger market until the others are able to change their prices. On the other hand, the punishment from deviating is less affected by the state of demand if punishments are meted out in the future, and demand tends to return to its normal level. Thus, when demand is high, the benefit from deviating from the output that maximizes joint profits may exceed the punishment a deviating firm can expect.

What should the oligopoly do when it cannot sustain the level of output that maximizes joint profits? It basically has two alternatives. The first is to give up any attempt to collude when demand is high. This leads to competitive outcomes in booms. Such competitive outcomes are basically price wars. The second, more profitable, alternative is to settle for the highest level of profits (lowest level of output) which is sustainable. As the oligopoly attempts to sustain lower profits, the benefits to a deviating firm fall. Thus, for a given punishment, there is always a level of profits low enough that no single firm finds it profitable to deviate. As demand increases, the oligopoly generally finds that the incentive to deviate is such that it must content itself with outcomes further and further away from those that maximize joint profits.

Our strongest results are for the case in which prices are the strategic variables and marginal costs are constant. Then, increases in demand beyond a certain point actually lower the oligopoly's prices monotonically. This occurs for the following reason: Suppose the oligopoly were to keep its prices constant and only increase output in response to higher demand. Then industry profits would increase when demand goes up. However, in this case, a deviating firm can capture the entire industry profits by shading its price slightly. Therefore, constant prices would increase the incentive to deviate. Reductions in price are needed to maintain implicit collusion.

It might be thought that if firms are capacity constrained in booms, they are essentially unable to deviate, so that the oligopoly doesn't have to cut prices in booms. Indeed, we find that when marginal costs increase with output, a more plausible way of capturing the importance of capacity, our results are weaker. Nonetheless, even in this case the equilibrium can be more competitive when demand is high, whether output or price is the strategic variable.

Any theory whose implication is that competitive behavior is more likely to occur in booms must confront the industrial organization folklore which is that price wars occur in recessions. This view is articulated for example in F. M. Scherer (1980). Our basis for questioning it is not only theoretical. Indeed, it is possible to construct models in which recessions induce price wars.[1,2] In a model with imperfect observability of demand, Edward Green and Porter (1984) show that price wars occur when demand is unexpectedly low. Then, firms switch to competition because they confuse the low price that prevails in equilibrium with cheating on the part of other firms.

Whether competition is more pervasive in booms or busts is an empirical question. While we do not conclusively settle this empirical issue, a brief analysis of some related facts seems to provide more support for our theory than for the industrial organization folklore.

First, at a very general level, it certainly appears that business cycles are related to sluggish adjustment of prices (see Rotemberg, 1982, for example). Prices rise too little in booms and fall too little in recessions. If recessions tended to produce massive price wars, this would be an unlikely finding. Second, more specifically, we find that both Scherer's evidence and our own study of the cyclical properties of price-cost margins are consistent with our theory. The ratio of prices to our measure of marginal cost tends to be countercyclical in more concentrated industries. Also the price wars purported to have happened in the automobile industry (Timothy Bresnahan, 1981) and the railroad industry (Porter, 1983b) occurred in periods of high demand. Finally, since Scherer singles out the cement industry as having repeated breakups of its cartel during recessions, we study the cyclical properties of cement prices. To our surprise, cement prices are strongly countercyclical, even though cement, as construction as a whole, has a procyclical level of output.

Up to this point we have focused on the effect of changes in demand like those that could be induced by business cycles on oligopolistic sectors. We go on to examine whether these oligopolistic responses to changes in demand themselves have aggregate consequences. In particular, we consider the general equilibrium effects of a shift in demand towards an oligopolistic sector. We show that in a very simplified two-sector model, the ensuing reduction in the oligopoly's price can lead the other sector to raise its output as well. This occurs in our model because the other sector, which is competitive, uses the oligopoly's output as an input.

The paper proceeds as follows. Section 1 presents our theory of oligopoly under fluctuating demand. Section 2 contains the empirical regularities which lend some plausibility to our theory. Section 3 considers the general equilibrium model which forms the basis of our discussion of macroeconomics, and conclusions are drawn in section 4.

1. Equilibrium in Oligopolistic Supergames with Demand Fluctuations

We consider N symmetric firms producing a homogeneous good in an infinite-horizon setting. It is well-known that infinitely lived oligopolies of this type are usually able to sustain outcomes in any period that strictly dominate the outcome in the corresponding one-period game, even if firms cannot sign binding contracts. In order to achieve this, the equilibrium strategies must involve a mechanism that deters an individual firm from "cheating" (by expanding output or by shading prices). One such mechanism, and one that has been fruitfully employed in theoretical models,[3] is the use of punishments against the defecting firm in periods following the defection. If these punishments are large enough to outweigh the gain from cheating, then the collusive outcome is sustainable.

In order for the equilibrium strategies to be sequentially rational,[4] however, it must be the case that if a defection actually occurs, the nondefecting firms are willing to mete out the proposed punishment. A simple and often employed way (see Green and Porter (1984), for example) to ensure sequential rationality is for punishments to involve playing the equilibrium strategies from the one-period game for some fixed period of time. We also restrict attention to strategies of this kind. In addition to their simplicity and conformity with the literature, they are also optimal punishments in some cases.[5] The major departure of our model from those that have previously been studied is that we allow for observable shifts in industry demand. We write the inverse demand function as $P(Q_t, \varepsilon_t)$ where Q_t is the industry output in period t and ε_t is the realization at t of $\tilde{\varepsilon}$, the random variable denoting the observable demand shock. We assume that P is increasing in ε_t, that $\tilde{\varepsilon}$ has domain $[\underline{\varepsilon}, \bar{\varepsilon}]$ and a distribution function $F(\varepsilon)$, and that these are the same across periods (i.e., shocks are independently and identically distributed). We denote firm i's output in period t by q_{it} so that

$$Q_t = \sum_{i=1}^{N} q_{it}$$

The timing of events is as follows: At the beginning of each period, all firms learn the realization of $\tilde{\varepsilon}$ (more precisely ε_t becomes common knowledge). Firms then simultaneously choose the level of their choice variable (price or quantity). These choices then determine the outcome for that period in a way that depends on the choice variable: in the case of quantities, the price clears the market given Q_t; in the case of prices, the firm with the lowest price sells as much as it wants at its quoted price; the firm with the second lowest price then supplies as much of the remaining demand at its quoted price as it wants, and so on. The strategic choices of all the firms then become common knowledge and this one-period game is repeated.

The effect of the observability of ε_t and the key to the difference between the model and its predecessors is the following: the punishments that firms face depend on the future realizations of $\tilde{\varepsilon}$. The expected value of such punishments therefore depends on the expected value of $\tilde{\varepsilon}$. However, the reward for cheating in any period depends on the observable ε_t. We show that for a wide variety of interesting cases, the reward for cheating from the joint profit-maximizing level is monotonically increasing in ε_t. If ε_t is large enough, the temptation to cheat outweighs the punishment.[6] The observability of ε_t allows the oligopoly to recognize this fact. Thus an implicitly colluding oligopoly may settle on a profit below the fully collusive level in periods of high demand to adequately reduce the temptation to cheat. Such moderation of its behavior tends to lower prices below what they would otherwise be, and may indeed cause them to be lower than for states with lower demand. We illustrate this phenomenon for both the case in which prices and the case in which quantities are the strategic variables.

1.1. Prices as strategic variables

We begin with an analysis of the case in which marginal costs (and average costs) are equal to a constant c. This is an appropriate assumption if capacity is very flexible in the short run, if firms produce at under capacity in all states, or if firms produce to order and can accumulate commitments for future deliveries. There always exists an equilibrium in which all the firms set $P = c$ in all periods. Firms then expect future profits to be zero whether they cooperate at time t or not. Accordingly the game at time t is essentially a one-shot game in which the unique equilibrium has all firms setting $P = c$. In what follows we concentrate instead on the equilibria that are optimal for the firms in the industry.

We begin by examining the oligopoly's options for each value of ε_t. Figure 1 shows the profits of each firm, Π, as a function of the aggregate output. Q_t, for a variety of values of ε_t. These profit loci are drawn assuming each firms supplies $1/N$ of Q_t. As ε_t increases, the price for each Q_t rises so that profits are increasing in ε_t. The term $\Pi^m(\varepsilon_t)$ denotes the profit of an individual firm in state ε_t if the firms each produce q^m which equals $1/N$ of the joint profit-maximizing output, Q_t^m. Notice that $\Pi^m(\varepsilon_t)$ is increasing in ε_t since profits are increasing in ε_t even holding Q_t constant.

If a firm deviates from this proposed outcome, it can earn approximately $N\Pi^m$ by cutting its price by an arbitrarily small amount and supplying the entire market demand. Firm i would therefore deviate from the joint profit-maximizing output if

$$N\Pi^m(\varepsilon_t) - K > \Pi^m(\varepsilon_t) \tag{1}$$

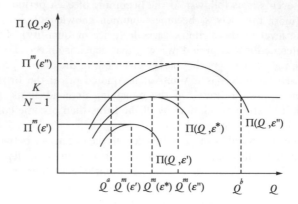

Figure 1.   Profits of the oligopoly

that is, if

$$\Pi^m(\varepsilon_t) > K/(N-1)$$

where K is the punishment inflicted on a firm in the future if it deviates at time t. It is thus the difference between the expected discounted value of profits from $t+1$ on, if the firm goes along, and the expected discounted value of profits if it deviates.

For the moment we will take K to be exogenous and independent of the value of ε_t at the point that cheating occurs. (We will prove the latter shortly and also endogenize K.)

Since $\Pi^m(\varepsilon_t)$ is increasing in ε_t there is some highest level of demand shock, $\varepsilon_t^*(K)$, for which $(N-1)\Pi^m(\varepsilon_t^*) = K$. We consider separately the cases in which ε_t is below and above ε_t^*. In the former case no individual firm has an incentive to deviate from the joint profit-maximizing outcome. Therefore, if we define $\Pi^s(\varepsilon_t, \varepsilon_t^*)$ to be the highest profits the oligopoly can obtain, $\Pi^s(\varepsilon_t, \varepsilon_t^*) = \Pi^m(\varepsilon_t)$. In the latter case, however, the monopoly profits are not sustainable since any individual firm would have an incentive to cheat. In this case the maximum sustainable profits are given by $(N-1)\Pi^s(\varepsilon_t, \varepsilon_t^*) = K$.

In summary,

$$\Pi^s(\varepsilon_t, \varepsilon_t^*) = \begin{cases} \Pi^m(\varepsilon_t) & \text{for } \varepsilon_t \leq \varepsilon_t^* \\ \Pi^m(\varepsilon_t^*) = \frac{K}{N-1} & \text{for } \varepsilon_t > \varepsilon_t^* \end{cases} \tag{2}$$

From (2) it is clear that the sustainable profits are higher, the higher is the punishment. Since we want to concern ourselves with equilibrium strategies that are optimal for the oligopoly, we concentrate on profits that are as large as possible. These involve the lowest possible present discounted value of profits if the firm deviates. Thus charging a price equal to c in all periods following a defection seems optimal, particularly since such punishments never need to be implemented in equilibrium.[7]

However, there are several related reasons why such infinite-length punishments are unlikely to be carried out in practice. First, once the punishment period has begun, the oligopoly would prefer to return to a more collusive arrangement. Second, if the industry members (whether they be firms or even management teams) change over time, shorter punishments seem more compelling. Finally, one can think the reason why firms succeed in punishing each other at all (even though punishments are costly) is because of the anger generated when a rival cheats on the implicit agreement. This anger, as any "irritational" emotion, may be short-lived.

The presence of relatively short punishments is important to our analysis because they make K low. Otherwise the inequality in (1) is always satisfied, that is, in all states of nature the punishment exceeds the benefits from cheating from the collusive price. This is particularly true if the length of the period in which a firm can undercut its competitor's price successfully is short. Thus the inequality in (1) is also more likely to be violated for high ε_t if firms are fairly committed to their current prices as they would be if adjusting prices were costly.

While short periods of punishment are realistic, infinite punishments are simpler. Thus we actually use infinite punishments and capture their relatively small importance by assuming that δ, the factor used to discount future profits, is small.[8] With price equal to marginal cost, the punishment is equal to the discounted present value of profits that the firm would have earned had it not deviated, or

$$K = \frac{\delta}{1-\delta} \int_{\underline{\varepsilon}}^{\bar{\varepsilon}} \Pi^s(\varepsilon, \varepsilon_t^*) dF(\varepsilon) \tag{3}$$

Even if we allow K to depend on ε_t, the right-hand side of (2) is independent of ε_t. Therefore the punishment is indeed independent of the state.[9] Using (2) we can rewrite equation (3) as

$$K(\varepsilon_t^*) = \frac{\delta}{1-\delta} \left[\int_{\underline{\varepsilon}}^{\varepsilon_t^*} \Pi^m(\varepsilon) dF(\varepsilon) + (1 - F(\varepsilon_t^*))\Pi^m(\varepsilon_t^*) \right] \tag{4}$$

This gives a mapping from the space of possible punishments into itself: a given punishment implies a cutoff ε_t^* from (2) which in turn implies a new punishment from (4).

The equilibria of the model are the fixed points of this mapping. The equilibrium that is optimal for the oligopoly is the one corresponding to the fixed point with the highest value of K.

It remains to provide sufficient conditions for the existence of a fixed point, that is, to show there exists an $\varepsilon^* \in (\underline{\varepsilon}, \bar{\varepsilon})$ for which (2) and (4) hold. Let ε_t' be a candidate for such an ε_t^* and define

$$g(\varepsilon_t') = \Pi^m(\varepsilon_t') - K(\varepsilon_t')/(N-1) \tag{5}$$

We need to show there exists an $\varepsilon_t' \in (\underline{\varepsilon}, \bar{\varepsilon})$ such that $g(\varepsilon_t') = 0$. Using (4) and (5):

$$g(\varepsilon) = \Pi^m(\varepsilon) \left(1 - \frac{\delta}{(1-\delta)(N-1)} \right)$$

which is negative if

$$N < 1/(1 - \delta) \tag{6}$$

In other words, for N small enough relative to the discount factor δ, it is possible to obtain the monopoly outcome in at least the lowest state of demand. As N gets bigger, or as firms discount the future more (δ smaller), the punishments become less important and (6) fails.

On the other hand:

$$g(\bar{\varepsilon}) = \Pi^m(\bar{\varepsilon}) - \delta/[(N-1)(1-\delta)] \times \int_{\underline{\varepsilon}}^{\bar{\varepsilon}} \Pi^m(\varepsilon)dF(\varepsilon)$$

which is positive if

$$\Pi^m(\bar{\varepsilon})/\int_{\underline{\varepsilon}}^{\bar{\varepsilon}} \Pi^m(\varepsilon)dF(\varepsilon) > \delta/[(1-\delta)(N-1)] \tag{7}$$

This condition ensures that the monopoly outcome is not the only solution in every state. This holds when there is sufficient dispersion in the distribution of profit-maximizing outputs. If there is no dispersion, the left-hand side of (7) equals one. Then (7) becomes $N > 1/(1 - \delta)$, the opposite of (6). So, in the absence of dispersion, if (6) holds there is never an incentive to cheat. When there is some dispersion, the left-hand side of (7) exceeds one, making it possible for (6) and (7) to hold simultaneously.

If conditions (6) and (7) are satisfied we have: (a) $g(\varepsilon'_t)$ is continuous, (b) $g(\bar{\varepsilon}) > 0$, and (c) $g(\underline{\varepsilon}) < 0$, which imply the existence of an $\varepsilon'_t \in (\underline{\varepsilon}_t, \bar{\varepsilon}_t)$ such that $g(\varepsilon'_t) = 0$ as required.

This equilibrium has several interesting features. In particular, for $\varepsilon_t > \varepsilon^*_t$ it can be shown that the higher is demand (the higher is ε_t), the higher is equilibrium output and the lower is the equilibrium price. When ε_t exceeds ε^*_t, $\Pi^s = Q_t(P_t - c)$ is constant. Also, Q_t must be as high as possible without reducing firm profits below the sustainable level. In other words, firms must be at Q^b_t in Figure 1 and not at Q^a_t. Otherwise a deviating firm can earn more than $N\Pi^s$ by cutting its price.

Since output is above Q^m_t, profits fall as Q_t rises as can be seen in Figure 1. On the other hand, for a constant Q_t, $Q_t(P_t - c)$ rises as ε_t rises since P_t is larger. Therefore an increase in ε_t must be accompanied by an increase in Q_t. Since increases in ε_t raise profits, increases in Q_t, which lower profits, are required to restore the original level of profits. Moreover, if $Q_t(P_t - c)$ is constant while Q_t rises, P_t must fall. So the oligopoly must actually lower its prices to deter deviations.

The model has some intuitive comparative statics. When N increases and when δ decreases, ε^*_t falls. In both cases, the gains from cheating rise relative to cooperative profits, either because the punishments are distributed among more firms, or because they are discounted more. Thus, the oligopoly must content itself with fewer states in which the monopolistic output is sustained. This can be seen by the following three-part argument.

First, the fact that $g(\bar{\varepsilon})$ is positive ensures that g is increasing in ε at the largest value of ε' for which $g(\varepsilon') = 0$. Second, for fixed Q_t and ε_t, the profits of a single firm are one-Nth of the total profits of the industry. Thus, for a fixed ε_t^*, equation (4) implies that K and $\Pi^m(\varepsilon_t^*)$ are inversely proportional to N. Therefore, increases in N raise g since they raise $\Pi^m(\varepsilon_t^*)$ relative to $K/(N-1)$, that is, the temptation to cheat increases. Similarly, a decrease in δ raises g since K falls. Finally, the increases in g brought about either by an increase in N or by a reduction in δ implies that ε_t^* must fall to restore equilibrium.

As mentioned above, punishments are never observed in equilibrium. Thus the oligopoly doesn't fluctuate between periods of cooperation and noncooperation as in the models of Green and Porter. To provide an analogous model, we would have to further restrict the strategy space so that the oligopoly can choose only between the joint monopoly price and the competitive price. Such a restriction is intuitively appealing since the resulting strategies are much simpler and less delicate. With this restriction on strategies, the firms know that when demand is high the monopoly outcome cannot be maintained. They therefore assume that the competitive outcome will emerge, which is sufficient to fulfill their prophecy. In many states of the world, the oligopoly will earn lower profits than under the optimal scheme we have analyzed. As a result, since punishments are lower, there will be fewer collusive states than before. There will still be some cutoff, ε_t^*, that delineates the cooperative and noncooperative regions. In contrast to the optimal model, however, the graph of price as a function of state will exhibit a sharp decline after ε_t^* with $P = c$ thereafter.

The above models impose no restrictions on the demand function except that it be downward sloping and that demand shocks move it outwards. However, the model does assume constant marginal costs. The case of increasing marginal cost is more complex than that of constant marginal costs for four reasons: 1) A firm that cheats by price cutting does not always want to supply the industry demand at the price it is charging. Specifically, it would never supply an output at which its marginal cost exceeded the price. 2) Cheating now pays off when $\Pi^d(\varepsilon_t, P) > \Pi^s(\varepsilon_t) + K$, where Π^d is the profit to the firm that defects when its opponents charge P. However, Π^d is no longer equal to $(N-1)\Pi^s$. Therefore, the sustainable profit varies by state. 3) With increasing marginal cost, cheating can occur by raising as well as by lowering prices. If its opponents are unwilling to supply all of demand at their quoted price, a defecting firm is able to sell some output at higher prices. 4) The one-shot game with increasing marginal cost does not have an equilibrium in which price is equal to marginal cost. Indeed the only equilibrium is a mixed-strategy equilibrium.[10]

A number of results can nonetheless be demonstrated for an example in which demand and marginal costs are linear:[11]

$$P = a + \varepsilon_t - bQ_t \tag{8}$$

$$c(q_{it}) = cq_{it} + dq_{it}^2/2 \tag{9}$$

It is straightforward to show that in this example, cheating becomes more desirable as ε_t rises.[12] So, as before, if the oligopoly is restricted to either collude or compete, high ε_ts generate price wars. Alternatively the oligopoly can pick prices P^s which just deter potentially deviating firms. These prices equate Π^s, the profits from going along, with $\Pi^d - K$ where K is the expected present value of Π^s minus the profits obtained when all firms revert to noncooperative behavior.

It is thus possible to calculate the P^ss, the sustainable prices, numerically. For a given value of K one first calculates in which states monopoly is not sustainable. For those states the sustainable price must then be calculated. Since both the sustainable profit. Π^s, and the profit to a deviating firm, Π^d, are quadratic in P^s, this involves solving a quadratic equation. The relevant root is the one that yields the highest value of Π^s that is consistent with the deviating firm planning to meet demand or equating price to marginal cost.

The resulting P^ss then enable us to calculate a new value for K: the one that corresponds to the calculated P^ss.[13] We can thus iterate numerically on K starting with a large number. Since larger values of K induce more cooperation, the first K which is a solution to the iterative procedure is the best equilibrium the oligopoly can enforce with competitive punishments. Figure 2 graphs these equilibrium prices and compares them to the monopoly prices as a function of states for a specific configuration of parameters. In particular ε_t is uniformly distributed over $\{0, 1, \ldots, 80\}$.

As before, the price rises monotonically to ε_t^* and then falls. The major difference here is that eventually the price begins to rise again. The explanation for this is straightforward. In a state with a high value of ε_t, a firm that deviates by shading its price slightly is unwilling to supply all that is demanded at its lower price. Instead, it will supply only to the point where its marginal cost and its price are equal. Now consider such a state and one with slightly more demand. If the oligopoly kept the same price in both states, an individual firm would find that its payoff from deviating is the same in both states (since it would supply to price equals marginal cost in both), but that its profits from going along are higher in the better state. Thus the oligopoly is able to sustain a higher price in the better state.

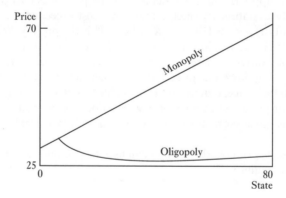

Figure 2.   Prices as strategic variables
Parameters: $a = 60, b = 1, c = 0, d = 1/3, \delta = 0.7, N = 5$

1.2. Quantities as strategic variables

There are two differences between the case in which quantities are used as strategic variables and the case in which prices are. First, when an individual firm considers deviations from the behavior favored by the oligopoly, it assumes that the other firms will keep their quantities constant. The residual demand curve is therefore obtained by shifting the original demand curve to the left by the amount of the rivals' combined output. Second, when firms are punishing each other the outcome in punishment periods is the Cournot equilibrium.

The results we obtain with quantities as strategic variables are somewhat weaker than those we obtained with prices. In particular, it is now not true that any increase in demand (even with constant marginal costs) leads to a bigger incentive to deviate from the collusive level of output. However, we show that when demand and marginal costs are linear, this is the case. We also show with that example that increases in demand can, as before, lead monotonically to "more competitive" behavior.

To see that increases in demand do not necessarily increase the incentive to deviate, we consider the following counterexample. Suppose that demand in states ε_t' and ε_t'' gives rise to the residual demand curves faced by an individual deviating firm in Figure 3. These demand curves are merely horizontal translations by $(N-1)q^m$ of the depicted residual demand curves. The monopoly price, P^m, is the same in both states because there is no demand at prices above P^m. Although these demand curves may seem somewhat contrived, they will suffice to establish a counterexample. They can be rationalized by supposing that there is a substitute good that is perfectly elastically supplied at price P^m.

A deviating firm chooses output to maximize profits given these residual demand curves. Suppose that the maximum profits are achieved at output D and price P^d for state ε_t''. For this to be a worthwhile deviation, it must be the case that the revenues from the extra sales due to cheating (CD) are greater than the loss in revenues on the old sales from the decrease in price from $P(Q^m, \cdot)$ to P^d. But (except for a horizontal translation) the firm faces the same residual demand curve in both states. Thus by selling at P^d, the extra sales due to cheating are the same at $\varepsilon_t'(AB)$ as at $\varepsilon_t''(CD)$. Moreover the loss in revenue on old sales is strictly smaller at ε_t'. Therefore the firm has a strictly greater incentive to deviate in state ε_t' than in state ε_t''.

The above counterexample exploits the assumed structure of demand only to establish that the collusive price is the same in both states. We have therefore also proved a related proposition: for any demand function, if the oligopoly keeps its price constant when ε_t

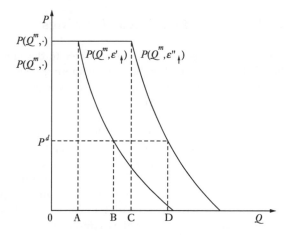

Figure 3. The incentive to deviate with quantities as strategic variables

increases (thus supplying all the increased demand), the incentive to cheat is reduced when demand shifts horizontally. This is why the oligopoly is always able to increase the price as the state improves.

Now consider the case in which demand and marginal costs are linear as in (8) and (9). There an increase in ε_t always leads to a bigger incentive to deviate from the collusive output.[14] As in the previous subsection, if the only options for the oligopoly are to either compete or collude, price wars emerge when demand is sufficiently high. Alternatively, the oligopoly can choose a level of output that will just deter firms from deviating when demand is high. The equilibrium levels of output can be obtained numerically in a manner analogous to the one used to calculate the equilibrium sustainable prices in the previous subsection.

Figure 4 plots the ratio of this equilibrium price to the monopoly price as a function of ε_t. While the equilibrium price rises as ε_t rises, it can be seen that beyond a certain ε_t the ratio of equilibrium price to monopoly price falls monotonically.

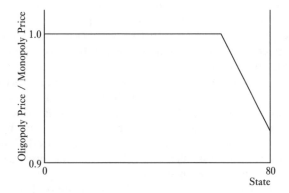

Figure 4.   Quantities as strategic variables
Parameters: $a = 60, b = 1, c = 0, d = 1/3, \delta = 0.7, N = 5$

2. A Survey of Related Empirical Findings

The theory presented in the previous section runs counter to the industrial organization folklore. This folklore is best articulated in Scherer, who says: "Yet it is precisely when business conditions really turn sour that price cutting runs most rampant among oligopolists with high fixed costs" (1980, p. 208).

Given the pervasiveness of this folklore, it is incumbent upon us to at least provide some fragments of evidence which are consistent with our theory. There are at least three kinds of data capable of shedding light on whether prices tend to be low in concentrated industries when their demand is high. First, there is the cyclical pattern of prices in concentrated industries relative to other prices. We can see whether these relative prices tend to be pro- or countercyclical. Second, a similar analysis can be applied to the cyclical pattern of prices in concentrated industries relative to their costs. Finally, there are the documented episodes of price wars. Here what is relevant is whether they occurred in periods of high or low demand. In this section, we reexamine existing data of all three types. It must be pointed out at the outset, however, that this analysis is not a direct empirical test of the model itself, but only a cursory analysis of its most striking implication. The need for such direct tests is suggested by our findings since they largely bear out this implication.

2.1. The cyclical properties of cement prices

Scherer cites three industries whose experience is presented as supporting the folklore: rayon, cement and steel. For rayon he cites a study by Jesse Markham (1952) which shows mainly that the nominal price of rayon fell during the Great Depression. Since broad price indices fell during this period this is hardly proof of a price war. Rayon has since been replaced by other materials making it difficult to use postwar data to check whether any real price-cutting took place during post-war recessions. For steel Scherer admits the following: "... up to 1968 and except for some episodes during the 1929–38 depression, it was more successful than either cement or rayon in avoiding widespread price deterioration, even when operating at less than 65% of capacity between 1958 and 1962" (1980, p. 210).

This leaves cement. We study the cyclical properties of real cement prices below. We collected data on the average price of portland cement from the *Minerals Yearbook* (Bureau of Mines). We then compare this price with the producer price index (PPI) and the price index of construction materials published by the Bureau of Labor Statistics. Regressions of the yearly rate of growth of real cement prices on the contemporaneous rate of growth of *GNP* are reported in Table 1.

As the table shows, the coefficient of the rate of growth of *GNP* is always meaningfully negative. A 1 percent increase in the rate of growth of *GNP* leads to a 0.5–1.0 percent fall in the price of cement. To test whether the coefficients are significant, the regression equations must be quasi differenced since their Durbin-Watson (*D-W*) statistics are small. Once this is done we find the coefficients are all significantly different from zero at the 5

Table 1   The cyclical properties of cement prices (yearly data from 1947 to 1981)[a]

Coefficient	Dependent variable			
	P^c/PPI	P^c/PPI	P^c/P^{con}	P^c/P^{con}
Constant	0.025	0.025	0.038	0.037
	(0.010)	(0.012)	(0.007)	(0.008)
GNP	−0.438	−0.456	−0.875	−0.876
	(0.236)	(0.197)	(0.161)	(0.149)
ρ		0.464		0.315
		(0.173)		(0.183)
R^2	0.10	0.15	0.48	0.52
$D-W$	1.03	1.73	1.28	1.92

[a] P^c is the price of cement, PPI is the producer price index, and P^{con} is the price index of construction materials. Standard errors are shown in parentheses.

percent level. More casually, the price of cement relative to the index of construction prices rose in the recession year 1954, while it fell in the boom year 1955. Similarly, it rose during the recession year 1958 and fell in 1959. These results show uniformly that the price of cement has a tendency to move countercyclically as our theory predicts for an oligopoly.

These results are of course not conclusive. First, it is possible that increases in *GNP* lower the demand for cement relative to that for other goods. Without a structural model, which is well beyond the scope of this paper, this question cannot be completely settled. However, the rate of growth of the output of the cement industry has a correlation of 0.69 with the rate of growth of *GNP*, and of 0.77 with the rate of growth of construction activity which is well known to be procyclical. Second, our regressions do not include all the variables one would expect to see in a reduced form. Thus the effect of *GNP* might be proxying for an excluded variable like the capacity of cement mines. This variable would probably be expected to exercise a negative effect on the real price of cement. It must be pointed out, however, that capacity itself is an endogenous variable which also responds to demand. It would thus be surprising if enough capacity were built in a boom to more than offset the increase in demand. If anything, the presence of costs of adjusting capacity would make capacity relatively unresponsive to increases in *GNP*.

2.2. *The cyclical properties of price-cost margins*

In the industrial organization literature there have been a number of studies that have attempted to measure the cyclical variations in price-cost margins. Usually these are measured by sales minus payroll and material costs divided by sales. This is a crude approximation to the Lerner Index which has the advantage of being easy to compute. Indeed, Scherer cites a number of studies which analyzed the cyclical variability of these margins in different industries. These studies have led to somewhat mixed conclusions. However, Scherer concludes: "The weight of the available statistical evidence suggests that concentrated industries do exhibit somewhat different pricing propensities over time than their atomistic counterparts. They reduce prices (and more importantly) price-cost margins by less in response to a demand slump and increase them by less in the boom phase" (1980, p. 357). This does not fit well with the folklore which would predict that, on average, prices would tend to fall more in recessions the more concentrated is the industry. On the other hand, a recent paper by Ian Domowitz, Glenn Hubbard, and Bruce Petersen (1986a) finds more procyclical movements of price-cost margins in concentrated industries.

Price-cost margins can only be interpreted as the Lerner Index if labor costs are proportional to output. However, there is a large fixed component to labor costs. Thus when output rises, the ratio of labor costs to revenues falls and, *ceteris paribus*, price-cost margins rise. Therefore, if the fixed labor cost tends to be higher in concentrated industries, one expects to find their price-cost margins to be relatively procyclical.

We therefore also study some independent evidence on margins. Michael Burda (1984) reports correlations between employment and real product wages in various 2-digit industries. These real product wages are given by the average hourly wage paid by the industry divided by the value-added deflator for the industry. They can be interpreted as a different crude measure of marginal cost over prices. Their disadvantage over the tradi-tional price-cost margin is that, unlike the latter, to interpret them in this way requires not only that materials be proportional to output, but also that materials costs be simply passed through as they would in a competitive industry with this cost structure. On the other hand, their advantage over the traditional measure is that they remain valid when some of the payroll expenditure is a fixed cost as long as, at the margin, labor has a constant marginal product. Moreover, it turns out that if the marginal product of labor actually falls as employment rises, our evidence provides even stronger support for our theory.

The correlations reported by Burda for the real product wage and employment using detrended yearly data from 1947 to 1978 are reported in Table 2, which also reports the average four-firm concentration ratio for each 2-digit industry. This average is obtained by weighting each 4-digit SIC code industry within a particular 2-digit SIC code industry by its sales in 1967. These weights were then applied to the 1967 four-firm concentration indices for each 4-digit SIC code industry obtained from the Census.[15]

At first glance it is clear from Table 2 that more concentrated industries like motor vehicles and electrical machinery tend to have positive correlations while less concentrated industries like leather, food, and wood products tend to have negative correlations. Statistical testing of this correlation with the concentration index is, however, somewhat delicate. That is because our theory does not predict that an industry which is 5 percent more concentrated than another will reduce prices more severely in a boom. On the contrary, a fully fledged monopoly will always charge the monopoly price which usually

Table 2   Concentration and the correlation between real wages and employment

SIC Number	Industry Designation	Correlation	Concentration
Durables Manufacturing			
24	Lumber and Wood Products	−0.33	17.6
25	Furniture and Fixtures	−0.18	21.6
32	Stone, Clay and Glass	0.39	37.4
33	Primary Metals	0.32	42.9
34	Fabricated Metal Industries	0.23	29.1
35	Machinery except Electrical	0.12	36.3
36	Electrical and Electronic Equipment	0.34	45.0
371	Motor Vehicles and Equipment	0.19	80.8
372–9	Other Transportation Equipment	0.02	50.1
38	Instruments and Related Products	−0.36	47.8
Nondurables Manufacturing			
20	Food and Kindred Products	−0.30	34.5
21	Tobacco Manufactures	−0.64	73.6
22	Textile Mill Products	0.04	34.1
23	Apparel and Related Products	−0.53	19.7
26	Paper and Allied Products	−0.42	31.2
27	Printing and Publishing	0.40	18.9
28	Chemical and Allied Products	−0.03	49.9
29	Petroleum and Coal Products	−0.48	32.9
30	Rubber	0.16	69.1
31	Leather and Leather Products	−0.44	24.5

increases when demand increases. All our theory says is, that as soon as an industry becomes an oligopoly it becomes likely that it will cut prices in booms.

Naturally the concentration index is not a perfect measure of whether an industry is an oligopoly. Indeed, printing has a low concentration index even though its large components are newspapers, books, and magazines that are in fact highly concentrated, once location in space or type is taken into account. Nonetheless, higher concentration indices are at least indicators of a smaller number of important sellers. Glass is undoubtedly a more oligopolistic industry than shoes. So we classify the sample into relatively unconcentrated and relatively concentrated and choose, somewhat arbitrarily, as the dividing line the median concentration of 35.4. This lies between food and nonelectrical machinery. Table 3 is the resulting 2×2 contingency table.

An alternative table can be obtained by neglecting the three observations whose correlations are effectively zero. These are sectors 22, 28, and 372–9. Their correlations are at most equal in absolute value to one-third of the next lowest correlation. Then the contingency table has, instead of the values 7: 3: 3: 7, the values 7: 2: 2: 6.

It is now natural to test whether concentrated and unconcentrated industries have the same ratio of positive correlations to negative ones against the alternative that this ratio is significantly higher for concentrated industries. The χ^2 test of independence actually only tests whether the values are unusual under the hypothesis of independence without focusing on our particular alternative. It rejects the hypothesis of independence with 92 percent confidence using the values of Table 3 and with 97 percent confidence using the values 7: 2: 2: 6. This test is, however, likely to be flawed for the small sample we consider. Fisher's test would appear more appropriate since it is an exact test against the alternative that more concentrated sectors have more positive correlations. With this test the hypothesis that the ratio of positive correlations is the same can be rejected with 91 percent confidence using the data of Table 3 and with 96 percent confidence using 7: 2: 2: 6.[16]

These regularities should be contrasted to the predictions of the standard theory of labor demand. In this theory, employment rises only when the real product wage falls. This occurs in both monopolistic and competitive industries as long as there are diminishing returns to labor. Therefore, the finding that the product wage rises when employment rises suggests the widespread price cutting our theory implies.

There is an alternative classical explanation for our findings. This explanation relies on technological shocks. These shocks can, in principle, either increase or decrease the demand for labor by a particular sector. If they increase the demand and the sector faces an upward-sloping labor supply function, employment and real wages can both increase. The difficulty with this alternative explanation is that the sectors with positive correlations do not appear to be those which a casual observer would characterize as having many technological shocks of this type. In particular, stone, clay and glass, printing

Table 3   Concentration/correlation contingency table

	Unconcentrated	Concentrated	Total
Negatively correlated	7	3	10
Positively correlated	3	7	10
Total	10	10	20

and publishing, and rubber appear to be sectors with fairly stagnant technologies. On the other hand, instruments and chemicals may well be among those whose technology has been changing the fastest.

2.3. Actual price wars

There have been two recent studies showing that some industries alternate between cooperative and noncooperative behavior. The first is due to Bresnahan (1981). He studies the automobile industry in 1954, 1955, and 1956, and attempts to evaluate the different interpretations of the events of 1955. That year production of automobiles climbed by 45 percent only to fall 44 percent the following year. Bresnahan formally models the automobile industry as choosing prices each year for a given set of models offered by each firm. He concludes that the competitive model of pricing fits the 1955 data taken by themselves while the collusive model fits the 1954 and 1956 data. Those two years exhibited at best sluggish GNP growth. GNP fell 1 percent in 1954 while it rose 2 percent in 1956. Instead, 1955 was a genuine boom with GNP growing 7 percent.[17] Insofar as cartels can only sustain either competitive or collusive outcomes, this is what our theory predicts. Indeed, in our model, the competitive outcomes will be observed only in booms.

Porter (1983b) studies the railroad cartel which operated in the 1880s on the Chicago-New York route. He uses time-series evidence to show that some weeks were collusive while others were not.

We present some of his findings in the first three columns of Table 4. The first column shows an index of cartel nonadherence estimated by Porter. He shows that this index parallels quite closely the discussions in the *Railway Review* and in the *Chicago Tribune* which are reported by Thomas Ulen (1978). The second column reports rail shipments of wheat from Chicago to New York. The third column shows the percentage of wheat shipped by rail from Chicago relative to the wheat shipped by both lake and rail. The fourth column presents the national production of grains estimated by the Department of Agriculture. Finally the last column represents the number of days between April 1 and December 31 that the Straits of Mackinac remained closed to navigation. (They were always closed between January 1 and March 31).

Table 4 Railroads in the 1880s

	Estimated Nonadherence	Rail Shipments (Million bushels)	Fraction Shippedby Rail	Total Grain Production (Billion Tons)[a,b]	Days Lakes Closed 4/1–12/31[a]
1880	0.00	4.73	22.1	2.70	35
1881	0.44	7.68	50.0	2.05	69
1882	0.21	2.39	13.8	2.69	35
1883	0.00	2.59	26.8	2.62	58
1884	0.40	5.90	34.0	2.98	58
1885	0.67	5.12	48.5	3.00	61
1886	0.06	2.21	17.4	2.83	50

[a] Obtained from the Chicago Board of Trade (1880–86).
[b] This total is constructed by adding the productions of wheat, corn, rye, oats, and barley in tons.

The three years in which the most severe price wars occurred were 1881, 1884, and 1885. Those are also the years in which rail shipments are the largest, both in absolute terms and relative to lake shipments. This certainly does not suggest that these wars occurred in periods of depressed demand. However, shipments may have been high only because the railroads were competing even though demand was low. To analyze this possibility, we report the values of two natural determinants of demand. The first is the length of time during which the lakes were closed. The longer the lakes remained closed, the larger was the demand for rail transport. The lakes were closed the longest in 1881 and 1885. These are also the years in which the index of cartel nonadherence is highest. In 1883 and 1884, the lakes remained closed only slightly less time than in 1885 and yet there were price wars only in 1884. The second natural determinant of demand, total grain production, readily explains the anomalous behavior of 1883. In 1883, total grain production was the second lowest in the entire period and in particular, was 12 percent lower than in 1884. This might have depressed demand so much that, in spite of the lake closings, total demand for rail transport was low enough to warrant cooperation.[18]

In summary, the years in which the cartel was unable to collude effectively were also years in which demand seems to have been high.

3. General Equilibrium Consequences

So far we have considered only the behavior of an oligopoly in isolation. To study the aggregate consequences of this behavior, we need to model the rest of the economy. We consider a two-sector general equilibrium model in which the first sector is competitive while the second is oligopolistic. There is also a competitive labor market. To keep the model simple, it is assumed that workers have a horizontal supply of labor at a wage equal to P_{1t}, the price of the competitive good. Since the model is homogeneous of degree zero in prices, the wage itself can be normalized to equal one. So the price of the good produced competitively must also equal one. This good can be produced with various combinations of labor and good 2. In particular the industrywide production function of good 1 is given by

$$Q_{1t} = \alpha Q_{21t} - \frac{\beta Q_{21t}^2}{2} + \gamma L_{1t} - \frac{\xi L_{1t}^2}{2} \tag{10}$$

where Q_{1t} is the output of the competitive sector at t, Q_{21t} is the amount of good 2 employed in the production of good 1 at t and L_{1t} is the amount of labor used in the production of good 1. Since the sector is competitive the price of each factor and its marginal revenue product are equated. Thus:

$$L_{1t} = (\gamma - 1)/\xi \tag{11}$$
$$P_{2t} = \alpha - \beta Q_{21t} \tag{12}$$

On the other hand the demand for good 2 by consumers is given by

$$P_{2t} = n - m Q_{2ct} + e_t$$

where Q_{2ct} is the quantity of good 2 purchased by consumers, n and m are parameters, and e_t is an independently and identically distributed random variable. Total demand for good 2, therefore, is given by

$$P_{2t} = a + \varepsilon_t - bQ_{2t}$$
$$a = (n\beta + m\alpha)/(m + \beta)$$
$$\varepsilon_t = e_t\beta/(m + \beta) \tag{13}$$
$$b = m\beta/(m + \beta)$$

Note that equation (13) is identical to equation (8). To continue the parallel with our sections on partial equilibrium, we assume that the labor requirement to produce Q_{2t} is

$$L_{2t} = cQ_{2t} + (d/2)Q_{2t}^2$$

which implies that, as before, marginal cost is $c + dQ_{2t}$. The model would be unaffected if good 1 were also an input into good 2 since P_{1t} is always equal to the wage. If sector 2 behaved competitively marginal cost would equal P_{2t}. Then output of good 2 would be Q_{2t}^c while price would be P_{2t}^c:

$$Q_{2t}^c = (a + \varepsilon_t - c)/(b + d)$$
$$P_{2t}^c = ((a + \varepsilon_t)d + bc)/(b + d)$$

An increase in ε_t raises both the competitive price and the competitive quantity of good 2. By (12), less of good 2 will be used in the production of good 1 thus leading to a fall in the output of good 1. So, a shift in tastes raises the output of one good and lowers that of the other. The economy implicitly has, given people's desire for leisure, a production possibility frontier.

Similarly, if sector 2 always behaves like a monopolist, increases in ε_t raise both P_{2t} and Q_{2t} thus lowering Q_{1t}. Once again shifts in demand are unable to change the levels of both outputs in the same direction. On the other hand, if the industry behaves like the oligopoly considered in the previous sections, an increase in ε_t can easily lead to a fall in the relative price of good 2.[19] This occurs in three out of the four scenarios considered in section 1. It occurs when the unsustainability of monopoly leads to competitive outcomes whether the strategic variable is price or output as long as increases in ε_t make monopoly harder to sustain. It also always occurs when the strategic variable is prices and the oligopoly plays an optimal supergame. The decrease in P_{2t} in turn leads firms in the first sector to demand more of good 2 as an input and to increase their output. So, a shift in demand towards the oligopolistic goods raises all outputs much as all outputs move together during business cycles.[20]

A number of comments deserve to be made about this model. First, our assumption that the real wage in terms of good 1 is constant does not play an important role. In equilibrium the reduction in P_{2t} raises real wages thus inducing workers to work more even if they have an upward-sloping supply schedule for labor. Whether this increased supply of labor would be sufficient to meet the increased demand for employees by sector 2 in unclear. If it wasn't, the wage would have to rise in terms of good 1. More interestingly, if the increased supply of labor was large, P_{1t} would have to rise thus increasing employment also in sector 1. This would lead to an expansion even if good 2 was not an input into good 1. This pattern of price movements is consistent with the evidence on the correlation between product wages and employment presented in section 2.

Second, the model can easily be made consistent with the procyclical variation of profits. Even though sector 2 reduces the margin between price and marginal cost as output expands, the difference between revenues and total costs can increase as long as there are fixed costs.

Third, the analysis leaves unexplained the causes of the shifts in sectoral demands. To make sense of actual business cycles, within the context of the models described here, one would have to relate these shifts in demand to changes in the money supply and interest rates which are highly correlated with cyclical fluctuations. While the connection between financial variables and shifts in demand is beyond the scope of this paper, it must be noted that such shifts form part of the popular discussion of the early stages of recoveries. At that point, consumers' desires for cars and other durables picks up.

Our model exhibits a variety of somewhat Keynesian features. First, changes in aggregate output are related to fluctuations in demand and not, unlike in classical models, to changes in supply conditions such as productivity or labor supply.[21] Second, the model has the potential for providing an explanation for the stickiness of prices discussed, for example, in Rotemberg (1982). Suppose that increases in ε_t are correlated with increases in the money supply. Then increases in output are correlated with increases in the money supply. As long as increases in output raise the demand for real money balances, increases in the money supply will be correlated with increases in real money balances. Prices do not rise equiproportionately. Third, we can discuss the multiplier in the context of our model. This concept reflects the idea that increases in demand lead output to rise which then leads to further increases in demand. Here a shift in demand towards an oligopolistic sector can raise that sector's output, lower its prices and thus raise national income. In turn, this increased national income can lead to increases in the demand for other goods produced in other oligopolistic markets, thus lowering their prices and raising their output as well.

4. Conclusions

The data we study show moderate support for the theories developed in this paper. This suggests that both the theories and their empirical validation deserve to be extended.

The theory of oligopoly might be extended to include also imperfectly observable demand shifts, prices and outputs of the type studies by Green and Porter. The advantage of introducing unobservable shifts in demand is that these can induce reversions to punishing behavior even when all firms are acting collusively. A natural question to ask is whether reversions to punishing behavior that result from unobservable shocks are more likely when everybody expects the demand curve to have shifted out. Unfortunately, this appears to be a very difficult question to answer. Even the features of the optimal supergame without observable shocks discussed in Porter (1983a) are hard to characterize. Adding the complication that both the length of the punishment period as well as the price that triggers a reversion depend on observable demand is a formidable task.

In this paper we considered only business cycles that are due to the tendency of oligopolists to act more competitively when demand shifts towards their products. An alternative and commonly held view is that business cycles are due to changes in aggregate demand which do not get reflected in nominal wages. In that case, a decrease in aggregate demand raises real wages, thereby reducing all outputs. In our theory of oligopoly, firms tend to collude more in these periods. Hence recessions are not only bad because output is low, but also because microeconomic distortions are greater. This suggests that stabilization of output at a high level is desirable because it reduces these distortions.

On the other hand, the business cycles discussed here do not necessarily warrant stabilization policy. While models of real business cycles merely feature ineffective stabilization policies, here such policies might actually be harmful. Booms occur because, occasionally, demand shifts towards oligopolistic products. In these periods the incentive to deviate from the collusive outcome is greatest, because the punishment will be felt in periods that, on average, have lower demand and hence lower profits. If, instead, future demand were also known to be high, the threat of losing the monopoly profits in those good periods might well be enough to induce the members of the oligopoly to collude now. So, if demand for the goods produced by oligopolies were stable they might collude always, leaving the economy in a permanent recession.[22] Therefore the merits of stabilization policy hinge crucially on whether business cycles are due to shifts in demand unaccompanied by nominal rigidities, or whether they are due to changes in aggregate demand accompanied by such rigidities. Disentangling the nature of the shifts in the demand faced by oligopolies therefore seems to be a promising line of research.

Much work also remains to be done empirically validating our model itself. In section 2 we presented a variety of simple tests capable of discriminating between the industrial organization folklore and our theory. Since none of them favored the folklore, it may well be without empirical content. On the other hand, our theory deserves to be tested more severely. First, a more disaggregated study of the cyclical properties of price-cost margins seems warranted. Unfortunately, data on value-added deflators do not appear to exist at a more disaggregated level so a different methodology will have to be employed. Second, our theory has strong implications for the behavior of structural models of specific industries. The study of such models ought to shed light on the extent to which observable shifts in demand affect the degree of collusion.

Finally, our theory can usefully be applied to other settings. Consider, in particular, the game between countries as they set their tariffs. In standard models, unilateral tariffs may be desirable either as devices to exercise monopsony power or, with fixed exchange rates, to increase employment. The noncooperative outcome in a game between the countries may have very little international trade. In a repeated game, more international trade can be sustained by the threat to curtail trade further. If unilateral trade barriers become more attractive in recessions (because the gains in employment they induce are valued more), the equilibrium will have trade wars in states of depressed demand.

Notes

1 If firms find borrowing difficult, recessions might be the ideal occasions for large established firms to elbow out their smaller competitors.

2   There are also two alternative reasons why prices may be lower when demand is high. First, firms may be charging the monopoly price in the face of short-run increasing returns to scale. The existence of such increasing returns strike us as unlikely. When production is curtailed this is usually done by temporary closings of plants or reductions of hours worked. These reductions would always start with the most inefficient plants and workers thus suggesting at most constant returns to labor in the short run. Second, as argued by Joseph Stiglitz (1984) using a setup similar to the incomplete information limit pricing model of Paul Milgrom and John Roberts (1982), limit pricing may be more salient in booms if the threat of potential entry is also greater at that time.

3   See, for example, Friedman (1971), Green and Porter (1984), and Roy Radner (1980).

4   Sequentially rational strategies are analyzed in games of incomplete information by David Kreps and Robert Wilson (1982). For the game of complete information that we analyze we use Reinhard Selten's concept of subgame perfection (1965).

5   When quantities are the strategic variable, Dilip Abreu (1982) shows that punishments can be more severe while still being credible. However, he requires that those firms which defect from the punishment be punished in turn, and so on. This considerably complicates the analysis.

6   In informal discussions, Moses Abramowitz (1938) and Mordecai Kurz (1979) recognize the link between short-run profitability and the sustainability of collusive outcomes. The relationship between profits, demand, and costs, however, is not made explicit.

7   Note that $P = c$ is the highest possible punishment for the oligopoly. If P is below c, firms make losses and will choose not to participate.

8   An infinite punishment period and low value of δ is only equivalent to a finite punishment period and high value of δ if the length of the punishment is independent of ε_t.

9   If, instead, the length of the punishment did depend on ε_t, naturally K would depend on ε_t as well.

10   See Eric Maskin (1984) for a proof that a mixed-strategy equilibrium exists.

11   In this case an increase in ε_t can directly be interpreted as either a shift outwards in demand or a reduction in c, that part of marginal cost which is independent of q. This results from the fact that the profit functions depend on ε_t only through $(a + \varepsilon_t - c)$.

12   The proof of this is contained in an appendix, available on request.

13   In order to do this, however, the profits accruing to firms during the punishment period must be calculated. Rather than attempting to solve for the mixed-strategy equilibria, we used the profits corresponding to price equal to marginal cost. In fact, those profits are lower than in the mixed-strategy equilibrium which means that actual punishments are less severe than we have assumed. However, as we show below, even in that case monopoly is often sustainable only in states of low demand. In any case, the qualitative features of the model are unaffected by this assumption, only the actual value of ε_t^* is affected.

14   The proof of this is also contained in the appendix available on request.

15   When constructing these aggregate concentration indices we systematically neglected the 4-digit SIC code industries which ended in 99. These contain miscellaneous or "not classified elsewhere" items whose concentration index does not measure market power in a relatively homogeneous market.

16   These results are consistent with evidence by Domowitz, Hubbard, and Petersen (1986b) which shows that value-added deflators tend to be more countercyclical in concentrated industries.

17   It must be noted that the focus of Bresnahan's study is the 1955 model year which doesn't coincide with the calendar year. Nonetheless his data on prices correspond to April 1955. By that time the boom was well under way.

18   Our analysis uses annual aggregates rather than the weekly data used by Porter (1985). As the estimate of cartel nonadherence in Table 2 shows, however, the price wars in 1881, 1884, and 1885 did not last the entire year. Indeed, in each of those years there were at least two separate

episodes of price wars. Using only annual data we are unable to show that each of the price wars occurred during a high demand period. Some relevant evidence is provided in a more recent study by Porter (1985). There, using weekly data, he finds that price wars were more likely to occur in any period the larger the quantity sold in the previous period. This suggests that price wars tended to begin when firms expected unusually high demand.

19 This fall in the price of a good in response to an increase in its demand would also characterize industries with increasing returns to scale which, for some reason, equated price to average costs.

20 Business cycles are persistent and thus cannot adequately be modeled as resulting from the independently and identically distributed shifts considered in previous sections. However, what is necessary for prices to be low when demand is high is only that the punishments for deviating be carried out mostly in states of lower demand. This is likely to happen even if demand follows a fairly general stationary process.

21 Keynesian models usually focus on changes in "aggregate demand" whereas our model hinges on changes in relative demand. However, in practice, when households demand more, they demand disproportionately more from certain oligopolistic sectors such as the consumer durables sector. Therefore, the distinction between the two types of changes in demand may not be very important.

22 For the examples in Figures 3 and 4, this occurs as long as $\delta \geq 0.8$ when prices are the strategic variables, or $\delta \geq 0.25$ when quantities are the strategic variables.

References

Abramowitz, Moses (1938): "Monopolistic Selling in a Changing Economy," *Quarterly Journal of Economics*, 52, February, 191–214.

Abreu, Dilip (1982): "Repeated Games with Discounting: A General Theory and an Application to Oligopoly," mimeo., Princeton University, December.

Bresnahan, Timothy F. (1981): "Competition and Collusion in the American Automobile Industry: The 1955 Price War," mimeo., Stanford University, February.

Burda, Michael C. (1984): "Dynamic Labor Demand Schedules Reconsidered: A Sectoral Approach," mimeo., Harvard University, June.

Bureau of Mines *Minerals Yearbook*, Washington, various years.

Chicago Board of Trade 1880–1886 *Annual Reports*, Chicago.

Domowitz, Ian, Hubbard, R. Glenn and Petersen, Bruce (1986a): "Business Cycles and the Relationship between Concentration and Price-Cost Margins," *Rand Journal of Economics*, 17, Spring, 1–17.

——, ——, and ——(1986b) "Cyclical Variation in Industry Price-Cost Margins: Price and Cost Channels," mimeo., Northwestern University.

Friedman, James W. (1971): "A Non-Cooperative Equilibrium for Supergames," *Review of Economic Studies*, 38, January, 1–12.

Green, Edward J. and Porter, Robert H. (1984): "Noncooperative Collusion under Imperfect Price Information," *Econometrica*, 52, January, 87–100.

Kreps, David and Wilson, Robert (1982): "Sequential Equilibrium," *Econometrica*, 50, July, 863–94.

Kurz, Mordecai (1979): "A Strategic Theory of Inflation," IMSSS Technical Report No. 283, April.

Markham, Jesse W. (1952): *Competition in the Rayon Industry*, Cambridge: Harvard University Press.

Maskin, Eric (1984): "Equilibrium with Price-Setting Duopolists," mimeo., MIT.

Milgrom, Paul and Roberts, John (1982): "Limit Pricing and Entry under Incomplete Information: An Equilibrium Analysis," *Econometrica*, 50, March, 443–60.

Porter, Robert H. (1983a): "Optimal Cartel Trigger-Price Strategies," *Journal of Economic Theory*, 29, April, 313–38.

—— (1983b): "A Study of Cartel Stability: The Joint Economic Committee, 1880–1886," *Bell Journal of Economics*, 14, Autumn, 301–14.

—— (1985): "On the Incidence and Duration of Price Wars," *Journal of Industrial Economics*, 33, June, 415–26.

Radner, Roy (1980): "Collusive Behavior in Noncooperative Epsilon-Equilibria of Oligopolies with Long but Finite Lives," *Journal of Economic Theory*, 22, April, 136–54.

Rotemberg, Julio J. (1982): "Sticky Prices in the United States," *Journal of Political Economy*, 90, December, 1187–211.

Scherer, F. M. (1980): *Industrial Market Structure and Economic Performance*, 2nd edn, Boston: Houghton-Mifflin.

Selten, Reinhard (1965): "Spieltheoretische Behandlung eines Oligopolsmodells mit Nachfrageträgheit," *Zeitschrift für die Gesamte Staatswissenschaft*, 121, 301–24 and 667–89.

Stiglitz, Joseph E. (1984): "Price Rigidities and Market Structure," *American Economic Review Proceedings*, 74, May, 350–5.

Ulen, Thomas S. (1978): "Cartels and Regulation," unpublished doctoral dissertation, Stanford University.

CHAPTER FIVE

Multimarket Contact and Collusive Behavior

B. Douglas Bernheim and Michael
D. Whinston
Source: *Rand Journal of Economics*, 1990, 21, 1–26.

In this article, we examine the effect of multimarket contact on the degree of cooperation that firms can sustain in settings of repeated competition. We isolate conditions under which multimarket contact facilitates collusion and show that these collusive gains are achieved through modes of behavior that have been identified in previous empirical studies of multimarket firms.

1. Introduction

Traditional analyses of industrial behavior typically link the exercise of market power in an industry to internal features such as demand conditions, concentration, and barriers-to-entry. Nevertheless, some economists have remained concerned that external factors may also play a significant role in determining the level of competitiveness in any particular industry. One aspect of this concern relates to the potential effects of multimarket contact between firms. The possibility that such contact could foster anticompetitive outcomes was first raised in 1955 by Corwin Edwards, who said

> When one large conglomerate enterprise competes with another, the two are likely to encounter each other in a considerable number of markets. The multiplicity of their contact may blunt the edge of their competition.[1]

This potential for "mutual forebearance" is not limited to conglomerates but exists for any multiproduct firms, including "single-product" firms that operate in a number of distinct geographic markets.

Despite the obvious prevalence of multimarket contact among firms, however, relatively little research has analyzed its effect on economic performance. Although a number of authors have recently attempted to study this issue empirically, the existing literature contains virtually no formal theoretical analyses.[2]

One recent exception is Bulow, Geanakoplos, and Klemperer (1985). These authors investigate the effects of cost- and demand-based linkages across markets in the context of static oligopolistic models. While these conditions give rise to linkages in strategic inter-action across markets, their analysis does not address the issue that multimarket contact may affect firms' abilities to sustain noncompetitive ("collusive") outcomes. The object of this article is to provide such an analysis. Given this aim, we focus on settings of repeated interactions between firms. Moreover, to highlight the strategic linkages between markets, we assume away the demand- and cost-based linkages that motivated their analysis.

In what follows, we examine the effect of multimarket contact on the degree of cooperation that firms can sustain in settings of repeated competition. In particular, we contrast the most collusive equilibrium outcomes that can be sustained in the presence of multimarket contact with those attainable when all products are produced by single-product firms. This exercise requires us to adopt a concept of strategic equilibrium. The most widely accepted concept is that of subgame perfection. The set of subgame perfect equilibria may also be viewed as the set of credible nonbinding agreements available to firms, since any element of this set specifies actions that are in each firm's individual self-interest at all times. Thus, following Abreu (1986, 1988), we investigate the effect of multimarket contact by contrasting the most collusive subgame perfect equilibria (those yielding Pareto-undominated payoffs for the firms) for these two settings.[3]

We begin section 2 by discussing some general aspects of the link between multimarket contact and collusive behavior. There, we point out that multimarket contact relaxes the incentive constraints governing the implicit agreements between firms, and that this has the potential to improve firms' abilities to sustain collusive outcomes.

To assess the effects of multimarket contact more fully, we then turn to an analysis of price competition with homogeneous products in each market. We begin section 3 by proving an irrelevance result: when markets are identical, firms are identical, and technology exhibits constant returns to scale, then multimarket contact does not enhance firms' abilities to sustain collusive prices. Nevertheless, certain natural conditions do give rise to collusive gains from multimarket contact. In sections 4 through 6 we investigate these conditions by successively relaxing each of the three assumptions which generate the irrelevance result, allowing in turn for differing markets, differing firms, and scale economies. Of particular interest is the fact that, in each of these cases, the gains from multimarket contact are achieved by using modes of behavior that have been identified in previous studies of multimarket firms. For instance, when firms differ in their costs of production across markets or when scale economies are present, multimarket contact allows the development of "spheres of influence," which enable firms to sustain higher levels of profits and prices. In addition, geographically based, reciprocal trades of output – a common practice in many industries in which transportation costs are high – may, in such circumstances, facilitate the maintenance of collusive prices. When markets are subject to imperfectly correlated random shocks, even risk-neutral firms will wish to diversify their multimarket holdings. For similar reasons, multimarket firms should prefer to operate simultaneously in both mature and rapidly growing industries.

In section 7 we extend our analysis to the case of heterogeneous products. This allows us to highlight several interesting issues that do not arise when products are homogeneous. Finally, section 8 summarizes our central conclusions and discusses their relations to the existing empirical literature.

2. General Aspects of Market Contact

When markets are not inherently linked, it is easy to see that multimarket contact cannot reduce firms' abilities to collude. Since firms can always treat each market in isolation, the set of subgame perfect equilibria cannot be reduced by the introduction of multimarket contact. It is somewhat more difficult to understand the mechanism through which multimarket contact can increase collusion. Edwards' view is the most commonly held:

> [Firms which compete against each other in many markets] may hesitate to fight local wars vigorously because the prospects of local gain are not worth the risk of general warfare... A prospect of advantage from vigorous competition in one market may be weighed against the danger of retaliatory forays by the competitor in other markets.[4]

Edwards' appealing assertion is that collusive outcomes are easier to sustain with multimarket contact because there is more scope for punishing deviations in any one market. The problem with this argument is that once a firm knows that it will be punished in every market, if it decides to cheat, it will do so in every market. This observation raises the possibility that increasing the number of markets over which firms have contact may simply proportionately raise the costs and benefits of an optimal deviation.

In fact, multimarket contact does generally alter the strategic environment in a substantive way. To see this, consider two markets, A and B, and two firms, 1 and 2, which operate in both markets. Let the strategy set of firm i in market k be S_{ik}. Firm i's static payoff function in market k is given by $\pi_{ik}(s_{ik}, s_{jk})$, where $s_{ik} \in S_{ik}$ and $s_{jk} \in S_{jk}$. Suppose that the optimal punishment of firm i in market k yields a discounted payoff to firm i of $\underline{v}_{ik}$, and, to keep things simple, consider only stationary equilibrium paths. If the firms treat the markets separately (act like single-product firms in each market), then strategies (s_{1k}, s_{2k}) are supportable as a perfect equilibrium outcome path in market k if and only if

$$\pi_{ik}(\hat{s}_{ik}(s_{jk}), s_{jk}) + \delta \underline{v}_{ik} \leq \left(\frac{1}{1-\delta}\right)\pi_{ik}(s_{ik}, s_{jk}) \tag{1}$$

for $i = 1, 2$, where $\hat{s}_{ik}(s_{jk})$ is firm i's static best response to s_{jk} and δ is the discount factor used by both firms. (See Abreu (1988).) In contrast, in any optimal multimarket collusive equilibrium, firms recognize that any deviation will be met with punishment in *both* markets (Abreu, 1988). As a result, if a firm decides to deviate, it will do so in *both* markets. Consequently, strategies $[(s_{1A}, s_{2A}), (s_{1B}, s_{2B})]$ are supportable as a perfect equilibrium outcome path if [5]

$$\sum_{k=A,B} \{\pi_{ik}(\hat{s}_{ik}(s_{jk}), s_{jk}) + \delta \underline{v}_{ik}\} \leq \left(\frac{1}{1-\delta}\right)\sum_{k=A,B} \pi_{ik}(s_{ik}, s_{jk}).$$

Thus, multimarket contact serves to *pool* the incentive constraints of the two markets.[6] This pooling can potentially relax binding incentive constraints, thereby increasing collusive profits. In order to gain a better understanding of the circumstances in which such gains are possible and of how firms act to take advantage of these gains, we next turn to an analysis of more structured models of oligopolistic pricing. In sections 3 through 6 we consider price-setting (Bertrand) models of repeated interactions with homogeneous products; in section 7 we investigate the heterogeneous product case.

For each of these models, we characterize and compare the most collusive equilibria with and without multimarket contact. Three points should be noted about this analysis. First, though our analysis follows that of Abreu (1988) in utilizing optimal punishments, our basic points would also apply for a variety of other punishments (e.g., reversion to the static equilibrium for some finite number of periods, T). Second, in analyzing situations with symmetrically positioned firms, we focus on equilibria which yield identical payoffs ("symmetric-payoff equilibria") to these firms; with asymmetrically positioned firms, we take a more agnostic position and examine the full Pareto frontier of equilibria. Third, for stationary models, we focus on stationary equilibria. We find these equilibria more plausible in such settings because they require less coordination between the firms. In many cases this additional restriction is without consequence, since the most collusive symmetric-payoff equilibrium is actually stationary. When this restriction is consequential, however, it does not drive our basic points regarding the gain in collusive ability that comes from multimarket contact.

3. A Simple Model of Multimarket Contact: An Irrelevance Result

We begin by introducing a simple model of multimarket contact with repeated (Bertrand) price competition. For expositional purposes, both here and in the following sections, we limit our discussion to a consideration of the gains from contact over two markets, which we label A and B. Trading in both markets occurs at the same set of points in discrete time, $\{t\}_{t=0}^{\infty}$. Demand in market k in each period is given by a decreasing continuous function, $Q(\cdot)$, of the price in market k, p_k. This demand relationship is identical for both markets.

Again, for expositional purposes, we shall suppose that two firms (labelled $i = 1, 2$) operate in both markets.[7] At every point in time, t, each firm i announces its current prices for the two markets, $\{p_{ik}(t)\}_{k=A,B}$. Consumers observe all announced prices and purchase each good from the firm with the lowest price. When different firms announce identical prices in the same market, consumers are indifferent between the suppliers, and we may resolve this indifference to achieve any desired division of demand.[8] We assume that each firm must meet all of the demand for its output at its announced price. Both firms produce output at some constant marginal (and average) cost, c, which is identical in both markets. For simplicity, we assume that industry profits, $(p - c)Q(p)$, are concave in price and denote the joint monopoly price by p^m. Finally, both firms have discount factor δ.

Abreu (1988) has shown that one can obtain all subgame perfect equilibrium paths in discounted, infinitely repeated games by considering strategies with a very simple structure. These strategies entail the use of optimal punishments that are applied whenever players deviate from the equilibrium path. The optimal punishment for each player is the perfect equilibrium which provides him with the lowest payoff that he receives in any perfect equilibrium. Since, in our model, firms always have the option to shut down, optimal punishments cannot be negative. Furthermore, there is a simple perfect equilibrium which yields discounted profits of zero to both players; this consists of the repeated static Bertrand solution, in which the price is set equal to the marginal cost by both firms. Consequently, we may describe an equilibrium as a path of prices and associated profits, $\{p_{ik}(t), \pi_{ik}(t)\}_{t=0}^{\infty}$, $i = 1, 2$, $k = A$, B, where it is understood that we punish any deviations from this path by retreating to the Bertrand solution forever.

For this simple model of multimarket contact, an irrelevance result holds.

PROPOSITION 1. When identical firms with identical constant-returns-to-scale technologies meet in identical markets, multimarket contact does not aid in sustaining collusive outcomes.

This irrelevance result holds not only for the case of stationary symmetric-payoff equilibria (which we discuss here), but also if we consider the entire set of subgame perfect equilibria. For completeness, we present the argument for the unrestricted case (including some extensions discussed below) in Appendix A.[9] We now turn to the case of stationary symmetric-payoff equilibria

PROOF. Consider first the single-market outcome. An outcome with stationary price $p \in [c, p^m]$ and equal market shares is sustainable if and only if, for $i = 1, 2$,

$$(p - c)Q(p) \leq \left(\frac{1}{1 - \delta}\right)(\tfrac{1}{2})(p - c)Q(p) \tag{2}$$

The left-hand side of (2) is firm i's discounted profit if it deviates (it slightly undercuts the price, p, and sells to the whole market; reversion to the Bertrand equilibrium then follows), while the right-hand side is firm i's discounted profit from abiding by the agreement. Simplifying (2) reveals that if $\delta < \frac{1}{2}$, no price above c is sustainable, while if $\delta \geq \frac{1}{2}$, there is a symmetric equilibrium that sustains the monopoly price.

Now consider multimarket equilibria. In searching for the most profitable stationary symmetric-payoff equilibrium, we can first restrict our attention to outcomes in which both firms name the same price in every period. To see this point, suppose that an equilibrium prescribes a lower price for firm 1 than for firm 2 in market k. If we adjust firm 2's prescribed price so that it equals firm 1's price and assign a zero market share to firm 2, both firms' profits are unchanged. Moreover, this change lowers firm 1's gain from deviation and leaves firm 2's unchanged. The revised strategies therefore constitute an equilibrium. Accordingly, we let p_k denote the price charged by the firms in market k and $(\lambda_{1k}, \lambda_{2k})$ denote the two firms' market shares in that market.

Next, note that we can also restrict our attention to those outcomes in which $p_k \in [c, p^m]$ for $k = A, B$: if either $p_k > p^m$ or $p_k < c$, then there exists a $\hat{p} \in [c, p^m]$ that results in equal or greater profits for both firms (keeping market shares fixed) and lower gains from deviating. Thus, if both firms name price $\hat{p}$, it would be sustainable as an equilibrium, and the firms would both earn (weakly) more than if they named p_k.[10]

Prices $(p_A, p_B) \in [c, p^m]^2$ and market shares $\{\lambda_{1k}, \lambda_{2k}\}_{k=A,B}$ are sustainable if and only if, for $i = 1, 2$,

$$\sum_{k=A,B} \left\{ \left[\left(\frac{1}{1-\delta} \right) \lambda_i (p_k - c) Q(p_k) \right] - [(p_k - c) Q(p_k)] \right\} \geq 0 \tag{3}$$

Summing (3) over $i = 1, 2$, we see that this requires that

$$\sum_{k=A,B} (p_k - c) Q(p_k) [\delta - \tfrac{1}{2}] \geq 0 \tag{4}$$

Thus, if $\delta < \frac{1}{2}$, it is again impossible to sustain any prices above c, so multimarket contact replicates the single-market outcome in *both* markets. If $\delta \geq \frac{1}{2}$, on the other hand, then a completely monopolistic outcome is possible even without multimarket contact.

QED

Thus, in this simple model, multimarket contact does not facilitate collusive behavior. As a prelude to the next several sections, it is worth emphasizing our three central assumptions: (i) markets are identical; (ii) firms are identical; and (iii) technology is constant returns to scale. The irrelevance of multimarket contact does not depend on all aspects of these assumptions. For example, if either demand or the level of (constant) marginal costs differs across markets, the same line of argument establishes irrelevance (just replace $Q(p)$ by $Q_k(p)$ and c by c_k above).[11] Nevertheless, certain aspects of these assumptions are critical. In the next three sections we consider several cases of special interest.

4. Differences Between Markets: Conglomeration and the Transfer of Market Power

The first central assumption in section 3 is that the markets are identical. In order to identify specific differences between markets that give rise to gains from multimarket contact, it is helpful to begin by thinking about stationary equilibria in a single market, k. By the same logic as in the previous section (parallel to condition (2)), if there are N identical firms, collusion is sustainable in a stationary symmetric-payoff equilibrium if and only if[12]

$$N \leq \frac{1}{1-\delta} \tag{5}$$

When this condition is satisfied strictly, firms have slack enforcement power in market k. If these firms also participate in a market in which this condition is violated, they may be able to put this slack enforcement power to use.

Recall that when markets are identical, differ in demand, or differ in marginal cost, then multimarket contact generates no gain in collusive ability. In essence, the pooling of incentive constraints does not help in such cases because either the incentive constraints in *both* markets can be satisfied individually at the monopoly price or *neither* can be satisfied individually at any price above cost. This is not true, however, when markets differ in terms of N or δ, and in such cases, multimarket contact may facilitate collusion. It is perhaps unnatural to assume that a firm uses different discount factors to value the net income streams associated with different activities. However, the importance of δ suggests a more general point: potential gains from multimarket contact may arise when firms attach more weight to future outcomes in some markets than in others. In the next two subsections, we explore these factors in greater detail.

Number of firms

For purposes of illustration, we consider a situation in which market A is a duopoly and market B consists of $N > 2$ competitors. To focus on the case of interest, we make the following three assumptions.

Assumption 1. $2(1 - \delta) < 1$.

Assumption 2. $N(1 - \delta) > 1$.

Assumption 3. $(N - 2)(1 - \delta) < 1$.

Assumption 1 implies that complete collusion can be sustained (strictly) in the duopolistic market, A. Assumption 2 implies that, in the absence of multimarket contact, the only outcome in the N-firm market, B, involves pricing at cost.[13] Finally, Assumption 3 implies that if market B had only $(N - 2)$ firms, then complete collusion would be sustainable.

Suppose now that each of the market A duopolists owns a market B firm. We again examine the set of optimal stationary symmetric-payoff equilibria. (These yield identical payoffs to identical firms, i.e., one payoff to each of the two conglomerates and another to each of the $N - 2$ market B firms.) It is not difficult to show that an optimal equilibrium within this class involves identical market shares in each market for the two conglomerates, and we impose this condition in the discussion that follows.[14]

Suppose then that the market A price is $p_A > c$, which yields aggregate profits in market A of $\Pi_A = (p_A - c)Q(p_A)$. By Assumption 1, the incentive constraint for each conglomerate in market A is nonbinding. In particular, the net gains of deviating for each conglomerate (given the worst possible punishments) are

$$\Pi_A \left[1 - \tfrac{1}{2} \left(\frac{1}{1 - \delta} \right) \right] < 0 \tag{6}$$

The conglomerates can potentially use this slack enforcement power to induce a partially or completely collusive outcome in market B.

This outcome occurs as follows. Each conglomerate sets output so that the market share of its market B subsidiary is less than $(1/N)$. This leaves a greater share of market B for the other $N - 2$ firms. A single-market firm, i, with market share λ_i will not undercut a price $p_B \in (c, p^m)$ if and only if

$$(p_B - c)Q(p_B) \leq \left(\frac{1}{1 - \delta} \right) \lambda_i (p_B - c)Q(p_B) \tag{7}$$

or

$$\lambda_i \geq (1 - \delta) \tag{8}$$

Thus, if the market share of each of these firms is at least $(1 - \delta)$, they will not undercut a collusive arrangement.

Of course, this strategy violates the market B incentive constraint for each conglomerate firm. Specifically, if the price in market B is p_B, then the net gains from deviating in market B (considered in isolation) for the two conglomerates, if they each have a market share of λ_c, are

$$\Pi_B \left[1 - \lambda_c \left(\frac{1}{1 - \delta} \right) \right] \tag{9}$$

where $\Pi_B = (p_B - c)Q(p_B)$ is the aggregate profit level in market B. The preceding discussion implies that $\lambda_c \leq [1 - (N - 2)(1 - \delta)]$, so (9) is strictly positive. However, as long as the sum of the expressions in (6) and (9) is nonpositive, neither conglomerate firm will deviate. Multimarket contact allows these firms to transfer the ability to collude from market A to market B by pooling their incentive constraints across markets.

The optimal collusive equilibrium is easily derived. Since both profits and the degree of surplus enforcement power rise with Π_A (recall condition (6)), the price in market A is set at its monopolistic level, p^m. Given the resulting slack enforcement power in market A and the conglomerate market shares in market B of $\lambda_c \leq [1 - (N - 2)(1 - \delta)]/2$, the highest sustainable level of aggregate profit in market B, $\Pi_B^*(\lambda_c)$, satisfies

$$(p^m - c)Q(p^m) \left[1 - \tfrac{1}{2} \left(\frac{1}{1 - \delta} \right) \right] + \Pi_B^*(\lambda_c) \left[1 - \lambda_c \left(\frac{1}{1 - \delta} \right) \right] = 0 \tag{10}$$

Note that as λ_c increases from zero to $[1 - (N - 2)(1 - \delta)]/2, \Pi_B^*(\lambda_c)$ increases. This raises conglomerate profits and, under Assumption 1, also increases the profits of the $(N - 2)$ market B firms, $(1 - 2\lambda_c)\Pi_B^*(\lambda_c)$. Thus, as long as the monopoly price cannot be sustained in market B for any λ_c, the optimal collusive outcome involves setting $\lambda_c = [1 - (N - 2)(1 - \delta)]/2$. (When the monopoly price can be sustained for some λ_c, there is a Pareto frontier of equilibria that corresponds to different levels of λ_c, all of which sustain $p_B = p_B^m$.)

Several aspects of this result deserve highlighting. First, contrary to conventional wisdom, the purchase of market B firms by "powerful" market A firms would lead to a decline in these firms' market shares – indeed, the conglomerate firms achieve a collusive outcome precisely through the contraction of their shares. Second, under Assumptions 1 through 3, multimarket contact *always* yields a potential gain, since $\Pi_B^*(\lambda_c)$ is always positive; that is, we can always sustain a price above cost in market B. Third, note that exactly the same points hold if we let either the demand or the level of (constant) marginal cost vary by market. Moreover, since the potential gains associated with multimarket contact depend upon the level of monopoly profits in market A (recall condition (10)), if the demand in market A is sufficiently large or the cost sufficiently low, multimarket contact leads to the complete monopolization of market B; that is, the firms can sustain $p_B = p_B^m$.

Growth rates, response lags, and fluctuations

In this subsection, we discuss three factors that may cause firms to attach more weight to future outcomes in some markets than in others. Since the analytics for all of the factors are similar, we present the first two informally, developing only the third in detail.

First, demand may grow more rapidly in one industry than in another. When one considers a single market in isolation, the addition of a geometric growth rate alters nothing of substance. Indeed, for analytical purposes, one can interpret δ as the product of a discount factor (ρ) and a growth factor (γ_k). Thus, it is easier to cartelize a rapidly growing market than one in which demand is stagnant. Intuitively, rapid growth makes the consequences of punishment (which occurs in the future) more important relative to the gain from deviating (which is immediate). This observation suggests that multimarket contact may serve as a device for shifting punishment power from rapidly to slowly growing markets.[15] Unfortunately, when one considers interactions over several markets, it is no longer valid to interpret δ as $\rho\gamma_k$, since differential growth causes the relative size of the two markets to change from period to period. One can nevertheless show that if N (the number of firms in both industries) is fixed, gains from multimarket contact are always available whenever

$$\rho\gamma_A > \left(1 - \frac{1}{N}\right) > \rho\gamma_B$$

(i.e., when collusion is sustainable in one market but not in the other).[16]

The tendency for established firms in mature industries to acquire subsidiaries in rapidly developing industries has often been attributed to the fact that established firms typically have high earnings but relatively poor internal investment opportunities, while rapidly growing firms have insufficient internal funds to finance all profitable projects. The present analysis suggests that the same tendency could arise in part from the desire to spread market power from one industry to another.

Second, firms may be able to respond more quickly to deviations from collusive agreements in some markets than in others. Actions may be directly observable and immediately punishable in some markets, while in others, defections may be detected and punishment initiated only with a lag or some statistical uncertainty. (See, for example, Green and Porter (1984).) As with growth rates, when one considers a single market in isolation, adding an explicit response lag (the amount of time required to initiate punishments subsequent to deviation) changes nothing of substance. Once again, we may interpret δ as a function of the discount factor and a market-specific response lag. Although this interpretation no longer holds when one considers interactions over several markets simultaneously (unless response lags are identical, the implied length of a single period differs between the two markets), one can nevertheless show that multimarket contact can create potential gains by allowing firms to shift enforcement power from a market in which responses are rapid to one in which they are sluggish.[17]

Finally, demand may fluctuate from period to period within each market. Rotemberg and Saloner (1986) have previously argued that when demand fluctuates in a single market, collusion should be countercyclical: the future seems more important relative to the present when demand is low than when it is high. Indeed, firms may have slack enforcement power in periods of low demand but may be unable to sustain collusion in periods of high demand. While firms cannot shift enforcement power across periods, they can shift it across markets. Thus, one would suspect that parallel mergers across industries would yield gains as long as the random shocks experienced by each market are not perfectly correlated. The tendency for conglomerate firms to diversify over markets which experience poorly correlated shocks (see Marshall, Yawitz, and Greenberg (1984)) has previously been attributed to risk aversion, taxes, and/or bankruptcy costs. Our analysis suggests that the ability to collude more effectively could also play a role.

We now formally illustrate this final point. As in section 3, we envision two firms, 1 and 2, operating simultaneously in two markets, A and B. We maintain all of our previous assumptions concerning demand and production costs, except that we now distinguish between two demand states for each market, signified by h (high) and l (low). We use $Q^s(\cdot)$ to denote demand (for either market) in state $s = h, l$, and assume that $Q^h(p) > Q^l(p)$ for all $p \geq 0$. As in Rotemberg and Saloner (1986), the realizations of these states are independent across periods. For illustrative purposes, we assume here that there is perfect negative correlation between the demand shocks in these two markets. Thus, with probability 0.5, market A is in state h and B is in state l, while with probability 0.5, the reverse is true. The general case is considered in Bernheim and Whinston (1987) and discussed briefly below.

In this model, optimal punishments consist of reverting to the static Bertrand solution in every period in every state – as before, this equilibrium yields net discounted profits of zero. A stationary equilibrium path specifies prices and market shares for each market for each state of nature. Once again, in looking for an optimal stationary symmetric-payoff equilibrium, we can restrict our focus to those equilibria that entail equal market shares within each market in all states. (This is also true of the single market case.) Furthermore, it is not difficult to show that we can also restrict ourselves to outcomes that treat the markets symmetrically. Consequently, an equilibrium is completely characterized by two prices, p_h and p_l. Both firms set prices equal to p_l in the low demand market and equal to p_h in the high demand market. Let π_s denote the corresponding profits for each firm in the market for which the realization is s. In the multimarket setting, by undercutting its opponent, either firm can temporarily capture all the business in both markets, earning profits that are arbitrarily close to $2(\pi_l + \pi_h)$. Thus, each firm's incentive constraint is

$$\frac{\delta}{1 - \delta} [\pi_h + \pi_l] \geq \pi_h + \pi_l$$

or $\delta \geq \frac{1}{2}$. As long as this condition is satisfied, the firms can jointly achieve monopoly profits in both markets. When $\delta < \frac{1}{2}$, no price above cost is feasible.

To gauge the gains from multimarket contact, we consider next the opportunities for cooperation in a single market, assuming that there are no conglomerate firms. This is essentially the problem treated by Rotemberg and Saloner (1986). In this case, stationary, symmetric equilibrium paths supported by Bertrand punishments are characterized by two prices, p_h and p_l, where p_s denotes the price quoted by both firms in state s. Again letting π_s be the associated level of profits for each firm, incentive compatibility requires that

$$\frac{\delta}{1-\delta}\left[\frac{\pi_h}{2}+\frac{\pi_l}{2}\right] \geq \max\{\pi_h, \pi_l\}$$

For $\delta < \frac{1}{2}$, the only nonnegative solution to this inequality is $\pi_h = \pi_l = 0$. For $\delta \geq \frac{1}{2}$, the most collusive outcome yields

$$\pi_l = \pi_l^m$$

and

$$\pi_h = \min\left\{\left[\frac{1-\delta}{2-3\delta}\right]\pi_l^m, \pi_h^m\right\}$$

where $2\pi_s^m$ is the aggregate monopoly profit in state s. Thus, in the single-market setting, firms can sustain full cooperation in both states only when $\delta \geq \delta^*$, where

$$\delta^* = \left[\frac{2\pi_h^m - \pi_l^m}{3\pi_h^m - \pi_l^m}\right] > \frac{1}{2}$$

For $\frac{1}{2} \leq \delta < \delta^*$, multimarket contact increases the ability to sustain collusive outcomes.

In Bernheim and Whinston (1987), we relax the assumption of perfect negative correlation. There we show that potential gains to multimarket contact exist as long as the coefficient of correlation between the demand shocks is less than unity. These gains rise monotonically as the correlation falls. Thus, firms should prefer to establish multimarket contact across markets for which the correlation of shocks is as low as possible.[18]

5. Differing Firms: Spheres of Influence and Reciprocal Exchanges

The second central assumption in section 3 is that firms are identical. In practice, of course, firms may have different production costs. Such differences may arise not only because of differing levels of technological knowledge and capability, but also, in markets where transportation costs are significant, due to differing plant locations.

In this section, we demonstrate that multimarket contact may facilitate collusion in the presence of such cost differences. Furthermore, we show that the firms' optimal behavior in such circumstances corresponds to patterns that have, in fact, been previously noted, i.e., the development of "spheres of influence" and the use of reciprocal trades of output.

The development of spheres of influence for multimarket firms was originally discussed by Edwards, who argued, "Each conglomerate competitor ... may informally recognize the other's primacy of interest in markets important to the other, in the expectation that its own important interests will be similarly respected."[19] Thus, when firms compete simultaneously in several different markets, each may come to specialize in some subset of these markets, and such specialization may help firms maintain high prices.

To illustrate these points, it is useful to distinguish between two cases of differing costs. First, firms may be in a situation of "symmetric advantage": each may be more efficient in some markets but less efficient in others. The most obvious example occurs when transportation costs are important and firms' plants are geographically separated, but symmetric advantage can clearly arise in other situations as well. The other case is that of "absolute advantage," in which one firm is more efficient in all markets. We now consider each of these cases in turn.

Symmetric advantage

Once again, consider a model with two markets (A and B), two firms (1 and 2), and homogeneous products within each market. Let firm 1's constant marginal cost of production in market A be $\underline{c}$, while firm 2's marginal cost is $\bar{c}$, where $\bar{c} > \underline{c}$. In market B, production costs are reversed, with firm 2 being more efficient than firm 1. In each market k, demand in every period is described by the function $Q(p_k)$. For expositional purposes, we again assume that $(p - c)Q(p)$ is concave in p for any level of constant marginal costs, $c \in [\underline{c}, \bar{c}]$, and we denote the monopoly price for cost level c by $p^m(c)$.

As a point of comparison, we begin by examining the optimal single-market outcome. (That is, we assume that the firms compete only in market A.) In this model, optimal punishments yield discounted payoffs of zero for both firms – the punishment for firm i entails both firms naming a price of $\underline{c}$ in every future period and firm 1 making all of the sales.[20]

Consider, first, the single-market stationary equilibria. Firm i will not cheat in market k when the price is $p_k \geq \bar{c}$ and its market share is λ_{ik} if and only if

$$\phi(p_k|c_{ik}) \leq \left(\frac{1}{1-\delta}\right)\lambda_{ik}(p_k - c_{ik})Q(p_k) \tag{11}$$

where c_{ik} is firm i's (constant) marginal cost in market k and $\phi(p|c) \equiv \max_{s \leq p}(s - c)Q(s)$. Noting that $\phi(p_k|c_{ik}) \geq (p_k - c_{ik})Q(p_k)$, we can sum (11) over $i = 1, 2$ and conclude that if $\delta < \frac{1}{2}$, then no price above $\bar{c}$ is sustainable. When $\delta \geq \frac{1}{2}$, firms can sustain collusive prices above $\bar{c}$. The crucial point for our purposes, however, is that some fraction of sales must be allocated to the inefficient firm to keep it from undercutting the collusive price. In particular, the inefficient firm must have a market share of at least $(1 - \delta)$.[21] If

$$\delta[p^m(\underline{c}) - \underline{c}] \geq (\bar{c} - \underline{c})Q(\bar{c})$$

then a collusive outcome Pareto dominates (from the firms' perspectives) the static equilibrium in which both firms name a price of $\bar{c}$ and the efficient firm makes all of the sales; abstracting from coordination difficulties, we would therefore expect to observe collusive behavior with a price $p \in [p^m(\underline{c}), p^m(\bar{c})]$ and a market share for the inefficient firm of at least $(1 - \delta)$. If this inequality is not satisfied, then the efficient firm prefers the static ("noncollusive") outcome, while the inefficient firm prefers the reverse.[22] In neither case, however, do the firms achieve the joint profit-maximizing outcome, since this involves a price of $p^m(\underline{c})$ and requires that the efficient firm makes all the sales.

Now, consider the most collusive outcome in the two market setting. For expositional purposes, we focus here on stationary equilibria that involve symmetric outcomes: a price p is charged in both markets by both firms, and the efficient firm receives a market share, λ, in each market. We argue below that the equilibria we derive are the optimal stationary symmetric-payoff equilibria, so this focus is unrestrictive.

As before, if a firm deviates, it receives a continuation payoff of zero. Thus, the optimal collusive outcome solves

$$\max_{\lambda, p \geq \bar{c}} \lambda(p - \underline{c})Q(p) + (1 - \lambda)(p - \bar{c})Q(p)$$

subject to

$$\phi(p \mid \underline{c}) + \phi(p \mid \bar{c}) \leq \left(\frac{1}{1 - \delta}\right)\{\lambda(p - \underline{c})Q(p) + (1 - \lambda)(p - \bar{c})Q(p)\} \qquad (12)$$

It is easy to see that any solution to this problem must involve $\lambda = 1$. That is, the less efficient firm *completely* withdraws from each market.[23,24] It is then clear that the solution never involves a price in excess of $p^m(\underline{c})$, the monopoly price level for a firm with cost level $\underline{c}$, since a price of $p^m(\underline{c})$ generates larger profits than any higher price and involves identical deviation profits. Now, when $\lambda = 1$, a price $p \leq p^m(\underline{c})$ is sustainable if and only if

$$(p - \bar{c}) \leq \left(\frac{\delta}{1 - \delta}\right)(p - \underline{c}) \qquad (13)$$

Two conclusions follow immediately. First, if $\delta \geq \frac{1}{2}$, complete monopolization is possible – the efficient firm sets price equal to $p^m(\underline{c})$ in each market. Second, for all $\delta \in (0, \frac{1}{2})$ at least *some* collusion is possible. The optimum involves a price such that (13) binds, unless $p^m(\underline{c})$ is sustainable, which occurs at some critical discount factor strictly less than $\frac{1}{2}$.[25]

The fact that the optimal collusive outcome here involves the development of spheres of influence is not terribly surprising, since such a move directly raises profits for the firms. What is interesting, however, is that the development of spheres of influence also enables firms to collude more effectively on price. By shifting sales toward the more efficient firm in each of the two markets, profits on the equilibrium path rise, while the possible gains from deviating fall. (A greater fraction of a firm's gain comes in the market where it has higher costs.) Both effects relax the incentive constraint associated with sustaining any given price p.[26]

An interesting comparison can be made between the effect of multimarket contact on the ability to collude and the effect of nonbinding side payments on collusion in a single-market setting.[27] In particular, the set of outcomes that can be sustained here through multimarket contact is identical to that which can be sustained with a scheme of non-binding side payments in a single-market context. Suppose, for example, that outcome

$(p, \underline{\lambda})$ is sustainable with multimarket contact; that is, it satisfies (12). Now, consider a single-market scheme in which in each period, the firms first name price p, receiving shares of $\underline{\lambda}$ and $(1 - \underline{\lambda})$, and then, if no one has deviated, one firm makes a payment to the other. If at any time a firm deviates, both firms revert to pricing at cost in all future periods, and no further side payments are made. It is easy to see that if the firm making the side payment is going to deviate, it will do so at the start of the period. (It will not name price p if it plans to refuse to make the side payment.) Let S denote the side payment given or received by the inefficient firm. (S is positive if the inefficient firm receives the side payment and negative if it makes a payment.) Then, the relevant incentive constraint for the efficient firm is

$$\phi(p|\underline{c}) \le \left(\frac{1}{1-\delta}\right)[\underline{\lambda}(p - \underline{c})Q(p) - S] \tag{14}$$

and the incentive constraint for the inefficient firm is

$$\phi(p \mid \bar{c}) \le \left(\frac{1}{1-\delta}\right)[(1 - \underline{\lambda})(p - \bar{c})Q(p) + S] \tag{15}$$

Since $(p, \underline{\lambda})$ satisfies (12), one can clearly find an S that satisfies both (14) and (15). ((12) is just the sum of (14) and (15).) More generally, when (nonbinding) side payments are allowed in a single-market context, their presence allows firms to effectively pool their incentive constraints in each period. (That is, they face an incentive constraint that is the sum of the individual firms' incentive constraints.) Thus, when firms differ across markets in a symmetric way (as is the case here), multimarket contact without side payments yields the same set of outcomes as does single-market interaction with side payments.[28]

The welfare implications of multimarket contact in this setting should also be noted. When collusion would arise in a single market (without side payments), multimarket contact unambiguously *improves* welfare, in contrast to the usual presumption; in this case, the movement toward spheres of influence both lowers costs (by setting $\underline{\lambda} = 1$) and (weakly) lowers prices (since the single-market collusive price lies in $[p^m(\underline{c}), p^m(\bar{c})]$). In contrast, if a collusive outcome would not arise in the single-market context (which is always the case whenever $\delta < \frac{1}{2}$), welfare is unambiguously impaired: in both the single- and multimarket situations, $\underline{\lambda} = 1$, but prices are higher in the multimarket case. Thus, multimarket contact may or may not reduce welfare, even when it has real effects.[29]

As we have seen, when firms differ in their costs across markets, multimarket contact can facilitate the maintenance of collusive prices through the development of spheres of influence. Nevertheless, if firms cannot coordinate such an arrangement tacitly, they may be reluctant to do so overtly given the Sherman Act's *per se* ban on market division agreements. In such circumstances, they may seek other lawful means of accomplishing the same ends. As we shall now demonstrate, in the case of geographic markets with high transportation costs, a frequently observed form of horizontal reciprocal output agreement can serve exactly this purpose.

Horizontal reciprocal output agreements are common in a number of industries in which transportation costs are significant.[30] In the typical reciprocal output agreement, a firm with a production facility in market A and a presence in market B will agree to swap output on a unit-for-unit basis with a firm whose production facility is in market B and who also sells in market A. Effectively, this provides output at a lower cost to the firm that is inefficient in each market.

Consider a situation in which the inefficient firm initially has a share, λ, in each market, and suppose that antitrust considerations preclude further specialization. Price $p \le p^m(\underline{c})$ is sustainable without a reciprocal agreement if and only if

$$[\lambda(p - \bar{c})Q(p) + (1 - \lambda)(p - \underline{c})Q(p)]$$
$$\le \left(\frac{\delta}{1 - \delta}\right)[\lambda(p - \underline{c})Q(p) + (1 - \lambda)(p - \bar{c})Q(p)] \qquad (16)$$

(This is the same constraint as in (12).) Now consider an agreement in which the efficient firm in each market provides the inefficient firm with $(1 - \lambda)Q(p)$ units of output in each period. In what follows, we distinguish contractual from noncontractual agreements.

Consider first a noncontractual agreement. To start, we suppose that in each period the firms first name their prices, and then they simultaneously announce whether they are willing to trade; a trade takes place only if both firms agree.[31] Optimal punishments in this setting involve a reversion to the single-market punishment and the cessation of all future trade. Clearly, neither firm will deviate and say "no" to trade if there has been no prior deviation, so we need only consider the incentive to undercut the collusive price. By not deviating, each firm earns a discounted payoff of

$$\left(\frac{1}{1 - \delta}\right)(p - \underline{c})Q(p)$$

while deviation yields $[(p - \underline{c})Q(p) + (p - \bar{c})Q(p)]$, since the output trade ceases in the period of deviation. Thus, price p is sustainable if and only if condition (13) is satisfied, i.e., under exactly the same conditions as those for the development of spheres of influence.

The ability of the firms to refuse to trade in period t if a firm has deviated in that period is important for this equivalence. If trade must occur either before or at the same time price choices are made, this lessens the effectiveness of the reciprocal output trade because a firm that undercuts the collusive price now benefits from the trade in the period of deviation. (See note 28.) Nevertheless, the reciprocal trade still increases the firms' abilities to collude on price. In this case, price p is sustainable if and only if

$$[\lambda(p - \bar{c})Q(p) + (1 - \lambda)(p - \underline{c})Q(p)] \le \left(\frac{\delta}{1 - \delta}\right)(p - \underline{c})Q(p) \qquad (17)$$

Finally, consider a contractual agreement in which the firms agree to trade in every future period. Once again, optimal punishments yield a payoff of zero in every period after the deviation. (Now both firms name prices equal to $\underline{c}$, and the inefficient firm sells $(1 - \lambda)Q(\underline{c})$ units of output in each period.) The condition under which a price, p, is sustainable with a contractual agreement is identical to (17).[32]

The key point is that the reciprocal agreement creates additional surplus for the firms that can be dissipated if either deviates from the collusive price.[33, 34] As with spheres of influence, the welfare implications of these agreements are ambiguous.

Absolute advantage

We now shift our attention to the case in which a single firm maintains a cost advantage over its competitor in two distinct markets. In particular, the efficient firm produces output at a cost $\underline{c}$ per unit, while the inefficient firm produces at $\bar{c} > \underline{c}$. As before, demand in each market k is given by $Q(p_k)$. Since we have already described the single-market outcomes, we turn immediately to the multimarket case.

Our goal is to show that multimarket contact expands the range of environments in which firms can sustain collusive equilibria. Accordingly, we assume that $\delta < \frac{1}{2}$, so that single-market outcomes are necessarily competitive. (See Proposition B2 in the Appendix.)

To construct a collusive multimarket equilibrium, we begin by fixing current output prices, $p_k \in [\bar{c}, p^m(\bar{c})]$, for each k. Without loss of generality, let $p_A \geq p_B$. Let $\underline{\lambda}_k$ denote the efficient firm's share of market k, and define

$$\underline{\pi}_k = (p_k - \underline{c})Q(p_k)$$

and

$$\bar{\pi}_k = (p_k - \bar{c})Q(p_k)$$

$k = A, B$. By deviating from the prescribed prices, the inefficient firm could obtain current profits arbitrarily close to $\bar{\pi}^d = \bar{\pi}_A + \bar{\pi}_B$. For the efficient firm, current period (deviation) profits are $\underline{\pi}^d \equiv \phi(p_A \mid \underline{c}) + \phi(p_B \mid \underline{c})$.

As before, we focus on stationary equilibria. Consider an allocation $(p_A, p_B, \underline{\lambda}_A, \underline{\lambda}_B)$. Since optimal punishments entail zero profits, this is sustainable if and only if

$$\bar{\pi}^d \leq (1 - \delta)^{-1}[\underline{\lambda}_A\underline{\pi}_A + \underline{\lambda}_B\underline{\pi}_B]$$

and

$$\underline{\pi}^d \leq (1 - \delta)^{-1}[(1 - \underline{\lambda}_A)\bar{\pi}_A + (1 - \underline{\lambda}_B)\bar{\pi}_B]$$

From these inequalities, it is easy to check that the set of sustainable collusive allocations is empty when $\delta < \frac{1}{2}$ and $p_A = p_B$. Henceforth, we take $p_A > p_B$. It is helpful to rewrite the incentive constraints as

$$\underline{\lambda}_A(\underline{\pi}_A/\underline{\pi}_B) + \underline{\lambda}_B \geq (1 - \delta)(\underline{\pi}^d/\underline{\pi}_B) \tag{18}$$

and

$$\underline{\lambda}_A(\bar{\pi}_A/\bar{\pi}_B) + \underline{\lambda}_B \leq (1 + \bar{\pi}_A/\bar{\pi}_B) \tag{19}$$

When $p_A > p_B$, it is straightforward to check that $\bar{\pi}_A/\bar{\pi}_B > \underline{\pi}_A/\underline{\pi}_B$. Accordingly, for fixed (p_A, p_B), we can graph the sustainable market shares. (See Figure 1.) $\underline{I}(\bar{I})$ represents the incentive constraint for the efficient (inefficient) firm. Equation (18) implies that for $\delta < \frac{1}{2}$, $\underline{I}$ must intersect the vertical axis above $\lambda_B = 1$. Thus, the set of sustainable market shares must look like the shaded area between the two incentive constraints. This suggests that the inefficient firm will have a tendency to specialize in the high-price market.

As δ rises, $\underline{I}$ shifts down, while $\bar{I}$ shifts up, so that the point of intersection, E, moves to the southeast. Some degree of collusion first becomes sustainable when the vertical coordinate of E reaches unity. (At this point, the horizontal component must exceed zero, since $\underline{I}$ crosses the vertical axis above $\lambda_B = 1$.) For the moment, we take $p_A \leq p^m(\underline{c})$. Using (18) and (19) to compute E, we find that it is possible to sustain the prices (p_A, p_B) in a stationary equilibrium if and only if

$$\delta \geq \delta^* \equiv [1 + (1 + \underline{\pi}_B/\underline{\pi}_A)(1 + \bar{\pi}_B/\bar{\pi}_A)^{-1}]^{-1}$$

Since $\underline{\pi}_A/\underline{\pi}_B < \bar{\pi}_A/\bar{\pi}_B$, it follows immediately that $\delta^* < \frac{1}{2}$. Thus, multimarket contact does expand the range of environments in which some collusion is sustainable.

More generally, for any fixed (p_A, p_B), we can say a bit more about the set of likely outcomes. Note that the efficient firm's isoprofit curves have slope $\underline{\pi}_A/\underline{\pi}_B$ and are therefore parallel to $\underline{I}$. Similarly, the inefficient firm's isoprofit curves have slope $\bar{\pi}_A/\bar{\pi}_B$, and are therefore parallel to $\bar{I}$. Thus, we can Pareto improve any allocation in the shaded area in Figure 1, unless that allocation lies on the northern frontier. It follows that the inefficient firm should completely specialize in the high-price market.

To summarize, when $\delta \in [\delta^*, \frac{1}{2}]$, it is possible to sustain some degree of collusion in the multimarket game. Firms set different prices in otherwise identical markets, and the

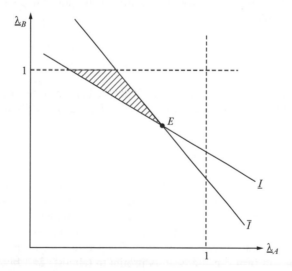

Figure 1 Sustainable market shares

inefficient firm specializes in the high-price market. Specialization again suggests the formation of spheres of influence. Note that this outcome entails both inefficient production and noncompetitive pricing.

When $\delta > \frac{1}{2}$, it is possible to sustain collusion even in a single-market game. However, any stationary equilibrium must involve a positive market share for the inefficient firm, and therefore, both firms can be made better off through the specialization that multimarket contact makes possible.[35]

6. Nonconvexities: Spheres of Influence

We now modify the model of section 3 by introducing a fixed cost of production, F. Thus, when firm i produces $q_{ik} > 0$ in market k, its total costs of production are given by $C(q_{ik}) = F + cq_{ik}$. We assume that firms bear this fixed cost only if they choose to produce, so $C(0) = 0$. Otherwise, we maintain all previous assumptions and notation. To avoid possible confusion, we note that π^m is defined as single-firm monopoly profits, $(p^m Q(p^m) - C(Q(p^m)))$, rather than the joint level of profits earned by two operating firms that collude fully, $(\pi^m - F)$. We assume that a single market can support both firms under a collusive arrangement, i.e., that $\pi^m > F$.

We begin our analysis by noting that the single-market, static price competition game has a unique equilibrium and that this equilibrium yields zero profits for both firms.[36] Repetition of this equilibrium generates optimal punishments for both firms; as in the previous sections, we may assume, without loss of generality, that firms revert to this equilibrium following any deviation from some proposed path.

Consider first the single-market (stationary symmetric-payoff) outcome. Let π denote the level of profits earned by each firm in each period along the equilibrium path (net of its fixed cost). An optimal deviation would yield current profits arbitrarily close to $2\pi + F$; subsequently, the deviator would earn zero profits in the punishment phase. On balance, deviation is unprofitable as long as

$$\delta \geq 1 - \frac{\pi}{2\pi + F} \equiv \delta^*(\pi)$$

Note that $\delta^*(\pi)$ is decreasing in π. Thus, it is (perhaps counterintuitively) easiest to sustain the fully collusive profit level, $(\pi^m - F)/2$. The required discount factor is

$$\tilde{\delta} \equiv \delta * ((\pi^m - F)/2) = \frac{1}{2} + \frac{F}{2\pi^m} > \frac{1}{2}$$

If $\delta < \tilde{\delta}$, no collusion is possible, while if $\delta \geq \tilde{\delta}$, a fully collusive outcome is sustainable.

Now consider the two-market case. Suppose firms attempt to sustain the global optimum by specializing. That is, each firm sets the monopoly price and meets all of the demand in its "home" market. In its competitor's home market, each firm sets a price strictly greater than p^m and produces nothing. Cooperation yields profits of π^m in each period. By deviating, a firm can increase its profits to (almost) $2\pi^m$ but will earn nothing thereafter. Accordingly, this collusive outcome is sustainable in equilibrium as long as

$\delta \geq \frac{1}{2}$; multimarket contact again expands the range of environments in which collusion is feasible. It is also possible to show that when $\delta < \frac{1}{2}$, all perfect equilibria yield zero profits.

Note that when $\delta < \frac{1}{2}$, multimarket contact has no effect on resource allocation. When $\frac{1}{2} \leq \delta < \tilde{\delta}$, multimarket contact leads to higher prices without improving productive efficiency and is therefore socially undesirable. On the other hand, if $\tilde{\delta} < \delta$, multimarket contact does not alter prices but does increase productive efficiency, and is therefore unambiguously desirable. Finally, note that, as in section 5, multimarket contact is associated with the development of "spheres of influence."

One might object to this analysis on the grounds that we have restricted our attention to stationary paths. For the single–market case, stationary equilibria are necessarily inefficient, since both firms must produce in every period. Nonstationary paths are of particular interest here, since they allow for the possibility that only one firm produces at a time. For analytic completeness, we have shown in Bernheim and Whinston (1987) that the consideration of nonstationary paths, which allow for the possibility that only one firm incurs the fixed cost in any period, does not qualitatively alter our results.

7. Differentiated Products

Up to this point, we have assumed that products are homogeneous within markets. In this section, we turn our attention to the case of differentiated products.[37] Our discussion focuses on two issues of interest that did not arise in the homogeneous product case.

Optimal allocation of market power

In the models with homogeneous products considered above, collusion in a single–market context was an all-or-nothing occurrence. If the discount factor was above a certain threshold level, then a fully monopolistic outcome was possible; if it was below this threshold, then no collusive price could be sustained. When markets differed, multimarket contact could increase profits only if firms could successfully cartelize one of the markets in isolation. Slack in the incentive constraints from this market could then be used to increase profits elsewhere.

Product heterogeneity within each market adds considerable complexity, since the maximum sustainable price typically increases continuously as the discount factor, δ, rises. At any given δ, the maximum degree of sustainable collusion may differ between markets, according to demand and cost conditions. Thus, even when firms cannot sustain a fully collusive outcome in any market, they may be able to gain by shifting market power between markets (i.e., lowering prices in one market and raising them in another).

To address this possibility, consider a simple model of symmetric product differentiation. Once again, there are two markets (A and B) and two firms (1 and 2). The sales of firm i in market k are given by the function $Q_k(p_{ik}, p_{jk})(j \neq i)$, which is symmetric in its arguments. The constant unit cost of production for both firms in market k is c_k. We assume that a firm's profits in market k, $(p_{ik} - c_k)Q_k(p_{ik}, p_{jk})$, are concave in (p_{ik}, p_{jk}) for $k = A, B$. Now define

$$\hat{\pi}_k(p) \equiv \max_z \ (z - c_k)Q_k(z, p)$$

and

$$\pi_k(p) \equiv (p - c_k)Q_k(p, p)$$

$\hat{\pi}_k(p)$ gives a firm's one-period deviation profits in market k when the price charged by its rival is p, while $\pi_k(p)$ is the firm's one-period profit when both firms charge a price of p. It is easy to verify that our concavity assumption implies that $\pi_k''(p) < 0$ and that $\hat{\pi}_k''(p) > 0$.

Under these assumptions the optimal symmetric-payoff equilibria in both the single- and multimarket settings can be shown to be symmetric and stationary (involve firms naming a single price in each market in every period).[38] The most profitable stationary equilibrium for the firms solves

$$\max_{p_A, p_B} \ [\pi_A(p_A) + \pi_B(p_B)]$$

subject to

$$[\hat{\pi}_A(p_A) + \hat{\pi}_B(p_B)] + \delta \underline{v} \leq \left(\frac{1}{1 - \delta}\right)[\pi_A(p_A) + \pi_B(p_B)]$$

Assuming that full collusion is not sustainable, we know that the constraint must bind, which implicitly defines p_B as a function of p_A. The feasible price frontier is depicted in Figure 2. The optimal collusive scheme finds the highest isoprofit contour that intersects this frontier. The solution is depicted in Figure 2 and satisfies the necessary condition[39]

$$\frac{\pi_A'(p_A^*)}{\hat{\pi}_A'(p_A^*)} = \frac{\pi_B'(p_B^*)}{\hat{\pi}_B'(p_B^*)}$$

Thus, the optimal collusive allocation equalizes the ratio of the marginal profit from collusion to the marginal profit from deviation across markets. Suppose, for example, that a monopolistic price is just sustainable (with no slack) in market A alone, but that complete cartelization of market B is not possible. Then, since $\pi_A' = 0$ at the single-market solution in market A, optimal multimarket collusion involves a decline in price in market A and an increase in price in market B. More generally, if $\hat{\pi}_k'' > 0$ for $k = A, B$, then multimarket contact leads to a price increase in the market in which the single-market outcome entails a higher value of $(\pi_k'/\hat{\pi}_k')$ and a price decrease in the other market.

It is of interest to note that, in contrast to the cases considered in section 4, multimarket contact across differing heterogeneous product markets may actually increase welfare when products are heterogeneous within markets, since price increases in some markets are offset by price decreases in others.[40]

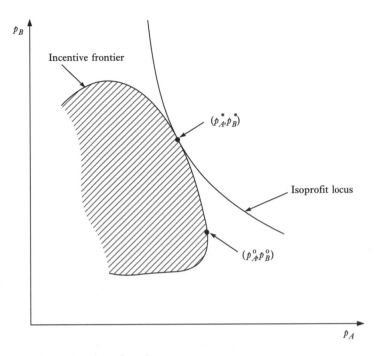

Figure 2   Optimal allocation of market power

Punishments

One issue that does not arise in the homogeneous product case is the effect of multimarket contact on punishments. Since optimal single-market punishments always yield zero profits, multimarket contact could not increase the severity of punishments.

With differentiated products, this is no longer the case. To see this, we consider once again a two-firm, two-market model with symmetric differentiation. Unfortunately, as Abreu (1986) discusses, globally optimal punishments are often intractable. We therefore restrict our attention here to the case of symmetric punishment paths, in which the firms charge the same prices within each market during any period (i.e., $p_{1k}(t) = p_{2k}(t) \equiv p_k(t)$ for all t). Following Abreu (1986), it is not difficult to show that when the optimal multimarket punishments yields positive profits, it involves a "stick–and–carrot" structure: firms first engage in a one-period price war and then revert to the most collusive symmetric price path.[41] The prices that prevail during the price war, (p_A, p_B), minimize $[\pi_A(p) + \pi_B(p)]$ subject to the constraint that

$$\sum_{k=A,B} \hat{\pi}_k(\underline{p}_k) + \delta[\pi_k(\underline{p}_k) + \delta\bar{v}_k] \le \sum_{k=A,B} [\pi_k(\underline{p}_k) + \delta\bar{v}_k]$$

where $\bar{v}_k$ is the discounted payoff from the most collusive symmetric path in market k. Differentiation once again yields the necessary condition that

$$[\pi'_A(p_A)/\hat{\pi}'_A(p_A)] = [\pi'_B(p_B)/\hat{\pi}'_B(p_B)]$$

which will not generally hold at the most severe single-market (symmetric) punishments. Thus, at least within the class of symmetric punishments, multimarket contact can enable firms to construct more severe punishments, which, in turn, further enhances collusive outcomes.

Finally, we argue that in the presence of multimarket contact, it is often possible to arrange more severe punishments for single-market competitors. To see this, consider first the globally optimal punishment in a single-market context with three symmetric firms. If firm 3 deviates, then the first-period prices along the optimal punishment path must solve

$$\min_{p_1, p_2, p_3} \pi(p_3 \mid p_1, p_2) \tag{20}$$

subject to

$$\hat{\pi}(p_2, p_3) - \pi(p_1 \mid p_2, p_3) \le \delta(u_1 - \underline{v}_1) \tag{21}$$

$$\hat{\pi}(p_1, p_3) - \pi(p_2 \mid p_1, p_3) \le \delta(u_2 - \underline{v}_2) \tag{22}$$

$$\hat{\pi}(p_1, p_2) - \pi(p_3 \mid p_1, p_2) \le \delta(u_3 - \underline{v}_3) \tag{23}$$

where u_i is firm i's continuation value on the punishment path, $\underline{v}_i$ is the value of the optimal punishment of firm i after it deviates, $\pi(p_i|p_j, p_l)$ is firm i's profit if it charges p_i and the other two firms charge p_j and p_l, and $\hat{\pi}(p_j, p_l)$ is firm i's one-shot deviation profit in that situation. If the punishment value to firm 3 is not zero, then either (21) or (22) – the incentive constraints for firms 1 and 2, respectively – must be binding at an optimum. Suppose not. By continuity, we can perturb p_1 and p_3 without violating (21) or (22). A small decrease in p_1 causes $\hat{\pi}(p_1, p_2)$ to fall. Since this relaxes constraint (23), we can choose p_3 appropriately to induce a lower value of $\pi(p_3|p_1, p_2)$.

Since either constraint (21) or (22) binds, it is clear that multimarket contact can make the punishment for firm 3 worse. To see this, suppose that firms 1 and 2 are involved in a second duopolistic market that can be completely cartelized. (The incentive constraint for this market is slack on the fully collusive path.) Then, if firm 3 deviates, firms 1 and 2 can shift into a punishment mode for the three-firm market *only*; therefore, while they are punishing firm 3, firms 1 and 2 continue to reap monopoly profits in the other market. If, however, either firm 1 or 2 subsequently deviates, it is punished as harshly as possible in *both* markets. The slack in the duopolistic market's incentive constraint relaxes constraints (21) and (22) and thereby facilitates a more severe punishment of firm 3.

8. Conclusion

In the preceding sections we have analyzed multimarket contact and collusive behavior in a variety of formal models. Three primary conclusions emerge from this investigation. First, multimarket contact can have real effects; in a wide range of circumstances, it relaxes the incentive constraints that limit the extent of collusion. Second, firms gain from multimarket contact by behaving in ways that have been noted in previous empirical discussions of multimarket firms. This suggests that multimarket contact may indeed have effects in practice. Third and finally, even when multimarket contact does have real effects, these effects are not necessarily socially undesirable.

Ultimately, the question of whether multimarket contact does have significant effects must be resolved through empirical research. Recently, there have been a number of attempts to address this empirical question. (See note 2.) Most of this work involves cross-sectional analyses of differences in performance (e.g., prices or profits) across industries, in which one or several measures of multimarket contact are included as explanatory variables.[42] These studies faced the formidable task of trying to distinguish between the effects of internal and external factors on performance. (Here, market definition is particularly critical.) In general, the literature has found a significant multimarket effect, although the sign of this effect has tended to vary across studies. One implication from our analysis, however, is that the effect of multimarket contact on the price or profits of any one industry depends greatly on the set of markets over which the firms have contact and on the characteristics of active (and potentially active) firms. For example, when firms are identical and markets differ, prices and profits may rise in some markets but fall in others as a result of multimarket contact. Similarly, when firms differ in their costs, multimarket contact can cause prices to either rise or fall (depending upon the discount factor). Thus, our analysis suggests that identifying the effects of multimarket contact on the price or profit level of an industry may require significantly more complex explanatory variables than have thus far been used in the literature.

A somewhat different approach was used in a recent experimental investigation conducted by Phillips and Mason (1988). Their study examined the effects of multimarket contact across two Cournot duopoly markets which fit into the class of markets covered in section 7 above. (See note 39.) Phillips and Mason's experimental procedure consists of running separate single-market experiments of the two markets and comparing these outcomes with those that arise in a multimarket setting. Interestingly, Phillips and Mason's findings correspond closely to our theoretical predictions: multimarket contact causes the price in their "monopolistic" market (low realized $\pi'/\hat{\pi}'$ ratio in the single-market experiment) to fall and the price in the other market to rise.

Our analysis also suggests other strategies for empirically examining the effects of multimarket contact. In particular, since market-specific events affect a multimarket incentive constraint, one would expect to observe correlations between prices in otherwise unrelated markets.[43] The identification of a large (independent) shock to one market could therefore offer a natural experiment for examining the theory.

In the preceding analysis, we have investigated the effects of multimarket contact by contrasting single-market outcomes with those arising in the presence of parallel diversification. It is worth inquiring about the extent to which parallel diversification is important to our results; that is, what is the effect of multimarket operation absent multimarket contact? To investigate this question, imagine that we have two markets and only one multimarket firm. Suppose, first, that this firm is a *monopolist* in one of the markets. Then the outcomes in the two markets would be no different than if all firms in both markets were single-product competitors. However, when the multiproduct firm faces single-product competitors in *both* markets, multiproduct operation pools the incentive constraints of the multiproduct firm. This can expand the set of possible outcomes, though to a lesser extent than with multimarket contact. For example, in section 4, firm 1 could still potentially transfer slack from market A to market B even if firm 2 operated only in market A. Note, though, that this would require that market A still revert to punishment mode in the event of a deviation in market B. In practice, the likelihood of this occurring in the presence of a significant number of single-product firms seems questionable in part because these firms may not even observe outcomes in market B. Thus, we are somewhat doubtful of the likelihood of effects arising from multimarket operation absent multimarket contact. Of course, the concern raised above can be a problem whenever single-market competitors are present. Thus, we suspect that in practice, the presence of significant single-market competitors will tend to retard the effects of multimarket contact. Clearly, further formal analysis of these issues seems desirable.

Appendix A

The proof of Proposition 1 for the unrestricted case follows.

Proof of Proposition 1 for the unrestricted case (including extensions). Consider any optimal multimarket equilibrium, $\{p_{ik}^0(t), \pi_{ik}^0(t)\}_{t=0}^{\infty}, i = 1, 2, k = A, B$. We construct two single-market equilibria, which together yield each firm exactly the profits it obtained in the multimarket equilibrium. This implies that multimarket contact yields no gain to the firms, since they may do equally well by treating each market in isolation. The important property shared by both the basic model and its extensions is that there exist positive constants (Θ_A, Θ_B) such that $\Theta_A + \Theta_B = 1$ and $\Pi_k^m(t) = \Theta_k[\Pi_A^m(t) + \Pi_B^m(t)]$ for $k = A, B$, where $\Pi_k^m(t)$ is the monopoly profit level in market k in period t.

Let $\pi_i^0(t) \equiv \pi_{iA}(t) + \pi_{iB}(t)$ and $\Pi^0(t) \equiv \pi_1^0(t) + \pi_2^0(t)$. Note that in any optimal collusive scheme, we must have $\pi_{ik}^0(t) \geq 0$ for all i, k, and t: if not, each firm's profits would be raised weakly, and one firm's profits would be raised strictly by setting both firm's prices equal to the cost in period t in market k. Since deviation profits would be unaffected, this change would satisfy each firms' incentive constraint.

To construct these single-market equilibria, we begin by choosing $\hat{p}_k(t)$ to be the lowest price that satisfies

$$[\hat{p}_k(t) - c_{kt}]Q_{kt}(\hat{p}_k(t)) = \Theta_k \Pi^0(t)$$

where c_{kt} is market k's marginal cost in period t and $Q_{kt}(\cdot)$ is market k's demand function in period t. Note that such a $\hat{p}_k(t)$ must exist and that, from the discussion in the previous paragraph, $\hat{p}_k(t) \geq c_{kt}$. Next, we choose $\hat{\lambda}_i(t) \equiv \pi_i^0(t)/\Pi^0(t)$. Note that $\hat{\lambda}_i(t)[\hat{p}_k(t) - c_{kt}]Q_{kt}(\hat{p}_k(t)) = \Theta_k \pi_i^0(t)$.

The equilibrium in market k has both firms naming price $\hat{p}_k(t)$ in period t and has firm i receiving a market share of $\hat{\lambda}_i(t)$ in period t in both markets. This outcome will be a single-market equilibrium in market k if and only if, for all t and $i = 1, 2$,

$$[\hat{p}_k(t) - c_{kt}]Q_{kt}(\hat{p}_k(t)) \leq \sum_{\tau=t}^{\infty} \hat{\lambda}_i(\tau)[\hat{p}_k(\tau) - c_{k\tau}]Q_{kt}(\hat{p}_k(\tau))\delta^{\tau-t} \tag{A1}$$

Substituting, we get

$$\Theta_k \Pi^0(t) \leq \sum_{\tau=t}^{\infty} \Theta_k \pi_i^0(\tau)\delta^{\tau-t} \tag{A2}$$

But, cancelling the Θ_k, we see that this condition is implied by the condition that must hold if $\{p_{ik}^0(t), \pi_{ik}^0(t)\}_{t=0}^\infty, i = 1, 2, k = A, B$ is a multimarket equilibrium. *QED*

Appendix B

Propositions B1, B2, B3, their proofs, and Corollary B1 follow.

Propositions B1. For the stationary multimarket models discussed in section 3 (including the extensions), there exists an optimal symmetric-payoff equilibrium that has stationary prices and stationary market shares.

Proof. The proof involves two steps. First, in any stationary model in which an optimal symmetric-payoff equilibrium satisfies these two conditions – (a) that equilibrium path actions can be restricted to a compact set and payoff functions are continuous functions of these variables, and (b) that the equilibrium involves equal payoffs for the two players in every period – there exists a *stationary* optimal symmetric-payoff equilibrium. The argument, which we omit here, closely parallels the proof of Theorem 9 in Abreu (1986). Second, these conditions are satisfied by the models in section 3. To see this, note first that for the reasons discussed in the text, there is always an optimal symmetric-payoff equilibrium in which $p_{ik}^*(t) = p_{jk}^*(t) \equiv p_k^*(t) \in [c_k, p_k^m]$ for all k and t. Letting $S = \{(p, p)|p \in [c_k, p_k^m]\}$, we can restrict the equilibrium path price choices of the two firms in market k to lie in this set. Since profits are continuous in the price vector on S, the first condition is satisfied. Now, if $\lambda_{ik}^*(t)$ is firm i's market share in market k at time t in this equilibrium, it must be that for all t and $i = 1, 2$,

$$\sum_{k=A,B} [p_k^*(t) - c_k] Q_k(p_k^*(t)) \le \sum_{k=A,B} \left\{ \sum_{\tau=t}^\infty \delta^\tau \lambda_{ik}^*(\tau)[p_k^*(\tau) - c_k] Q_k(p_k^*(\tau)) \right\} \tag{A3}$$

Summing over i implies that

$$\sum_{k=A,B} [p_k^*(t) - c_k] Q_k(p_k^*(t)) \le \sum_{k=A,B} \left\{ \sum_{\tau=t}^\infty \delta^\tau (\tfrac{1}{2})[p_k^*(\tau) - c_k] Q_k(p_k^*(\tau)) \right\} \tag{A4}$$

But (A4) is exactly the incentive constraint that applies if we alter the market shares to give each firm half of each market in every period (while not altering the prices). Thus, an optimal symmetric-payoff equilibrium exists that involves equal payoffs for the two players in every period, so the second condition is also satisfied. *QED*

Proposition B2. Consider a single market with N firms, $i = 1, \ldots N$. Firm i has a constant marginal cost of production of c_i, where $c_N \ge c_{N-1} \ge \ldots \ge c_1$, and there are no fixed costs. Then, for all $n \le N$ if $\delta < \frac{n-1}{n}$, no subgame perfect equilibrium has sales at a price greater than c_n in any period. *Proof.* Suppose not. Let $p_t \equiv \min\{p_i(t)\}_{i=1}^N$ for all t, and define $\bar{p} \equiv \sup p_t$. Then, $\bar{p} > c_N$. Now, if we have a perfect equilibrium, $\{p_i(t), \pi_i(t)\}_{t=0}^\infty (i = 1, \ldots, N)$, with associated output shares in period t of $\{\lambda_i(t)\}_{i=1}^N$, then the following condition must hold in every period t for $i = 1, \ldots, n$:

$$\phi(p_t|c_i) \le \sum_{\tau=t}^\infty \delta^{\tau-t}(p_\tau - c_i) Q(p_\tau) \lambda_i(\tau) \tag{A5}$$

where $\phi(p_t|c_i) \equiv \max_{s \le p} (s - c_i) Q(s)$. Note that $\phi(\cdot)$ is continuous. (A5) implies that

$$\phi(p_t|c_i) \le \sum_{\tau=t}^{\infty} \delta^{\tau-t}\phi(p_\tau \mid c_i)(p_\tau)\lambda_i(\tau) \tag{A6}$$

Since $\phi_i(\cdot)$ is nondecreasing and $\phi_i(\bar{p}) > 0$, we then have

$$\frac{\phi(p_t|c_i)}{\phi(\bar{p}|c_i)} \le \sum_{\tau=t}^{\infty} \delta^{\tau-t}\lambda_i(\tau) \tag{A7}$$

Summing over $i = 1, \ldots, n$ and noting that $\sum_{i=1}^{n} \lambda_i(\tau) \le 1$ yields

$$\sum_{i=1}^{n} \frac{\phi(p_t|c_i)}{\phi(\bar{p}|c_i)} \le \frac{1}{1-\delta} \tag{A8}$$

By the definition of $\bar{p}$, the left-hand side of (A8) can be made arbitrarily close to n by choosing t appropriately. When $\delta \le \frac{n-1}{n}$, however, $\frac{1}{1-\delta} < n$, so we must have a contradiction to (A8) for some t.

$$QED$$

Corollary B1. Consider a single market with N identical firms with constant marginal costs and no fixed costs. If $\delta < \frac{N-1}{N}$, then any subgame perfect equilibrium gives every firm zero discounted profits.

Proposition B3. In the model of section 5, any price above $\bar{c}$ arising in a stationary symmetric-payoff equilibrium must satisfy condition (13) in the text.

Proof. Consider an equilibrium with outcome $(p_A, p_B, \underline{\lambda}_A, \underline{\lambda}_B)$ where, without loss of generality, $p_A \ge p_B$ and $P_A \in (\bar{c}, p^m(\bar{c})]$. The incentive constraints for the two firms are

$$(1-\delta)[\phi(p_A|\underline{c}) + \phi(p_B|\bar{c})] \le [\underline{\lambda}_A(P_A - \underline{c})Q(p_A) + (1-\underline{\lambda}_B)(p_B - \bar{c})Q(p_B)] \quad \text{(firm1)}$$

and

$$(1-\delta)[\phi(p_A|\bar{c}) + \phi(p_B|\underline{c})] \le [(1-\underline{\lambda}_A)(p_A - \bar{c})Q(p_A) + \underline{\lambda}_B(p_B - \underline{c})Q(p_B)] \quad \text{(firm2)}$$

In a symmetric-payoff equilibrium we must have that

$$\underline{\lambda}_A(p_A - \hat{c})Q(p_A) - \underline{\lambda}_B(p_B - \hat{c})Q(p_B) = \tfrac{1}{2}[(p_A) - \bar{c})Q(p_A) - (p_B - \bar{c})Q(p_B)] \tag{A9}$$

where $\hat{c} \equiv (\underline{c}/2) + (\bar{c}/2)$. Now, consider the change in the firms' payoffs when $\underline{\lambda}_A$ and $\underline{\lambda}_B$ are raised keeping prices fixed and the firms' payoffs equal. Using (A9) to determine the change in $\underline{\lambda}_A$ that is required when $\underline{\lambda}_B$ is raised, we can calculate the change in firm 2's profit per period, π_2, to be

$$\frac{d\pi_2}{d\underline{\lambda}_B} = Q(p_B)\left[\left(\frac{p_B - \underline{c}}{p_A - \bar{c}}\right) - \left(\frac{p_B - \hat{c}}{p_A - \hat{c}}\right)\right](p_A - \bar{c}) > 0$$

Thus, raising $\underline{\lambda}_B$ and $\underline{\lambda}_A$ in this manner raises profits and therefore also satisfies the incentive constraints. Furthermore, this implies that a necessary condition for sustaining prices (p_A, p_B) is that the firms' incentive constraints are satisfied when $\underline{\lambda}_B = 1$ and that

$$\underline{\lambda}_A = \left[\frac{(p_A - \bar{c})Q(p_A) + (p_B - \underline{c})Q(p_B)}{2(p_A - \hat{c})Q(p_A)} \right] \equiv \underline{\hat{\lambda}}_A$$

the level implied by (A9) when $\lambda_B = 1$. (Note that this may imply a $\underline{\lambda}_A > 1$; although this is not actually feasible, the necessary condition we derive is still valid.) Now, if firm 2's incentive constraint is satisfied when $\underline{\lambda}_A = \underline{\hat{\lambda}}_A$ and $\lambda_B = 1$, then, by the definition of $\phi(\cdot|\cdot)$, it must be that

$$(1 - \delta)[(p_A - \bar{c})Q(p_A) + (p_B - \underline{c})Q(p_B)] \leq -\underline{\hat{\lambda}}_A(p_A - \bar{c})Q(p_A) + [(p_A - \underline{c})Q(p_A) \\ + (p_B - \underline{c})Q(p_B)]$$

Substituting for $\bar{\lambda}_A$ and rearranging yields

$$\frac{(p_A - \bar{c})Q(p_A)}{2(p_A - \hat{c})Q(p_A)} \leq \delta$$

or

$$(p_A - \bar{c}) \leq \left(\frac{\delta}{1 - \delta} \right)(p_A - \underline{c})$$

which is condition (13) in the text.   QED

Notes

1 Corwin Edwards, as quoted in Scherer (1980, p. 340).
2 Existing empirical work includes Mueller (1977), Heggestad and Rhoades (1978), Whitehead and Luytjes (1983), Whitehead (1978), Scott (1982), Rhoades and Heggestad (1985), Mester (1985), and Gelfand and Spiller (1986). We discuss this work in section 8.
3 One might want to impose further restrictions on the set of equilibrium outcomes. In fact, as we discuss later, we focus on stationary outcomes in the text (for stationary models) because these require relatively little coordination between the firms. An alternative that we do not pursue here is to consider group incentive constraints, i.e., "collective dynamic consistency" or "renegotiation–proofness," as in Bernheim and Ray (1989), Farrell and Maskin (1989), or more general coalitional incentive constraints, as in Bernheim, Peleg, and Whinston (1987).
4 Corwin Edwards, as quoted in Scherer (1980, p. 340).
5 For expositional simplicity, we are ignoring the effect that multimarket contact may have on punishments. We consider this issue in section 7.
6 Telser (1980) briefly considers this aspect of multiproduct operation toward the end of his discussion of self-enforcing agreements.
7 The result of this section is unaffected by the number of firms assumed. Note, however, that we do implicitly assume that entry is blocked. This could, for example, be due to patents. Alternatively, this may be due to the existence of sunk costs associated with entry that make entry unprofitable even when it is followed by collusion. In addition, potential entrants may fear that their entry into the industry will upset the collusive nature of industry pricing.
8 We shall make use of this freedom to divide the market when prices are equal. One useful way to think about this is to imagine a market in which products are almost perfectly homogeneous. In particular, firm i's demand function is given by

$q_i(p_i, p_j) = 0$ if $p_i > p_j + e$

by

$Q(p_i)$ if $p_i < p_j - e$

and by

$q(p_j - p_i)$ if $p_i \in [p_j - e, p_j + e]$

where $q(p_j - p_i)$ is an increasing continuous function mapping to $[0, \, Q(p_i)]$. Then, for sufficiently small e, the firms can achieve any split of market demand they desire with almost no effect on profits.

9   It is also worth noting that once one restricts attention to symmetric-payoff equilibria, stationarity is optimal. This is shown in Proposition B1 in Appendix B.

10 These two arguments also apply for the models considered in sections 4 and 6, and so we shall make use of these restrictions in our analysis there without further comment. In section 5, where firms differ in their costs, we can, without loss of generality, restrict our attention to equilibria in which firms name identical prices, which lie above the lowest-cost level and below the high-cost monopoly price.

11 The irrelevance result (for the unrestricted equilibrium set) also holds if we allow certain forms of nonstationarity. In particular, we can let demand in market k be a function of time and can let (constant) marginal costs vary with time as well, as long as there exists a constant, Θ, such that $\Pi_A^m(t)/\Pi_B^m(t) = \Theta$, where $\Pi_k^m(t)$ is the monopoly profit level in market k in period t. This is established formally in Appendix A in the course of proving Proposition A1 for the unrestricted case.

12 Proposition B2 and Corollary B1 in Appendix B establish that when $N < (1 - \delta)^{-1}$, all subgame perfect equilibria yield a discounted payoff of zero to every firm. Thus, by demonstrating that multimarket contact can sustain stationary collusive outcomes when this inequality holds, we also establish that this contact yields gains even when we allow for nonstationary outcomes.

13 The reader may wonder about the consistency of Assumption 2 with our implicit assumption that entry is blockaded; that is, why did these N firms spend money to enter an industry in which they would earn nothing? This can be justified in several ways. For example, the N firms may be those that, *ex post*, were successful in stochastic R&D programs. Alternatively, the firms may have originally expected demand to grow rapidly (we argue in section 4 that this would make supracompetitive prices possible), but, *ex post*, demand has been stationary.

14 The argument parallels that of the second step of the proof of Proposition B1 in Appendix B.

15 Harrington (1986) establishes a similar result. He considers two finite-horizon industries, one of which terminates before the other. Due to the existence of multiple static equilibria, one can enforce collusion in a single market until some critical period prior to termination. If multimarket firms operate in both industries, they may be able to maintain collusive outcomes in the short-horizon industry through its terminal period by shifting enforcement power from the long-horizon industry.

16 In fact, under this condition, it is always possible to eventually sustain complete collusion in both industries; since market A becomes extremely large relative to market B, slack enforcement power in market A must eventually exceed the net gains from deviating from a monopolistic outcome in market B.

17 Tirole (1988) provides a simple example that illustrates this basic idea, in which in one market, firms choose prices every period, while in the other, they choose prices every other period.

18 Evidence indicating that conglomerate firms tend to diversify over poorly correlated markets does not, of course, differentiate between our explanation of this phenomenon and the alternatives mentioned earlier. However, it may be possible to test between these two competing explanations by examining other collateral implications. For example, our model implies that the variability of total profits in each market is higher when multimarket contact is present. (Contact does not affect profits in state l but raises them in state h.) We doubt that this prediction also follows from any of the alternatives.

19 Corwin Edwards, as quoted in Scherer (1980, p. 340).

20 While this punishment is subgame perfect, it does have the unattractive feature that firm 2 plays a weakly dominated strategy. It is not difficult, however, to construct other punishment paths that yield the deviator a discounted payoff of zero and that do not involve weakly dominated strategies. (These have a "stick and carrot" structures as in Abreu (1986).) In any case, our basic points regarding the effect of multimarket contact do not rely in any way on the use of optimal punishments.

21 Proposition B2 in Appendix B shows that when $\delta < \frac{1}{2}$, sales never occur at a price above $\bar{c}$ in any period of a subgame perfect equilibrium. Our focus on stationary equilibria is therefore unrestrictive for such discount factors. When $\delta > \frac{1}{2}$, however, this focus may be restrictive since, as Schmalensee (1987) has shown, the set of payoffs achievable by market sharing is nonconvex. (So, profits may be increased by allowing the firms to alternate production between them.) Even so, for any $\delta < 1$, some production must be allocated to the inefficient firm. As a result, the firms still cannot achieve the joint profit-maximizing solution. In contrast, multimarket contact (as we show in the text) can allow them to achieve this outcome.

22 Note, however, that if punishments consisted of reversion to the static outcome, then a collusive price could *only* arise if $\delta[p^m(\underline{c}) - \underline{c}] \geq (\bar{c} - \underline{c})Q(\bar{c})$.

23 The reader may perceive a tension between the assumption that entry is blockaded (see note 7), and the supposition that each incumbent firm can freely enter the other's market even after complete withdrawal. Implicitly, we assume that each incumbent has an advantage over potential entrants in both markets and that it retains at least a portion of this advantage even if it terminates operations in some market. For example, the advantage could arise from a patent, knowledge, or other sunk assets that are useful in both markets. Alternatively, patents or assets may be market specific, but the firms may be legally barred from trading them so as to also prevent each other's entry.

24 Note that while this highly stylized model involves *complete* withdrawal of the less efficient firm, this need not happen with more general cost structures. If, for example, the marginal costs of production for the less efficient firm were $\underline{c}$ up to some quantity $\bar{q}$ but were $\bar{c}$ thereafter, then an optimal collusive arrangement would involve the less efficient firm producing $\bar{q}$ units. More generally, the optimal stationary market share allotment for any given price minimizes industry production costs; as in the case analyzed in the text, this share allotment allows firms to collude more effectively on prices. It is worth noting, however, that there may be advantages to complete withdrawal arising from factors not present in our model. Withdrawal may, for example, improve the quality of monitoring. (For example, in geographic markets, it may be easier to detect a rival's entry into a city than to monitor its price if it is selling there.)

25 Clearly, when $p^m(\underline{c})$ can be sustained, this stationary symmetric equilibrium is an optimal stationary symmetric-payoff equilibrium (since it yields the joint monopoly outcome). This is also true, however, when $p = p^m(\underline{c})$ does not satisfy (13). In particular, we show in Proposition B3 of Appendix B that in any stationary symmetric-payoff equilibrium, the highest price that can be sustained in either market must satisfy (13), and therefore no stationary symmetric-payoff equilibrium can yield larger profits than those derived in the text.

26   An additional and distinct way in which multimarket contact can facilitate collusion is by
     eliminating the bargaining problems associated with single-market asymmetries. For example,
     we have noted that a collusive price might not arise in the single-market case even when it could
     ($\delta \geq \frac{1}{2}$) because both firms might not benefit from this outcome. Multimarket contact can allow
     each firm to gain from collusion that raises aggregate profits by allowing each to gain in one
     market.

27   We would like to thank Ken Hendricks and Paul Klemperer for suggesting that we think about
     this issue.

28   Note that we could alternatively model side payments as occurring simultaneously with price
     choices. Which choice is more appropriate depends on the structure of the market that we are
     trying to capture. For example, if competition occurs in discrete lumps (as in government
     procurement auctions) but side payments can occur at any time, then the timing described in
     the text is appropriate. Alternatively, if the delay in reaction to a deviation occurs because
     changing prices takes time, while making side payments does not, then our assumed timing is
     again appropriate. If, on the other hand, the delay in punishment occurs because of a detection
     lag, then simultaneous modeling is more appropriate. With simultaneous modeling the equiva-
     lence discussed in the text does not hold. In particular, side payments no longer completely pool
     incentive constraints in the single-market context because the payment also appears on the left-
     hand side of either (14) or (15). (Whichever firm receives the side payment still receives it in the
     period in which it first deviates.)

29   Note, though, that in the case of geographic markets with high transportation costs, there is no
     simple policy, such as prevention of mergers, that can eliminate the effects of multimarket
     contact. (The essence of this situation is that differing costs arise precisely because firms do not
     have a plant in each market.)

30   See *Blue Bell Co. v. Frontier Refining Co.*, 213 F. 2d 354 (10th Cir. 1954) for an example in the
     oil industry and, in the corrugated container industry, Baker (1986).

31   We ignore any difficulties in enforcing the trade if both parties say "yes." In a sense, our
     "contractual" versus "noncontractual" distinction really represents long-term (many-period)
     versus short-term (single-period) contracting.

32   This illustrates that a breakdown in a noncontractual agreement is actually inessential to our
     result when trade is simultaneous with price choices. The surplus can be dissipated equally well
     through price choices. Likewise, although we have assumed that the contractual agreement
     remains in force, in principle, we could allow the firms to tear up the agreement and get the
     same result. The only important point about the contractual agreement is that it precludes the
     cessation of trade in the same period as a deviation, since the deviator can refuse to tear up
     the agreement.

33   Baker (1986) quotes a former paper industry executive as indicating that the threat of exclusion
     from the existing network of linerboard exchanges was an effective means of enforcing co-
     operation in the corrugated container industry. It is interesting to note that our analysis also
     suggests a theory of detente, in which gains from trade can help sustain more cooperative
     behavior in the military sphere. For a development of this idea, see Alt and Eichengreen (1987).

34   It should be clear that similar benefits can be had from supply agreements in a single-market
     context. Indeed, the outcomes that can arise with "at cost" supply arrangements are equivalent
     to those when nonbinding side payments occur. While such supply arrangements would
     typically raise a concern with antitrust authorities in a single-market context because of their
     "appearance" of being like side payments, reciprocal output agreements – which yield identical
     results here – are typically allowed.

35   For sufficiently large δ, however, there are nonstationary single-market equilibria which mimic
     the multimarket solutions. In essence, price alternates between a high and low value, and each
     firm produces most or all of the output in every other period.

36 Specifically, each firm announces the price p^c defined implicitly by the following single-firm, zero-profit condition: $(p^c - c)Q(p^c) - F = 0$. Consumers resolve their indifference by demanding all output from the same firm. Consequently, both firms earn zero profits, and neither has an incentive to deviate. One might object to this zero-profit equilibrium on the grounds that the convenient coordination of consumers' decisions is implausible. However, one can view the game here as a limiting approximation, either along the lines discussed in note 8, or alternatively by interpreting the continuous strategy space as approximating a large but finite number of strategies. With discrete price choices, for example, one could sustain an approximate zero-profit equilibrium without encountering the coordination problem: simply have one firm set the lowest price that yields nonnegative profits and have the other firm set its price "one penny" higher.

37 The points we cover in this section also apply to the case of quantity (Cournot) competition with homogeneous products. In fact, an earlier version of this article (Bernheim and Whinston (1986)) analyzed the Cournot case.

38 The symmetry of price choices within each market derives from the concavity assumption. In particular, if $\{(p_{1A}(t), p_{2A}(t), p_{1B}(t), p_{2B}(t))\}_{t=0}^{\infty}$ is a sustainable sequence of prices that yields symmetric payoffs, then $\{(\hat{p}_A(t), \hat{p}_A(t)), (\hat{p}_B(t), \hat{p}_B(t))\}_{t=0}^{\infty}$, where $\hat{p}_k(t) \equiv \frac{1}{2}[p_{1k}(t) + p_{2k}(t)]$ $(k = A, B)$ is a sustainable sequence that yields (weakly) larger symmetric payoffs. (Profits rise, while deviation profits fall.) Stationarity is demonstrated using an argument parallel to that in Abreu (1986).

39 $\hat{\pi}_k'' > 0 (k = A, B)$ implies that this condition is also sufficient for a profit maximum. (The frontier in Figure 2 will be strictly convex.)

40 Unfortunately, it is difficult to say anything general about the welfare effect of the movement from the single-market outcomes to the multimarket solution. We did perform some limited simulations using demands (x_1, x_2) generated by a representative consumer with quasi-linear preferences over x_1, x_2, and income (I) of the form $u(x_1, x_2, I) = I + \alpha(x_1 + x_2) - (\lambda/2)[x_1^2 + x_2^2] - \beta x_1 x_2$. We found multimarket contact to have a small positive effect on welfare (less than a 3% increase in all cases). The changes in prices due to this contact, however, were in some cases quite large. The difference between the prices in the two markets decreased by as much as 80% after the establishment of multimarket contact.

41 More precisely, a sufficient condition for the one-period punishment is that $\lim_{p \to 0} Q_k(p, p) = \infty$.

42 Of the various articles listed in note 2, only Gelfand and Spiller (1986) was not a cross-sectional study. They analyzed time series data on two interrelated Uruguayan banking markets (U.S. dollar and new pesos loans) and found multimarket effects. Examples of typical measures of multimarket contact can be found in Heggestad and Rhoades (1978) and in Scott (1982).

43 The closest article to this sort of test is that of Gelfand and Spiller (1986).

References

Abreu, D. (1986): "Extremal Equilibria of Oligopolistic Supergames," *Journal of Economic Theory*, 39, 191–225.

—— (1988): "On the Theory of Infinitely Repeated Games with Discounting," *Econometrica*, 56, 383–96.

Alt, J. E. and Eichengreen, B. (1987): "Overlapping and Simultaneous Games: Theory and Applications," mimeo, Harvard University.

Baker, B. J. (1986): *Price Collusion in the Paper Industry*, senior thesis, Harvard University.

Bernheim, B. D. and Ray, D. (1989): "Collective Dynamic Consistency in Repeated Games," *Games and Economic Behavior*, 1, 295–326.

——and Whinston, M. D. (1987): "Multimarket Contact and Collusive Behavior," Discussion Paper No. 1317, Harvard Institute of Economic Research, Harvard University.

——and—— (1986): "Multimarket Contact and Collusive Behavior," mimeo, Stanford University

—— Peleg, B., and Whinston, M. D. (1987): "Coalition-Proof Nash Equilibria: I. Concepts," *Journal of Economic Theory*, 42, 1–12.

Bulow, J., Geanakoplos, J., and Klemperer, P. (1985): "Multimarket Oligopoly: Strategic Substitutes and Complements," *Journal of Political Economy*, 93, 388–511.

Edwards, C. D. (1955): "Conglomerate Bigness as a Source of Power," In *Business Concentration and Price Policy*, NBER conference report, Princeton: Princeton University Press.

Farrell, J. and Maskin, E. (1989): "Renegotiation in Repeated Games," *Games and Economic Behavior*, 1, 327–60.

Gelfand, M. and Spiller, P. (1986): "Entry Barriers and Multiproduct Oligopolies: Do They Forbear or Spoil?" mimeo.

Green, E. and Porter, R. (1984): "Noncooperative Collusion under Imperfect Price Information," *Econometrica*, 52, 87–100.

Harrington, J. E. (1986): "Collusion in Multiproduct Oligopoly Games under a Finite Horizon," mimeo, Johns Hopkins University.

Heggestad, A. and Rhoades, S. (1978): "Multimarket Interdependence and Local Market Competition in Banking," *Review of Economics and Statistics*, 60, 523–32.

Marshall, W. J., Yawitz, J. B., and Greenberg, E. (1984): "Incentives for Diversification and the Structure of the Conglomerate Firm," *Southern Economic Journal*, 51, 1–22.

Mester, L. (1985): "The Effects of Multimarket Contact on Savings and Loan Behavior," research paper no. 85–13, Federal Reserve Bank of Philadelphia.

Mueller, D. C. (1977): "The Effects of Conglomerate Mergers: A Survey of the Empirical Evidence," *Journal of Banking and Finance*, 1, 315–47.

Phillips, O. R. and Mason, C. F. (1988): "Mutual Forbearance in a Conglomerate Game," mimeo, University of Wyoming.

Rhoades, S. A. and Heggestad, A. (1985): "Multimarket Interdependence and Performance in Banking: Two Tests," *The Antitrust Bulletin*, 30, 975–95.

Rotemberg, J. and Saloner, G. (1986): "A Supergame-Theoretic Model of Price Wars during Booms," *American Economic Review*, 76, 390–407.

Scherer, F. M. (1980): *Industrial Market Structure and Economic Performance*. Boston: Houghton Mifflin Company.

Schmalensee, R. (1987): "Competitive Advantage and Collusive Optima," *International Journal of Industrial Organization*, 5, 351–68.

Scott, J. T. (1982): "Multimarket Contact and Economic Performance," *Review of Economics and Statistics*, 64, 368–75.

Telser, L. G. (1980): "A Theory of Self-Enforcing Agreements," *Journal of Business*, 53, 27–44.

Tirole, J. (1988): *The Theory of Industrial Organization*. Cambridge, Mass.: M.I.T. Press.

Whithhead, D. (1978): "An Empirical Test of the Linked Oligopoly Theory: An Analysis of Florida Holding Companies," Working Paper, Federal Reserve Bank of Atlanta.

——and Luytjes, J. November (1983): "An Empirical Test of the Linked Oligopoly Theory: An Analysis of Florida Holding Companies Revisited," paper presented at the Southern Economics Association Meeting, 20–23.

PART III
Product Differentiation

Introduction

Part I of this reader introduced the "paradox" that results from contrasting assumptions and results of the Cournot and Bertrand models. Capacity constraints were then proposed as a first possible solution to the "paradox." In part 2, a second solution was proposed: repeated interaction. A third possible solution to the Cournot–Bertrand "paradox" is given by product differentiation. In particular, the result that price competition leads to pricing at the level of marginal cost depends crucially on the assumption (common to the Cournot and Bertrand models) of product homogeneity.

The first attempt to formally model competition with differentiated products is due to Hotelling (1929). Hotelling went futher than the issue of equilibrium pricing with product differentiation. He was also interested in the equilibrium choice of products, in particular the equilibrium degree of product differentiation.[1] Hotelling considered a model where consumers are uniformly distributed along a segment and pay a total cost given by price plus transportation cost to the seller's location. Hotelling concluded that, in equilibrium, firms choose to locate very close to each other, in the middle of the segment – thence the principle of *minimum product differentiation*.

D'Aspremont, Gabszewicz and Thisse (1979) show that Hotelling's equilibrium derivation is incorrect. In fact, for the case considered by Hotelling, no price equilibrium in pure strategies exists when the firms' products are similar. D'Aspremont et al. consider a slightly different version of the Hotelling model (quadratic transportation costs instead of linear transportation costs) and show that the equilibrium corresponds to firms *maximizing*, not minimizing, the degree of product differentiation. The importance of d'Aspremont et al.'s contribution lies more in the methodology (completely and correctly solving the two-period model) than in the result itself (maximum differentiation). In fact, as de Palma et al. (1985) have shown, Hotelling's principle of minimum differentiation holds under sufficient consumer heterogeneity.

On a slightly more technical note, one interesting problem raised by the Hotelling model is that of equilibrium existence. Important results pertaining to a class of models that includes Hotelling were developed by Caplin and Nalebuff (1991).[2]

A distinction is normally made between horizontal and vertical differentiation. The Hotelling model is one of *horizontal* product differentiation: different consumers have different valuations for different products. Some consumers prefer A to B, other consumers prefer B to A. An example is given by the sweetness of a cola drink: different consumers have different ideas of what the ideal sugar content is, and so a little more sugar is a good thing for some consumers and a bad thing for other consumers. In contrast, when all consumers agree that, conditional on price, product A is better than product B, then we have a case of *vertical* product differentiation. The durability of a battery might be an example: all consumers agree that longer lasting batteries are better.

The first models to examine the issue of competition with vertical product differentiation are Gabszewicz and Thisse (1979) and Shaked and Sutton (1982). Gabszewicz and Thisse determine the price equilibrium for exogenously given product qualities. Shaked and Sutton examine in addition the endogenous choice of quality levels.[3]

Since these seminal papers in the late 1970s and early 1980s, a large amount of research has been devoted to modeling oligopoly competition with product differentiation. Many of these models are extensions or variations of the horizontal or vertical differentiation models. Specifically, Salop (1979) considers a version of the Hotelling model where consumers are located along a circumference – not a segment – an alternative modeling strategy that has come to play an important role in economic analysis. Many of the models in this line of research are concerned with the issue of endogenous choice of the degree of product differentiation. However, in light of the ambiguity evidenced in the paper by de Palma et al. (1985), the value added by this literature seems questionable.

For all their differences, the vertical and the horizontal product differentiation models have one aspect in common: They are both "address" models. Each firm is located at a given "address," and has at most two direct competitors, its direct neighbors. A radically different approach to modeling product differentiation is that of "non-address" models. Under the latter approach, each product competes directly with all other products. Important contributions to this literature include Spence (1976) and Dixit and Stiglitz (1977). One question these authors are concerned with is the comparison of the equilibrium number of product varieties to the socially optimal number of product varieties. The answer is – it depends. More on this in part 5.

The address and the non-address approaches are both very extreme. The address approach exaggerates the extent of neighborhood effects. The non-address approach assumes no neighborhood effects. Reality is clearly somewhere in between. For this reason, a promising line of research is that of models based on the characteristics approach. Each products is defined by a number of characteristics, normally a number greater than one. Each consumer is defined by valuations for each of the product characteristics and maximizes the difference between utility and price. This approach, which dates back to at least Lancaster (1979), has been developed, inter alia, by Anderson et al. (1989). The approach has two advantages. First, it encompasses the models considered earlier in this part. For example, vertical product differentiation obtains when there is one characteristic only. Second, it has shown promising results in terms of empirical application, as we will see in part 4.

Notes

1 This is another instance of the framework analyzed by Fudenberg and Tirole in the paper included in part 1.
2 An even more general set of results regarding existence of Nash equilibrium, with applications to a series of IO models, was developed by Dasgupta and Maskin (1986). The seminal contribution is, of course, Nash (1951).
3 One of the interesting results in Shaked and Sutton is that, with two competitors, the profits of the lower-quality firm decrease as the firm increases its quality, *even if quality is costless* – a result that runs counter to the "principle of minimum differentiation."

References

Anderson, Simon P, André de Palma and Jacques-François Thisse (1989): "Demand for Differentiated Products, Discrete Choice Models and the Characteristics Approach," *Review of Economic Studies*, 56, 21–35.

Caplin, Andrew and Barry Nalebuff (1991): "Aggregation and Imperfect Competition: On the Existence of Equilibrium," *Econometrica*, 59, 25–59.

Dasgupta, Partha and Eric Maskin (1986): "The Existence of Equilibrium in Discontinuous Economic Games," *Review of Economic Studies*, 53, 1–41.

d'Aspremont, Claude, J. Jaskold Gabszewicz and Jacques-François Thisse (1979): "On Hotelling's 'Stability of Competition'," *Econometrica*, 47, 1145–50.

de Palma, A., V. Ginsburgh, Y. Y. Papageorgiou and J.-F. Thisse (1985): "The Principle of Minimum Differentiation Holds Under Sufficient Heterogeneity," *Econometrica*, 53, 767–81.

Dixit, Avinash and Joseph Stiglitz (1977): "Monopolistic Competition and Optimum Product Diversity," *American Economic Review*, 67, 297–308.

Gabszewicz, Jaskold and Jacques-François Thisse (1979): "Price Competition, Quality and Income Disparities," *Journal of Economic Theory*, 2, 340–59.

Hotelling, Harold (1929): "Stability in Competition," *Economic Journal*, 39, 41–57.

Lancaster, Kelvin (1979): *Variety, Equity and Efficiency*. Oxford: Basil Blackwell.

Nash, John (1951): "Non-Cooperative Games," *Annals of Mathematics*, 54, 286–95.

Salop, Steven C. (1979): "Monopolistic Competition with Outside Goods," *Bell Journal of Economics*, 10, 141–56.

Shaked, Avner and John Sutton (1982): "Relaxing Price Competition Through Product Differentiation," *Review of Economic Studies*, 49, 3–13.

Spence, Michael (1976): "Product Selection, Fixed Costs and Monopolistic Competition," *Review of Economic Studies*, 43, 217–36.

CHAPTER SIX

On Hotelling's "Stability in Competition"

CLAUDE D'ASPREMONT, J. JASKOLD GABSZEWICZ, AND
JACQUES-FRANÇOIS THISSE

Source: *Econometrica*, 1979, 47, 1145–50.

The purpose of this note is to show that the so-called *Principle of Minimum Differentiation*, as based on Hotelling's 1929 celebrated paper (Hotelling [4]), is invalid. Firstly, we assert that, contrary to the statement formulated by Hotelling in his model, nothing can be said about the tendency of both sellers to agglomerate at the center of the market. The reason is that no equilibrium price solution will exist when both sellers are not far enough from each other. Secondly, we consider a slightly modified version of Hotelling's example, for which there exists a price equilibrium solution everywhere. We show however that, for this version, there is a tendency for both sellers to maximize their differentiation. This example thus constitutes a counterexample to Hotelling's conclusions.

We shall first recall Hotelling's model and notations. On a line of length l, two sellers A and B of a homogeneous product, with zero production cost, are located at respective distances a and b from the ends of this line ($a + b \leq l$; $a \geq 0, b \geq 0$). Customers are evenly distributed along the line, and each customer consumes exactly a single unit of this commodity per unit of time, irrespective of its price. Since the product is homogeneous, a customer will buy from the seller who quotes the least delivered price, namely the mill price plus transportation cost, which is assumed linear with respect to the distance. Let p_1 and p_2 denote, respectively, the mill price of A and B and let c denote the transportation rate.

The situation described above gives rise to a two-person game with *players* A and B, *strategies* $p_1 \in S_1 \underset{def}{=} [0, \infty[$, and $p_2 \in S_2 = S_1$, and *payoff functions* given by the profit functions:

$$
\begin{aligned}
\pi_1(p_1, p_2) &= ap_1 + \tfrac{1}{2}(l - a - b)p_1 + \tfrac{1}{2c} p_1 p_2 - \tfrac{1}{2c} p_1^2 && \text{if } |p_1 - p_2| \leq c(l - a - b) \\
&= lp_1 && \text{if } p_1 < p_2 - c(l - a - b) \\
&= 0 && \text{if } p_1 > p_2 + c(l - a - b)
\end{aligned}
$$

$$\pi_2(p_1, p_2) = bp_2 + \tfrac{1}{2}(l - a - b)p_2 + \tfrac{1}{2c}p_1 p_2 - \tfrac{1}{2c}p_2^2 \quad \text{if}\, |p_1 - p_2| \le c(l - a - b)$$
$$= lp_2 \qquad\qquad\qquad\qquad\qquad\qquad \text{if}\, p_2 < p_1 - c(l - a - b)$$
$$= 0 \qquad\qquad\qquad\qquad\qquad\qquad\quad \text{if}\, p_2 > p_1 + c(l - a - b)$$

The profit function of seller A is illustrated in Figure 1 for a fixed value $\bar{p}_2$.

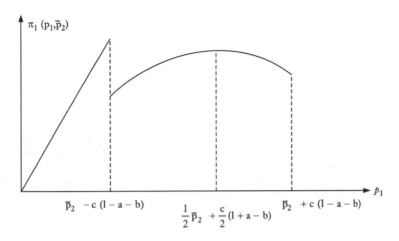

Figure 1

Clearly a particular feature of these profit functions is the presence of two discontinuities which appear at the price where a whole group of buyers is indifferent between the two sellers.

A strategy p_1 of player A is a *best reply against* a strategy p_2 of player B when it maximizes $\pi_1(\cdot, p_2)$ on the whole S_1 for the given p_2. Similarly for player B. A *Nash-Cournot equilibrium point* is a pair (p_1^*, p_2^*) such that p_1^* is a best reply against p_2^* and vice-versa.

In the following proposition we shall treat the problem of existence of such an equilibrium for every location a and b. More specifically, we shall derive necessary and sufficient conditions on a and b for such an equilibrium to exist, and compute all equilibrium points.

PROPOSITION: *For $a + b = l$, the unique equilibrium point is given by $p_1^* = p_2^* = 0$. For $a + b < l$, there is an equilibrium point if, and only if*

$$\left(1 + \frac{a - b}{3}\right)^2 \ge \tfrac{4}{3}l(a + 2b) \tag{1}$$

$$\left(1 + \frac{b - a}{3}\right)^2 \ge \tfrac{4}{3}l(b + 2a) \tag{2}$$

and, whenever it exists, an equilibrium point is uniquely determined by

$$p_1^* = c\left(l + \frac{a-b}{3}\right) \tag{3}$$

$$p_2^* = c\left(l - \frac{a-b}{3}\right) \tag{4}$$

PROOF: The case $a + b = l$ is immediate. Then both sellers are located at the same place and, as in Bertrand [1], there always exists an equilibrium uniquely determined by $p_1^* = p_2^* = 0$. So let $a + b < l$. We shall begin by showing that any equilibrium must satisfy the condition $|p_1^* - p_2^*| < c(l - a - b)$.

Suppose first on the contrary that (p_1^*, p_2^*) is an equilibrium but $|p_1^* - p_2^*| > c(l - a - b)$. Then, one of the two sellers – the one who charges the strictly larger (and hence positive) price – gets a null profit and so may gain by charging a positive price equal to the delivered price of the other. But this contradicts the fact that (p_1^*, p_2^*) is an equilibrium. Suppose now that $|p_1^* - p_2^*| = c(l - a - b)$, say, for instance, $p_2^* - p_1^* = c(l - a - b)$. If $p_1^* = 0$, then the profit of A is zero and so he would profit by charging a positive price less than $p_2^* + c(l - a - b)$. If $p_1^* > 0$, two cases may arise. Either A gets the whole market and so B, who charges a positive price, can increase his profit by decreasing his price. Or A gets only a fraction of the market, i.e. $q_1 < l$, and it is then sufficient for A to charge a slightly lower price to capture the whole market and make a larger profit: indeed for $0 < \varepsilon < (l - q_1)p_1^*/l$ we have $\pi_1(p_1^* - \varepsilon, p_2^*) = l(p_1^* - \varepsilon) > q_1 p_1^* = \pi_1(p_1^*, p_2^*)$. In any case we always get a contradiction. Accordingly any equilibrium (p_1^*, p_2^*) must satisfy the condition $|p_1^* - p_2^*| < c(l - a - b)$.

A consequence of this condition is that, for any equilibrium (p_1^*, p_2^*), p_1^* must maximize $a p_1 + \frac{1}{2}(l - a - b)p_1 + (\frac{1}{2c})p_2^* p_1 - (\frac{1}{2c})p_1^2$ in the open interval $]p_2^* - c(l - a - b)$, $p_2^* + c(l - a - b)[$, and similarly for p_2^*. Taking first order conditions we get (3) and (4). Hence, we shall now verify that the pair of prices given by (3) and (4) is indeed an equilibrium. Recall that to be an equilibrium strategy p_1^* must maximize $\pi_1(p_1, p_2^*)$ not only in the above interval but on the whole domain S_1, and similarly for p_2^*. Let us see that this is true only on a restricted set of possible locations. Indeed, given a and b, for p_2^* to be an equilibrium strategy against p_2^*, we must have in particular that, for any $\varepsilon > 0$,

$$\pi_1(p_1^*, p_2^*) = \frac{c}{2}\left[l + \frac{a-b}{3}\right]^2 \geq l[p_2^* - c(l - a - b) - \varepsilon]. \tag{*}$$

The right-hand side of the inequality is the profit of A, should he quote a delivered price slightly smaller than p_2^*. But condition $(*)$ can be rewritten as (1). By symmetry we get condition (2).

To show that conditions (1) and (2) are also sufficient for (p_1^*, p_2^*) to be an equilibrium it remains only to check that they imply $|p_1^* - p_2^*| < c(l - a - b)$. This completes the proof of our proposition.

Note in passing that if we consider only symmetric locations around the center $(a = b)$, then the necessary and sufficient conditions (1) and (2) reduce to $a = b \leq l/4$. In other words, both the duopolists must be located outside the quartiles to get a Cournot equilibrium in prices.

If conditions (1) and (2) are strictly verified, then, as noted by Hotelling, both $\partial\pi_1(p_1^*,p_2^*)/\partial a$ and $\partial\pi_2(p_1^*,p_2^*)/\partial b$ are strictly positive, which implies a tendency of both sellers towards the center. But a major consequence of the preceding proposition is that, as far as the Cournot equilibrium is taken as the market solution, nothing can be said on this solution when conditions (1) and (2) are violated. Hotelling seems to be unaware of this difficulty while deriving the implications of his model, and in particular the tendency of both sellers to agglomerate at the center of the market.[1] Indeed should conditions (1) and (2) be violated, i.e., should the firms be located relatively close to each other, the Cournot equilibrium could no longer serve as a reference point since it no longer exists![2]

Having reached this negative outcome, it seems natural to work out an example, which is as close as possible to Hotelling's one, but avoiding the difficulty exhibited above.[3] If, for this alternative example, the principle of minimal differentiation could be retrieved, the defect in Hotelling's argumentation would be immaterial. Unfortunately, this principle is invalidated by the following reexamination.

A slightly modified version of Hotelling's example for which there exists a price equilibrium solution for *any* pair of locations (a, b) obtains if, in place of considering linear transportation costs we assume that these costs are quadratic with respect to the distance, i.e., for any distance x, transportation costs are given by cx^2. Under this assumption, an easy computation leads to the following expressions for the demand and profit functions:

$$q_1(p_1, p_2) = a + \frac{p_2 - p_2}{2c(l - a - b)} + \frac{l - a - b}{2} \quad \text{if } 0 \leq a + \frac{p_2 - p_1}{2c(l - a - b)} + \frac{l - a - b}{2} \leq l$$

$$= l \quad \text{if } a + \frac{p_2 - p_1}{2c(l - a - b)} + \frac{l - a - b}{2} > l$$

$$= 0 \quad \text{if } a + \frac{p_2 - p_1}{2c(l - a - b)} + \frac{l - a - b}{2} < 0$$

$$q_1(p_1, p_2) = b + \frac{p_1 - p_2}{2c(l - a - b)} + \frac{l - a - b}{2} \quad \text{if } 0 \leq b + \frac{p_1 - p_2}{2c(l - a - b)} + \frac{l - a - b}{2} \leq l$$

$$= l \quad \text{if } b + \frac{p_1 - p_2}{2c(l - a - b)} + \frac{l - a - b}{2} > l$$

$$= 0 \quad \text{if } b + \frac{p_1 - p_2}{2c(l - a - b)} + \frac{l - a - b}{2} < 0$$

$\pi_1(p_1, p_2) = p_1 \cdot q_1(p_1, p_2)$ and $\pi_2(p_1, p_2) = p_2 \cdot q_2(p_1, p_2)$. These profit functions ensure the existence of a price equilibrium, *whatever the locations a and b may be*. It is indeed easily checked that the pair of prices (p_1^*, p_2^*) defined by

$$p_1^* = c(l - a - b)\left(l + \frac{a - b}{3}\right) \tag{5}$$

$$p_2^* = c(l - a - b)\left(l + \frac{b - a}{3}\right) \tag{6}$$

is the unique Nash–Cournot equilibrium point for fixed a and b, and that this is true without any condition on these location parameters. We verify however that, if we substitute these equilibrium prices in the profit functions of both players, both $\partial \pi_1(p_1^*, p_2^*)/\partial a$ and $\partial \pi_2(p_1^*, p_2^*)/\partial b$ are negative! Consequently, at any given pair of locations, each merchant gains an advantage from moving away as far as possible from the other.[4]

The preceding example, far from confirming the minimal differentiation principle, suggests that this principle cannot be based on spatial competition. Certainly many comments derived from Hotelling's contribution should be carefully reexamined before taking them as granted. The outcome of this note should not however be considered as too negative. Indeed, although Hotelling's example suggested the contrary, one should expect intuitively that product differentiation must be an important component of oligopolistic competition. It seems to be clear that oligopolists should gain an advantage by dividing the market into submarkets in each of which some degree of monopoloy would reappear.[5] But this important subject would need more imagination.

Notes

1   In footnote (8) of his paper, Hotelling remarks however that, for some values of a and b, the pair of prices defined by (3) and (4) cannot be an equilibrium, but proposes then another pair of prices as an equilibrium. By our proposition, we know that they are not. It seems that Hotelling has neglected to consider strategies through which a merchant undercuts the delivered price of the other, and attracts to him the whole market. These strategies are particularly advantageous when both merchants are close to each other.

2   Here we only consider equilibrium with price strategies. However, it is easily verified that if each seller's strategy is a price location pair, which has to be chosen simultaneously, then again no Nash equilibrium exists.

3   This example is particularly illustrative in regard to footnote (9) of Hotelling's paper.

4   In other terms, for the game where the strategies are the locations and the payoff functions the profits $\pi_1(p_1^*(a, b), p_2^*(a, b))$ and $\pi_2(p_1^*(a, b), p_2^*(a, b))$ – which can be viewed as a sequential game where first locations, and then prices, are chosen – the equilibrium locations are the two extremes. As a referee pointed out to us, Hay [3] and Prescott and Visscher [5] use a similar sequential approach. In particular, Prescott and Visscher analyze the existence problem by numerical methods in a revised Hotelling problem and find equilibrium locations "far apart." We should stress however that the existence is not restored simply because the discontinuities of the demand functions are eliminated as, for example, by introducing the assumption of strictly convex transportation costs. We have indeed worked out an example which verifies the latter assumption and does not possess any equilibrium prices.

5   An example of this advantage is studied in Gabszewicz and Thisse [2] and Salop [6].

References

1   Bertrand, J. (1883): "Théorie mathématique de la richesse sociale," *Journal des Savants*, 48, 499–508.

2   Gabszewicz Jaskold, J., and J.-F. Thisse: "Price Competition, Quality, and Income Disparities," *Journal of Economic Theory*, forthcoming.

3   Hay, D. A. (1976): "Sequential Entry and Entry-Deterring Strategies," *Oxford Economic Papers*, 28, 240–57.

4   Hotelling, H. (1928): "Stability in Competition," *Economic Journal*, 39, 41–57.

5   Prescott, E. C., and M. Visscher (1977): "Sequential Location among Firms with Foresight," *The Bell Journal of Economics*, 8, 378–93.

6   Salop, S. (1977): "Monopolistic Competition Reconstituted or – Circular Fashions in Economic Thought," mimeo, Federal Reserve Board, Washington, D.C.

CHAPTER SEVEN

Relaxing Price Competition Through Product Differentiation

AVNER SHAKED AND JOHN SUTTON

Source: Review of Economic Studies, 1982, 49, 3–13.

The notion of a Perfect Equilibrium in a multi-stage game is used to characterize industry equilibrium under Monopolistic Competition, where products are differentiated by quality.

Central to the problem of providing adequate foundations for the analysis of monopolistic competition, is the problem of describing market equilibria in which firms choose both the specification of their respective products, and their prices. The present paper is concerned with a – very particular – model of such a market equilibrium. In this equilibrium, exactly two potential entrants will choose to enter the industry; they will choose to produce differentiated products; and both will make positive profits.

1. The Equilibrium Concept

Our present analysis is based on a three-stage non-cooperative game. In the first stage, firms choose whether or not to enter the industry. At the end of the first stage, each firm observes which firms have entered, and which have not. In the second stage each firm chooses the quality of its product. Then, having observed its rivals' qualities, in the final stage of the game, each firm chooses its price. This three-stage process is intended to capture the notion that the price can in practice be varied at will, but a change in the specification of a product involves modification of the appropriate production facilities; while entry to the industry requires construction of a plant.

The strategies of firms specify actions to be taken in each of the three stages.

Thus a (pure) strategy takes one of two forms, "don't enter", or else "enter; choose a level of quality, dependent on the number of firms who have entered; and set price, dependent both on the number of entrants and on the quality of their respective products".

The payoffs will be defined in terms of a model of consumer choice between the alternative products, in section 2 below. They will be identified with the profit earned by the firm, less a "cost of entry" of $\epsilon > 0$, for those who enter; and zero for non-entrants.

We may now define the solution concept. As in any non-cooperative game, we might investigate the set of Nash Equilibria. Here, as is often the case, that set may be very large. We therefore introduce the now familiar concept of a Perfect Equilibrium (Selten (1975)).

An n-tuple of strategies is a Perfect Equilibrium in this three-stage game, if, after any stage, that part of the firms strategies pertaining to the game consisting of those stages which remain, form a Nash Equilibrium in that game.

It follows immediately from this that, after any stage, that part of the firms' strategies pertaining to the game consisting of those stages which remain, in fact form a Perfect Equilibrium in that game.

Thus, for example, when firms have decided whether to enter, and have chosen their qualities, we require that their price strategies are a Nash Equilibrium, i.e. a non-cooperative price equilibrium, in the single remaining stage of the game.

To study such a Perfect Equilibrium, we begin, therefore, by analysing the final stage of the game – being the choice of price, given the number of entrants and the qualities of their respective products (section 2). We will then proceed, in section 3, to examine the choice of quality by firms, and in section 4 we consider the entry decision. Section 5 contains a summary of the argument, and develops some conclusions.

2. Price Competition

Consider a number of firms producing distinct, substitute goods.[1] We label their respective products by an index $k = 1, \ldots, n$ where firm k sells product k at price p_k.

Assume a continuum of consumers identical in tastes but differing in income; incomes are uniformly distributed, viz. the density equals unity on some support $0 < a \leqq t \leqq b$.

Consumers make indivisible and mutually exclusive purchases from among these n goods, in the sense that a consumer either makes no purchase, or else buys exactly one unit from one of the n firms.[2] We denote by $U(t, k)$ the utility achieved by consuming one unit of product k and t units of "income" (the latter may be thought of as a Hicksian "composite commodity", measured as a continuous variable); and by $U(t, 0)$ the utility derived from consuming t units of income only.

Assume that the utility function takes the form

$$U(t, k) = u_k \cdot t \tag{1}$$

with $u_0 < u_1 < \ldots < u_n$ (i.e. the products are labeled in increasing order of quality).

Let

$$C_k = \frac{u_k}{u_k - u_{k-1}}$$

(whence $C_k > 1$). Then we may define the income level t_k such that a consumer with income t_k is indifferent between good k at price p_k and good $k - 1$ at price p_{k-1}, viz.

$$U(t_k - p_k, k) = U(t_k - p_{k-1}, k - 1)$$

whence

$$t_1 = p_1 C_1$$

and

$$t_k = p_{k-1}(1 - C_k) + p_k C_k \tag{2}$$

This is easily checked by reference to (1).

Now it follows immediately on inspection of (1) that consumers with income $t > t_k$ strictly prefer good k at price p_k to good $k - 1$ at p_{k-1}, and conversely, whence consumers are partitioned into segments corresponding to the successive market shares of rival firms.

Assuming zero costs the profit (revenue) of the k-th firm is:

$$R_1 = \begin{cases} p_1(t_2 - a) & t_1 \leq a \\ p_1(t_2 - t_1) & t_1 \geq b \end{cases}$$
$$R_k = p_k(t_{k-1} - t_k) \quad 1 < k < n \tag{3}$$
$$R_n = p_n(b - t_n)$$

Now, at equilibrium (if it exists), it follows trivially that the top quality product will enjoy a positive market share; moreover if any product has zero market share, so also do all lower quality products.

Now where n products co-exist at equilibrium (i.e. each of these n goods has a positive market share) the first-order necessary conditions for profit (revenue) maximization take the form,

for $k = 1$

$$t_2 - a - p_1(C_2 - 1) \quad = 0 \qquad t_1 \leq a$$
$$t_2 - t_1 - p_1[(C_2 - 1) + C_1] \quad = 0 \qquad t_1 \geq a$$

for $k = 2, \ldots, n - 1$

$$t_{t-1} - t_k - p_k[(C_{k-1} - 1) + C_k] = 0 \tag{4}$$

for $k = n$

$$b - t_n - p_n C_n \quad = 0$$

We may now proceed to establish:

LEMMA 1. *Let $b < 4a$. Then for any Nash Equilibrium involving the distinct goods $n, n - 1$, $\ldots, 1$ at most two products (the top two) have a positive market share at equilibrium.*

PROOF.   Assume that there exists a Nash Equilibrium in which three or more products have a positive market share at equilibrium. From inspection of the necessary conditions for profit maximization (4), and remembering $C_k > 1$, it follows that, for $k > 1$, and $k = n$, respectively, by rewriting the first-order conditions and using the definition of t_k,

$$t_{k+1} - 2t_k - p_k(C_{k+1} - 1) - p_{k-1}(C_k - 1) = 0$$
$$b - 2t_n - p_{n-1}(C_n - 1) = 0$$

whence

$$b > 2t_n \quad t_{k+1} > 2t_k$$

whence

$$4t_{n-1} < b$$

Now by assumption $b < 4a$, so that $t_{n-1} < a$ i.e. the top two firms cover the market. Thus equilibrium involves at most two products. ‖
    The idea here is that price competition between "high quality" products drives their prices down to a level at which not even the poorest consumer would prefer to buy certain lower quality products even at price zero. Clearly, the number of products which can survive at equilibrium depends on the distribution of income. Lemma 1 provides a restriction, that $b < 4a$, which is sufficient to limit this number to *at most* two; we shall in fact be concerned with this case in what follows.
    It will be convenient at this point, then, to cite the special form of the revenue functions and the first-order conditions for the case where $n = 2$, i.e. where exactly two firms enjoy a positive market share.
    We define

$$V = \frac{u_2 - u_0}{u_2 - u_1} = \frac{C_2 - 1}{C_1} + 1 \tag{5}$$

being a measure of the relative qualities of goods 1 and 2, and the residual good 0.
    Applying equation (2) we have here that

$$p_1 = \frac{t_1}{C_1} \quad \text{and} \quad p_2 = \frac{t_2 + t_1(V - 1)}{C_2} \tag{6}$$

Using equations (5), (6) we may rewrite the first-order conditions for profit maximization in terms of t_1, t_2, V, viz.

firm 1:

$$\begin{aligned} t_2 \qquad &= a + t_1(V - 1) \quad t_1 \leqq a \\ t_2 \qquad &= t_1(V + 1) \qquad t_1 \geqq a \end{aligned} \tag{7}$$

firm 2:

$$b - 2t_2 = \qquad t_1(V-1) \qquad\qquad (8)$$

We identify three regions as illustrated in Figure 1. For a certain range of p_2 chosen by firm 2, the optimal reply of firm 1 leads to an outcome (t_1, t_2) in region II, i.e. $t_1 = a, aV \leqq t_2 \leqq a(V+1)$. Over this range firm 1 leaves its price constant as p_2 varies; at the price p_1 it chooses, the poorest consumer is just willing to buy good 1. Firm 1 faces a demand schedule which is kinked at this price level (given p_2); and either raising or lowering price reduces revenue. Thus we have a corner solution, and the equalities of (7) are replaced by a pair of inequalities.

Equation (8) describes a decreasing function of t_1,

$$t_2 = \tfrac{1}{2}\left[b - t_1(V-1) \right]$$

The intersection of (7), (8) defines the unique equilibrium pair (t_1, t_2), and so the equilibrium pair (p_1, p_2).

Whether the solution lies in region I, II or III depends on where the decreasing function (8) cuts the vertical $t_1 = a$, viz.

region I if $\qquad V \geqq \dfrac{b+a}{3a}$

region II if $\dfrac{b+a}{3a} \geqq V \geqq \dfrac{b-a}{3a}$

region III if $\qquad V \leqq \dfrac{b-a}{3a}$

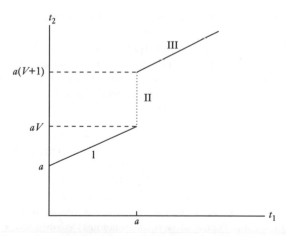

Figure 1   The first order conditions for profit maximization by firm 1

Thus the solution lies in region I when the qualities are "close", and in region III when the qualities are "far apart".

If the solution lies in region III, then $t_1 > a$ and some consumers purchase neither good. If the solution lies in region II then all consumers purchase one or other good – the market is "covered", and the poorest consumer is indifferent between buying the low quality product 1 or not. In region I the market is again covered, but now the poorest consumer strictly prefers to purchase product 1.

Moreover, we note from equations (7), (8) that,

in region I:

$$t_1 = \frac{b - 2a}{3(V - 1)} \qquad t_2 = \frac{b + a}{3} \tag{9}$$

while

in region II:

$$t_1 = a \qquad\qquad t_2 = \tfrac{1}{2}[b - a(V - 1)] \tag{10}$$

We are now in a position to strengthen our earlier result.

LEMMA 2.   *Let $2a < b < 4a$. Then of any n firms offering distinct products, exactly two will have positive market shares at equilibrium. Moreover, at equilibrium, the market is covered (i.e. the equilibrium is not in region III).*

PROOF.   From Lemma 1 only two goods (at most) will survive with positive market shares and positive price. Hence we may write the equations for this case as developed above.

We note from Figure 1 that the decreasing function (8) lies above a for $t_1 = 0$ (Note $t_2(0) = b/2 > a$).

Hence the two functions (7), (8) intersect at a point such that $t_1 > 0, t_2 > a$, so that the two products coexist with positive market shares.

To verify that this solution is indeed an equilibrium, it must further be shown that the second-order conditions are satisfied, i.e. the revenue function of firm 1, given p_2, is concave, over all p_1; and conversely. This may be verified in a straightforward manner. Moreover, since $b < 4a, (b - a)/3a < 1$ and the condition for the solution to be in region III cannot be met (as $V > 1$) so the market is covered.   ‖

From this point forward we shall assume that $2a < b < 4a$.

The preceding discussion establishes the existence of a unique price pair which forms a Nash Equilibrium in prices, for any two distinct levels of product quality. Moreover, both firms enjoy strictly positive revenue. If on the other hand the firms choose the same level of quality, our use of a non-cooperative price equilibrium ensures that both prices become zero (the Bertrand duopoly case); so that both firms have revenue zero at equilibrium. In either case, the equilibrium vector of payoffs (revenues) is uniquely determined via our preceding discussion.

We now turn to the case where more than two firms enter the industry. Still assuming, as always, that $2a < b < 4a$, we distinguish two cases. If one firm has a quality lower than either of its rivals, it has a zero market share, and so revenue zero, as shown in Lemma 1. If two (or three) firms have an equal lowest quality, then the price of this lowest quality product is zero at equilibrium (again from the usual Bertrand argument). In either case, any firm setting the lowest, or equal lowest, quality, has revenue zero at equilibrium. Thus, the equilibrium vector of payoffs (revenues) of the firms present in the industry is uniquely determined via our preceding characterization.

3. Competition in Quality

We now turn to the preceding stage of the process, in which firms choose quality. Let k denote the number of firms who have entered. We introduce the notation G^k to denote the two-stage game in which quality is first chosen, and then price.

Finding a perfect equilibrium in G^k is equivalent to finding a Nash equilibrium in qualities, the payoffs arising from any vector of qualities being defined by the (unique) equilibrium vector of revenues in the "choice of price" game of the preceding section.

We suppose for the moment that the number of firms is exactly two, deferring the question of further "potential entrants" until later.

Each firm chooses a level of quality, being a value $u_i, u_0 < u_i < \bar{u}$, where $\bar{u}$ is an exogenously given upper bound on quality.

We introduce the notation $R(u; v)$ to denote the revenue of a firm whose product is of quality u, its rival's product being of quality v, at a Nash equilibrium in prices.

We will establish the existence of an equilibrium involving differentiated products, as a consequence of two properties of the revenue function $R(u; v)$. The first property, stated in Lemma 3, is that, at equilibrium, the revenue of the firm offering the higher quality product is greater. The second property (Lemma 4) states that the revenue of both firms increases as the quality of the better product improves. The latter property reflects the effect of the lessening of price competition as qualities diverge, and is the key to the existence of an equilibrium with differentiated products in the present analysis. (This runs counter to the classic Hotelling "Principle of Minimal Differentiation", of course (Hotelling (1928), d'Aspremont, Gabszewicz and Thisse (1979)).

LEMMA 3. *For any two qualities $u > v$, the top quality firm enjoys greater revenue than its rival, i.e.*

$$R(u; v) > R(v; u)$$

PROOF. Let the pair of prices p, q for u and v respectively be a Nash Equilibrium in prices. Trivially, $p > q$. But one strategy open to the top firm is to set its price equal to q, (whereupon the low quality firm has sales zero) and its sales clearly exceed those of its rival in the initial equilibrium. Hence our result follows immediately. ‖

LEMMA 4. *The revenues of both firms increase as the quality of the better product improves, i.e. $R(v; u)$ and $R(u; v)$ are increasing in u for $u \geqq v$.*

PROOF.   We establish the result separately for the two cases where the outcome is in region I, and in region II, respectively.

We begin by writing down the revenue of both firms in region I. We have from (9) that the revenue of firm 1 is

$$R(u_1; u_2) = p_1(t_2 - a) = \frac{t_1}{C_1}\left(\frac{b - 2a}{3}\right) = \left(\frac{b - 2a}{3}\right)^2 \frac{1}{(V - 1)C_1} = \left(\frac{b - 2a}{3}\right)^2 \frac{u_2 - u_1}{u_1}$$

$$(11)$$

while the revenue of firm 2 is

$$R(u_2; u_1) = p_2(b - t_2) = \left(\frac{2b - a}{3}\right)^2 \frac{1}{C_2} = \left(\frac{2b - a}{3}\right)^2 \left(\frac{u_2 - u_1}{u_2}\right) \tag{12}$$

Both these expressions increase with u_2, for $u_2 \geqq u_1$, whence our result follows.

In region II we have from (10) that

$$R(u_1; u_2) = p_1(t_2 - a) = \frac{a[b - a(V + 1)]}{2C_1}$$

$$R(u_2; u_1) = p_2(b - t_2) = \frac{[b + a(V - 1)]^2}{4C_2}$$

That $R(u_1; u_2)$ increases in u_2 follows on noting that V falls as u_2 increases (note C_1 is independent of u_2).

For $R(u_2; u_1)$, we note that, by definition of C_1, C_2, V we have

$$C_2 = C_1(V - 1) + 1$$

whence the logarithmic derivative of $R(u_2; u_1)$ w.r.t. V is

$$\frac{2a}{b + a(V - 1)} - \frac{C_1}{C_1(V - 1) + 1} = \frac{aC_1(V - 1) + 2a - C_1 b}{[b + a(V - 1)][C_1(V - 1) + 1]}$$

where, for region II,

$$\frac{b - a}{3a} \leqq V \leqq \frac{b + a}{3a}$$

The denominator is positive since $V > 1$ so the sign coincides with that of the numerator. We wish to establish therefore, that the numerator is negative; but since it is a linear increasing function of V it suffices to show that it is negative when V takes its maximum value in region II i.e. $V = (b + a)/3a$.

But here the numerator is

$$C_1\left(\frac{b-2a}{3}\right) + 2a - C_1 b = 2a - \tfrac{2}{3}C_1(a+b) < 2a(1-C_1) < 0$$

where we have used the fact that $b > 2a$. Thus $R(u_2; u_1)$ decreases with increasing V, i.e. is increasing in u_2.   ‖

We now define the "optimal reply from below" as follows. Let one firm set quality u. Then, of all qualities on the restricted range $[u_0, u]$ we choose that level v which maximizes the revenue $R(v, u)$. Since $R(v; u)$ is continuous in v it follows that for any u, $R(v; u)$ takes a maximum over v in the closed set $[u_0, u]$. Moreover, for $v = u$, $R(v; u) = 0$, while for $u_o < v < u$, $R(v; u) > 0$; so that the maximum is attained at a quality strictly less than u.

We define the set[3] of optimal replies

$$\rho(u) = \{v \mid R(v; u) = \max R(s; u); u_0 \leqq s \leqq u\}$$

and our preceding remarks imply that $\rho(u) \neq \phi$ and $u \notin \rho(u)$ for $u_0 < u$.

We may now establish[4]

PROPOSITION 1.   *The game G^2 has a perfect equilibrium in pure strategies; the outcome involves distinct qualities, and both firms earn positive revenue (profits) at equilibrium.*

PROOF.   We demonstrate the existence of such an equilibrium as follows. Choose a $v \in \rho(\bar{u})$. Then we will show that the pair $(\bar{u}, v)$ is a Nash Equilibrium in the "choice of quality" game, with the payoffs defined as the revenue obtained in the "choice of price" game of the preceding sections, and so is a Perfect Equilibrium in G^2.

Let the firm setting $\bar{u}$ be labeled 2, and its rival 1. To show that $(\bar{u}, v)$ is a Nash Equilibrium, we note that, given a choice of $\bar{u}$ by firm 2, then the choice of v by firm 1 is optimal, by definition of $\rho(u)$.

To complete our proof we show that, given a choice of v by firm 1, $\bar{u}$ is an optimal choice for firm 2.

We divide the argument into two parts. First note that $\bar{u}$ is preferred to any $u \geqq v$ by virtue of Lemma 4. Secondly, consider the payoff to firm 2 if it chooses any quality u_2 where $u_0 \leqq u_2 < v$.

Then we have

$$R(u_2; v) \leqq R(u_2; \bar{u}) \hspace{4cm} \text{by Lemma 4.}$$

But

$$R(u_2; \bar{u}) \leqq R(v; \bar{u}) \hspace{4cm} \text{as } v \in \rho(\bar{u}).$$

While

$$R(v; \bar{u}) \leqq R(\bar{u}; v) \hspace{4cm} \text{by Lemma 3.}$$

Hence

$$R(u_2; v) \leqq R(\bar{u}; v)$$

and the choice of $\bar{u}$ is indeed optimal for firm 2 as required.   ‖

We have thus established that with two firms present, a Nash Equilibrium in qualities exists, which is a Perfect Equilibrium in the two-stage game ("choice of quality, choice of price").

We now consider the outcome if $k > 2$ firms are present. We aim to show here, (i) that the choice of $\bar{u}$ by all firms is a Nash Equilibrium,[5] and (ii) that for *any* Nash Equilibrium, all firms have revenue zero. (Up to this point we have confined our attention to equilibria in pure strategies. In fact the proof of (ii) extends trivially to mixed strategies, and we will establish the result in this more general setting below.)

PROPOSITION 2.

(i) *The game* $G^k, k > 2$ *has a Nash Equilibrium*

$$u_i = \bar{u}, \ 1 \leqq i \leqq k$$

(ii) *For every Nash Equilibrium of* G^k *the payoff for each firm is zero.*

PROOF.   (i) Suppose all firms but one choose $\bar{u}$. Then at least two firms sell an identical product of quality $\bar{u}$; following the familiar Bertrand argument for a non-cooperative price equilibrium between two firms selling an identical product, we have immediately that each of these firms sets price zero. Hence our remaining firm earns payoff zero for any choice $u \leqq \bar{u}$; for either its price is zero (at $u = \bar{u}$) or its sales are zero (at $u < \bar{u}$). Hence G^k has a Nash Equilibrium, $u_i = \bar{u}, 1 < i < k$.

(ii) In order to establish this, we show that in every Perfect Equilibrium at least two firms adopt the pure strategy $\bar{u}$; whence the result follows immediately.

Let μ^i be a probability measure on $[u_0, \bar{u}]$ and let $\{\mu^i\}$ be a Nash Equilibrium for G^k. Let V_i be the lim inf of the support of μ^i. Assume $V_1 \leqq V_2 \leqq \ldots \leqq V_k$, and furthermore assume that if any of the μ^i has an atom at V_1 then we label the firms so as to denote it (or one such firm) as 1.

First we show that the payoff of 1 is zero. If V_1 is an atom of μ^1 then the pure strategy V_1 yields payoff zero to firm 1 (given $\mu^2, \ldots, \mu^k$); for here the probability is zero that firm 1 offers the (sole) highest quality; or the (sole) second highest quality, product, whence from the analysis of the non-cooperative price equilibrium it earns payoff zero.

If, on the other hand, μ^1 does not have an atom at V_1 then there is a descending sequence of points in the support of μ^1 with limit V_1. The payoff of all these points as pure strategies is the same, but it tends to zero in the limit where quality approaches V_1: for the probability of the limit point V_1 being the (sole) highest quality, or the (sole) second highest quality, is zero (none of the μ^i has an atom at V_1). Thus the payoff to firm 1 is zero.

We may now deduce that at least two firms adopt the pure strategy $\bar{u}$. Suppose firstly that none of the strategies $\mu^1, \ldots, \mu^k$ is the pure strategy $\bar{u}$. Then there is a neighbourhood of $\bar{u}$, and an $\varepsilon > 0$, such that with probability $\varepsilon > 0$ none of the firms $2, \ldots, k$ choose a quality in that neighborhood. Now we have just shown that the payoff to firm 1 is zero; we now note that μ^1 can not be an optimal strategy, for by choosing the pure strategy $\bar{u}$ firm 1 can now achieve a strictly positive payoff.

Thus at least one of the strategies $\mu^1, \ldots, \mu^k$ is the pure strategy $\bar{u}$. Denote it μ^k. Assume that no other firm adopts this strategy. Then there is a neighborhood of $\bar{u}$, and an $\varepsilon > 0$, such that with probability $\varepsilon > 0$ none of the firms $2, \ldots, k-1$ choose a quality in this neighborhood. Firm 1 can thus earn a strictly positive payoff by choosing its quality in this interval.

Hence at least two of the $\mu^1, \ldots, \mu^k$ are the pure strategy $\bar{u}$. Hence all payoffs are zero. ‖

4. Entry

We have now shown how, in the present model, only two firms can survive with positive prices, and positive market shares, at equilibrium; and how the entry of further firms leads to a configuration in which the top quality product is available at price zero, while all firms earn zero revenue (profits).

We now consider the analysis of entry to the industry. We introduce a "small" cost[6] of entry $\varepsilon > 0$; our results in fact are independent of the size of ε. We define the game G_ε^k as the game G^k introduced above, with ϵ subtracted from all payoffs. Let there be n potential entrants; they play the three-stage game E_ε^n as follows. At the first stage each firm decides whether to enter or not; according as the number who choose to enter is k, these k firms then play the game G_ε^k. Those firms who choose not to enter receive payoff zero.

We establish:

PROPOSITION 3. *For any $\varepsilon > 0$ (sufficiently small), and any number $n > 2$ of potential entrants*

  (i) *there exists a Perfect Equilibrium in which two firms enter; and in which they produce distinct products, and have positive revenues (profits);*

  (ii) *no Perfect Equilibrium exists in which $k > 2$ firms enter.*

PROOF. Corresponding to any pair[7] of firms drawn from n potential entrants, given a decision by these two firms to enter, the payoff to each of the other firms from not entering is zero, while the payoff from entering is $-\varepsilon$ by virtue of Proposition 2. This establishes (ii). Where exactly two firms enter however, each earns a positive payoff (since ε is "small"); and then (i) follows immediately from Proposition 1. ‖

5. Summary and Conclusions

We have here described a perfect equilibrium of a three-stage game in which a number of firms choose firstly, whether to entry an industry; secondly, the quality of their respective products, and thirdly, their prices.

At the final stage of the game, in a non-cooperative price equilibrium, there is an upper bound to the number of firms which enjoy positive market shares, at positive prices (production costs being assumed zero). This reflects the fact that competition between the surviving "high quality" products drives their prices down to a point at which not even the poorest consumer prefers the (excluded) low quality products even at price zero. This number reflects inter alia the utility functions of consumers and the shape of the income distribution. We have here taken a particular form of utility function and assumed a uniform distribution of incomes on $[a,b]$ where $2a < b < 4a$; whence our upper bound is 2. It can be shown by extending our discussion in a natural way, that this upper bound rises as the range of incomes increases.

We establish two results which form the core of the analysis.

(a) We show that where the number of firms equals 2, these two firms will choose distinct qualities, and both will enjoy positive profit at equilibrium. The intuitive idea behind this result is that, as their qualities become close, price competition between the increasingly similar products reduces the profit of both firms.

(b) We show that if three or more firms are present, competition in choice of quality drives all firms to set the same "top" level of quality permitted while prices, and so profits, become zero. This reflects the fact that no one of the three firms will now prefer to set its quality lower than that of its two rivals, as it would thereby certainly earn revenue zero at equilibrium.

Combining (a) and (b) and introducing a small cost of entry ε, we deduce that *the only Perfect Equilibrium in the three stage game is one in which exactly two firms enter; in which they produce distinct products, and earn positive profits at equilibrium.* Moreover, this equilibrium configuration is independent of ε.

A natural question concerns the extension of this model to cases where the upper bound on the number of products which can survive exceeds two. This remains an open question; while property (b) generalizes readily, we have not succeeded in generalizing property (a). Our present argument does not generalize in an obvious manner here.

Notes

1   The model of consumer choice over alternative products described here follows Gabszewicz and Thisse (1979, 1980). These authors analyze a non-cooperative price equilibrium between firms, the quality of whose products is fixed exogenously. This corresponds to the last stage of our present three-stage process.

2   Thus our consumer buys *either* this product, or that. Contrast Dixit and Stiglitz (1977).

3   In fact a lengthy development shows that the optimal reply from below, $\rho(u)$, is unique, but this is not required for our present purposes.

4   It may be shown indirectly using the Lemma of Roberts and Sonnenschein (1976), that an equilibrium exists in the present model, but the present direct proof is much shorter.

5   We repeat that a perfect equilibrium in G^k is equivalent to a Nash Equilibrium in qualities, the payoffs arising from any vector of qualities being defined by the (unique) equilibrium values of revenue in the "choice of price" game.

6   Trivially, if ε is sufficiently large, no firm will enter.

7   Of course *any* pair of firms may enter. Similarly, in the "choice of quality" stage, we have, corresponding to the equilibrium $(\bar{u}, v)$, its mirror image $(v, \bar{u})$. The question of *which* firm enters, or sets the higher quality, is outside the scope of this type of model.

References

d'Aspremont, C., Gabszewicz, Jaskold J., and Thisse, J.-F. (1979): "On Hotelling's 'Stability in Competition'", *Econometrica*, 47, 1145–50.

Dixit, A. and Stiglitz, J. E. (1977): "Monopolistic Competition and Optimum Product Diversity", *American Economic Review*, 67, 297–308.

Gabszewicz, Jaskold J. and Thisse, J.-F. (1979): "Price Competition, Quality and Income Disparities", *Journal of Economic Theory*, 20, 340–59.

Gabszewicz, Jaskold J. and Thisse, J.-F. (1980): "Entry (and Exit) in a Differentiated Industry", *Journal of Economic Theory*, 22, 327–38.

Hotelling, H. (1928): "Stability in Competition", *Economic Journal*, 39, 41–57.

Roberts, J. and Sonnenschein, H. (1976): "On the Existence of Cournot Equilibrium without Concave Profit Functions", *Journal of Economic Theory*, 13, 112–17.

Selten, R. (1975): "Re-examination of the Perfectness Concept for Equilibrium Points in Extensive Games", *International Journal of Game Theory*, 4, 25–55.

CHAPTER EIGHT

Monopolistic Competition and Optimum Product Diversity

AVINASH K. DIXIT AND JOSEPH E. STIGLITZ

Source: *American Economic Review*, 1997, 67, 297–308.

The basic issue concerning production in welfare economics is whether a market solution will yield the socially optimum kinds and quantities of commodities. It is well known that problems can arise for three broad reasons: distributive justice; external effects; and scale economies. This paper is concerned with the last of these.

The basic principle is easily stated.[1] A commodity should be produced if the costs can be covered by the sum of revenues and a properly defined measure of consumer's surplus. The optimum amount is then found by equating the demand price and the marginal cost. Such an optimum can be realized in a market if perfectly discriminatory pricing is possible. Otherwise we face conflicting problems. A competitive market fulfilling the marginal condition would be unsustainable because total profits would be negative. An element of monopoly would allow positive profits, but would violate the marginal condition.[2] Thus we expect a market solution to be suboptimal. However, a much more precise structure must be put on the problem if we are to understand the nature of the bias involved.

It is useful to think of the question as one of quantity versus diversity. With scale economies, resources can be saved by producing fewer goods and larger quantities of each. However, this leaves less variety, which entails some welfare loss. It is easy and probably not too unrealistic to model scale economies by supposing that each potential commodity involves some fixed set-up cost and has a constant marginal cost. Modeling the desirability of variety has been thought to be difficult, and several indirect approaches have been adopted. The Hotelling spatial model, Lancaster's product characteristics approach, and the mean-variance portfolio selection model have all been put to use.[3] These lead to results involving transport costs or correlations among commodities or securities, and are hard to interpret in general terms. We therefore take a direct route, noting that the convexity of indifference surfaces of a conventional utility function defined over the quantities of all potential commodities already embodies the desirability of variety. Thus, a consumer who is indifferent between the quantities (1,0) and (0,1) of two commodities prefers the mix (1/2, 1/2) to either extreme. The advantage of this view is that the results involve the familiar own- and cross-elasticities of demand functions, and are therefore easier to comprehend.

There is one case of particular interest on which we concentrate. This is where potential commodities in a group or sector or industry are good substitutes among themselves, but poor substitutes for the other commodities in the economy. Then we are led to examining the market solution in relation to an optimum, both as regards biases within the group, and between the group and the rest of the economy. We expect the answer to depend on the intra- and intersector elasticities of substitution. To demonstrate the point as simply as possible, we shall aggregate the rest of the economy into one good labeled 0, chosen as the numeraire. The economy's endowment of it is normalized at unity; it can be thought of as the time at the disposal of the consumers.

The potential range of related products is labeled 1, 2, 3, ... Writing the amounts of the various commodities as x_0 and $x = (x_1, x_2, x_3, \ldots$, we assume a separable utility function with convex indifference surfaces:

$$u = U(x_0, V(x_1, x_2, x_3, \ldots)) \tag{1}$$

In sections 1 and 2 we simplify further by assuming that V is a symmetric function, and that all commodities in the group have equal fixed and marginal costs. Then the actual labels given to commodities are immaterial, even though the total number n being produced is relevant. We can thus label these commodities $1, 2, \ldots, n$, where the potential products $(n + 1), (n + 2), \ldots$ are not being produced. This is a restrictive assumption, for in such problems we often have a natural asymmetry owing to graduated physical differences in commodities, with a pair close together being better mutual substitutes than a pair farther apart. However, even the symmetric case yields some interesting results. In section 3, we consider some aspects of asymmetry.

We also assume that all commodities have unit income elasticities. This differs from a similar recent formulation by Michael Spence, who assumes U linear in x_0, so that the industry is amenable to partial equilibrium analysis. Our approach allows a better treatment of the intersectoral substitution, but the other results are very similar to those of Spence.

We consider two special cases of (1). In section 1, V is given a *CES* form, but U is allowed to be arbitrary. In section 2, U is taken to be Cobb-Douglas, but V has a more general additive form. Thus the former allows more general intersector relations, and the latter more general intra-sector substitution, highlighting different results.

Income distribution problems are neglected. Thus U can be regarded as representing Samuelsonian social indifference curves, or (assuming the appropriate aggregation conditions to be fulfilled) as a multiple of a representative consumer's utility. Product diversity can then be interpreted either as different consumers using different varieties, or as diversification on the part of each consumer.

1. Constant-Elasticity Case

1.1. Demand functions

The utility function in this section is

$$u = U\left(x_0, \left\{ \sum_i x_i^{\rho} \right\}^{1/\rho} \right) \tag{2}$$

For concavity, we need $\rho < 1$. Further, since we want to allow a situation where several of the x_i are zero, we need $\rho > 0$. We also assume U homothetic in its arguments.

The budget constraint is

$$x_0 + \sum_{i=1}^{n} p_i x_i = I \tag{3}$$

where p_i are prices of the goods being produced, and I is income in terms of the numeraire, i.e., the endowment which has been set at 1 plus the profits of the firms distributed to the consumers, or minus the lump sum deductions to cover the losses, as the case may be.

In this case, a two-stage budgeting procedure is valid.[4] Thus we define dual quantity and price indices

$$y = \left\{ \sum_{i=1}^{n} x_i^{\rho} \right\}^{1/\rho} \qquad q = \left\{ \sum_{i=1}^{n} p_i^{-1/\beta} \right\}^{-\beta} \tag{4}$$

where $\beta = (1 - \rho)/\rho$, which is positive since $0 < \rho < 1$. Then it can be shown[5] that in the first stage,

$$y = I \frac{s(q)}{q} \qquad x_0 = I(1 - s(q)) \tag{5}$$

for a function s which depends on the form of U. Writing $\sigma(q)$ for the elasticity of substitution between x_0 and y, we define $\theta(q)$ as the elasticity of the function s, i.e., $qs'(q)/s(q)$. Then we find

$$\theta(q) = \{1 - \sigma(q)\}\{1 - s(q)\} < 1 \tag{6}$$

but $\theta(q)$ can be negative as $\sigma(q)$ can exceed 1.

Turning to the second stage of the problem, it is easy to show that for each i,

$$x_i = y \left[\frac{q}{p_i} \right]^{1/(1-\rho)} \tag{7}$$

where y is defined by (4). Consider the effect of a change in p_i alone. This affects x_i directly, and also through q; thence through y as well. Now from (4) we have the elasticity

$$\frac{\partial \, log q}{\partial \, log p_i} = \left(\frac{q}{p_i}\right)^{1/\beta} \tag{8}$$

So long as the prices of the products in the group are not of different orders of magnitude, this is of the order $(1/n)$. We shall assume that n is reasonably large, and accordingly neglect the effect of each p_i on q; thus the indirect effects on x_i. This leaves us with the elasticity

$$\frac{\partial \, log x_i}{\partial \, log p_i} = \frac{-1}{(1-\rho)} = \frac{-(1+\beta)}{\beta} \tag{9}$$

In the Chamberlinian terminology, this is the elasticity of the *dd* curve, i.e., the curve relating the demand for each product type to its own price with all other prices held constant.

In our large group case, we also see that for $i \neq j$, the cross elasticity $\partial log x_i / \partial log p_j$ is negligible. However, if all prices in the group move together, the individually small effects add to a significant amount. This corresponds to the Chamberlinian *DD* curve. Consider a symmetric situation where $x_i = x$ and $p_i = p$ for all i from 1 to n. We have

$$y = xn^{1/\rho} = xn^{1+\beta}$$
$$q = pn^{-\beta} = pn^{-(1-\rho)/\rho} \tag{10}$$

and then from (5) and (7),

$$x = \frac{Is(q)}{pn} \tag{11}$$

The elasticity of this is easy to calculate; we find

$$\frac{\partial \, log x}{\partial \, log p} = -[1 - \theta(q)] \tag{12}$$

Then (6) shows that the *DD* curve slopes downward. The conventional condition that the *dd* curve be more elastic is seen from (9) and (12) to be

$$\frac{1}{\beta} + \theta(q) > 0 \tag{13}$$

Finally, we observe that for $i \neq j$,

$$\frac{x_i}{x_j} = \left[\frac{p_j}{p_i}\right]^{1/(1-\rho)} \tag{14}$$

Thus $1/(1 - \rho)$ is the elasticity of substitution between any two products within the group.

1.2. Market equilibrium

It can be shown that each commodity is produced by one firm. Each firm attempts to maximize its profit, and entry occurs until the marginal firm can only just break even. Thus our market equilibrium is the familiar case of Chamberlinian monopolistic competition, where the question of quantity versus diversity has often been raised.[6] Previous analyses have failed to consider the desirability of variety in an explicit form, and have neglected various intra- and intersector interactions in demand. As a result, much vague presumption that such an equilibrium involves excessive diversity has built up at the back of the minds of many economists. Our analysis will challenge several of these ideas.

The profit-maximization condition for each firm acting on its own is the familiar equality of marginal revenue and marginal cost. Writing c for the common marginal cost, and noting that the elasticity of demand for each firm is $(1 + \beta)/\beta$, we have for each active firm:

$$p_i\left(1 - \frac{\beta}{1 + \beta}\right) = c$$

Writing p_e for the common equilibrium price for each variety being produced, we have

$$p_e = c(1 + \beta) = \frac{c}{\rho} \tag{15}$$

The second condition for equilibrium is that firms enter until the next potential entrant would make a loss. If n is large enough so that 1 is a small increment, we can assume that the marginal firm is exactly breaking even, i.e., $(p_n - c)x_n = a$, where x_n is obtained from the demand function and a is the fixed cost. With symmetry, this implies zero profit for all intramarginal firms as well. Then $I = 1$, and using (11) and (15) we can write the condition so as to yield the number n_e of active firms:

$$\frac{s(p_e n_e^{-\beta})}{p_e n_e} = \frac{a}{\beta c} \tag{16}$$

Equilibrium is unique provided $s(p_e n^{-\beta})/p_e n$ is a monotonic function of n. This relates to our earlier discussion about the two demand curves. From (11) we see that the behavior of $s(pn^{-\beta})/pn$ as n increases tells us how the demand curve DD for each firm shifts as the number of firms increases. It is natural to assume that it shifts to the left, i.e., the function above decreases as n increases for each fixed p. The condition for this in elasticity form is easily seen to be

$$1 + \beta\theta(q) > 0 \tag{17}$$

This is exactly the same as (13), the condition for the *dd* curve to be more elastic than the *DD* curve, and we shall assume that it holds.

The condition can be violated if $\sigma(q)$ is sufficiently higher than one. In this case, an increase in n lowers q, and shifts demand towards the monopolistic sector to such an extent that the demand curve for each firm shifts to the right. However, this is rather implausible.

Conventional Chamberlinian analysis assumes a fixed demand curve for the group as a whole. This amounts to assuming that $n \cdot x$ is independent of n, i.e., that $s(pn^{-\beta})$ is independent of n. This will be so if $\beta = 0$, or if $\sigma(q) = 1$ for all q. The former is equivalent to assuming that $\rho = 1$, when all products in the group are perfect substitutes, i.e., diversity is not valued at all. That would be contrary to the intent of the whole analysis. Thus, implicitly, conventional analysis assumes $\sigma(q) = 1$. This gives a constant budget share for the monopolistically competitive sector. Note that in our parametric formulation, this implies a unit-elastic *DD* curve, (17) holds, and so equilibrium is unique.

Finally, using (7), (11), and (16), we can calculate the equilibrium output for each active firm:

$$x_e = \frac{a}{\beta c} \qquad (18)$$

We can also write an expression for the budget share of the group as a whole:

$$s_e \quad s(q_e) \qquad (19)$$

where $\quad q_e \quad p_e n_e^{-\beta}$

These will be useful for subsequent comparisons.

1.3. Constrained optimum

The next task is to compare the equilibrium with a social optimum. With economies of scale, the first best or unconstrained (really constrained only by technology and resource availability) optimum requires pricing below average cost, and therefore lump sum transfers to firms to cover losses. The conceptual and practical difficulties of doing so are clearly formidable. It would therefore appear that a more appropriate notion of optimality is a constrained one, where each firm must have nonnegative profits. This may be achieved by regulation, or by excise or franchise taxes or subsidies. The important restriction is that lump sum subsidies are not available.

We begin with such a constrained optimum. The aim is to choose n, p_i, and x_i so as to maximize utility, satisfying the demand functions and keeping the profit for each firm nonnegative. The problem is somewhat simplified by the result that all active firms should have the same output levels and prices, and should make exactly zero profit. We omit the proof. Then we can set $I = 1$, and use (5) to express utility as a function of q alone. This is of course a decreasing function. Thus the problem of maximizing u becomes that of minimizing q, i.e.,

$$\min_{n, p} pn^{-\beta}$$

subject to

$$(p - c)\frac{s(pn^{-\beta})}{pn} = a \tag{20}$$

To solve this, we calculate the logarithmic marginal rate of substitution along a level curve of the objective, the similar rate of transformation along the constraint, and equate the two. This yields the condition

$$\frac{\dfrac{c}{p-c} + \theta(q)}{1 + \beta\theta(q)} = \frac{1}{\beta} \tag{21}$$

The second-order condition can be shown to hold, and (21) simplifies to yield the price for each commodity produced in the constrained optimum, p_c, as

$$p_c = c(1 + \beta) \tag{22}$$

Comparing (15) and (22), we see that the two solutions have the same price. Since they face the same break-even constraint, they have the same number of firms as well, and the values for all other variables can be calculated from these two. Thus we have a rather surprising case where the monopolistic competition equilibrium is identical with the optimum constrained by the lack of lump sum subsidies. Chamberlin once suggested that such an equilibrium was "a sort of ideal"; our analysis shows when and in what sense this can be true.

1.4. Unconstrained optimum

These solutions can in turn be compared to the unconstrained or first best optimum. Considerations of convexity again establish that all active firms should produce the same output. Thus we are to choose n firms each producing output x in order to maximize

$$u = U(1 - n(a + cx), xn^{1+\beta}) \tag{23}$$

where we have used the economy's resource balance condition and (10). The first-order conditions are

$$-ncU_0 + n^{1+\beta}U_y = 0 \tag{24}$$

$$-(a + cx)U_0 + (1 + \beta)xn^{\beta}U_y = 0 \tag{25}$$

From the first stage of the budgeting problem, we know that $q = U_y/U_0$. Using (24) and (10), we find the price charged by each active firm in the unconstrained optimum, p_u, equal to marginal cost

$$p_u = c \tag{26}$$

This, of course, is no surprise. Also from the first-order conditions, we have

$$x_u = \frac{a}{c\beta} \tag{27}$$

Finally, with (26), each active firm covers its variable cost exactly. The lump sum transfers to firms then equal an, and therefore $I = 1 - an$, and

$$x = (1 - an)\frac{s(pn^{-\beta})}{pn}$$

The number of firms n_u is then defined by

$$\frac{s(cn_u^{-\beta})}{n_u} = \frac{a/\beta}{1 - an_u} \tag{28}$$

We can now compare these magnitudes with the corresponding ones in the equilibrium or the constrained optimum. The most remarkable result is that the output of each active firm is the same in the two situations. The fact that in a Chamberlinian equilibrium each firm operates to the left of the point of minimum average cost has been conventionally described by saying that there is excess capacity. However, when variety is desirable, i.e., when the different products are not perfect substitutes, it is not in general optimum to push the output of each firm to the point where all economies of scale are exhausted.[7] We have shown in one case that is not an extreme one, that the first best optimum does not exploit economies of scale beyond the extent achieved in the equilibrium. We can then easily conceive of cases where the equilibrium exploits economies of scale too far from the point of view of social optimality. Thus our results undermine the validity of the folklore of excess capacity, from the point of view of the unconstrained optimum as well as the constrained one.

A direct comparison of the numbers of firms from (16) and (28) would be difficult, but an indirect argument turns out to be simple. It is clear that the unconstrained optimum has higher utility than the constrained optimum. Also, the level of lump sum income in it is less than that in the latter. It must therefore be the case that

$$q_u < q_c = q_e \tag{29}$$

Further, the difference must be large enough that the budget constraint for x_0 and the quantity index y in the unconstrained case must lie outside that in the constrained case in the relevant region, as shown in Figure 1. Let C be the constrained optimum, A the unconstrained optimum, and let B be the point where the line joining the origin to C meets the indifference curve in the unconstrained case. By homotheticity the indifference curve at B is parallel to that at C, so each of the moves from C to B and from B to A increases the value of y. Since the value of x is the same in the two optima, we must have

$$n_u > n_c = n_e \tag{30}$$

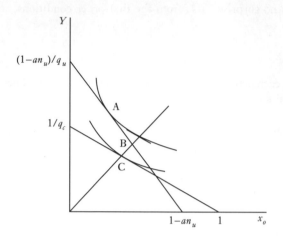

Figure 1

Thus the unconstrained optimum actually allows more variety than the constrained optimum and the equilibrium; this is another point contradicting the folklore on excessive diversity.

Using (29) we can easily compare the budget shares. In the notation we have been using, we find $s_u \gtreqless s_c$ as $\theta(q) \gtreqless 0$, i.e., as $\sigma(q) \gtreqless 1$ providing these hold over the entire relevant range of q.

It is not possible to have a general result concerning the relative magnitudes of x_0 in the two situations; an inspection of Figure 1 shows this. However, we have a sufficient condition:

$$x_{0u} = (1 - an_u)(1 - s_u) < 1 - s_u \leq 1 - s_c$$
$$= x_{0c} \qquad\qquad\qquad\qquad \text{if } \sigma(q) \geq 1$$

In this case the equilibrium or the constrained optimum use more of the numeraire resource than the unconstrained optimum. On the other hand, if $\sigma(q) = 0$ we have L-shaped isoquants, and in Figure 1, points A and B coincide giving the opposite conclusion.

In this section we have seen that with a constant intrasector elasticity of substitution, the market equilibrium coincides with the constrained optimum. We have also shown that the unconstrained optimum has a greater number of firms, each of the same size. Finally, the resource allocation between the sectors is shown to depend on the intersector elasticity of substitution. This elasticity also governs conditions for uniqueness of equilibrium and the second-order conditions for an optimum.

Henceforth we will achieve some analytic simplicity by making a particular assumption about intersector substitution. In return, we will allow a more general form of intrasector substitution.

2. Variable Elasticity Case

The utility function is now

$$u = x_0^{1-\gamma} \left\{ \sum_i v(x_i) \right\}^\gamma \tag{31}$$

with v increasing and concave, $0 < \gamma < 1$. This is somewhat like assuming a unit inter-sector elasticity of substitution. However, this is not rigorous since the group utility $V(\underline{x}) = \sum_i v(x_i)$ is not homothetic and therefore two-stage budgeting is not applicable.

It can be shown that the elasticity of the *dd* curve in the large group case is

$$-\frac{\partial \log x_i}{\partial \log p_i} = -\frac{v'(x_i)}{x_i v''(x_i)} \quad \text{for any } i \tag{32}$$

This differs from the case of section 1 in being a function of x_i. To highlight the similarities and the differences, we define $\beta(x)$ by

$$\frac{1 + \beta(x)}{\beta(x)} = -\frac{v'(x)}{x v''(x)} \tag{33}$$

Next, setting $x_i = x$ and $p_i = p$ for $i = 1, 2, \ldots, n$, we can write the *DD* curve and the demand for the numeraire as

$$x = \frac{1}{np} \omega(x) \quad x_0 = I[1 - \omega(x)] \tag{34}$$

where

$$\begin{aligned} \omega(x) &= \frac{\gamma \rho(x)}{[\gamma \rho(x) + (1 - \gamma)]} \\ \rho(x) &= \frac{x v'(x)}{v(x)} \end{aligned} \tag{35}$$

We assume that $0 < \rho(x) < 1$, and therefore have $0 < \omega(x) < 1$.

Now consider the Chamberlinian equilibrium. The profit-maximization condition for each active firm yields the common equilibrium price p_e in terms of the common equilibrium output x_e as

$$p_e = c[1 + \beta(x_e)] \tag{36}$$

Note the analogy with (15). Substituting (36) in the zero pure profit condition, we have x_e defined by

$$\frac{cx_e}{a + cx_e} = \frac{1}{1 + \beta(x_e)} \tag{37}$$

Finally, the number of firms can be calculated using the *DD* curve and the break-even condition, as

$$n_e = \frac{\omega(x_e)}{a + cx_e} \tag{38}$$

For uniqueness of equilibrium we once again use the conditions that the *dd* curve is more elastic than the *DD* curve, and that entry shifts the *DD* curve to the left. However, these conditions are rather involved and opaque, so we omit them.

Let us turn to the constrained optimum. We wish to choose n and x to maximize u, subject to (34) and the break-even condition $px = a + cx$. Substituting, we can express u as a function of x alone:

$$u = \gamma^{\gamma}(1 - \gamma)^{(1-\gamma)} \frac{\left[\frac{\rho(x)v(x)}{a + cx}\right]^{\gamma}}{\gamma\rho(x) + (1 - \gamma)} \tag{39}$$

The first-order condition defines x_c:

$$\frac{cx_c}{a + cx_c} = \frac{1}{1 + \beta(x_c)} - \frac{\omega(x_c)x_c\rho'(x_c)}{\gamma\rho(x_c)} \tag{40}$$

Comparing this with (37) and using the second-order condition, it can be shown that provided $\rho'(x)$ is one-signed for all x,

$$x_c \gtrless x_e \text{ according as } \rho'(x) \lessgtr 0 \tag{41}$$

With zero pure profit in each case, the points (x_e, p_e) and (x_c, p_c) lie on the same declining average cost curve, and therefore

$$p_c \lessgtr p_e \text{ according as } x_c \gtrless x_e \tag{42}$$

Next we note that the *dd* curve is tangent to the average cost curve at (x_e, p_e) and the *DD* curve is steeper. Consider the case $x_c > x_e$. Now the point (x_c, p_c) must lie on a *DD* curve further to the right than (x_e, p_e), and therefore must correspond to a smaller number of firms. The opposite happens if $x_c < x_e$. Thus,

$$n_c \lessgtr n_e \text{ according as } x_c \gtrless x_e \tag{43}$$

Finally, (41) shows that in both cases that arise there, $\rho(x_c) < \rho(x_e)$. Then $\omega(x_c) < \omega(x_e)$, and from (34),

$$x_{0c} > x_{0e} \tag{44}$$

A smaller degree of intersectoral substitution could have reversed the result, as in section 1.

An intuitive reason for these results can be given as follows. With our large group assumptions, the revenue of each firm is proportional to $xv'(x)$. However, the contribution of its output to group utility is $v(x)$. The ratio of the two is $\rho(x)$. Therefore, if $\rho'(x) > 0$, then at the margin each firm finds it more profitable to expand than what would be socially desirable, so $x_e > x_c$. Given the break-even constraint, this leads to there being fewer firms.

Note that the relevant magnitude is the elasticity of utility, and not the elasticity of demand. The two are related, since

$$x\frac{\rho'(x)}{\rho(x)} = \frac{1}{1 + \beta(x)} - \rho(x) \tag{45}$$

Thus, if $\rho(x)$ is constant over an interval, so is $\beta(x)$ and we have $1/(1 + \beta) = \rho$, which is the case of section 1. However, if $\rho(x)$ varies, we cannot infer a relation between the signs of $\rho'(x)$ and $\beta'(x)$. Thus the variation in the elasticity of demand is not in general the relevant consideration. However, for important families of utility functions there is a relationship. For example, for $v(x) = (k + mx)^j$, with $m > 0$ and $0 < j < 1$, we find that $-xv''/v'$ and xv'/v are positively related. Now we would normally expect that as the number of commodities produced increases, the elasticity of substitution between any pair of them should increase. In the symmetric equilibrium, this is just the inverse of the elasticity of marginal utility. Then a higher x would correspond to a lower n, and therefore a lower elasticity of substitution, higher $-xv''/v'$ and higher xv'/v. Thus we are led to expect that $\rho'(x) > 0$, i.e., that the equilibrium involves fewer and bigger firms than the constrained optimum. Once again the common view concerning excess capacity and excessive diversity in monopolistic competition is called into question.

The unconstrained optimum problem is to choose n and x to maximize

$$u = [nv(x)]^\gamma [1 - n(a + cx)]^{1-\gamma} \tag{46}$$

It is easy to show that the solution has

$$p_u = c \tag{47}$$

$$\frac{cx_u}{a + cx_u} = \rho(x_u) \tag{48}$$

$$n_u = \frac{\gamma}{a + cx_u} \tag{49}$$

Then we can use the second-order condition to show that

$$x_u \lessgtr x_c \text{ according as } \rho'(x) \gtrless 0 \tag{41}$$

This is in each case transitive with (41), and therefore yields similar output comparisons between the equilibrium and the unconstrained optimum.

The price in the unconstrained optimum is of course the lowest of the three. As to the number of firms, we note

$$n_c = \frac{\omega(x_c)}{a + cx_c} < \frac{\gamma}{a + cx_c}$$

and therefore we have a one-way comparison:

If $x_u < x_c$, then $n_u > n_c$ \hfill (51)

Similarly for the equilibrium. These leave open the possibility that the unconstrained optimum has both bigger and more firms. That is not unreasonable; after all the unconstrained optimum uses resources more efficiently.

3. Asymmetric Cases

The discussion so far imposed symmetry within the group. Thus the number of varieties being produced was relevant, but any group of n was just as good as any other group of n. The next important modification is to remove this restriction. It is easy to see how interrelations within the group of commodities can lead to biases. Thus, if no sugar is being produced, the demand for coffee may be so low as to make its production unprofitable when there are set-up costs. However, this is open to the objection that with complementary commodities, there is an incentive for one entrant to produce both. However, problems exist even when all the commodities are substitutes. We illustrate this by considering an industry which will produce commodities from one of two groups, and examine whether the choice of the wrong group is possible.[8]

Suppose there are two sets of commodities beside the numeraire, the two being perfect substitutes for each other and each having a constant elasticity subutility function. Further, we assume a constant budget share for the numeraire. Thus the utility function is

$$u = x_0^{1-s} \left\{ \left[\sum_{i_1=1}^{n} x_{i_1}^{\rho 1} \right]^{1/\rho 1} + \left[\sum_{i_2=1}^{n_2} x_i^{\rho 2} \right]^{1/\rho 2} \right\}^s \hfill (52)$$

We assume that each firm in group i has a fixed cost a_i and a constant marginal cost c_i.

Consider two types of equilibria, only one commodity group being produced in each. These are given by

$$\bar{x}_1 = \frac{a_1}{c_1 \beta_1} \quad \bar{x}_2 = 0 \hfill (53a)$$

$$\bar{p}_1 = c_1(1 + \beta_1)$$

$$\bar{n}_1 = \frac{s\beta_1}{a_1(1+\beta_1)}$$

$$\bar{q}_1 = \bar{p}_1\bar{n}_1^{-\beta_1} = c_1(1+\beta_1)^{1+\beta_1}\left(\frac{a_1}{s}\right)^{\beta_1}$$

$$\bar{u}_1 = s^s(1-s)^{1-s}\bar{q}_1^{-s}$$

$$\bar{x}_2 = \frac{a_2}{c_2\beta_2} \quad \bar{x}_1 = 0 \tag{53b}$$

$$\bar{p}_2 = c_2(1+\beta_2)$$

$$\bar{n}_2 = \frac{s\beta_2}{a_2(1+\beta_2)}$$

$$\bar{q}_2 = \bar{p}_2\bar{n}_2^{-\beta_2} = c_2(1+\beta_2)^{1+\beta_2}\left(\frac{a_2}{s}\right)^{\beta_2}$$

$$\bar{u}_2 = s^s(1-s)^{1-s}\bar{q}_2^{-s}$$

Equation (53a) is a Nash equilibrium if and only if it does not pay a firm to produce a commodity of the second group. The demand for such a commodity is

$$x_2 = \begin{cases} 0 & \text{for } p_2 \geq \bar{q}_1 \\ s/p_2 & \text{for } p_2 < \bar{q}_1 \end{cases}$$

Hence we require

$$\max_{p_2}(p_2 - c_2)x_2 = s\left(1 - \frac{c_2}{\bar{q}_1}\right) < a_2$$

or

$$\bar{q}_1 < \frac{sc_2}{s - a_2} \tag{54}$$

Similarly, (53b) is a Nash equilibrium if and only if

$$\bar{q}_2 < \frac{sc_1}{s - a_1} \tag{55}$$

Now consider the optimum. Both the objective and the constraint are such as to lead the optimum to the production of commodities from only one group. Thus, suppose n_i commodities from group i are being produced at levels x_i each, and offered at prices p_i. The utility level is given by

$$u = x_0^{1-s}\left\{x_1 n_1^{1+\beta_1} + x_2 n_2^{1+\beta_2}\right\}^s \tag{56}$$

and the resource availability constraint is

$$x_0 + n_1(a_1 + c_1 x_1) + n_2(a_2 + c_2 x_2) = 1 \tag{57}$$

Given the values of the other variables, the level curves of u in (n_1, n_2) space are concave to the origin, while the constraint is linear. We must therefore have a corner optimum. (As for the break-even constraint, unless the two $q_i = p_i n_i^{-\beta_i}$ are equal, the demand for commodities in one group is zero, and there is no possibility of avoiding a loss there.)

Note that we have structured our example so that if the correct group is chosen, the equilibrium will not introduce any further biases in relation to the constrained optimum. Therefore, to find the constrained optimum, we only have to look at the values of $\bar{u}_i$ in (53a) and (53b) and see which is the greater. In other words, we have to see which $\bar{q}_i$ is the smaller, and choose the situation (which may or may not be a Nash equilibrium) defined in (53a) and (53b) corresponding to it.

Figure 2 is drawn to depict the possible equilibria and optima. Given all the relevant parameters, we calculate $(\bar{q}_1, \bar{q}_2)$ from (53a) and (53b). Then (54) and (55) tell us whether either or both of the situations are possible equilibria, while a simple comparison of the magnitudes of $\bar{q}_1$ and $\bar{q}_2$ tells us which is the constrained optimum. In the figure, the nonnegative quadrant is split into regions in each of which we have one combination of equilibria and optima. We only have to locate the point $(\bar{q}_1, \bar{q}_2)$ in this space to know the result for the given parameter values. Moreover, we can compare the location of the points corresponding to different parameter values and thus do some comparative statics.

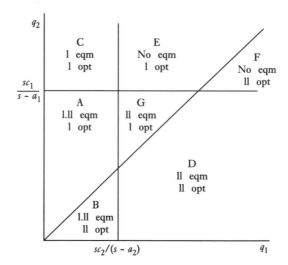

Figure 2 Solutions labeled 1 refer to equation (53a); solutions labeled 11 refer to equation (53b)

To understand the results, we must examine how $\bar{q}_i$ depends on the relevant parameters. It is easy to see that each is an increasing function of a_i and c_i. We also find

$$\frac{\partial \log \bar{q}_i}{\partial \beta_i} = -\log \bar{n}_i \tag{58}$$

and we expect this to be large and negative. Further, we see from (9) that a higher β_i corresponds to a lower own-price elasticity of demand for each commodity in that group. Thus $\bar{q}_i$ is an increasing function of this elasticity.

Consider initially a symmetric situation, with $sc_1/(s - a_1) = sc_2/(s - a_2), \beta_1 = \beta_2$ (the region G vanishes then), and suppose the point $(\bar{q}_1, \bar{q}_2)$ is on the boundary between regions A and B. Now consider a change in one parameter, say, a higher own-elasticity for commodities in group 2. This raises $\bar{q}_2$, moving the point into region A, and it becomes optimal to produce commodities from group 1 alone. However, both (53a) and (53b) are possible Nash equilibria, and it is therefore possible that *the high elasticity group is produced in equilibrium when the low elasticity one should have been.* If the difference in elasticities is large enough, the point moves into region C, where (53b) is no longer a Nash equilibrium. But, owing to the existence of a fixed cost, a significant difference in elasticities is necessary before entry from group 1 commodities threatens to destroy the "wrong" equilibrium. Similar remarks apply to regions B and D.

Next, begin with symmetry once again, and consider a higher c_1 or a_1. This increases $\bar{q}_1$ and moves the point into region B, making it optimal to produce the low-cost group alone while leaving both (53a) and (53b) as possible equilibria, until the difference in costs is large enough to take the point to region D. The change also moves the boundary between A and C upward, opening up a larger region G, but that is not of significance here.

If both $\bar{q}_1$ and $\bar{q}_2$ are large, each group is threatened by profitable entry from the other, and no Nash equilibrium exists, as in regions E and F. However, the criterion of constrained optimality remains as before. Thus we have a case where it may be necessary to prohibit entry in order to sustain the constrained optimum.

If we combine a case where $c_1 > c_2$ (or $a_1 > a_2$) and $\beta_1 > \beta_2$, i.e., where commodities in group 2 are more elastic and have lower costs, we face a still worse possibility. For the point $(\bar{q}_1, \bar{q}_2)$ may then lie in region G, where only (53b) is a possible equilibrium and only (53a) is constrained optimum, i.e., the market can produce only a low cost, high demand elasticity group of commodities when a high cost, low demand elasticity group should have been produced.

Very roughly, the point is that although commodities in inelastic demand have the potential for earning revenues in excess of variable costs, they also have significant consumers' surpluses associated with them. Thus it is not immediately obvious whether the market will be biased in favor of them or against them as compared with an optimum. Here we find the latter, and independent findings of Michael Spence in other contexts confirm this. Similar remarks apply to differences in marginal costs.

In the interpretation of the model with heterogenous consumers and social indifference curves, inelastically demanded commodities will be the ones which are intensively desired by a few consumers. Thus we have an "economic" reason why the market will lead to a bias against opera relative to football matches, and a justification for subsidization of the former and a tax on the latter, provided the distribution of income is optimum.

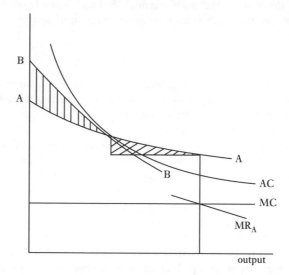

Figure 3

Even when cross elasticities are zero, there may be an incorrect choice of commodities to be produced (relative either to an unconstrained or constrained optimum) as Figure 3 illustrates. Figure 3 illustrates a case where commodity A has a more elastic demand curve than commodity B; A is produced in monopolistically competitive equilibrium, while B is not. But clearly, it is socially desirable to produce B, since ignoring consumer's surplus it is just marginal. Thus, the commodities that are not produced but ought to be are those with inelastic demands. Indeed, if, as in the usual analysis of monopolistic competition, eliminating one firm shifts the demand curve for the other firms to the right (i.e., increases the demand for other firms), if the consumer surplus from A (at its equilibrium level of output) is less than that from B (i.e., the cross hatched area exceeds the striped area), then constrained Pareto optimality entails restricting the production of the commodity with the more elastic demand.

A similar analysis applies to commodities with the same demand curves but different cost structures. Commodity A is assumed to have the lower fixed cost but the higher marginal cost. Thus, the average cost curves cross but once, as in Figure 4. Commodity A is produced in monopolistically competitive equilibrium, commodity B is not (although it is just at the margin of being produced). But again, observe that B should be produced, since there is a large consumer's surplus; indeed, since were it to be produced, B would produce at a much higher level than A, there is a much larger consumer's surplus. Thus if the government were to forbid the production of A, B would be viable, and social welfare would increase.

In the comparison between constrained Pareto optimality and the monopolistically competitive equilibrium, we have observed that in the former, we replace some low fixed cost-high marginal cost commodities with high fixed cost-low marginal cost commodities, and we replace some commodities with elastic demands with commodities with inelastic demands.

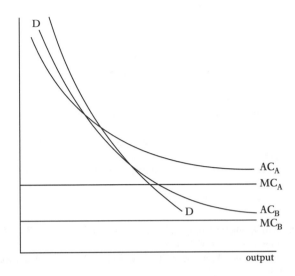

Figure 4

4. Concluding Remarks

We have constructed in this paper some models to study various aspects of the relation-ship between market and optimal resource allocation in the presence of some nonconvex-ities. The following general conclusions seem worth pointing out.

The monopoly power, which is a necessary ingredient of markets with nonconvexities, is usually considered to distort resources away from the sector concerned. However, in our analysis monopoly power enables firms to pay fixed costs, and entry cannot be prevented, so the relationship between monopoly power and the direction of market distortion is no longer obvious.

In the central case of a constant elasticity utility function, the market solution was constrained Pareto optimal, regardless of the value of that elasticity (and thus the implied elasticity of the demand functions). With variable elasticities, the bias could go either way, and the direction of the bias depended not on how the elasticity of demand changed, but on how the elasticity of utility changed. We suggested that there was some presumption that the market solution would be characterized by too few firms in the monopolistically competitive sector.

With asymmetric demand and cost conditions we also observed a bias against commod-ities with inelastic demands and high costs.

The general principle behind these results is that a market solution considers profit at the appropriate margin, while a social optimum takes into account the consumer's surplus. However, applications of this principle come to depend on details of cost and demand functions. We hope that the cases presented here, in conjunction with other studies cited, offer some useful and new insights.

Notes

1 See also the exposition by Michael Spence (1996).
2 A simple exposition is given by Peter Diamond and Daniel McFadden (1974).
3 See the articles by Harold Hotelling (1929), Nicholas Stern (1972), Kelvin Lancaster (1972), and Stiglitz (1975).
4 See p. 21 of John Green (1964).
5 These details and several others are omitted to save space, but can be found in Dixit and Stiglitz (1975).
6 See Edwin Chamberlin (1950), Nicholas Kaldor (1934), and Robert Bishop (1967).
7 See David Starrett (1974).
8 For an alternative approach using partial equilibrium methods, see Spence (1976).

References

Bishop, R. L. (1967): "Monopolistic Competition and Welfare Economics," in Robert Kuenne, ed., *Monopolistic Competition Theory*, New York.

Chamberlin, E. (1950): "Product Heterogeneity and Public Policy," *American Economic Review Proceedings*, May, 40, 85–92.

Diamond, P. A. and McFadden, D. L. (1974): "Some Uses of the Expenditure Function In Public Finance," *Journal of Public Economy*, 82, February, 1–23.

Dixit, A. K. and Stiglitz, J. E. (1975): "Monopolistic Competition and Optimum Product Differentiation," economics research paper no. 64, University of Warwick, UK.

Green, H. A. John (1964): *Aggregation in Economic Analysis*, Princeton.

Hotelling, H. (1929): "Stability in Competition," *Economic Journal*, 39, March, 41–57.

Kaldor, N. (1934): "Market Imperfection and Excess Capacity," *Economica*, 2, February, 33–50.

Lancaster, K. (1975): "Socially Optimal Product Differentiation," *American Economic Review*, 65, September, 567–85.

Spence, A. M. (1976): "Product Selection, Fixed Costs, and Monopolistic Competition," *Review Economy Studies*, 43, June, 217–35.

Starrett, D. A. (1974): "Principles of Optimal Location in a Large Homogeneous Area," *Journal of Economic Theory*, 9, December, 418–48.

Stern, N. H. (1972): "The Optimal Size of Market Areas," *Journal of Economic Theory*, 4, April, 159–73.

Stiglitz, J. E. (1975): "Monopolistic Competition in the Capital Market," technical report no. 16, IMSS, Stanford University, February.

PART IV
Empirical Analysis of Oligopoly

Introduction

Introduction

It is fair to say that empirical work has lagged behind IO theory in the past twenty-five years or so. To some extent, the "renaissance" of empirical IO, as it was once labeled, is still under way. This makes the task of selecting representative articles more difficult. To this is added the fact that there is less consensus about the main contributions than in the case of IO theory.

One of the main goals of empirical IO has been the estimation of market power. Until the 1970s, this was primarily done by means of cross-sectoral studies, that is, studies that pool data from various industries. However, this approach was plagued by the economic and econometric problems of estimating reduced-form models and combining data from different industries. By contrast, the "New Empirical Industrial Organization" attempts to estimate the degree of market power in a particular industry and based on a structural model of oligopoly competition.

Estimating the degree of market power raises interesting identification problems. Suppose, for example, that there is a one-unit shift in the demand intercept and that demand is linear and sloped -1. A 0.5 shift in price is then consistent with both (a) monopoly pricing and constant marginal cost; and (b) competitive pricing and increasing marginal cost (such that the supply function has a slope of 1). Is it possible to identify the degree of market power based on demand and cost data?[1] Bresnahan (1982) provides a set of conditions under which the answer is positive. In a companion paper, Lau (1982) generalizes these conditions.

In terms of applications, the literature on identification of market power goes back at least to Iwata (1974). Bresnahan (1982), however, was the first to tackle the problem in a systematic way. Since then, many applications of his framework and variations thereon have been performed with data from different industries and different countries.

For all their variety, most of these applications have the common feature of being static models. Porter (1983) provides the first attempt at estimating an econometric model that is inspired by a dynamic model, specifically, the model developed in Green and Porter (1984). As seen in part 2, this is a game of collusion with price wars, that is, with phases of "cooperative" pricing and phases of "non-cooperative" pricing. Obviously, a model of this sort cannot be estimated based on an econometric specification that implies a unique (static) solution. Porter's (1983) model has become a source of inspiration for other attempts at estimation of dynamic models. The number of such attempts is still relatively low; it includes Ellison (1994) (an extension of Porter's (1983) paper, based on the same dataset), Bresnahan (1987), Roberts and Samuelson (1988) and Slade (1992), among others.

In part 3, we depicted the dilemma between address and non-address models of product differentiation, concluding that empirical analysis should be the way forward – based on models following the characteristics approach. That is what Berry, Levinson and Pakes (1995) do, together with the contemporaneous Goldberg (1995). The Berry–Levinson–Pakes framework, which follows an earlier contribution by Berry (1994), has spawned a respectable number of similar applications to other industries. These empirical models of product differentiation have been used to address a number of important issues where theory has essentially reached its limits; for example, the question of selection bias in the provision of differentiated products (cf the papers by Spence, and Dixit and Stiglitz, cited in part 3).

One of the troublesome features of oligopoly theory is the variety of solutions that can be supported as an equilibrium; and the sensitivity of equilibria to apparently small changes in the assumptions. Witness, for example, the contrast between Green and Porter (1984) and Rotemberg and Saloner (1986).[2] For empirical economists, this implies the choice between two possible paths. One is to study individual industries, determining their particular institutional features and estimating specialized models. Porter (1983) would be an example of this. An alternative path is to look for empirical implications of oligopoly theory that are sufficiently robust, that is, common to a reasonably wide class of models.

Prominent among the second path is the "bounds" approach, pioneered by Sutton (1991) and extended in Sutton (1999). The idea of this approach is to derive the set of empirical observations that are consistent with theory, and to test whether the data are consistent with the theory. A related line of research is that of Bresnahan and Reiss (1991) who, like Sutton, look at the relation between market size and market structure.

Another strand of recent empirical IO literature pertains to competitive industry dynamics. Strictly speaking, this would not fit under the current section heading, as most of this literature assumes competitive markets, not oligopoly competition. However, it forms part of the "renaissance" of empirical IO, and is thus worth mentioning. This new literature is possible thanks to the availability of novel, comprehensive firm-level or plant-level datasets, together with the remarkable improvement in computing resources. The result is a series of studies that document important regularities regarding firm entry, growth and exit. To cite only a few: Dunne, Roberts and Samuelson (1988), Evans (1987) and Hall (1987).

Unusually for Economics, this is an area where theoretical work trails behind empirical work. Some of the theoretical contributions are reviewed in the last part of part 5. I would expect them to occupy an entire new section in a future edition of this reader.

Notes

1   The above is not a great example since the change in output together with the change in price would select between (a) and (b). However, it illustrates the fact that variable market power introduces an added degree of freedom that has to be taken into account in econometric estimation.

2   The problem is especially apparent in the context of repeated-game oligopoly theory, but is true more generally.

References

Berry, Steven (1994): "Estimating Discrete Choice Models of Product Differentiation," *Rand Journal of Economics*, 25, 242–62.

Berry, Steven, James Levinson and Ariel Pakes (1995): "Automobile Prices in Market Equilibrium," *Econometrica*, 63, 841–90.

Bresnahan, Timothy (1982): "The Oligopoly Solution is Identified," *Economics Letters*, 10, 87–92.

Bresnahan, Timothy (1987): "Competition and Collusion in the American Automobile Industry: The 1955 Price War," *Journal of Industrial Economics*, 35, 457–82.

Bresnahan, Timothy F., and Peter C. Reiss (1991): "Entry and Competition in Concentrated Markets," *Journal of Political Economy*, 99, 977–1009.

Dunne, Timothy, Mark J. Roberts and Larry Samuelson (1988): "Patterns of Firm Entry and Exit in U. S. Manufacturing Industries," *Rand Journal of Economics*, 19, 495–515.

Ellison, Glenn (1994): "Theories of Cartel Stability and the Joint Executive Committee," *Rand Journal of Economics*, 25, 37–57.

Evans, David (1987): "The Relation Between Firm Growth, Size, and Age: Estimates for 100 Manufacturing Industries," *Journal of Industrial Economics*, 35, 567–81.

Goldberg, Pinelopi Koujianou (1995): "Product Differentiation and Oligopoly in International Markets: The Case of the U. S. Automobile Industry," *Econometrica*, 63, 891–951.

Green, Ed and Robert H. Porter (1984): "Noncooperative Collusion Under Imperfect Price Information," *Econometrica*, 52, 87–100.

Hall, Bronwyn (1987): "The Relationship Between Firm Size and Firm Growth in the U. S. Manufacturing Sector," *Journal of Industrial Economics*, 35, 583–606.

Iwata, G. (1974): "Measurement of Conjectural Variations in Oligopoly," *Econometrica*, 42, 947–66.

Lau, Lawrence J. (1982): "On Identifying the Degree of Competitiveness From Industry Price and Output Data," *Economics Letters*, 10, 93–9.

Porter, Robert H. (1983): "A Study of Cartel Stability: the Joint Executive Committee, 1880–1886," *Bell Journal of Economics*, 14, 301–14.

Roberts, Mark J. and Larry Samuelson (1988): "An Empirical Analysis of Dynamic, Nonprice Competition in an Oligopolistic Industry," *Rand Journal of Economics*, 19, 200–20.

Rotemberg, Julio and Garth Saloner (1986): "A Supergame-Theoretic Model of Price Wars During Booms," *American Economic Review*, 76, 390–407.

Slade, Margaret (1992): "Vancouver's Gasoline-Price Wars: An Empirical Exercise in Uncovering Supergame Strategies," *Review of Economic Studies*, 59, 257–76.

Sutton, John (1991): *Sunk Costs and Market Structure*, Cambridge, Mass.: MIT Press.

Sutton, John (1999): *Technology and Market Structure*, Cambridge, Mass.: MIT Press.

CHAPTER NINE

The Oligopoly Solution Concept is Identified

TIMOTHY F. BRESNAHAN

Source: *Economics Letters*, 1982, 10, 87–92.

Oligopoly theory predicts that market price will be at least as high as the competitive price and no higher than the monopoly price. Particular oligopoly solution concepts offer more exact predictions, but it is difficult to know which solution concept holds in any real market. This paper shows that the oligopoly solution concept can be estimated econometrically.

1. Introduction

Recent case studies of concentrated industries have attempted to use structural econometric models to tell Cournot from Bertrand from Collusion. (See Bresnahan (1981) for a bibliography.) This note shows that the theoretical underpinnings of these studies are sound. A parameter indexing the oligopoly solution concept is econometrically identified. It is identified by standard econometric methods, even when no cost or profit data are available, and even when the demand and cost curves must be estimated as well. That is, the comparative statics of equilibrium, as price and quantity are moved by exogenous variables, reveal the degree of market power.

The models we treat will all have market price and quantity determined by the intersection of demand function and a supply relation. The demand function presumes price-taking buyers. The supply relation may be a supply function, a solution of $P = MC$. More general supply relations arise where the sellers may have some market power. They take the form $MR_p = MC$, perceived marginal revenue equals marginal cost. When $MR_p = P$, competition is present. When $MR_p = MR$, sellers are changing the monopoly price. When $MR_p < P$, there is some element of market power. The question here is whether observations on industry prices and quantities can reveal whether price or some smaller number is being set equal to MC, given that the demand function and the cost function are unknown *a priori*.

2. The Model

Let buyers have a typical demand function:

$$Q = D(P, Y, \alpha) + \varepsilon \tag{1}$$

where Q is quantity, P price, Y an exogenous variable, and α parameters of the demand system to be estimated. ε is the econometric error term. The selling side of the market equilibrium model is more complex. When sellers are price-takers, we can write

$$P = c(Q, W, \beta) + \eta \tag{2}$$

where W are exogenous variables on the supply side, β the supply-function parameters, and η the supply error. $c(\cdot)$ is marginal cost. When firms are *not* price-takers, perceived marginal revenue, not price, will be equal to marginal cost. This in general will take the form

$$P = c(Q, W, \beta) - \lambda \cdot h(Q, Y, \alpha) + \eta \tag{2'}$$

where $P + h(\cdot)$ is marginal revenue, and $P + \lambda h(\cdot)$ is *MR* as perceived by the firm. The demand-side parameters and exogenous variables are in $h(\cdot)$ because they affect marginal revenue. λ is a new parameter indexing the degree of market power. $\lambda = 0$ is perfect competition, $\lambda = 1$ is a perfect cartel, and intermediate λs correspond to other oligopoly solution concepts. For example, Cournot equilibrium has $\lambda = 1/n$.[1] In general, the econometrician will estimate (1) and (2') simultaneously, treating both price and quantity as endogenous in both. The formal question is then whether λ is identified in (1) (2'). This is the question: Are competition and a cartel observationally distinct?

The problem

Let demand and *MC* be linear. The demand function is now

$$Q = \alpha_0 + \alpha_1 P + \alpha_2 Y + \varepsilon \tag{3}$$

and the marginal-cost function is

$$MC = \beta_0 + \beta_1 Q + \beta_2 W \tag{4}$$

The supply relation is

$$P = \lambda(-Q/\alpha_1) + \beta_0 + \beta_1 Q + \beta_2 W + \eta \tag{5}$$

since $MR = P - Q/\alpha_1$.

The demand equation is identified no matter which form the supply relation takes. The demand equation (3) has only one included endogenous variable, P, and there is an excluded exogenous variable, W, so the equation is identified.

The supply relation is also identified. But the degree of market power is not. To see the first assertion, rewrite (5) as

$$P = \beta_0 + \gamma Q + \beta_2 W + \eta \tag{6}$$

where $\gamma = \beta_1 - \lambda/\alpha_1$. Clearly (6) is identified. Only Q is included and endogenous, while Y is excluded. But how would we know whether we were tracing out $P = MC$ or $MR = MC$? The thing we can estimate, γ, depends on both β_1 and λ. We cannot determine both of these from knowledge of γ, even though we can treat α_1 as known (since the demand curve can be estimated).

Figure 1 may clarify the issues. Look first at D_1, MR_1 and E_1. The demand curve is linear, so the MR is linear and twice as steep. Note that E_1 could be an equilibrium either for a cartel or monopolist with cost MC^m (by $MR_1 = MC^m$), or for a perfectly competitive industry with cost MC^c (by $P = MC^c$). Increase Y to shift the demand curve out to D_2, and note that *both* the monopoly *and* the competitive equilibria move to (P_2, Q_2). In fact, MC^c is the supply relation either for the competitor for whom MC^c is marginal cost, or for the cartel with the lower, flatter marginal cost MC^m. Unless we know marginal costs, for this example there is no observable distinction between the hypotheses of competition and monopoly.

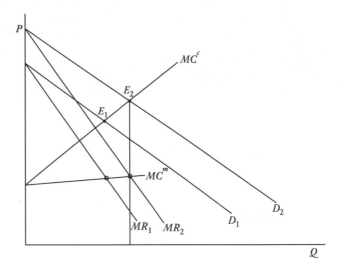

Figure 1

3. Solution

Solving the problem posed involves generalizing the demand function so that movements in the exogenous variables do more than shift its intercept up and down. Some exogenous variables must also be capable of changing the demand slope.

The argument is made graphically in figure 2. The demand system $D_1 - MR_1$ and the two cost curves are as before. But now instead of shifting the demand curve vertically (to get $D_2 - MR_2$ in figure 1) we rotate it around E_1 to get $D_3 - MR_3$. If the supply relation is a supply curve, then this will have no effect on the equilibrium. That is, if MC^c is the marginal cost curve and competition is perfect, E_1 should be the equilibrium under either D_1 or D_3. But if MC^m were the marginal cost curve, and supply were monopoly, then equilibrium shifts to E_3, where $MR_3 = MC^m$. Thus, if we can rotate as well as shift the demand function, the hypotheses of competition and monopoly are observationally distinct.

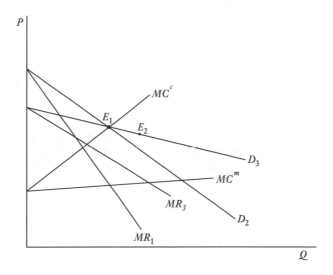

Figure 2

Formally, change the demand equation to

$$Q = \alpha_0 + \alpha_1 P + \alpha_2 Y + \alpha_3 PZ + \alpha_4 Z + \epsilon \tag{7}$$

where Z is a new demand-side exogenous variable. The key feature is that Z enters interactively with P, so that changes in Y and Z combine elements both of rotation and of vertical shifts in demand. Z might best be viewed as the price of a substitute good, which makes the interaction natural, while Y might be interpreted as income.

Now the supply relation has been altered to be

$$P = \frac{-\lambda}{\alpha_1 + \alpha_3 Z} \cdot Q + \beta_0 + \beta_1 Q + \beta_2 W + \eta \tag{8}$$

Clearly λ is identified. The demand side is still identified. So in attempting to disentangle λ and β_1 in (8), we treat α_1 and α_3 as known. Writing $Q^* = -Q/(\alpha_1 + \alpha_3 Z)$, there are two included exogenous variables, Q and Q^*. And there are two excluded exogenous variables Z and W. Thus, λ is identified as the coefficient of Q^*.

The logic of this argument holds up even if the curves are not linear. Translation of the demand curve will always trace out the supply relation. Rotations of the demand curve around the equilibrium point will reveal the degree of market power. Conditions on the demand system in which movements in the exogenous variables can do this have been worked out exactly. See the companion paper by Lau (1981). In general, such rotations will have no effect on the equilibrium if pricing is competitive, but will have an effect if there is market power. Thus the hypotheses of competition and monopoly are distinct. In any applied study the model of supply and demand will be more complex than that here. Considerations of product differentiation or of the fixity of capital, for example, might enter. The logic of the result here seems likely to be robust to such considerations.

Notes

1   Applied work has often concentrated on models in which each individual firm has its own λ. In this way Stackelberg, dominant firm, etc., can be handled.

References

Bresnahan, Timothy F., (1981): "*Identification of Market Power.*" Research paper no. 15, Stanford Workshop on Factor Markets (Department of Economics, Stanford University, Stanford, CA).
Lau, Lawrence J., (1981): "On Identifying the Degree of Competitiveness from Industry Price and Output Data" *Economic Letters*, 10.

CHAPTER TEN

A Study of Cartel Stability: The Joint Executive Committee, 1880–1886

Robert H. Porter

Source: *Bell Journal of Economics*, 1983, 14, 301–14.

This article employs weekly time series data on the Joint Executive Committee railroad cartel from 1880 to 1886 to test empirically the proposition that observed prices reflected switches from collusive to noncooperative behavior. An equilibrium model of dynamic oligopoly with asymmetric firms, together with explicit functional form assumptions about costs and demand, determines the estimating equations and stochastic structure of the econometric model. The hypothesis that no switch took place, so that price and quantity movements were solely attributable to exogenous shifts in the demand and cost functions, is then tested against this alternative and rejected.

1. Introduction

Industrial organization economists have recognized for some time that the problem of distinguishing empirically between collusive and noncooperative behavior, in the absence of a "smoking gun," is a difficult one. This article exploits the model proposed in Green and Porter (1984). They consider an explicitly dynamic model in which the firms of an industry are faced with the problem of detecting and deterring cheating on an agreement. In particular, they assume that firms set their own production level and observe the market price, but do not know the quantity produced by any other firm. Firms' output is assumed to be of homogeneous quality, so they face a common market price. If the market demand curve has a stochastic component, an unexpectedly low price may signal either deviations from collusive output levels or a "downward" demand shock. Under these circumstances participating firms can deter deviations from collusive output levels by threatening to produce at Cournot quantities for a period of fixed duration whenever they observe market price below some trigger price. A firm which considers a secret expansion of output above the collusive level must trade off immediate profit gains with the increased probability that the market price will fall below the trigger price, thereby increasing the likelihood of lower profits when the industry reverts to Cournot output levels. Green and Porter offer an explanation that what looks like collusive behavior at a point in time is actually the non-cooperative outcome of a regularly repeated market game. For small enough discount rates, an output vector which yields profits in excess of the Cournot vector can be supported as a noncooperative equilibrium. Thus the results of Friedman (1977) and Telser (1972) extend to uncertain environments. In equilibrium, firms maximize expected discounted profits by producing at collusive output levels, so that any price wars which are observed should occur after unexpected drops in demand, rather than after actual cheating by member firms. Thus price wars can be the occasional equilibrium outcome of a dynamic non-cooperative market game.

There are many such equilibria, as a number of output vectors can be supported by appropriately chosen (trigger price, punishment period length) pairs as noncooperative equilibria. However, such a cartel may be expected to select an enforcement mechanism which maximizes expected discounted profits, subject to the constraint that producing at collusive levels is individually rational. In equilibrium, the marginal gains from cheating in cooperative periods must be exactly offset by the marginal losses implicit in the increased probability of an industry reversion to Cournot behavior. The marginal gains from cheating increase as output in cooperative periods decreases towards perfectly collusive levels, so expected marginal losses must be increased by increasing the trigger price or the length of reversionary episodes. Expected discounted industry profits will be maximized at output levels in cooperative periods which exceed those which maximize single-period expected joint net returns, as long as the variance of the demand shock is positive (Porter, 1983).

This article adopts econometric techniques which employ aggregate time series price and quantity data for a particular industry, and which are designed to detect the behavioral switches implied by such an enforcement mechanism. I exploit the fact that there will be periodic switches or reversions between the Cournot and collusive output levels when such a noncooperative equilibrium exists. These reversions serve to identify periods of collusive behavior in a simultaneous equation switching regressions model. There is no explicit test of whether this sort of enforcement mechanism is employed. Instead, the econometric model is designed to test whether significant switches in supplier behavior occurred, and to identify the periods in which they took place. One can then determine whether the pattern of these switches is consistent with an equilibrium of the Green and Porter model. Thus the theoretical model is exploited to the extent that it predicts that such switches will occur, and that they should follow a certain pattern. (Of course, this sort of outcome may also arise if there are external supply shocks which are not observed by the econometrician. I can only state whether the econometric results are consistent with the theoretical model.) The model also predicts that optimally selected output levels in cooperative periods will exceed those which would maximize static joint net returns. The econometric model allows me to determine whether this is in fact the case.

2. The Joint Executive Committee

This section contains a description of the Joint Executive Committee, henceforth referred to as the JEC, with emphasis on the period from 1880 to 1886. Readers who are interested in a more complete history should refer to MacAvoy (1965) and Ulen (1978). Much of the material in this section is drawn from these studies.

The JEC was a cartel which controlled eastbound freight shipments from Chicago to the Atlantic seaboard in the 1880s. It was formed in April 1879 by an agreement of the railroads involved in the market. The firms involved publicly acknowledged this agreement, as it preceded the passage of the Sherman Act (1890) and the formation of the Interstate Commerce Commission (1887). A separate agreement was reached for westbound shipments on the same railroad lines, primarily because of the essential physical differences of the products being transported.

The internal enforcement mechanism adopted by the JEC was a variant of a trigger price strategy. According to Ulen, there were several instances in which the cartel thought that cheating had occurred, cut prices for a time, and then returned to the collusive price.

Through-shipments of grain accounted for 73 per cent of all dead freight tonnage handled by the JEC. The railroads also handled eastbound shipments of flour and provisions, but the prices charged for transporting these commodities were tied to the grain rate. None of these commodities is easily perishable, so speed of delivery was probably not an important factor by which firms could have differentiated their products. Furthermore, while different railroads shipped grain to different port cities, most of the wheat handled by the cartel was subsequently exported overseas, and the rates charged by different firms adjusted to compensate for differences in ocean shipping rates. Thus, the assumption that a homogeneous good was sold seems to have been approximately satisfied, and attention can be focused on the movement of grain with little loss of generality.

Price, rather than quantity, has typically been thought to be the strategic variable of firms in the rail-freight industry. In particular, the specification of Green and Porter (1984) that industry conduct during reversionary periods was Cournot might be considered unrealistic. Econometrically, it is not very difficult to modify the model so that firms revert from collusive to Bertrand behavior (as they would if they were price setters). If firms are price setters, then the inference problem they face in detecting cheating is quite similar to that originally posed by Stigler (1964). In the case of the JEC, the cartel agreement took the form of market share allotments rather than absolute amounts of quantities shipped. Firms set their rates individually, and the JEC office took weekly accounts so that each railroad could see the total amount transported. Total demand was quite variable, and the actual market share of any particular firm depended on both the prices charged by all the firms and unpredictable stochastic forces. Thus, the problem faced by the members of the JEC seems to be comparable to that posed by Green and Porter. Indeed, Brock and Scheinkman (1981) have shown that noncooperative equilibria with similar properties exist in supergames involving price-setting firms which face capacity constraints.

In their model Green and Porter explicitly rule out the possibility of entry into the market. In the case of the JEC, entry occurred twice between 1880 and 1886. It appears that the cartel passively accepted the entrants, allocated them market shares, and thereby allowed the collusive agreement to continue. The reason for this is undoubtedly that when a firm entered the rail freight industry in the late nineteenth century, it faced a "no-exit" constraint. To put it briefly, bankrupt railroads were relieved by the courts of most of their fixed costs and instructed to cut prices to increase business (Ulen, 1978, pp. 70–74). As a result, I deal with the actual entry which occurred during the sample period by appropriately modifying the nature of collusive and noncooperative outcomes, before and after entry, with the expectation that, *ceteris paribus*, reversionary periods should not have been precipitated by entry. Of course, entry to the industry may have increased the likelihood of future price wars.

Lake steamers and sailships were the principal source of competition for the railroads, but at no point did they enter into an agreement with the JEC. The predictable fluctuations in demand that resulted from the annual opening and closing of the Great Lakes to shipping did not disrupt industry conduct. Rather, rates adjusted systematically with the lake navigation season.

Therefore, the conduct of the JEC from 1880 to 1886 is largely consistent with the collusive equilibrium described by Green and Porter, as price wars were caused by unpredictable disturbances, rather than by entry or predictable fluctuations in demand.

3. The Econometric Model

This section is concerned with the possibility of estimating a model of the Nash equilibrium proposed by Green and Porter, suitably altered to reflect the structure of the JEC, by using time series data on price and aggregate output levels. A simultaneous equation switching regression model is proposed, in which the parameters of the demand and cost functions are estimated, and in which the regime classification is unknown.

Denote the market price in period t by p_t. Then the total quantity demanded is assumed to be a loglinear function of price,

$$\log Q_t = \alpha_0 + \alpha_1 \log p_t + \alpha_2 L_t + U_{1t} \tag{1}$$

where L_t is a dummy variable equal to one if the Great Lakes were open to navigation, and $\{U_{11}, U_{12}, \ldots, U_{1T}\}$ is a sequence of independently distributed normal variables with zero mean and variance σ_1^2. Here α_1 is the price elasticity of demand, and presumably negative. Also α_2 should be negative, reflecting a decrease in demand when the lake steamers were operating.

The N active firms in the industry are assumed to be asymmetric, in that they each face a different cost function. The cost of producing output q_{it} for firm i in period t is given by

$$C_i(q_{it}) = a_i q_{it}^\delta + F_i \quad \text{for } i = 1, \ldots, N$$

where δ, the (constant) elasticity of variable costs with respect to output, must exceed one if an equilibrium is to exist. Here a_i is a firm-specific shift parameter, and F_i the fixed cost faced by firm i. These fixed costs are assumed to be small enough that firms have positive discounted expected profits in equilibrium.

Since the products provided by these firms are of approximately homogeneous quality, all firms will charge equal prices in equilibrium. The actions of firms under different behavioral assumptions can then be summarized by

$$p_t(1 + \theta_{it}/\alpha_1) = MC_i(q_{it}) \text{ for } i = 1, \dots, N$$

where MC_i is the marginal cost function of firm i. If firms choose price noncooperatively in each period, they price at marginal cost as Bertrand predicted, and so θ_{it} equals zero for all i and t. If instead they maximize joint profits, θ_{it} equals one for all i and t. If firms produce at Cournot output levels, θ_{it} equals $s_{it} = q_{it}/Q_t$, the market share of firm i in period t.

For estimation purposes, I employ aggregate data. The individual supply equations are weighted by market shares in time t, s_{it}, and added up. Then we get the industry supply relationship

$$p_t(1 + \theta_t/\alpha_1) = \sum_i s_{it} MC_i(q_{it})$$

where $\theta_t = \sum_i s_{it}\theta_{it}$.

It can be shown that, given these functional forms for the market demand and cost functions, the market share of firm i in period t will be

$$s_{it} = \frac{a_i^{1/(1-\delta)}}{\sum_j a_j^{1/(1-\delta)}} \equiv s_i$$

in each of the three cases above. Thus the market share of each firm will be constant over time and invariant across changes in industry conduct. Note that the higher the value of the firm-specific variable cost shift parameter, a_i, the lower is the market share of firm i.

The supply relationship can now be written as

$$p_t(1 + \theta_t/\alpha_1) = DQ_t^{\delta-1}$$

where

$$D = \delta\left(\sum_i a_i^{1/(1-\delta)}\right)^{1-\delta}$$

Note that D depends only on the parameters of the cost functions of the firms. Here θ equals zero, H, or 1 for Bertrand, Cournot, or perfectly collusive firms, respectively. H is the Herfindahl index, $H = \sum_i s_i^2$, and is invariant across time, as long as the number of firms remains unchanged. Suppose I_t is an indicator variable which equals one when the industry is in a cooperative regime and equals zero when the industry witnesses a reversionary episode. Then the supply relationship of the industry is given by

$$\log p_t = \beta_0 + \beta_1 \log Q_t + \beta_2 S_t + \beta_3 I_t + U_{2t} \tag{2}$$

If reversionary periods are Bertrand, $\beta_0 = \log D$ and $\beta_1 = \delta - 1$. Since δ is assumed to be greater than one, β_1 should be positive. Here S_t is a vector of structural dummies which reflect entry and acquisitions in the industry. Recall that, for the JEC, entry does not seem to have caused reversions to noncooperative behavior. Then entry should not result in a regime change, only a shift in the parameter D. Also, $\{U_{21}, \ldots, U_{2T}\}$ is assumed to be a sequence of independent normal variables, with mean zero, variance σ_2^2, and Cov $(U_{1t}, U_{2t}) = \sigma_{12}$.

If firms behaved in cooperative periods to maximize single-period expected joint net returns, then β_3 would equal $\log(\alpha_1/(1+\alpha_1))$. However, as I discussed in the introduction, if a cartel selects an optimal trigger price strategy, output in cooperative periods will exceed perfectly collusive levels. While the industry structure described in this article differs from that of Green and Porter, there is some reason to suspect that the same sort of equilibrium will result. To repeat, the larger the profits in cooperative periods, the greater the marginal benefit to secretly cutting price. Then cheating will be deterred only if reversionary periods are of greater length, or more likely to occur. An optimal enforcement mechanism will trade off short-run profits for increased future cartel stability. Thus the value of β_3 will not be restricted, but instead estimated independently. Since market price should be higher in cooperative periods, β_3 should be positive but less than $\log(\alpha_1/(1+\alpha_1))$.

If the sequence $\{I_1, \ldots, I_T\}$ is known, then the estimation of the parameters of the demand and supply functions is straightforward, as two-stage least squares can be employed to obtain consistent estimates. If instead I_t is unknown, but assumed to be governed by the Bernoulli distribution

$$I_t = \begin{cases} 1 & \text{with probability } \lambda \\ 0 & \text{with probability } 1 - \lambda \end{cases} \tag{3}$$

then we have a simultaneous equations switching regression problem, where the "switch" is reflected solely by the constant term in the supply function. The parameters of the demand and supply functions, as well as the switch probability λ, can be estimated by appropriately generalizing a technique first proposed by Kiefer (1980), which adapts the E-M algorithm to models of this sort.

We can summarize equations (1) and (2) by writing

$$By_t = \Gamma X_t + \Delta I_t + U_t \tag{4}$$

where

$$y_t = \begin{pmatrix} \log Q_t \\ \log p_t \end{pmatrix} \quad X_t = \begin{pmatrix} 1 \\ L_t \\ S_t \end{pmatrix} \quad U_t = \begin{pmatrix} U_{1t} \\ U_{2t} \end{pmatrix}$$

and where

$$B = \begin{pmatrix} 1 & -\alpha_1 \\ -\beta_1 & 1 \end{pmatrix} \quad \Delta = \begin{pmatrix} 0 \\ \beta_3 \end{pmatrix} \quad \text{and} \quad \Gamma = \begin{pmatrix} \alpha_0 & \alpha_2 & 0 \\ \beta_0 & 0 & \beta_2 \end{pmatrix}$$

Here U_t is identically and independently distributed $N(0, \Sigma)$, where

$$\Sigma = \begin{pmatrix} \sigma_1^2 & \sigma_{12} \\ \sigma_{12} & \sigma_2^2 \end{pmatrix}$$

The probability density function of y_t, given I_t, is then

$$h(y_t|I_t) = (2\pi)^{-1}|\Sigma|^{-1/2}\|B\|\exp\{-\tfrac{1}{2}(By_t - \Gamma X_t - \Delta I_t)'\Sigma^{-1}(By_t - \Gamma X_t - \Delta I_t)\}$$

and the likelihood function, if there are T observations, is

$$L(I_t, \ldots, I_T) = \Pi_{t=1}^T h(y_t|I_t)$$

If the $\{I_t\}$ sequence is known, then we can obtain estimates of $B, \Gamma, \Delta,$ and Σ by maximizing $L(I_t, \ldots, I_T)$. When the $\{I_t\}$ series is unknown and governed by equation (3), then the probability density function of y_t is given by

$$f(y_t) = (2\pi)^{-1/2}|\Sigma|^{-1/2}\|B\| \times \big[\lambda \exp\{-\tfrac{1}{2}(By_t - \Gamma X_t - \Delta)'\Sigma^{-1}(By_t - \Gamma X_t - \Delta)\} \\ + (1-\lambda)\exp\{-\tfrac{1}{2}(By_t - \Gamma X_t)'\Sigma^{-1}(By_t - \Gamma X_t)\}\big]$$

and the likelihood function by

$$L = \Pi_{t=1}^T f(y_t) \tag{5}$$

Given an initial estimate of the regime classification sequence, say $\{w_1^0, \ldots, w_T^0\}$, where w_t^0 is an estimate of $\Pr\{I_t = 1\}$, we can obtain an initial estimate of λ by using

$$\lambda^0 = \Sigma_t w_t^0 / T$$

and initial estimates of $\Delta, \Sigma, B,$ and Γ by maximizing $L(w_1^0, \ldots, w_T^0)$. Denote these estimates by $\Omega^0 = (\Delta^0, \Sigma^0, B^0, I^0)$. Kiefer's algorithm then updates the w_t^0 series by Bayes' rule, so that

$$w_t^1 = \Pr\{I_t = 1 \,|\, y_t, X_t, \Omega^0, \lambda^0\}$$

$$= \frac{\lambda^0 h(y_t \,|\, X_t, \Omega^0, I_t = 1)}{\lambda^0 h(y_t \,|\, X_t, \Omega^0, I_t = 1) + (1 - \lambda^0) h(y_t \,|\, X_t, \Omega^0, I_t = 0)}$$

Given the new regime classification series $\{w_1^1, \ldots, w_T^1\}$, new estimates of $(\Delta, \Sigma, B, \Gamma)$, say Ω^1, can be obtained by maximizing $L(w_1^1, \ldots, w_T^1)$ with respect to Ω. Our new estimates of λ will be $\lambda^1 = \Sigma_t w_t^1 / T$. This iterative procedure is continued until convergence occurs, say at $(\hat{w}_1, \ldots, \hat{w}_T), \hat{\lambda} = \Sigma_t \hat{w}_t / T$, and $\hat{\Omega}$. The stopping criterion was that the correlation between the estimated w_t sequences of two successive iterations exceed 0.999. As Kiefer shows, $\hat{\lambda}$ and $\hat{\Omega}$ will be the maximum likelihood estimates of λ and Ω. Thus $\hat{\lambda}$ and $\hat{\Omega}$ maximize the likelihood function L of equation (5). (This is generally true for the E-M algorithm.)

Once estimation is completed, the sample can be classified into collusive and reversionary periods. Lee and Porter (1984) show that if $\hat{w}_t$ exceeds 0.5, period t should be classified as collusive. This rule minimizes the total probability of misclassification in the sample. Thus $(\hat{w}_1, \ldots, \hat{w}_T)$ generates the classification series $\hat{I}_t$, where

$$\hat{I}_t = 1 \quad \text{if} \quad \hat{w}_t > 0.5$$
$$\quad\ = 0 \quad \text{otherwise}$$

The Kiefer estimation scheme does not constrain the estimated $\hat{I}_t$ series to follow any particular process. If trigger price strategies of the sort described by Green and Porter actually occur, then the $\hat{I}_t$ sequence should follow a Markov process of order equal to the length of reversionary periods. Rather than attempt to estimate subject to a constraint of this sort, which would be relatively difficult, I have chosen to employ Kiefer's technique. (Note also that one would expect the duration of reversionary episodes to vary within the sample, as firms solve a new constrained-optimization problem in response to entry.) Green and Porter (1984) show that, when the number of reversionary episodes is small relative to the sample size (as is the case for the JEC data), the bias which arises from treating the endogenous Markov process as exogenous will plausibly be slight.

To see how sensitive the estimation scheme is to the specified functional forms, I also estimated the model with a linear specification of equation (4), that is, where $y_t' = [Q_t, p_t]$. These results were not significantly different from those reported in this article, and are documented in Porter (1982).

4. The Data

A principal function of the JEC was information gathering and dissemination to member firms. Weekly accounts were kept to keep members abreast of developments in the industry. In this section, I document the data set which is employed in this study, and mention some of its features. A list of variables is contained in Table 1. Some summary statistics are provided in Table 2.

Table 1 List of variables*

GR	grain rate, in dollars per 100 lbs
TQG	total quantity of grain shipped, in tons
LAKES	dummy variable; = 1 if Great Lakes were open to navigation; = 0 otherwise
PO	cheating dummy variable; = 1 if colluding reported by *Railway Review*; = 0 otherwise
PN	estimated cheating dummy variable
DM1	= 1 from week 28 in 1880 to week 10 in 1883; = 0 otherwise; reflecting entry by the Grand Trunk Railway
DM2	= 1 from week 11 to week 25 in 1883; = 0 otherwise; reflecting an addition to New York Central
DM3	= 1 from week 26 in 1883 to week 11 in 1886; = 0 otherwise; reflecting entry by the Chicago and Atlantic
DM4	= 1 from week 12 to week 16 in 1886; = 0 otherwise; reflecting departure of the Chicago and Atlantic from the JEC

* The sample is from week 1 in 1880 to week 16 in 1886.

Table 2 Summary statistics

Variable	Mean	Standard deviation	Minimum value	Maximum value
GR	0.2465	0.06653	0.125	0.40
TQG	25384	11632	4810	76407
LAKES	0.5732	0.4954	0	1
PO	0.6189	0.4864	0	1

The quantity variable, *TQG* is the total tonnage of grain shipped by JEC members. It varied dramatically over the sample period, but does not appear to follow any significant trend.

The price variable, *GR*, is somewhat suspect. The JEC polled member firms and provided an index of prices charged. There is some reason to expect that secret price cuts would not be reflected by this index, since there is a moral hazard problem in reporting actual prices. Therefore, any price wars precipitated by secret price cutting may have been recorded with a lag. On the other hand, the existence of this sort of information structure is necessary if an enforcement mechanism involving reversions to noncooperative behavior, or price wars, is to be witnessed. It is of crucial importance that firms monitor some variable (in this case their own market share) which imperfectly reflects the actions of other firms. Here firms knew what prices they charged their own customers, but the *GR* series would not be of much use in determining whether other firms were secretly cutting price.

While the *LAKES* variable documents when the JEC faced its main source of competition, it would be preferable if the prices charged by the lake steamers has also been used in the econometric work. Unfortunately, this series was not available.

The *PO* series equals one unless the *Railway Review*, a trade magazine, reported that a price war was occurring. This series concurred with the reports of the *Chicago Tribune* and other accounts in this period. The *PN* series is the $\hat{I}_t$ sequence, the estimated classification index which indicates whether industry conduct in period *t* is cooperative, and which should mirror the *PO* series if the latter is at all accurate. One reason for estimating a *PN* series is that *PO*, reported by Ulen (1978), conflicts sharply with an index of cartel adherence created by MacAvoy (1965).

The various *DM* dummy variables proxy structural change caused by entry, departures from the JEC, or additions to existing networks. (In 1886, the Chicago and Atlantic temporarily left the JEC because of a dispute with the railroad which provided them access to the eastern seaboard. This railroad (the Erie) was not a JEC member.) In each case, these changes are presumed to result in a once-and-for-all shift in the constant term of the supply relationship, which is consistent with the algebra of the previous section.

Finally, I also employed dummy variables to capture seasonal aspects of market demand and supply. Each year was segmented into thirteen four-week segments, and so twelve "monthly" dummies entered both the demand and the supply equations.

One assumption of the econometric model of the previous section is that the output shares of JEC members are relatively stable across episodes of reversionary conduct. These shares are allowed to vary when structural change occurs. There are five distinct periods in the sample, as reflected by the *DM* variables. *DM1* and *DM3* correspond to the longest periods (281 of 328 sample points), and all reversionary episodes occurred during these intervals. Within these intervals, the average sum (across firms) of squared deviations from allocated market shares was roughly the same in cooperative and reversionary periods. Thus, the assumption of approximately constant market shares seems reasonable, between times of structural change. (This is also borne out by data on the Herfindahl index.) While MacAvoy's (1965) results indicate significant fluctuations from trend shares, he does not examine deviations from allotted shares.

5. Results and Interpretation

This section contains an interpretive discussion of the econometric results. The regression coefficients obtained when two-stage least squares are applied to the system of equations (4), taking the *PO* series to be an accurate classification of regimes, are displayed in the left-hand columns of Table 3. Both single equation R^2 statistics and standard errors of the regression are displayed. Generally speaking, all variables have coefficients of the anticipated sign significantly different from zero, but the "fits" are not particularly good.

In the demand equation the predicted quantity is much lower when the lakes were open. The price elasticity is negative and less than one in absolute value. Thus, the marginal revenue associated with the industry demand curve is negative. This fact is not consistent with single-period profit maximization, which stipulates that industry marginal revenue equal a weighted average of the marginal costs of individual firms, a positive number.

The supply equation is also sensible. Price was significantly higher in cooperative periods. The predicted price of suppliers is an increasing function of quantity shipped, but the elasticity is of minor magnitude and only significantly different from zero at a 15 per cent significance level. Given the presumed cost and demand functions, this might be taken as evidence of weak diseconomies of scale, at least locally. (Of course, these diseconomies might be offset by large fixed costs.) The coefficients of the structural dummies are also reasonable. Entry led to a fall in market price, *ceteris paribus*, as the coefficient of *DM1* is negative, and that of *DM3* is less than that of *DM2*.

Table 3 Estimation results*

Variable	Two-stage least squares (Employing PO)		Maximum likelihood (Yielding PN)**	
	Demand	Supply	Demand	Supply
C	9.169	−3.944	9.090	−2.416
	(0.184)	(1.760)	(0.149)	(0.710)
LAKES	−0.437		−0.430	
	(0.120)		(0.120)	
GR	−0.742		−0.800	
	(0.121)		(0.091)	
DM1		−0.201		−0.165
		(0.055)		(0.024)
DM2		−0.172		−0.209
		(0.080)		(0.036)
DM3		−0.322		−0.284
		(0.064)		(0.027)
DM4		−0.208		−0.298
		(0.170)		(0.073)
PO/PN		0.382		0.545
		(0.059)		(0.032)
TQG		0.251		0.090
		(0.171)		(0.068)
R^2	0.312	0.320	0.307	0.863
s	0.398	0.243	0.399	0.109

*Monthly dummy variables are employed. To economize on space, their estimated coefficients are not reported. Estimated standard errors are in parentheses.
**PN is the regime classification series $(\hat{I}, \ldots, \hat{I}_T)$. The coefficient attributed to PN is the estimate of β_3.

The right-hand columns of Table 3 display the results of applying Kiefer's iterative technique. (This algorithm converged to these estimates from several disparate starting points.) The coefficient attributed to PN is the estimate of β_3, i.e., the difference between the intercept of the supply relationship in cooperative and noncooperative periods. The obvious difference between the results of Table 3 is that measures of goodness of fit of the supply equation are dramatically better for the E-M algorithm.

For practical purposes, the demand equations of Table 3 are identical. Again, the demand curve is inelastic. The real differences are reflected in the supply relationships. The coefficient attributed to the PN series, β_3, is larger and with about half the standard error. If we assume that $\beta_3 = -\log(1 + \theta/\alpha_1)$ for some constant θ, then the value of θ implied by the estimates of β_3 and α_1 is 0.336. This is roughly consistent with Cournot behavior in cooperative periods. The witnessing of approximately Cournot behavior is by itself of no special significance. What matters is that cooperative period prices exceed those implied by competitive price setting, but are less than those consistent with static joint profit maximizing, as predicted by Porter (1983).

If we set all explanatory variables equal to their sample mean, with the exception of the *LAKES* and *PN* dummy variables, then the maximum likelihood estimates displayed in Table 3 imply the reduced-form estimates shown in Table 4. Thus, in equilibrium, price was 66 percent higher in cooperative periods, and quantity 33 percent lower. Similarly, price was 4.5 percent lower when the lakes were open, and quantity 33 percent lower. The total revenue figure is twenty times the product of *GR* and *TQG*, and so in dollars (20 × $ per 100 lbs. × tons). Thus, the cartel as a whole could expect to earn 11 percent higher revenues in cooperative periods, a difference of about $11,000 per week. (Recall that these are 1880 dollars.) This is the revenue earned on grain shipments, which represented between 70 and 80 percent of total revenues from eastbound freight shipments by the JEC. Finally, revenues were about 35 percent lower when the lakes were navigable.

Table 4   Price, quantity, and total revenue for different values of *LAKES* and *PN**

	PN	LAKES	
		0	1
Price	0	0.1673	0.1612
	1	0.2780	0.2679
Quantity	0	38680	25904
	1	25775	17261
Total Revenue**	0	129423	83514
	1	143309	92484

* Computed from the reduced form of the maximum likelihood estimates of Table 3, with all other explanatory variables set at their sample means.
** Total Revenue = 20 (Price × Quantity), to yield dollars per week.

The *PO* and *PN* series are depicted, together with *GR*, in Figure 1, which shows when noncooperative episodes were predicted by the two series. Both series are similar to the extent that noncooperative periods averaged about 10 weeks in duration, and primarily occurred in 1881, 1884, and 1885. In several instances, *PO* reflects a price war before *PN*, and both switch back to unity together, which is consistent with *GR* not picking up secret price cuts. For either series, a regression of price war length on the realization of the demand equation residual error term in the period before the beginning of the episode had little predictive power. Of course, the demand equation is marred by a missing variable problem (namely, the price charged by lake steamers), so there is not much reason to think that the demand residuals would accurately reflect unexpected disturbances. (Some people have suggested that optimal price war length might depend on the magnitude of the demand shock.) More importantly, since JEC firms were price setters, price wars may not have necessarily been triggered by adverse demand shocks. As predicted by Stigler (1964), unpredictable fluctuations in market shares were probably more decisive. In this sample,

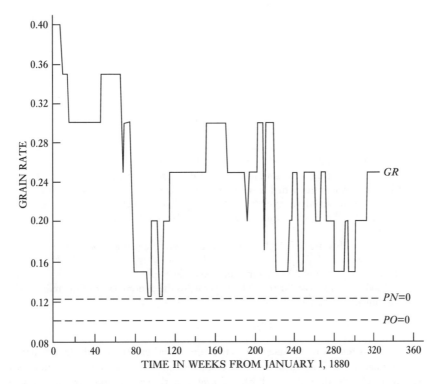

Figure 1   Plot of *GR*, *PO*, *PN* as a function of time

price wars (as measured by either *PO* or *PN*) were not preceded by large negative demand residuals.

The 1881 and 1884 incidents both began about 40 weeks after the entry of the Grand Trunk and the Chicago and Atlantic, respectively. While entry may not have immediately caused reversion to noncooperative behavior, it is quite plausible that it increased the probability of its incidence in the future, as cartel enforcement problems typically increase with the number of participating firms. In the sample, reversions were more frequent when the number of firms increased. (They were also shorter, on average.)

The *PO* series collected by Ulen (1978) differs markedly from an index of cartel nonadherence created by MacAvoy (1965). These series, as well as *PN*, are summarized in Table 5. The "Reported" and "Estimated" columns show the fraction of weeks in each year in which *PO* and *PN* were equal to zero, respectively. Since the *PN* series was in no way constrained to resemble *PO*, it is evident that *PN* supports the documentation of the *Railway Review* and *Chicago Tribune*, rather than MacAvoy's results.

To conclude this section, I consider the statistical evidence that switches actually occurred and were significant. First, the coefficient of *PO* and that attributed to *PN* are significantly greater than zero, so that periods of cooperation involved a significantly higher price.

Table 5   Index of cartel nonadherence[1]

Year	MacAvoy[2]	Reported[3]	Estimated[4]
1880	26	0.00	0.00
1881	14	0.67	0.44
1882	18	0.06	0.21
1883	6	0.10	0.00
1884	16	0.58	0.40
1885	10	0.77	0.67
1886[5]	15	0.50	0.06

[1] Columns 1 and 2 are taken from Ulen (1978, p. 336).
[2] The number of months, summed over all cartel members, for which the difference between the actual market share and "trend" share of tonnage was greater than the standard error from the "trend" share regression of each member road. The greater this number of months, the less stable the cartel is likely to be.
[3] For year i, this index is $\Sigma(1 - PO(t))/52$, where the summation is over t in year i.
[4] This index is $\Sigma(1 - \hat{I}_t)/52$, summing over t in year i.
[5] PO and PN only exist for the first 16 weeks, so the denominator of the indices is 16 rather than 52.

Likelihood ratio tests can be used to determine whether structural change has in fact occurred. The natural null hypothesis to be tested is that only cooperative or noncooperative behavior is observed, but not both. These are the respective implications of the equilibria described by Friedman (1977) and Telser (1972), or of a Nash open-loop strategy equilibrium. The value of the likelihood function, given the Kiefer estimation technique, can be compared to that when L is maximized subject to the constraint that $\Delta = 0$.

Suppose that L_1 is the maximized value of the log likelihood function for the specification of Table 3 when Kiefer's technique is used, and $(\hat{B}_1, \hat{\Sigma}_1)$ the corresponding estimates of (B, Σ). Further, suppose that L_0 is the maximized value of the log likelihood function for this specification when Δ equals zero, and that $(\hat{B}_0, \hat{\Sigma}_0)$ are the estimates of (B, Σ). Then

$$L_1 - L_0 = (\log \|\hat{B}_1\| - \tfrac{1}{2}\log |\hat{\Sigma}_1|) - (\log\|\hat{B}_0\| - \tfrac{1}{2}\log |\hat{\Sigma}_0|)$$

Under the null hypothesis that no regime change is observed, $2T(L_1 - L_0)$ has a chi-squared distribution with one degree of freedom. For the JEC sample, $2T(L_1 - L_0)$ is 554.1. Thus I can overwhelmingly reject the hypothesis that no switch occurred, given the specifications adopted. Price and quantity changes cannot be attributed solely to exogenous changes in demand and structural conditions. The similarity of the estimated PN series and the PO series indicate that some price changes can be attributed to periods of noncooperative behavior, and that the incidence of alleged switches in behavior cannot be explained by missing data problems.

The conclusions of this section are quite robust, as they are obtained under a variety of different specifications and functional forms.

6. Summary

The econometric evidence presented in the previous section indicates that reversions to noncooperative behavior did occur in the JEC, with a significant decrease in market price in these periods. The econometric results indicating that these episodes were concentrated in 1881, 1884, and 1885 are in keeping with the behavior of the JEC that was reported at that time. The question remaining, however, is what the causes of these reversions were.

Traditionally, breakdowns in cartel discipline have been attributed to demand slumps, both within the JEC as well as in other cartels. What distinguishes the theoretical model of Green and Porter (1984) from other theories of cartel stability is that reversionary episodes, or price wars, are caused by an unanticipated change in demand, in this case reflected by an unusually low market share for at least one firm, rather than by a prolonged drop in total market demand. Trying to determine which model best describes the observed behavior of the JEC from 1880 to 1886 is not an easy task, but I can refer to two pieces of evidence which may support the Green and Porter paradigm. First, the reduced-form estimates predict that price was lower and quantity higher in reversionary periods, *ceteris paribus*. Of course, this could merely reflect the fact that demand was quite elastic with respect to price changes, a fact at least partially refuted by the estimated price elasticity of demand. Second, one can look at total grain shipments from Chicago to see what fraction is accounted for by the JEC. Annual data showing the amount of grain shipped by lake steamers versus railroads are presented in Table 6. Of the years in the sample, 1880 is a boom year, which would account for the unusually high prices charged then. Of the remaining years, the annual variation in total shipments is not correlated with measures of cartel nonadherence. The distinguishing feature of the "breakdown" years of 1881, 1884, and 1885 is the much higher market share captured by the JEC as a whole in the intermodal competition to ship wheat. This is an indication that JEC price wars were not concurrent with lake steamer price wars, and also that JEC price wars did not always

Table 6   Annual eastbound shipments of wheat from Chicago by lake and rail*

Year	Lake		Rail		Total Shipments
	Total	Percentage	Total	Percentage	
1880	16.69	77.9	4.728	22.1	21.42
1881	7.688	50.0	7.680	50.0	15.37
1882	14.94	86.2	2.389	13.8	17.33
1883	7.067	73.2	2.590	26.8	9.66
1884	11.52	66.0	5.928	34.0	17.45
1885	5.436	51.5	5.116	48.5	10.55
1886	10.51	82.6	2.209	17.4	12.72

* in millions of bushels.

occur in years when total demand was unusually low. Thus, while some observers have claimed that price wars will be triggered by the unexpected tapering off of demand, which is consistent with the paradigm of Green and Porter, the JEC seems to be a case where this was not necessarily true of periods in which demand was low *per se*. Further support of this contention is that the *PO* and *PN* series are not systematically related to the opening or closing of the lake steamer shipping season. Finally, the fact that the frequency of reversionary periods increased as the number of market participants increased is consistent with a story of dynamic cartel enforcement mechanisms, especially since the "no-exit" constraint faced by railroads deterred predatory reactions to entry.

References

Brock, W. A. and Scheinkman, J. A. (1981): "Price-Setting Supergames with Capacity Constraints," SSRI Paper No. 8130, University of Wisconsin–Madison.

Friedman, J. W. (1977): *Oligopoly and the Theory of Games*. Amsterdam: North-Holland.

Green, E. J. and Porter, R. H. (1984): "Noncooperative Collusion under Imperfect Price Information," *Econometrica*, January.

Kiefer, N. M. (1980): "A Note on Switching Regressions and Logistic Discrimination," *Econometrica*, 48, May, 1065–9.

Lee, L. F. and Porter, R. H. (1984): "Switching Regression Models with Imperfect Sample Separation Information – With an Application on Cartel Stability," *Econometrica*, 52, January.

MacAvoy, P. W. (1965): *The Economic Effects of Regulation*. Cambridge: M.I.T. Press.

Porter, R. H. (1982): "A Study of Cartel Stability: The Joint Executive Committee, 1880–1886," C.E.R. Discussion Paper No. 82–158, University of Minnesota.

——. (1983): "Optimal Cartel Trigger Price Strategies," *Journal of Economic Theory*, 29, April, 313–38.

Stigler, G. J. (1964): "A Theory of Oligopoly," *Journal of Political Economy*, 72, February, 44–61.

Telser, L. G. (1972): *Competition, Collusion, and Game Theory*. Chicago: Aldine-Atherton.

Ulen, T. S. (1978): *Cartels and Regulation*. Unpublished Ph.D. dissertation, Stanford University.

CHAPTER ELEVEN

Automobile Prices in Market Equilibrium

STEVEN BERRY, JAMES LEVINSOHN, AND ARIEL PAKES

Source: *Econometrica*, 1995, 63, 841–90.

1. Introduction

This paper develops techniques for empirically analyzing demand and supply in differentiated products markets and then applies these techniques to analyze equilibrium in the U.S. automobile industry. Our primary goal is to present a framework that enables one to obtain estimates of demand and cost parameters for a class of oligopolistic differentiated products markets. Estimates from our framework can be obtained using only widely available product-level and aggregate consumer-level data, and they are consistent with a structural model of equilibrium in an oligopolistic industry. When we apply the techniques developed here to the U.S. automobile market, we obtain cost and demand parameters for (essentially) all models marketed over a twenty-year period. On the cost side, we estimate cost as a function of product characteristics. On the demand side, we estimate own- and cross-price elasticities as well as elasticities of demand with respect to vehicle attributes (such as weight or fuel efficiency). These elasticities, together with the cost-side parameters, play central roles in the analysis of many policy and descriptive issues (see, e.g., Pakes, Berry, and Levinsohn (1993) and Berry and Pakes (1993)).

Our general approach posits a distribution of consumer preferences over products. These preferences are then explicitly aggregated into a market-level demand system that, in turn, is combined with an assumption on cost functions and on pricing behavior to generate equilibrium prices and quantities. The primitives to be estimated are parameters describing the firms' marginal costs and the distribution of consumer tastes. The distribution of tastes determines elasticities, and these, together with marginal cost and a Nash assumption, determine equilibrium prices.

A familiar alternative is to posit a simple functional form for the market-level demand system. This requires some aggregation over products, since, for example, a constant elasticity demand system for 100 products would require estimating 10,000 elasticities. This problem is frequently alleviated by aggregating and/or nesting products into groups, with justification often given by representative consumer theory. Even apart from the appropriateness of the implied restrictions, aggregation methods that might seem useful for one policy experiment are unlikely to be useful for another. For example, an applied researcher investigating tariffs might be tempted to aggregate all foreign and all domestic cars. However the resulting model is unlikely to prove useful when investigating domestic competition or pollution taxes. Further problems associated with the market-level demand approach include an inability to evaluate the impact of the introduction of new goods on demand and the difficulty of incorporating more micro information on the distribution of consumers into a representative agent framework.

One extensively used alternative to the market-level approach is a system that represents consumer preferences over products as a function of individual characteristics and of the attributes of those products (an approach that dates back at least to Lancaster (1971)). Advances in the discrete choice literature over the last two decades have generated much of the econometric methodology needed to use micro level data to estimate the parameters determining individual demands from this characteristics approach (e.g., McFadden (1973) and the literature he cites in his 1986 review article). Moreover a few studies have, by using convenient (but restrictive) assumptions, been able to aggregate the individual demands generated by this approach into a market-level demand system (e.g., Berkovec (1985), Morrison and Winston (1989)). Finally, there is a literature that integrates very simple discrete choice demand systems with an oligopolistic price setting model in a way that allows use of aggregate data to estimate the parameters of marginal cost and demand (Bresnahan (1987)).

We follow in this tradition, consider two problems that arise quite naturally in this framework, and provide computationally tractable methods for solving them. The first of the two problems concerns the imposed functional form of utility and the resulting pattern of cross-price elasticities. We show how, using only aggregate data, to interact consumer and product characteristics, thereby allowing for plausible substitution patterns. The second problem involves the correlation between prices, which are observed by the econometrician, and product characteristics, some of which are observed by the consumer but not by the econometrician, and the bias in estimated elasticities that this induces. This is just the differentiated products analog of the traditional simultaneous equations problem in homogeneous product markets (the classic reference being Working (1926)). The resulting estimation strategy involves solving an aggregation problem in moving from the individual to aggregate demands (solved via simulation, as suggested by Pakes (1986)), and solving a nonlinear simultaneous equations problem to account for endogenous prices (solved via an inversion routine as suggested by Berry (1994)). Both these techniques have precursors in the literature. McFadden, et al. (1977) use simulation to generate aggregate predictions from micro parameter estimates. Hotz and Miller (1993) use a related inversion technique to estimate a dynamic model, and Bresnahan (1987) allows prices to be correlated with a linear disturbance in an equilibrium pricing equation but does not explicitly model the correlation between prices and unobserved characteristics.

Because we rely on mostly aggregate data, we do not have the degrees of freedom associated with more micro-level studies. This naturally raises concerns about obtaining precise estimates of the parameters of interest. We have two suggestions for ameliorating any precision problems that may arise. First, we show how to use widely available data on the distribution of consumer characteristics to augment market level information. Second, we use recent results to describe and compute an approximation to the efficient instrumental variables estimator for our system (Chamberlain (1986), Newey (1990), and Pakes (1994)).

Our framework is based upon: (i) a joint distribution of consumer characteristics and product attributes that determines preferences over the products marketed; (ii) price taking assumptions on the part of consumers; and (iii) Nash equilibrium assumptions on the part of producers. This a very rich framework which we have not fully exploited. In particular, to generate our instruments we use a strong assumption on the orthogonality of observed and unobserved product characteristics. Though we think this is a natural starting place, it is an assumption that can be relaxed in future work. Relatedly, and perhaps more interesting, the framework is rich enough to incorporate nontrivial dynamics and endogenize the distribution of product attributes. We discuss these extensions in section 8 below.

1.1. The automobile industry

Few industries have been studied as intensively as the auto industry and with good reason. With sales topping $150 billion in 1989, the auto market is one of the largest in the U.S. and has ramifications for entire state economies. Moreover it is often at the heart of policy debates (in fields once as diverse as international trade and environmental regulation) and it is a market that has evolved in important ways.

Early work treated autos as a homogeneous product and estimated aggregate demand (e.g. Suits (1958)). Griliches (1971) and later work by Ohta and Griliches (1976) adopted the hedonic approach. Their work was among the first to consider the automobile market at the level of the individual product, a feature that set the tone for much future research (examples include Berkovec and Rust (1985), Toder et al. (1978), and Levinsohn (1988)). None of these studies gave much consideration to the production side of the model, although many of them used consumer micro data (a point we address below).

Perhaps the first attempt at simultaneously modeling and estimating the demand and oligopoly pricing sides of the market was Bresnahan's (1987) study. In that paper, Bresnahan adopted a vertical differentiation model and assumed a uniform density of consumers over the quality line. Feenstra and Levinsohn (1995) extend Bresnahan's work and allow products to be differentiated in multiple dimensions, but retain his assumption of the uniform density of consumers. Manski (1983) investigates the (perfectly competitive) supply side and demand side of the Israeli automobile market. Our goal is to estimate a model that allows for products that are differentiated in multiple dimensions, richer distributions of taste parameters, and unobserved (to the econometrician) product characteristics. We attempt to integrate and extend the advances in this literature, thereby taking a step towards a more detailed understanding of behavior in the auto market. (For a more detailed comparison to previous studies, see section 2.3.)

1.2. A road map

The next two sections describe our theoretical model. Section 2 discusses utility and demand, while section 3 models firm behavior and derives industry equilibrium. Section 4 introduces our instruments, section 5 formally defines the estimators and describes their properties, while section 6 provides the required computational techniques. The data and estimation results are discussed in section 7. This section also provides a quick review of alternative models and compares our estimates to those of some alternative models. We conclude and discuss extensions in section 8.

2. Theory: Utility and Demand

Our demand system is obtained by aggregating a discrete choice model of individual consumer behavior.[1] We then combine this demand system with a cost function, and embed these two primitives into a model of price setting behavior in differentiated products markets. The demand and pricing equations that this model generates give us the system of equations that we take to the data.

Most of this paper assumes that we do not have data that matches individual characteristics to the products those individuals purchased. Consequently we proceed (as does much of the prior literature on the empirical analysis of *equilibrium* in markets for differentiated products[2]) by considering the problem of estimating all the parameters of the demand system from product level data (i.e. from information on prices, quantities, and the measurable characteristics of the products). We then extend the discussion to allow for the possibility of incorporating exogenous (and frequently available) information on the *distribution* of individual characteristics (e.g., the distribution of income and/or family size). Only in the extensions section do we come back to the advantages of having data that matches consumer characteristics to the products those consumers purchased.

Our specification posits that the level of utility that a consumer derives from a given product is a function of both a vector of individual characteristics, say ζ, and a vector of product characteristics, say (x, ξ, p). Here p represents the price of the product, and x and ξ are, respectively, observed and unobserved (by the econometrician) product attributes. That is, the utility derived by consumer i from consuming product j is given by the scalar value

$$U(\zeta_i, p_j, x_j, \xi_j; \theta)$$

where θ is a k-vector of parameters to be estimated.

Consumers with different ζ make different choices, and to derive the aggregate demand system we integrate out the choice function over the distribution of ζ in the population. Throughout we will take ζ to have a *known* distribution. This distribution may either be the *empirical* distribution of a characteristic, or a standardized distribution whose standardization parameters are estimated (unit normals for example, whose standardization parameters are a mean vector and covariance matrix). For notational simplicity, we will let θ include any parameters determining the distribution of consumer characteristics, as well as the parameters that describe the utility surface conditional on these characteristics.

Consumer i chooses good j if and only if

$$U(\zeta_i, p_j, x_j, \xi_j; \theta) \geq U(\zeta_i, p_r, x_r, \xi_r; \theta) \quad \text{for} \quad r = 0, 1, \ldots, \mathcal{J}$$

where alternatives $r = 1, \ldots, \mathcal{J}$ represent purchases of the competing differentiated products. Alternative zero, or the outside alternative, represents the option of not purchasing any of those products (and allocating all expenditures to other commodities). It is the presence of this outside alternative that allows us to model aggregate demand for autos as a function of prices and auto characteristics. Let

$$A_j = \left\{ \zeta : U(\zeta, p_j, x_j, \xi_j; \theta) \geq U(\zeta, p_r, x_r, \xi_r; \theta) \right\} \quad \text{for} \quad r = 0, 1, \ldots, \mathcal{J} \tag{2.1}$$

That is, A_j is the set of values for ζ that induces the choice of good "j". Then, assuming ties occur with zero probability, and that $P_0(d\zeta)$ provides the density of ζ in the population, the market share of good "j" as a function of the characteristics of all the goods competing in the market is given by

$$s_j(p, x, \xi; \theta) = \int_{\zeta \in A_j} P_0(d\zeta) \tag{2.2}$$

Denote the $\mathcal{J}$-element vector of functions whose "jth" component is given by (2.2) as $s(\cdot)$. Then, if M is the number of consumers in the market, the $\mathcal{J}$-vector of demands is $Ms(p, x, \xi; \theta)$.

2.1. Functional forms and substitution patterns

This subsection begins by discussing alternative functional forms for the consumer decision problem and then aggregates over consumers to obtain market demand.

A special case of the model in (2.1) and (2.2) is

$$U(\zeta_i, p_j, x_j, \xi_j; \theta) \equiv x_j \beta - \alpha p_j + \xi_j + \epsilon_{i,j} \equiv \delta_j + \epsilon_{ij} \tag{2.3}$$

where

$$\delta_j = x_j \beta - \alpha p_j + \xi_j$$

and the mean of the ϵ vector in the population of consumers is assumed to be zero so that for each j, ξ_j is the mean (across consumers) of the unobserved component of utility, $f(\nu_i, \zeta_i)$, while δ_j is the mean of the utility from good j. In (2.3), the ϵ are the only elements of the vector of consumer characteristics, ζ.

This specification is particularly tractable if the unobserved characteristic $\xi_j = 0$ and the vector ϵ_{ij} is distributed independently across both consumers and products. Note that this implies that the distribution of ϵ_{ij} is independent of the observed characteristics, x_j. The tractability of combining (2.3) with an i.i.d. assumption on the distribution of the ϵ follows from the ease of computing market shares from

$$s_j = \int_\epsilon \prod_{q \neq j} P(\delta_j - \delta_q + \epsilon) P(d\epsilon) \qquad (2.4)$$

Equation (2.4) shows that this computation requires, at most, evaluating a unidimensional integral. We note that if the ϵ are distributed multivariate extreme value (the logit model) then there is a closed form for (2.4) and there is no need to compute any integral.

Despite this computational simplicity, the assumption that the utility function is additively separable into two terms, one determined entirely by the product characteristics (the δ_j in (2.3)) and one determined by the consumer characteristics (the ϵ_{ij} in (2.3)), is problematic. This is because (2.3) generates aggregate substitution patterns, and hence a set of (cross and own) price derivatives, as well as responses to the introduction of new products, that *cannot* possess many of the features that we expect them to have.

Before considering the implications of (2.3) in detail, it may be worthwhile to note that the additive separability assumption just discussed is stronger than the assumptions used in many models of individual consumer behavior. These models often assume i.i.d. additive utility errors, an assumption that has been critiqued extensively in the literature, at least since Debreu's (1960) discussion of the "independence of irrelevant alternatives" property in the logit model. However, consumer level studies *do* often interact observed consumer characteristics with product characteristics. These interactions mean that market shares do not take the simple form of (2.4) and hence do not have the unnatural implications on demand patterns which we now discuss.

An implication of (2.3) is that all substitution effects depend only on the δ_js. Since there is a unique vector of market shares associated with each δ-vector, the additively separable specification implies that the cross-price elasticities between any two products, or, for that matter, the similarity in their price and demand responses to the introduction of a new third product, depend only on their market shares. That is, conditional on market shares, substitution patterns do not depend on the observable characteristics of the product.

Thus, if we were using the specification in (2.3) to analyze an automobile market in which an inexpensive Yugo and an expensive Mercedes had the same market shares, then the parameter estimates would have to imply that the two cars have the same cross-price derivative with respect to *any* third car. In particular, the model would necessarily predict that an increase in the price of a BMW would generate equal increases in the demand for Yugos and for Mercedes. This contradicts the intuition which suggests that couples of goods whose characteristics are more "similar" should have higher cross-price elasticities. We expect this to happen because the consumers who would have chosen a BMW at the old prices, but now do not, have a preference for large cars and are therefore likely to move to another large car. Similarly, when a new car enters the market, we expect it to have a large effect on the demand for cars with similar characteristics. Additive separability plus i.i.d. ϵs, on the other hand, imply that a consumer who substitutes away from any given choice will tend to substitute toward other popular products, not to other similar products. Note that this does not depend on any specific distribution for the ϵs (e.g. logit).

For analogous reasons, the specification in (2.3) implies that two products with the same market share will have the same own-price demand derivatives. For example, if a Jaguar and a Yugo have the same market share, the specification in (2.3) implies that they must have the same own-price derivative. In an oligopoly context, this is troubling for it implies (assuming single-product firms) that the two products must have the same markup over marginal cost. Intuitively, however, we expect markups to be determined by more than market shares. They ought also to be determined by the number of competing products that are "close" in product space, and, because consumers who buy more expensive goods are likely to have lower marginal utilities of income, by the price of the product.[3]

We now consider ways of allowing for interaction between individual and product characteristics. A familiar starting point is to allow each individual to have a different preference for each different observable characteristic. This generates the traditional random coefficients model

$$U(\zeta_i, p_j, x_j, \xi_j; \theta) = x_j \bar{\beta} - \alpha p_j + \xi_j + \sum_k \sigma_k x_{jk} \nu_{ik} + \epsilon_{ij} \qquad (2.5)$$

where $(\zeta_i, \epsilon_i) = (\nu_{i1}, \nu_{i2}, \ldots, \nu_{iK}, \epsilon_{i0}, \epsilon_{i1}, \ldots, \epsilon_{iJ})$ is a mean zero vector of random variables with (a known) distribution function. Now the contribution of x_k units of the kth product characteristic to the utility of individual i is $(\bar{\beta}_k + \sigma_k \nu_{ik}) x_k$, which varies over consumers. We scale ν_{ik} such that $E(\nu_{ik}^2) = 1$, so that the mean and variance of the marginal utilities associated with characteristic k are $\bar{\beta}_k$ and σ_k^2 respectively.[4] This specification is particularly tractable if ϵ_i consists of i.i.d. extreme value deviates.

The utility obtained from consuming good j can still be decomposed into a mean

$$\delta_j = x_j \bar{\beta} - \alpha p_j + \xi_j$$

and a deviation from that mean

$$\mu_{ij} = \sum_k \sigma_k x_{jk} \nu_{ik} + \varepsilon_{ij}$$

but now μ_{ij} depends on the interaction between consumer preferences and product characteristics. As a result, consumers who have a preference for size will tend to attach high utility to all large cars, and this will induce large substitution effects between large cars.

Note, however, that though this specification allows for more realistic cross-price elasticities, it re-introduces the problem of computing the integral (in 2.2) that defines market shares as a function of the parameters of the model. We solve this computational problem via aggregation by simulation, a technique introduced by Pakes (1986).

Though familiar, the random coefficients specification in (2.5) is not really suitable for our purposes. We prefer a specification that makes it easy for us to incorporate prior information on both the distribution of the relevant consumer characteristics, and on the functional form of the interaction between those characteristics and product attributes. This is because we have additional information on the distribution of income across households, and a theoretical rationale for the form of the interaction between income and price.

To this end, we now nest the random coefficients specification into a Cobb-Douglas utility function in expenditures on other goods and services and characteristics of the good purchased:

$$U(\zeta_i, p_j, x_j, \xi_j; \theta) = (y_i - p_j)^\alpha G(x_j, \xi_j, \nu_i) e^{\epsilon(i,j)} \tag{2.6}$$

where y is income, and ϵ provides the effect of the interactions of unobserved product and individual characteristics.

In our empirical example we assume that $G(\cdot)$ is linear in logs and has the random coefficient specification discussed above, so that if $u_{ij} = \log[U_{ij}]$, then

$$u_{ij} = \alpha \log(y_i - p_j) + x_j \bar{\beta} + \xi_j + \sum_k \sigma_k x_{jk} \nu_{ik} + \epsilon_{ij} \tag{2.7a}$$

for $j = 1, \cdots, \mathcal{J}$, while

$$u_{i0} = \alpha \log(y_i) + \xi_0 + \sigma_0 \nu_{i0} + \epsilon_{i0} \tag{2.7b}$$

Note, first, that our current data set does not have information on differences in the value of the outside alternative (differences that would be generated by, among other factors, differences in access to public transportation and differences in used car holdings). Thus, to account for the possibility that there is more unobserved variance in the idiosyncratic component of the outside than of the inside alternatives, we allow for an extra unobserved term in the determination of u_{i0} (the ν_{i0}).[5]

Second, note that the consumer terms that interact with product characteristics are now

$$\nu_i = (y_i, \nu_{i1}, \dots, \nu_{iK})$$

We have used special notation for income here both because it enters the utility function in a special way, and because it is a variable whose distribution can be estimated from the March Current Population Survey. As a result, if one assumes a parametric form for the distribution of ν_i conditional on y_i, we can use the CPS to determine the distribution of y_i in our population and reduce the number of parameters that are estimated from our auto data.

Two characteristics of (2.7) are central to the rest of this paper: it allows for interactions between consumer and product characteristics and it allows us to make use of exogenous data on the distribution of income in a natural and parsimonious way. The first characteristic enables us to model reasonable substitution patterns, while the second allows us to get more precise parameter estimates.[6]

2.2.　Endogenous prices

If producers know the values of the unobserved characteristics, ξ, even though we do not, then prices are likely to be correlated with them. This generates a differentiated products analog to the classic simultaneity problem in the analysis of demand and supply in homogeneous product markets.[7] The simultaneity problem is complicated by both the discrete choice set for each individual and the interaction of individual and product characteristics. These together make aggregate demand a complicated nonlinear function of product characteristics. Berry (1994) suggests one approach to obtaining estimates of the demand parameters, and proves its viability under certain restrictions. This subsection begins by discussing the importance of unobserved demand characteristics and the resulting endogeneity of prices, then reviews Berry's approach, and finally extends it to allow for the random coefficients in (2.7). The computation section will provide a contraction mapping that allows us to compute the unobserved components and hence use them in estimation.

Much empirical work on discrete choice models of demand (both aggregate and consumer level studies) has specified that the unobserved component in the utility function for each alternative is mean zero and independent across agents.[8] This specification assumes away the simultaneity problem. It also leads to an embarrassing "over fitting" problem on aggregate data (see, for example, Toder et al. (1978)). That is, if there is no "structural" disturbance in the market share equation, then only sampling error can explain differences between the data and the predictions of the model. For sample sizes as large as those typically found in aggregate studies, this variance is just too small to account for any noticeable discrepancy between the data and the model (so that a χ^2 test of the model's restrictions on the multinomial proportions is rejected with probability close to one).[9]

In contrast, aggregate demand in homogeneous product markets is typically specified to have a nonzero disturbance that is generally associated with unobserved determinants of demand that are correlated across consumers in a market. If these disturbances are known to the producers and the consumers (and if demand depends upon them, one expects this to be so), and if there is any equilibrating mechanism in the market, then equilibrium quantities and prices will depend upon the disturbances. It is this relationship between the disturbance and price that generates the simultaneity problem and the need for alternatives to ordinary least squares estimation techniques.

All the utility specifications in the last subsection had disturbances with a product specific mean, ξ, which is the analog of the disturbance in the aggregate demand system in homogeneous product markets. In the automobile example, ξ reflects the difficult to quantify aspects of style, prestige, reputation, and past experience that affect the demand for different products, as well as the effects of quantifiable characteristics of the car that we simply do not have in our data. As one might expect, the introduction of ξ will alleviate the overfitting problem. However, our primary concern is that if unobserved characteristics are important, and our data indicate that they are, prices will be correlated with them, and the estimates of price effects will be biased. This is precisely the same logic that leads to biased O.L.S. estimates of price effects in traditional demand systems.

As in traditional homogeneous goods models, we will assume that ξ is mean independent of some set of exogenous instruments and then derive estimators from the orthogonality conditions those assumptions imply. This procedure requires only the same assumptions needed for instrumental variable estimators of demand parameters in homogeneous product markets. In particular we do not require an explicit assumption on the distribution of the ξ, just that they be mean independent of the instruments. Furthermore, the procedure does not depend on the exact form of the pricing rule. On the other hand, since the pricing rule depends in equilibrium on the true values of the demand parameters, joint estimation of the pricing and demand equations should increase efficiency as long as the model is correctly specified.

The difference between our case and the homogeneous product case is that the demand of a given individual, and hence market demand, becomes a nonlinear function of the ξ;

i.e. $q_j = Ms_j(x, \xi, p; \theta)$. Consequently the orthogonality between ξ and the x-vector cannot be used for estimation without first transforming the observed quantity, price, and characteristic data into a linear function of ξ. It is this transformation that is the focus of Berry's (1994) paper and we return to it in the computational section. There remains the important issue of the choice of instruments, an issue we come back to after describing the pricing equation.

2.3. Previous approaches to demand estimation

Variations on the logit model, discussed at length above, have often formed the basis for micro-data studies of the automobile industry (that is, studies that match consumers to the cars they purchased). The authors of those studies frequently have been aware of the problems that we discuss here: the endogeneity of prices and the need to generate reasonable substitution patterns. With micro-data, there were alternatives to our proposed solutions. In particular, it is possible to interact product characteristics with *observed* consumer characteristics and many studies have done so (for example, Berkovec (1985)). Also, there is a possibility of using nested logit, which in our framework can be shown to be a restricted version of a model with random coefficients on a set of dummy variables that define groups (or "nests") of products (Ben-Akiva (1973), McFadden (1978), and Berkovec and Rust (1985), Goldberg (1993)). Note that this requires *a priori* information on the order and the contents of the nests. Finally, given recent advances in simulation methodology, one could use a random coefficients specification similar to ours and simulate choice probabilities. Note that the ν_i in the micro model (equation 2.7) underlying our aggregate specification could potentially reflect any combination of observed and unobserved consumer characteristics.

Micro-data does not by itself solve the problem of unobserved product characteristics that are correlated with prices. It does, however, allow one to introduce product-specific dummies to control for unobserved attributes. These dummies correspond to our δ_j s. Note first that this approach runs into an efficiency problem due to the relatively large number of automobile models. For example, there are on average more than 100 products in a given year of our sample, a number that might be compared to the approximately 500 new car purchases observed annually in the Consumer Expenditure Survey (which is on the order of the largest publicly available survey that includes detailed information on automobile purchases).[10] Thus, it is not surprising that we do not know of a study of automobile demand that estimates choice-specific constants, except when choices are artificially aggregated into a small number of alternatives, such as small, medium, and large cars (for more detail, see Train (1986) and his review of the literature on estimating auto demand). In addition, even if product specific dummies could be estimated, these dummies will contain the linear utility components of product characteristics and prices (as in our equation (2.3)). Therefore, to calculate price and characteristic elasticities we would need to separate out the effects of price, x and ξ on the product specific constants. This separation requires additional assumptions – the sort of assumptions that we make here to justify our instrumental variable approach.

With only aggregate data, previous authors have adopted other specifications for utility. In his study, Bresnahan (1987) adopts a pure vertical differentiation model (Shaked and Sutton (1982)). In this model, there is only one characteristic, the marginal valuation of either price or "quality," that varies across consumers. This greatly restricts substitution patterns. In particular, the pattern of cross-price elasticities is determined exclusively by market shares and the rank-order of prices, not by the value of other product characteristics such as size, power, etc. Products have nonzero cross-price elasticities only with the two other products that are adjacent to it in the ranking of prices. Consider, for example, the possibility that the price ranking contains, in order, a \$24,998 family station wagon, a \$24,999 sports car, and another family station wagon priced at \$25,000. In this case the vertical model guarantees that the wagons are *not* substitutes for one another, but that the sports car is. A solution to this is to allow products to be differentiated in multiple dimensions. Feenstra and Levinsohn (1995) adopt this approach while maintaining the rest of Bresnahan's framework.

3. Cost Functions and the Pricing Problem of the Multiproduct Firm

We take as given that there are F firms, each of which produce some subset, say $\mathcal{T}_f$, of the J products. For simplicity we begin by assuming that the marginal cost of producing the goods marketed is both independent of output levels and log linear in a vector of cost characteristics. These assumptions are made only for expositional convenience and we relax them in our investigation of the robustness of our empirical results.

The cost characteristics are decomposed into a subset which are observed by the econometrician, the vector w_j for model j, and an unobserved component, ω_j. Note that we might expect the observed product characteristics, the x_j, to be part of the w_j, and ω_j to be correlated with ξ_j. This is because larger cars, or cars with a larger unobserved quality index, might be more costly to produce, a possibility we will account for in our estimation algorithm.

Given these assumptions the marginal cost of good j, say mc_j, is written as

$$\ln(mc_j) = w_j\gamma + \omega_j \tag{3.1}$$

where γ is a vector of parameters to be estimated.

Given the demand system in (2.1) and (2.2), the profits of firm f, say Π_f, are

$$\Pi_f = \sum_{j \in \mathcal{T}_f}(p_j - mc_j)Ms_j(p, x, \xi; \theta) \tag{3.2}$$

with mc_j given by (3.1). Each firm is assumed to choose prices that maximize its profit given the attributes of its products and the prices and attributes of competing products.[11]

Given our assumptions, any product produced by firm f, or any $j \in \mathcal{T}_f$, must have a price, p_j, that satisfies the first-order conditions

$$s_j(p, x, \xi; \theta) + \sum_{r \in \mathcal{T}_f}(p_r - mc_r)\frac{\partial s_r(p, x, \xi; \theta)}{\partial p_j} = 0 \tag{3.3}$$

The $\mathcal{J}$ first-order conditions in (3.3) imply price-cost markups $(p_j - mc_j)$ for each good. To obtain these, define a new $\mathcal{J}$-by-$\mathcal{J}$ matrix, Δ, whose (j, r) element is given by:

$$\Delta_{jr} = \begin{cases} \dfrac{-\partial s_r}{\partial p_j} & \text{if } r \text{ and } j \text{ are produced by the same firm} \\ 0 & \text{otherwise} \end{cases} \tag{3.4}$$

In vector notation the first-order conditions can then be written as

$$s(p, x, \xi : \theta) - \Delta(p, x, \xi; \theta)[p - mc] = 0$$

Solving for the price-cost markup gives

$$p = mc + \Delta(p, x, \xi; \theta)^{-1} s(p, x, \xi; \theta)$$

Note that prices are additively separable in marginal cost and the markup defined as

$$b(p, x, \xi; \theta) \equiv \Delta(p, x, \xi; \theta)^{-1} s(p, x, \xi; \theta) \tag{3.5}$$

The vector of markups in (3.5) depends only on the parameters of the demand system and the equilibrium price vector. However, since p is a function of ω, $b(p, x, \xi; \theta)$ is a function of ω, and cannot be assumed to be uncorrelated with it (the correlation of ξ with ω also generates a dependence between the markups and ω). Substituting in the expression for marginal cost, we obtain the pricing equation we take to the data:

$$\ln(p - b(p, x, \xi; \theta)) = w\gamma + \omega \tag{3.6}$$

Just as in estimating demand, estimates of the parameters of (3.6) can be obtained if one assumes orthogonality conditions between ω and appropriate instruments. We now move on to a discussion of appropriate instruments.

4. Instruments

We need to specify instruments for both the demand and pricing equations. Any factors that are correlated with specific functions of the observed data, but are not correlated with the demand or supply disturbances, ξ and ω, will be appropriate instruments. Our procedure is to specify a list of variables that are mean independent of ξ and ω and use the logic of the estimation procedure to derive appropriate instruments.

Our mean independence assumption is that the supply and demand unobservables are mean independent of both observed product characteristics and cost shifters. Formally, if $z_j = [x_j, w_j]$ and $z = [z_1, \ldots, z_{\mathcal{J}}]$, then

$$E[\xi_j \mid z] = E[\omega_j \mid z] = 0 \tag{4.1}$$

Note first that we do not include price or quantity in the conditioning vector, z. This is because our model implies that price and quantity are determined in part by ξ and ω. In contrast, we do not model the determination of product characteristics and cost shifters.

On the other hand, one might think that there is a "true" underlying model which jointly determines both observed and unobserved product characteristics. Assumption (4.1) will only be correct if that model has very specific properties. It is relatively easy to formulate other assumptions that would also formally identify the model. For example, with a panel data set such as ours, one could assume that the ξ and ω of a given auto model evolve as a first-order Markov process, with the innovation in that process independent of the auto's initial characteristics. It is possible to modify our procedures to use this assumption as the basis of our estimation algorithm. However, this modified procedure would be much more demanding of the data. As a result, we started with the simpler assumption in (4.1).

Given (4.1) and some additional regularity conditions, we show in section 5 that the model generates an optimal set of instruments. While those instruments are hard to compute, we suggest an approximation to them. It is important to realize that the instruments associated with product j include functions of the characteristics and cost shifters of all other products. The intuition here follows from a natural feature of oligopoly pricing: products that face good substitutes will tend to have low markups, whereas other products will have high markups and thus high prices relative to cost. Similarly, because Nash markups will respond differently to own and rival products, the optimal instruments will distinguish between the characteristics of products produced by the same multi-product firm versus the characteristics of products produced by rival firms. Similar intuition has been used to motivate identification assumptions in several previous models, e.g. Bresnahan (1987).

Given the fact that demand for any product is, via the functional form of the demand system, a function of the characteristics of all products, our instruments cannot rely on "exclusion" restrictions. However, in our model the utility of consuming product j depends only on the characteristics of that product. Given this restriction, it is natural that the number of utility parameters grows with the dimension of the product characteristics space and not with the number of products. For example, if we approximated utility via a polynomial in characteristics, the number of utility parameters would be determined solely by the order of the polynomial and the number of characteristics. This restriction, combined with specific functional form and distributional assumptions, is what allows us to identify the demand system even in the absence of cost shifters that are excluded from the x vector.[12]

We turn now to a formal description of the estimation algorithm.

5. The Estimation Algorithm

To keep the exposition simple, we begin by maintaining some simplifying assumptions that we later remove. In particular, although we will actually use panel data, we start by assuming that our data consist of a single cross-section of the autos marketed in a given year. If $\mathcal{J}$ is the number of autos marketed, the data set then contains $\mathcal{J}$ vectors (x_j, w_j, p_j, q_j), and a number of households sampled, n, which, when combined with the information on purchases, can be used to compute the share of the outside alternative. Thus, the observed vector of sampled market shares, denoted s^n, belongs to the $\mathcal{J} + 1$ dimensional unit simplex. (This includes the share of the outside alternative).

The assumptions on the data generating process are as follows. Market shares are calculated from the purchases of a random sample of n consumers from a population with a distribution of characteristics, ν, given by $P_0(\cdot)$. This population abides by the model's decision rules at $\theta = \theta_0$. Letting s^0 denote the vector of shares in the underlying population, the multinomial sampling process implies that s^n converges to s^0 at rate $\sqrt{n}$, or $(s^n - s^0) = O_p(1/\sqrt{n})$. The $(\xi_j, \omega_j, x_j, w_j)$ vectors that characterize the primitive product characteristics are independent draws from some larger population of possible characteristic vectors.[13] The distribution of these vectors in this population has the mean independence property of (4.1), namely that $E[\xi_j|z] = E[\omega_j|z] = 0$.[14] We also assume that

$$E\big[(\xi_j, \omega_j)'(\xi_j, w_j)|z\big] = \Omega(z_j) \tag{5.1}$$

with $\Omega(z_j)$ finite for almost every z_j.

The logic behind the estimation procedure is simple enough. Appendix I shows that given the data on the prices and the observed characteristics of the products, *any* choice of a triple consisting of an observed vector of positive market shares, say s, a distribution of consumer characteristics, say P, and the parameters of the model, say θ, implies a unique sequence of estimates for the two unobserved characteristics of our products, say $\{(\xi_j(\theta, s, P), \omega_j(\theta, s, P)\}_{j=1}^{\mathcal{J}}$. Assume, temporarily, that we can actually calculate $\{(\xi_j(\theta, s^0, P_0), \omega_j(\theta, s^0, P_0)\}_{j=1}^{\mathcal{J}}$ for alternative values of θ. In fact, we do not actually observe s^0 (though we do observe s^n), and for most of the models we consider we cannot actually compute the disturbances generated by P_0, but rather only from a (simulation) estimator of it. So our actual estimation procedure will be based on substituting estimates of s^0 and of P_0 into the algorithm we now develop.

Assuming we can compute $\{\xi_j(\theta, s^0, P_0), \omega_j(\theta, s^0, P_0)\}$, then at $\theta = \theta_0$ our computation will reproduce the true values of the unobserved car characteristics. Consequently, the conditional moment restrictions in (4.1) imply that any function of z must be uncorrelated with the vector $\{\xi(\theta, s^0, P_0), \omega(\theta, s^0, P_0)]\}$ when that vector is evaluated at $\theta = \theta_0$. As in Hansen (1982), we can use this fact to generate a method of moments estimator of θ_0. That is, we can form the sample analog to some set of covariance restrictions and find that value of θ that sets this sample analog "as close as possible" to zero (see below).

To be more precise let $T(z_j)$ be a 2-by-2 matrix of functions of z_j, and $H_j(z)$ be an L-by-2 matrix of functions of z (the j index here indicates that the function may differ with the observation). The matrix $T(\cdot)$ is introduced to standardize $[\xi(\theta_0), \omega(\theta_0)]$; so we will assume that

$$T(z)'T(z) = \Omega(z)^{-1} \tag{5.2}$$

$H_j(\cdot)$ is a matrix of instruments for two standardized disturbances. Now define

$$G^{\mathcal{J}}(\theta) = E\left[H_j(z)T(z_j)\begin{pmatrix} \xi_j(\theta, s^0, P_0) \\ w_j(\theta, s^0, P_0) \end{pmatrix}\right] \tag{5.3}$$

and note that (4.1) guarantees $G^{\mathcal{J}}(\theta_0) = 0$. So form

$$
G_j(\theta; s^0, P_0) = \frac{1}{\mathcal{J}} \sum_{j=1}^{\mathcal{J}} H_j(z) T(z_j) \begin{pmatrix} \xi_j(\theta, s^0, P_0) \\ \omega_j(\theta, s^0, P_0) \end{pmatrix} \tag{5.4}
$$

and choose, as an estimate of θ, the value that minimizes, up to a term of $O_p(1/\sqrt{\mathcal{J}})$,

$$
\|G_{\mathcal{J}}(\theta; s^0, P_0)\|
$$

where for any vector y, $\|y\| = y'y$.

We need to account for the fact that we cannot actually compute the moment conditions, $G_{\mathcal{J}}(\theta; s^0, P_0)$, needed to minimize the objective function. There are two separate problems here. The first is that we do not observe s^0 but just s^n, so for any P we actually calculate $G_{\mathcal{J}}(\theta, s^n, P)$. Second, for most of our models we will not be able to calculate $G_{\mathcal{J}}(\theta; s, P_0)$ explicitly but will have to suffice with a simulation estimator of it. We show in section 6 that this is equivalent to using $(G_{\mathcal{J}}(\theta; s, P_{ns})$ where P_{ns} provides the empirical distribution of ns simulation draws from P_0.[15] Consequently, the objective function that our estimator θ minimizes is

$$
\|G_{\mathcal{J}}(\theta, s^n, P_{ns})\| \tag{5.5}
$$

In a separate paper, Berry and Pakes (in process) provide conditions that ensure that our estimate is consistent and asymptotically normal. Three problems arise in deriving the limiting properties of this estimator. First, the interdependence implicit in the demand system generates dependence in the quantities that we average over to form moment conditions. Indeed these quantities are not mean independent at values of θ different from θ_0, so consistency requires us to bound the moment conditions away from zero uniformly for θ different from θ_0. Given consistency, asymptotic normality follows from mean independence and smoothness of the objective function at θ_0. Second, the quantities entering the moment conditions are nonlinear functions of the disturbances generated by the consumer sampling and simulation processes. As a result, consistency requires both the number of simulation draws, ns, and the size of the consumer sample, n, to grow large. In addition, both the consumer sampling and simulation processes generate disturbances whose effects on the variance of our parameter estimates we want to quantify. Third, as $\mathcal{J}$ goes to infinity all but a finite number of the choice probabilities must go to zero, which makes it particularly difficult to evaluate the impact of the simulation and sampling errors on the inverse market share function that defines ξ. To accommodate these last two points more detailed assumptions must be made on the rate at which n and ns grow with respect to $\mathcal{J}$.

The covariance matrix, provided in Berry and Pakes (in process), for our estimator is[16]

$$
(\Gamma'\Gamma)^{-1}\Gamma'\left(\sum_{i=1}^{3} V_i\right)\Gamma(\Gamma'\Gamma)^{-1} \tag{5.6}
$$

Here

$$\Gamma = \lim_{\mathcal{J} \to \infty} \frac{\partial E[G_{\mathcal{J}}(\theta, s^0, P_0)]}{\partial \theta'}\bigg|_{\theta=\theta_0}$$

while if

$$V_1^{\mathcal{J}} = E_z\left[H_j(z)T(z_j)\begin{pmatrix} \xi_j(\theta_0, s^0, P_0) \\ \omega_j(\theta_0, s^0, P_0) \end{pmatrix}\begin{pmatrix} \xi_j(\theta_0, s^0, P_0) \\ \omega_j(\theta_0, s^0, P_0) \end{pmatrix}' T(z_j)'H_j(z)'\right]$$

$$V_2^{\mathcal{J}} = \frac{\mathcal{J}}{n}E(\sqrt{n}[G_{\mathcal{J}}(\theta_0, s^0, P_0) - G_{\mathcal{J}}(\theta_0, s^n, P_0)] \times \sqrt{n}[G_{\mathcal{J}}(\theta_0, s^0, P_0) - G_{\mathcal{J}}(\theta_0, s^n, P_0)]')$$

$$V_3^{\mathcal{J}} = \frac{\mathcal{J}}{ns}E(\sqrt{ns}[G_{\mathcal{J}}(\theta_0, s^n, P_{ns}) - G_{\mathcal{J}}(\theta_0, s^n, P_0)]$$
$$\times \sqrt{ns}[G_{\mathcal{J}}(\theta_0, s^n, P_{ns}) - G_{\mathcal{J}}(\theta_0, s^n, P_0)]'|s^n)$$

then

$$V_1 = \lim_{\mathcal{J} \to \infty} V_1^{\mathcal{J}} \quad V_2 = \lim_{\mathcal{J} \to \infty} V_2^{\mathcal{J}} \quad \text{and} \quad V_3 = \lim_{\mathcal{J} \to \infty} V_3^{\mathcal{J}}$$

The matrices V_1, V_2, and V_3 arise from the three independent sampling processes. V_1 arises from the process generating the product characteristics (the (x, w, ξ, ω)), V_2 from the consumer sampling process (which generates the difference between S^n and S^0) and V_3 from the simulation process (which generates the difference between P_{ns} and P_0).

From the utility specification used here, the results in Berry and Pakes (in process) require n and ns to grow quite rapidly, on the order of $\mathcal{J}^3$. Despite this, the fact that n in our sample is so large (the number of households in the U.S. economy is of the order of 100 million) implies that V_2 is negligible in our problem. On the other hand, we are concerned about the variance due to simulation error. Section 6 develops variance reduction techniques that enable us to use relatively efficient simulation techniques for our problem. Even so, we found that with a reasonable number of simulation draws the contribution of the simulation error to the variance in our estimates (V_3) is not negligible.

To calculate standard errors, we estimate V_1 by substituting $\theta_{\mathcal{J}}$ for θ_0 and taking the sample analog of the expression above. To estimate V_3, we substitute $\theta_{\mathcal{J}}$ for θ_0 and employ a Monte Carlo procedure. Specifically, we draw P_{ns} independently times. For each of these samples, we calculate the vector of moment conditions (5.4) and use the empirical variance of these moment conditions as our estimate. Correcting for the variance due to simulation increases our reported standard errors in table 4 of section 7 by about 5–20 percent (with the exception of one parameter, whose reported standard error doubles).

5.1. Optimal instruments

In section 4, we propose using as instruments functions of z, the cost and demand characteristics of all products in a given year. In this section we consider the form of those functions. Because we use only market level data and are therefore concerned with efficiency, we are guided in our choice by the optimal instrument literature.

Using an i.i.d. sampling scheme and other mild regularity conditions Chamberlain (1986) shows that the efficient set of instruments when we have only conditional moment restrictions is equal to the conditional expectation of the derivative of the conditional moment condition with respect to the parameter vector (conditioning on the same set of variables that condition the moment restriction, and evaluated at θ_0). The analogous instruments for our case are

$$
H_j(z) = E\left[\frac{\partial \xi_j(\theta_0, s^0, P_0)}{\partial \theta}, \frac{\partial \omega_j(\theta_0, s^0, P_0)}{\partial \theta}\Big|z\right] T(z_j) \equiv D_j(z)T(z_j) \tag{5.7}
$$

in which case the variance covariance matrix of the estimated parameter vector is

$$
\{E_z[D_j(z)\Omega(z_j)^{-1}D_j(z)']\}^{-1}
$$

The formula in (5.7) is very intuitive: larger weights should be given to the observations that generate disturbances whose computed values are very sensitive to the choice of θ (at $\theta = \theta_0$). Unfortunately $D_j(z)$ is typically very difficult, if not impossible, to compute. To calculate $D_j(z)$ we would have to calculate the pricing equilibrium for different $\{\xi_j, \omega_j\}$ sequences, take derivatives at the equilibrium prices, and then integrate out over the distribution of such sequences. In addition, this would require an assumption that chooses among multiple equilibria when they exist, and either additional assumptions on the joint distribution of (ξ, ω), or a method for estimating that distribution.[17]

Newey (1990) considers the special case where $T(z) = T$ (for all z), and shows that, again under mild regularity conditions, one can circumvent the problem of computing $D_j(z)$ by using a semiparametric estimator of it, and still generate an estimator whose limiting variance-covariance matrix is $\{E_z[D_j(z)\Omega^{-1}D_j(z)']\}^{-1}$ (see also the related work on feasible GLS by Robinson (1987); and the literature cited in both of these articles). The first stage of this procedure uses an initial consistent estimate of θ_0 to compute a nonparametric estimate of $H_j(z)$. Newey (1990) provides results from a Monte Carlo experiment that shows that this procedure tends to work well when a polynomial series approximation to the efficient instrument vector is used.

Though polynomial approximations are easy to compute, there is a dimensionality problem in using them to approximate functions whose arguments include the characteristics of all competing products. An unrestricted polynomial series approximation of a given order will have a number of basis functions that grows polynomially in the number of products in the market, J. In our case J is also the limiting dimension of the problem. This implies that the dimension of the basis needed for the approximation grows polynomially in sample size. This in turn both creates a practical problem in forming the estimator and violates the regularity conditions required for the consistency of the first stage estimator of the efficient instruments.

As shown in Pakes (1994) this dimensionality problem can be circumvented if ξ and ω are symmetric, or more precisely exchangeable, in some of their arguments. By exchangeable we mean that we can permute the order in which those variables enter a function without changing the value of that function. Recall that ξ and ω are determined by the demand function, the cost function, and the pricing assumption. By construction, both the demand and the cost functions for product j are exchangeable in vectors of characteristics of all other products. This is true trivially of cost functions that only depend on own-product characteristics, and is true for any differentiated products demand system in which the demand for a product does not depend on the ordering of rival products but just on their characteristics.

The pricing function for a given firm's product will change, however, if we permute the order of a product produced by the given firm and a product produced by a rival firm. So this function is not exchangeable in the characteristics of all other products. On the other hand, any unique Nash equilibrium is still partially exchangeable: that is, exchangeable in the characteristics of the firm's other products and exchangeable in the state vectors of its competitors products. In fact, a unique Nash equilibrium would imply the following three forms of exchangeability for the ξ and ω functions:

(i) exchangeable in the order of the competing firms (e.g., the prices of GM's products would not change if instead of listing the characteristics of Ford's products before Chrysler's, we listed the characteristics of Chrysler's products before Ford's)

(ii) for a given competitor, exchangeable in the order of that competitors products, and

(iii) for a given product, exchangeable in the order of the other products marketed by the same firm.

Theorem 32 in Pakes (1994) shows that the dimension of the basis for polynomials of a given order that are partially exchangeable is independent of the number of exchangeable arguments. For example, given the properties above, the first-order basis functions associated with characteristic z_{jk}, the kth characteristic of product j produced by firm f, are

$$z_{jk} \sum_{r \neq j, r \in \mathcal{T}_f} z_{rk} \sum_{r \neq j, r \notin \mathcal{T}_f} z_{rk} \tag{5.8}$$

(Remember that $\mathcal{T}_f$ is the set of products produced by firm f). Note that the dimension of the first-order terms in this basis is $3K$, where K is the dimension of z_j. In contrast, the dimension of the first-order terms in the unrestricted basis is JK.

For each of the separate cost and demand characteristics in our model, we compute the three terms in (5.8) and include these three terms as potential instruments. For example, if one of our characteristics is the size of a car, then the instrument vector for product j includes the size of car j, the sum of size across own-firm products, and the sum of size across rival-firm products. Note the two sums vary across products in our sample because

(i) they exclude different own-products j,

(ii) different firms produce different sets of products, and

(iii) there is variation across time in the products in our panel data set.

Note also that one of our characteristics is a constant term, so that the number of own-firm products and rival-firm products become instruments.

We could also include second-and higher-order basis functions, but in practice we found these extra terms to be nearly collinear with the terms in (5.8). In fact, the entire matrix of these linear terms is also nearly not of full rank. We faced a somewhat arbitrary choice of what terms to leave out, but given the near multicollinearity the choice should not greatly affect our estimates.

In constructing a set of instruments to interact with the demand error, ξ_j, we began with the three terms in (5.8) for each of the five demand variables described in the data section below, as it seemed reasonable to ensure that x_j entered the demand side moment conditions. The two variables that in our specification enter cost but not demand (miles per gallon and a trend) could be added to this list, but we found them to be so nearly collinear as to cause numerical problems in inversion and therefore we left them out, giving 15 demand-side instruments. To construct a list of variables to interact with ω, we began with the three terms of (5.8) for each of the six elements of w_j, giving at least eighteen cost side instruments. We were able to add the excluded demand variable, miles per dollar, to this list without causing a problem with near collinearity. Therefore, there are nineteen cost side instruments, giving a total of $34(= 15 + 19)$ sample moment restrictions.

5.2. Other details

The method outlined by Newey (1990) would suggest projecting the derivatives in (5.7) onto the basis functions in (5.8). Instead, we enter the basis functions directly into the instrument vector. To see why, let $f_j(z) \in R^R$ provide the values of the basis functions in (5.8) for the jth observation, let $\otimes$ be the Kronecker product operator, and let I_2 be an identity matrix of order two. It is helpful to consider the special case in which $T(z) = T$ and the conditional expectation of the derivative matrix, $D_j(z)$, is a linear function of a finite dimensional basis. That is, $D_j(z)$ exactly equals $(f_j'(z) \otimes I_2) B$ for some matrix B. In this case algebraic manipulation shows that the estimator found by first projecting the derivatives in (5.7) onto $(f_j'(z) \otimes I_2)$, and then using the fitted values from this projection as the estimate of $D_j(z)$, has the same limiting distribution as the generalized method of moments (or GMM) estimator (Hansen (1982)) that uses $\{[\xi(\theta), \omega(\theta)]' \otimes f_j(z)\}$ as moments and a consistent estimate of $E(\{[\xi(\theta), \omega(\theta)]' \otimes f_j(z)\}\{[\xi(\theta), \omega(\theta)]' \otimes f_j(z)\}')$ as its weighting matrix. Since the method of moments estimator is easier to compute, we use it in the actual estimation subroutine.[18]

Finally, note that the data we actually use are not a single cross-section, but a panel data set that follows car models over all years they are marketed. It is likely that the demand and cost disturbances of a given model are more similar across years than are the disturbances of different models (so model–year combinations are not exchangeable). Though correlation in the disturbances of a given model marketed in different years does not alter the consistency or asymptotic normality of the parameter estimates from our algorithm, it does affect their variance-covariance matrix. As a result, we use estimators that treat the sum of the moment restrictions of a given model over time as a single observation from an exchangeable population of models. That is, replacing product index j by indices for model m and year t, we define the sample moment condition associated with a single model as

$$g_m(\theta) \equiv \sum_t [f_{mt}(z)' \otimes I_2] \begin{bmatrix} \xi_{mt}(\theta) \\ w_{mt}(\theta) \end{bmatrix}$$

and then obtain our GMM estimator by minimizing our quadratic form in the average of these moment conditions across models. Although this is probably not the most efficient method for dealing with correlation across years for a given model, it does produce standard errors that allow for arbitrary correlation across years for a given model and arbitrary heteroskedasticity across models.

6. Computation

The method of moments estimation algorithm outlined in the last section requires computation of the moments, $G_{\mathcal{I}}(\theta, s^n, P_{ns})$, for different values of θ. Most of this section is devoted to providing an algorithm that computes the $G_{\mathcal{I}}(\theta, s^n, P_{ns})$. The reader who is not interested in computational details can go directly to the empirical results in section 7.

We focus throughout on two special cases. The first is the pure logit model, while the second adds interactions between consumer and product characteristics as in (2.7). The advantages of carrying along the logit model, despite its unreasonable substitution patterns, stem from its computational simplicity. This makes it easy to use the logit model to illustrate both the logic of the overall estimation procedure and the likely importance of unobserved product characteristics.

There are four steps to each evaluation of $G_{\mathcal{I}}(\theta, s^n, P_{ns})$ in both models. For each θ:

    (i) estimate (via simulation) the market shares implied by the model;
    (ii) solve for the vector of demand unobservables [i.e. $\xi(\theta, s^n, P_{ns})$] implied by the simulated and observed market shares;
    (iii) calculate the cost-side unobservable, $\omega(\theta, s^n, P_{ns})$, from the difference between price and the markups computed from the shares; and finally
    (iv) calculate the optimal instruments and interact them with the computed cost- and demand-side unobservables (as in (5.3)) to produce $G_{\mathcal{I}}(\theta, s^n, P_{ns})$.

Both models are nested to the utility specification,

$$u_{ij} = \delta(x_j, p_j, \xi_j, \theta_1) + \mu(x_j, p_j, \nu_i, \theta_2) + \epsilon_{ij} \tag{6.1}$$

where the ϵ_{ij} are draws from independent extreme value distributions (independent over both i and j). Here $\delta_j = \delta(x_j, p_j, \xi_j; \theta_1)$ is a product-specific component that does not vary with consumer characteristics, while $\mu_{ij} = \mu(x_j, p_j, \nu_i; \theta_2)$ contains the interactions between product specific and consumer characteristics. We begin with the logit model.

6.1. The logit model

Our first model will assume no interaction effects: i.e. $\mu_{ij} = 0$. Given that we are assuming that ϵ_{ij} has the Weibull (or type I extreme value) distribution function, $\exp[-\exp(-\epsilon)]$, the assumption that $\mu_{ij} \equiv 0$ gives us the traditional logit model for market shares. In addition we assume that the mean utility level is linear in product characteristics, or

$$\delta_j = x_j \beta - \alpha p_j + \xi_j \tag{6.2}$$

so that $u_{ij} = x_j \beta - \alpha p_j + \xi_j + \epsilon_{ij}$. Since $\mu_{io} = \epsilon_{io}$ (that is, we normalize δ_0 to zero), the market-share functions are given by

$$s_j(p, x, \xi, \theta, P_0) = \frac{e^{\delta_j}}{\left(1 + \sum_{j=1}^{\mathcal{J}} e^{\delta_j}\right)} \tag{6.3}$$

for $j = 0, 1, \ldots, \mathcal{J}$ (McFadden (1973)).
   Also, since (6.3) implies that

$$\delta_j = \ln(s_j) - \ln(s_0) \tag{6.4}$$

our estimate of δ_j for the logit model is $\ln(s_j^n) - \ln(s_0^n)$, and, consequently, our estimate of the demand-side unobservable is

$$\xi(s^n, p, x, \theta, P_0) = \ln(s_j^n) - \ln(s_0^n) - x_j \beta + \alpha p_j \tag{6.5}$$

That is, there are analytic formulae for both the market share and the inverse functions for the logit model (see (i) and (ii) above).
   The demand-side parameters can be estimated by interacting the demand-side unobservables from (6.5) with instruments and applying a method of moments procedure to the resulting moment conditions. For joint estimation of the demand and pricing equations we also need to compute the markups (see (iii) above) from the logit demand system and then use them to compute the cost-side unobservables (as in (3.6)).

6.2. A model with interactions

We now reintroduce a nontrivial interaction term $\mu = \mu(x_j, p_j, \nu_i, \theta_2)$. For the reasons noted, we focus on the "Cobb-Douglas" specification in (2.7).[19]
   For this model, it is useful to obtain the market share function in two stages. First, condition on the ν and integrate out over the extreme value deviates to obtain the conditional (on ν) market shares as

$$f_j(\nu_i, \delta, p, x, \theta) = \frac{e^{\delta_j + \mu(x_j, p_j, \nu_i, \theta_2)}}{1 + \sum_{j=1}^{\mathcal{J}} e^{\delta_j + \mu(x_j, p_j, \nu_i, \theta_2)}} \tag{6.6}$$

Second, integrate out over the distribution of ν to obtain the market shares conditional only on product characteristics as

$$s_j(p, x, \xi, \theta, P_0) = \int f_j(\nu_i, \delta(x, p, \xi), p, x, \theta) P_0(d\nu) \qquad (6.7)$$

Note that (6.6) has a closed form, while (6.7) does not. Since we cannot compute (6.7) exactly we will substitute a simulation estimator of its value into the estimation algorithm. Integrating out the ϵ analytically in the first stage allows us to limit the variance in the estimator of $s_j(p, x, \xi, \theta, P_0)$ to the variance induced by the ν. It also produces simulated market shares that are: positive, sum to one, and are smooth functions of their argument. We come back to the problem of efficiently simulating (6.7) in the next subsection; for now we simply assume we have a good simulation estimator and label the vector of simulated shares $s(p, x, \delta, P_{ns}; \theta)$.

Next we have to combine our estimates of the market share function with the observed market shares to solve for δ as a function of θ (see (ii) above). Once we add the interaction term we cannot solve for δ analytically, so we will have to solve for it numerically each time we evaluate the objective function at a different θ. Recall that δ solves the nonlinear system $s^n = s(p, x, \delta, P_{ns}, \theta)$, or equivalently

$$\delta = \delta + \ln(s^n) - \ln[s(p, x, \delta, P_{ns}; \theta)]$$

In Appendix I, we show that for any triple (s, θ, P), such that s is in the interior of the $\mathcal{J} + 1$ dimensional unit simplex, $\theta \in \Theta \subset R^k$, and P is a proper distribution for ν, the operator $T(s, \theta, P) : R^{\mathcal{J}} \to R^{\mathcal{J}}$ defined pointwise by

$$T(s, \theta, P)[\delta_j] = \delta_j + \ln(s_j) - \ln[s_j(p, x, \delta, P; \theta)] \qquad (6.8)$$

is a contraction mapping with modulus less than one. This implies that we can solve for δ recursively. That is, we begin by evaluating the right-hand side of (6.8) at some initial guess for δ, obtain a new δ' as the output of this calculation, substitute δ' back into the right-hand side of (6.8), and repeat this process until convergence.

Given $\delta_j(\theta, s, P)$, it is easy to solve for the demand-side unobservable as $\xi_j(\theta, s, P) = \delta_j(\theta, s, P) - x_j\beta$. Next we calculate the cost-side unobservable. To do so, we need to solve for the markup, which in turn requires the derivatives of the market share function with respect to price. Equation (6.7) implies that those derivatives are

$$\partial s_j(p, x, \xi, \theta, P_0)/\partial p_j = \int f_j(\nu, \delta, x, p, \theta)(1 - f_j(\nu, \delta, x, p, \theta))[\partial \mu_{ij}/\partial p_j] P_0(d\nu) \qquad (6.9a)$$

$$\partial s_j(p, x, \xi, \theta, P_0)/\partial p_q = \int -f_j(\nu, \xi, x, p, \theta) f_q(\nu, \delta, x, p, \theta)[\partial \mu_{ij}/\partial p_q] P_0(d\nu) \qquad (6.9b)$$

6.3. *Simulators for market shares*

The integral in (6.7) becomes difficult to calculate as the dimension of the consumer characteristic grows much beyond two or three. As a result we form a simulation estimator of that integral and use it in the estimation algorithm. One simple simulation estimator would replace the population density, $P_0(d\nu)$ in (6.7), with the empirical distribution obtained from a set of ns pseudo-random draws from P_0, say, $(\nu_1, \cdots, \nu_{ns})$ and calculate

$$s_j(p, x, \xi, \theta, P_{ns}) \equiv \frac{1}{ns} \sum_{i=1}^{ns} f_j(\nu_i, \delta, p, x, \theta) \tag{6.10}$$

The derivatives of market shares have similar, simple analytic forms. Although this simulation estimator does have a smaller variance than the standard frequency simulator, we looked for a simulator with yet smaller variance.

The importance sampling literature notes that we can often reduce the sampling variance of a simulation estimator of an integral by transforming both the integrand and the density we are drawing from in a way that reduces the variance of a simulation draw but leaves its expectation unchanged (see Rubinstein (1981), and the literature cited there). To see this take any function $h(\cdot, \theta)$ that is strictly positive on the support of P_0, and note that the integral in (6.7) can be rewritten as

$$s_j(\theta, P_0) = \int \left[\frac{f_j(\nu, \theta)}{h(\nu, \theta)} p_0(\nu) h(\nu, \theta) \right] d\nu \equiv \int f_{hj}(\nu, \theta) P_{hj}(d\nu, \theta) \equiv s_j(\theta, P_{hj}) \tag{6.11}$$

where

$$P_{hj}(d\nu, \theta) \equiv h(\nu, \theta) d\nu \text{ and}$$
$$f_{hj}(\nu, \theta) \equiv \left[f_j(\nu, \theta) p_0(\nu) \right] / h(\nu, \theta)$$

and we have assumed, for simplicity, that P_0 has a density with respect to Lebesgue measure (denoted by p_0).

Let $s_j(\theta, P_{hj,ns})$ be the $h(\cdot)$-based unbiased estimator of $s_j(\theta, P_0)$ formed from a simulated analogue to (6.11). Since there are many feasible $h(\cdot)$ the literature has focused on finding an $s_j(\theta, P_{hj,ns})$ with minimum variance. The solution is to set

$$P_{hj}^*(d\nu, \theta) = \left[f_j(\nu, \theta) p_0(\nu) d\nu \right] / s_j(\theta, P_0) \tag{6.12}$$

as, in this case, $s_j(\theta, P_{hj,ns})$ equals $s_j(\theta, P_0)$ exactly (no matter ns). Intuitively, $P_{hj}^*(d\nu, \theta)$ places proportionately higher weight (relative to P_0) on draws of ν that result in larger values of the integrand. That is, we over sample consumers whose characteristics would lead them to buy product j.

Unfortunately, the optimal importance sampling simulator cannot be used directly. The most obvious problem with it is that to use it we need to know the integral itself, i.e.,

$s_j(\theta, P_0)$. Also, it depends on θ, while the limit properties of simulation estimators (and indeed the performance of the search algorithms used to find them) require the use of simulation draws that do not change as the minimization algorithm varies θ (see Pakes and Pollard (1989)). Finally, the contraction property that allows us to solve for the unobservables as a function of θ requires the vector of simulated shares to sum to one. However, the optimal importance sampling estimator changes with the share we are trying to simulate. If we use draws that change across shares in this way, it is difficult to guarantee that the shares sum to one.

Though these problems make direct use of the simulator in (6.12) impossible, that formula does suggest how to build an importance sampling simulator with low variance. First, note that though we do not know $P_{hj}^*(d\nu, \theta)$, we can obtain a consistent estimator of it, at least about $\theta = \theta_0$, by taking an initial consistent estimate of θ_0, say θ', calculating a good estimate of the share at θ', say $s_j(\theta', P_{nsi})$, and then drawing from $[f_j(\nu, \theta')p_0(\nu)d\nu]/s_j(\theta', P_{nsi})$. Note that the estimate $s_j(\theta', P_{nsi})$ is calculated only once, so nsi (the number of simulation draws for the initial step) can be quite large without imposing too much of a computational burden.

To implement this suggestion we need a way of drawing from $[f_j(\nu, \theta')p_0(\nu)d\nu]/s_j(\theta', P_{nsi})$. A simple *acceptance/rejection* procedure which accomplishes this is to draw ν from P_0 and "accept" it with probability $f_j(\nu, \theta')$. It is easy to use Bayes Rule to show that the accepted draws have the required density.

Lastly, to ensure that the vector of simulated market shares sums to one, we used the same simulation draws to calculate each market share. Thus, we had to base the importance sampling estimators for the shares of all choices on the market share for a particular choice. We focus on the share of households who purchase automobiles, that is, on $\bar{s}(\theta) = [1 - s_o(\theta)] = \sum_{j=1}^{J} s_j$.

Thus we proceed as follows. We obtain an initial estimator of θ_o, say θ', using the simple smooth simulator in (6.10). Next we draw ν from P_0 and accept it with probability $\bar{f}(\nu, \theta') = \sum_{j=1}^{J} f_j(\nu, \theta')$. The vector of simulated market shares are then calculated as

$$s_j[\theta, P_h^*(\theta')_{ns}] = \sum_{i=1}^{ns} \frac{\bar{s}(\theta', P_0)}{\bar{f}(\nu_i, \theta')} f_j(\nu_i, \theta) \tag{6.13}$$

where the sum is over accepted ν draws. This oversamples (relative to P_0) the νs that are more likely to lead to (some) auto being purchased and then weights the purchase probabilities, f_j, by $s(\theta', P_0)/\bar{f}(\nu_i, \theta')$, the inverse of the sampling weights.

6.4. The empirical distribution of income and the final form of the simulator

Recall that consumer preferences in our interactive "Cobb-Douglas" model of (2.7) are determined by the marginal utility of characteristics [the vectors $\nu_i' = (\nu_{i0}, \ldots, \nu_{ik})$] and income (y_i). We assume that the ν_i are random draws from a normal distribution with mean vector zero and an identity covariance matrix independent of the level of consumer's income (y_i). The income distribution is assumed to be lognormal and we estimate its parameters from the March Current Population Survey (CPS) for each year of our panel (we denote the estimated mean by m_t and the estimated standard deviation by $\hat{\sigma}_y$). This allows us to use the exogenously available information on the income distribution to increase the efficiency of our estimation procedure.[20]

Using this procedure our utility model is written as

$$u_{itj} = \alpha \ln\left(e^{m_t + \hat{\sigma}_y \nu_{iy}} - p_{jt}\right) + x_{jt}\bar{\beta} + \xi_{jt} + \sum_k \sigma_k x_{jkt}\nu_{ik} + \epsilon_{ijt} \tag{6.14a}$$

$$u_{i0t} = \alpha \ln(e^{m_t + \hat{\sigma}_y \nu_{iy}}) + \xi_{0t} + \sigma_0 \nu_{i0} + \epsilon_{i0t} \tag{6.14b}$$

where the vectors $(\nu_{iy}, \nu_{i0}, \ldots, \nu_{ik})$ are random draws from a multivariate normal distribution with mean 0 and an identity covariance matrix. Note that we held the vector of characteristics $(\nu_{iy}, \nu_{i0}, \ldots, \nu_{ik})$ fixed over the time period of the panel.

6.5. Minimization

Finally, we need a minimization routine that searches to find the value of θ that minimizes the objective function in (5.5). The minimization routine can be simplified by noting that the first-order conditions for a minimum to (5.5) for our specifications are linear in β and γ for any given (α, σ). As a result β and γ can be "concentrated out" of those conditions, allowing us to confine the nonlinear search to a search over (α, σ) couples. This search was performed using the Nelder-Mead (1965) nonderivative "simplex" search routine.

7. Data and Results

7.1. The data

We use data on product characteristics obtained from annual issues of the *Automotive News Market Data Book*.[21] Product characteristics for which we have data include the number of cylinders, number of doors, weight, engine displacement, horsepower, length, width, wheelbase, EPA miles per gallon rating (MPG), and dummy variables for whether the car has front wheel drive, automatic transmission, power steering, and air conditioning as standard equipment.

The price variable is the list retail price (in $1000s) for the base model. This is clearly not ideal; we would prefer transaction prices, but these are not easy to find. All prices are in 1983 dollars. (We used the Consumer Price Index to deflate.) The sales variable corresponds to U.S. sales (in 1000s) by name plate.[22] The product characteristics correspond to the characteristics of the base model for the given name plate.

The data set includes this information on (essentially) all models marketed during the 20-year period beginning in 1971 and ending in 1990 (the only models excluded are "exotic" models with extremely small market shares, such as the Ferrari and the Rolls Royce). Since models both appear and exit over this period, this gives us an unbalanced panel. Treating a model/year as an observation, the total sample size is 2217. Throughout we shall assume that two observations in adjacent years represent the same model if (a) they have the same name; and (b) their horsepower, width, length, or wheelbase do not change by more than ten percent. With these definitions the 2217 model/years represent 997 distinct models (as noted in section 5, different models are assumed to have unobservables whose conditional distributions are independent of one another, but the unobservables for different years of the same model are allowed to be freely correlated).

Aside from these product characteristics, we obtain additional data from a variety of sources. Because the cost of driving may matter to consumers (as opposed to just the MPG rating), we gathered data on the price of gasoline (the real price of unleaded gasoline as reported by the U.S. Department of Commerce in *Business Statistics*, 1961–1988). One of our product characteristics is then miles per dollar (MP$), calculated as MPG divided by price per gallon. Also, our measure of market size (M) was the number of households in the U.S. and this was taken for each year from the *Statistical Abstract of the U.S.*, while, as noted in the computation section, the parameters of the distribution of household income were estimated from the annual March Current Population Surveys. We also obtained *Consumer Reports* reliability ratings. This variable is a relative index that ranges from 1 (poor reliability) to 5 (highest reliability).[23]

The multi-product pricing problem requires us to distinguish which firms produce which models. We assume that different branches of the same parent company comprise a single firm. For example, Buick, Oldsmobile, Cadillac, Chevrolet, and Pontiac are all part of one firm, General Motors. This follows Bresnahan (1981) and Feenstra and Levinsohn (1995). For some results, we also assign a country of origin to each model, which is simply the country associated with the producing firm.[24]

Tables 1 and 2 provide some summary descriptive statistics of variables that are used in the specifications we discuss below. These variables include quantity (in units of 1000), price (in $1000 units), dummies for where the firm that produced the car is headquartered, the ratio of horsepower to weight (in HP per 10 lbs.), a dummy for whether air conditioning is standard (1 if standard, 0 otherwise), the number of ten-mile increments one could drive for $1 worth of gasoline (*MP$*), tens of miles per gallon (*MPG*), and size (measured as length times width).

Table 1 gives sales-weighted means. Several interesting trends are evident. The number of products available generally rises from a low of 72 in 1974 to its high of 150 in 1988. Sales per model, on the other hand trend downward (though here there is some movement about the trend). In real terms, the sales-weighted average list price of autos has risen almost 50 percent during the 1980s after having remained about constant during the 1970s. On the other hand, the characteristics of the cars marketed are also changing (so the cost of a car with a given vector of characteristics need not be increasing). The ratio of horsepower to weight fell in the early 1970s and has since trended upward. Most of the changes in this ratio are attributable to changes in weight as horsepower has remained remarkably constant. It appears that prior to the first oil price shock, cars were becoming heavier, while after the mid-1970s cars became lighter. Along with the change in the ratio of horsepower to weight, cars have also become more fuel cost-efficient. In 1971, the average new car drove 18.50 miles on a (1983) dollar of gasoline, while by 1990 that figure was 28.52 miles. Also, while no cars had air conditioning as standard equipment at the start of the sample, 30.8 percent had it by the end. This is indicative of a general trend

Table 1 Descriptive statistics

Year	No. of Models	Quantity	Price	Domestic	Japan	European	HP/Wt	Size	Air	MPG	MPS
1971	92	86.892	7.868	0.866	0.057	0.077	0.490	1.496	0.000	1.662	1.850
1972	89	91.763	7.979	0.892	0.042	0.066	0.391	1.510	0.014	1.619	1.875
1973	86	92.785	7.535	0.932	0.040	0.028	0.364	1.529	0.022	1.589	1.819
1974	72	105.119	7.506	0.887	0.050	0.064	0.347	1.510	0.026	1.568	1.453
1975	93	84.775	7.821	0.853	0.083	0.064	0.337	1.479	0.054	1.584	1.503
1976	99	93.382	7.787	0.876	0.081	0.043	0.338	1.508	0.059	1.759	1.696
1977	95	97.727	7.651	0.837	0.112	0.051	0.340	1.467	0.032	1.947	1.835
1978	95	99.444	7.645	0.855	0.107	0.039	0.346	1.405	0.034	1.982	1.929
1979	102	82.742	7.599	0.803	0.158	0.038	0.348	1.343	0.047	2.061	1.657
1980	103	71.567	7.718	0.773	0.191	0.036	0.350	1.296	0.078	2.215	1.466
1981	116	62.030	8.349	0.741	0.213	0.046	0.349	1.286	0.094	2.363	1.559
1982	110	61.893	8.831	0.714	0.235	0.051	0.347	1.277	0.134	2.440	1.817
1983	115	67.878	8.821	0.734	0.215	0.051	0.351	1.276	0.126	2.601	2.087
1984	113	85.933	8.870	0.783	0.179	0.038	0.361	1.293	0.129	2.469	2.117
1985	136	78.143	8.938	0.761	0.191	0.048	0.372	1.265	0.140	2.261	2.024
1986	130	83.756	9.382	0.733	0.216	0.050	0.379	1.249	0.176	2.416	2.856
1987	143	67.667	9.965	0.702	0.245	0.052	0.395	1.246	0.229	2.327	2.789
1988	150	67.078	10.069	0.717	0.237	0.045	0.396	1.251	0.237	2.334	2.919
1989	147	62.914	10.321	0.690	0.261	0.049	0.406	1.259	0.289	2.310	2.806
1990	131	66.377	10.337	0.682	0.276	0.043	0.419	1.270	0.308	2.270	2.852
All	2217	78.804	8.604	0.790	0.161	0.049	0.372	1.357	0.116	2.099	2.086

Note: The entry in each cell of the last nine columns is the sales weighted mean.

Table 2 The range of continuous demand characteristics (and associated models)

	Percentile				
Variable	0	25	50	75	100
Price	90 Yugo	79 Mercury Capri	87 Buick Skylark	71 Ford T–Bird	89 Porsche 911 Cabriolet
	3.393	6.711	8.728	13.074	68.597
Sales	73 Toyota 1600 CR	72 Porsche Rdstr	77 Plym. Arrow	82 Buick LeSabre	71 Chevy Impala
	0.049	15.479	47.345	109.002	577.313
HP/Wt.	85 Plym. Gran Fury	85 Suburu DH	86 Plym. Caravelle	89 Toyota Camry	89 Porsche 911 Turbo
	0.170	0.337	0.375	0.428	0.948
Size	73 Honda Civic	77 Renault GTL	89 Hyundai Sonata	81 Pontiac F–Bird	73 Imperial
	0.756	1.131	1.270	1.453	1.888
MP$	74 Cad. Eldorado	78 Buick Skyhawk	82 Mazda 626	84 Pontiac 2000	89 Geo Metro
	8.46	15.57	20.10	24.86	64.37
MPG	74 Cad. Eldorado	79 BMW 528i	81 Dodge Challenger	75 Suburu DL	89 Geo Metro
	9	17	20	25	53

Note: The top entry for each cell gives the model name and the number directly below it gives the value of the variable for this model.

toward more extensive standard equipment. The market share of domestic cars has fallen from a 1973 high of 93.2 percent to a 1990 low of 68.2 percent. European market share has been fairly constant since the demise of the popular VW Beetle in the mid-1970s hovering around 4 to 5 percent. The Japanese market share has risen from a low of 4.0 percent in 1973 to a high of 27.6 percent in 1990. An automobile's size, given by its length times width trends generally downward with this measure falling about 17 percent over the sample.

Table 2 associates some names with the numbers. This table provides an indication of the range of the continuous product attributes by presenting the quartiles of their distribution. The least expensive car in the sample is the 1990 Yugo at $3393 (1983 dollars) while the top-of-the-line Porsche 911 Turbo Cabriolet costs $68,597. The 1989 Geo Metro has the highest MPG and MP$ while the 1974 Cadillac Eldorado has the lowest. The ratio of horsepower to weight varies tremendously from 0.170 for the (questionably named) 1985 Plymouth Gran Fury to 0.948 for the Porsche 911 Turbo. The smallest car in the sample was the 1973 Honda Civic.

7.2. Some results

We will report three basic sets of results together with some auxiliary calculations. These are a simple logit specification, an instrumental variables logit specification, and the Cobb-Douglas specification in (6.14) above. For simplicity, we will refer to the first as logit, the second as IV logit, and the third as BLP.

The logit model, discussed first, provides an easy to compute reference point. One advantage of presenting logit results is that we can explore the effects of controlling for the endogeneity of prices in a very simple framework. The IV logit maintains the restrictive functional form of the logit (and hence must generate the restrictive substitution patterns that this form implies), but allows for unobserved product attributes that are correlated with price, and therefore corrects for the simultaneity problem that this correlation induces. The BLP results allow both for unobserved product characteristics and a more flexible set of substitution patterns. Results from each specification will be discussed in turn.

7.3. The logit and the IV logit

The first set of results are based on the simplest logit specification for the utility function. They are obtained from an ordinary least squares regression of $\ln(s_j) - \ln(s_0)$ on product characteristics and price (see (5.5)).

The choice of which attributes to include in the utility function is, of course, ad hoc. For the BLP specification, computational constraints dictate a parsimonious list. Since we wish to compare results across different specifications, we adopt a short list of included attributes in the logit specifications also. Included characteristics are the ratio of horsepower to weight (*HPWT*), a dummy for whether air conditioning is standard, miles per dollar (*MP$*), size, and a constant. Horsepower over weight and *MP$* are obvious measures of power and fuel efficiency, while air conditioning proxies for a measure of luxury. Size is intended as a measure of both itself and safety. Other measures of size such as interior room are not available for much of the sample period while government crash test results are only available for a small subsample of the data. Though there are surely solid arguments for including excluded attributes, their force is somewhat diminished by our explicit treatment of product attributes unobserved by the econometrician but known to the market participants. Still, we investigate how robust results are to the choice of included attributes in sensitivity analyses that are presented below.

In the first column of Table 3, we report the results of OLS applied to the logit utility specification. Most coefficients are of the expected sign, although the (imprecisely estimated) negative coefficients on air conditioning and size are anomalies, as one would expect these attributes to yield positive marginal utility. On the other hand these estimates have a distinctly implausible set of implications on own price elasticities. The estimated coefficient on price in Table 3 implies that 1494 of the 2217 models have inelastic demands. This is inconsistent with profit maximizing price choices. Moreover this is not simply a problem generated by an imprecise estimate of the price coefficient. Adding and subtracting two times the estimate of the standard deviation of the price coefficient to its value and recalculating the price elasticities still leaves 1429 and 1617 inelastic demands respectively.

In the second column of Table 3, we re-estimate the logit utility specification, this time allowing for unobservable product attributes that are known to the market participants (and hence can be used to set prices), but not to the econometrician. To account for the possible correlation between the price variable and the unobserved characteristics, we

Table 3   Results with logit demand and marginal cost pricing (2217 observations)

Variable	OLS logit demand	IV logit demand	OLS ln (price) on w
Constant	−10.068	−9.273	1.882
	(0.253)	(0.493)	(0.119)
HP/Weight*	−0.121	1.965	0.520
	(0.277)	(0.909)	(0.035)
Air	−0.035	1.289	0.680
	(0.073)	(0.248)	(0.019)
MP$	0.263	0.052	–
	(0.043)	(0.086)	–
MPG*	–	–	−0.471
			(0.049)
Size*	2.341	2.355	0.125
	(0.125)	(0.247)	(0.063)
Trend	–	–	0.013
			(0.002)
Price	−0.089	−0.216	–
	(0.004)	(0.123)	
No. inelastic demands	1494	22	n.a.
(+/ − 2s.e.)	(1429–1617)	(7–101)	
R^2	0.387	n.a.	0.656

Notes: The standard errors are reported in parentheses.

* The continuous product characteristics – hp/weight, size, and fuel efficiency (MP$ or MPG) – enter the demand equations in levels, but enter the column 3 price regression in natural logs.

use an instrumental variable estimation technique, using the instruments discussed at the end of section 5.1.

The use of instruments generates substantial changes in several of the parameter estimates. All characteristics now enter utility positively and all but $MP\$$ are statistically significant. Moreover, just as the simultaneity story predicts, the coefficient on price increases in absolute value (indeed it more than doubles). Our interpretation of this finding is familiar: products with higher unmeasured quality components sell at higher prices. Note that now only 22 products have inelastic demands – a significant improvement from the OLS results. Seven to 101 demands are estimated to be inelastic when we evaluate elasticities at plus and minus two standard deviations of the parameter estimate.

These results seem to indicate that correcting for the endogeneity of prices matters. One can also see the importance of unobservable characteristics by examining the fit of the logit demand equation. The simple logit specification gives an R^2 of 0.387. This implies that 61 percent of the variance in mean utility levels is due to the unobserved characteristics.

As noted in section 2, the separability, in product and consumer characteristics, of the logit functional form applied to aggregate data implies that neither the IV nor the simple logit estimates can possibly generate plausible cross price elasticities, or for that matter differences in markups across products. Thus, the IV logit estimates reported in Table 3 imply that all models have about the same mark-up (ranging from \$4630 for the BMW to \$4805 for the Chevy Cavalier). Markups are related to the model's market share (which, as noted, are about equal in absolute terms for all products) and how many products are made by the same parent firm. GM produces the most models and therefore its estimated markups are highest, while BMW produces the fewest models and its estimated markups are, quite counter-intuitively, the lowest.[25]

Table 3 also presents results from a very simple model of "supply." For the purposes of Table 3 we assume marginal cost pricing, with the specification for marginal cost found in (3.1). The marginal cost pricing equation is obtained by setting the markup term in our pricing equation (3.6) to zero, and regressing log price on w (the characteristics that shift the cost surface).[26]

The third column of Table 3 presents the results of this simple regression. In Table 3 (and in subsequent cost-side results), included cost shifters (w_j) are the same attributes that appear in utility with three modifications. First, miles per gallon replaces miles per dollar, as the production cost of fuel efficient vehicles presumably does not change with the retail price of gasoline (at least in the short run). Second, we include a trend term to capture technical change and other trending influences (e.g. government regulation) on real marginal cost. Third, we use the log of continuous attributes, not their level, in the cost function. Thus the cost function parameters have the interpretation of elasticities of marginal cost with respect to associated product characteristics.

Note that the cost function adopted here is both simple and restrictive. In particular, it implies a constant elasticity of marginal cost with respect to all attributes and does not permit marginal cost to vary with output. Though our robustness tests provide some results with more flexible cost functions (see Table 9), we hesitate to use a more detailed specification of the cost surface without having more direct information on costs.

As is typical in similarly estimated hedonic pricing regressions, each of the coefficients on characteristics (except MPG) is estimated to be positive and all are significantly different from zero. (We comment on the *MPG* coefficient below). For example, a 10 percent increase in the ratio of horsepower to weight is associated with a 5.2 percent increase in prices (and, in this context, in marginal costs). Also familiar from hedonic results is the fact that the R^2 from this regression is fairly high (at 0.66); simple functions of observable characteristics seem to be much better able to explain differences in the log of prices, than they are able to explain differences in the mean utility levels that rationalize the logit demand structure.

We turn now to results from our full model.

7.4. Results from the full model

The demand system for the full model is derived from the utility function in (5.14). The attributes that enter the utility function (the *x*-vector) for our base case scenario are the same as in Table 3. Now, the marginal utility of each attribute varies across consumers so that we estimate a mean and a variance for each of them.[27] The pricing equation is given in (3.6) and the cost-side variables (the *w*-vector) are the same as in the third column of Table 3.

The results from jointly estimating the demand and pricing equations from our specification are provided in Table 4.[28] As noted, the reported standard errors have been corrected for simulation error and for serial correlation of unobserved characteristics within models across years (but not for any correlation across models). The first and second panels of the table provide the estimates of the means and standard deviations of

Table 4 Estimated parameters of the demand and pricing equations: BLP specification, 2217 observations

Demand-side parameters	Variable	Parameter estimate	Standard error	Parameter estimate	Standard error
Means ($\bar{\beta}$s)	Constant	−7.061	0.941	−7.304	0.746
	HP/Weight	2.883	2.019	2.185	0.896
	Air	1.521	0.891	0.579	0.632
	MP$	−0.122	0.320	−0.049	0.164
	Size	3.460	0.610	2.604	0.285
Std. deviations (σ'_{β}s)	Constant	3.612	1.485	2.009	1.017
	HP/Weight	4.628	1.885	1.586	1.186
	Air	1.818	1.695	1.215	1.149
	MP$	1.050	0.272	0.670	0.168
	Size	2.056	0.585	1.510	0.297
Term on price (α)	$\ln(y - p)$	43.501	6.427	23.710	4.079
Cost-side parameters	Constant	0.952	0.194	0.726	0.285
	$\ln(HP/Weight)$	0.477	0.056	0.313	0.071
	Air	0.619	0.038	0.290	0.052
	$\ln(MPG)$	−0.415	0.055	0.293	0.091
	$\ln(Size)$	−0.046	0.081	1.499	0.139
	Trend	0.019	0.002	0.026	0.004
	$\ln(q)$			−0.387	0.029

the taste distribution of each attribute, respectively. The third panel provides the estimate of the coefficient of ln $(y - p)$, and the last panel provides the estimates of the parameters of the cost functions.

We begin with a discussion of the cost-side parameters. The coefficients on ln $(HP/$ Weight$)$, Air, and the constant are positive and significantly different from zero. The term on trend is also positive and significant. The coefficient on ln(size) is not significantly different from zero. The coefficient on MPG is negative and significant, just as it is in the regression of log price on product characteristics reported in Table 3.

Indeed, recall that our pricing equation is essentially an instrumental variable regression of ln $[p - b(p, x, \xi; \theta)]$ on the cost-side characteristics, where $b(p, x, \xi; \theta)$ is the markup (see (3.5)). Since ln$[p - b(p, x, \xi; \theta)] \cong \ln(p) - b(p, x, \xi; \theta)/p$, if our model is correct, the marginal cost pricing, or "hedonic," regression should, by the traditional omitted variable formula, produce coefficients that are approximately the sum of the effect of the characteristic on marginal cost and the coefficient obtained from the auxiliary regression of the percentage markup on the characteristics. Comparing the cost-side parameters in Table 4 with the hedonic regression in Table 3 we find that the only two coefficients that seem to differ a great deal between tables are the constant term and the coefficient on size. The fall in these two coefficients tells us that there is a positive average percentage markup, and that this markup tends to increase in size.

The coefficients on MPG and size may be a result of our constant returns to scale assumption. Note that, due to data limitations, neither sales nor production enter the cost function. Almost all domestic production is sold in the U.S., hence domestic sales is an excellent proxy for production. The same is not true for foreign production, and we do not have data on model-level production for foreign automobiles. The negative coefficient on MPG may result because the best selling cars are also those that have high MPG. By imposing constant returns to scale, we may force these cars to have a smaller marginal cost than they actually do. Due, to the positive correlation between both MPG and size and sales, conditional on other attributes, the coefficients on MPG and size are driven down. We can attempt to investigate the accuracy of this story by including ln(sales) in the cost function, keeping in mind that for foreign cars this is not necessarily well measured. (Note, though, in Table 1 that about 80 percent of the cars in our sample are domestic). When we include ln(q), so that the cost function is given by

$$\ln(c_j) = w_j \gamma_w + \gamma_q \ln(q_j) + \omega_j$$

and re-estimate with the same instruments, all cost shifters are positive and significantly different from zero. These estimates are presented in the last two columns of Table 4. The coefficient on ln(q) is very significantly negative, giving implied returns to scale that seem implausibly high. Adding higher-order terms in ln(q) reduces this problem, but we hesitate to take this approach too far since the data are inaccurate for about a fifth of our sample.

Our estimate of the variance of the cost-side unobservable, ω, implies that it accounts for about 22 percent of the estimated variance in log marginal cost. Thus, though our estimates do imply that there are some differences in "productivity" across firms, most of the differences in (the log of) marginal costs can be accounted for by a simple linear function of observed characteristics. As one might expect, the correlation between the demand-side error, ξ, and ω is positive implying that products with more unmeasured quality were more costly to produce. On the other hand, that correlation was only 0.17, implying that most of the (substantial) variance in ξ could not be accounted for by a linear function of differences in *marginal* costs of production.

Before discussing the demand-side coefficients in the first three panels of Table 4, we briefly review the structure of purchases in a discrete-choice model. Recall that these are driven by the maximum, and not by the mean, of the utilities associated with the given products. Thus there are, in general, two ways to explain why, say, products with high levels of horsepower to weight (*HPWT*), are popular. One can explain this by either positing a high mean for the distribution of tastes for *HPWT*, or by positing a large variance of that same distribution, for both an increase in the mean and an increase in the variance of tastes will increase the share of consumers who purchase cars with high *HPWT*. However, the two explanations have different implications for substitution patterns, and thus different implications for how market share will change with product attributes and prices. If there were, for example, a zero standard deviation for the distribution of marginal utilities of *HPWT*, we would find that when a high *HPWT* car increases its price, consumers who substitute away from that car have the same marginal utilities for *HPWT* as any other consumer and hence will not tend to substitute disproportionately toward other high *HPWT* cars. If, on the other hand, the standard deviation of tastes for *HPWT* was relatively large, the consumers who substitute away from the high *HPWT* cars will tend to be consumers who placed a relatively high marginal utility on *HPWT* originally, and hence should tend to substitute disproportionately towards other high *HPWT* cars.[29]

We now move on to the estimates of the means, $\bar{\beta}_k$, and the standard deviations, σ_k, of the marginal utility distributions. For expositional simplicity, we will focus on the estimates in the first two columns. The demand-side estimates in the nonconstant returns to scale case imply elasticities and substitution patterns similar to the constant returns case. We find that the means ($\bar{\beta}$s) on *Air* and *Size* are positive and are estimated precisely enough to be significant at traditional significance levels. The estimate of the constant is precise and negative, while the mean utility levels associated with *HPWT* and *MP\$* are insignificantly different from zero. On the other hand, the estimate of the standard deviations of the distribution of marginal utilities for *HPWT* and *MP\$* are substantial and estimated precisely enough to be considered significant at reasonable significance levels. Thus, each of the included attributes is estimated to have either a significantly positive effect on the mean of the distribution of utilities, or a significant positive effect on the standard deviation of that distribution (and in the case of *Size* on both). We turn next to providing some figures on the economic magnitude of these effects.

Table 5 presents estimates of elasticities of demand with respect to the continuous attributes, including prices. Each row in this table corresponds to a model. The top number in each cell is the actual value of that attribute for that model, while the bottom number is the elasticity of demand with respect to the attribute. For example, the Mazda 323 has a *HP / weight* ratio of 0.366 and its elasticity of market share with respect to *HP / weight* is 0.458.

The elasticities with respect to *MP\$* illustrate the importance of considering both the mean and standard deviation of the distribution of tastes for a characteristic. The results here are quite intuitive. The elasticity of demand with respect to *MP\$* declines almost

Table 5   A sample from 1990 of estimated demand elasticities with respect to attributes and price (based on Table 4 (CRTS) estimates)

Model	Value of Attribute/Price Elasticity of demand with respect to:				
	HP/Weight	Air	MP$	Size	Price
Mazda323	0.366	0.000	3.645	1.075	5.049
	0.458	0.000	1.010	1.338	6.358
Sentra	0.391	0.000	3.645	1.092	5.661
	0.440	0.000	0.905	1.194	6.528
Escort	0.401	0.000	4.022	1.116	5.663
	0.449	0.000	1.132	1.176	6.031
Cavalier	0.385	0.000	3.142	1.179	5.797
	0.423	0.000	0.524	1.360	6.433
Accord	0.457	0.000	3.016	1.255	9.292
	0.282	0.000	0.126	0.873	4.798
Taurus	0.304	0.000	2.262	1.334	9.671
	0.180	0.000	−0.139	1.304	4.220
Century	0.387	1.000	2.890	1.312	10.138
	0.326	0.701	0.077	1.123	6.755
Maxima	0.518	1.000	2.513	1.300	13.695
	0.322	0.396	−0.136	0.932	4.845
Legend	0.510	1.000	2.388	1.292	18.944
	0.167	0.237	−0.070	0.596	4.134
TownCar	0.373	1.000	2.136	1.720	21.412
	0.089	0.211	−0.122	0.883	4.320
Seville	0.517	1.000	2.011	1.374	24.353
	0.092	0.116	−0.053	0.416	3.973
LS400	0.665	1.000	2.262	1.410	27.544
	0.073	0.037	−0.007	0.149	3.085
BMW 735i	0.542	1.000	1.885	1.403	37.490
	0.061	0.011	−0.016	0.174	3.515

Notes: The value of the attribute or, in the case of the last column, price, is the top number and the number below it is the elasticity of demand with respect to the attribute (or, in the last column, price.)

monotonically with the car's MP$ rating. While a 10 percent increase in MP$ increases sales of the Mazda 323, Sentra, and Escort by about 10 percent, the demand for the cars with low MP$ are actually falling with an increase in MP$. The decreases, though, are quite close to zero. Hence, we conclude that consumers who purchase the high mileage cars care a great deal about fuel economy while those who purchase cars like the BMW 735i or Lexus LS400 are not concerned with fuel economy. Similarly, the demand elasticities with respect to size are generally declining as cars get larger.

   The elasticity of demand with respect to *HP/Weight*, our proxy for acceleration, is also small (about 0.1) for the largest cars in the sample, the Lincoln, Cadillac, Lexus, and BMW. On the other hand, it appears that consumers who purchase the smallest cars place a greater value on increased acceleration. For the Mazda 323, Sentra, and Escort, a 10 percent increase in *HP / weight* increases demand by about 4.5 percent. The relationship between the elasticities and the value of *HP/weight* is not monotonic though. For midsize cars, the elasticities are varied. The Maxima (a fairly sporty midsize car) has a relatively high elasticity (0.322) while the similarly sized but more sedate Taurus has an elasticity of 0.180.

The term on $\ln(y - p), \alpha$, is of the expected sign and is measured precisely enough to be highly significant. Its magnitude is most easily interpreted by examining the elasticities and markups it, together with the other estimated coefficients, imply. We note first that the estimates imply that demands for *all* 2217 models in our sample are elastic. The last column of Table 5 lists prices and price elasticities of demand for our subsample of 1990 models. We find that the most elastically demanded products are those that are in the most "crowded" market segments – the compact and subcompact models. (The Buick Century is an exception to this pattern.) The Sentra and Mazda 323 face demand elasticities of 6.4 and 6.5 respectively, while the $37,490 BMW and $27,544 (in 1983 dollars) Lexus face demand elasticities of 3.5 and 3.0 respectively.

Table 6 presents a sample of own and cross price semi-elasticities. Each semi-elasticity gives the percentage change in market share of the row car associated with a $1000 increase in the price of the column car. Looking down the first column, for example, we note that a thousand dollar increase in the price of a Mazda 323 increases the market share of a Nissan Sentra by 0.705 percent but has almost no effect on the market share of a Lincoln Town Car, Cadillac Seville, Lexus LS400, or a BMW 735i.

In general, Table 6 shows cross-price elasticities that are large for cars with similar characteristics. Perhaps not surprisingly, the magnitudes of the effects of a $1000 price increase of the higher priced cars are much smaller than they are for the lower priced cars. The general pattern of cross-price semi-elasticities accords well with intuition. For example, the Lexus is the closest substitute (measured by magnitude of cross-price semi-elasticities) to the BMW 735, the Cadillac is the closest substitute to the Lincoln, and the Accord is the closest substitute to the Taurus. Since the demand elasticities will play a crucial role in policy analysis, the sensible elasticities in Table 6 are encouraging.

Next we consider the substitutability of our auto models with the "outside good," that is ds_0/dp_j. To give some idea of the magnitude of this derivative, we express it as a percentage of the absolute value of the own-price derivative:

$$\frac{100 * (ds_0/dp_j)}{|ds_j/dp_j|}$$

For a small increase in the price of product j, this gives the number of consumers who substitute from j to the outside good, as a percentage of the total number of consumers who substitute away from j. The results of this exercise are given in Table 7. There we report results concerning substitution to the outside good for our subsample of 1990 models under both the logit and the BLP specifications. The first column in Table 7 indicates that for every model, about 90 percent of the consumers who substitute away from a model opt instead for the outside good. This figure is just $s_0/(1 - s_j)$. The results under the BLP specification are not nearly as uniform across models. Here, the numbers still seem a bit large to us, which may point to the need for improvements in our treatment

Table 6 A sample from 1990 of estimated own- and cross-price semi-elasticities: based on Table 4 (CRTS) estimates

	Mazda 323	Nissan Sentra	Ford Escort	Chevy Cavalier	Honda Accord	Ford Taurus	Buick Century	Nissan Maxima	Acura Legend	Lincoln Town Car	Cadillac Seville	Lexus LS400	BMW 735i
323	-125.933	1.518	8.954	9.680	2.185	0.852	0.485	0.056	0.009	0.012	0.002	0.002	0.000
Sentra	0.705	-115.319	8.024	8.435	2.473	0.909	0.516	0.093	0.015	0.019	0.003	0.003	0.000
Escort	0.713	1.375	-106.497	7.570	2.298	0.708	0.445	0.082	0.015	0.015	0.003	0.003	0.000
Cavalier	0.754	1.414	7.406	-110.972	2.291	1.083	0.646	0.087	0.015	0.023	0.004	0.003	0.000
Accord	0.120	0.293	1.590	1.621	-51.637	1.532	0.463	0.310	0.095	0.169	0.034	0.030	0.005
Taurus	0.063	0.144	0.653	1.020	2.041	-43.634	0.335	0.245	0.091	0.291	0.045	0.024	0.006
Century	0.099	0.228	1.146	1.700	1.722	0.937	-66.635	0.773	0.152	0.278	0.039	0.029	0.005
Maxima	0.013	0.046	0.236	0.256	1.293	0.768	0.866	-35.378	0.271	0.579	0.116	0.115	0.020
Legend	0.004	0.014	0.083	0.084	0.736	0.532	0.318	0.506	-21.820	0.775	0.183	0.210	0.043
TownCar	0.002	0.006	0.029	0.046	0.475	0.614	0.210	0.389	0.280	-20.175	0.226	0.168	0.048
Seville	0.001	0.005	0.026	0.035	0.425	0.420	0.131	0.351	0.296	1.011	-16.313	0.263	0.068
LS400	0.001	0.003	0.018	0.019	0.302	0.185	0.079	0.280	0.274	0.606	0.212	-11.199	0.086
735i	0.000	0.002	0.009	0.012	0.203	0.176	0.050	0.190	0.223	0.685	0.215	0.336	-9.376

Note: Cell entries i, j, where i indexes row and j column, give the percentage change in market share of i with a \$1000 change in the price of j.

Table 7 Substitution to the outside good

Model	Given a price increase, the percentage who substitute to the outside good (as a percentage of all who substitute away.)	
	Logit	BLP
Mazda 323	90.870	27.123
Nissan Sentra	90.843	26.133
Ford Escort	90.592	27.996
Chevy Cavalier	90.585	26.389
Honda Accord	90.458	21.839
Ford Taurus	90.566	25.214
Buick Century	90.777	25.402
Nissan Maxima	90.790	21.738
Acura Legend	90.838	20.786
Lincoln Town Car	90.739	20.309
Cadillac Seville	90.860	16.734
Lexus LS400	90.851	10.090
BMW 735i	90.883	10.101

of the outside good (see the extensions section below). However, our estimates are much smaller than the corresponding figures for the logit model. Our results also show the expected pattern that consumers of lower priced cars are more likely to stay with the outside good when the price of their most preferred model increases.

Table 8 presents the estimated price-marginal cost markups implied by the estimates of the constant returns to scale case reported in Table 4. In 1990, the average markup is $3,753 and the average ratio of markup to retail price is 0.239.[30] The pattern and magnitudes of the markups reported in Table 8 are quite plausible. The models with the lowest markups are the Mazda ($801), Sentra ($880), and Escort ($1077). At the other extreme, the Lexus and BMW have estimated markups of $9,030 and $10,975 respectively. In general, markups rise almost monotonically with price.

In the third column of Table 8, we list variable profits for each model (since marginal costs are assumed to be constant in output, variable profits are just sales multiplied by price minus marginal cost). Given our estimates, large markups do not necessarily mean large profits, as the sales of some of the high markup cars are quite small. The models that, according to our estimates, are the most profitable (by a factor of two, relative to the other models reported in the table) are the Honda Accord and the Ford Taurus. Both are widely regarded as essential to each firm's financial well-being.

It seems to us that Tables 4 through 8 demonstrate that allowing more flexible utility specifications generates a more realistic picture of equilibrium in the U.S. automobile industry. Conditional on allowing for a more flexible utility specification, there are, however, a number of different variables one might include in the utility and cost functions. We now ask how sensitive our results are to our admittedly ad hoc choice of included variables. Table 9 begins to address this issue.

There are many ways one might summarize the implications of the estimated parameters. We choose to report the estimated price-marginal cost markups that result from

Table 8   A sample from 1990 of estimated price-marginal cost markups and variable profits: based on Table 6 (CRTS) estimates

	Price	Markup over MC $(p - MC)$	Variable profits (in $'000s) $q * (p - MC)$
Mazda 323	$5,049	$801	$18,407
Nissan Sentra	$5,661	$880	$43,554
Ford Escort	$5,663	$1,077	$311,068
Chevy Cavalier	$5,797	$1,302	$384,263
Honda Accord	$9,292	$1,992	$830,842
Ford Taurus	$9,671	$2,577	$807,212
Buick Century	$10,138	$2,420	$271,446
Nissan Maxima	$13,695	$2,881	$288,291
Acura Legend	$18,944	$4,671	$250,695
Lincoln Town Car	$21,412	$5,596	$832,082
Cadillac Seville	$24,353	$7,500	$249,195
Lexus LS400	$27,544	$9,030	$371,123
BMW 735i	$37,490	$10,975	$114,802

Table 9   Results from some alternative specifications: price-marginal cost markups

	Base case (reported in Table 8)	Include $ln(q)$ in cost function	Use AT instead of AIR	Weight and HP instead of HP/Wt	Include interaction terms in cost function	Use 3 region dummies and add Reliability	Add weight and include interactions in cost function
Mazda 323	$801	$1,616	$1,012	$1,073	$828	$1,125	$1,389
Nissan Sentra	$880	$1,769	$1,153	$1,271	$912	$1,308	$1,487
Ford Escort	$1,077	$2,043	$1,326	$1,470	$1,111	$2,094	$1,690
Chevy Cavalier	$1,302	$2,490	$1,729	$1,655	$1,329	$2,593	$2,020
Honda Accord	$1,992	$3,059	$2,629	$2,703	$2,059	$3,839	$2,327
Ford Taurus	$2,577	$3,721	$2,528	$3,344	$2,585	$4,094	$2,898
Buick Century	$2,420	$4,162	$3,161	$2,939	$2,405	$4,030	$3,321
Nissan Maxima	$2,881	$4,674	$4,565	$2,085	$2,911	$6,941	$3,513
Acura Legend	$4,671	$7,105	$6,563	$3,059	$4,661	$8,305	$5,081
Lincoln Town Car	$5,596	$8,029	$6,778	$4,765	$5,508	$7,114	$6,518
Cadillac Seville	$7,500	$10,733	$8,635	$4,863	$7,439	$9,182	$8,015
Lexus LS400	$9,030	$10,510	$8,411	$4,791	$8,585	$10,925	$7,398
BMW 735i	$10,975	$13,646	$9,122	$7,605	$10,713	$12,153	$12,202
No. of demand-side variables significant at 95% level[a]	5 of 5	4 of 5	4 of 5	6 of 6	4 of 5	8 of 8	4 of 6

[a] A demand-side variable is considered significant if *either* its mean or standard deviation (σ_β) is significant. See text for details.

alternative specifications, since these markups embody information from both the cost and demand sides of the model, and they are easily interpretable. The first column of Table 9 replicates the results in Table 8 and is included to make comparisons more convenient. In the second column, we report the markups that result when we include the natural log of output in the cost function. The vector of other cost-shifters, w, is unchanged from the base case. This is the specification reported in the last two columns of Table 4 and, as previously noted, the quantity variable is problematic. Nonetheless, the markups follow the same pattern in the base case. The main difference is that the markups are uniformly higher. This results from the decreasing returns to scale. The markups over average variable cost (not reported) are much lower. Indeed, without higher order-terms in $\ln(q)$ entering the cost function, the markups over average variable cost are implausibly low. Of all the alternate specifications we investigated, this one yielded the highest price-marginal cost markups, and yet even these markups are not extraordinarily high. For this and all the other alternate specifications, we also report the number of demand-side variables whose means or σs are significantly different from zero at standard levels.

In the Table 4 results, the σ associated with air conditioning was not significantly different from zero. We believe the *AIR* variable is proxying for a degree of luxury. It is possible that there really is little disagreement in the population about this attribute, but perhaps it is a poor proxy. In column 3 of Table 9, we report the markups that result from using another proxy – whether automatic transmission is standard equipment. The pattern and magnitudes of the markups are quite similar to the base case results. Markups are slightly higher for the less expensive cars and slightly lower for the high-end cars, but not dramatically so.

In the fourth column of Table 9, we report the results from a specification that replaces the ratio of horsepower to weight with the two variables entered separately and linearly. Of all the alternative specifications investigated, this one gave the largest change in estimated markups. While the patterns of markups is the same, this specification gave implausibly low markups for the more costly cars. This might result if cost were not linear in horsepower and weight, since these cars have large values of each attribute, hence forcing marginal cost to be higher than it perhaps actually is.

In our model, adding additional terms to the cost function is computationally cheap, while adding additional demand-side random coefficients is computationally demanding. In column 5 of Table 9, we include interaction terms in the cost function between all the continuous characteristics. This captures the notion that the cost of a characteristic may depend on the level of another characteristic. The results of this exercise give markups very similar to our base case results. For most models, the markups are within a few percent of one another. We found that most interaction terms were statistically significant at the usual levels and the elasticities of marginal cost with respect to the continuous attributes were virtually identical to those that resulted with no interaction terms in the cost function. Further, the parameters associated with one of the five demand-side variables was no longer significantly different from zero.

In the sixth column of Table 9, we report the markups that result when we replace the constant in the utility function with a set of dummy variables indicating whether the car was built by a firm from the U.S., Japan, or Europe. We also include the Consumer Reports reliability rating. Problems with this variable are noted above, but we include it in this particular specification because we suspect that the region dummies may be highly correlated with reliability. If we did not include a measure of reliability, it would mean that an instrument would be correlated with the unobservables, contrary to the assumptions we need for the consistency of our estimator. In this specification there is a separate mean and variance for the dummy associated with each region. Once again, the markups exhibit the same pattern as in the other specifications. We do find, though, that the markups for a number of the models in the middle of the price range are substantially higher. Since these models are not from just one region, it is not clear what drives this change.

In the final column of Table 9, we report the results when we add *weight* to the list of regressors (instead of sufficing with the ratios of horsepower to weight), and then allow for interactions in all the cost-side variables. Here the linear coefficient of the *weight* variable came in insignificant on the cost side with a significant mean and insignificant standard deviation on the demand side. The pattern and magnitude of markups was quite similar to the base case results.

8. Applications, Problems, and Extensions

8.1. *Applications*

Our model is defined in terms of four primitives and a Nash equilibrium assumption in prices. The primitives are the utility surface that assigns values to different possible combinations of product characteristics as a function of consumer characteristics, a cost function which determines the production cost associated with different combinations of product characteristics, a distribution of consumer characteristics, and a distribution of product characteristics. Conditional on these primitives the model can solve for the distribution of prices, quantities, variable profits, and consumer welfare. There are, therefore, at least two ways one might use the estimated parameters. One is to investigate changes in one of the primitives *assuming* that the others are held fixed, while the other is to determine the extent that changes in the various primitives can account for historical movements in the data. The first corresponds to traditional policy analysis, while the second provides an interpretation of the changes that have occurred in the industry.

It is easy to list policy questions that our estimates might be used to help analyze. These include: trade policy (e.g., the effect of import restrictions), merger policy, environmental policy (e.g., carbon and gas guzzler taxes as well as Auto Emission and Corporate Average Fuel Efficiency Standards) and the construction of price indices. For a start on these issues, see Berry, Levinsohn, and Pakes (1994) and Berry and Pakes (1993) for the first two and Pakes, Berry, and Levinsohn (1993) for the last two. Demand elasticities play a crucial role in each of these issues and hence the methods developed in this paper might provide more realistic analyses than some more traditional models.

On the other hand, all of the models, including our own, are limited in that they provide only a "conditional" analysis of each issue. That is, to do policy analysis we will have to perturb a small number of parameters and compute new equilibria conditional on the other primitives of the model remaining unchanged. In fact in many cases these other "primitives" will change in response to a change in policy or in the environment.

For example, Pakes, Berry, and Levinsohn (1993) used our model's estimates to predict the effect of the 1973 gas price hike on the average MPG of new cars sold in subsequent years. We found that our model predicted 1974 and 1975 average MPG almost exactly. This is because the characteristics of cars, treated as fixed in our predictions, did not change much in the first two years after the gas price hike and our model did well in predicting responses conditional on the characteristics of cars sold. However, by 1976 new small fuel efficient models began to be introduced and our predictions, based on fixed characteristics, became markedly worse and deteriorated further over time. We return to the problem of endogenizing characteristics in the next subsection.

8.2. Extensions

Our methods have been developed on the premise that consumer and producer level data are not always available. This seems an important concession to the realities facing empirical researchers investigating many, but not all, markets. We do note that information on the distribution of many of the relevant consumer characteristics is generally available and we illustrate how to make use of the empirical distribution of this information in the estimation algorithm. (In addition to income, consumer characteristics that might be expected to interact with product attributes and for which distributional information is available include household size, geographic region in which the household resides, and age of head of household.)

There are, however, several industries in which some consumer and/or producer-level micro data are available, and the auto industry is one of them. Though production costs for autos are not publicly available at the product-level, the Longitudinal Research Data (LRD) maintained by the Bureau of the Census do contain plant-level cost data. Since industry publications link automotive models to specific plants, we are exploring the possibility of using this information to improve our estimates. Note that separate information on costs would allow for a more detailed examination of the relationship of prices to marginal costs, and, therefore, for a more detailed analysis of the nature of the appropriate equilibrium in the spot market for current output. The cost information would also enable a more flexible analysis of functional forms for the cost surface, and, perhaps, an analysis of how that surface has changed over time in response to changes in both R&D investments and in government policies. As noted above, there is also consumer survey information on automobile purchases and we are investigating how to integrate survey data with the aggregate data used here.

The other, perhaps more important and certainly more difficult, direction for future work is incorporating a realistic treatment of dynamics. On the producer side there are two aspects of this problem. The first and possibly easier one is obtaining consistent estimates of the parameters of the static profit function while allowing for a correlation between observed and unobserved characteristics. This correlation may result from the fact that both sets of characteristics are, in part, determined by related decision-making processes. The second, and richer, part of the problem is to endogenize the actual choice of the characteristics of the models marketed. Even the more detailed models of dynamic industry equilibrium (see, for example, the theory in Ericson and Pakes (1995) and the computational algorithm in Pakes and McGuire (1994)) still have to be enriched before we can provide a realistic approximation to the multiproduct, multi-characteristic nature of the auto industry.

On the consumer side, a complete model of dynamic decision making would incorporate both the transaction costs of buying and selling a car and uncertainty about the future. In particular, a dynamic model of consumer decision making would highlight the important role played by our outside alternative, which for many consumers is simply an older model car. Treating the outside alternative in a realistic way would require building a demand system for durable goods and incorporating a used car market.

Appendix I: The Contraction Mapping

In this appendix, we will establish the contraction argument used in the computational algorithm. We will show that the function (6.8) has a unique fixed point. Furthermore, we want to establish that (6.8) is a contraction mapping. In fact, our proof will require us to impose an upper bound on the value taken by the function in (6.8), although in practice we never had to impose this bound. (This upper bound appears in the definition of f in the statement of the following theorem.)

THEOREM: *Consider the metric space (R^K, d) with $d(x, y) = \|x - y\|$ (where $\| \cdot \|$ is the sup-norm). Let $f : R^K \to R^K$ have the properties:*

(1)   *$\forall\, x \in R^K$, $f(x)$ is continuously differentiable, with, $\forall j$ and k,*

$$\partial f_j(x)/\partial x_k \geq 0$$

and

$$\sum_{k=1}^{K} \partial f_j(x)/\partial x_k < 1$$

(2)   *$\min_j \inf_x f(x) \equiv x > -\infty$*
(3)   *There is a value, $\bar{x}$, with the property that if for any $j, x_j \geq \bar{x}$, then for some k (not necessarily equal to j), $f_k(x) < x_k$.*

Then, there is a unique fixed point, x_0, to f in R^K. Further, let the set $X = [\underline{x}, \bar{x}]^k$, and define the truncated function, $\hat{f} : X \to X$, as $\hat{f}_j(x) = \min\{f_j(x), \bar{x}\}$. Then, $\hat{f}(\hat{x})$ is a contraction of modulus less than one on X.

PROOF: We will first show the contraction mapping property that $\exists \beta, < 1$ such that $\forall x$ and $x' \epsilon X$, $\|\hat{f}(x) - \hat{f}(x')\| \leq \beta \|x - x'\|$. To see this, choose any x and x' in X and define the scalar $\lambda = \|x - x'\|$. Consider the jth element of $\hat{f}$, $\hat{f}_j(x)$ and WLOG assume $\hat{f}_j(x') - \hat{f}_j(x) \geq 0$. Then, $x + \lambda \geq x'$ implies

$$\hat{f}_j(x') - \hat{f}_j(x) \leq \hat{f}_j(x + \lambda) - \hat{f}_j(x) \leq f_j(x + \lambda) - f_j(x) = \int_0^\lambda \left[\sum_{k=1}^{K} \partial f_i(x + z)/\partial x_k \right] dz \leq \beta \lambda$$

where

$$\beta \equiv \max_j \max_{x \in W} \sum_{k=1}^{K} \partial f_j(x)/\partial x_k$$

and the set W is defined as

$$W = \{y \in R^K : y = (x + z), x \in X, z \in [0, \bar{x} - \underline{x}]\}$$

The second inequality follows from the fact that $\hat{f}_j(x + \lambda) \le f_j(x + \lambda)$, while $\hat{f}_j(x) = f_j(x)$. The scalar β exists, as it is the maximum of a continuous function over a compact set. β is the maximum value of the integrand over the set of $(x + z)$ values that can possibly be reached when $x \in X$ and the scalar z is less than the possible difference between any two points in the set X. The final inequality and the fact that $\beta < 1$ follow from Assumption (1).

We have now established that $\hat{f}$ is a contraction of modulus $\beta < 1$ on X. Therefore, there is a unique fixed point, x_0, to $\hat{f}$ on X and for any x in X, the sequence $\hat{f}^n(x)$ converges to x_0. Assumptions (2)–(3) rule out the existence of fixed points to either f or $\hat{f}$ that are outside the interior of X. Thus, x_0 cannot be on the boundary of X; x_0 is a fixed point of f and there can be no other fixed point to f.   *QED*

We will now show that the function $f(\delta) = \delta + \ln(s) - \ln(s(\delta))$ satisfies the hypotheses of the theorem. The function f is differentiable by the differentiability of the function $s(\delta)$. To check the monotonicity condition of Assumption 1 note that

$$\partial f_j(\delta)/\partial \delta_j = 1 - \frac{1}{s_j} \frac{\partial s_j}{\partial \delta_j}$$

while for $k \ne j$,

$$\partial f_j(\delta)/\partial \delta_k = -\frac{1}{s_j} \frac{\partial s_j}{\partial \delta_k}$$

By differentiating our specific market share function, it is easy to show that both $\partial f_j/\partial \delta_j$ and $\partial f_j/\partial \delta_k$ are positive and that $\Sigma_{k=1}^{J} \partial s_j/\partial \delta_k < s_j$. This in turn establishes that the derivatives of f sum to less than one, establishing all the conditions of Assumption 1.

It is easy to find the lower bound for f (Assumption 2). First note that we can rewrite $s_j(\delta)$ as

$$s_j(\delta) = e^{\delta_j} D_j(\delta)$$

where

$$D_j(\delta) \equiv \int \frac{e^{\mu_i}}{1 + \sum_k e^{\delta_k + \mu_i}} d\Phi(\mu)$$

Plugging this into the definition of f gives

$$f_j(\delta) = \ln(s_j) - \ln(D_j(\delta))$$

Note that D_j is declining in all the δ_k. As all of the δ_k approach $-\infty$, $D_j(\delta)$ goes to $\int e^{\mu_i} d\Phi(\mu)$. Thus a lower bound for f_j is $\underline{\delta}_j \equiv \ln(s_j) - \ln(\int e^{\mu_i} d\Phi(\mu))$. This is the value of δ_j that would explain a market share for good j of s_j if all the other market shares (other than the outside good) were equal to zero.

Unfortunately, $f(\delta)$ is increasing in δ_j without bound. Berry (1994) does, however, show how to establish the existence of a value, $\bar{\delta}$, such that if any element of $\underline{\delta}$ is greater than $\bar{\delta}$, then there is some k such that $s_k(\delta) > s_k$. The vector with each element equal to $\bar{\delta}$ then satisfies the requirements of $\bar{x}$ in Assumption (3), for if $s_k(\delta) > s_k$, then $f_k(\delta) < \delta_k$.

Berry (1994) shows that an appropriate $\bar{\delta}$ is found as follows. For product j, define $\bar{\delta}_j$ as the value of $-\delta_j$ that would explain the market share of the outside good, s_0, when $\delta_0 = 0$ and all the other $\delta_k = -\infty$. Then set $\bar{\delta} > \max_j \bar{\delta}_j$.

Notes

1   For background on demand systems obtained in this manner see McFadden (1981) and the literature cited there as well as the product differentiation literature cited in Shaked and Sutton (1982), Sattinger (1984), Perloff and Salop (1985), Bresnahan (1987), and Anderson, de Palma, and Thisse (1989), among others.

2   For examples see Bresnahan (1987) and Feenstra and Levinsohn (1995).

3   For earlier discussions of the implications of related specifications on aggregate demand patterns see the Appendix to Hausman (1975), McFadden (1981), and Schmalensee (1985). Note also that (2.4) assumes more than additive separability. It also assumes that δ_j is a linear function of product characteristics and that the distributions of the ϵ_{ij} are identical across "j"; but these assumptions are primarily for expositional simplicity. They can be relaxed with only minor modifications to the discussion that follows (see below).

4   We will assume that the distribution of the $[v(i, 1), \ldots, v(i, K)]$ factors into a product of independent densities. This is for expositional convenience; with the addition of some notation we could easily allow for patterns of correlation among them.

5   Note that since market shares depend only on differences in utilities, the actual estimation an algorithm ends up subtracting the $u(i, 0)$ in (2.7b) from the $u(i, j)$, and estimating a model where the outside alternative is "normalized" to zero. Given (2.7b), this implies there is a random coefficient on the constant term in the utility function for the inside goods.

6   There are also a number of restrictive assumptions in (2.7), including both the decomposition of the interaction of unobserved individual and product characteristics into $\xi_j + \epsilon_{ij}$ with the ϵ_{ij} i.i.d over both i and j, and the separability implied by log-linearity. We are exploring some of these restrictions in related work using more disaggregated data.

7   For a history of the econometrics of demand and supply analysis in homogeneous product markets, see Morgan (1990, Ch. 2).

8   One exception is Berry's (1991) study of airline hubbing, which includes an aggregate market-specific demand error that is correlated with prices. However, that paper uses a very restrictive functional form for utility.

9   Similar overfitting phenomena have been a source of concern in the biometrics literature for some time; see, for example, Haseman and Kuper (1979) or Williams (1982). Though they do not worry about simultaneity, their conceptual solution to the overfitting problem is similar to the one we shall use (allowing for unobserved determinants of the cell probabilities).

10 This suggests the possible advantages of combining consumer and market-level data, an approach that we are currently pursuing.

11 We assume that a Nash equilibrium to this pricing game exists, and that the equilibrium prices are in the interior of the firm's strategy sets (the positive orthant). While Caplin and Nalebuff (1991) provide a set of conditions for the existence of equilibrium for related models of single product firms, their theorems do not easily generalize to the multiproduct case. However, we

are able to check numerically whether our final estimates are consistent with the existence of an equilibrium. Note that none of the properties of the estimates require uniqueness of equilibrium, although without uniqueness it is not clear how to use our estimates to examine the effects of policy and environmental changes.

12 Note, however, that we use identification in an informal sense; a formal identification argument requires further regularity conditions.

13 In fact all we require is that the draws on $y_j = (\xi_j, \omega_j, z_j)$ be exchangeable draws from some population. That is, if the joint distribution of $\{y_j\}$ is $f[\mathcal{J}](\cdot)$, then we require that

$$f[\mathcal{J}][y_1, \ldots, y_{\mathcal{J}}] = f[\mathcal{J}][y_{\pi(1)}, \ldots, y_{\pi(\mathcal{J})}]$$

for any permutation $[\pi(1), \ldots, \pi(\mathcal{J})]$ of $[1, \ldots, \mathcal{J}]$. A reason for using this assumption (rather than the more restrictive assumption of independence) is to allow the (at least in part, chosen) characteristics of a product to be related to the characteristics of other products, and to allow for the outcomes of environmental processes that are likely to affect many products. The assumption that we can permute the y vector without changing our model [i.e., $f(\cdot)$] amounts to assuming that the y-vectors include all characteristics that are determinants of the choices made (a strong, but not unfamiliar, assumption in applied work, especially given our allowance for the unobservables, ξ and ω).

14 In reference to the representation in the last note, we note that exchangeability implies the existence of a random variable, say $q(\mathcal{J})$, and distribution functions, say $g[\mathcal{J}](\cdot)$ such that the $\{y_j\}$ are independent conditional on (the "aggregate") random variable $q(\mathcal{J})$ or $f[\mathcal{J}](y_1, \ldots, y_j) = \Pi_j g[\mathcal{J}](y_j|q)$ (see Kingman (1978)). One can place (different sets of) restrictions on this representation that imply (4.1) and (5.1), though this returns us to the discussion in section 4.

15 Actually for increased efficiency we use an importance sampling simulator; see equation (5.3).

16 Berry and Pakes (in process) provide expressions for V_2 and V_3 in terms of the model's primitives. The conditions in their paper include an identification condition, conditions which ensure the existence of limits, a condition on the form of the covariance matrix for a single draw of the simulation process as $\mathcal{J}$ goes to ∞, conditions on the rate at which the derivatives of the market share vector with respect to ξ go to zero as $\mathcal{J}$ goes to ∞, conditions on the rate at which ns and n grow as $\mathcal{J}$ goes to ∞ and smoothness conditions on the map from $\Theta \times R^{\mathcal{J}}$ to $s(\theta, \xi, P_0)$.

17 In an early version of this paper, we proposed alternative ways of approximating $H_j(z)$ and we have found some of these useful in subsequent work; see Berry, Levinsohn, and Pakes (1994).

18 Additionally, if $T(z) \neq T$ we do not know of a proof which ensures that the two-step estimator is more efficient than this GMM estimator.

19 The computational techniques provided here generalize to handle a variety of other cases. For example, at an additional computational cost we can allow for an interaction between unobserved product (ξ_j) and consumer (ν_i) characteristics, and/or do away with the extreme value, or idiosyncratic, error (the ϵ_{ij}). Also it is straightforward to generalize to less restrictive functional forms for utility (at least subject to mild regularity conditions).

20 We could have taken ns draws from the CPS for each year and used these draws directly to simulate the market shares. This places fewer restrictions on the empirical distribution of income, but is inefficient if the true income distribution is in fact lognormal. We found the less restrictive procedure led to quite imprecise simulators (it did a particularly bad job of estimating changes in the upper tail of the income distribution), and, as a result, we kept the lognormal assumption. Also, we did not attempt to estimate a different standard deviation of income in each year because such estimates were imprecise.

21   The data set combines data collected by us with a similar data set graciously made available to us by Ernie Berndt of MIT.

22   We do not observe fleet sales, which include sales to rental car companies. In ignoring fleet sales, we effectively assume that fleet purchasers are acting as agents for households.

23   Unfortunately, this variable is not available for every product in our sample and, more importantly, the rating was rescaled in every year of our sample. For example, the absolute level of reliability of a "3" rating changes every year in an unreported way, as does the absolute increment in reliability represented by a one point increase in the index.

24   For example, we treat Hondas as Japanese and VWs as German, although, by the end of our sample, some of each were produced in the U.S.

25   A referee has noted that we could generate variation in markups by putting $\ln(p)$ instead of p into the logit utility function, which might also more closely match the $\ln(y - p)$ specification in the full model. We implemented this suggestion and found that markups are indeed more reasonable, but that substitution patterns are still quite unreasonable.

26   The hedonic pricing literature, e.g. Griliches (1971), frequently presents similar regressions of log price on product characteristics. Of course, these regressions are motivated much differently from the marginal cost pricing argument we give here.

27   In this context, we remind the reader that a positive variance of the random coefficient on the constant term implies that the distribution of the outside good has more idiosyncratic variance than that of the extreme value deviates generating idiosyncratic variance for the inside alternatives.

28   We should note here that we have also estimated the demand side of our specification separately, and that we have run specifications that allowed for firm specific dummy variables on both the demand and cost side. Since there are 22 firms in our data set this latter specification generates 66 additional parameters (a mean and variance for each firm on the demand side, and one cost elasticity on the supply side). Neither of these changes generated point estimates that were much different from the point estimates in Table 4, but both generated much larger estimated standard errors.

29   This same reasoning leads to an interesting set of questions regarding the nonparametric identification of the parameters of the taste distribution, which we have not yet begun to investigate. We should note, however, that we had much more difficulty estimating separate mean and variance terms from a single cross-section than we did from the panel; indeed, this was one motivation for using a panel data set.

30   Interestingly, while the pattern of markups differs considerably between the logit case and the BLP specification, the average level of markups is similar across the two sets of results.

References

Anderson, S., A. de Palma and F. Thisse (1989): "Demand for Differentiated Products, Discrete Choice Models, and the Characteristics Approach," *Review of Economics Studies*, 56, 21–35.

Ben-Akiva, M. (1973): "Structure of Passenger Travel Demand Models," Ph.D. dissertation, Department of Civil Engineering, MIT.

Berkovec, J. (1985): "New Car Sales and Used Car Stocks: A Model of the Automobile Market," *RAND Journal of Economics*, 16, 195–214.

Berkovec, J. and J. Rust (1985): "A Nested Logit Model of Automobile Holdings for One Vehicle Households," *Transportation Research*, 19B, 275–85.

Berry, S. (1991): "Airport Presence as Product Differentiation," *American Economic Review, Papers and Proceedings*, 80, 394–9.

——(1994): "Estimating Discrete Choice Models of Product Differentiation," *RAND Journal of Economics*, 25, 242–62.

Berry, S. and A. Pakes (1993): "Some Applications and Limitations of Recent Advances in Empirical Industrial Organization: Merger Analysis," *American Economic Review, Papers and Proceedings*, 83, 247–52.

——(in process): "The Limit Properties of an Estimator for Differentiated Products Demand Systems as the Number of Products Grows Large," mimeo, Yale University.

Berry, S., J. Levinsohn, and A. Pakes (1994): "Voluntary Export Restraints on Automobiles: Evaluating a Strategic Trade Policy," mimeo.

Bresnahan, T. (1981): "Departures from Marginal-Cost Pricing in the American Automobile Industry," *Journal of Econometrics*, 17, 201–27.

——(1987): "Competition and Collusion in the American Automobile Oligopoly: The 1955 Price War," *Journal of Industrial Economics*, 35, 457–82.

Caplin, A. and B. Nalebuff (1991): "Aggregation and Imperfect Competition: On the Existence of Equilibrium," *Econometrica*, 59, 26–61.

Chamberlain, G. (1986): "Asymptotic Efficiency in Estimation with Conditional Moment Restrictions," *Journal of Econometrics*, 33, 305–34.

Debreu, G. (1960): "Review of R. D. Luce Individual Choice Behavior," *American Economic Review*, 50, 186–8.

Ericson, R. and A. Pakes (1995): "Markov Perfect Industry Dynamics: A Framework for Empirical Work," *Review of Economic Studies*, 62, 53–82.

Feenstra, R. and J. Levinsohn (1995): "Estimating Markups and Market Conduct with Multidimensional Product Attributes," *Review of Economic Studies*, 62, 19–52.

Goldberg, P. (1993): "Product Differentiation and Oligopoly in International Markets: The Case of the U.S. Automobile Industry," mimeo, Princeton University.

Griliches, Z. (1971): "Hedonic Price Indices for Automobiles: an Econometric Analysis of Quality Change," in *Price Indices and Quality Change*, ed. by Z. Griliches. Cambridge: Harvard University Press.

Hansen, L. (1982): "Large Sample Properties of Generalized Method of Moments Estimators," *Econometrica*, 50, 1029–54.

Haseman, J. and L. Kuper (1979): "Analysis of Dichotomous Response Data from Certain Toxicological Experiments," *Biometrics*, 35, 281–93.

Hausman, J. (1975): "Project Independence Report: An Appraisal of U.S. Energy Needs Up to 1985," *BELL Journal of Economics*, 6, 517–51.

Hotz, V. J. and R. Miller (1993): "Conditional Choice Probabilities and the Estimation or Dynamic Models," *Review of Economic Studies*, 60, 497–529.

Kingman, J. F. C. (1978): "The 1977 Wald Memorial Lectures," *The Annals of Probability*, 6, 183–97.

Lancaster, K. J. (1971): *Consumer Demand: A New Approach*. New York: Columbia University Press.

Levinsohn, J. (1988): "Empirics of Taxes on Differentiated Products: The Case of Tariffs in the U.S. Automobile Industry," in *Trade Policy Issues and Empirical Analysis*, ed. by R. Baldwin. Chicago: University of Chicago Press.

Manski, C. (1983): "Analysis of Equilibrium Automobile Holdings in Israel with Aggregate Discrete Choice Models," *Transportation Research*, 17B, 373–89.

McFadden, D. (1973): "Conditional Logit Analysis of Qualitative Choice Behavior," in *Frontiers of Econometrics*, ed. by P. Zarembka. New York: Academic Press.

——(1978): "Modelling the Choice of Residential Location," in *Spatial Interaction Theory and Planning Models*, ed. by A. Karlvist et al. Amsterdam: North Holland, 75–96.

——(1981): "Econometric Models of Probabilistic Choice," in *Structural Analysis of Discrete Data with Econometric Applications*, ed. by C. Manski and D. McFadden. Cambridge: MIT Press.

——(1986): "Econometric Analysis of Qualitative Response Models," in *Handbook of Econometrics, Volume III*, ed. by Z. Griliches and M. Intriligator. Amsterdam: North Holland.

McFadden, D., A. Talvitie and Associates (1977): *Demand Model Estimation and Validation*. Berkeley: The Institute of Transportation Studies, University of California, Berkeley and Irvine.

Morgan, M. (1990): *The History of Econometric Ideas*. New York: Cambridge University Press.

Morrison, S. and C. Winston (1989): "Enhancing the Performance of the Deregulated Air Transportation System," *Brookings Papers on Economic Activity: Microeconomics*, 2, 61–112.

Nelder, J., and R. Mead (1965): "A Simplex Method for Function Minimization," *Computer Journal*, 7, 308–13.

Newey, W. (1990): "Efficient Instrumental Variables Estimation of Nonlinear Models," *Econometrica*, 58, 809–39.

Ohta, M. and Z. Griliches (1976): "Automobile Prices Revisited: Extensions of the Hedonic Hypothesis," in *Household Production and Consumption*, ed. by N. Terlecky. New York: NBER.

Pakes, A. (1986): "Patents as Options: Some Estimates of the Value of Holding European Patent Stocks," *Econometrica*, 54, 755–84.

—— (1994): "Dynamic Structural Models, Problems and Prospects: Mixed Continuous Discrete Controls and Market Interactions," in *Advances in Econometrics: The Sixth World Congress of the Econometric Society, Vol. II*, ed. by J.-J. Laffont and C. Sims. New York: Cambridge University Press, pp. 171–260.

Pakes, A. and P. McGuire (1994): "Computation of Markov Perfect Nash Equilibria I: Numerical Implications of a Dynamic Product Model," *RAND Journal of Economics*, 25, 555–89.

Pakes, A. and D. Pollard (1989): "Simulation and the Asymptotics of Optimization Estimators," *Econometrica*, 57, 1027–57.

Pakes, A. S. Berry and J. Levinsohn (1993): "Applications and Limitations of Some Recent Advances in Empirical Industrial Organization: Price Indexes and the Analysis of Environmental Change," *American Economic Review, Papers and Proceedings*, 83, 240–6.

Perloff, J. and S. Salop (1985): "Equilibrium with Product Differentiation," *Review of Economic Studies*, 52, 107–20.

Robinson, P. (1987): "Asymptotically Efficient Estimation in the Presence of Heteroskedasticity of Unknown Form," *Econometrica*, 55, 875–91.

Rubinstein, R. (1981): *Simulation and the Monte Carlo Method*. New York: Wiley.

Sattinger, M. (1984): "Value of an Additional Firm in Monopolistic Competition," *Review of Economic Studies*, 49, 3–13.

Schmalensee, R. (1985): "Econometric Diagnosis of Competitive Localization," *International Journal of Industrial Organization*, 57–70.

Shaked, A. and J. Sutton (1982): "Relaxing Price Competition Through Product Differentiation," *Review of Economic Studies*, 49, 3–13.

Suits, D. (1958): "The Demand for Automobiles in the United States," *Review of Economics and Statistics*, 40, 273–80.

Toder, E., with N. Cardell and E. Burton (1978): *Trade Policy and the U. S. Automobile Industry*. New York: Praeger.

Train, K. (1986): *Qualitative Choice Analysis: Theory, Econometrics and an Application to Automobile Demand*. Cambridge: MIT Press.

Williams, D. (1982): "Extra-binomial Variation in Logistic Linear Models," *Applied Statistics*, 31, 144–8.

Working, E. (1926): "What Do Statistical Demand Curves Show?" *Quarterly Journal of Economics*, 41, 212–35.

PART V

Entry

Introduction

Monopolies are more profitable than oligopolies. This simple fact provides the motivation for the strategy of entry preemption. Incumbent monopolists will do all they can to maintain their dominant position. In a seminal work, Sylos-Labini (1962) proposed the strategy of limit pricing as a positive theory of entry preemption (the idea goes back at least to Bain (1949)). By setting a low price, an incumbent discourages entry by potential rivals. The latter, taking the incumbent's price as given, finds it unprofitable to enter. The incumbent, in turn, sacrifices short-run profits (lower than monopoly price) for the maintenance of a monopoly situation.

How can low prices be an entry deterrent? After all, once entry is a *fait accompli*, the incumbent will find out that it is in its best interest to raise price to more reasonable levels. In other words, if the incumbent cannot commit to set a low price for a long period, then low prices should not be a entry deterrent. The game-theoretic development of this idea owes much to the work of Selten (1965), who argues that the threat of maintaining low prices after entry is not a credible threat.

As a reaction to this criticism, Spence (1977) proposed a reinterpretation of the Sylos-Labini model whereby the incumbent expands its capacity, possibly to the point of holding excess capacity, and threatens to use such excess capacity were entry to take place. This seems like a more credible strategy. After all, capacity costs are mostly sunk; it would thus seem that the monopolist has an incentive to use its capacity were entry to take place.

Not necessarily, argues Dixit (1980). In a model with linear demand and costs, Dixit shows that an incumbent may increase capacity to (successfully) deter entry. However, the incumbent never holds excess capacity in equilibrium. Bulow et al. (1985) qualify this assertion: if demand is nonlinear (constant elasticity, for example), then excess capacity may indeed be an equilibrium entry deterring strategy, as suggested by Spence (1977).

Sunk capacity costs are not the only source of credible commitment.[1] Schmalensee (1978), for example, shows that product proliferation may deter entry in a similar way. Another important instance of credible deterrence is given by contracts. For example, in anticipation of the expiry of its patent, Monsanto (the producer of Nutrasweet) signed long-term contracts with its main customers (Coca-Cola and Pepsi-Cola), making life more difficult for entrant Holland Sweetner Company. On the eve of entry deregulation in

Portuguese TV broadcasting, the incumbent monopolist signed a series of contracts with suppliers of movie and sports programs, the most important items – financially speaking – in TV broadcasting.

Can such an outcome result from rational behavior on the part of customers and suppliers? Why didn't Coca-Cola, for example, wait for Holland Sweetner to enter the market and then benefit from lower prices resulting from duopoly competition? Aghion and Bolton (1987) make the point that a long-term contract of the sort considered above may be in the joint-interest of incumbent and buyer (or incumbent and supplier); that is, it can be an equilibrium phenomenon. Suppose the entrant's cost is unknown to incumbent and buyer. When the entrant's cost is lower than the incumbent's, entry takes place absent any contract between incumbent and buyer. In this case, the entrant prices below the incumbent's cost and makes a profit. It is precisely because of this "entrant's surplus" that incumbent and buyer find it optimal to write a contract. Such contract, including a liquidated damages clause (if the buyer decides to switch to the entrant) effectively extracts some of the entrant's surplus, to the benefit of incumbent and buyer. The inefficiency that the contract causes (deterred entry when the incumbent is less efficient) is analogous to the inefficiency caused by monopoly pricing. In fact, crucial to the Aghion–Bolton result is the fact that the entrant's cost is unknown to the incumbent, just like a monopolist lacks information on each buyer's valuation.

Another question of interest in the context of entry is whether the equilibrium number of entrants is too small or too large from a social welfare point of view. In a seminal paper, von Weizsacker (1980) showed that entry barriers may be welfare enhancing, for otherwise the equilibrium number of entrants would be too large from a social welfare point of view. A more general analysis of this problem was developed by Mankiw and Whinston (1986), who characterize an important externality in the entry decision – the "business stealing" effect. The idea is that, when there is market power, part of the profits earned by an entrant correspond to earnings transfered from incumbent firms, earnings which do not correspond to an increase in social welfare. A analysis similar to Mankiw–Whinston's is presented by Suzumura and Kiyone (1987).

In the context of free entry with product differentiation, early attempts at solving the free-entry-and-welfare question include Spence (1976) and Dixit and Stiglitz (1977) (cf part 3). An important recent contribution is Anderson et al. (1995). A general feature of all these models is that there is a conflict between the business-stealing effect and the opposite externality that an entrant is only able to capture a fraction of the consumer surplus it generates. General results regarding the relative weight of these two effects seem difficult to obtain. The way forward would seem to be empirical analysis (see the third paper in part 4).

Not every industry has "large" incumbent firms playing strategies of entry preemption. At the opposite extreme of the spectrum, we have perfect competition, where entry is "easy" and incumbent firms' profits are zero in the long-run equilibrium. The problem with the perfect competition "story" is that it does not fit the data. In theory, we should observe entry *or* exit, depending on whether the number of firms is lower or greater than the long-run equilibrium, respectively. But typically one observes both entry *and* exit in any given industry or time period. A first attempt at a model that is consistent with price-taking equilibrium behavior and with the above stylized fact was developed by Jovanovic (1982). Jovanovic's seminal paper has spawned an interesting literature on industry dynamics, including important contributions by Hopenhayn (1992) and Ericson and Pakes (1995).

Notes

1 In fact, aside from Dupont's strategy of capacity expansion in the market for Titanium Dioxide in the 1970s, it is remarkably difficult to find an example of preemption by capacity expansion.

References

Aghion, Philippe and Patrick Bolton (1987): "Contracts as a Barrier to Entry," *American Economic Review*, 77, 38–401.

Anderson, Simon P., André de Palma and Yurii Nesterov (1995): "Oligopolistic Competition and the Optimal Provision of Products," *Econometrica*, 63, 1281–301.

Bain, J. (1949): "A Note on Pricing in Monopoly and Oligopoly," *American Economic Review*, 39, 448–64.

Bulow, Jeremy, John Geanakoplos and Paul Klemperer (1985): "Multimarket Oligopoly: Strategic Substitutes and Complements," *Journal of Political Economy*, 93, 488–511.

Dixit, A. (1980): "The Role of Investment in Entry Deterrence," *Economic Journal*, 90, 95–106.

Dixit, Avinash and Joseph Stiglitz (1977): "Monopolistic Competition and Optimum Product Diversity," *American Economic Review*, 67, 297–308.

Ericson, Richard and Ariel Pakes (1995): "Markov-Perfect Industry Dynamics: A Framework for Empirical Work," *Review of Economics Studies*, 62, 53–82.

Hopenhayn, Hugo (1992): "Entry, Exit, and Firm Dynamics in Long Run Equilibrium," *Econometrica*, 60, 1127–50.

Jovanovic, Boyan (1982): "Selection and Evolution of Industry," *Econometrica*, 50, 649–70.

Mankiw, N. Gregory and Michael D. Whinston (1986): "Free Entry and Social Inefficiency," *Rand Journal of Economics*, 17, 48–58.

Schmalensee, Richard (1978): "Entry Deterrence in the Ready-to-eat Breakfast Cereal Industry," *Bell Journal of Economics*, 9, 305–27.

Selten, Reinhard (1965): "Spieltheoretische Behandlung eines Oligopolmodells mit Nachfrageträgheit," *Zeitschrift für die gesamte Staatswissenschaft*, 121, 301–24, 667–89.

Spence, Michael (1976): "Product Selection, Fixed Costs and Monopolistic Competition," *Review of Economic Studies*, 43, 217–36.

Spence, Michael (1977): "Entry, Investment and Oligopolistic Pricing," *Bell Journal of Economics*, 8, 534–44.

Suzumura, Kotaro and Dazuharu Kiyone (1987): "Entry Barriers and Economic Welfare," *Review of Economic Studies*, 54, 157–67.

Sylos-Labini, P. (1962): *Oligopoly and Technical Progress*. Cambridge, Mass: Harvard University Press.

von Weizsacker, C. C. (1980): "A Welfare Analysis of Barriers to Entry," *Bell Journal of Economics*, 11, 399–420.

CHAPTER TWELVE

The Role of Investment in Entry-Deterrence

Avinash K. Dixit

Source: *Economic Journal*, 1980, 90, 95–106.

The theory of large-scale entry into an industry is made complicated by its game-theoretic aspects. Even in the simplest case of one established firm facing one prospective entrant, there are some subtle strategic interactions. The established firm's pre-entry decisions can influence the prospective entrant's view of what will happen if he enters, and the established firm will try to exploit this possibility to its own advantage.

The earliest treatments met these problems by adopting the Bain-Sylos postulate, where the prospective entrant was assumed to believe that the established firm would maintain the same output after entry as its actual pre-entry output. Then the established firm naturally acquired a Stackelberg leadership role. However, the assumption is dubious on two opposing counts. First, faced with an irrevocable fact of entry, the established firm will usually find it best to make an accommodating output reduction. On the other hand, it would like to threaten to respond to entry with a predatory increase in output. Its problem is to make the latter threat credible given the prospective entrant's knowledge of the former fact. (A detailed exposition of the Bain–Sylos model and its critique can be found in Scherer (1970, ch. 8).)

In a seminal treatment of games involving such conflicts, Schelling (1960, ch. 2) suggested that a threat which is costly to carry out can be made credible by entering into an advance commitment which makes its fulfilment optimal or even necessary. This was applied to the question of entry by Spence (1977), who recognised that the established firm's prior and irrevocable investment decisions could be a commitment of this kind. He assumed that the prospective entrant would believe that the established firm's post-entry output would equal its pre-entry capacity. In the interests of entry-deterrence, the established firm may set capacity at such a high level that in the pre-entry phase it would not want to utilise it all, i.e. excess capacity would be observed.

The Bain-Sylos and Spence analyses were extended in Dixit (1979) by considering whether the established firm will find it best to prevent entry or to allow it to occur. However, the basic assumptions concerning the post-entry developments were maintained.

Since it is at best unclear whether such assumptions will be valid, it seems useful to study the consequences of some alternatives. In reality, there may be no agreement about the rules of the post-entry game, and there may be periods of disequilibrium before any order is established. Financial positions of the firms may then acquire an important role. However, even when the two have a common understanding of the rules of the post-entry duopoly, there are several possibilities. An obvious case is where a Nash equilibrium will be established after entry, either in quantities as in Cournot (see also Wenders (1971)) or in prices as in Bertrand. Yet another case is where the entrant is destined to take over Stackelberg leadership in setting quantities (see Salop (1978)).

In this paper I examine some of these possibilities. The basic point is that although the *rules* of the post-entry game are taken to be exogenous, the established firm can alter the *outcome* to its advantage by changing the initial conditions. In particular, an irrevocable choice of investment allows it to alter its post-entry marginal cost curve, and thereby the post-entry equilibrium under any specified rule. It will be seen that it can use this privilege to exercise limited leadership.

1. The Model

The basic point is most easily seen in a simplified model. I shall reduce the dynamic aspects to the barest essentials by ignoring all lags. Either entry does not occur at all, in which case the established firm continues in a stationary state, or else it occurs at once, and the post-entry equilibrium is also established at once, so that the resulting duopoly continues in its stationary state. It is as if the two players see through the whole problem and implement the solution immediately.[1] The result is that we can confine attention to the constant streams of profits, avoiding the complication of reducing a varying pair of profit flows to discounted present values. However, once the underlying principle is understood, an added complication in this respect is not difficult to admit in principle.

The second simplification made in the main body of the analysis is with regard to the costs of production. Let the subscript 1 denote the established firm and 2 the prospective entrant. Each firm will be supposed to have a constant average variable cost of output, and a constant unit cost of capacity expansion, and a set-up cost. If firm i has capacity k_i and is producing output x_i (with $x_i \leq k_i$), its cost per period will be

$$C_i = f_i + w_i x_i + r_i k_i \tag{1}$$

where f_i is the fixed set-up cost, r_i the constant cost per unit of capacity (both expressed in per period or flow terms), and w_i the constant average variable cost for output. The possibility that the two firms have the same cost functions ($f_1 = f_2$, etc.) is not excluded. The special form (1) has some analytical and empirical merit; I examine a more general cost function in section 3.

The revenues per period for the two firms will be functions $R^i(x_1, x_2)$. Each will be increasing and concave in that firm's output. Also, each firm's total and marginal revenue will be decreasing in the other's output.

The rules of the game are as follows. The established firm chooses a pre-entry capacity level $\bar{k}_1$. This may subsequently be increased, but cannot be reduced. If the other firm decides to enter, the two will achieve a duopoly Cournot–Nash equilibrium with quantity-setting. Otherwise the established firm will prevail as a monopoly.

First suppose that firm I has installed capacity $\bar{k}_1$. If it is producing output within this limit, i.e. if $x_1 \leq \bar{k}_1$, its total costs are

$$C_1 = f_1 + r_1\bar{k}_1 + w_1 x_1$$

However, if it wishes to produce greater output, it must acquire additional capacity. If $x_1 > \bar{k}_1$, therefore,

$$C_1 = f_1 + (w_1 + r_1)x_1$$

Correspondingly, firm 1's marginal cost is w_1 so long as its output does not exceed $\bar{k}_1$, and $(w_1 + r_1)$ thereafter. Firm 2 has no prior commitment in capacity. For all positive levels of output x_2, it acquires capacity k_2 to match, yielding

$$C_2 = f_2 + (w_2 + r_2)x_2$$

and a marginal cost of $(w_2 + r_2)$. The choice of $\bar{k}_1$ thus affects the shape of the marginal cost curve of firm 1, which in turn affects its reaction curve. When the two firms interact, the resulting duopoly equilibrium depends on $\bar{k}_1$, and therefore so do the profits of the two firms in it. If the profits for the second firm are positive, it will enter; otherwise it will not. Bearing this in mind, firm 1 will choose that $\bar{k}_1$ which maximises its profit. Whether this is done by preventing entry or by allowing it to occur remains to be seen. However, I shall assume for simplicity of exposition that the established firm's maximum profit is positive, i.e. exit is not its best policy.

The analysis follows the scheme just outlined. For a given $\bar{k}_1$, Figure 1 shows the marginal cost curve for the established firm, MC_1, as the heavy kinked line. It equals w_1, the marginal cost when there is spare capacity, up to the output level $\bar{k}_1$ and $(w_1 + r_1)$, the marginal cost including capacity expansion cost, thereafter. On this we superimpose the marginal revenue curve, the position of which depends on the assumed output level x_2 of the other firm. For a sufficiently low value of x_2, the curve is in a position like the one labelled MR_1, and the first firm's profit-maximising choice of x_1 lies to the right of its previously fixed capacity level. For successively higher levels of x_2, the marginal revenue curve shifts downwards to occupy positions like MR_1' and MR_1'', yielding choices of x_1 at, or below, the capacity level. This response of x_1 to x_2 is just the established firm's reaction function to the entrant's output.

This function can be shown in a more familiar direct manner in the space of two quantities, and this is done in Figure 2. I have shown two 'reference' curves MM' and NN'. The first becomes the reaction function if capacity expansion costs matter, and the second if there is spare capacity. Therefore the first is relevant for outputs above k_1 and the second for outputs below this level. For fixed $\bar{k}_1$, then, the reaction function is the kinked curve shown in heavy lines.

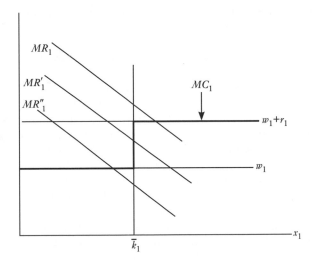

Figure 1

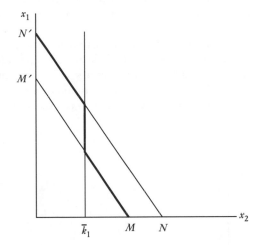

Figure 2

Let the points M and N have respective coordinates $(M_1, 0)$ and $(N_1, 0)$. The quantities M_1 and N_1 can be interpreted as follows. Both are profit-maximising quantity choices of firm 1 when the output level of firm 2 is held fixed at zero, i.e. when the possibility of entry is ignored. However, M_1 is the choice when capacity expansion costs matter, and N_1 is relevant when there is sufficient capacity already installed and only variable costs matter.

Since firm 2 has no prior commitment in capacity, its reaction function RR' is straightforward. I assume that it intersects both MM' and NN' in a way that corresponds to the usual 'stable' Cournot solution, in order to minimise complications other than those of immediate interest (see Figure 3).

For given $\bar{k}_1$, we have a duopoly Nash equilibrium at the intersection of the two reaction functions. However, the established firm has the privilege of choosing $\bar{k}_1$ in advance, and thus determining which reaction function it will present in the post-entry duopoly. Suppose firm 2's reaction function meets MM' at $T = (T_1, T_2)$ and NN' at $V = (V_1, V_2)$ as shown in Figure 3. Clearly T and V can be interpreted as Nash equilibria under alternative extreme circumstances, T when capacity expansion costs matter for firm 1, and V when they do not. It is then evident on comparing Figures 2 and 3 that for a choice of $\bar{k}_1 \leq T_1$, the post-entry equilibrium will be at T, while for $\bar{k}_1 \geq V_1$, it will occur at V. Most importantly, for $T_1 \leq \bar{k}_1 \leq V_1$, it will occur at the appropriate point on the heavy line segment of the entrant's reaction function lying between T and V. Here the established firm will produce output $x_1 = \bar{k}_1$, and the entrant will produce the same output as would a Stackelberg follower faced with this x_1. It is in this sense that, even when the post-entry game is accepted as leading to a Nash equilibrium, the established firm can exercise leadership over a limited range by using its capacity choice to manipulate the initial conditions of that game.

However, the qualification of the limited range is important. In particular, it means that capacity levels above V_1 are not credible threats of entry-deterrence. When a prospective entrant is confident of its ability to sustain a Nash equilibrium in the post-entry game, it does not fear such levels. And when the established firm knows this, it does not try out the costly and empty threats.

Since $N_1 > V_1$, we see *a fortiori* the futility of maintaining capacity levels above N_1 as threats to deter entry. Nor are such capacity levels justified by considerations of pre-entry production; in fact a monopolist saddled with capacity above N_1 will choose to leave the excess idle. Under the rules of the game assumed here, therefore, we will not observe the established firm installing capacity above N_1. The Spence excess capacity strategy will not be employed.

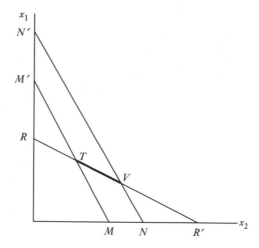

Figure 3

Nor will we ever see the established firm installing pre-entry capacity of less than T_1: if entry is to occur it will want more capacity, and if entry is not to occur it will want capacity of at least $M_1 > T_1$.

In the model used by Spence, it is simply assumed that a prospective entrant expects the established firm will respond to entry by producing an output level equal to its pre-entry capacity, no matter how high that may be. It is then possible that constrained monopoly profits made by keeping capacity at the entry-deterring level and producing at N exceed what is possible with a lower capacity leading to a Stackelberg duopoly equilibrium. This is the excess capacity strategy of entry prevention. When the credibility of the threat is questioned, matters can be different, and the above argument shows that they are indeed different under the particular modification of the rules of the game.

2. Classification of Outcomes

The discussion so far was confined to the post-entry duopoly, i.e. both firms were assumed to have incurred the set-up costs. When we come to the *ex ante* decision about whether to enter, set-up costs matter, and the choice is governed by the sign of the profits net of them. (Dixit (1979) uses an alternative geometric approach involving discontinuous reaction functions.)

We have seen above that at all points that are ever going to be observed without or with entry, the established firm will be producing an output equal to its chosen pre-entry capacity. Therefore we may write the profits of the two firms as functions of their outputs alone, i.e.

$$\pi_i(x_1, x_2) = R^i(x_1, x_2) - f_i - (w_i + r_i)x_i$$

It will often be convenient to indicate the point of evaluation (x_1, x_2) by a letter label such as that used in the corresponding figure. I have assumed that the maximum value of π_1 is always positive. Depending on the sign of π_2, various cases arise. Note that along firm 2's reaction function, its profit decreases monotonically from T to V. Therefore we can classify the possibilities as follows.

CASE 1. $\pi_2(T) < 0$. Now the prospective entrant cannot make a profit in any post-entry equilibrium. So it will not try to enter the industry at all. Entry being irrelevant, the established firm will enjoy a pure monopoly by setting its capacity and output at M_1.

CASE 2. $\pi_2(V) > 0$. Here the prospective entrant will make a positive profit in any post-entry equilibrium, so the established firm cannot hope to prevent entry. It can only seek the best available duopoly position. To this end, it will compute its profit along the segment TV. Since all these choices involve output equal to capacity, we can simply use the conventional iso-π_1 contours in (x_1, x_2) space and find the highest contour along the segment TV. If there is a Stackelberg tangency to the left of V, that is firm 1's best choice. However, if the conventional tangency occurs to the right of V, we now have a corner solution at V, which can then be thought of as a sort of generalised Stackelberg leadership point.

CASE 3. $\pi_2(T) > 0 > \pi_2(V)$.   This presents the richest set of possibilities. Now there is a point $B = (B_1, B_2)$ along such TV that $\pi_2(B) = 0$. If the established firm sets its capacity above B_1, the prospective entrant will reckon on making a negative profit in the post-entry Nash equilibrium, and therefore will not enter. Thus the capacity level B_1 is the entry-barring level. Knowing this, firm 1 wants to know whether it is worth its while to prevent entry.

SUB-CASE I.   If $B_1 < M_1$, then the established firm's monopoly choice is automatically sufficient to deter entry. In Bain's terminology, entry can be said to be blockaded.

If $B_1 > M_1$, the established firm can only bar entry by maintaining capacity (and output) at a level greater than it would want to as a monopolist; thus it is faced with a calculation of the costs and benefits of entry-prevention. To prevent entry, it needs a capacity of just greater than B_1. Since $B_1 < V_1 < N_1$, we know that it will want to use all this capacity in its monopoly choice of output, so its profit will be $\pi_1(B_1, 0)$. The alternative is to allow entry and settle for the best duopoly point, which may be a tangency in the segment TV, or a corner solution at V. Whichever it is, call it the generalised Stackelberg point S, with coordinates (S_1, S_2). Then we have:

SUB-CASE II. $\pi_1(S) < \pi_1(B_1, 0)$, when it is better to prevent entry by choosing a limit-capacity or limit-output at B_1. There is a corresponding limit-price. In Bain's usage, entry is effectively impeded. Incidentally, for this sub-case to arise, it is sufficient to have $S_1 \geq B_1$. For, with $B_1 > M_1$, we have $\pi_1(S_1, S_2) < \pi_1(S_1, 0) \leq \pi_1(B_1, 0)$.

SUB-CASE III. $\pi_1(S) > \pi_1(B_1, 0)$, when it is better to allow entry, i.e. entry is ineffectively impeded, and a duopoly solution is observed at S. Remember that S is the post-entry Nash equilibrium.

An alternative way of distinguishing between the sub-cases II and III is to draw the iso-π_1 contour through S and see if it intersects the x_1-axis to the right or the left of B_1. This would follow Dixit (1979), except for one new feature: the Stackelberg point S can be at the corner solution V.

For particular demand functions, we can evaluate all these profit expressions explicitly, and thereby express the classification of outcomes in terms of the underlying parameters.

3. Extensions and Modifications

Of the numerous extensions conceivable, I consider three. The first involves an alternative and rather extreme post-entry equilibrium, where the rules of the game are that the entrant acquires the role of quantity leadership (see Salop (1978)). Thus firm 2 chooses a point on firm 1's post-entry reaction function to maximise its own profit. However, firm 1, by its initial commitment to capacity, can decide which reaction function to present to the entrant, and can manipulate this choice to its own advantage.

Figure 4 shows the possibilities. The notation is the same as in Figure 3, with some additions. Let $F = (F_1, F_2)$ be the ordinary Stackelberg point where firm 2 is the leader

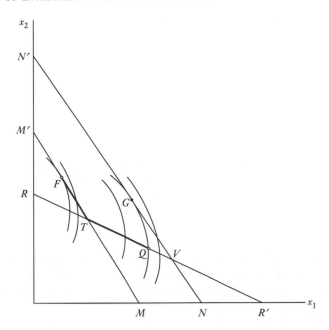

Figure 4

and firm 1 the follower, taking into account capacity expansion costs, i.e. using the reference curve MM'. If firm 1 sets its capacity $\bar{k}_1$ at a level less than F_1, then its reaction function as drawn in Figure 2 will drop from NN' to MM' at $\bar{k}_1$ to the left of F. Firm 2's profit will then be maximised on this reaction function at the tangency point F. For $\bar{k}_1$ between F_1 and T_1, there will be a maximum at the kink in firm 1's reaction function where it meets MM', yielding an equilibrium at the appropriate point along the segment FT. For a while to the right of T, we will have a tangency solution along TV, an iso-π_2 contour being tangential to the vertical portion of firm 1's reaction function. Let G be the point where an iso-π_2 contour is tangential to NN', and let this contour meet RR' at $Q = (Q_1, Q_2)$. Then the vertical tangency will be the best choice for firm 2 so long as $\bar{k}_1 \leq Q_1$. For $\bar{k}_1 > Q_1$, however, it will prefer the tangency at G.

By its choice of $\bar{k}_1$, the established firm can therefore secure as the post-entry equilibrium any point along the kinked line segment FTQ, shown in heavy in in the figure, and the isolated point G. In other words, even though the rules of the game require it to surrender post-entry quantity leadership, the established firm can use its commitment to capacity to seize a limited initiative back from the entrant. It remains to choose the best available point. Now G is clearly inferior from the point of view of firm 1 to the point directly below it on the segment TQ. Similarly, all points along FT are worse than T. However, there is a genuine choice to be made, i.e. leadership exercised, along the segment TQ. This is smaller than the segment TV which was available when the post-entry rules led to a Nash equilibrium. But the qualitative features are unchanged, and all of my earlier analysis applies on replacing V by Q throughout.

The second extension I consider allows a more general cost function. The form (1), up to the given capacity level, has marginal cost constant at the level ω_1, and since capacity cannot be exceeded, the marginal cost of output can be said to jump to infinity where output hits capacity. An increase in capacity then lowers marginal cost from infinity to ω_1 over the added range. Now I replace this by a form which has a more flexible notion of capacity. Let

$$C_1 = C^1(x_1, k_1) \tag{2}$$

This will be increasing in x_1, and convex at least beyond a certain point. For each x_1 there will be a cost-minimising choice of k_1, so C^1 will be decreasing in k_1 up to this level and increasing thereafter. Finally, a higher level of k_1 will lower marginal cost of output, i.e.

$$C^1_{x_1 k_1} < 0 \tag{3}$$

with subscripts denoting partial derivatives in the usual way. All this follows the theory of the familiar textbook short-run cost functions. This is similar to the more general model in Spence (1977) except that price discipline does not break down completely after entry.

Begin with the post-entry Nash equilibrium given that firm 1 has set its capacity variable at the level $\bar{k}_1$. Firm 2's reaction function is again straightforward. That for firm 1 is found by choosing x_1 to maximise

$$R^1(x_1, x_2) - C^1(x_1, \bar{k}_1)$$

for given x_2 and $\bar{k}_1$. This has the first-order condition

$$R^1_{x_1}(x_1, x_2) - C^1_{x_1}(x_1, \bar{k}_1) = 0 \tag{4}$$

and the second-order condition

$$R^1_{x_1 x_1}(x_1, x_2) - C^1_{x_1 x_1}(x_1, \bar{k}_1) < 0 \tag{5}$$

Equation (4) defines firm 1's post-entry reaction function, and also tells us how it shifts as $\bar{k}_1$ changes. Total differentiation gives

$$dx_1 = [-R^1_{x_1 x_2}/(R^1_{x_1 x_1} - C^1_{x_1 x_1})]dx_2 + [C^1_{x_1 x_1}/(R^1_{x_1 x_1} - C^1_{x_1 x_1})]d\bar{k}_1$$

Given our assumption that the commodities are substitutes in the sense that an increased quantity of the second lowers the marginal revenue for the first, and using (5), we see that the reaction function slopes downward. Also, using (3) and (5), we see that it shifts to the right as $\bar{k}_1$ increases.

Figure 5 shows a collection of firm 1's reaction functions for different choices of $\bar{k}_1$, as a set of dashed lines. Where each meets firm 2's reaction function RR', there is a post-entry

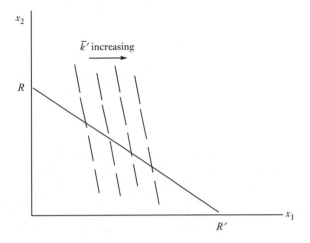

Figure 5

Nash equilibrium for the appropriate choice of $\bar{k}_1$. Thus, once again, firm 1 by its choice of capacity can achieve any one of a range of points along firm 2's reaction function. This is almost as if it acquired the privilege of quantity leadership. There are two limitations. First, the possible reaction functions found by varying $\bar{k}_1$ may trace out only a limited part of firm 2's reaction function, as happened in the case of section 1. Second, in any post-entry Nash equilibrium, the $\bar{k}_1$ which achieves it is not the ideal choice for producing the x_1 that prevails there; so the policy involves a cost that does not appear in straightforward quantity leadership. To see this, we must examine the equilibrium in more detail. Firm 2 maximises $R^2(x_1, x_2) - C^2(x_2)$ in obvious notation, so its reaction function is given by

$$R^2_{x_2}(x_1, x_2) - C^2_{x_2}(x_2) = 0 \tag{6}$$

Then (4) and (6) define the duopoly equilibrium as a function of $\bar{k}_1$. Differentiating the equations totally, we have

$$\begin{bmatrix} R^1_{x_1x_1} - C^1_{x_1x_1} & R^1_{x_1x_2} \\ R^2_{x_1x_2} & R^2_{x_2x_2} - C^2_{x_2x_2} \end{bmatrix} \begin{bmatrix} dx_1 \\ dx_2 \end{bmatrix} = \begin{bmatrix} C^1_{x_1k_1} d\bar{k}_1 \\ 0 \end{bmatrix} \tag{7}$$

Write Δ for the determinant of the coefficient matrix; it is positive by the stability condition for the equilibrium. Then we have the solution

$$\begin{bmatrix} dx_1 \\ dx_2 \end{bmatrix} = \frac{1}{\Delta} \begin{bmatrix} R^2_{x_2x_2} - C^2_{x_2x_2} \\ -R^1_{x_1x_2} \end{bmatrix} C^1_{x_1k_1} d\bar{k}_1 \tag{8}$$

Firm 1 uses this in its choice to $\bar{k}_1$ to maximise its profit, therefore

$$d\pi_1 = (R^1_{x_1} - C^1_{x_1})dx_1 + R^1_{x_2}dx_2 - C^1_{k_1}d\bar{k}_1$$
$$= -(R^1_{x_2}R^2_{x_1x_2}C^1_{x_1k_1}/\Delta + C^1_{k_1})d\bar{k}_1 \tag{9}$$

At the best duopoly point, the coefficient of $d\bar{k}_1$ in (9) is zero. Since all three factors in the numerator of the first term are negative while Δ is positive, we see that at this point,

$$C^1_{k_1} > 0$$

i.e. firm 1 carries its capacity to a point beyond what is optimum for producing its output.

Once again the analysis can be completed by examining the sign of firm 2's profits, and the desirability of entry-prevention for firm 1. This more flexible notion of capacity can be interpreted in terms of other types of investment such as dealer networks and advertising, and this provides a basis for arguments that such expenditures can be used by an established firm in its efforts to deter entry. This counters recent expressions of pessimism (e.g. Needham (1978) pp. 177–9) concerning the effectiveness of such tactics.

For the last modification, I revert to a rigid concept of capacity, but consider price-setting in the post-entry duopoly, the solution rule being the Bertrand-Nash equilibrium. Some added complications can arise due to possible non-convexities even with reasonable demand and cost functions, but I ignore these and show the simplest possible case. This is done in Figure 6, with notation analogous to the corresponding quantity-setting case of Figure 3. The prospective entrant's reaction function is RR'. For the established firm, we have two reference curves MM' and NN', the former when capacity expansion costs matter and the latter when they do not. Their relative positions are naturally reversed as compared to the quantity-setting case. The former is relevant for $x_1 \geq \bar{k}_1$ and the latter for $x_1 \leq \bar{k}_1$, where x_1 is found from the demand function $D^1(p_1, p_2)$. The boundary curve $x_1 = \bar{k}_1$ is shown for a particular $\bar{k}_1$, and the corresponding reaction function for the

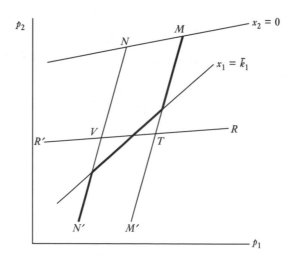

Figure 6

established firm is shown by the heavy lines. It is then clear that by varying $\bar{k}_1$, the established firm can secure any point along the segment TV of the prospective entrant's reaction function as the post-entry Nash equilibrium. Once again, we observe a limited leadership possibility arise by virtue of the established firm's advantage in being the first to make a commitment to capacity.

4. Concluding comments

The theme of the paper is that the role of an irrevocable commitment of investment in entry-deterrence is to alter the initial conditions of the post-entry game to the advantage of the established firm, for any fixed rule under which that game is to be played. This was illustrated in several simple models. Prominent among the conclusions was the observation that if the post-entry game is agreed to be played according to Nash rules, the established firm will not wish to install capacity that would be left idle in the pre-entry phase. This contrasts with the results of Spence (1977), where the post-entry game involves leadership by the established firm, and its threat of producing at a level equal to its pre-entry capacity is assumed to be believed by the prospective entrant. It is not possible to claim universal validity for either of these models. However, in the absence of any asymmetrical advantage possessed by the established firm in the post-entry phase, the Nash solution has considerable appeal.

Salop (1979) provides some examples of similar prior commitments that create an advantage for the established firm. Spence (1979) can be thought of as developing the same theme. In this model, capacity can only be acquired slowly, and the two firms differ in their abilities in this regard. This difference governs how the industry evolves, including issues of whether the second firm will enter, and what kind of equilibrium will result if it does. Much of the interesting dynamics is lost in my formulation, but the compensating advantage is that the basic idea becomes much more transparent. It is hoped that the distinction between the *rules* of the post-entry game and its *initial conditions* will prove useful in future work. I have assumed the rules to be understood and accepted by both firms. Investment then helps deter entry by changing the initial conditions. Within this framework, there is scope for several extensions: several periods and firms could be introduced, and constraints arising from capital markets could be imposed. The question of whether one firm can change the rules in its own favour is more interesting, but much more difficult.

Notes

1   Compare the exchange between Moriarty and Holmes in *The Final Problem*: 'All that I have to say has already crossed your mind', said he. 'Then possibly my answer has crossed yours', I replied.

References

Dixit, A. (1979): "A Model of Duopoly Suggesting a Theory of Entry Barriers." *Bell Journal of Economics*, 10(1), Spring, 20–32.

Needham, D. (1978): *The Economics of Industrial Structure, Conduct and Performance*. London: Holt, Rinehart and Winston.

Salop, S. (1978): "A Note on Self-enforcing Threats and Entry Deterrence". University of Pennsylvania, Discussion Paper No. 14.

——(1979): "Strategic Entry Deterrence." *American Economic Review*, Papers and Proceedings.

Schelling, T. C. (1960): *The Strategy of Conflict*. Cambridge, Mass.: Harvard University Press.

Scherer, F. M. (1970): *Industrial Market Structure and Economic Performance*. Chicago: Rand-McNally.

Spence, M. (1977): "Entry, Investment and Oligopolistic Pricing." *Bell Journal of Economics*, 8(2), Autumn, 534–44.

——(1979): "Investment, Strategy and Growth in a New Market." *Bell Journal of Economics*, 10(1), Spring, 1–19.

Wenders, T. (1971): "Collusion and Entry." *Journal of Political Economy*, 79(6), November–December, 1258–77.

CHAPTER THIRTEEN

Contracts as a Barrier to Entry

PHILIPPE AGHION AND PATRICK BOLTON

Source: *American Economic Review*, 1984, 77, 338–401.

It is shown that an incumbent seller who faces a threat of entry into his or her market will sign long-term contracts that prevent the entry of some lower-cost producers even though they do not preclude entry completely. Moreover, when a seller possesses superior information about the likelihood of entry, it is shown that the length of the contract may act as a signal of the true probability of entry.

Most of the literature on entry prevention deals with the case of two duopolists (the established firm and the potential entrant) who compete with each other to share a market, where one of the duopolists (the incumbent) has a first-move advantage.[1] This basic paradigm has been studied under various assumptions: about the strategy space of the players; the information structure of the game; and the time horizon. Recently, the model has been enlarged to allow for several entrants, several incumbents, several markets, and third parties.[2]

We propose here to extend the entry-prevention model in one other direction, which to our knowledge has not yet been formalized; namely, we consider whether optimal contracts between buyers and sellers deter entry and whether they are suboptimal from a welfare point of view. It has been pointed out by many economists that contracts between buyers and sellers in intermediate-good industries may have significant entry-prevention effects and that such contracts may be bad from a welfare point of view.[3]

On the other hand, it is a widespread opinion among antitrust practitioners that contracts between buyers and sellers are socially efficient.[4] There have been a number of antitrust cases involving exclusive dealing contracts and often the decision reached by the judge has lead to considerable controversy. One famous case, *United States v. United Shoe Machinery Corporation* (1922), illustrates quite clearly the nature of the debate: the

United Shoe Machinery Corporation controlled 85 percent of the shoe-machinery market and had developed a complex leasing system of its machines to shoe manufacturers, a leasing system against which, it was thought, other machinery manufacturers would have difficulty competing. The judge ruled that these leasing contracts were in violation of the Sherman Act; his decision has been repeatedly criticized by leading antitrust experts (see Richard Posner, 1976, and Robert Bork, 1978). The main argument against the decision has been expressed by Posner: "The point I particularly want to emphasize is that the customers of United would be unlikely to participate in a campaign to strengthen United's monopoly position without insisting on being compensated for the loss of alternative and less costly (because competitive) sources of supply" (p. 203). Exactly the same point is made by Bork (p. 140), who concludes that when we find exclusive dealing contracts in practice, then these contracts could not have been signed for entry-deterrence reasons.

Both Posner and Bork are right in pointing out that the buyer is better off when there is entry and that he (she) will tend to reject exclusive dealing contracts that reduce the likelihood of entry unless the seller compensates him (her) by offering an advantageous deal. Nevertheless, we show that contracts between buyers and sellers will be signed for entry-prevention purposes.

When the buyer and the seller sign a contract, they have a monopoly power over the entrant. They can jointly determine what fee the entrant must pay in order to be able to trade with the buyer; that is to say, if the buyer signs an exclusive contract with the seller and then trades with the entrant, he must pay damages to the seller. Thus he will only trade with the entrant if the latter charges a price which is lower than the seller's price minus the damages he pays to the seller. These damages, which are determined in the original contract (liquidated damages), act as an entry fee the entrant must pay to the seller. We show that the buyer and the seller set this entry fee in the same way that a monopoly would set its price, when it cannot observe the willingness to pay of its customers. Thus, the main reason for signing exclusive contracts, in our model, is to extract some of the surplus an entrant would get if he entered the seller's market.

These contracts introduce a social cost, for they sometimes block the entry of firms that may be more efficient than the incumbent seller. Entry is blocked because the contract imposes an entry cost on potential competitors. This cost takes two different forms: an entrant must either wait until contracts expire, or induce the customers to break their contract with the incumbent by paying their liquidated damages.

The waiting cost is larger, other things being equal, the longer the contract. We are thus led to study the question of the optimal length of the contract. It is a well-known principle in economics that if agents engage in mutually advantageous trade, it is in their best interest to sign the longest possible contract. A long-term contract can always replicate what a sequence of short-term contracts achieves.

This principle, however, sharply contrasts empirical evidence: In practice most contracts are of an explicit finite duration. Many economists have been puzzled by this obvious discrepancy between the theory and empirical evidence, and several authors have attempted to provide an explanation for why contracts are of a finite duration; most notably Oliver Williamson (1975, 1979) and Milton Harris and Bengt Holmström (1983).

We argue here that looking only at the length of a contract is misleading. What is important is to what extent a contract of a given length locks the parties into a relationship. Thus we are led to make the distinction between the *nominal length* of the contract (the length that is specified in the contract) and the *effective length* of the contract (the actual length that the parties expect the relationship to last at the time of signing). Liquidated damages constitute an implicit measure of the effective length of the contract.

The paper is organized as follows: section 1 looks at optimal contracts between a single buyer and the incumbent seller, when both parties have the same information about the likelihood of entry. Section 2 analyzes optimal contracts when there is asymmetric information about the probability of entry. Section 3 deals with optimal contracts when there are several buyers. Finally, section 4 offers some concluding comments.

1. Optimal Contracts Between One Buyer and the Incumbent Seller

We consider a two-period model, where a single producer supplies one unit to a buyer. The latter has a reservation price, $P = 1$, and buys at most one unit. The seller faces a threat of entry, which is modeled as follows: At the time of contracting the seller's unit cost is $c = \frac{1}{2}$, while the entrant's cost of producing the same homogeneous good is not known. For simplicity we assume that the entrant's cost, c_e, is uniformly distributed in [0, 1].[5] Furthermore, if entry occurs and no contract has been signed between the incumbent and the buyer, both suppliers compete in prices, so that the Bertrand equilibrium price is given by $P = \max\{\frac{1}{2}, c_e\}$. When there is no entry, the potential entrant makes zero profits. Thus entry will only occur if $c_e \leq \frac{1}{2}$ and the probability of entry is given by

$$\phi = Pr(c_e \leq \tfrac{1}{2}) = \tfrac{1}{2} \tag{1}$$

We attempt here to model in the simplest way the view of the world where there are many investors at each period of time who try to invest their funds in the markets where they hope to get the highest returns. The distribution of profits across markets, however, changes stochastically over time. Therefore entry into a given market may also be stochastic. In this story it is implicitly assumed that investors do not have an unlimited access to funds and/or that there are diminishing returns to managing more investment projects. If neither of these assumptions hold, then investment will take place until the marginal return on the last investment project is equal to the interest rate. Many good reasons have been given for why investors only have a limited access to funds (see for example, Joseph Stiglitz and Andrew Weiss, 1981, or Williamson, 1971).

The timing of the game is as follows: At date 1 the incumbent seller and the buyer negotiate a contract, then entry either takes place or does not. Finally at date 2, there is production and trade.[6] We assume that the entrant's cost, c_e, is *not observable* but the parties to the contract know the distribution function of c_e. Therefore, contracts contingent on c_e cannot be written.[7]

If no contract is signed at date 1, the buyer's expected payoff is given by

$$(1 - \phi) \cdot 0 + \phi \cdot \tfrac{1}{2} = \tfrac{1}{2} \cdot \tfrac{1}{2} = \tfrac{1}{4} \tag{2}$$

That is, with probability $(1 - \phi)$ there is no entry and the seller sets the price equal to one. Hence, the buyer gets no surplus. With probability ϕ, entry occurs and Bertrand competition drives the price down to the incumbent's unit cost $c = \tfrac{1}{2}$. Now, Posner's point simply was that any contract that is acceptable to the buyer must give him an expected surplus of at least $\tfrac{1}{4}$ (assuming that the buyer is risk neutral). We shall show that even though the seller faces this constraint, there are gains to signing long-term contracts and in preventing entry.

The buyer and the incumbent seller could conceivably sign very complicated contracts even in this simple setting. For example, the price specified in the contract may be contingent on the event of entry or even contingent on the entrant's offer.[8] We shall, however, restrict ourselves to simple contracts of the form $c = \{P, P_0\}$ and show that there is no loss of generality in considering only this type of contract. Here P is the price of the good when the buyer trades with the incumbent and P_0 is the price the buyer must pay if he does not trade with the incumbent. In other words, P_0 represents *liquidated damages*.

When a contract $c = \{P, P_0\}$ is signed, the buyer gets a surplus of $1 - P$ if there is no entry. Furthermore, if there is entry, he will only switch to the entrant if the latter offers a surplus of at least $1 - P$. We shall assume that when the buyer is indifferent between switching and not switching, he trades with the entrant. Thus in the post-entry equilibrium, the buyer also gets a surplus of $1 - P$. Then a contract $c = \{P, P_0\}$ is acceptable to the buyer only if

$$1 - P \geq \tfrac{1}{4} \tag{3}$$

Next, an entrant can only attract the buyer if he sets a price $\tilde{P}$, such that

$$\tilde{P} \leq P - P_0 \tag{4}$$

(in equilibrium the entrant sets, $\tilde{P} = P - P_0$). And entry only occurs if the entrant makes positive profits:

$$\tilde{P} - c_e \geq 0 \tag{5}$$

Thus, when a contract $c = \{P, P_0\}$ is signed the probability of entry becomes

$$\phi' = \max\{0; P - P_0\} \tag{6}$$

The incumbent now faces the following program:

$$\max_{P, P_0} \phi' \cdot P_0 + (1 - \phi')(P - c) \tag{7}$$

subject to

$$1 - P \geq \tfrac{1}{4}$$

It is straightforward to verify that the optimal contract is then given by $c = \{\tfrac{3}{4}; \tfrac{1}{2}\}$.

There are several conclusions to be drawn. First, the incumbent's expected payoff of signing the contract $c = \{\tfrac{3}{4}, \tfrac{1}{2}\}$ is given by $\pi = \tfrac{1}{16} + \tfrac{1}{4}$. If he had not signed a contract, or if he had signed a contract that completely blocks entry, his expected payoff would be $\tfrac{1}{4}$. Hence he is strictly better off signing this contract and the buyer is not worse off.

Second, when $c = \{\tfrac{3}{4}, \tfrac{1}{2}\}$ is signed, the probability of entry is $\phi' = \tfrac{3}{4} - \tfrac{1}{2} = \tfrac{1}{4}$. Thus the optimal contract prevents entry to some extent but does not preclude entry completely. The contract $c = \{P, P_0\}$ changes the entry game in a subtle way. On the one hand, it sets a large entry fee, P_0, to the entrant. This reduces the likelihood of entry. But $P_0 = \tfrac{1}{2}$, does not completely eliminate entry, since the contract commits the incumbent to set a price $P = \tfrac{3}{4}$. Thus all entrants with costs $c_e \leq \tfrac{1}{4}$ will find it profitable to enter. Furthermore, even if the incumbent had the opportunity of lowering the price P below $\tfrac{3}{4}$ in the post-entry game, he would not want to do this. *The incumbent is strictly better off when the buyer switches to the entrant* in the post-entry game, for then he gets a surplus of $\tfrac{1}{2}$ compared with a maximum surplus of $P - c = \tfrac{1}{4}$, if he retained the buyer.

By signing a contract, the incumbent and the buyer form a coalition which acts like a nondiscriminating monopolist with respect to the entrant. The coalition sets P_0 like a monopolist sets its price when it cannot discriminate between buyers with different willingness to pay.[9] If c_e were observable, the contract could specify P_0 as a function of c_e and the coalition would be able to extract all of the entrant's surplus ($P_0 = \tfrac{1}{2} - c_e$).

The idea that the incumbent and the buyer can get together and extract some of the entrant's rent is very general. It does not depend, for instance, on the assumption that the seller sets the contract. Peter Diamond and Eric Maskin (1979) have obtained a similar result in the context of a model of search with breach of contract, where neither the buyer nor the seller has the power of making take-it-or-leave-it offers. Rather, Diamond and Maskin assume that the outcome of the bargaining game between a buyer and a seller is given by the Nash-bargaining solution.

Given that the incumbent and the buyer can only act as nondiscriminating monopolists, with respect to potential entrants, the optimal contract introduces a *social cost*, for it sometimes blocks the entry of a firm with a lower cost of production than the incumbent. When an optimal contract is signed, entrants with costs $c_e \in [\tfrac{1}{4}; \tfrac{1}{2}]$ do not enter.

To close this section we explain why the buyer and the seller can restrict themselves to simple contracts, $c = \{P, P_0\}$. The buyer and the seller can form a coalition whose value is $\tfrac{1}{2}$ when they do not allow entry into the market (the buyer's reservation price is 1 and the incumbent's cost is $c = \tfrac{1}{2}$). They can raise their payoff by allowing entry and making the entrant pay a fee, which in general will be a function of the entrant's cost, c_e. But the entrant's cost is private information so that the coalition faces a revelation of information problem. Now, a direct mechanism would specify a transfer from the entrant to the coalition, which is a function of the entrant's cost report: $t(c_e)$. This function $t(c_e)$ must satisfy the incentive-compatibility (*IC*) constraints: for all $c_e \in [0, 1]$,

$$\pi(c_e) - t(c_e) \geq \pi(c_e) - t(\hat{c}_e) \quad \text{for all } \hat{c}_e \in [0,1] \tag{IC}$$

where $\pi(c_e)$ is the entrant's rent when his cost is c_e. The IC constraints imply that $t(c_e) = t$ for all $c_e \in [0,1]$. In other words, the entry fee is independent of the entrant's cost.

Next, the entrant's rent is given by the difference between the incumbent's cost and his cost, c_e (i.e., $\pi(c_e) = \frac{1}{2} - c_e$). The coalition chooses t to maximize:

$$\begin{aligned} t \cdot Pr(\pi(c_e) \geq t) &= t \cdot Pr(\tfrac{1}{2} - c_e \geq t) \\ &= t(\tfrac{1}{2} - t) \end{aligned}$$

Then the optimal transfer is $t^* = \frac{1}{4}$ and the expected surplus raised is $\frac{1}{16}$. Notice that the optimal contract $c = \{P = \frac{3}{4}; P_0 = \frac{1}{2}\}$ also raises a surplus of $\frac{1}{16}$ from the entrant. We can now appeal to the revelation principle (Dasgupta, Peter Hammond, and Maskin, 1979), which says that no indirect mechanism does better than the best direct mechanism. That is, no other contract exists that raises a higher surplus than $\frac{1}{16}$. Therefore there is no loss in restricting the contracts to be of the form $c = \{P, P_0\}$.[10]

2. Asymmetric Information About the Probability of Entry

In section 1 it was assumed that both the incumbent and the buyer know the true probability of entry. This is not always realistic and one would expect that often the incumbent is better informed about the possibility of entry than the buyer. For example, if the incumbent is a high-tech firm and is the only one to have the know-how to produce a given intermediate good, then it is likely to be much better informed than its customers about the ability of a potential competitor in acquiring this know-how and thus produce the intermediate good. Hence, in this section we assume that the incumbent has some private information about the likelihood of entry.[11]

Asymmetric information has important consequences for the determination of the optimal nominal length of the contract. Under symmetric information, there is no incentive for writing a contract of finite nominal length. On the contrary, the incumbent always gains by locking the buyer into a contract in every period, for then an entrant cannot avoid paying the entry fee by entering at a time when the buyer is not bound by a contract to the incumbent. Under asymmetric information, on the other hand, the seller may wish to sign a contract of finite nominal length in order to signal to the buyer that entry is unlikely. Of course, the seller could also signal his information by offering a contract with lower liquidated damages, P_0. Such a contract would reduce the buyer's switching cost and could only profitably be offered by a seller facing a low probability of entry. We show however, that under certain conditions, signaling through the length of the contract is strictly better than signaling through liquidated damages.

To keep the analysis simple, we shall assume that the probability of entry is either "high" or "low." The incumbent knows the true probability but the buyer does not. Furthermore, as in section 1, the incumbent makes the contract offer. The situation described here is akin to an "informed Principal" problem (see Roger Myerson, 1983, and Maskin and Jean Tirole, 1985).

As in section 1, we shall assume that the entrant's costs are uniformly distributed on $[0,1]$. The incumbent's cost, on the other hand, is either $c = \frac{1}{2}$ or $c = k$, where $0 < k < \frac{1}{2}$. Then the probability of entry is low when $c = k$ and it is high when $c = \frac{1}{2}$, since when $c = k$, we have

$$\underline{\phi} \equiv Pr(c_e \leq k) = k < \frac{1}{2} \tag{8}$$

and when $c = \frac{1}{2}$, we have

$$\bar{\phi} \equiv Pr(c_e \leq \frac{1}{2}) = \frac{1}{2} \tag{9}$$

The buyer's prior beliefs about the incumbent's costs are given by $m = Pr(c = k)$.

Under asymmetric information, it is no longer true that the seller can restrict himself with no loss to simple contracts, $c = \{P, P_0\}$. In fact, we show in our earlier paper that the incumbent seller can achieve the symmetric information optimal outcome by offering contracts of the form $c = \{P, P^e, P_0\}$ where P_0 is defined as in the previous section, P is the price the buyer pays if he trades with the incumbent and entry did not occur and P^e is the price the buyer pays if he trades with the incumbent and entry took place. Alternatively, when the incumbent only offers contracts of the form $c = \{P, P_0\}$, he can never attain the symmetric information optimal outcome. Thus simple contracts $c = \{P, P_0\}$ are suboptimal under asymmetric information. Thus, if the more general contracts $c = \{P, P^e, P_0\}$ are feasible asymmetric information puts no restrictions on the nominal length of the contract.

We give the following argument for why such contracts may not be feasible: First, "entry" may be a very complicated event to describe, when a firm can enter with a non-homogeneous good. The incumbent must then decide what commodities qualify as "entrants" and, even if a list of such commodities can be defined, an entrant would have an incentive to produce a good which is not on that list whenever $P > P^e$. Alternatively, if $P^e > P$, there would be an incentive for the incumbent to claim that entry has occurred whenever there is an ambiguity about the event of entry. In short, the event of entry may be difficult to observe, let alone to verify.

Second, when $P > P^e$, the buyer could bribe someone to "enter" only to force the incumbent to lower his price. Vice versa, when $P < P^e$, the incumbent may want to bribe someone to enter.

When only simple contracts $c = \{P, P_0\}$ are feasible, asymmetric information can put restrictions on both the liquidated damages P_0, and the length of the contract. In the present model, contract length is somewhat artificially defined since production and trade take place only once. It should however be clear from what follows that the conclusions reached here carry over to a model with N periods of production and trade $(N \geq 2)$ where entry can take place in any of these N periods.

Here we compare the asymmetric information-contracting solution with the no-contracting solution and show that when the difference between high and low costs is sufficiently large, the low-cost incumbent is better off not signing a contract and leaving options open until the entry decision is taken by the potential competitor. In a model with N periods, this result would be modified and the low-cost incumbent would be better off signing a *shorter* contract than the high-cost incumbent.

When the seller makes a contract offer $c = \{P, P_0\}$, he conveys information about his type, so that the buyer's beliefs change.

Let the buyer's posterior beliefs be

$$\beta(c) = Pr(\phi = \bar{\phi}/c) \tag{10}$$

The buyer will only accept the contract if

$$1 - P \geq \beta(c)\bar{\phi}/2 + (1 - \beta(c))\underline{\phi}(1 - k) \tag{11}$$

From (8) and (9) we can rewrite (11) as

$$1 - P \geq (\beta(c)/4) + (1 - \beta(c))k(1 - k) \tag{12}$$

When the incumbent signs a contract $c = \{P, P_0\}$, the probability of entry is given by

$$Pr(c_e \leq P - P_0) = P - P_0 \tag{13}$$

Thus, the incumbent's payoff when he is respectively of type $\bar{\phi}$ or $\underline{\phi}$ is given by

$$\begin{aligned} V(c, \bar{\phi}) &= (P - P_0)(P_0 - P + \tfrac{1}{2}) + P - \tfrac{1}{2} \\ V(c, \underline{\phi}) &= (P - P_0)(P_0 - P + k) + P - k \end{aligned} \tag{14}$$

for $P > P_0$, (otherwise $V(c, \bar{\phi}) = P - \tfrac{1}{2}$ and $V(c, \underline{\phi}) = P - k$). It is straightforward to verify that the Spence–Mirrlees condition is satisfied:

$$d/dk[-\partial V/\partial P/\partial V/\partial P_0] < 0 \tag{15}.$$

In other words, it is more costly for an incumbent facing a higher probability of entry to lower P_0 than it is for an incumbent facing a lower probability of entry. Given condition (12) we can draw Figure 1 where $\bar{c}^* = \{P = \tfrac{3}{4}; P_0 = \tfrac{1}{2}\}$ is the optimal symmetric information contract when $\phi = \phi$. Notice that this contract will always be accepted by the buyer since the right-hand side in (12) is increasing in β and when $\beta = 1$ (12) becomes

$$1 - P \geq \tfrac{1}{4} \tag{16}$$

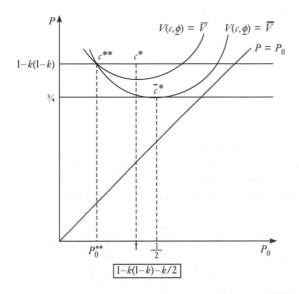

Figure 1

In addition, the contract $\bar{c}^*$ is the best contract for the high-cost incumbent, among the class of contracts which generate beliefs $\beta(c) = 1$. It is common in signaling models to obtain a plethora of equilibria and our model is no exception to this rule. Any pair of contracts $(c, \bar{c}^*)$ where c is such that $P = 1 - k(1 - k)$ and $0 \leq P_0 \leq P_0^*$ (see Figure 1) constitutes a separating equilibrium. Furthermore, any point in the shaded area in the diagram may be a pooling or semiseparating equilibrium of the signaling game. Following David Kreps (1984), however, we can refine the Bayesian equilibrium concept by using dominance and stability arguments and thus single out the best separating equilibrium $(c^{**}, \bar{c}^*)$ where c^{**} is defined as $c^{**} = \{P = 1 - k(1 - k); P_0 = P_0^*\}$. How is P_0^* determined? It is the solution to the equation

$$V(c^{**}, \bar{\phi}) = V(\bar{c}^*, \bar{\phi})$$

which can be rewritten as

$$(P - P_0)(P_0 - P + \tfrac{1}{2}) + P - \tfrac{1}{2} = \tfrac{1}{16} + \tfrac{1}{4} \tag{17}$$

where $P = 1 - k(1 - k)$.

Now P_0^* is the smaller root of this quadratic equation (see Figure 1) and is given by

$$P_0^* = ((2P - \tfrac{1}{2}) - \sqrt{4P - 3})/2 \tag{18}$$

How does the optimal contract for the low-cost incumbent under asymmetric information compare with the optimal symmetric information contract given by $\underline{c}^* = \{P = 1 - k(1 - k); P_0 = (2P - k)/2\}$?

The optimal contract under asymmetric information, c^{**} specifies the same price P as c^*, but it specifies lower liquidated damages: $P_0^* < P_0$. It is straightforward to compute that $P_0^* < P_0$ reduces to

$$1 + 4k^2 > 5k - \tfrac{1}{2} \tag{19}$$

And for all $0 < k < \tfrac{1}{2}$ this inequality is verified.

Intuitively, the incumbent with low costs signals his type by offering to reduce liquidated damages below the first-best level. His information is credibly transmitted since it is too costly for the high-cost incumbent to reduce P_0 to that level and thereby induce too much entry.

We now show that for small k, the low-cost incumbent is better off not signing a contract than signing c^{**}. If the low-cost seller does not sign a contract, his expected profits are given by

$$(1 - \underline{\phi})(1 - k) = (1 - k)^2 \tag{20}$$

If he signs c^{**} he gets

$$V(c^{**}, \underline{\phi}) = (P - P_0^*)(k - (P - P_0^*)) + P - k \tag{21}$$

where

$$P = 1 - k(1 - k)$$

and

$$P - P_0^* = \tfrac{1}{4} + \tfrac{1}{2}\sqrt{4(1 - k(1 - k)) - 3}$$

It remains to show that for small k, we have

$$[\tfrac{1}{4} + \tfrac{1}{2}\sqrt{4(1 - k(1 - k)) - 3}\,]k$$
$$- [\tfrac{1}{4} + \tfrac{1}{2}\sqrt{4(1 - k(1 - k)) - 3}\,]^2 + 1 - k(1 - k) - k \le (1 - k)^2 \tag{22}$$

And (22) reduces to

$$k \le \tfrac{1}{4} + \tfrac{1}{2}\sqrt{4(1 - k(1 - k)) - 3} \tag{23}$$

which is clearly verified for small k. Also, for k close to $\frac{1}{2}$, (23) is not satisfied. We summarize the above discussion in the following proposition:

PROPOSITION 1: *Under asymmetric information about the probability of entry (or equivalently about the incumbent's costs), the optimal contracting solution is such that*

(a) *the high-cost incumbent signs the optimal symmetric information contract* $\bar{c}^* = \{P = \frac{3}{4}; P_0 = \frac{1}{2}\}$.

(b) *the low-cost incumbent either signs the second-best contract*

$$c^{**} = \left\{ P = 1 - k(1-k); P_0^* = P - \frac{1}{4} - \frac{1}{2}\sqrt{4P-3} \right\}$$

(when k is close to $\frac{1}{2}$) or does not sign a long-term contract at all (when k is close to zero).

(c) c^{**} *is characterized by the property that liquidated damages (P_0^*) are lower than in the optimal symmetric information contract,*

$$\underline{c}^* = \{P = 1 - k(1-k); P_0 = P - (k/2)\}$$

One can explain Proposition 1(b) as follows. As k becomes smaller the price $P = 1 - k(1-k)$ rises, which makes it more attractive for the high-cost firm to mimic the low-cost firm's behavior. In order to discourage the high-cost firm from cheating, the low-cost firm must therefore increase the gap $P - P_0 = [\frac{1}{4} + \frac{1}{2}(4(1-k(1-k))-3)^{1/2}]$. But this is equivalent to raising the probability of entry after a contract has been signed (see equation (13)). There comes a point where $\phi' = P - P_0 \geq \underline{\phi} = k$; that is, by raising $P - P_0$, the low-cost firm raises the *ex post probability of entry* (ϕ') above the *ex ante probability of entry* $(\underline{\phi})$ (see (23)). This essentially involves subsidizing some inefficient entrants to enter the market. The incumbent then gets a negative transfer from the entrant. He can do strictly better by not offering any transfer (i.e., by not signing a contract at all).

We have thus established that the *nominal* length of the contract may serve as a signal of the probability of entry. This result confirms the following basic intuition:

The buyer reasons as follows when he is offered a contract: "If the incumbent wants to sign a contract of a long duration he must be worried about entry, so that I infer from this that the probability of entry is high and I will only accept to sign this contract if he charges a low price. If, on the other hand, the incumbent offers a short-term contract, he reveals that he is not much preoccupied about entry, so that I will be willing to accept a higher price."

The result obtained in Proposition 1(c) implies that the social cost is smaller in the asymmetric information case than in the symmetric information case. That is, liquidated damages (P_0*) are smaller in c^{**} than in $\underline{c}*$; therefore fewer efficient firms will be kept out of the market. It is worth emphasizing this point, since one usually thinks of asymmetric information as a constraint that prevents agents from reaching a socially efficient outcome (a first-best optimum). This is a general theme in Agency theory (see Oliver Hart and Holmström, 1985). Here, on the contrary, asymmetric information about the incumbent's costs may actually force agents to choose the socially efficient outcome (whenever the condition in (23) is verified). *The informational asymmetry constrains the monopoly power of the incumbent and the buyer with respect to the entrant.* There is another interpretation of this result. Remember that the incumbent and the buyer are constrained in the first place by the informational asymmetry about the entrant's costs. Then, the conclusion reached here is that if there exists another informational asymmetry between the buyer and the incumbent (about the latter's cost) *the two informational constraints may cancel each other out.*

This is an important observation for agency theory. Informational constraints do not necessarily add up; they may cancel out.

3. Optimal Contracts with Several Buyers

One may wonder to what extent the results obtained in sections 1 and 2 depend on the assumption that there is only one incumbent seller and one buyer? This section attempts to give a partial answer to this question. We compare in turn the situation where there is one buyer but several incumbent sellers, and the situation where there is one incumbent seller but several buyers. All the results established in section 1 are valid in each case. Moreover, new interesting features are introduced in the latter situation, where a single incumbent negotiates with several buyers.

Consider first the situation where there are two or more identical sellers but only one buyer. Then, Bertrand competition essentially gives all the bargaining power to the buyer; he gets all of the surplus but the form of the optimal contract does not change. The buyer sets P_0 in the same way as the seller does, when the seller makes the contract offer.

The interesting situation is when there are several buyers and one seller. In this case, the entrant's profits depend on how many customers he can serve in the post-entry game. What is crucial, however, is how the size of the entrant's potential market affects the probability of entry. If the probability of entry is independent of the size of the market, then the case of several buyers reduces to the case of one buyer. In general, however, the size of the market will affect the probability of entry. For example, if the entrant must pay a fixed cost of entry, then his average cost is decreasing in the number of customers served and the probability of entry is increasing in the number of customers.

In this latter case, when one buyer signs a long-term contract with the incumbent, he imposes a negative externality on all other buyers. By locking himself into a long-run relation with the seller, he reduces the size of the entrant's potential market so that, *ceteris paribus*, the probability of entry will be smaller. As a result, the other buyers will have to accept higher prices. We show that the incumbent can exploit this negative externality to extract more (possibly all) surplus out of each buyer. In some cases, the seller can impose the monopoly price ($P = 1$) on each buyer, even though the *ex ante* probability of entry is arbitrarily close to one (*ex ante* refers to the no-contract situation). In addition, the seller can extract part of the entrant's surplus by choosing damages (P_0) appropriately, so that we get the paradoxical result that a seller facing a threat of entry may be better off than a natural monopoly. To reach this conclusion, we must push the logic of the game to its limits. This result is thus interesting mainly for illustrative purposes.

We will only consider the case of two buyers and one seller.[12] Both buyers are identical and have a reservation price $P = 1$. The incumbent is as described in section 1. The entrant has the same unit costs as in section 1; in addition, he may face a fixed cost of entry, $F \geq 0$. We shall first consider the problem where F is strictly positive. Then, in the absence of any contract, the entrant's profit is given by

$$\pi_e = 2(\tfrac{1}{2} - c_e) - F \tag{24}$$

Thus, the *ex ante* probability of entry is given by

$$\phi = Pr(\pi_e \geq 0) = (1 - F)/2 \tag{25}$$

Suppose now that one of the buyers signs a contract with the incumbent where $P_0 = +\infty$. Then in the post-entry game, this buyer will never switch to the entrant. The latter can now hope to get at most:

$$\hat{\pi}_e = \tfrac{1}{2} - c_e - F \tag{26}$$

The other buyer therefore faces a lower likelihood of entry given by

$$\hat{\phi} = Pr(\hat{\pi}_e \geq 0) = (1 - 2F)/2 \tag{27}$$

More generally, whenever one buyer signs a contract with the incumbent of the form $c = \{P, P_0\}$, the other buyer faces a new probability of entry given by

$$\hat{\phi} = \max\left\{\frac{P - P_0 + \tfrac{1}{2} - F}{2}; \frac{1 - 2F}{2}\right\} \tag{28}$$

We will analyze the negotiation game where the incumbent makes simultaneous contract offers to both buyers. The case where the incumbent makes sequential offers is considered in our earlier paper. There we establish that the timin of offers does not matter. The same outcome is obtained in the simultaneous offers case as in the sequential offers case.

The incumbent can without loss restrict the set of contracts to be of the form $c = \{P, P_0, P^r, P_0^r\}$, where

$P =$ the price a buyer must pay if he trades with the incumbent and the other buyer has signed a long-term contract;

$P_0 =$ the damages a buyer must pay if he switches to the entrant and the other buyer has signed a contract with the incumbent;

$P^r =$ the price a buyer must pay if he trades with the incumbent and the other buyer did not sign a contract;

$P_0^r =$ the damages a buyer must pay if he trades with the entrant and the other buyer did not sign a contract with the incumbent.

It is implicitly assumed here that all contracts are publicly observable. This is a strong assumption. In practice, all contracts are not observable. As a result, one can never be certain when a contract is observed, whether there does not exist a hidden contract which cancels the effects of the observed contract. In our model, however, the incumbent has an incentive to publicize all of his contracts, as will become clear below. Thus, hidden contracts are not a problem.

When the seller makes a contract offer $c = \{P, P_0, P^r, P_0^r\}$ to each buyer, B_1 and B_2, the latter play a noncooperative game where they have two pure strategies: "accept" and "reject." The payoff matrix of this game is represented in Table 1.

Table 1 – B_1

	Accept		Reject	
	$1 - P$		$1 - P^r$	
Accept		$1 - P$		$\hat{\phi}/2$
	$\hat{\phi}/2$		$\phi/2$	
Reject		$1 - P^r$		$\phi/2$

By choosing P^r and P_0^r appropriately, the incumbent can ensure that $\hat{\phi} = (1 - 2F)/2$. Essentially, this involves choosing P_0^r large enough so that the buyer who accepted a contract will not switch to the entrant. Now, accept is a (weakly) dominant strategy when

$$1 - P \geq \hat{\phi}/2 = (1 - 2F)/4 \qquad (29)$$

$$1 - P^r > \phi/2 \qquad (30)$$

When the incumbent offers a contract to both buyers such that (29) and (30) are satisfied (and such that $\hat{\phi} = (1 - 2F)/2$), the unique Nash equilibrium is for both buyers to accept the contract offer. As a result, both buyers receive a strictly lower payoff in equilibrium than if they both rejected the contract, since $\hat{\phi} < \phi$.

Thus when there are several buyers contracting with the incumbent, there is another reason why rational buyers are willing to perpetuate the monopoly position of the seller. As Steven Salop puts it, contracts "...are valued by each buyer individually even while they create an external cost to all other buyers" (1986, p. 273). He calls this situation a *"free-rider effect in reverse"* (emphasis added).

In addition to this effect, the seller can set P_0 appropriately so as to extract the maximum expected surplus from the entrant. To summarize, in this simple model with simultaneous offers, the set of optimal contracts is given by

$$c^* = \left\{ P = 1 - \frac{(1 - 2F)}{4}; \; P_0 = P - \frac{F + 1}{4}; \; P^r < 1 - \frac{\phi}{2}; \; P_0^r > P^r + \tfrac{1}{2} + F \right\} \qquad (31)$$

And at the optimum the incumbent's expected payoff is given by

$$\pi = \left(2(P - P_0) - F\right)\left(2\left(P_0 - P + \tfrac{1}{2}\right)\right) + 2\left(P - \tfrac{1}{2}\right)$$

$$= \frac{(1 - F)^2}{2} + 1 - \frac{(1 - 2F)}{2} \tag{32}$$

Suppose now that $F \geq \tfrac{1}{2}$, then $\hat{\phi} = 0$ and the incumbent is able to impose the monopoly price $(P = 1)$ on the buyer. His expected payoff at the optimum is then given by

$$\pi = \left((1 - F)^2/2\right) + 1 \tag{33}$$

Thus the incumbent does strictly better than a natural monopoly, since he can also extract some of the potential entrant's surplus. On the other hand, when $F = 0$, we have $\hat{\phi} = \phi = \tfrac{1}{2}$, and the "free-rider effect in reverse" disappears, so that the two–buyers case reduces to a one-buyer case, where the customer purchases two units rather than one. In other words, when the probability of entry is independent of the size of the market, competition among buyers does not matter.

Thus the principles established in the one-buyer–one-seller case remain valid when we allow for either more than one buyer or more than one seller. The analysis is somewhat incomplete since we did not deal with the several-buyers–several-sellers case. The results obtained in section 1 carry through to this more general model (see Diamond and Maskin 1979). As far as the results in this section are concerned, it is likely that sellers will not be able to exploit to the same extent the free-rider effect in reverse.

4. Conclusion

The principles formalized in this paper are very general. What is basically required for contracts to constitute a barrier to entry is that post-entry profits for the incumbent in the absence of any contract be lower than pre-entry profits (and vice versa for consumers). In addition, it is necessary that the incumbent cannot discriminate between entrants of various levels of efficiency. This is a rather mild assumption if one interprets the entrant's cost as an opportunity cost of entry as in our earlier paper. Throughout the paper we interpreted P_0 to be "liquidated damages," but P_0 may also represent down payments, deposits, collateral, future discounts, and benefits, etc. Thus, the analysis developed here has potentially a wide range of applicability.

Casual empiricism suggests that "endogenous switching costs" for customers are a widespread phenomenon. In the housing market, for example, advance deposits in rental contracts can be interpreted as serving this function (there are, of course, also moral hazard reasons for requiring deposits). Paul Klemperer (1986) provides a number of examples of endogenous switching costs, like frequently flyer programs, trading stamps, deferred rebates by shipping firms, etc. Also, fixed fees in franchise contracts may be used to extract some rent from a potential competitor. The contract between Automatic Radio Manufacturing Co. and Hazeltine Research (see *Automatic Radio Manufacturing Co. v. Hazeltine Research Inc.*, 1950) is a good example. Automatic Radio had to pay a fixed fee irrespective of whether it exploited the patents licensed by Hazeltine. Any new licensor therefore faced an entry barrier equal to the amount of this fee. Another striking example is the case of Bell Laboratories when it invented the transistor. There were other research institutes competing with Bell Laboratories. In order to preempt them, Bell Labs offered to publicize the technology to any potential licensee, in exchange for a fixed fee of $25,000. This fee served the same function as P_0, in the contract above. Moreover Bell Lab's strategy was to become the industry standard. Thus any individual licensee would have to take into account the additional switching cost of not being standardized (see E. Braun and S. Macdonald, 1978). Our analysis provides a rationale for the practices described here and explains why rational customers cooperate with firms in these anticompetitive practices. Unfortunately, the variety and potential complexity of these contractual clauses makes the task for antitrust authorities very difficult.

A rapidly growing literature on exogenous switching costs is related to our present study (see Klemperer for a recent thorough exposition). The welfare conclusions obtained in this research are radically different from ours. For example, in Klemperer, entry may be socially inefficient because consumers dissipate the gains from entry (in terms of lower prices and higher output) by incurring the socially wasteful switching costs. In our model, the social cost comes from insufficient entry; when entry occurs it is always welfare improving. Salop also studies the effect of various clauses, such as the "meeting the competition clause" or the "clause of the most favored nation" on competition. His emphasis is more on cartel coordination than entry prevention. In our model a "meeting the competition clause" would preclude entry since the entrant could never undercut the incumbent. *We have shown, however, that it is optimal not to eliminate entry completely.* Therefore, such clauses will never be adopted for entry-deterrence purposes; they may however be useful to facilitate cartel coordination, as Salop shows, since they increase the cost of price cutting.

Our theory of contract length is a substantial departure from existing theories. Most explanations have emphasized the idea that contract length is determined as a tradeoff between recontracting costs and the costs associated with the incompleteness of the contract (see Williamson, 1975, 1985; Ronald Dye, 1985a; Jo Anna Gray, 1976). A notable exception is Harris and Holmström. In practice, uncertainty about the future and the cost of writing complete contracts are without doubt important elements in the determination of contract length. The difficulty from a theoretical perspective is however that uncertainty about the future and "transaction costs" are notoriously vague categories. If contracts are to be incomplete what contingencies should the parties leave out of the contract? This is a very difficult question which has only received partial answers (see Dye, 1985b, and Hart and Holmström 1985). Explanations of contract length based on contractual incompleteness crucially depend on how one answers this question (see Dye, 1985b). In this paper we have sidestepped the difficulty to provide a story based on asymmetric information. We believe that signaling aspects are important in the determination of contract length and view our explanation as complementary to the existing theories.

Recently, Benjamin Hermalin (1986) has developed another theory of contract length based on asymmetric information. He considers a competitive labor market where initially workers have private information about productivity but where in a later stage this information becomes public (for example, through output observations). He shows that by varying contract length, it is impossible for firms to *profitably* screen out low-productivity workers from high-productivity workers. Ideally, a firm wants to retain only high-productivity workers, but long-term contracts are most attractive to low-productivity workers. Thus, by screening out workers, the firm achieves the opposite of what it wants: it offers long contracts to low-productivity workers and short contracts to high-productivity workers. In equilibrium, either firms offer only short-term contracts, or they offer "trivial" long-term contracts that replicate the outcome achieved with short-term contracts. In our model, on the contrary, signaling (or screening) works. Moreover, when it is optimal for the low-cost incumbent to sign a short-term contract, there does not exist an alternative trivial long-term contract. One can view our explanation and Hermalin's as dual: in his model the high-productivity sellers do not want to be locked in a long-term contract; here it is the buyer who does not want to forego future opportunities.

Notes

1 See, for example, the seminal contributions by Michael Spence (1977) and Avinash Dixit (1979, 1980).

2 For a recent survey, see Drew Fudenberg and Jean Tirole (1986).

3 Spence (1977, p. 544), for example, briefly mentioned contracts as a method for impeding entry; see also Oliver Williamson (1979). Furthermore, there is a literature on barriers to entry and vertical integration that is relevant to our discussion, since most of the time what vertical integration achieves in this literature can also be done through an appropriate contract. (See Roger Blair and David Kaserman, 1983.)

4 This position has been forcefully defended by Robert Bork (1978), for example.

5 The choice of a uniform distribution is entirely for the sake of computational simplicity. In our 1985 paper, we show that the qualitative results obtained here are valid for any continuous density $f(x)$ with a support such that the lower bound is finite and that contains the interval $[0\frac{1}{2}]$.

6 When production takes place before entry, the analysis is slightly modified. When the buyer switches to the entrant, the incumbent must now incur a loss of $c = \frac{1}{2}$. Thus the Bertrand equilibrium in the post-entry game now is $P = c_e$, so that entry will be precluded (since the entrant always makes nonpositive profits). To avoid an outcome where *ex post* competition (after entry) drives out *ex ante* competition (see Partha Dasgupta and Stiglitz, 1984), we then need to assume that the entrant sometimes makes losses when he does not enter into the incumbent's market. In other words, the entrant sometimes has a negative opportunity cost (see our earlier paper).

7 In general, what matters is not the actual unit cost of the entrant but his opportunity cost of not entering. If one takes this interpretation, then nonobservability of the entrant's opportunity cost is a mild assumption.

8 One often observes contracts where a retailer provides a minimum price warranty of the form: "If the buyer is offered a lower price by another retailer for the same good, within t periods, he can then claim back the difference between the high and the low price." These are examples of contracts which are contingent on the entrant's offer. Of course, if such contracts are written then entry is precluded (since the entrant makes zero profits). See our discussion of these contracts in section 4.

9 An interesting feature of the optimal contract is that if the probability of entry ϕ increases, then the optimal price P_0 may decrease. For example if the incumbent's unit cost is k then $\phi = k$ and $P_0^* = 1 - k(1 - k) - k/2$. Thus $dP_0^*/dk < 0$ for $k < \frac{3}{4}$.

10   In the above discussion we have restricted ourselves to deterministic mechanisms. Since all agents are assumed to be risk neutral, there is no loss of generality in considering only deterministic mechanisms (see Maskin, 1981).
11   One can think of situations where the buyer is better informed about the probability of entry. Then we have a classic self-selection problem and all the results obtained in this section would also apply to this case.
12   We deal with the generalization to n buyers $(n \geq 2)$ in our earlier paper.

References

Aghion, Philippe and Bolton, Patrick (1985): "Entry-Prevention through Contracts with Customers," unpublished.

Automatic Radio Manufacturing Co. v. Hazeltine Research Inc., 339 U.S. 827, 834, 1950.

Blair, Roger D. and Kaserman, David L. (1983): *Law and Economics of Vertical Integration and Control*, New York: Academic Press.

Bork, Robert H. (1978): *The Antitrust Paradox*, New York: Basic Books.

Braun, E. and Macdonald, S. (1978): *Revolution in Miniature: The History and Impact of Semiconductor Electronics*, New York: Cambridge University Press.

Dasgupta, Partha and Stiglitz, Joseph (1984): "Sun Costs and Competition," mimeo., Princeton University.

——, Hammond, Peter and Maskin, Eric (1979): "The Implementation of Social Choice Rules: Some General Results on Incentive Compatability," *Review of Economic Studies*, 46, April, 185–206.

Diamond, Peter A. and Maskin, Eric (1979): "An Equilibrium Analysis of Search and Breach of Contract, I: Steady States," *Bell Journal of Economics*, 10, Spring, 282–316.

Dixit, Avinash (1979): "A Model of Duopoly Suggesting a Theory of Entry-Barriers," *Bell Journal of Economics*, 10, Spring, 20–32.

—— (1980): "The Role of Investment in Entry Deterrence," *Economic Journal*, 90, March, 95–106.

Dye, Ronald (1985a): "Costly Contract Contingencies," *International Economic Review*, 26, February, 233–50.

—— (1985b): "Optimal Length of Labor Contracts," *International Economic Review*, 26, February, 251–70.

Fudenberg, Drew and Tirole, Jean (1986): "Dynamic Models of Oligopoly," in J. Lesourne and H. Sonnenschein (eds), *Fundamentals of Pure and Applied Economics*, New York: Harwood Academic Press.

Gray, Jo Anna (1976): "Wage Indexation: A Macro-economic Approach," *Journal of Monetary Economics*, 2, April, 221–35.

Harris, Milton and Holmström, Bengt (1983): "On the Duration of Agreements," mimeo., IMSSS, Stanford University.

Hart, Oliver and Holmström, Bengt (1985): "The Theory of Contracts," in T. Bewley (ed.), *Advances in Economic Theory*, New York: Cambridge University Press.

Hermalin, Benjamin (1986): "Adverse Selection and Contract Length," mimeo., MIT.

Klemperer, Paul (1986): "Markets with Consumer Switching Costs," unpublished doctoral dissertation, Graduate School of Business, Stanford University.

Kreps, David M. (1984): "Signaling Games and Stable Equilibrium," mimeo., Stanford University.

Maskin, Eric (1981): "Randomization in Incentive Problems," mimeo.

—— and Tirole, Jean (1985): "Principals with Private Information, II: Dependent Values," lecture notes.

Myerson, Roger B. (1983): "Mechanism Design by an Informed Principal," *Econometrica*, 51, November, 1767–97.

Posner, Richard A. (1976): *Antitrust Law: An Economic Perspective*, Chicago: University of Chicago Press.;

Salop, Steven (1986): "Practices that (credibly) Facilitate Oligopoly Coordination," in J. Stiglitz and F. Mathewson (eds), *New Developments in the Analysis of Market Structure*, Cambridge: MIT Press.

Spence, A. Michael (1977): "Entry, Capacity, Investment and Oligopolistic Pricing," *Bell Journal of Economics*, 8, Autumn, 534–44.

Stiglitz, Joseph and Weiss, Andrew (1981): "Credit Rationing in Markets with Imperfect Information," *American Economic Review*, 71, June, 393–409.

United States v. United Shoe Machinery Corporation, 258 U.S. 451, 1922.

Williamson, Oliver E. (1971): "The Vertical Integration of Production: Market Failure Considerations," *American Economic Review*, 61, March, 112–23.

—— (1975): *Markets and Hierarchies: Analysis and Antitrust Implications*, New York: Free Press.

—— (1979): "Assessing Vertical Market Restrictions: Antitrust Ramifications of the Transaction-Cost Approach," *University of Pennsylvania Law Review*, 127, April, 953–93.

—— (1985): *The Economic Institutions of Capitalism*, New York: Free Press.

CHAPTER FOURTEEN

Free Entry and Social Inefficiency

N. Gregory Mankiw and Michael D. Whinston

Source: *Rand Journal of Economics*, 1986, 17, 48–58.

Previous articles have noted the possibility of socially inefficient levels of entry in markets in which firms must incur fixed set-up costs upon entry. This article identifies the fundamental and intuitive forces that lie behind these entry biases. If an entrant causes incumbent firms to reduce output, entry is more desirable to the entrant than it is to society. There is therefore a tendency toward excessive entry in homogeneous product markets. The roles of product diversity and the integer constraint on the number of firms are also examined.

1. Introduction

Economists typically presume that free entry is desirable for social efficiency. As several articles have shown, however, when firms must incur fixed set-up costs upon entry, the number of firms entering a market need not equal the socially desirable number. Spence (1976a) and Dixit and Stiglitz (1977), for example, demonstrate that in a monopolistically competitive market, free entry can result in *too little* entry relative to the social optimum. In more recent work von Weizsäcker (1980) and Perry (1984) point to a tendency for *excessive* entry in homogeneous product markets. Nevertheless, despite these findings, many economists continue to hold the presumption that free entry is desirable, in part, it seems, because the fundamental economic forces underlying these various entry biases remain somewhat mysterious.

Our goal is to provide a simple, yet general, exposition of the conditions under which the number of entrants in a free-entry equilibrium is excessive, insufficient, or optimal. Our analysis compares the number of firms that enter a market when there is free entry with the number that would be desired by a social planner who is unable to control the behavior of firms once they are in the market. That is, we consider the second-best problem of choosing the welfare-maximizing number of firms, while we take as given their noncompetitive behavior after entry.

We demonstrate that the crucial conditions for establishing the presence of an entry bias can be stated quite simply in terms of the outcome of the postentry game played by entrants. In contrast to previous work, we do not need to model this postentry game explicitly. This approach has two advantages. First, it uncovers the fundamental and intuitive reasons behind the presence of entry biases. Second, it provides a set of properties that can be readily checked for any particular application.

We focus extensively on the central roles played by two aspects of the postentry game in producing an entry bias: imperfect competition and what we call the "business-stealing effect." The business-stealing effect exists when the equilibrium strategic response of existing firms to new entry results in their having a lower volume of sales – that is, when a new entrant "steals business" from incumbent firms. Put differently, a business-stealing effect is present if the equilibrium output per firm declines as the number of firms grows. Intuitively, it would seem that most markets would be characterized by such an effect.[1] As we shall demonstrate, in the presence of imperfect competition (so that firms do not act as price-takers after entry), the business-stealing effect is a critical determinant of the direction of entry bias.

After formally specifying our model in section 2, we begin our analysis in section 3 by considering a homogeneous product market. Ignoring the integer constraint on the number of firms (as has been done in most of the previous literature), we demonstrate that if the postentry price exceeds marginal cost and if a business-stealing effect exists, then free entry leads to excessive entry from a social standpoint (Proposition 1). Intuitively, business stealing by a marginal entrant drives a wedge between the entrant's evaluation of the desirability of his entry and the planner's: the marginal entrant's contribution to social surplus is (except for second-order effects) equal to his profits *less* the social value of the output lost owing to the output restriction he engenders in other firms. The business-stealing effect therefore makes entry more attractive than is socially warranted.[2] We show by example that the resulting bias can, in fact, be dramatic: the equilibrium number of firms can exceed the socially optimal number by a very large margin.

We then consider the role of the integer constraint on the number of firms. In Proposition 2 we prove the fully rigorous result: Under the conditions described above, the free-entry number of firms can be less than the welfare-maximizing number, but not by more than one firm. This result relates to the common observation that a monopolist does not capture all of the social surplus generated by his product. It is interesting that even in oligopolistic (homogeneous product) markets, this consideration cannot bias entry by more than one firm. Of course, this finding does not imply that the welfare losses associated with such occurrences are unimportant; as we show by example, they can, in fact, be substantial.

In section 4 we examine the implications of product diversity for the nature of entry biases. We show that product differentiation can reverse the tendency toward excessive entry that is found in homogeneous product markets. Intuitively, the presence of heterogeneity introduces another factor that biases entry: the marginal entrant creates surplus by increasing product variety that he does not capture as profits. The product diversity and business-stealing effects thus work in opposite directions. With the functional form (constant elasticity of substitution) and equilibrium notion used by Spence (1976a), this new effect always dominates the business-stealing effect, and the result is insufficient entry. This need not be the case, however, and we give examples in which the contrary result holds with the business-stealing effect always dominating the product diversity effect.

The results of sections 3 and 4 indicate that when firms must incur fixed set-up costs, the regulation of entry is often desirable. In section 5 we explore the limiting case in which the fixed cost approaches zero. Simple examples illustrate that the entry bias may get infinitely large as the fixed cost grows small: the difference between the equilibrium and optimal number of firms may approach infinity. Nonetheless, we prove that the welfare loss caused by having the wrong number of firms approaches zero if firms act approximately as price-takers as their numbers grow large. Thus, the regulation of entry becomes unnecessary as an industry comes close to the ideal of no fixed costs.

Finally, section 6 provides concluding remarks.

2. The Model

We wish to compare the number of firms that enter a market in a "free-entry equilibrium" with the number that a welfare-maximizing social planner would desire. We model the entry process as a two-stage game. In the first stage a large (infinite) number of identical potential entrants exists, each of whom must decide whether to enter the industry. Should a firm decide to enter, it must incur set-up costs of K. Stage two is the production period. In this stage those firms that have entered and have sunk the set-up costs play some oligopoly game, the details of which we do not need to specify. Each entrant possesses a technology given by the cost function $c(q)$, where $c(\cdot)$ is continuous, $c(0) = 0, c'(\cdot) \geq 0$, and $c''(\cdot) \geq 0$ for all $q \geq 0$. We assume that the equilibrium in this stage is symmetric, and we define q_N to be the equilibrium output per firm, given that N firms have entered the industry. Typically q_N is not the competitive output level, because the firms that enter do not act as price-takers, but rather behave strategically. We also define π_N as the equilibrium profits per firm, given that N firms have entered.

We denote the free-entry equilibrium number of firms by N^e.[3] The necessary and sufficient conditions for N^e to be the free-entry equilibrium number of firms are: (i) $\pi_{N^e} \geq 0$ and (ii) $\pi_{N^e+1} < 0$.[4] Condition (i) ensures that no firm that has entered would have been better off not entering. Condition (ii) requires that no firm that has not entered would have found it worthwhile to have entered.

We consider the second-best problem faced by a social planner who can control the number of firms that enter the industry but not their oligopolistic behavior once they have entered. As Scherer (1980, p. 525) notes, "Oligopolists refraining from price competition merely because they recognize the likelihood of rival retaliation do not violate the law as long as their decisions are taken independently." Thus, we assume that the social planner cannot affect the market outcome for any given number of firms. In particular, the planner cannot ensure that the active firms behave as price-takers.

Finally, we further suppose that the objective of the planner is to select the number of firms that maximizes the total surplus in the market.[5]

3. Homogeneous Product Markets

We begin our analysis with consideration of a simple homogeneous product market. Denote the inverse market demand function for the product by $P(Q)$, where Q is aggregate output in the market, and assume that $P'(Q) < 0$ at all Q. Given this inverse demand function, we can then define the equilibrium profits per firm when N firms have entered, π_N, by $\pi_N \equiv P(Nq_N)q_N - c(q_N) - K$ and the socially optimal number of firms, N^*, as the number of firms that solves:

$$\max_{N} W(N) \equiv \int_0^{Nq_N} P(s)ds - Nc(q_N) - NK$$

Our basic result characterizes the relationship between N^e (the free-entry equilibrium number of firms) and N^* (the socially optimal number of firms) for postentry behavior that satisfies the following three assumptions.

ASSUMPTION 1. $Nq_N > \hat{N}q_{\hat{N}}$ for all $N > \hat{N}$ and $\lim_{N \to \infty} Nq_N = M < \infty$

ASSUMPTION 2. $q_N < q_{\hat{N}}$ for all $N > \hat{N}$

ASSUMPTION 3. $P(Nq_N) - c'(q_N) \geq 0$ for all N

Assumption 1 simply says that (postentry) equilibrium aggregate output rises with the number of firms entering the industry and approaches some finite bound. This assumption guarantees that the free-entry equilibrium number of firms (N^e) is well defined. Assumption 2 requires that output per firm fall as the number of firms in the industry increases, that is, that a business-stealing effect is present. Finally, Assumption 3 requires that for any number of entrants, the resulting equilibrium price is not below marginal cost.

We begin our analysis by ignoring the integer constraint on the number of firms. Although we do this primarily for expositional purposes, this simplification also facilitates comparisons with previous results in the literature. Thus, we assume that the free-entry equilibrium number of firms exactly satisfies the zero-profit condition,

$$\pi_{N^e} = 0$$

while the socially optimal number of firms exactly satisfies the first-order condition,

$$W'(N^*) = 0$$

In what follows we also assume that q_N is a differentiable function of N.

PROPOSITION 1. Suppose that Assumptions 1–3 hold. Then, when we ignore the integer constraint, the free-entry equilibrium number of firms is not less than the socially optimal number; that is, $N^e \geq N^*$. Furthermore, if the inequality in Assumption 3 holds strictly, then the equilibrium number of firms strictly exceeds the optimal number, that is, $N^e > N^*$.

PROOF.   Differentiating the expression for social surplus, $W(N)$, with respect to the number of firms yields for all N:

$$W'(N) = P(Nq_N)\left[N\frac{\partial q_N}{\partial N} + q_N\right] - c(q_N) - N'c(q_N)\frac{\partial q_N}{\partial N} - K \tag{1}$$

Rearranging terms and recalling the expression for equilibrium profits per firm, π_N, yield

$$W'(N) = \pi_N + N[P(Nq_N) - c'(q_N)]\frac{\partial q_N}{\partial N} \tag{2}$$

for all N. Under Assumptions 2 and 3, the second term on the right-hand side of equation (2) is nonpositive, and it is strictly negative if the inequality in Assumption 3 holds strictly. Therefore, for all N, $W'(N) \leq \pi_N$. Thus, $\pi_{N^*} \geq 0$.

We can now complete the argument by showing that profits per firm fall as N increases, since then $\pi_{N^e} = 0$ implies that $N^e \geq N^*$. The derivative of π_N with respect to N is given by

$$\frac{\partial \pi_N}{\partial N} = [P(Nq_N) - c'(qN)]\frac{\partial q_N}{\partial N} + q_N P'(Nq_N)\frac{\partial(Nq_N)}{\partial N} \tag{3}$$

which is negative under our assumptions. Thus, $N^e \geq N^*$.

Finally, note that if the inequality in Assumption 3 holds strictly, then $\pi_{N^*} > 0$, which implies that $N^e > N^*$.   *QED*

Equation (2) helps to provide the intuition for this result. The (first-order) change in social welfare attributable to a marginal entrant is composed of two terms. First, the new entrant contributes directly to social surplus through his profits. Second, the entrant causes all existing firms to contract their output levels, which results in an aggregate contraction equal to $N(\partial q_N/\partial N)$. This causes a reduction in social surplus of

$$[P(Nq_N) - c'(q_N)]N(\partial q_N/\partial N)$$

Thus, the presence of the business-stealing effect drives a wedge between the marginal entrant's evaluation of the desirability of entry and the social planner's. If entry does not change the output of existing firms, then equation (2) reduces to

$$W'(N) = \pi_N \qquad \text{for all } N \tag{4}$$

and the level of entry resulting from a situation of free entry is socially efficient.

As a final remark on Proposition 1, note that if firms act as price-takers after entry, then (again when we ignore the integer constraint) free entry results in exactly the socially efficient number of firms, despite the presence of a business-stealing effect. The reason is that the output contraction caused by a marginal entrant no longer has any net social value. We summarize this in the following corollary.

COROLLARY 1. Suppose that Assumptions 1 and 2 hold and that $P(Nq_N) - c'(q_N) = 0$ for all N. Then, when we ignore the integer constraint on the number of firms, the free-entry number of firms exactly equals the socially efficient number (i.e., $N^e = N^*$).[6]

Proposition 1 provides very general and intuitive conditions under which free entry leads to excessive entry.[7] Furthermore, as the following examples demonstrate, the bias toward excessive entry can be extremely large.

EXAMPLE 1. Consider a linear market structure in which firms behave as Cournot oligopolists in the production period. That is, suppose that the inverse demand function is given by $P(Q) = a - bQ$ and that $c(q) = cq$. It is easy to show that the equilibrium output per firm is given by:

$$q_N = \left(\frac{1}{N+1}\right)\left(\frac{a-c}{b}\right) \tag{5}$$

Using this fact, one can show that the free-entry equilibrium number of firms, N^e, satisfies (when we ignore the integer constraint):

$$(N^e + 1)^2 = \frac{(a-c)^2}{bK}$$

while the socially optimal number of firms, N^*, satisfies (when we again ignore the integer constraint):

$$(N^* + 1)^3 = \frac{(a-c)^2}{bK}$$

Thus, in a linear market, if the socially optimal number of firms is three, then *seven* firms actually enter the market under free entry; if the social optimum has five firms, then *thirteen* firms enter; and if the social optimum has eight firms, then *twenty-six* firms enter. Clearly, the bias toward excessive entry under free entry can be very large, although, of course, the difference in the number of firms is not the correct measure of the welfare loss.[8] In this market the government would achieve a welfare improvement by raising the private cost of entry through an entry tax (e.g., a licensing fee). Furthermore, if the government found that artificial restrictions on entry were present in this market, it is possible that their removal would lead to a welfare loss.

EXAMPLE 2. Though it is perhaps easiest to think of q_N as resulting from noncooperative behavior, our result does not depend upon any such assumption. For example, suppose that in the linear market described above, firms that enter the industry behave as a cartel rather than as Cournot oligopolists.[9] In this case we would have $Nq_N = (a-c)/2b$ (the monopoly output) for all N. Since aggregate output is invariant to the number of firms in the industry, if the market should exist at all, the social optimum is to have only one firm (so as to pay K only once). Yet, if the number of firms is continuous, firms enter until *all* of the collusive monopoly profits are dissipated into set-up costs. The welfare losses caused by free entry in this example are similiar to those Posner (1975) describes in his discussion of competition for monopoly positions. In both cases rent-seeking turns monopoly profits into deadweight social losses.[10]

Proposition 1 and the previous two examples indicate that the presence of a business-stealing effect creates a strong bias toward excessive entry. The avoidance, up to this point, of the integer constraint on the number of firms, however, is not satisfactory. In Example 2, for instance, consideration of integer constraints reveals that the level of entry is actually *insufficient* whenever $(a - c)^2/4bK \in [\frac{2}{3}, 1)$. In these cases, no firm enters the industry, even though a monopoly is the socially optimal outcome.[11] This occurs because, as is well known, a monopolist does not capture the full social surplus generated by his entry.

The following result explicitly takes account of the integer constraint.

PROPOSITION 2.   Suppose that Assumptions 1–3 hold. Then $N^e \geq (N^* - 1)$.

PROOF.   See the Appendix.

Proposition 2 modifies the very strong result of Proposition 1. In particular, in the presence of a business-stealing effect, entry may be insufficient, although never by more than one firm. Although Proposition 2 and our previous examples still suggest a tendency toward excessive entry in homogeneous markets, it is important to recognize that the welfare losses in cases of insufficient entry can be substantial.[12] The following example makes this clear.

EXAMPLE 3.   Consider a linear market as above in which a single firm acts as a monopolist but two firms act as Bertrand competitors. For any value of K, duopolists earn negative profits. If $K \leq (a - c)^2/4b$, a monopolist earns nonnegative profits: hence, $N^e = 1$. When $K \leq (a - c)^2/8b$, however, duopoly is socially optimal.[13] As K becomes small, the social loss due to one too few firms approaches 25 per cent of the potential surplus in the market (the area between the demand curve and the marginal cost curve).

4. Product Diversity

We now explore how the presence of product diversity affects the direction of the entry bias identified in section 3. Following Spence (1976a), we specify gross consumer benefits to be of the form

$$G\left[\sum_{i=1}^{\infty} f(q^i) \right] \tag{6}$$

where q^i is firm i's output level, $f(0) = 0$, $f'(\cdot) > 0$, and $f''(\cdot) \le 0$ for all $q \ge 0$, and $G'(z) > 0$ and $G''(z) < 0$ for all $z \ge 0$. These assumptions imply that consumers prefer variety and that the outputs of various firms are substitutes for one another.

The objective of the social planner in this market is therefore to select N to solve (here we impose symmetry again):

$$\max_{N} W(N) \equiv G[Nf(q_N)] - Nc(q_N) - NK \tag{7}$$

To derive equilibrium profits per firm, note that when N firms have entered the industry, consumer maximization implies that each firm's equilibrium price is exactly equal to $G''[Nf(q_N)] f'(q_N)$. We then have

$$\pi_N \equiv G'[Nf(q_N)] f'(q_N) q_N - c(q_N) - K \tag{8}$$

To understand the effects of product diversity on entry biases, we again begin by differentiating $W(N)$ (equation (7)). Omitting arguments of some functions for notational simplicity, this yields

$$W'(N) = G'\left\{ Nf' \frac{\partial q_N}{\partial N} + f \right\} - c(q_N) - Nc'(q_N) \frac{\partial q_N}{\partial N} - K \tag{9}$$

Adding and subtracting $G''f'q_N$ and rearranging terms give

$$W'(N) = \pi_N + N[G'f' - c'] \frac{\partial q_N}{\partial N} + G'[f - f'q_N] \tag{10}$$

Equation (10) is the generalization of equation (2) of section 3 to the case of product diversity. Now there are two different terms that can drive a wedge between the private and social evaluation of marginal entry: the second and third terms on the right-hand side of equation (10). The first of these is identical to that in equation (2) of section 3: it is negative if the equilibrium price exceeds marginal cost and a business-stealing effect is present.[14] The second term is new and represents the effect of product diversity – it is positive if $f'' < 0$ (consumer prefer variety). More specifically, when consumers have a preference for variety, a marginal entrant, by increasing variety, increases surplus but does not capture this gain in profits. The last term in (10) captures this diversity effect since $G'f$ is the marginal entrant's contribution to gross social surplus, while $G'f'q_N$ is his revenue.

Given these two separate effects that work in opposite directions, it is not possible to sign unambiguously the direction of the entry bias: entry can be excessive, insufficient, or even optimal.[15] Spence (1976a) demonstrates that if $f(q) \equiv q^\beta (\beta < 1)$ and if firms choose quantities and act as price-takers with respect to the "market price" G' (that is, they take G' as given when choosing their quantities), then free entry results in *insufficient entry*. In fact, it is not difficult to show that under this set of assumptions

$$N[G'f' - c']\frac{\partial q_N}{\partial N} + G'[f - f'q_N] > 0$$

for all N: the product diversity term always dominates the business-stealing effect. Thus, by equation (10), $W'(N) > \pi_N$ for all N, so that $N^e < N^*$.[16]

This direction of entry bias need not always hold, however. Koenker and Perry (1981), for example, show that if one replaces Spence's postentry price-taking assumption with a postentry conjectural variation model (with the functional form of f unchanged), then there exist ranges of values for β and the conjectural variation such that Spence's result is reversed: excessive entry occurs.

Using equation (10), we can also find other functional forms such that entry is excessive even under Spence's price-taking assumption. In Mankiw and Whinston (1985), for example, we demonstrate that if

$$G(z) \equiv -\frac{1}{z}$$

$$f(q) \equiv aq - \left(\frac{b}{2}\right)q^2$$

$$c(q) \equiv cq; \quad c > \left(\frac{a}{2}\right)$$

then the business-stealing effect always dominates – that is,

$$N[G'f' - c']\frac{\partial q_N}{\partial N} + G'[f - f'q_N] < 0$$

for all N. Thus, here we find that $N^e > N^*$.

One can also explicitly recognize the integer constraint here as we did in section 3. Such considerations do not affect the basic points made above regarding the effects of product heterogeneity.[17]

5. Small Set-up Costs and the Regulation of Entry

The results of the previous two sections indicate that when firms must incur fixed set-up costs upon entry, free entry typically does not result in the socially optimal number of firms. One might hope, however, that as set-up costs become small, the regulation of entry becomes unimportant. For instance, in the linear Cournot example of section 3, the welfare loss due to free entry falls as the set-up cost falls, even though the excessive number of firms grows infinitely large (see note 8).

The cartel example (Example 2) of section 3 shows, however, that some further qualification is necessary if we wish to obtain such a limiting result. In that example the loss due to free entry does not fall to zero as the set-up cost falls, since firms enter until all monopoly rents are dissipated. To obtain a limiting result, we assume that as the number of entrants grows large, firms come to act approximately as price-takers.

Let N_K^* and N_K^e denote, respectively, the socially optimal and free-entry number of firms when set-up costs are K. Denote the associated levels of welfare by W_K^* and W_K^e, respectively. The following proposition examines the difference between the social optimum and free-entry welfare as K approaches zero.

PROPOSITION 3. Suppose that Assumption 2 and the following assumptions hold.

ASSUMPTION 1a.

$$G'[Nf(q_N)]f'(q_N) < G'[\hat{N}f(q\hat{N})]f'(q\hat{N}) \qquad \text{for all } N > \hat{N}$$

and

$$\lim_{n \to \infty} Nf(q_N) = M < \infty$$

ASSUMPTION 3a. $\{G'[Nf(q_N)]f'(q_N) - c'(q_N)\} > 0$ for all N

ASSUMPTION 4. $\lim_{N \to \infty} \{G'[Nf(q_N)]f'(q_N) - c'(q_N)\} = 0$

Then the welfare loss due to free entry goes to zero as K gets small; that is,

$$\lim_{K \to 0} (W_K^* - W_K^e) = 0$$

Assumptions 1a and 3a are the natural generalizations of Assumptions 1 and 3 to a heterogeneous product setting.[18] Assumption 4 requires that price approach marginal cost as the number of firms grows infinitely large. As we now demonstrate, under these four assumptions, the welfare loss due to free entry disappears as the set-up cost K approaches zero.

PROOF. Define

$$W* = \lim_{N \to \infty} \{G[Nf(q_N)] - Nc(q_N)\}$$

It is not difficult to show that, under our assumptions, W^* is the socially optimal level of welfare when the set-up cost is zero, and further, that this level is finite.[19] Then the following set of inequalities clearly must hold for any K:

$$\infty > W^* \geq W_K^* \geq W_K^e$$

The result can therefore be established by showing that $\lim_{K \to 0} W_K^e = W^*$.

First, we note that $N_K^e \to \infty$ as $K \to 0$. To see this, suppose instead that $N_K^e \to (\bar{N} - 1) < \infty$. Then, since

$$G'[\bar{N}f(q_{\bar{N}})]\,f'(q_{\bar{N}})q_{\bar{N}} - c(q_{\bar{N}}) \geq G'[\bar{N}f(q_{\bar{N}})]\,f'(q_{\bar{N}})q_{\bar{N}} - c'(q_{\bar{N}})q_{\bar{N}}$$
$$= \{G'[\bar{N}f(q_{\bar{N}})]\,f'(q_{\bar{N}}) - c'(q_{\bar{N}})\}q_{\bar{N}} > 0$$

there exists a $\bar{K} > 0$ small enough that entry by an $\bar{N}$th firm would be profitable.

Since $N_K^e \to \infty$, it is clear from the definition of W_K^e that $W_K^e \to W^*$ if and only if $N_K^e K \to 0$. Now, by the definition of N_K^e we know that

$$G'[N_K^e f(q_{N_K^e})]\,f'(q_{N_K^e})q_{N_K^e} - c(q_{N_K^e}) \geq K$$

so that (when we ignore the subscript of N_K^e for notational simplicity):

$$G'[N^e f(q_{N^e})]f'(q_{N^e})N^e q_{N^e} - N^e c(q_{N^e}) \geq N^e K$$

or

$$\left\{G'[N^e f(q_{N^e})]f'(q_{N^e}) - \frac{c(q_{N^e})}{q_{N^e}}\right\}N^e q_{N^e} \geq N^e K$$

But, since $N_K^e \to \infty$, it must be true that $q_{N_K^e} \to 0$ since $Nf(q_N) \to M < \infty$. Thus, $c(q_{N^e})/q_{N^e} \to c'(0)$. But, $\lim_{N\to\infty}c'(q_N) = c'(0)$. Thus,

$$\lim_{N^e \to \infty}\left\{G'[N^e f(q_{N^e})]\,f'(q_{N^e}) - \frac{c(q_{N^e})}{q_{N^e}}\right\} = \lim_{N\to\infty}\{G'[Nf(q_N)]f'(q_N) - c'(q_N)\} = 0$$

Finally, $N^e f(q_{N^e}) \to M < \infty$ implies that $N^e q_{N^e}$ is also bounded under our assumptions since $f(q_{N^e}) \geq f'(q_{N^e})q_{N^e}$ and $f'(0) > 0$. Thus, $\lim_{K\to 0}N_K^e K = 0$.   *QED*

The idea behind the proof is as follows. First, as K approaches zero, in both the free-entry equilibrium and the optimum, N approaches infinity, and thus price approaches marginal cost. The only welfare difference between the equilibrium and the optimum might be excessive entry, that is, $(N^e - N^*)K$. But since industry output is bounded and price is approaching cost, operating profits (and thus $N^e K$) are approaching zero. Thus, the welfare cost of excessive entry must be approaching zero as well.

The assumption that price strictly exceeds marginal cost for all finite N is for this result. To see this, consider again Example 3 of section 3. There, price falls to marginal cost for $N \geq 2$, and as K grows small, the loss due to free entry persists.

Both Hart (1979) and Novshek (1980) prove results that are similar in spirit to Proposition 3. Both of these articles show that as the efficient scale of firms grows small (in Hart's case this is done in *per capita* terms), free-entry Cournot equilibrium converges to a first-best allocation.[20] There are two basic differences between our result and theirs. First, and most important, although these authors assume Cournot behavior and *derive* that price approaches marginal cost, we *assume* that pricing becomes competitive as the number of firms grows, but we do not need to be specific about the nature of postentry interaction. Second, we specify a two-stage entry process as opposed to the simultaneous (Cournot) entry-quantity decision posited in their models.[21]

6. Conclusion

Economists have long believed that unencumbered entry is desirable for social efficiency. This view has persisted despite the illustration in several recent articles of the inefficiencies that can arise from free entry in the presence of fixed set-up costs. In this article we have attempted to elucidate the fundamental and intuitive forces that lie behind these entry biases.

In homogeneous product markets the existence of imperfect competition and a business-stealing effect always creates a bias toward excessive entry: when we ignore the integer constraint on the number of firms, marginal entry is more desirable to the entrant than it is to society because of the output reduction entry causes in other firms. Hence, in a homogeneous market entry restrictions are often socially desirable, although, as we show, they become unnecessary as the fixed set-up cost becomes small.

The introduction of product diversity, however, can reverse this bias toward excessive entry. Intuitively, a marginal entrant adds to variety, but does not capture the resulting gain in social surplus as profits. Hence, in heterogeneous product markets the direction of any entry bias is generally unclear, although efficient levels of entry remain an unlikely occurrence.

Appendix

The proof of Proposition 2 follows.
Proof of Proposition 2. The result is trivial for $N^* \leq 1$. Suppose now that $N^* > 1$. We first show that profits per firm are nonegative when $(N^* - 1)$ firms are in the industry, i.e., that $\pi_{N^*-1} \geq 0$. To see this, note first that by the definition of N^* we have $W(N^*) \geq W(N^* - 1)$, or

$$\int_{Q_{N^*-1}}^{Q_{N^*-1}} P(s)ds - N^*c(q_{N^*}) + (N^*-1)c(q_{N^*} - 1) \geq K \qquad (A1)$$

where $Q_N \equiv Nq_N$. We can rearrange (A1) to yield

$$\pi_{N^*-1} \geq P(Q_{N^*-1})q_N^{*-1} - \int_{Q_{N^*-1}}^{Q_{N^*}} P(s)ds + N^*[c(q_{N*}) - c(q_{N^*-1})] \qquad (A2)$$

Since $P'(\cdot) < 0$ and Assumption 1 holds, this implies that

$$\pi_{N^*-1} \geq P(Q_{N^*-1})[q_{N^*-1} - Q_{N^*} + Q_{N^*-1}] + N^*[c(q_{N*}) - c(q_{N^*-1})] \qquad (A3)$$

Since $c''(\cdot) \geq 0$, we know that

$$c'(q_{N^*-1})[q_{N^*} - q_{N^*-1}] \leq c(q_{N*}) - c(q_{N^*-1}) \qquad (A4)$$

Substituting (A4) into (A3) yields

$$\pi_{N^*-1} \ge [P(Q_{N^*-1}) - c'(q_{N^*-1})][N^*(q_{N^*-1} - q_{N^*})] \qquad (A5)$$

But by Assumption 3 the first bracketed expression on the right-hand side is nonnegative, and by Assumption 2 the second bracketed expression is also nonnegative. Thus, $\pi_{N^*-1} \ge 0$.

If π_N is decreasing in N, then $\pi_{N^*-1} \ge 0$ implies that $N^e \ge N^* - 1$. To see that this is the case, note that

$$\pi_N - \pi_{N-1} = [P(Q_N)q_N - c(q_N)] - [P(Q_{N-1})q_{N-1} - c(q_{N-1})] \qquad (A6)$$

$$\le P(Q_{N-1})[q_N - q_{N-1}] - [c(q_N) - c(q_{N-1})] \qquad (A7)$$

$$\le [P(Q_{N-1}) - c'(q_{N-1})](q_N - q_{N-1}) \qquad (A8)$$

where the first inequality follows from Assumption 1 and the second by applying equation (A4). Thus, Assumptions 2 and 3 imply that $\pi_{N-1} \ge \pi_N$ for all N. $\qquad QED$

Notes

1   Seade (1980) examines the conditions under which business stealing does and does not characterize markets operating under conjectural variation equilibrium. Business stealing also relates to the concept of "strategic substitutes" discussed by Bulow, Geanakoplos, and Klemperer (1985).

2   Spence (1976b, p. 410) suggests the importance of such firm interaction for the social evaluation of entry.

3   N^e need not, in general, be unique. Our assumptions below, however, guarantee its uniqueness.

4   We assume that firms do, in fact, enter when they are indifferent about entering.

5   Throughout we assume that a partial equilibrium approach is justified, that is, that income effects can be ignored.

6   Note that the second-best social optimum here is first-best.

7   Note, though, that if the inequality in Assumption 2 is reversed – that is, if entry is "business augumenting" – then free entry results in an insufficient level of entry.

8   It is interesting that in this example the welfare loss due to free entry declines as the socially optimal number of firms increases. As a percentage of the total area between the demand and marginal cost curves, the loss is 7.8 percent, 5.2 percent, and 3.8 percent, for the three cases. We say more about this below in section 5.

9   Of course, the relevance of the social planning problem we consider depends upon the planner's having no control over this behavior. Some industries, however, seem to behave collusively without any explicit conspiratorial behavior that can be attacked in the courts.

10 In this example free entry results in a 50 percent welfare loss (again, measured as a percentage of the total area between the demand and marginal cost curves) as K grows small.

11 It is easy to verify that in Example 2 excessive entry occurs for all parameter values such that $(a - c)^2/4bK \ge 2$.

12 Perry (1984) performs numerical simulations assuming constant elasticity cost and demand curves and Cournot equilibrium (his Table 1). His results suggest that the integer constraint is important only if the number of firms in the free-entry equilibrium is small, that is, one or two firms.

13 In this example a business-stealing effect only weakly holds, that is, $q_1 = q_2 = (a - c)/2b$. This does not, however, affect the point being made – just suppose, instead, that demand is equal to $(a - c - \epsilon)/b$ for all $P \leq c + \epsilon$, where ϵ is a small positive number.

14 Note that demand substitutability is neither a necessary nor a sufficient condition for the presence of a business-stealing effect.

15 Note that a business-augmenting effect would reverse the sign of $N[G'f' - c'](\partial q_N/\partial N)$ in equation (10), and it would lead to insufficient entry.

16 This assumes that N^e is well defined. A sufficient condition for this is that $\partial\{G'[Nf(q_N)]f'(q_N)\}/\partial N < 0$.

17 The interested reader is referred to Mankiw and Whinston (1985).

18 Note the $\lim_{N \to \infty} Nq_N < \infty$ implies that $\lim_{N \to \infty} Nf(q_N) < \infty$ as long as $f'(0) < \infty$.

19 The first part of this claim is established by showing that $\{G[Nf(q_N)] - Nc(q_N)\}$ is increasing in N, while the latter part follows from the assumption that $\lim_{N \to \infty} Nf(q_N) = M < \infty$.

20 We would like to thank Andreu Mas-Colell for helpful discussion regarding these issues.

21 A third difference actually exists: as K grows small in our model, minimum average cost falls. In contrast, in Hart (1979) and Novshek (1980) the limiting process keeps minimum average cost unchanged (in *per capita* units in Hart's case). It is not difficult, however, to adapt Novshek's argument to the case of a limiting process of our type. We would like to thank a referee for calling our attention to this fact.

References

Bulow, J. I., Geanakoplos, J. D., and Klemperer, P. D. (1985): "Multimarket Oligopoly: Strategic Substitutes and Complements." *Journal of Political Economy*, 93, 488–511.

Dixit, A. K. and Stiglitz, J. E. (1977): "Monopolistic Competition and Optimal Product Diversity." *American Economic Review*, 67, 297–308.

Hart, O. D. (1979): "Monopolistic Competition in a Large Economy with Differentiated Commodities." *Review of Economic Studies*, 46, 1–30.

Koenker, R. W. and Perry, M. K. (1981): "Product Differentiation, Monopolistic Competition, and Public Policy." *Bell Journal of Economics*, 12, 217–31.

Mankiw, N. G. and Whinston, M. D. (1985): "Free Entry and Social Inefficiency." Harvard Institute of Economic Research Discussion Paper No. 1125.

Novshek, W. (1980): "Cournot Equilibrium with Free Entry." *Review of Economic Studies*, 47, 473–87.

Perry, M. K. (1984): "Scale Economies, Imperfect Competition, and Public Policy." *Journal of Industrial Economics*, 32, 313–30.

Posner, R. (1975): "The Social Costs of Monopoly and Regulation." *Journal of Political Economy*, 83, 807–27.

Scherer, F. M. (1980): *Industrial Market Structure and Economic Performance*, 2nd edn. Boston: Houghton Mifflin.

Seade, J. (1980): "On the Effects of Entry." *Econometrica*, 4, 479–90.

Spence, A. M. (1976a): "Product Selection, Fixed Costs, and Monopolistic Competition." *Review of Economic Studies*, 43, 217–36.

—— (1976b): "Product Differentiation and Welfare." *American Economic Review*, 66, 407–14.

von Weizsäcker, C. C. (1980): "A Welfare Analysis of Barriers to Entry." *Bell Journal of Economics*, 11, 399–420.

CHAPTER FIFTEEN

Selection and the Evolution of Industry

BOYAN JOVANOVIC

Source: *Econometrica*, 1982, 50, 649–70.

Recent evidence shows that within an industry, smaller firms grow faster and are more likely to fail than large firms. This paper provides a theory of selection with incomplete information that is consistent with these and other findings. Firms learn about their efficiency as they operate in the industry. The efficient grow and survive; the inefficient decline and fail. A perfect foresight equilibrium is proved by means of showing that it is a unique maximum to discounted net surplus. The maximization problem is not standard, and some mathematical results might be of independent interest.

1. Theory and Evidence on the Growth and Survival of Firms

Do small firms grow faster than large firms? Are they less likely to survive? Early studies found no relation between the size of firms and their growth rates [8, 14, 16]. The growth of firms seemed to be proportional to their size. In later work, adjustment costs with constant returns to scale were shown to imply that firms *should* grow in proportion to their size [10, 11].

Recent evidence from larger samples tells a different story. Mansfield [13] finds that smaller firms have *higher* and *more variable* growth rates. Du Rietz [6], in a sample of Swedish firms, again finds that smaller firms grow faster, and that they *are* less likely to survive [6, 8, 13]. These findings conflict with the adjustment costs theory in which all firms grow at the same rate, and in which failure does not happen.

To explain these deviations from the proportional growth law, I propose a theory of "noisy" selection. Efficient firms grow and survive; inefficient firms decline and fail. Firms differ in size not because of the fixity of capital, but because some discover that they are more efficient than others. The model gives rise to entry, growth, and exit behavior that agrees, broadly, with the evidence.

The model also agrees with some more tentative findings. First, firm size and concentration seem to be positively related to rates of return.[1] Second, the correlation *over time* of rates of return is higher for larger firms and in the concentrated industries [15, 17]. Third, the variability of rates of return *at a point in time* is higher in the concentrated industries [17]. Finally, higher concentration is associated with higher profits for the larger firms, but *not* for the smaller firms [4].

Enduring differences in size and in growth are no doubt caused in part by the fixity of capital. This paper shows, I think, that selection matters too.

2. A Brief Description of the Model

The model deals with a small industry to which factors are supplied at a constant price. The product is homogeneous and the time-path of the demand for the product is deterministic and known.

Costs are random, and different among firms. For each firm, the mean of its costs may be thought of as the firm's "true cost." The *distribution* of true costs among the potential firms is known to all, but no firm knows what *its* true cost is. All firms have the same prior beliefs, and each firm regards itself as a random draw from the population distribution of true costs. This "prior" distribution is then updated as evidence comes in.

If the firm has low true costs, it is likely that the evidence will be favorable, and the firm will survive. If its costs are high and the evidence adverse, the firm may not wait too long before withdrawing from the industry.

The number of firms in the industry is always infinite – each firm is of measure zero so that it is too small to affect price. With uncertainty at the individual level but with no *aggregate* uncertainty, the path of output prices is deterministic and is assumed to be self-fulfilling in equilibrium.

Firms and potential entrants know the entire equilibrium price sequence, and based on it, they make entry, production, and exit decisions. A one-time entry cost is borne at the time of entry. Thereafter, only production costs are incurred. In equilibrium, the net present value of entry cannot be positive, for if it were, more firms would enter.

In the next section, the model is presented, and the firm's optimization problem is defined. Some of the properties of the model then become clear. Figure 1 portrays them concisely: efficient firms grow and survive; the inefficient decline and fail. Toward the end of the section, results are described which are obtained in the later, mathematical sections of the paper. The implications are compared to the empirical evidence. The perfect foresight equilibrium is defined in section 4. Section 5 is devoted to proving that equilibrium exists, is unique, and is, in a sense, socially optimal. The proof involves showing that equilibrium coincides with the unique maximum of the discounted sum of consumer plus producer surplus. Two theorems that describe the equilibrium appear in section 6, and some of the longer proofs are contained in the Appendix.

A curious feature of the paper is that proofs of "obvious" results are complicated. The reader may be eager – on the first reading at least – to take such results on trust. So, the remainder of the paper is arranged into two distinct parts. The next section contains a discussion of all the results. If the reader is not interested in the mathematics, he can stop there, for the discussion is self-contained. Sections 4 and beyond are devoted to the formal

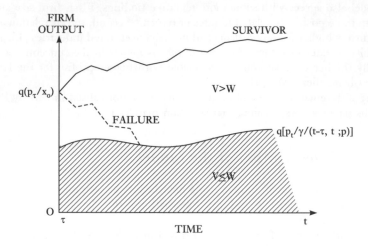

Figure 1

development, which is interesting in its own right. Proving that equilibrium is a maximum is not new, of course. But the problem of maximizing discounted surplus here does not fit a regular mold. Similar problems will no doubt arise again and results proved here could then be useful. A description of the nature of the problem being solved and of how it differs from other work on stochastic optimization is contained at the beginning of section 5.

3. The Model

In an industry with a homogeneous output, firms differ in efficiency. Some are more efficient than others at *all* levels of output. Let q be the output of a firm, and $c(q)$ a cost function which satisfies

$$c(0) = 0, \qquad c'(0) = 0, \qquad c'(q) > 0, \qquad c''(q) > 0 \qquad \text{and} \qquad \lim_{q \to \infty} c'(q) = \infty$$

Total costs are $c(q_t)x_t$ where x_t is a random variable independent across firms. For the firm of type θ, let $x_t = \xi(\eta_t)$ where $\xi(\cdot)$ is a positive, strictly increasing, and continuous function with $\lim_{\eta_t \to -\infty} \xi(\eta_t) = \alpha_1 > 0$ and $\lim_{\eta_t \to \infty} \xi(\eta_t) = \alpha_2 \leq \infty$, and where

$$\eta_t = \theta + \epsilon_t, \qquad \epsilon_t \sim N(0, \sigma^2) \text{iid}$$

Firms with large values of θ will generate larger x_t, and be less efficient at all levels of output. The ϵ_t are firm-specific shocks, independent over time and across firms.

Among potential firms, θ is normally distributed with mean $\bar{\theta}$ and variance σ_θ^2. An entrant does not know his own θ, but he knows that he is a random draw from $N(\bar{\theta}, \sigma_\theta^2)$. He also knows the variance of ϵ_t, as well as the exact form of $\xi(\cdot)$ so that observing his own costs at t allows him to infer η_t.

The firm is too small to affect price. It chooses q_t so as to maximize expected profits:

$$\max_{q_t} \left[p_t q_t - c(q_t) x_t^* \right]$$

where x_t* is the expectation of x_t conditional upon information received prior to t. The output decision is made *before* x_t is observed, and is denoted by $q(p_t/x_t^*)$. As one would expect, it is decreasing in x:

$$\frac{\partial q}{\partial x_t^*} = \frac{-c'}{x_t^* c''} < 0 \quad \text{and} \quad \frac{\partial^2 q}{\partial x_t^{*2}} = \frac{1}{x_t^*} \left[\frac{c' c'''}{(c'')^2} - 2 \right] \frac{\partial q}{\partial x_t^*} \tag{3.1}$$

3.1. The exit decision

Let $W > 0$ be the expected present value of the firms' fixed factor (its "managerial ability" or "advantageous location") if it is employed in a different activity. The value of W is the same for all firms in the industry *regardless of how successful they are in that industry*. In other words, if the firm learns that it is efficient in this industry, this does not increase its estimated efficiency anywhere else. This assumption may seem restrictive, but it could be relaxed to allow for correlation in firms' efficiencies in different industries, without changing the nature of the results. What really matters is that if favorable information about a firm's costs in an industry raises its expected earnings *in that industry* by one dollar, its expected earnings elsewhere increase by *less* than a dollar. Here it is assumed that new information about θ leaves expected alternative earnings unchanged.

A cost of entry, k, is borne by the firm when it enters – the cost of establishing a particular location for example. And θ might be the degree of suitability of the location. The firm learns about θ with the passage of time.

The firm has an infinite horizon and a constant discount rate, r. At time t, if the firm is in the industry, it will have a pair of sufficient statistics $(\bar{\eta}_n, n)$ which characterize its beliefs about its parameter θ. Here n is the number of periods that the firm has been in the market (the age of the firm) and $\bar{\eta}_n = \sum^n \eta_i / n$. These two statistics are sufficient for the posterior distribution on θ, as this distribution is normal [20, p. 15].

In spite of the infinite horizon and the constant discount rate, the present value of earnings will depend on t too, because the price path, $\{p_t\}_0^\infty$, treated as given by the firm, is in general not constant over time. Therefore, once $\{p_t\}_0^\infty$ is given, t determines where one is along the price sequence.

Since $x_t^* = \int \xi(\eta) P^0(d\eta \mid \bar{\eta}_n, n)$ (where $P^0(\cdot | \bar{\eta}_n, n)$ is the normal posterior distribution of η_t with variance which depends only on n), and since $\xi(\eta)$ is strictly increasing, x_t* is strictly increasing in $\bar{\eta}_n$ for each n. Therefore the pair (x_t^*, n) is also a sufficient statistic.

Let $\pi(p_t, x) \equiv p_t q(p_t/x) - c[q(p_t/x)]x$ be the expected value of profits maximized with respect to q when $x_t* = x$. For a bounded price sequence $p \equiv \{p_t\}_0^\infty$, let $V(x, n, t; p)$ be the value, at t, of staying in the industry for one period and then behaving optimally, when the information is *(x, n)* and when the price sequence is p. Then V statisfies[2]

$$V(x, n, t; p) = \pi(p_t, x) + \beta \int \max[W, V(z, n+1, t+1; p)] P(dz | x, n) \tag{3.2}$$

At entry, when the firm has only its prior information, $x = x_0 \equiv$ prior mean of x_t, and $V(x_0, 0, t; p) - k$ is the net value of entry at t. The following simple result is proved in the Appendix.

THEOREM 1:   (i) *A unique, bounded and continuous solution for V in equation* (3.2) *exists and* (ii) *V is strictly decreasing in x.*

Thus firms with higher expected costs have a lower value of staying in the industry. Let $\gamma(n, t; p)$ be the level of x_t* at which the firm is *indifferent* between staying in the industry and leaving it. Then $\gamma(\cdot)$ is the solution for x to the equation[3]

$$V(x, n, t; p) = W \tag{3.3}$$

As V is strictly decreasing in $x, \gamma(\cdot)$ is uniquely defined. Consequently, the level of output below which the firm will not produce (but will exit instead) is $q[p_t/\gamma(n, t; p)]$. It is drawn in Figure 1. Here τ is the time at which the firm enters the industry, so $n = t - \tau$. For any price sequence, the boundary defines an "exit" region in which $V \leq W$ (shaded area) and a "continuation" region, in which $V > W$.

The firm's output sequence, $q(p_t/x_t^*)$, is a random process which starts from $q(p_\tau/x_0)$. The x_t^* sequence is a Martingale: $E_t x_{t+k}^* = x_t^*$ for any $k \geq 0$ [7, p. 212]. If output remains above the shaded area, the firm stays in the industry. Therefore the firms that survive are larger than the firms that fail – at the point of failure, the firm is smaller than all surviving members of its cohort.

The x_t^* sequences are independent across firms. They tend to *diverge*, as do the output sequences. Each firm is of measure zero, so the number of firms is always infinite, and the concentration *ratio* always zero. But a popular measure of concentration is the Gini coefficient. The greater the dispersion of x_t^* across firms, the greater the dispersion of firm size. At $t = 0$, all firms are of the same size, and the Gini coefficient is zero. As the x_t^* diverge, so do the outputs, and the Gini coefficient increases over time. But the increase need not be monotonic. And this is *exactly* the type of increase the Gini coefficient has exhibited at the economy-wide level in the U.K. [8].

Average profits also rise as the industry matures – at least they do if the equilibrium price sequence is constant (the latter possibility is the subject of Theorem 3 and is discussed below as well). The reason is simple. Since the unprofitable firms leave while profitable firms stay, the profits of the survivors as a group will increase so long as the price of the product does not fall. If it does not, profits increase with the age of the industry, as does concentration. In this sense then, the model predicts a positive relation between profits and concentration. But if the equilibrium price sequence falls over time, it may offset the upward "selection effect" on profits, and nothing can then be said about the time path of profits.

Why does concentration increase the profits of the large firms but not of the small firms? A high Gini coefficient results from high inequality in firm size in the industry. And the latter is caused by more inequality in efficiency. This means that some firms – large firms – earn higher rents. But the marginal firms – small firms – do not earn rents; there is no reason to expect a positive relation between concentration and the profits of these firms.

As for the positive relation between concentration and the *variability* of profits, take the case where $\sigma_t^2 = 0$ – all firms are equally efficient, and all are equal in size. The variability of profits is zero, as is the Gini coefficient. Since both profits and output decrease with x, there is a *one-to-one* relation between the relative dispersion in profits and in size.

Another implication is that unusually high profits today lead to unusually high growth between today and tomorrow. The reason is that the firm's *revision* of x_t^* depends on *realized* profits. Since $\pi_t = p_t q_t - c(q_t) x_t$,

$$\pi_t - E_t \pi_t = -c(q_t)(x_t - x_t^*)$$

So if profits at t are large compared to average profits *for that size of firm*, it means that x_t is unusually low. And this leads to a downward revision of expected marginal costs: $x_{t+1}^* < x_t^*$. But then next period's output – and growth – will be higher than usual. So, high profits are transformed into high growth. Of course, the standard "explanation" has relied on imperfect capital markets: constraints on borrowing lead to higher growth for firms that can finance it internally.

Fluctuations in output occur in any industry. What fraction is due to changes in the output of existing firms as opposed to changes – through entry or exit – in the number of firms? If demand changes are erratic and unforeseen, one might expect the existing firms to meet a large proportion of such changes. But in this paper, all the demand changes are foreseen. Holding constant the behavior of demand, a lot hinges on whether $q(\cdot)$ is concave in x or not (see (3.1) for the concavity condition). Why should this matter? Suppose for the moment that price is constant, say at $\bar{p}$. Since x_t^* is a Martingale, concavity and Jensen's inequality imply that $E_t q(\bar{p}/x_{t+1}^*) < q(\bar{p}/x_t^*)$. So when the output price does not increase, the existing firms would produce *less* in each successive period. This is only re-inforced by the reduction of output due to exit of some of the existing firms. So, if $q(\cdot)$ is concave in x, increases in demand should be met by new entrants. Theorem 3 proves that when demand is non-decreasing and $q(\cdot)$ concave in x, the unique equilibrium is one in which price is constant over time and in which entry and exit occur in every period.

No technological progress takes place in this model. Yet it seems possible (but I cannot prove it) that even if demand is constantly shifting to the right, equilibrium price will constantly decline. Since the efficient survive while the inefficient fail, the average efficiency of the survivors improves from period to period. Convexity of $q(\cdot)$ in x is a necessary condition for such an equilibrium to occur. On the other hand, prices cannot monotonically increase, as the net value to entry would become positive.

What can be proved is that equilibrium *always* coincides with the unique maximum to the discounted consumer surplus (Theorem 2). This is not surprising – firms take prices as given and there are no externalities. Still, as background to the current work on oligopolistic entry-deterrence, it is useful to know that at least when numbers are large, entry – and exit – occurs neither too early nor too late.

Some specialized results can also be proved. The variability of growth rates will be largest among the young (and therefore smaller) firms. But for mature firms that have survived for a long time, x_t^* converges to a constant. Therefore, if growth rates are to be equal among *mature* firms (and there is some empirical basis for this: samples of *large* firms were used in [14 and 16]), one must have, for each x,

$$\frac{1}{q}\frac{dq}{dp_t} = k(p_t)$$

where $k(p_t)$ is some function which does not depend on firm size and is therefore independent of x.

Solving this differential equation under the constraint that q is a function only of the ratio p_t/x,

$$q(p_t/x) = \delta_t \left[\frac{p_t}{x}\right]^\delta \tag{3.4}$$

where δ_1 and δ are positive constants. This can only happen if $c(q)$ assumes the Cobb–Douglas form

$$c(q) = \beta_1 q^{\beta_2} \qquad \text{with} \qquad \beta_2 = 1/\delta + 1$$

and with

$$\beta_1 = \delta_1^{-1/\delta}\left[\frac{\delta}{1+\delta}\right]$$

Since the restriction in (3.4) applies to *all* firms, the growth rate of any given firm is

$$\left[\frac{p_{t+1}}{p_t}\right]^\delta \left[\frac{x_t^*}{x_{t+1}^*}\right]^\delta - 1$$

In the sections that follow, we shall *not* restrict the cost function to be Cobb–Douglas. But it is instructive to pursue further the implications of the existence of approximately equal expected growth rates of firms of a given vintage. Let $z_t \equiv x_t^*/x_{t+1}^*$. If (3.5) holds, a weak form of the proportional growth law requires that $E_t z_t^\delta$ be the same for all x_t^*. A strong form requires that the entire distribution of z_t (conditional on information at t) be the same for all firms. The strong form of the law has been empirically rejected, and we now show that it cannot hold within the framework of this model: since the Martingale x_t^* has decreasing incremental variance as the precision on θ grows, two firms with the same x_t^* but different precisions could not have the same distribution for z_t. However, z_t can have the same distribution for firms in the same age cohort. Since one may write $x_{t+1}^* = x_t^*(1 + u_t)$ where u_t has mean zero due to the Martingale property, $z_t = 1/(1 + u_t)$ will be identically distributed for each firm in the cohort so long as the distribution of u_t does not depend on x_t^*. Then $\xi(\eta)$ may be chosen so that this property holds. Let $x_t - \alpha_1$ be log-normally distributed so that $\xi(\eta) = \alpha_1 + e^\eta$. Let θ_n and ν_n denote the posterior mean and variance on θ when n observations $\{\eta_i\}_{i=0}^{n-1}$ are available. Then,

$$x_t^* = \alpha_1 + \exp\left\{\theta_{t-\tau} + \tfrac{1}{2}(\nu_{t-\tau} + \sigma^2)\right\}$$

As $\alpha_1 \to 0$,

$$z_t \to \frac{1}{1 + u_t} = \frac{x_t^*}{x_{t+1}^*} = \exp\left\{(\theta_{t-\tau} - \theta_{t+1-\tau}) + \tfrac{1}{2}(\nu_{t-\tau} - \nu_{t+1-\tau})\right\}$$

and since the distribution of $\theta_{t-\tau} - \theta_{t+1-\tau}$ (conditional on information available at t) is normal with mean zero and variance that does *not* depend on $\bar{\eta}_n$, only on $t - \tau$, the variable $1/(1 + u_t)$ does not depend on x_t^*.

Since the variance of u_t declines as the firm becomes more mature, younger firms have more variability in their growth rates. They will also grow faster than the older firms. This follows from the convexity of x_t^*/x_{t+1}^* and the application of Jensen's inequality: $E_t(x_t^*/x_{t+1}^*) > x_t^*/E_t x_{t+1}^* = 1$. So even the weak form of the law cannot hold except within a single age cohort.

The implication that smaller firms should have higher and more variable growth rates is in accord with evidence. But there is a selection bias in the data. Smaller firms are more likely to fail and the model implies (see Figure 1) that the firms which fail are exactly those which otherwise would have grown more slowly. If, as is done in practice, all failures are omitted from the sample, one overestimates the growth rate of small firms relative to that of large firms. The model implies that even if one were to eliminate this bias by an appropriate choice of statistical technique, the results should show a higher growth-rate for smaller firms.

4. Equilibrium

Before defining equilibrium, the industry supply and demand functions are defined. Let

$$\Psi(x|t, \tau; p) = \text{Prob } x_s^* < \gamma(s - \tau, s; p), s = \tau + 1, \ldots, t - 1, \text{ and } x_t^* < \min$$
$$[x, \gamma(t \quad \tau, t; p)] \text{ given } x_\tau^* = x_0 \text{ and given that entry occurred at}$$
$$\tau (\tau < t)]$$

Ψ is the probability that the firm which enters at τ, and follows its optimal stopping policy, is still in the industry at t, at which time its $x_t^* \leq x$. (Note that since s runs from $\tau + 1$, *immediate* exit is not feasible – it is not feasible for the firm to exit without having spent at least one period in the industry.) Then,

$$\phi(t, \tau; p) \equiv \int q(p_t/x)\Psi(dx|t, \tau; p) \tag{4.2}$$

is the expected output at t of a firm of vintage τ. If y_τ is the measure of entrants at time τ, the output of these firms at t is $y_\tau \phi(t, \tau; p)$. This output is deterministic, as each firm is of measure zero. Let Q_t be the aggregate industry output at t. Then, the industry *supply function* is

$$Q_t = \sum_{\tau=0}^{t} y_\tau \phi(t,\tau;p) \equiv Q_t(p,y)$$

where $y \equiv \{y_\tau\}_0^\infty$ is a sequence of entry. So $Q_t(p,y)$ is the industry output at t which results if the firms are faced with an *arbitrary* pair of price and entry sequences (p, y), and if they make optimal output and exit decisions in response to the price sequence p.

A deterministic *demand function* $D[Q_t, t]$ is given for each t. For each t, $D(\cdot)$ is strictly decreasing in Q_t.

A perfect foresight equilibrium has the property that if firms and prospective entrants behave on the assumption that a particular price sequence will occur, then their behavior does in fact give rise to this price sequence. In other words, the equilibrium price sequence is self-fulfilling.

4.1. Definition of Equilibrium

Equilibrium is of a pair of functions $q(\cdot)$ and $\Psi(\cdot)$ that characterize optimal output and exit behavior of firms, and a pair of nonnegative sequences (p, y) such that for all $t = 0, 1, \ldots,$

$$p_t = D\{Q_t(p,y), t\} \tag{D1}$$

$$V(x_0, 0, t; p) - k = W \text{ if } y_t > 0$$

$$V(x_0, 0, t; p) - k \leq W \text{ if } y_t = 0 \tag{D2}$$

where $Q_t(p, y)]$ is defined in (4.3).

Condition D.1 expresses the self-fulfilling property of the equilibrium price sequence. Condition D.2 states that at each t, the net present value to entry cannot be positive, for if it were, more firms would enter, so that this could not be an equilibrium. The value to entry may be negative in some of the periods, in which case no firm would enter.

5. Existence, Uniqueness, and Optimality of Equilibrium

We prove the existence and uniqueness of the equilibrium by showing that it is a unique maximum to a particular functional – the discounted consumer plus producer surplus. The equilibrium is an optimum in this sense.

Before plunging into the algebra, let us review the elements of the argument. A benevolent planner chooses an industry output sequence $\{Q_t\} \equiv Q$ so as to maximize the discounted sum of surplus. He has exactly the same amount of information as is collectively available to firms. He assigns the entry and exit in each time period, as well as the output of each firm. The benevolent planner is concerned only with one industry and shadow prices in other industries are held constant both through time and with respect to the industry output level.

One possible approach could have been to use dynamic programming. But the state space is too large here: a firm is characterized by its expected cost and its age (this is the basis for (3.1)) while the industry is described by a *measure* over (x_t^*, n) – the measure of firms, at t, with those characteristics. Because of the dimensionality of the state space, we take the route of direct optimization subject to constraints. There are problems with this approach too, because the horizon is infinite. The constraint space is ℓ_∞, and linear functionals in the dual of ℓ_∞ do not assume a simple form (see (5.8)). The key result is in Lemma 5 (which is probably of independent interest) where it is shown that – essentially because of discounting – the class of linear functionals in the dual of ℓ_∞ can be reduced to a "manageable" subclass.

The cheapest way (for the planner) of producing an aggregate output sequence Q, is defined as $K(Q)$. The hard part of the proof is showing that $K(Q)$ is well-defined (Lemma 2), convex, and differentiable (Lemma 7).

Having established the relevant properties of $K(Q)$, we proceed to compare the necessary conditions for $S(Q)$ to be at a maximum, with the necessary conditions for the actions of firms to be optimal in the perfect foresight equilibrium. This comparison turns out to be easier if an alternative representation for the value of entry is used. This representation is derived (at the outset) in equation (5.2). We now proceed with the analysis.

In view of equation (4.1), another representation for the value of entry at $\tau, V(x_0, 0, \tau; p)$ is

$$V(x_0, 0, \tau; p) = \sum_{t=\tau}^{\infty} \beta^{t-\tau} \int_{\alpha_1}^{\alpha_2} \pi(p_t, x) \Psi(dx|t, \tau; p)$$
$$+ \sum_{t=\tau}^{\infty} \beta^{t-\tau} W\{\Psi(\alpha_2|t-1, \tau; p) - \Psi(\alpha_2|t, \tau; p)\} \qquad (5.1)$$

because the expression in curly brackets is just the probability of exit exactly at t. (Here we define $\Psi(\alpha_2|\tau - 1, \tau; p) = 1$.) Writing $\psi_t \equiv \Psi(\alpha_2|t, \tau; p)$ (since α_2, τ, and p are fixed), the second part of equation (5.1) may be written as

$$W \sum_{t=\tau}^{\infty} \beta^{t-\tau}(\psi_t - \psi_{t-1}) = W \left[\psi_{\tau-1} + \beta \sum_{t=\tau}^{\infty} \beta^{t-\tau}\psi_t - \sum_{t=\tau}^{\infty} \beta^{t-\tau}\psi_t \right]$$
$$= -(1 - \beta)W \sum_{t-\tau}^{\infty} \beta^{t-\tau}\psi_t + W$$

(because $\psi_{\tau-1} = 1$). Therefore,

$$V(x_0, 0, \tau; p) = W + \sum_{t=\tau}^{\infty} \beta^{t-\tau} \int_{\alpha_1}^{\alpha_2} [\pi(p_t, x) - (1 - \beta)W] \Psi(dx|t, \tau; p) \qquad (5.2)$$

(The intuition here is that $(1 - \beta)W$ is the per-unit time expected foregone income for the firm while it is in the industry.)

Now let $\gamma \equiv \{\gamma_t\}_{t=1}^{\infty}$ be a particular sequence bounded above by α_2 and below by α_1. Any such sequence γ represents a *feasible* exit policy. Let Γ be the set of all such sequences. That is,

$$\Gamma = \{\gamma : \gamma_t \in [\alpha_1, \alpha_2], t = 1, \ldots\}$$

Then, analogously to equation (4.1), for any $\gamma \in \Gamma$, let

$$\hat{\Psi}_\gamma(x|t, \tau) = \text{Prob}\ [x_s^* < \gamma_{s-\tau}, s = \tau + 1, \ldots, t, \text{ and } x_t^* < \min\ (x, \gamma_{t-\tau})$$
$$\text{given } x_\tau = x_0 \text{ and entry occurred at } \tau]$$

In words, $\hat{\Psi}_\gamma(\cdot)$ is the distribution of x at t (for vintage-τ firms) if they follow the feasible policy characterized by γ.

LEMMA 1:   *The density $\hat{\psi}_\gamma(x|t, \tau) = \partial \hat{\Psi}_\gamma(x|t, \tau)/\partial x$ exists for all γ, and $t > \tau$, and any $x \in (\alpha_1, \alpha_2)$. Furthermore, $\hat{\Psi}_\gamma$ is differentiable in each element, γ_j, of the sequence γ, for all $j \geq 1$.*

PROOF: Contained in the Appendix.

Now let $\gamma(p, \tau) \equiv \{\gamma(t - \tau, t; p)\}_{t=\tau}^{t=\infty}$ [the latter is defined in (3.3)]. Then $\gamma(p, \tau) \in \Gamma$. Therefore $\Psi(x|t, \tau; p)$ [defined in (4.1)] has density $\psi(x|t, \tau; p)$. Then $\psi(x|t, \tau; p)$ is the solution to the problem

$$\max_{\gamma \in \Gamma} \left\{ W + \sum_{t=\tau}^{\infty} \beta^{t-\tau} \int_{\alpha_1}^{\alpha_2} [\pi(p_t, x) - (1 - \beta)W] \hat{\psi}_\gamma(x|t, \tau) dx \right\} \tag{5.3}$$

because the optimal "cutoff" sequence $\gamma(p, \tau)$ is contained in Γ. Of course, $\psi(x|t, \tau; p) = \hat{\psi}_{\gamma(p, \tau)}(x|t, \tau)$. Writing $\gamma_j(p, \tau)$ for the jth member of the optimal sequence, since $\gamma_j(p, \tau) \in [\alpha_1, \alpha_2]$, the necessary conditions for optimality may be written for $j = 1, \cdots,$

$$\left\{ \sum_{t=\tau}^{\infty} \beta^{t-\tau} \int_{\alpha_1}^{\alpha_2} [\pi(p_t, x) - (1 - \beta)W] \frac{\partial \psi}{\partial \gamma_j}(x|t, \tau; p) dx \right\} \times [\gamma_j - \gamma_j(p, \tau)] \leq 0 \tag{5.4}$$

for all $\gamma_j \in [\alpha_1, \alpha_2]$.

Let $Q \equiv \{Q_t\}_0^{\infty}$ be a bounded output sequence. Let ℓ_∞ denote the set of bounded infinite sequences. We now define the social benefit functional $S : \ell_\infty \to R$ as

$$S(Q) = \sum_{t=0}^{\infty} \beta^t \int_0^{Q_t} D(z, t) dz - K(Q) \tag{5.5}$$

where $K : \ell_\infty \to R$ is the present value of the minimized cost of producing the output sequence Q.

The problem of attaining $K(Q)$ will be referred to as the "planner's cost minimization problem." We shall assume that the planner possesses all of the information available to each firm. He chooses an entry sequence[4] $y \equiv \{y_t\}_0^\infty \in A_1$, where $A_1 = \{y : 0 \le y_t \le \tilde{y}_t,$ where $\sum_{t=0}^\infty \tilde{y}_t < \infty\}$, and for firms of vintage τ he chooses an exit policy $\gamma(\tau) \equiv \{\gamma_j(\tau)\}_{j=1}^\infty \in \Gamma$. Finally he assigns a nonnegative output level $\hat{q}(x, t)$ to a firm which at t has $x_t^* = x$. Let $A_2 = \{\hat{q}(x, t):$ each t and $x \in [\alpha_1, \alpha_2], 0 \le \hat{q}(x, t) \le b(x)$, with $b(x)$ Lebesgue integrable$\}$. By Tychonoff's theorem on product spaces, A_1, Γ, and A_2 are compact sets in their product topology. Let $\Gamma^\infty = \Gamma \times \Gamma \times \cdots$, and let $\gamma \equiv \{\gamma(\tau)\}_{\tau=0}^\infty$, so that $\gamma \in \Gamma^\infty$. Similarly, let $A_2^\infty = A \times A \times \cdots$ and let $\hat{q} \equiv \{\hat{q}(\cdot, t)\}_{t=0}^\infty$, so that $\hat{q} \in A_2^\infty$. Finally let $s \equiv (y, \gamma, \hat{q}) \in A_1 \times \Gamma^\infty \times A_2^\infty \equiv \Omega$. Again, Ω is a product of compact spaces and is therefore compact in its product topology. Then one may write

$$K(Q) = \inf_{s \in \Omega} f(s) \qquad \text{subject to} \qquad G_t(s, Q_t) \le 0$$

for $t = 0, 1, \ldots$, where

$$f(s) = \sum_{t=0}^\infty \beta^t \left\{ \sum_{\tau=0}^t y_\tau \int_{\alpha_1}^{\alpha_2} (c[\hat{q}(x, t)]x + (1 - \beta)W)\hat{\psi}_{\gamma(\tau)}(x|t, \tau)dx + ky_t \right\}$$

and where

$$G_t(s, Q_t) = -\sum_{\tau=0}^t y_\tau \int_{\alpha_1}^{\alpha_2} \hat{q}(x, t)\hat{\psi}_{\gamma(\tau)}(x|t, \tau)dx + Q_t$$

so that $f : \Omega \to R^1$ and $G_t : \Omega \times \ell_\infty \to R^1$. The meaning of the constraint $G_t(s, Q_t) \le 0$ is that the planner is required to produce *no less* than the target output Q_t at t. This constraint holds at each t.

Let $G(s, Q) \equiv \{G_t(s, Q_t)\}_{t=0}^\infty$. Since G_t is bounded (uniformly in t), $G : \Omega \times \ell_\infty \to \ell_\infty$. The constraint may then be written as $G(s, Q) \le 0$.

LEMMA 2:   *There exists a constrained minimum for f on Ω.*

PROOF: Contained in the Appendix.

Simplifying the notation slightly, we write $G(s) \le 0$ for the constraint, dropping Q from the notation. We now define the Gateaux differentials $\delta f(s_0, s_1)$ $= df[s_0 + \alpha(s_1 - s_0)]/d\alpha$ and $\delta G(s_0, s_1) = dG[s_0 + \alpha(s_1 - s_0)]/d\alpha$ for $s_0, s_1, \in \Omega$. They are differentials at the point s_0, with increment $(s_1 - s_0)$. We have $\delta f : \Omega \to R$ and $\delta G : \Omega \to \ell_\infty$. Since Ω is convex, the point $s_1 + \alpha(s_1 - s_0)(= (1 - \alpha)s_0 + \alpha s_1) \in \Omega$ for all $\alpha \in [0, 1]$.

Definition: A point $s_0 \in \Omega$ is said to be a regular point of the inequality $G(s) \le 0$ if $G(s_0) \le 0$ and there exists a point $s_1 \in \Omega$ such that

$G(s_0) + \delta G(s_0, s_1) < 0[12, \text{p. } 248]$. The inequality is strict at each coordinate, i.e., $G_t(s_0) + \delta G_t(s_0, s_1) < 0$ for each t.

LEMMA 3:   *Let $f(s_0) = \min f(s)$ subject to $G(s) \leq 0$. Then if $Q_t > 0$ (each t), s_0 is a regular point.*

PROOF: Contained in the Appendix. Of course, the condition that the maximum occurs at a regular point is the analogue of the Kuhn–Tucker constraint qualification in the finite dimensional case.

Let P be the positive cone of ℓ_∞. Then P contains an interior point (any bounded, strictly positive sequence which is bounded away from zero is an interior point of P). Let ℓ_∞^* be the dual space of ℓ_∞, that is, the space of bounded linear functionals on ℓ_∞. Let $\lambda \in \ell_\infty^*$ be a particular functional. Its value at the point $z \in \ell_\infty$ will be denoted by $\lambda(z)$. We then have the following lemma.

LEMMA 4:   *If s_0 minimizes f on Ω subject to $G(s) \leq 0$, then there exists a functional $\lambda^* \in \ell_\infty^*$ such that if $Q > 0$,*

$$\delta f(s_0; s) + \lambda^*[\delta G(s_0; s)] \geq 0 \quad \text{for all } s \in \Omega \tag{5.6}$$

and such that $\lambda^* > 0$ and

$$\lambda^*[G(s_0)] = 0 \tag{5.7}$$

PROOF: [12, pp. 249–50]: (His proof relies on s_0 being regular (and this we have established in Lemma 3) and on the interior point property of P.)

We now proceed to characterize λ^*. Since $\lambda^* \in \ell_\infty^*$, it is representable in the following way: for any sequence $\eta \in \ell_\infty$:

$$\lambda^*(\eta) = \sum_{t=0}^{\infty} \lambda_t^* \eta_t + \int \eta d\hat{\lambda}^* \tag{5.8}$$

where $\hat{\lambda}^*$ is a bounded and *purely finitely additive* measure on the set of all possible subsets of the positive integers [9, p. 870; 19, p. 52] and where $\sum |\lambda_t^*| < \infty$. The purely finitely additive property implies $\int \eta d\hat{\lambda}^* = 0$ for all $\eta \in \ell_\infty$ such that only finitely many elements of the sequence η are nonzero. We now prove that $\lambda_t^* > 0$ (each t) and that $\int \eta d\hat{\lambda}^* = 0$, for all $\eta \in \ell_\infty$.

At the optimal solution, $s_0, G_t(s_0) = 0$. For if $G_t(s_0) < 0$, one could reduce f by reducing $\hat{q}^0(x, t)$ (for t only) on a set of positive measure without violating the constraint at t, and leaving all the other constraints unaffected. If s_1 differs from s_0 only in as much as $\hat{q}^1(x, t) \neq \hat{q}^0(x, t)$ for some x and for *fixed* t, only the constraint at t is affected. More precisely $\delta G_i(s_0; s_1)$ is zero except for $i = t$. Hence, for such variations, $\lambda^*[\delta G(s_0; s_1)] = \lambda_t^* \delta G_t(s_0; s_1)$ (in view of (5.8)). Equation (5.6) then implies

$$\sum_{\tau=0}^{t} y_\tau^0 \int \left\{ \beta^t c' [\hat{q}^0(x,t)]x - \lambda_t^* \right\} [\hat{q}^1(x,t) - \hat{q}^0(x,t)] \hat{\psi}_{\gamma_{(\tau)}^0} (x|t,\tau) dx \geq 0 \qquad (5.9)$$

for all $\hat{q}^1$ which are integrable. (We shall refer to "sets on which

$$\sum_{\tau=0}^{t} y_\tau^0 \hat{\psi}_{\gamma_{(\tau)}^0} (x|t,\tau)$$

is of positive Lebesgue measure" as sets of positive measure. Clearly, variations in $\hat{q}$ on sets of measure zero in this sense are immaterial since they affect neither f nor G.) Since $Q_t > 0, \hat{q}^0(x,t) > 0$ on a set of positive measure, so that $c'[\hat{q}^0(\cdot)] > 0$ on these sets. But then $\lambda_t^* > 0$, or else there would exist an admissible variation which would violate equation (5.9). Also, if $\hat{q}^0(x,t) = 0$ on some set of positive measure, it is readily seen that since $c'(0) = 0$, equation (5.9) would again be violated by an admissible variation. Therefore $\hat{q}^0 > 0$, which implies that except on sets of measure zero, for each t,

$$\lambda_t^* = \beta^t c' [\hat{q}^0(x,t)]x > 0 \qquad (5.10)$$

We are now able to prove the following lemma.

LEMMA 5: $\int \eta d\hat{\lambda}^* = 0$ for all $\eta \in \ell_\infty$.

PROOF: Contained in the Appendix.

Lemma 5 establishes that the second expression on the right-hand side of equation (5.8) is equal to zero. Now let $s_1 = s_0$ except that $y_t^1 \neq y_t^0$ for some t. Then equation (5.6) reads (in view of Lemma 5)

$$\left\{ \frac{\partial f}{\partial y_t} + \sum_{j=t}^{\infty} \lambda_j^* \frac{\partial G_j}{\partial y_t} \right\} (y_t^1 - y_t^0) \geq 0$$

for all y_t^1. Therefore, if $y_t^0 > 0, \partial f/\partial y_t + \sum_{j=t}^{\infty} \lambda_j^* \partial G_j/\partial y_t = 0$ while if $y_t^0 = 0$, then $\partial f/\partial y_t + \sum_{j=t}^{\infty} \lambda_j^* \partial G_j/\partial y_t \geq 0$. This implies that

$$\sum_{j=t}^{\infty} \int \left\{ \beta^j [c(\hat{q}^0)x + W(1-\beta)] - \lambda_j^* \hat{q}^0 \right\} \hat{\psi}_{\gamma^0(t)} (x|j,t) dx + \beta^t k \gtreqqless 0 \text{ as } y_t^0 \gtreqqless 0 \qquad (5.11)$$

Finally we consider the variation for which $s_1 = s_0$, except that $\gamma_i^1(\tau) \neq \gamma_i^0(\tau)$ for some $i \geq 1$ and some $\tau \geq 0$. Applying Lemma 5, equation (5.6) reads

$$\left\{ \frac{\partial f}{\partial \gamma_i(\tau)} + \sum_{j=\tau+i}^{\infty} \lambda_j^* \frac{\partial G_j}{\partial \gamma_i(\tau)} \right\} [\gamma_i^1(\tau) - \gamma_i^0(t)] \geq 0 \qquad (5.12)$$

(note that a change in $\gamma_i(\tau)$ does not affect G_t for $t < \tau + i$). Then equation (5.12) implies that for all $\gamma_i^1(\tau) \in [\alpha_1, \alpha_2]$,

$$
\left\{ \sum_{j=\tau+i}^{\infty} \int \left\{ \beta^j [c(\hat{q}^0)x + W(1-\beta)] - \lambda_j^* q^0 \right\} \frac{\partial \hat{\psi}_\gamma^0(\tau)}{\partial \gamma_i(\tau)} (x|t, \tau) dx \right\}
$$

$$
\times y_\tau^0 [\gamma_i^1(\tau) - \gamma_i^0(\tau)] \geq 0 \tag{5.13}
$$

If $y_\tau^0 = 0$, this inequality is automatically satisfied – there are no firms of vintage τ.

LEMMA 6:   *The Lagrangean* $L(s, \lambda^*) = f(s) + \lambda^* [G(s)]$ *is minimized over* s *at* (s_0, λ^*) *satisfying equations* (5.10), (5.11), *and* (5.13). *The point* $f(s_0)$ *is a global constrained minimum.*

PROOF: Contained in the Appendix. Lemma 6 ensures that the minimum attained at s_0 is indeed the global minimum.

LEMMA 7: $K(Q)$ *is convex in* Q, *and is differentiable in the elements of* Q, *with* $\partial K / \partial Q_t = \lambda_t^*$.

PROOF: Contained in the Appendix.

The social marginal cost is λ_t^*, in present value terms. From equation (5.10) this is also the discounted expected marginal cost of each firm.

We recall that the derived properties of $K(Q)$ hold only for sequences Q which are bounded away from zero by some positive ϵ. However, for each such ϵ, λ_t^* is bounded uniformly in $Q \in \ell_\infty$. Let $\bar{\lambda}$ be the upper bound on λ. The following assumption on demand ensures that marginal benefits exceed marginal costs at some sufficiently small level of output at each t: we assume that for some $\epsilon > 0$ sufficiently small,

$$
D(\epsilon, t) > \bar{\lambda} \text{ all } t \tag{5.14}
$$

Secondly, in order to ensure that the socially optimal output sequence is bounded, we assume that for each t

$$
\int_0^\infty D(z, t) dz < A \tag{5.15}
$$

for some A sufficiently large and independent of t.

PROPOSITION 1:   *There is exactly one bounded sequence* $\{Q_t^*\}$ *which maximizes* $S(Q)$ *in equation* (5.5), *and it satisfies*

$$
\beta^t D[Q_t^*, t] = \lambda_t^*, \qquad t = 0, 1, \ldots \tag{5.16}
$$

PROOF: Equation (5.15) implies that Q_t^* is bounded. Equation (5.14) ensures that Q_t^* is bounded away from zero. Each decision Q_t then belongs to a compact set, and $S(Q)$ is strictly concave in Q, because $D(Q_t, t)$ is downward sloping. Therefore the maximum exists and is unique. Since $S(Q)$ is also differentiable, one has $\partial S/\partial Q_t = 0$ at the optimum, which implies that equation (5.16) holds, and the proof is complete.

Let $\hat{q}^*(x, t)$ and $\hat{\psi}_{\gamma^*(\tau)}(x|t, \tau)$ denote the optimal $\hat{q}$ and $\hat{\psi}$ for minimizing f when $Q = Q^*$. We may now state:

THEOREM 2   (Existence, Uniqueness, Optimality): *There is exactly one equilibrium price sequence $\tilde{p}$ and entry sequence $\tilde{y}$ satisfying D1 and D2 in section 4. The price sequence is given by $\tilde{p}_t = \beta^{-t}\lambda_t^*$. The social benefit functional $S(Q)$ is at a maximum with $Q_t^* = Q_t(\tilde{p}, \tilde{y})$, where $\hat{q}^*(x, t) = q(\tilde{p}_t/x)$ and where $\hat{\psi}_{\gamma^*(\tau)}(x|t, \tau) = \hat{\psi}_\gamma(\tilde{p}, \tau)(x|t, \tau)$.*

PROOF: From equation (5.10) it is seen that $\hat{q}^*(x, t) = q(\tilde{p}_t/x)$. Substituting this for $\hat{q}^*$ into equation (5.13), this condition becomes identical to equation (5.4) when the latter is evaluated at $\psi(x|t, \tau; \tilde{p})$. Therefore $\hat{\psi}_{\gamma^*(t)} = \psi(x|t, \tau; \tilde{p})$ as asserted. Substituting for $\hat{q}^*$ and $\hat{\psi}_{\gamma^*(t)}$ in equation (5.11), this condition is identical to condition D2. Finally, from Lemma 8, $D[Q_t(\tilde{p}, \tilde{y}), t] = p_t^*$ so that condition D1 is satisfied. Therefore, the maximum is necessarily an equilibrium. This establishes existence. For uniqueness and optimality, note that since any candidate equilibrium price and entry sequence, $(\tilde{p}, \tilde{y})$ satisfies $\tilde{p}_t = \beta^{-t}(\partial K/\partial Q_t)[Q_t(\tilde{p}, \tilde{y})]$, condition D1 requires that $\tilde{p}_t = D[Q_t(\tilde{p}, \tilde{y}), t]$. This requires that $S(Q)$ be maximized by $Q_t(\tilde{p}, \tilde{y})$. By lemma 7 this maximum is unique. Therefore $Q(\tilde{p}, \tilde{y}) = Q^*$, and $\tilde{p}_t = \beta^{-t}\lambda_t^*$, so that the equilibrium $(\tilde{p}, \tilde{y})$ is necessarily a maximum. This completes the proof of the theorem.

6. Two Characterization Theorems

This section gives some characterization of the behavior of entry and prices in equilibrium. Much depends on whether $q(p_t/x)$ is convex in x. This is made precise in the following theorem.

THEOREM 3:   *Assume that $D[Q_t, x]$ is nondecreasing in t (demand grows monotonically). If $q(p/x)$ is a strictly concave function of x [see equation (3.1)], then the equilibrium price sequence is constant, with $p_t^* = \bar{p}$ for each t, and entry occurs at each $t(y_t^* > 0)$ while $\sum_0^\infty y_t^* < \infty$, and $V(x_0, 0, t; \bar{p}) - k = W$ for each t.*

PROOF: Since D2 must hold, profits to entry must be zero at each t. Suppose the optimal exit policies of firms are such that no firm exits under any circumstance. Since x_t^* is a martingale, strict concavity of $q(\cdot)$ in x implies (by Jensen's inequality) $E_t q(\bar{p}/x_{t+1}^*) < q(\bar{p}/x_t^*)$. This implies that $\phi(t, \tau; p^*) > \phi(t + 1, \tau; p^*)$ for each $t \geq \tau$. This inequality is only reinforced by firms making an exit under some contingencies. In other words, if the price is constant at $\bar{p}$, the output of the survivors (of any given vintage) would decline with time *even if none were to exit*. It follows that it will decline even more if some do exit. Define $A_t(\bar{p})$ by $\bar{p} = D[A_t(\bar{p}), t]$. In other words, $A_t(\bar{p})$ is the amount of output which must be forthcoming at t if price is to be kept constant at $\bar{p}$. Then since demand is nondecreasing in t, the sequence $\{A_t(\bar{p})\}$ is also nondecreasing in t. Since for each t, ϕ declines in t, the output of the survivors is declining. Therefore $y_t^* > 0$ for each t because if $y_t^* = 0$ for some t, price at t would be strictly greater than in the previous period. Finally, since $A_t(\bar{p})$ is bounded, one has $\sum_0^\infty y_t^* < \infty$ if $\inf_{t,\tau}\phi(t,\tau;p^*) > 0$. For this it is sufficient to show that for each τ, $\lim_{t\to\infty}\Psi(\alpha_2|t,\tau;p^*) > 0$, that is, the probability of permanent survival is positive for firms of each vintage. To prove that this is so, consider the policy: "stay in for one more period, then exit no matter what." The expected reward from this policy is $\pi(\bar{p}, x) + \beta W$. Therefore the firm will not exit if this reward is greater than W, or equivalently, if $\pi(\bar{p}, x) > (1 - \beta)W$. Let $\hat{x}$ be such that $\pi(\bar{p}, \hat{x}) = (1 - \beta)W$, so that the firm stays in if $x_t^* < \hat{x}$. Of course, $\hat{x} > \alpha_1$, otherwise the net value of entry at all t would be negative. For each firm of age n (see section 3), $x_t^* = E(x|\bar{\eta}_n, n)$. Let $\bar{\eta}_n$ be such that $\hat{x} = E(x|\bar{\eta}_n, n)$. Since $\hat{x} > \alpha_1$, $\hat{\eta}_n$ is bounded from below. Therefore exit does not occur so long as $\bar{\eta}_n < \hat{\eta}_n$. But the probability that a normal posterior mean does not ever reach a boundary that is *bounded* is strictly positive (Chernoff [3]). Therefore $\lim_{t\to\infty}\Psi(\alpha_2|t,\tau;p^*) > 0$ for all τ, and $\sum_0^\infty y_t^* < \infty$. This completes the proof of the theorem.

The concavity of $q(\cdot)$ in x is (under conditions of increasing demand) sufficient to imply a constant-price equilibrium. But it is not necessary. The concavity of q in x was, in the proof of Theorem 3, used only to prove that $\phi(t + 1, \tau; p^*) < \phi(t, \tau; p^*)$. If q is convex in x, this means that the collective output of the *surviving* firms is larger at $t + 1$ than it was at t. But the subtraction from the total output due to firms' exit might still be larger than this increase, resulting, on net, in a decrease in ϕ.

It seems possible that after withdrawals have occurred, the surviving firms will increase their output by *more* than the increase in the quantity demanded (at an unchanged price), thereby making it necessary for price to fall over time. In view of Theorem 3, convexity of q in x is a *necessary* condition for such an equilibrium to occur.

THEOREM 4: $K(Q)$ *is homogeneous to degree one: for any* $\alpha > 0, \alpha K(Q) = K(\alpha Q)$. *An equiproportional shift to the right of demand (for all t) brings about an increase in Q_t in the same proportion for all t. Equilibrium prices remain unchanged.*

PROOF: IF $(y^0, \hat{q}^0, \gamma^0)$ MINIMIZES f WHEN THE CONSTRAINT IS Q_0, THEN $(\alpha y^0, \hat{q}^0, \gamma^0)$ MINIMIZES IT WHEN THE CONSTRAINT IS αQ_0: SINCE f IS LINEAR HOMOGENEOUS IN y, THIS PROVES $(Q) = K(\alpha Q)$ FOR ALL q. NOW INTRODUCE THE DEMAND-SHIFT-PARAMETER μ, SUCH THAT $D[Q_t, t, u] = D[\mu Q_t, t]$. EQUILIBRIUM REQUIRES THAT $\beta^t D[\mu Q_t(\mu), t] = \partial K[Q(\mu)]/\partial Q_t$, WHERE $\{Q_t(\mu)\}$ IS THE EQUILIBRIUM QUANTITY SEQUENCE INDEXED BY μ. WE NEED TO SHOW THAT $Q(\mu) = Q(1)/\mu$. BY HOMOGENEITY OF K, $\alpha\partial K(Q)/\partial Q_t = \alpha\partial K(\alpha Q)/\partial Q_t$ FOR ALL $\alpha > 0$ AND Q, SO THAT $\partial K(Q)/\partial Q_t = \partial K(\alpha Q)/\partial Q_t$. LETTING $Q = Q(1)$ AND $\alpha = 1/\mu$, THE RESULT FOLLOWS.

Appendix

PROOF OF THEOREM 1:   Part (i): The proof of this part consists of an application of Theorem 5 of [2]. Let T denote the operator which defines V as the fixed point of the equation (3.2) $V = TV$. First it needs to be shown that T transforms continuous, bounded functions into other continuous, bounded functions. Boundedness follows if $\pi(p_t, x_t^*)$ is bounded – the latter is true because (a) p_t is bounded, (b) $x_t^* \geq \alpha_1 > 0$, and (c) $\lim_{q \to \infty} c'(q) = \infty$, so that the necessary condition $p_t - c'(q_t)x_t^*$ is always satisfied at a bounded output level. To prove that T preserves continuity, note firstly that $\pi(\cdot)$ is continuous in x_t^*, as is P. Therefore T preserves boundedness and continuity.

Secondly, T is a monotone (increasing) operator. That is, for two functions f_1 and f_2, if $f_1 \geq f_2$ everywhere, then $Tf_1 \geq Tf_2$ everywhere.

Finally, for any function f and any constant $c > 0$, $T(f + c) \leq Tf + \beta c$.

Therefore T is a contraction operator with modulus $\beta < 1$, and the Banach fixed-point theorem may be applied to yield assertion (i) of the theorem.

Part (ii): The proof is in two steps. We first prove that V is nonincreasing in x and then use this to prove that it is strictly decreasing.

Let T denote the operator in equation (3.2) so that V is the unique solution to the equation $V = TV$. Since T is a contraction operator, we have $V = \lim_{n \to \infty} T^n g$ for *any* bounded, continuous function g [where $T^n g \equiv T(T^{n-1}g)$]. Any monotonicity properties of *each* member of the sequence $T^n g$ are preserved (weakly) by the limit function V. We shall now show that if g is decreasing in x, so is Tg. If $g(z)$ is decreasing in z, then so is the function $\max[W, g(z)]$. Then, since $P(z|x, n)$ is increasing in x, $\int \max[W, g(z)]P(dz|x, n)$ is decreasing in x. By induction, these properties carry over to the limit function V which is therefore nonincreasing in x. But then $\int \max[W, V(z, n + 1, t + 1; p)]P(dz|x, n)$ is nonincreasing in x. But π is strictly decreasing in x and therefore so is V.

PROOF OF LEMMA 1:   One has

$$\hat{\Psi}_\gamma(x|t, \tau) = \int_{\alpha_1}^{\alpha_2} H[\min(x, \gamma_{t-\tau})|z, t - 1 - \tau]\hat{\Psi}_\gamma(dz|t - 1, \tau)$$

where $H(z'|z, n)$ is the (one-step) transition probability that $x_t^* \leq z'$ given the pair of sufficient statistics $x_{t-1}^* = z$ and $n = t - 1 - \tau$. But H is a continuous transform of the normal CDF, and is differentiable in z' for $z' \in (\alpha_1, \alpha_2)$. Therefore if $\hat{\Psi}$ is continuous at t, then it is also differentiable at $t + 1$. Thus if $\hat{\Psi}$ is differentiable when $t = \tau + 1$, it is differentiable for all $t > \tau$. But $\hat{\Psi}(x|\tau + 1, \tau) = H[\min(x, \gamma_1|x_0, 0)]$ if $x_0 < \gamma_0$, while if $x_0 \geq \gamma_0$, $\hat{\Psi}(x|\tau + 1, \tau) = 0$, so that $\hat{\Psi}$ is differentiable when $t = \tau + 1$. Furthermore since H is continuously differentiable, so is $\hat{\Psi}$, except at the point $x = \gamma_{t-\tau}$, (where the derivative is in general discontinuous as it becomes zero for $x > \gamma_{t-\tau}$) so that the density $\hat{\psi}$ exists and is piecewise continuous. Turning to differentiability of $\hat{\psi}$ in γ_j, note that $\hat{\psi}_\gamma(x|t, \tau)$ does not depend on γ_j if $j > t - \tau$. For any $j < t - \tau$, $H[\cdot]$ does not depend on γ_j, and therefore if $\hat{\psi}$ is differentiable at t, it is differentiable at $t + 1$. Since this is true for any t, it is sufficient to show that $\hat{\psi}$ is differentiable at $t = \tau + j$, where

$$\hat{\Psi}_\gamma(x|\tau + j, \tau) = \int_{\alpha_1}^{\alpha_2} H[\min(x, \gamma_j)|z, j + \tau - 1]\hat{\psi}_\gamma(z|\tau + j - 1, \tau)dz$$

and where $\hat{\psi}_\gamma(z|\tau + j - 1, \tau)$ does not depend on γ_j. Then the cross-derivative $\partial^2 \hat{\Psi}/\partial x \partial \gamma_j$ exists, and this completes the proof of the lemma.

PROOF OF LEMMA 2:   Let $\Omega(Q) = \{s : G(s, Q) \leq 0\} \subseteq \Omega$. We need to show that f is continuous on $\Omega(Q)$ and that $\Omega(Q)$ is compact [1, p. 69]. In the product topology, sequences $\{s_i\}_0^\infty (s_i \in \Omega)$ converge to s_0 *weakly* [5, p. 32]. That is, $s_1 \to s_0$ if and only if

$y_t^1 \to y_t^0$ each t, $\hat{q}^1(x,t) \to \hat{q}^0(x,t)$ for each t except on a set of Lebesgue measure zero, and $\gamma_j^1(\tau) \to \gamma_j^0(\tau)$ for each j. Suppose then that $|f(s_1) - f(s_0)| \to \delta > 0$ as $s_1 \to s_0$, so that f is not continuous at s_0. Write $f(s)$ as $\sum_{t=0}^{\infty} \beta^t f_t(s)$. Since $f_t(s)$ is bounded on Ω, one may choose $T(\delta) < \infty$ such that $\sum_{t=T(\delta)}^{\infty} \beta^t |f_t(s_1) - f_t(s_0)| < (\delta/2) \forall s_1 \in \Omega$. Then

$$|f(s_1) - f(s_0)| \leq \sum_{t=0}^{T(\delta)-1} \beta^t |f_t(s_1) - f_t(s_0)| + \frac{\delta}{2}$$

$$\leq [T(\delta) - 1]_{0 \leq t \leq T(\delta)-1}^{\max} |f_t(s_1) - f_t(s_0)| + \frac{\delta}{2}$$

But for any $t < \infty$, $\hat{\psi}_\gamma(\tau)(x|t,\tau)$ depends only upon $\gamma_j(\tau)$ for $j = 1, \ldots, t - \tau$ and is continuous in γ_j, so that for each $t > \tau$, and each x, $\hat{\psi}_{\gamma^1(\tau)} \to \hat{\psi}_{\gamma^0(\tau)}$ as $s_1 \to s_0$ so that $|f_t(s_1) - f_t(s_0)| \to 0$ as $s_1 \to s_0$. But then $|f(s_1) - f(s_0)| \to (\delta/2) < \delta$, a contradiction. Therefore f is continuous on Ω.

Compactness of $\Omega(Q)$ is assured if $\Omega(Q)$ is closed, because a closed subset of a compact space is compact [1, p. 68]. $\Omega(Q)$ is closed if its complement is open. Consider then a point $s_0 \in \Omega$ such that $G_t(s_0, Q_t) > 0$ for each t. One must show that there exists an open neighborhood of s_0, $N(s_0)$, such that $G(s, Q) > 0$ for all $s \in N(s_0)$. Let $G_t(s, Q_t) = -\sum_0^t y_i z_i(\hat{q}, \gamma) + Q_t$. Then let $G(s_0, Q) > 0$. For any $s \in \Omega$, since y_t and z_t are bounded,

$$G_t(s, Q_t) - G_t(s_0, Q_t) = -\sum_0^t y_i(z_i - z_i^0) - \sum_0^t (y_i - y_i^0) z_i^0$$

Since $\sum_0^t y_i < \infty$, and $y_i \geq 0$, one has $\sum_T^{\infty} y_t \to 0$ as $T \to \infty$. Then one may choose $T = T(\delta)$ sufficiently large such that $\sum_{T(\delta)}^t y_i |z_i - z_i^0| + \sum_{T(\delta)}^t |y_i - y_i^0| z_i^0 < (\delta/2)$ for all $t \geq T(\delta)$. Then for any $t \geq T(\delta)$,

$$|G_t(s, Q_t) - G_t(s_0, Q_t)| \leq \sum_{i=0}^{T(\delta)-1} (y_i|z_i - z_i^0| + |y_i - y_i^0|z_i^0) + \frac{\delta}{2}$$

$$\leq [T(\delta)-] \Big(c_1 \, {}_{0 \leq i \leq T(\delta)-1}^{\max} |z_i - z_i^0|$$

$$+ c_2 \, {}_{0 \leq i \leq T(\delta)-1}^{\max} |y_i - y_i^0| \Big) + \frac{\delta}{2}$$

where the second inequality follows as both y_i and z_i are bounded. But for any $t < \infty$, $|z_i - z_i^0| \to 0$ and $|y_i - y_i^0| \to 0$ as $s \to s_0$. Since this is true for any $\delta > 0$, one has, for any t, that $G_t(s, Q_t) \to G_t(s_0, Q_t)$ as $s \to s_0$. This is true for each t; therefore $G(s, Q)$ converges to $G(s_0, Q)$, so that G is a continuous mapping. Therefore the set $\{s : G(s, Q) > 0\}$ is open. But s_0 is a member of this set (since by assumption $G(s_0, Q) > 0$). Therefore $\Omega(Q)$ is closed and the proof of Lemma 2 is complete.

PROOF OF LEMMA 3:   The $s_1 = (y^1, \gamma^0, \hat{q}^0)$ and $s_0 = (y^0, \gamma^0, \hat{q}^0)$. That is s_1 differs from s_0 only in the entry sequence y. Then,

$$\delta G_t(s_0; s_1) = -\sum_{\tau=0}^t (y_\tau^1 - y_\tau^0) \int \hat{q}^0(x,t) \hat{\psi}_{\gamma^0(\tau)}(x|t,\tau) dx$$

Since $G_t(s_0) \leq 0$, one need only show that $\delta G_t < 0$ (each t) for some $s_1 \in \Omega$. Since $Q_t > 0$, one has $\sum_0^t y_\tau^0 \int \hat{q}^0 \hat{\psi}_\gamma^0 dx > 0$ for each t. But then one may set $y_\tau^1 - y_\tau^0 = \alpha y_\tau^0 (\alpha > 0)$ in which case $\delta G_t(s_0; s_1) < 0$ for each t. Since $\sum^\infty y_\tau^0$ is finite, so is $(1 + \alpha) \sum^\infty y_\tau^0$ so that $s_1 \in \Omega$ and Lemma 3 has been proved.

PROOF OF LEMMA 5:   Suppose $\exists \, \eta \in \ell_\infty$ such that $|\int \eta d\hat{\lambda}^*| = \epsilon_1 > 0$. Then for any ϵ_2 no matter how small, $|\int \epsilon_2 \eta d\hat{\lambda}^*| = \epsilon_2 \epsilon_1 > 0$. Let $T > 0$ be given, and let

$$\eta_t^T = \begin{cases} \eta_t & \text{if } t \geq T \\ 0 & \text{if } 0 \leq t < T \end{cases} \quad \text{and} \quad \eta_t^1 = \begin{cases} 0 & \text{if } t \geq T \\ \eta_t & \text{if } 0 \leq t < T \end{cases}$$

By linearity, $\int \epsilon_2 \eta d\hat{\lambda}^* = \epsilon_2 \int (\eta^1 + \eta) d\hat{\lambda}^* = \epsilon_2 \int \eta^T d\hat{\lambda}^*$, where the second equality is due to the purely finitely additive property of λ^*. Next we show that $\exists \, s_1, s_2 \in \Omega$ such that $\delta G(s_0; s_1) = \epsilon_2 \eta^T$ and $\delta G(s_0; s_2) = -\epsilon_2 \eta^T$. For the first equality one may choose s_1 the same as s_0 except that $\hat{q}^1 = \hat{q}^0 (1 + \epsilon_2 \eta_t^T / Q_t)$ for each x, t. This is a feasible variation, since $\exists \, \epsilon > 0$ such that $Q_t \geq \epsilon \forall t$ so that one may set ϵ_2 sufficiently small such that $\epsilon_2 \bar{\eta}/\epsilon \leq 1$ (where $\bar{\eta}$ is such that $\eta_t \leq \bar{\eta} \forall \eta \in \ell_\infty$). Similarly, to obtain the second equality one sets $\hat{q}^1 = \hat{q}^0 (1 - \epsilon_2 \eta_t^T / Q_t)$. For each $\eta, \| \eta^T \| \to 0$ unless $\lim_{t \to \infty} \eta_t = 0$. But if $\lim_{t \to \infty} \eta_t = 0$, then the lemma is true [9, p. 872]. Suppose then that $\| \eta^T \| \to \epsilon_3 > 0$. (The limit must exist because $\| \eta^T \|$ is nonincreasing in T and positive.) Clearly, $\lim_{T \to \infty} \delta f (s_0; s_0 + \epsilon_2 \eta^T) = 0$, and $\lim_{T \to \infty} \sum_{t=0}^\infty \lambda_t^* \delta G_t(s_0; s_0 + \epsilon_2 \eta^t) = 0$, while for T no matter how large, $|\int \epsilon_2 \eta^T d\lambda^*| = \epsilon_2 \epsilon_1 = |\int -\epsilon_2 \eta^T d\lambda^*| > 0$. By linearity, therefore, there is a feasible variation for which $\delta f + \lambda^*(\delta G) < 0$, a contradiction to equation (5.6). This completes the proof of the lemma.

PROOF OF LEMMA 6:   If the Lagrangean is minimized at s_0, then the global minimum property follows from [12, p. 220, Theorem 1], and from the fact that $G(s_0) = 0$. It then remains to be shown that $L(s, \lambda^*) \geq L(s_0, \lambda^*)$ for $s \in \Omega$.   Since $c(\cdot)$ is   convex,   one   has $c(\hat{q}) \geq c(\hat{q}^0)$ $+ c'(\hat{q}^0)(\hat{q} - \hat{q}^0) = c(\hat{q}^0) + x^{-1}\beta^{-t}\lambda_t^*(\hat{q} - \hat{q}^0)$. Therefore, for $s \in \Omega$,

$$f(s) + \lambda^*[G(s)]$$

$$\geq \sum_{t=0}^\infty \left[\int \{ \beta^t [c(\hat{q}^0)x + \beta^{-t}\lambda_t^*(\hat{q} - \hat{q}^0) + (1-\beta)W] - \lambda_t^*\hat{q} \} \right.$$

$$\left. \times \sum_{\tau=0}^t \psi_{\gamma(\tau)} y_\tau dx + \beta^t k y_t + \lambda_t^* Q_t \right]$$

$$= \sum_{t=0}^\infty \int \beta^t [c(\hat{q}^0)x - \beta^{-t}\lambda_t^*\hat{q}^0 + (1-\beta)W] \sum_{\tau=0}^\infty \hat{\psi}_{\gamma(\tau)} y_\tau dx + \beta^t k y_t + \lambda_t^* Q_t$$

$$= \sum_{\tau=0}^\infty y_\tau \left\{ \sum_{t=\tau}^\infty \beta^t \int [c(\hat{q}^0)x - \beta^{-t}\lambda_t^*\hat{q}^0 + (1-\beta)W] \hat{\psi}_{\gamma(\tau)} dx \right\} + \beta^\tau k y_\tau + \lambda_\tau^* Q_\tau.$$

However, $c(\hat{q}^0)x - \beta^{-t}\lambda_t^*\hat{q}^0 = \pi(\beta^{-t}\lambda_t^*, x)$. Therefore, in view of equation (5.3), the expression in curly brackets is minimized by $\gamma(\{\beta^{-t}\lambda_t^*\}_0^\infty, \tau)$ (see the first line following equation (5.3)). But the necessary conditions for this to occur in equation (5.4) are identical to those of equation (5.13) (when one sets $p_t = \beta^{-t}\lambda_t^*$ in equation (5.4)). Therefore, the expression in curly brackets is minimized for each τ, by $\psi_{\gamma^0(\tau)}$. Therefore,

$$f(s) + \lambda^*[G(s)] \geq \sum_0^\infty y_\tau r_\tau + \sum_0^\infty \lambda_\tau^* Q_\tau$$

where

$$r_\tau = \sum_{t=\tau}^\infty \beta^t \int [c(\hat{q}^0)x - \beta^{-t}\lambda_t^*\hat{q}^0 + (1-\beta)W]\hat{\psi}_{\gamma^0(\tau)}dx + \beta^t k$$

Therefore,

$$f(s) + \lambda^*[G(s)] \geq \sum y_t^0 r_t + \sum(y_t - y_t^0)r_t + \sum \lambda_t^* Q_t$$
$$= f(s_0) + \lambda^*[G(s_0)] + \sum(y_t - y_t^0)r_t$$

But equality implies that $r_t(y_t - y_t^0) \geq 0 \; \forall t$, implying that $f(s) + \lambda^*[G(s)] \geq f(s_0) + \lambda^*[G(s_0)]$, for $s \in \Omega$. The lemma has been proved.

PROOF OF LEMMA 7: Let s_0 be optimal when $Q = Q_0$, and let s_1 be optimal when $Q = Q_1$. $f(s_0) + \lambda^*[G(s_0, Q_0)] \leq f(s_1) + \lambda^*[G(s_1, Q_0)]$ (using   Lemma   6).   Therefore $f(s_1) - f(s_0) \geq \lambda^*[G(s_0, Q_0) - G(s_1, Q_0)]$. But $G(s_0, Q_0) = 0$. Also, $G(s_1, Q_1) = 0$. Therefore $G(s_1, Q_0) = -Q_1 + Q_0$. Therefore $K(Q_1) - K(Q_0) = f(x_1) - f(x_0) \geq \lambda^*[Q_1 - Q_0]$. Next let Q_1, Q_2 be given and let $Q_\rho \equiv \rho Q_1 + (1-\rho)Q_2$. Then

$$K(Q_1) - K(Q_\rho) \geq \lambda^*[Q_1 - Q_\rho] \quad \text{and} \quad K(Q_2) - K(Q_\rho) \geq \lambda^*[Q_2 - Q_\rho]$$

Multiplying these expressions by ρ and by $1 - \rho$ respectively, and adding them together, one obtains

$$\rho K(Q_1) + (1-\rho)K(Q_2) - K(Q_\rho) \geq \lambda^*[\rho(Q_1 - Q_\rho) + (1-\rho)(Q_2 - Q_\rho)]$$
$$= \lambda^*[\rho Q_1 + (1-\rho)Q_2 - Q_\rho] = 0$$

so that K is convex in Q. Turning to differentiability, let $Q_1 = Q_0$ except that $Q_t^1 = (1+\epsilon)Q_t$ where $\epsilon > 0$. Let s_1 be optimal when $Q = Q_1$. Then $f(s_1) \leq f(\tilde{s}_1)$, where $\tilde{s}_1 = s_0$ except that $\hat{q}^1(x,t) = (1+\epsilon)\hat{q}^0(x,t)$. Then $\tilde{s}_1$ meets all the constraints, and

$$f(s_1) - f(s_0) \leq f(\tilde{s}_1) - f(s_0)$$
$$= \beta^t \sum_{\tau=0}^t y_\tau \int \{c'[\hat{q}^0(x,t)]x\epsilon\hat{q}^0(x,t)\}\hat{\psi}_{\gamma^0(\tau)}(x|t,\tau)dx + o(\epsilon)$$
$$= Q_t^0 \lambda_t^* \epsilon + o(\epsilon)$$

where the last equality follows from equation (5.10) and the definition of $G_t(s_0, Q)$. But $K(Q_1) - K(Q_0) \geq \lambda^*[Q_1 - Q_0] = \lambda_t^* \epsilon Q_t^0$. Together with equation (A.1) this implies $Q_t^0 \lambda_t^* \epsilon + o(\epsilon) \geq K(Q_1) - K(Q_0) = \lambda_t^* \epsilon Q_t^0$. Dividing by ϵ and taking the limit as $\epsilon \to 0$ establishes that the right-derivative $\partial K/\partial Q_t$ exists and is equal to λ_t^*. A parallel argument taking $\epsilon < 0$ establishes the same property for the left-derivative. The proof is complete.

Notes

1 Weiss [18] summarizes a number of studies that report this finding. Two exceptions are Stigler [17] who found no relation and Samuels and Smyth [15] who found a negative relation.

2 In equation (3.2), $P(z|x, n)$ is the probability that $x_{t+1}^* \leq z$ given that $x_t^* = x$, and given that the firm has been in the industry for n periods.

3 If $V < W$ for all $x \in [\alpha_1, \alpha_2]$, we set $\gamma = \alpha_1$, while if $V > W$ for all $x \in [\alpha_1, \alpha_2]$, we set $\gamma = \alpha_2$.

4 The restriction that $\sum y_t$ be bounded is stated for analytical convenience. The optimal entry sequence is bounded because at the optimum one must have $G_t = 0$ for all t. For if $G_t < 0$, the planner could reduce $\hat{q}(x, t)$ for some firms, thereby reducing f without violating any of the constraints. Rewriting G_t as $-\sum_{\tau=0}^{t} y_\tau \hat{\phi}(t, \tau) + Q_t \leq 0$, one then has that $\sum_{\tau=0}^{t} y_\tau \hat{\phi}(t, \tau)$ is bounded because Q_t is bounded. Then, if $\sum^t y_\tau$ did not converge, one would have output per entrant

$$\lim_{t \to \infty} (t > T) \frac{\sum_{\tau=T}^{t} \hat{\phi}(t, \tau) y_\tau}{\sum_{\tau=T}^{t} y_\tau} = 0$$

for every $T < \infty$, which cannot be optimal. It is of relevance, however, that one may have entry at each point in time ($y_t > 0$ each t) while $\sum^{\infty} y_t < \infty$. In fact, this may well happen in equilibrium (Theorem 3).

References

1 Berge, C. (1963): *Topological Spaces*. New York: MacMillan.

2 Blackwell, D. (1965): "Discounted Dynamic Programming," *Annals of Mathematical Statistics*, 36, 226–35.

3 Chernoff, H. (1968): "Stochastic Control," *Sankhyā*, Ser. A, 43, 111–42.

4 Demsetz, H. (1973): "Industry Structure, Market Rivalry and Public Policy," *Journal of Law and Economics*, 16, 1–9.

5 Dunford, N. and J. T. Schwartz (1958): *Linear Operators*, Part I. New York: Interscience Publishers.

6 Du Reitz, G. (1975): "New Firm Entry in Swedish Manufacturing Industries during the Post-War Period," doctoral dissertation, Stockholm.

7 Feller, W. (1971): *Introduction to Probability*, II (2nd edn), New York: John Wiley and Sons.

8 Hart, P. E. and S. J. Prais (1956): "The Analysis of Business Concentration: A Statistical Approach," *Journal of the Royal Statistical Society*, 119, 2, 150–91.

9 Hilderbrandt, T. H. (1948): "On Bounded Functional Operations," *Transactions of the American Mathematical Society*, 64, 868–75.

10 —— (1978): "On the Size Distribution of Business Firms," *Bell Journal of Economics*, 9, 508–23.

11 Lucas, R. E. and E. C. Prescott (1971): "Investment Under Uncertainty," *Econometrica*, 39, 659–81.

12 Luenberger, D. G. (1969): *Optimization by Vector Space Methods*. New York: John Wiley and Sons.

13 Mansfield, E. (1962): "Entry, Gibrat's Law, Innovation, and the Growth of Firms," *American Economic Review*, 52, 1023–51.

14 Pashigian, P. and S. Hymer (1962): "Firm Size and Rate of Growth," *Journal of Political Economy*, 52, 556–69.

15 Samuels, J. M. and D. J. Smyth (1968): "Profits, Variability of Profits and Firm Size," *Economica*, 35, 127–39.
16 Simon, H. E. and C. P. Bonini (1958): "The Size Distribution of Business Firms," *American Economic Review*, 48, 607–17.
17 Stigler, G. J. (1963): *Capital and Rates of Return in Manufacturing Industries*. Princeton: Princeton University Press (for NBER).
18 Weiss, L. (1971): "Quantitative Studies of Industrial Organization," in *Frontiers of Quantitative Economics*, ed. by M. D. Intrilligator. Amsterdam: North-Holland.
19 Yosida, K. and E. Hewitt (1952): "Finitely Additive Measures," *Transactions of the American Mathematical Society*, 72, 46–66.
20 Zellner, A. (1971): *An Introduction to Bayesian Inference in Econometrics*. New York: John Wiley and Sons.

Introduction

Considering how important technical progress is, considering the dramatic impact that new products and production processes can have on industry structure, it is surprising how little attention IO has devoted to this issue. One of the central points of the Schumpeterian school (and, to some extent, of the Chicago school) is that economists pay too much attention to the problem of (static) market power. Because of technical progress and entry, market power is inherently a temporary phenomenon. Or is it?

This question motivates an analysis that goes beyond the measurement of market power and instead focuses on the *persistence* of market power. Do dominant firms tend to maintain, or even increase, their market dominance? Is market power temporary or is it permanent?

R&D-intensive industries are a natural context in which to address this question. New products or production processes provide a channel through which new firms might supplant old ones. This could then justify Schumpeter's assertion that technical progress is nothing but a process of *creative destruction* in which firms have at most transitory market power.

Gilbert and Newbery (1982) develop a strong argument against this view. Although their paper is posed in a particular context (the incentive of an incumbent monopolist to acquire "sleeping patents"), their point is more general: a monopolist has more to lose from letting competition in than a potential entrant has from challenging the monopolist. As a result, the tendency should be towards persistence, not alternation, of market dominance.

Reinganum (1982) makes the point that Gilbert and Newbery's (1982) result depends on their assumptions, especially the assumption that there is no uncertainty in the R&D process. Under uncertainty, with positive probability, the potential entrant does not succeed in inventing a new product, even though it invests a positive amount. When this happens, a successful incumbent would only be replacing its monopoly product with another monopoly product. This is basically Arrow's (1962) "replacement" effect. Arrow argues that, because of this effect, a monopolist has less incentive to engage in R&D that a competitive firm has. Along the same lines, Reinganum (1982) shows that, with uncertainty, there are cases when the probability the monopolist is replaced by an entrant is greater than the probability of persistence.

Gilbert and Newbery (1982) and Reinganum's (1982) models are static models. Even though the latter introduces time (the time before an invention is made), they only consider one innovation. But the problem of the persistence of dominance is an inherently dynamic one. A potential entrant that challenges the monopolist should take into account that, if successful, it will be playing the same game that the monopolist is playing now – including the fact that it will be challenged.

Cabral and Riordan (1994) develop a "truly" dynamic model where two duopolists compete in an infinite series of periods. Technology dynamics are given by a learning curve, a particular but important case of R&D where R&D is complementary with production. They provide sufficient conditions for increasing dominance to hold, that is, for the probability that the leader gets ahead to be greater than 50 per cent. A similar set of conditions is presented in Budd et al. (1993). Early contributions to the literature on competition with a learning curve include Spence (1976) and Fudenberg and Tirole (1985), who consider two-period models.

It is not enough for technologies to be developed. They also need to be employed. Fudenberg and Tirole (1985) analyze the strategic issues involved in the adoption of a new technology. One of the stylized facts of technology adoption is that of diffusion: not all firms adopt a new technology at the same time. Many authors attribute this feature to adopter heterogeneity: not all firms have the same incentive to adopt a given technology. Fudenberg and Tirole (1985) propose an explanation for diffusion based on strategic behavior by adopters who compete in the product market. Under some conditions, equilibrium implies that two otherwise symmetric firms decide to adopt a new technology at different times.

The paper by Fudenberg and Tirole (1985) is also interesting for the methodological contribution it makes to the study of games in continuous time. Previous research, e.g., Reinganum (1981), considered a solution where firms precommit to an adoption time (open-loop solution). Fudenberg and Tirole (1985) consider the alternative case when firms can react instantaneously to the other firm's moves. Several papers have extended this methodology in the context of technology adoption games, e.g., Riordan (1992).

References

Arrow, Kenneth J. (1962): "Economic Welfare and the Allocation of Resources for Invention," in National Bureau of Economic Research, *The Rate and Direction of Inventive Activity*, Princeton: Princeton University Press.

Budd, Christopher, Christopher Harris and John Vickers (1993): "A Model of the Evolution of Duopoly: Does the Asymmetry Between Firms Tend to Increase or Decrease?" *Review of Economic Studies*, 60, 543–74.

Cabral, Luís and Michael H. Riordan (1994): "The Learning Curve, Market Dominance, and Predatory Pricing," *Econometrica*, 62, 1115–40.

Fudenberg, Drew and Jean Tirole (1985): "Preemption and Rent Equalization in the Adoption of New Technology," *Review of Economic Studies*, 52, 383–401.

Gilbert, Richard J. and David M. G. Newbery (1982): "Preemptive Patenting and the Persistence of Monopoly Power," *American Economic Review*, 72, 514–26.

Reinganum, Jennifer F. (1981): "On the Diffusion of New Technology: A Game-Theoretic Approach," *Review of Economic Studies*, 153, 395–406.

Reinganum, Jennifer F. (1982): "Uncertain Innovation and the Persistence of Monopoly," *American Economic Review*, 73, 741–8.

Riordan, Michael H. (1992): Regulation and Preemptive Technology Adoption, *Rand Journal of Economics*, 23, 334–49.

Spence, Michael (1976): "The Learning Curve and Competition," *Bell Journal of Economics*, 12, 49–70.

CHAPTER SIXTEEN

Preemptive Patenting and the Persistence of Monopoly

RICHARD J. GILBERT AND DAVID M. G. NEWBERY

Source: *American Economic Review*, 1982, 72, 514–26.

The problem of dominant firms has received much attention in the antitrust literature. One strand of thought, exemplified by George Stigler (1968), argues that the forces of natural selection are strong and that firms which stay dominant are firms with superior managerial or technological performance. Others, notably Oliver Williamson (1977a), have argued that market imperfections and chance events contribute to the persistence of dominant firms. This paper takes a different tack and inquires whether institutions such as the patent system create opportunities for firms with monopoly power to maintain their monopoly power. The results apply to other situations such as brand identification, spatial location, and capacity expansion, which share the characteristic that early, or preemptive, actions may lower the returns to potential competitors.

Preemptive invention is not without topical interest. In a recent antitrust case – the longest jury trial on record in the federal courts – the SCM Corporation sought more than $500 million in damages on its claim that the Xerox Corporation, among other alleged anticompetitive behavior, had maintained a "patent thicket" where some inventions were used while others were neither used nor licensed to others.[1]

This paper shows that, under certain conditions, a firm with monopoly power has an incentive to maintain its monopoly power by patenting new technologies before potential competitors and that this activity can lead to patents that are neither used nor licensed to others (sometimes called "sleeping patents"). Section 1 examines the incentives for preemptive invention in an illustrative market model with an existing monopolist and a single patentable substitute technology. While highly simplified, the example serves to identify the incentives for preemptive patenting. The monopolist will preempt if the cost is less than the profits gained by preventing entry, which follows whenever entry brings about an anticipated reduction of total industry profits below the monopoly level.

Section 2 examines several questions that arise in the context of the simple example, such as threat credibility, the occurrence of sleeping patents, and limits to the span of control by the monopolistic firm. Section 3 develops a more general model that permits analysis of the interaction of patenting and strategic investment activity, the consequences of limited patent protection and many potentially patentable technologies, and the effects of uncertainty on the preemption decision. These considerations significantly affect attainable monopoly profits with and without patenting, but they do not necessarily destroy incentives for preemption.

Although patents serve to illustrate incentives for preemptive activity, the complexities of $R\&D$ limit preemptive patenting to exceptional circumstances. Patent protection is typically quite limited and even modest prospects for developing new products can make the cost of entry deterrence by preemptive patenting excessively costly.[2] In addition, complementarities between patentable product components encourage cross-licensing agreements and discourage restrictive patent enforcement. Preemptive patenting may be unnecessary if potential entrants can be deterred more cheaply by other behavior, such as capacity expansion. Preemption is too costly if an established firm has a sufficient comparative disadvantage in research or production; and uncertainty about the expectations and resulting investment activities of potential rivals may lead an established firm to choose an $R\&D$ strategy that allows entry by optimistic firms.

The existence of patent rights is neither necessary nor sufficient for preemptive activity. The crucial element is that the rewards from acting first must be sufficiently large relative to the gains to subsequent investors. Patents provide a vivid example where the award goes only to the first firm, although in practice the advantage offered by patent protection is typically small. The acquisition of technical know-how, with or without patent protection, provides the significant returns from accelerated investments in research and development.

Several examples of preemptive competition have appeared recently. Preemptive brand proliferation is discussed by Richard Schmalensee (1978). One-dimensional spatial location models where preemption may occur are described by B. Curtis Eaton (1976), Edward Prescott and Michael Visscher (1977), and Robert Reynolds (1978); these are similar in structure to the problem discussed by Nicholas Kaldor (1935). Examples of preemption by accelerated investment in new plant capacity appear in Gilbert and Harris (1980), A. Michael Spence (1977, 1979), and Ram Rao and David Rutenberg (1979).

1. The Elements of Preemptive Patenting

The incentives for preemptive patenting emerge most clearly in a simple model. Suppose an established firm has a monopoly position in the sale or manufacture of a product (labelled product 1). The monopoly may be the consequence of an earlier patent or unique access to factors of production or distribution. Entry into the monopolized industry can take place only through the invention and patenting of a single patentable substitute for the monopolist's product. The cost of inventing the substitute (labelled product 2) depends only on the expected lag before a patentable design can be produced. In its simplest representation the date of invention, T, is a deterministic function of the time path of expenditures. The present value of an optimal expenditure path defines a cost function $C(T)$, that is a decreasing function of the invention date.[3] The cost function is the same for all firms engaged in research and development for the substitute product.

The strategy space for each firm is restricted to the $R\&D$ expenditure on product 2 and the price(s) the firm charges for the product(s) it sells. Let P^j represent the product price ($j = 1, 2$). Product 1 is sold only by the established firm (i.e., the monopolist); either the monopolist (labelled $i = m$) or an entrant ($i = e$) can patent product 2. Demand is known with certainty and is unchanging over time.

Before patenting of the substitute product, the monopolist earns profits at the rate $\pi_m(P^1_m)$. If the monopolist patents the substitute, profits are $\pi_m(P^1_m, P^2_m)$. If an entrant patents the substitute, the former monopolist's profit is $\pi_m(P^1_m, P^2_e)$ and the entrant earns profits at the rate $\pi_e(P^1_m, P^2_e)$. Profits are written as independent of time, which implicitly assumes any capital expenditures are included as fully amortized costs. In all cases $P^j_i (j = 1, 2; i = m, e)$ denotes firm i's maximizing choice of price for product j, given the prevailing market structure.

The monopolist has the option of patenting the substitute technology or allowing entry to occur. We allow the monopolist to choose a patent date under the assumption that competitors will patent at the date determined by free entry into the patent competition. Questions relating to the credibility of the preemption threat are deferred until section 2. The return to the monopolist from patenting is the difference between monopoly profits with the patent and profits when entry is allowed to occur. The firm should patent the substitute product and preempt potential entrants whenever this difference exceeds the cost of securing the patent. A simple comparison of profit streams shows that, under a general set of conditions, the monopolist will always gain by spending more on inventive activity than the present value of returns a rival can expect to earn from the new product. Specifically, the monopolist will spend more on $R\&D$ than rival firms *if entry results in any reduction of total profits below the joint-maximizing level.*

The demonstration of this result is straightforward. Let r represent the rate of interest (the same for all firms). The reward to any entrant depends on the price set by the former monopolist for product 1, P^1_m, and the price set by the entrant, P^2_e, as well as the entry date, T. Free entry into the patent race will dissipate profits so that

$$C(T) = \int_T^\infty \pi_e(P^1_m, P^2_e)e^{-rt}dt \tag{1}$$

If equation (1) is satisfied for more than one invention date T, competition for the patent will select the earliest date. When entry occurs at the competitive entry date, the former monopolist's profits are

$$V_e = \int_0^T \pi_m(P^1_m)e^{-rt}dt + \int_T^\infty \pi_m(P^1_m, P^2_e)e^{-rt}dt \tag{2}$$

Now suppose the monopolist takes the competitive invention date as determined by equation (1) and considers inventing before this date. If the cost of invention is continuous at date T, the monopolist can preempt rivals (i.e., invent at a date $T - \varepsilon$ for some arbitrarily small positive ε) by spending an amount $C(T) + \delta(\varepsilon)$. The firm remains a monopolist and earns

$$V_p = \int_0^{T-e} \pi_m(P_m^1)e^{-rt}dt + \int_{T-e}^{\infty} \pi_m(P_m^1, P_m^2)e^{-rt}dt - [C(T) + \delta] \tag{3}$$

The difference between profits with preemption and profits with entry is, in the limit as δ and δ approach zero,

$$V_p - V_e = \int_T^{\infty} \pi_m(P_m^1, P_m^2)e^{-rt}dt - \int_T^{\infty} \pi_m(P_m^1, P_e^2)e^{-rt}dt - C(T) \tag{4}$$

Note that the monopolist's price of product 1 with entry may differ from the price the monopolist sets when entry is preempted. Indeed, the monopolist need not even produce the patented substitute technology.

Substituting equation (1) for $C(T)$ gives an alternative expression for the relative benefits of preemptive patenting:

$$V_p - V_e = \int_T^{\infty} \{\pi_m(P_m^1, P_m^2) - [\pi_m(P_m^1, P_e^2) + \pi_e(P_m^1, P_e^2)]\}e^{-rt}dt \tag{5}$$

The monopoly profits from preemptive patenting strictly exceed the monopolist's profits with entry if

$$\pi_m(P_m^1, P_m^2) > \pi_m(P_m^1, P_e^2) + \pi_e(P_m^1, P_e^2) \tag{6}$$

The left-hand side of equation (6) is the maximum monopoly profit attainable with both product 1 and product 2, while the right-hand side is the total industry profit earned when a rival patents. The former will exceed the latter whenever entry results in some reduction in total profits, provided the monopolist suffers no diseconomies in the production of the substitute relative to production by a rival firm.[4] Moreover, the same argument holds if competition for the patent is less intense, so that the potential entrant anticipates positive profits instead of the zero profits implied by equation (1).[5]

Kenneth Arrow (1962) observed that, with patent protection, the incentive to invest in $R\&D$ is less under monopoly than under competitive conditions, which would suggest that monopolistic firms would be slower than competitors in developing new products or processes, *ceteris paribus*. This does not contradict the arguments in section 1 because Arrow assumed that entry was blockaded in the monopoly case. This paper does show that allowing for the possibility of entry can have a marked effect on monopoly incentives for $R\&D$.

2. Comments on the Simple Model

The preceding example illustrates the source of incentives for preemptive patenting. The incentives are not the result of market failures which Williamson (1977a) describes as shielding dominant firms from the forces of competition. In the preemption example, markets operate efficiently except for the assumed prior existence of a firm with substantial monopoly power. The firm can sustain its monopoly if potential entrants rationally expect that rivalry will erode total industry profits. This does require some foresight on the part of potential entrants, and it implicitly assumes entrants are large enough to have some effect on total industry profits.

The example ignores several potentially significant complications. Those which can be addressed without a more general model are discussed below, while more involved issues are deferred to the next section.

2.1. Monopoly expenditure on R&D

The monopolist prevents entry by patenting before the competitive date. If a potential competitor knows this strategy is rational for the monopolist, entry through R&D will not occur. This raises the question of whether the monopolist actually has to carry out an R&D plan which produces a patent before the competitive date. The preemption threat would be credible if the monopolist could accelerate R&D activity in response to R&D spending by potential rivals without incurring significant additional costs or delays. In this case, the potential of entry does not alter the behavior of the monopolist, and the monopolist invests in R&D as if entry were blockaded. Potential competitors do not invest in R&D because they know it is rational for the monopolist to accelerate his research if any competitor enters the patent race.

Conversely, if the monopolist incurs substantial costs by speeding up R&D in response to the inventive activities of rivals, the monopolist may be forced to play the preemption threat. This would be rational if the cost of waiting for a competitor to begin an R&D program exceeded the return from preemption. In this circumstance, research is carried out at the intensity determined by competitive forces, but it is the monopolist who performs the research (as, indeed, Joseph Schumpeter (1942) argued).

The remainder of this paper assumes the monopolist must play the preemption threat. A formal model of the patent competition is that of an auction market. Each firm enters a bid which is the maximum present-value amount that the firm will spend on R&D. (Firms can be thought of as bidding for R&D services.) With free entry, competitors will bid up R&D expenditures to the level determined by equation (1). At this level of investment in R&D, monopoly profits are strictly higher if the monopolist patents and if equation (6) is satisfied. Hence the established firm will enter a slightly higher bid which preempts the competitive patent date. Preemption is a Nash equilibrium of this bidding game.

2.2. Preemption and "sleeping patents"

A sleeping patent is an invention that is not put to commercial use. In a world of certainty, a monopolist protected from entry would never invest resources to produce a sleeping patent, since the monopolist could postpone the patent date until the best moment for innovation and reduce present discounted costs.[6] Yet a sleeping patent may occur as the consequence of preemptive patenting by the monopolist. As an illustration, consider the case where the patented substitute product has the same production cost and the same demand characteristics as the product controlled by the monopolist, except that development of the substitute from the patented design to the production state is costly. This means that any revenue stream can be earned at lower cost by producing product 1 than by developing and producing the substitute product. In particular, when amortized development costs are deducted from profits,

$$\pi_m(P_m^1, P_m^2) < \pi_m(P_m^1) \tag{7}$$

for any P_m^2 at which demand and production of the substitute is positive.[7]

With these assumptions a profit-maximizing monopolist will never choose to produce the substitute product, but might the monopolist patent the substitute and let it sleep? If entry of a rival is profitable, the argument developed in the simple model is still valid and the monopolist will preemptively patent the substitute whenever entry is expected to lower total industry profits.

The possibility of sleeping patents strengthens the argument for preemptive patenting by the monopolist. The monopolist's decision to let a patent sleep is efficient given the monopolist's choice of output(s). If a rival uses the patent, the effect of entry is to lower industry profits by using an inefficient production technology as well as possibly lowering profits through price competition. Both effects serve as incentives for preemptive patenting.

The monopolist must patent before potential competitors to deter entry, and this determines the invention date. The date at which the monopolist actually uses the patent depends on the characteristics of the new technology and the characteristics of the monopolist's existing capital stock. In this illustration the monopolist will never use the patent, but more generally Yoram Barzel (1968) and Dasgupta et al. (1982) show that a monopolist's optimal date for use of a patented technology will be later than the date determined by competition (the preemption date).

2.3. Managerial diseconomies

Managerial diseconomies exist if the monopolist cannot conduct a research program or production plan as efficiently as any rival. Formally, managerial diseconomies make no difference to the monopolist's decision problem. Preemption is a rational strategy if the cost of securing the patent is less than the difference between monopoly profits with the patent and the profits when entry is allowed to occur. Obviously if managerial diseconomies are significant, preemption is less likely to occur. What is more important is that in such cases the monopolist may dissipate much of the producers' surplus potentially available to the most efficient research group. For it may still pay the monopolist to preempt more efficient rivals, perhaps at the expense of almost all the potential profit.

3. Strategic Behavior, Uncertainty, and Multiple Competitive Threats

The illustrative example described in section 1 was sufficient to introduce the monopolist's decision problem and show the incentives for preemptive patenting. The general problem is much more complex. The monopolist can pursue strategic activities that lower the profitability of the patent to a potential competitor. The value of a patent and the process of invention are clouded by uncertainty. The assumption of a single patentable substitute for the monopolized product is clearly extreme, and in practice the protection afforded by a patent is limited by the ability to invent around and imitate the patent.

This section shows that these additional considerations do not destroy the incentives for preemptive patenting. The monopolist should take advantage of entry-deterring strategies, but these strategies should be used as complements to preemptive patenting, unless the strategies used alone efficiently impede entry. With uncertainty, preemption remains desirable if the expectations of potential entrants are known, but without this knowledge, optimistic competitors may succeed in patenting before the monopolist. The existence of more than one patentable substitute will generally have a large effect on the monopolist's maximum attainable profits, but these multiple potential patents need not alter the desirability of preemptive activity.

3.1. Strategic behavior

In the simple example, firms' strategies were limited to setting a price and producing sufficient quantities to meet demand at that price. This ignores the possibility of strategic behavior by an incumbent firm with the objective of either deterring entry or reducing the losses from competition. This section shows that in the case of a single competitive threat, strategic behavior does not alter the incentive for preemption. Strategies that lower the expected profits to potential entrants make preemption more attractive by lowering the cost of an $R\&D$ program designed to patent before rivals. Strategic investments and preemption generally go hand-in-hand as components of the incumbent firm's business strategies, although investments can be so effective in preventing entry as to make preemptive patenting unnecessary.

We choose an illustrative example of strategic investment following the analysis in Avinash Dixit (1980) where a dominant firm acts as a Stackelberg leader in the choice of capacity. Investment in capacity may benefit the incumbent firm by increasing profits in the event of entry and by possibly delaying the date at which entry occurs. The latter follows in our patenting model because the date of entry (patenting) depends directly on anticipated profits through the cost of invention function. In particular, firms may abandon the patent race if the returns from entry are sufficiently small.

Industry capacity affects the profits of both the incumbent and entering firm directly through costs and indirectly through the selection of product prices. We assume strategic behavior takes place only in the selection of production capacity by the incumbent for the manufacture of product 1 and we amend the notation for profits to include this capacity choice, represented by K. For simplicity the choice of production capacities for product 2, which should be conditional on K, is suppressed in the notation.

One result emerges immediately. Suppose in the absence of preemptive patenting the incumbent firm chooses a strategy that results in entry at date T when capacity is K. If monopoly profits exceed total profits with entry, *the incumbent firm is at least as well off choosing the same investment strategy and patenting before date T.* The proof of this result is exactly the same as in section 1 where only pricing decisions were considered. Note that the argument in section 1 holds for any market environment described by demands, technology, and capacities, provided the environment is the same whether or not preemption occurs. What remains unanswered is the effect of preemption on the choice of strategic investment. Consider equation (5), the difference between incumbent profits with and without preemption, augmented to include capacity choice. Technically we should write profits as the time dependent flow of net revenues corresponding to a particular investment strategy, but we shall simply append the variable K to represent the actual capacity at the date of entry and omit time as an explicit argument of the profit functions. If capacity choice is the same with and without preemption, the difference in incumbent profits is

$$(V_p - V_e) = \int_T^\infty \left\{ \pi_m(P_m^1, P_m^2, K) - \left[\pi_m(P_m^1, P_e^2, K) + \pi_e(P_m^1, P_e^2, K) \right] \right\} e^{-rt} dt \tag{8}$$

The entry date T depends on the choice of K through the straightforward extension of equation (1) to include the effect of capacity on entrant profits.

Let P denote the price vector (P_m^1, P_m^2, P_e^2) and define

$$\Delta(P, K) = \pi_m(P_m^1, P_m^2, K) - \left[\pi_m(P_m^1, P_e^2, K) + \pi_e(P_m^1, P_e^2, K) \right] \tag{9}$$

the difference between monopoly and competitive profits, or the loss from competition given capacity choice and prices at a particular (suppressed) date. Assuming continuity of the entry date and profits, differentiating equation (9) with respect to K gives the relative effect of a local change in capacity on incumbent profits with and without preemption.

$$\frac{d}{dK}(V_p - V_e) = \int_T^\infty \frac{d\Delta(P, K)}{dK} e^{-rt} dt - \Delta(P, K) e^{-rT} \frac{dT}{dK} \tag{10}$$

The first term in equation (10) is the change in the loss from competition due to a change in the level of capacity. Since the loss from competition is the incentive to preempt conditional on a capacity choice, if this increases (decreases) with capacity, it increases (decreases) the marginal value of capacity in the preemption decision. The second term represents the effect on the preemption decision of a change in the entry date due to a change in the capacity choice. This term is always nonpositive because T is a nondecreasing function of K and $\Delta(P, K)$ is nonnegative ($\Delta(P, K)$ is evaluated at date T in equation (10)).[8] Hence a sufficient condition for

$$\frac{d}{dK}(V_p - V_e) < 0 \tag{11}$$

is that the loss from competition decrease with an increase in capacity investment by the dominant firm. Simple models show that the loss from competition may increase or decrease with capacity, although it should be noted that a decrease is not necessary for the marginal value of capacity in the preemption decision to be less than the marginal value of capacity in strategic entry deterrence without preemption.

The opportunity to preempt competitors alters incentives for strategic investment in capacity. Preemption profits exceed profits without preemption whenever the loss from competition is positive. If the loss from competition does not increase with capacity, the marginal value of capacity is lower in the preemption decision. Then at least in the neighborhood of the capacity choice without preemption, allowing for preemption reduces the optimal capacity choice. If incumbent profits are a concave function of capacity, then the optimal capacity choice with preemption is less than the optimal choice without preemption when inequality (11) holds.

It could be the case that the capacity choice without preemption blockades entry, corresponding to $T \rightarrow \infty$. Preemption is unnecessary if entry never occurs, hence profits with and without preemption are identical. One can show that reducing capacity below the level that blockades entry and preemptively patenting is a preferred strategy if the entry date is a continuous function of the capacity choice. The intuition here is that the cost of preemption is negligible if the entry date is sufficiently distant, and at any finite entry date preemption is desirable. If a small change in the capacity choice leads to a discontinuous change in the entry date, the gain from avoiding rivalry may be offset by the nonnegligible cost of preemption. In this case blockading entry through strategic investment in capacity can prove superior to preemptive patenting.

3.2. Uncertainty

Several sources of uncertainty may affect the preemption decision. The invention process, the characteristics of the invention and the market, the competitive strategies of an entrant, and the appropriate response by the original monopolist are all more or less uncertain. Uncertainty in the invention process means that the patent date is not a deterministic function of the expenditure on $R\&D$. Uncertainty in the characteristics of the invention and in the strategies used by competitors after entry affect the value of the new technology after it is patented.

Consider first the implications of a patent with an uncertain value. If all agents are risk neutral, the analysis is essentially unchanged. The preceding results hold with the profit terms replaced by their expected values, conditional on those actions (price, capacity, etc.) under the control of the firm.

Preemption is desirable only if the expected loss from competition is positive for every potential entrant. Define the expectations of the monopolist and a potential entrant as consistent if the sum of the returns expected by each firm with entry are no greater than the monopolist's expected return without entry. The monopolist is better off preempting if expectations are consistent for the most optimistic entrant. If expectations are not consistent, either the monopolist or the entrant is unduly optimistic. In the former case, the monopolist's realized profits would be greater with preemption. The latter case is an example of the winner's curse; the entrant's realized profits fall short of expectations and may fail to cover the costs of product development.

Of course the monopolist need not know and may not be able to infer the expectations of potential rivals. Even if all expectations are consistent, uncertainty about competitors' expectations may lead the monopolist to choose a strategy that allows entry with positive probability. For example, suppose profits expected by an entrant of $100 are consistent, but the monopolist thinks it is unlikely that any rival expects to earn more than $50. An investment program that preempts only those rivals with profit expectations of no more than $50 costs less than a program that preempts all rivals with consistent expectations, and it would have higher expected profits if the probability that any entrant expects to earn more than $50 is sufficiently small.

The presence of risk aversion alters incentives for preemptive activity, as suggested by the analysis of Spence and Porter (1978). Risk aversion has consequences similar to managerial diseconomies, in that both imply a lower expected return from a given level of effort.

Similar results are obtained when the assumption of a deterministic patent date is replaced by a more general stochastic function which describes the probability of invention at date T conditional on a particular $R\&D$ plan. Various authors have constructed models which suggest that the competitive equilibrium will be one in which several firms pursue research programs, each expecting to make sufficient profits if successful in the patent race to offset the risks of failure.[9] It might be thought that such models imply that the monopolist cannot guarantee successful preemption, but this is not so, at least on our present set of assumptions. If expectations are consistent, $R\&D$ inputs are observable, and there are no managerial diseconomies, the monopolist can guarantee negative expected profits to any potential entrant, and knowing this, firms would not invest in $R\&D$.

The argument is the same as before, except that the monopolist has to set up the correct number of rival research teams – the same number as the number of firms who would choose to enter under competitive conditions. If the monopolist is able to do so (the assumption of no managerial economies, that he is as good at research as anyone else) then no extra firms will be tempted to enter and compete.[10]

3.3. Multiple competitive threats

The assumption that entry can be blockaded by a single patent is a convenient simplification to emphasize the strategic value of patents as barriers to entry, but it remains to be seen whether the results in sections 1 and 2 extend to more realistic situations. Typically, many different design routes lead to the development of products with similar market characteristics. Patents may not be effective in preventing potential competitors from making relatively minor design changes which avoid infringement. The cost of an infringement suit relative to the potential gains from patent enforcement may be so large as to discourage legal proceedings. In addition, potential competitors are often dependent on each other for the use of patented technology. This encourages cross licensing of patents and discourages attempts at restrictive patent enforcement. Finally, any monopoly power afforded by patent protection may be ephemeral or trivial if the firm does not continue to introduce improved technology and develop a range of products necessary to capture a substantial market.

This section examines the preemption decision in the situation where entry can occur over time by developing any of several technologies with or without patent protection. The problems of cross licensing and developing new and improved technology are ignored, and in order to focus on the questions of entry deterrence, all patentable technologies are assumed perfectly substitutable with each other and with the monopolist's existing technology. This removes any incentive for a monopolist to engage in $R\&D$ for reasons other than entry deterrence. Let t index discrete time periods ($t = 0, 1, \ldots, T$), and assume there exists a mapping from the time path of investments into a statistic $A(t)$, which provides all relevant information pertaining to cumulative $R\&D$ knowledge at date

t. Given the current state of knowledge, the firm has an estimate of the number of new technologies that can be developed and patented. The estimate can change over time and may decrease as well as increase. For simplicity, assume the number of new $R\&D$ paths can only increase, and let $\sigma(n|A(t), t)$ denote the probability that n new paths will be discovered at date t given $A(t)$.[11]

Assume, as in section 1, that the monopolist has no strategic choices other than preemptive patenting. This permits specifying the monopoly return as conditional only on whether entry occurs. Since patentable designs are perfect substitutes, the value of a patent to a potential entrant should be the same for all patentable designs. (Alternatively, entrants might place different values on different designs, provided the highest valuation by any entrant is the same for all designs.) Let π_m represent the monopolist's amortized profit per period if no rival firm patents a new design, and let π_0 be the profit if a rival patents. The per period return to a rival who wins a patent is π_e. The present value of rival profits with an interest rate r and discount factor $\beta = 1/1 + r$ equals $\pi_e/(1 - \beta)$, which determines the cost of preempting each patent, provided all firms have access to the same $R\&D$ technology.

An attempt to blockade entry by preemptive patenting may prove excessively costly. Even if a firm succeeds in patenting all product innovations, the patents may not seriously encumber potential competitors who can invent around and imitate new designs.[12] Since patenting cannot prevent this activity, it is convenient to include the effect of imitators in the profit terms, π_m and π_0. This convention permits a distinction between competitors who invent around existing patents and competitors who develop new patented designs. A rival may patent a new design first if the monopolist overlooks a patentable design or fails to develop ideas which could lead to new patents. Let $\mu(A(t), t)$ represent the probability that a preemption strategy fails to prevent entry because the monopolist missed a patentable design and a rival succeeds in patenting. The probability depends on cumulative $R\&D$ experience and could decrease with $A(t)$ if the firm is able to cast a wider net with more experience, or could increase with $A(t)$ if the $R\&D$ experience spills over to potential competitors and generates opportunities for product innovation external to the firm.

If $C = \pi_e/(1 - \beta)$ is the cost of preempting each patent, the expected returns from a preemption strategy in the current period is

$$(1 - \mu(A(t), t))\pi_m + \mu(A(t), t)\pi_0 - \sum_{n=0}^{\infty} \sigma(n|A(t), t)nC \equiv \pi_p(A(t), t) \tag{12}$$

Let $V(A(t), t)$ represent the present value of profits when the monopolist chooses an optimal strategy. The strategy could call for preemption only up to some date, after which the firm no longer attempts to prevent entry. The general expression for $V(A(t), t)$ is

$$V(A(t), t) = \max\{[\pi_p(A(t), t) + (1 - \mu(A(t), t))\beta V(A(t + 1), t + 1) \\ + \mu(A(t), t)\beta\pi_0/(1 - \beta)]; \pi_0/(1 - \beta)\} \tag{13}$$

The term in the square brackets is the present value of a preemption strategy. The current return from preemption is $\pi_p(A(t), t)$; with probability $(1 - \mu(A(t), t))$, no rival firm will patent and the monopolist can choose in the next period whether to continue preemption or allow entry to occur. This explains the term $(1 - \mu(A(t), t))\beta V(A(t + 1), t + 1)$. With probability $\mu(A(t), t)$, a rival will patent and the former monopolist's profits next period, discounted to the present, are $\beta\pi_0/(1 - \beta)$, which accounts for the third term in the square brackets. The last term is the present value of profits if entry occurs, and this equals the return if no attempt is made to preempt rivals.

A general solution for the monopolist's optimal policy is straightforward but cumbersome. Simplifying the dependence of the probabilities μ and σ offers insight into the determinants of the preemption decision without detailed computations. Assume the probability, μ, of a breakthrough by a competitor is constant and the expected number of new $R\&D$ paths in each period,

$$\bar{n}(A(t), t) = \sum_{n=0}^{\infty} \sigma(n|A(t), t)n \tag{14}$$

is also a constant. The present value of a preemption strategy for this case is

$$\bar{V} = \pi_p + (1 - \mu)\beta\bar{V} + \mu\beta\pi_0/(1 - \beta) \tag{15}$$

where $\pi_p = (1 - \mu)\pi_m + \mu\pi_0 - \bar{n}\pi_e/(1 - \beta)$. Rearranging terms gives

$$\bar{V} = \frac{\pi_0}{1 - \beta} + \frac{1}{1 - (1 - \mu)\beta} \times \left[(1 - \mu)(\pi_m - \pi_0) - \frac{\bar{n}}{1 - \beta}\pi_e\right] \tag{16}$$

Since $\pi_0/(1 - \beta)$ is the present value of profits when the firm does not attempt a preemption strategy, the expected profits from preemption are positive only if

$$\pi_m - \pi_0 > \frac{\bar{n}}{(1 - \beta)(1 - \mu)}\pi_e \tag{17}$$

This condition is much more restrictive than the requirement that monopoly profits exceed the industry profits if entry occurs, as determined in section 1. Entrant profits in equation (18) are multiplied by the factor $\bar{n}/(1 - \beta)(1 - \mu)$. The term $\bar{n}\pi_e/(1 - \beta)$ is the present value cost of continued entry deterrence, and this is divided by $(1 - \mu)$, the probability that deterrence is successful. Even modest prospects for new $R\&D$ opportunities cause a significant increase in the cost of entry deterrence. It is not difficult to see that a preemption strategy would be futile in a technologically progressive industry, where both $\bar{n}$ and μ are relatively large.

Furthermore, even if the factor $\bar{n}/(1 - \beta)(1 - \mu)$ is close to one, inequality (17) is not equivalent to the condition that monopoly profits exceed profits with competition because the profit, π_m, is defined to include the impacts of imitating firms. This is less than pure monopoly profits by an amount equal to the sum of the profits of imitating firms plus the losses from imitative competition. Hence, even if the monopolist could succeed in preempting all patentable substitute technologies, this does not assure that a preemptive strategy would yield a higher net return.

Although these results imply that patenting may be an ineffective means to deter entry in most industries, other strategies may be used preemptively to erect barriers to entry. A monopolist may accelerate investment in new capacity in order to accumulate a capital stock large enough to serve as an entry deterrent. The effectiveness of preemptive capacity construction depends, as Dixit (1979, 1980) has argued, on the relation between a firm's capacity level (the threat level in game-theoretic terms) and the firm's production decision after entry occurs (i.e., the credibility of the threat). With free entry, a monopolist has an incentive to preemptively build capacity to deter entry, provided the capacity will be used if entry occurs (see Spence, 1977; Williamson, 1977b; and Gilbert and Harris, 1980).

4. Concluding Remarks

While several conditions limit the efficacy of preemptive activity, the analysis in this paper shows that in some circumstances a firm can maintain a monopoly through preemptive activity despite the potential of entry. The conclusion is in agreement with that of Williamson (1977a), but for different reasons. Williamson attributes the persistence of dominant firms at least partly to market imperfections. We do not disagree with Williamson's arguments that market imperfections contribute to the persistence of dominant firms. We do disagree with the contrafactual statement that in the absence of market imperfections potential competition would eliminate dominant firms. Our results show that without market imperfections (except for an initial monopoly), incentives exist to maintain a monopoly position. Indeed, a perfect market for $R\&D$ inputs gives the monopolist a credible threat that it would overtake any rival undertaking a competitive research program, which reduces the cost of preemption to nil and makes the preservation of his monopoly position costless and hence doubly attractive.

The undesirable consequences of preemptive activity are evident. A firm may sustain its monopoly power through preemption. The firm may spend resources on the development of new technologies, and then deny society the use of these technologies. Resources are expended on $R\&D$ only to produce "sleeping patents" which are withheld from use, and the firm with monopoly power maintains its monopoly position. However, prohibiting preemptive activity need not lead to an increase in economic surplus even in those extreme situations where resources are expended primarily for entry deterrence rather than for product development.

The problem that may arise is implicit in the analysis of strategic behavior in section 3. Preemptive $R\&D$ is only one of many actions which, in the language of Joe Bain, may impede the entry of rivals or at least mitigate the profit loss from competition. In the absence of preemption, alternative entry-deterring behavior could incur private and social costs that exceed the social cost of monopoly sustained by preemptive activity. Section 3 showed conditions where strategic capital investment is lower when combined with preemptive $R\&D$. If preemptive activity were prohibited, strategic capital investment, with its associated costs, would increase and the net cost in terms of economic surplus could be larger.

Preemption would be very hard to identify in any practical situation because it is difficult to distinguish product development that is the result of superior foresight and technological capabilities from development that is motivated by entry deterrence. This may be just as well since preemption need not have adverse consequences for economic welfare. Preemption requires investment in product development with only a probability of successful entry deterrence. Society gains from the development of new technology at a pace at least as rapid as would occur with more competition, and in all but rare instances the technology would be put to use. If entry deterrence is not successful, the burden of monopoly would be removed or reduced. Since entry at some date is inevitable, to the extent that preemption does occur it is a phase in the Schumpeterian process of creative destruction.

Notes

1   *New York Times*, "Damages Denied in Xerox Case," December 30, 1978. The case reference is 463 F. Supp. 983 (1978). Other cases involving alleged anticompetitive *R&D* include the *U.S. v. IBM* and the *U.S. v. AT & T.*

2   The survey by Chris T. Taylor and Z. Aubrey Silberston (1973) reveals the scope of patent protection in the United Kingdom.

3   Although studies by Edwin Mansfield (1968) and others suggest a positive relation between perceived profitability and the commitment of funds to *R&D*, the relation between *R&D* expenditures and the timing of product development and patenting is more difficult to substantiate. R. G. Richels and J. L. Plummer (1977) cite an example of the cost-time tradeoff in the development of the nuclear breeder reactor. The cost should be a strictly decreasing function of the invention date with any positive discount rate if it is possible to postpone expenditures.

4   Clearly there is no incentive for preemption if production of product 2 has no effect on the profits from product 1. Also, if the entrant's profit-maximizing price for product 2 results in zero profits for the former monopolist, then $\pi_m(P_m^1, P_m^2) = \pi_e(P_m^1, P_e^2)$ and again there is no incentive for preemptive patenting.

5   A potential competitor may patent with the expectation of bargaining with the monopolist for a share of the difference between monopoly profits with and without competition. This does not change the incentive to preempt provided the rival expects his share of monopoly profits to be less than unity.

6   A monopolist protected from entry may hold a sleeping patent if the patent represents a step in the development of a more advanced technology or if the patent is a joint product from another line of research. Sleeping patents are not limited to monopoly since, as Partha Dasgupta, Gilbert, and Joseph Stiglitz (1982) show, free entry can lead to sleeping patents in a competitive *R&D* market.

7   Peter Swan (1970) argued that a monopolist would use any new technology that a competitor would use, but his argument required the assumption of convex cost functions, which is ruled out by consideration of development costs.

8   Output is a nondecreasing function of capacity if capacity lowers, or does not increase, marginal production cost. Thus entrant profits are a nonincreasing function of incumbent firm capacity, and lower profits imply a later entry date.

9   Stiglitz (1971), Glenn Loury (1979), and Dasgupta and Stiglitz (1978) characterize equilibrium research for patent rights with stochastic returns.

10 The reason why these models predict more than one firm undertaking research is that there are essentially U-shaped costs curves to a particular research laboratory, and hence an optimum level at which to run a given program. Rather than putting more eggs into one basket, it is argued that it pays to pursue several parallel lines each at the optimum rate. Our argument is that, if this is a rational way to organize *R&D*, the monopolist could replicate it, and perhaps

improve on it by having more exchange of ideas between rival laboratories. If, on the other hand, monopolies are bad at optimally subdividing research tasks between competing teams and choose to have just one research team, they could be described as being relatively inefficient, and suffering from managerial diseconomies.

11   This assumption, to the extent that it is significant exaggerates the cost of preemptive patenting, and should lead to an underestimate of the value of a preemption strategy.

12   Milton Kamien and Nancy Schwartz (1978) construct a descriptive model of imitative research.

References

Arrow, Kenneth J. (1962): "Economic Welfare and the Allocation of Resources for Invention," in *The Rate and Direction of Inventive Activity: Economic and Social Factors*, Conference No. 13, Universities-National Bureau of Economic Research, Princeton: Princeton University Press.

Bain, Joe (1962): *Barriers to New Competition*, Cambridge.

Barzel, Yoram (1968): "Optimal Timing of Innovation," *Review of Economic Statistics*, 50, August, 348–55.

Dasgupta, Partha and Stiglitz, Joseph E. (1978): "Market Structure and Research and Development," mimeo., Oxford University.

——, Gilbert, Richard J., and Stiglitz, Joseph E. (1982), "Invention and Innovation Under Alternative Market Structures: The Case of Natural Resources," *Review of Economic Studies*, 49 (4), October, 567–82.

Dixit, Avinash K. (1979): "A Model of Duopoly Suggesting a Theory of Entry Barriers," *Bell Journal of Economics*, 10, Spring, 20–32.

—— (1980): "The Role of Investment in Entry-Deterrence," *Economic Journal*, 90, March, 95–106.

Eaton, B. Curtis (1976): "The Theory of Spatial Preemption: Location as a Barrier to Entry, discussion paper no. 208. Queen's University.

Gilbert, Richard J. and Harris, Richard G. (1980): "Lumpy Investments and 'Destructive' Competition," presented at the NSF-NBER Conference on Industrial Organization and Public Policy, University of California-Berkeley, May.

Kaldor, Nicholas (1935): "Market Imperfections and Excess Capacity," *Economica*, 2, February, 35–50.

Kamien, Milton I., and Schwartz, Nancy L. (1978): "Potential Rivalry, Monopoly Profits and the Pace of Inventive Activity," *Review of Economic Studies*, 45, October, 547–58.

Loury, Glenn, (1979): "Market Structure and Innovation," *Quarterly Journal of Economics*, 93, August, 395–410.

Mansfield, Edwin (1968): *Industrial Research and Technological Innovation*, New York: Norton.

New York Times (1978): "Damages Denied in Xerox Case," December 30, 25–6.

Prescott, Edward C. and Visscher, Michael (1977): "Sequential Location Among Firms with Foresight," *Bell Journal of Economics*, 8, Autumn, 378–93.

Rao, Ram and Rutenberg, David (1979): "Preempting an Alert Rival: Strategic Timing of the First Plant by Analysis of Sophisticated Rivalry," *Bell Journal of Economics*, 10, Autumn, 412–28.

Reynolds, Robert (1978): "Location and Entry Deterrence," discussion paper, U.S. Dept. of Justice.

Richels, Richard G. and Plummer, James L. (1977): "Optimal Timing of the US Breeder," *Energy Policy*, 5, June, 106–21.

Schmalensee, Richard (1978): "Entry Deterrence in the Ready-to-Eat Breakfast Cereal Industry," *Bell Journal of Economics*, 9, Autumn, 305–27.

Schumpeter, Joseph (1942): *Capitalism, Socialism, and Democracy*, New York: Harper and Brothers.

SCM Corp. v. Xerox Corp. (1978): 463 F. Supp. 983.

Spence, A. Michael (1977): "Entry, Capacity, Investment and Oligopolistic Pricing," *Bell Journal of Economics*, 8, Autumn, 534–44.

——(1979): "Investment Strategy and Growth in a New Market," *Bell Journal of Economics*, 10, Spring, 1–19.

——and Porter, Michael (1978): "The Capacity Expansion Process in a Growing Oligopoly: The Case of Corn Wet Miling," discussion paper no. 670, Harvard Institute of Economic Research, November.

Stigler, George (1968): *Industrial Organization*, Homewood: Richard D. Irwin.

Stiglitz, Joseph E. (1971): "Perfect and Imperfect Capital Markets," presented at the Econometric Society Meeting, New Orleans.

Swan, Peter L. (1970): "Market Structure and Technological Progress: The Influence of Monopoly on Product Innovation," *Quarterly Journal of Economics*, 84, November, 627–38.

Taylor, Chris T. and Silberston, Z. Aubrey (1973): *The Economic Impact of the Patent System*, Cambridge.

United States v. American Telephone & Telegraph Corp. (1982): Civil Action No. 74–1698 (District D.C.), dismissed January 8.

United States v. IBM Corp. (1982): 60 FRD 654, 658 (S.D. NY 1973), dismissed January 8.

Williamson, Oliver E. (1977a): *Markets and Hierarchies*, New York.

——(1977b): "Predatory Pricing – A Strategic and Welfare Analysis," *Yale Law Journal*, 87, December, 284–340.

CHAPTER SEVENTEEN

Uncertain Innovation and the Persistence of Monopoly

JENNIFER F. REINGANUM

Source: *American Economic Review*, 1982, 73, 741–8.

A topic of long-standing interest in industrial organization is the effect of monopoly power upon incentives to engage in innovative activity. More recently, the concept of monopoly has been replaced with incumbency, so that explicit account may be taken of the existence of potential (and actual) rivals. According to F. M. Scherer:

> There is abundant evidence from case studies to support the view that actual and potential new entrants play a crucial role in stimulating technical progress, both as direct sources of innovation and as spurs to existing industry members. ... new entrants contribute a disproportionately high share of all really revolutionary new industrial products and processes. [1980, pp. 437–38]

In a recent paper published in this *Review* (1982), Richard J. Gilbert and David M. G. Newbery show that, because an incumbent firm enjoys greater marginal incentives to engage in *R&D* (under their assumption of deterministic invention), the incumbent firm will engage in preemptive patenting. Thus the industry will tend to remain monopolized, and by the same firm.

In this paper, I present a model in which an incumbent firm and a challenger engage in a game of innovation in which the inventive process is stochastic. I show that when the first successful innovator captures a sufficiently high share of the post-innovation market (i.e., when the innovation is sufficiently revolutionary), then in a Nash equilibrium the incumbent firm invests less on a given project than the challenger. Under an alternative specification, in a Nash equilibrium an incumbent firm conducts fewer parallel projects than would a challenger. In either case, the incumbent is less likely to patent the innovation than is the challenger.

The intuition for this result is relatively straightforward, at least in the case where the first successful innovator captures the entire post-innovation market. When the inventive process is stochastic, the incumbent firm continues to receive flow profits during the time preceding innovation. This period is of random length but is stochastically shorter the greater the firms' investments in *R&D*. Since a successful incumbent merely "replaces himself" (albeit with a more profitable product), the incumbent firm has a lower marginal incentive to invest in *R&D* than does the challenger.

Thus this paper provides a theoretical model that embodies Scherer's empirical observations: entrants stimulate progress both through their own innovative behavior and through their provocation of incumbent firms. Moreover, in equilibrium they contribute a disproportionate share of important innovations. I also attempt to isolate the causes of the discrepancy between my results and those of Gilbert and Newbery, and to integrate the two into a coherent theory consistent with the empirical observations.

1. Related Literature

For simplicity, consider a case of cost-reducing innovation in an industry with constant returns to scale. Let $\bar{c}$ denote the incumbent firm's initial unit cost, and let $c < \bar{c}$ be the unit cost associated with the new technology. Let the relevant profit rates be $R =$ the current revenue flow to the incumbent firm; $\Pi(c) =$ the present value of monopoly profits using the new technology; also the present value of profits to the current incumbent if the incumbent receives a patent on the new technology; $\pi_I(c) =$ the present value of Nash–Cournot profits to the current incumbent firm if the challenger receives a patent on the new technology; and $\pi_C(c) =$ the present value of Nash–Cournot profits to the challenger if the challenger receives a patent on the new technology.

ASSUMPTION 1: *The functions* $\Pi(c), \pi_I(c),$ *and* $\pi_C(c)$ *are continuous, and piecewise continuously differentiable. Moreover,* $\Pi(c)$ *and* $\pi_C(c)$ *are nonincreasing in* c *while* $\pi_I(c)$ *is nondecreasing in* c.

That is, if the incumbent patents the new technology, its profits will be lower the higher is the unit cost associated with the new technology. On the other hand, if the challenger patents the new technology (and the incumbent continues to use the old one), then the challenger's profits will be lower and the incumbent's higher the higher is the unit cost associated with the new technology.

DEFINITION 1: The innovation will be termed *drastic* if $c \leq c_0$, where c_0 is assumed to exist and to be uniquely defined as the maximum value of c such that $\pi_I(c) = 0$.

The important feature of the constant returns to scale assumption is that if profits are zero, so is output. Thus if $c \leq c_0$, then the current incumbent's output will be zero after the challenger patents the innovation. In this event, the challenger is a monopolist and $\pi_C(c) = \Pi(c)$. Note that $\Pi(c) \geq \pi_I(c) + \pi_C(c)$ with strict inequality whenever the innovation is not drastic.

REMARK 1: Since $c < \bar{c}$, the present value of monopoly profits after innovation $\Pi(c)$ always exceeds the present value of monopoly profits without the innovation, R/r, where r

is the discount rate. Furthermore, $R/r > \pi_I(c)$ for all $c < \bar{c}$. This is because $R/r = \Pi(\bar{c}) > \pi_I(\bar{c}) \geq \pi_I(c)$ for all $c < \bar{c}$ by Assumption 1.

The following example illustrates the preceding discussion and Assumption 1. If the demand curve is linear, $P = a - bQ$, then the functions above are $\Pi(c) = (a - c)^2/4rb$, $\pi_I(c) = (a - 2\bar{c} + c)^2/9rb$ and $\pi_C(c) = (a - 2c + \bar{c})^2/9rb$, whenever the expressions in parentheses are nonnegative; otherwise the relevant value for the function is zero. Each of these functions is continuously differentiable except at the point at which the expression in parentheses becomes zero, and continuity is preserved at that point. The innovation is drastic whenever $c \leq c_0$, where $a - 2\bar{c} + c_0 = 0$. From this equality, it is easy to see that $\Pi(c_0) = \pi_C(c_0)$ and $\pi_I(c_0) = 0$.

Gilbert and Newbery argue as follows. If the inventive process is deterministic, then whoever is willing to bid most for the new technology receives the patent first with probability 1. The challenger will be willing to bid up to $\pi_C(c)$, while the incumbent will be willing to bid up to $\Pi(c) - \pi_I(c)$. Since $\Pi(c) \geq \pi_I(c) + \pi_C(c)$, with strict inequality for $c > c_0$, the incumbent preemptively patents the new technology. Only if the innovation is drastic will the incumbent and the challenger invest an equal amount. Consequently, preemption is the Nash equilibrium outcome in the bidding game. Thus the industry will remain monopolized and in the hands of the current incumbent.

This is clearly true when there is no uncertainty in the innovation process. The natural extension of this result to the case of uncertain innovation is that the incumbent is *more likely* to patent the innovation than is the challenger.[1] In the next section, a simple model is presented which incorporates uncertainty. It is found that, for drastic innovations, the incumbent always invests less than the challenger, so that the incumbency changes hands *more often than not*. Due to the continuity of the equilibrium investment rates in the unit cost associated with the new technology, there will be an open neighborhood of c_0, representing innovations which are not drastic, for which the incumbent still invests less than the challenger. In section 3, I briefly report results from a more general model in which firms are allowed to choose both the number of parallel projects to undertake, and the rate of investment on each project. Again there is a nontrivial set of innovations which the incumbent is less likely to patent than is the challenger.

2. A Model Incorporating Uncertainty

The model developed in this section is a generalization of that of Tom Lee and Louis Wilde (1980) (which is itself based upon a model by Glenn Loury (1979)). An incumbent and a challenger are simultaneously attempting to perfect a particular cost-reducing technology. Technological uncertainty takes the form of a stochastic relationship between the rate of investment and the eventual date of successful completion of the new technology. If x_I represents the rate of investment of the incumbent, and $\tau_I(x_I)$ the random success date of the incumbent, then $Pr\{\tau_I(x_I) \leq t\} = 1 - e^{-h(x_I)t}$, for $t \in [0, \infty)$. Similarly, if x_C and $\tau_C(x_C)$ represent the investment rate and the random success date for the challenger, then $Pr\{\tau_C(x_C) \leq t\} = 1 - e^{-h(x_C)t}$. The expected success date for firm $i (i = I, C)$ is $1/h(x_i)$, where the function $h(\cdot)$ is the hazard function used in much of the recent literature on patent races. In particular, following Loury (1979), Lee and Wilde (1980), and Partha Dasgupta and Joseph Stiglitz (1980), I assume:

Assumption 2: *The hazard function $h(\cdot)$ is twice continuously differentiable, with $h'(x) > 0$ and $h''(x) < 0$ for all $x \in [0, \infty)$. Furthermore,*

$$h(0) = 0 = \lim_{x \to \infty} h'(x)$$

Thus the technology exhibits decreasing returns to scale.

Suppose that the new technology is patentable so that the race ends with the first success. The expected profit to the incumbent for any pair of investment rates (x_I, x_C) is

$$V^I(x_I, x_C) = \int_0^\infty e^{-rt} e^{-(h(x_I)+h(x_C))t} \times [h(x_I)\Pi(c) + h(x_C)\pi_I(c) + R - x_I] dt$$
$$= [h(x_I)\Pi(c) + h(x_C)\pi_I(c) + R - x_I]/[r + h(x_I) + h(x_C)]$$

That is, the incumbent receives $\Pi(c)$ at t if the challenger has not yet succeeded and the incumbent succeeds at t; this event has probability density $h(x_I)e^{-(h(x_I)+h(x_C))t}$. The incumbent receives $\pi_I(c)$ at t if the incumbent has not yet succeeded and the challenger succeeds at t; this event has probability density $h(x_C)e^{-(h(x_I)+h(x_C))t}$. Finally, the incumbent receives flow profits of R and pays flow costs of x_I so long as no firm has succeeded; this event has probability $e^{-(h(x_I)+h(x_C))t}$.

The challenger's payoff is analogous.

$$V^C(x_I, x_C) = \int_0^\infty e^{-rt} e^{-(h(x_i)+h(x_C))t} \times [h(x_C)\pi_C(c) - x_C] dt$$
$$= [h(x_C)\pi_C(c) - x_C]/[r + h(x_I) + h(x_C)]$$

The differences between these payoffs arise from the incumbent's current profit flow and the fact that it shares the market in the event of successful innovation by the challenger.

Definition 2: A *strategy* for the incumbent (challenger) is an investment rate $x_I(x_C)$. The *payoff* to the incumbent (challenger) is $V^I(x_I, x_C)(V^C(x_I, x_C))$.

Definition 3: A *best response function for the incumbent* is a function $\phi_I : [0, \infty) \to [0, \infty)$ such that, for each x_C, $V^I(\phi_I(x_C), x_C) \geq V^I(x_I, x_C)$ for all $x_I \in [0, \infty)$. Similarly, a *best response function for the challenger* is a function $\phi_C : [0, \infty) \to [0, \infty)$ such that, for each x_I, $V^C(x_I, \phi_C(x_I)) \geq V^C(x_I, x_C)$ for all $x_C \in [0, \infty)$. The best response functions will also depend upon the parameters (c, R).

Definition 4: A strategy pair (x_I^*, x_C^*) is a *Nash equilibrium* if $x_I^* = \phi_I(x_C^*)$ and $x_C^* = \phi_C(x_I^*)$. That is, each firm's investment rate is a best response to the other's.

The proof of the following proposition can be found in the Appendix.

PROPOSITION 1: *If* $h'(0) \geq \max \{1/[\Pi(c) - R/r], 1/\pi_C(c)\}$, *then there exists a best response function[2] for the incumbent* $\phi_I(x_C; c, R)$ *which satisfies the first-order condition* $\partial V^I(\phi_I, x_C)/\partial x_I = 0$ *and the second-order condition* $\partial^2 V^I(\phi_I, x_C)/\partial x_I^2 < 0$. *The function* ϕ_I *is continuously differentiable in its argument* x_C *and continuous in the parameters c, R. Similarly, there exists a best response function for the challenger* $\phi_C(x_I; c)$ *which satisfies the analogous first- and second-order conditions, and is continuously differentiable in its argument* x_I *and continuous in the parameter c. Moreover, there exists a pair of Nash equilibrium strategies* $x_I^*(c, R)$ *and* $x_C^*(c, R)$; *each is continuous in the parameters c, R.*

The first-order conditions which implicitly define the best response functions are

$$\partial V^I(\phi_I, x_C)/\partial x_I \propto [r + h(\phi_I) + h(x_C)][h'(\phi_I)\Pi(c) - 1] - [h(\phi_I)\Pi(c) \\ + h(x_C)\pi_I(c) + R - \phi_I]h'(\phi_I) = 0 \tag{1}$$

$$\partial V^C(x_I, \phi_C)/\partial x_C \propto [r + h(x_I) + h(\phi_C)][h'(\phi_C)\pi_C(c) - 1] \\ - [h(\phi_C)\pi_C(c) - \phi_C]h'(\phi_C) = 0 \tag{2}$$

Rearranging terms and noting the definitions of $V^I(\phi_I, x_C)$ and $V^C(x_I, \phi_C)$ yields

$$V^I(\phi_I, x_C) = [h'(\phi_I)\Pi(c) - 1]/h'(\phi_I) \tag{3}$$

$$V^C(x_I, \phi_C) = [h'(\phi_C)\pi_C(c) - 1]/h'(\phi_C) \tag{4}$$

REMARK 2: Since the individual firm payoffs must be nonnegative, particularly when the firms play best responses, it follows that $h'(\phi_I)\Pi(c) - 1 \geq 0$ and $h'(\phi_C)\pi_C(c) - 1 \geq 0$.

LEMMA 1: $\partial\phi_I(x_C; c, R)/\partial x_C > 0$ and $\partial\phi_C(x_I; c)/\partial x_I \geq 0$. *Thus the existence of the challenger provokes the incumbent to invest more than it otherwise would on the innovation.*

PROOF: By the implicit function theorem,

$$\partial\phi_I/\partial x_C = -[\partial^2 V^I(\phi_I, x_C)/\partial x_C\partial x_I]/[\partial^2 V^I(\phi_I, x_C)/\partial x_I^2]$$

The denominator is negative by the second-order condition. The numerator is

$$-h'(x_C)[h'(\phi_I)(\Pi(c) - \pi_I(c)) - 1] = -h'(x_C)h'(\phi_I)[V^I(\phi_I, x_C) - \pi_I(c)]$$

by equation (3). Since ϕ_I is a best response to $x_C, V^I(\phi_I, x_C) \geq V^I(0, x_C)$; but $V^I(0, x_C) - \pi_I(c) = [R - r\pi_I(c)]/[r + h(x_C)] > 0$ by Remark 1. Thus $V^I(\phi_I, x_C) - \pi_I(c) > 0$ for all x_C. It follows that $\partial\phi_I/\partial x_C > 0$ for all x_C.

By the implicit function theorem,

$$\partial\phi_C/\partial x_I = -[\partial^2 V^C(x_I, \phi_C)/\partial x_I\partial x_C]/[\partial^2 V^C(x_I, \phi_C)/\partial x_C^2]$$

The denominator is negative by the second-order condition, while the numerator is $-h'(x_I)[h'(\phi_C)\pi_C(c) - 1]$, which is nonpositive by Remark 2.

LEMMA 2: *If the innovation is drastic and $R > 0$, then $\phi_I(x; c, R) < \phi_c(x; c)$ for all x, c.*

PROOF: Recall that if the innovation is drastic, $\pi_C(c) = \Pi(c)$ and $\pi_I(c) = 0$. Then the only difference between equations (1) and (2), which implicitly define the best response functions ϕ_I and ϕ_C, is the term R, representing current profit flows to the incumbent firm. If $R = 0$, and the innovation is drastic, then $\phi_I(x; c, 0) = \phi_C(x; c)$ for all x, c. Again using the implicit function theorem, we see that

$$\partial \phi_I / \partial R = -\left[\partial^2 V^I(\phi_I, x)/\partial R \partial x_I\right] / \left[\partial^2 V^I(\phi_I, x)/\partial x_I^2\right]$$

Since the denominator is negative and the numerator is $h'(\phi_I)$ which is positive, we have $\phi_I(x; c, R) < \phi_I(x; c, 0) = \phi_C(x; c)$ for all $R > 0$, and all x, c.

PROPOSITION 2: *If the innovation is drastic and $R > 0$, then in a Nash equilibrium, the incumbent invests less than the challenger; that is, $x_I^*(c, R) < x_c^*(c, R)$.*

PROOF: Suppose, contrary to the proposition, that $x_I^*(c, R) \geq x_C^*(c, R)$. Then Lemmas 1 and 2 and the definition of a Nash equilibrium imply that

$$x_C^*(c, R) = \phi_C(x_I^*(c, R); c) \geq \phi_C(x_C^*(c, R); c) > \phi_I^*(x_C^*(c, R); c, R) = x_I^*(c, R)$$

But this is a contradiction. Thus $x_I^*(c, R) < x_C^*(c, R)$.

COROLLARY 1: *If $R > 0$, then there exists an open neighborhood of c_0 (which may depend on R), denoted $N(c_0; R)$, such that if the technology is not drastic, but $c \in N(c_0; R)$, then $x_I^*(c, R) < x_C^*(c, R)$.*

PROOF: This follows immediately from Proposition 2 and the continuity of the Nash equilibrium investment rates $x_I^*(c, R)$ and $x_C^*(c, R)$ in the parameter c.

Thus I have concluded that for sufficiently radical innovations (i.e., for technologies in the set $N(c_0; R)$), it is precisely the assumption of certainty versus. uncertainty which is responsible for the discrepancy between my results and those of Gilbert and Newbery. To see the economics of the issue, consider what happens in my model with drastic innovation if the incumbent were to consider investing a tiny bit less. It would suffer a slightly increased probability of losing the patent to the challenger and a slightly decreased chance of collecting the patent itself, but would spend a bit less and would receive the flow revenue R stochastically longer. The challenger, by investing a bit less, suffers a slightly increased probability of losing the patent to the incumbent and a slightly decreased probability of collecting the patent for itself; on the other hand, it spends a bit less. Since it *does not* collect any additional current revenue, its marginal benefits due to investing a bit less are lower than those of the incumbent, and hence in equilibrium the challenger invests more than the incumbent. Consider the same question under the assumption of certainty. What happens in the certainty model if the incumbent were to consider investing a tiny bit less? If the incumbent still invests more than the challenger, then the incumbent collects revenues R with probability 1 and suffers no threat of losing the patent to the challenger. If the incumbent was investing less than the challenger, then further reductions have no impact on their profits. The only important case is when the incumbent considers reducing its investment from above that of the challenger to below that of the challenger. This results in the incumbent receiving R for an infinitesimally short additional time, and losing the noninfinitesimal difference between the present values of monopoly profits and Nash–Cournot profits when the challenger patents the new technology. Consequently, the incumbent is always willing to invest more than the challenger when the innovation process is deterministic.

3. A Model with Parallel Projects

In this section, I report briefly on a model in which firms are allowed to select both the number of parallel projects to undertake, denoted n_I and n_C for incumbent and challenger, respectively, and the rate of investment on each project, x_I and x_C, respectively.[3] The conjecture is that the incumbent is more likely than the challenger to patent the innovation. However, it can be shown that both firms will select the same level of investment per project; that is, $x_I^* = x_C^*$. Thus each firm varies its "scale" by choosing the number of (statistically independent) projects. Moreover, it can be shown that if the innovation is drastic and $R > 0$, then $n_I^* < n_C^*$; that is, the incumbent invests in fewer parallel projects than does the challenger. Again by the continuity of these equilibrium strategies in the parameters R, c, there exists an open set of innovations which are not drastic, for which the incumbent still operates fewer parallel projects than does the challenger.

Thus the alternative form of the conjecture is also false for an open set of innovations – those which are sufficiently revolutionary. It fails for essentially the same reason as before; the incumbent has a lower marginal incentive to hasten the date of innovation, since it continues to receive the flow profit R until innovation, while the challenger does not.

4. Conclusion

It seems clear that the assumption of certainty in the inventive process is not an innocuous one, particularly when one compares the policy implications of these two models. The Gilbert–Newbery model suggests that one ought to be very worried about the development of entrenched monopolies via preemptive patenting. This study suggests that one can reasonably worry far less on this score when the inventive process is stochastic.

It seems reasonable that the degree of cost reduction and the degree of associated uncertainty are related. That is, more drastic innovations may also be subject to greater uncertainty. Thus one can reconcile the Gilbert and Newbery (1982) paper with Scherer's observations (1980) by suggesting that the certainty model is most appropriate for incremental innovations.

Of course, the models discussed in this paper also rely upon simplifying assumptions. The assumption of constant returns to scale in the output production function is particularly useful, since it allows us to use simple parametric expressions for the post-innovation profit functions. Taken together, this paper and that of Gilbert and Newbery (1982) indicate that the influence of monopoly power on the persistence of monopoly is considerably more complicated than either paper taken alone might suggest.

Appendix: Proof of Proposition 1

The method of proof is as follows. I first show that there is a finite investment level for each firm such that the firm's best response never exceeds this level, regardless of its rival's investment. Then we can restrict the firm to strategies within this interval without any loss of generality. Next it is shown that the firm's payoff function is single peaked in its own investment level, and reaches this peak on the aforementioned compact interval. Finally, we need to show that this peak is a stationary point and that the payoff function is locally concave at this point. This suffices to define the firm's best response function. A fixed-point argument completes the proof.

$$\partial V^I / \partial x_I = \left[h'(x_I) \left(\Pi(c) r - R + h(x_C)(\Pi(c) - \pi_I(c)) + x_I \right) - B \right] / B^2$$

where $B = r + h(x_I) + h(x_C)$. Let

$$f_I(x_I, x_C) = h'(x_I)[\Pi(c)r - R + h(x_C)(\Pi(c) - \pi_I(c)) + x_I] - B$$

Note that sgn $\partial V^I / \partial x_I =$ sgnf_I. Under the assumption that $h'(0) \geq \max\{1/(\Pi(c) - R/r),$ $1/\pi_C(c)\}$, it can be seen that $f_I(0, x_C) \geq 0$ for all x_C. Moreover, $f_I(\hat{x}_I(c, R), x_C) \leq 0$ for all x_C, where

$$\hat{x}_I(c, R) = \min\{x \in [0, \infty) \mid h'(x) \leq \min\{1/(\Pi(c) - \pi_I(c)), 1/(\Pi(c) - R/r)\}\}$$

This value exists and is finite since $\lim_{x \to \infty} h'(x) = 0$. Since

$$\partial f_I / \partial x_I = h''(x_I)[\Pi(c)r - R + h(x_C)(\Pi(c) - \pi_I(c)) + x_I]$$

is strictly negative, the function V^I is first increasing, eventually peaks, and subsequently declines. Consequently, V^I is single peaked and reaches its peak at or before $\hat{x}_I(c, R)$ for all x_C.

The value of x_I which provides the peak is $\phi_I(x_C; c, R)$, the unique best response for the incumbent to x_C. Moreover, since V^I is twice differentiable in (x_I, x_C) and continuous in (c, R), and since

$$\partial^2 V^I(\phi_I, x_C) / \partial x_I^2 = h''(\phi_I)[\Pi(c)r - R + h(x_C)(\Pi(c) - \pi_I(c)) + \phi_I] / B^2 < 0$$

ϕ_I is implicitly defined as a continuously differentiable function of x_C (and a continuous function of (c, R)) by the first-order condition $\partial V^I / \partial x_I = 0$. A similar argument establishes the analogous result for ϕ_C.

Define the composite function $\omega = \phi_I \circ \phi_C : [0, \hat{x}_I(c, R)] \to [0, \hat{x}_I(c, R)]$ (holding c and R fixed). The function $\omega(x; c, R)$ is continuously differentiable in x on a compact, convex and nonempty domain. Hence it has a fixed point $x_I^*(c, R)$ by Brouwer's theorem; that is, there is a point $x_I^*(c, R)$ such that $\omega(x_I^*(c, R); c, R) - x_I^*(c, R) = 0$. Under the assumption that $x_I^*(c, R)$ is not a critical point of $\omega(x; c, R) - x$ (i.e., $\partial \omega(x_I^*(c, R); c, R) / \partial x \neq 1$), there exists a neighborhood of c in which the implicit function $x_I^*(c, R)$ is continuous (see Magnus Hestenes (1980, p. 22, Theorem 7.1)). Let $x_C^*(c, R) = \phi_C(x_I^*(c, R); c)$. The strategies $x_I^*(c, R)$ and $x_C^*(c, R)$ constitute a Nash equilibrium, and they are continuous in the parameter c.

Notes

1   Gilbert subsequently argues; "Uncertainty in the invention process does not greatly change the deterministic analysis of preemption, provided R and D expenditures are sensitive to the expected returns and the established firm is no more averse to risk than rivals" (1981, p. 299). In a laudatory comment on the Gilbert paper, Richard Craswell continues: "Assuming any form of direct relationship between the amount spent on R and D and the likelihood of making the invention first, the incumbent will end up with the patent more often than not, and his monopoly will be maintained. In fact, the incumbent will usually end up with the patent even if he is less efficient at R and D than are his rivals, so long as his inefficiency does not completely negate the advantage due to his larger expenditure on R and D" (1981, p. 272).
    To summarize, Gilbert and Craswell evidently believe that the result that the incumbent invests more than the challenger extends straightforwardly to the case of uncertainty. A somewhat different argument is offered by Gilbert and Newbery in support of the same basic claim: "Similar results are obtained when the assumption of a deterministic patent date is replaced by a more general stochastic function which describes the probability of invention at date T conditional on a particular R and D plan. ... The argument is the same as before, except that the monopolist has to set up the correct number of rival research teams ... " (1982, p. 521). Thus the implied claim is that, if allowed to select the number of parallel projects to be undertaken, an incumbent firm would choose a larger number than would a challenger.
2   The hypothesis of this proposition ensures that each firm's payoff function is initially nondecreasing in that firm's investment level. Without this assumption, it is possible that the firm may have two (widely separated) best responses.
3   Since it would seem to add little to the essential intuition of the previous section, the analysis of this more general model is not included here; a technical appendix to this paper which contains the analysis of this more general model is available from the author upon request.

References

Craswell, Richard (1981): "Patents, Sleeping Patents and Entry Deterrence: Comments," in Steven C. Salop (ed.), *Strategy, Predation and Antitrust Analysis*, Federal Trade Commission, September, 271–85.

Dasgupta, Partha and Stiglitz, Joseph (1980): "Uncertainty, Industrial Structure and the Speed of R and D," *Bell Journal of Economics*, 11, Autumn, 1–28.

Gilbert, Richard J. (1981): "Patents, Sleeping Patents and Entry Deterrence," in Steven C. Salop (ed.), *Strategy, Predation and Antitrust Analysis*, Federal Trade Commission, September, 205–69.

—— and Newbery, David M. G. (1982): "Preemptive Patenting and the Persistence of Monopoly," *American Economic Review*, 72, June, 514–26.

Hestenes, Magnus R. (1980): *Calculus of Variations and Optimal Control Theory*, Huntington: Robert E. Krieger.

Lee, Tom and Wilde, Louis L. (1980): "Market Structure and Innovation: A Reformulation," *Quarterly Journal of Economics*, 94, March, 429–36.

Loury, Glenn C. (1979): "Market Structure and Innovation," *Quarterly Journal of Economics*, 93, August, 395–410.

Scherer, F. M. (1980): *Industrial Market Structure and Economic Performance*, 2nd edn, Chicago: Rand McNally Co.

CHAPTER EIGHTEEN

The Learning Curve, Market Dominance, and Predatory Pricing

Luís M. B. Cabral and Michael H. Riordan

Source: *Econometrica*, 1994, 62, 1115–40.

Strategic implications of the learning curve hypothesis are analyzed in a model of a price-setting, differentiated duopoly selling to a sequence of heterogeneous buyers with uncertain demands. A unique and symmetric Markov perfect equilibrium is characterized, and two concepts of self-reinforcing market dominance investigated. One is increasing dominance (ID), whereby the leading firm has a greater probability of winning the next sale; the other is increasing increasing dominance (IID), whereby a firm's probability of winning the next sale increases with the length of its lead. Sufficient conditions for IID (and thus for ID) are that the discount factor is sufficiently low or sufficiently high. Other sufficient conditions for ID and IID are given in the case of two-step learning, in which a firm reaches the bottom of its learning curve after just two sales. However, examples are also constructed for the two-step learning case in which neither ID nor IID holds. It is also shown that, in equilibrium, IID implies that learning is privately disadvantageous, although it is socially advantageous. Finally, introducing avoidable fixed costs and possible exit into the model yields a new theory of predatory pricing based on the learning curve hypothesis.

1. Introduction

There are several strategic implications of the hypothesis that a firm's unit cost declines with its cumulative production – the learning curve hypothesis. First, by moving down the learning curve faster than its rivals a firm gains a strategic advantage.[1] Second, recognizing this potential for strategic advantage, firms compete aggressively, and perhaps even unprofitably, to move down their learning curves. Third, even a mature firm might compete aggressively to prevent a rival from moving down its learning curve. Fourth, the strategic advantage conferred by learning may drive rivals from the market, creating an incentive for predatory pricing. We study these strategic issues in a dynamic duopoly model.

The learning curve hypothesis is not new, and has been studied in many industries. These include airframes (Wright (1936), Asher (1956), Alchian (1963)), machine tools (Hirsch (1952)), metal products (Dudley (1972)), nuclear power plants (Zimmerman (1982), Joskow and Rozanski (1979)), chemical processing (Lieberman (1984)), shipbuilding (Searle and Goody (1945), Argote, Beckman, and Epple (1990)), and semiconductors (Webbink (1977)). There is also casual evidence that learning by doing matters for how firms compete. For example, in discussing the semiconductor market, *The Economist* (October 13, 1990) states that chip makers "almost bankrupted themselves" selling early generations of memory chips. Newhouse (1982) makes similar remarks about airframe manufacturers in discussing competition between the Boeing 747, the Lockheed L1011, and the McDonnell-Douglas DC10 beginning in the late 1960s.

The industrial organization literature on the strategic implications of the learning curve is sparse.[2] Lee (1975) argued that learning might raise entry barriers in a dynamic limit pricing model. Spence (1981) showed with numerical examples how, in a Cournot quantity-setting model, a learning curve creates entry barriers against late entrants; Ghemawat and Spence (1985) elaborated how industry spillovers mitigate this effect. An extreme form of spillovers, industry-wide learning, was analyzed by Stokey (1986). Fudenberg and Tirole (1983) showed that, in a linear two-period Cournot model: (i) firms' outputs might decrease with learning, (ii) learning is socially beneficial, and (iii) a balanced-budget tax-subsidy scheme can improve welfare. Ross (1986) demonstrated numerically how learning enhanced a Stackelberg advantage, and Dasgupta and Stiglitz (1988) showed how learning might enhance other (possibly small) exogenous strategic advantages. Gilbert and Harris (1981) discuss how a learning curve for investment enables an incumbent to preempt entrants repeatedly by installing lumpy new capacity anticipating demand growth. Mookherjee and Ray (1991) analyzed how learning curves facilitate oligopoly collusion in a dynamic Bertrand model.

The Dasgupta–Stiglitz article is perhaps closest in theme to our own approach, being concerned with how learning influences the evolution of market structure. Adapting Fudenberg and Tirole's linear Cournot model, Dasgupta and Stiglitz showed how granting one firm a small initial cost advantage can lead to increasing market concentration as learning proceeds. Indeed, they demonstrated that, if firms are sufficiently myopic and learning proceeds fast enough, then an oligopoly with initially asymmetric costs eventually becomes monopolized. They also showed how in a homogeneous product Bertrand model a learning curve yields a monopoly market structure if one firm has a customer loyalty advantage.

Our approach to the strategic implications of the learning curve is distinct in several ways. First, our model of dynamic oligopoly is different. We assume a price setting duopoly selling to a sequence of heterogeneous buyers with uncertain preferences for one product over the other. The previous literature has focused mostly on homogeneous products, deterministic demand, and quantity-setting.[3] We think our model better captures the market for commercial airframes, for example. This market operates on the basis of closed competitive price negotiations, and product differentiation and demand uncertainty clearly matter (Newhouse (1982)). A virtue of our approach is that it enables us to study the endogenous evolution of market shares arising from asymmetries generated by demand realizations.

Second, our modeling approach relies on general functional forms, although admittedly it is specialized in other respects. In contrast, most previous oligopoly learning curve models have relied on special functional forms and specific parameter values. Our approach characterizes equilibrium by a two-dimensional system of difference equations. The two dimensions define the "state of the system" which is given by the cumulative previous sales of both firms.

Third, we address questions new to the learning curve literature. It is a familiar idea in industrial organization (e.g., Flaherty (1980), Gilbert and Newbery (1982), Vickers (1986), Budd, Harris, and Vickers (1993)), and quite clear from the theory of races (e.g., Harris and Vickers (1985, 1987)), that, once ahead, a leader might tend to stay ahead. In our model, this "increasing dominance" property means that a leader has a greater probability of selling to the next buyer. We provide sufficient conditions for increasing dominance and show it implies learning is privately disadvantageous, i.e. symmetric firms would be better off if no learning were possible. We also obtain sufficient conditions for an even stronger property of "increasing increasing dominance" meaning that a leader's probability of winning the next competition increases with the length of its lead.[4]

Furthermore, we extend our model to include avoidable fixed costs and develop a new theory of predatory pricing based on the learning curve hypothesis. In contrast to previous formal models (Ordover and Saloner (1989), Roberts (1987)), ours relies neither on financial market imperfections nor on asymmetric information. We argue that: (i) entry and subsequent exit can be an equilibrium outcome, (ii) the possibility of a rival's exit induces more aggressive pricing, which, in turn, increases the probability of exit, and (iii) such predatory pricing might be socially beneficial. We also show that predatory and nonpredatory equilibria can coexist, and prices below marginal cost need not indicate a predatory intent except for a mature incumbent.

The sequel is organized as follows. Section 2 presents our model and characterizes a unique and symmetric Markov perfect equilibrium. Section 3 presents our results about market dominance, and section 4 presents our results about predatory pricing. Section 5 discusses some normative implications of the learning curve hypothesis, and section 6 concludes by summarizing and indicating some open directions for future research.

2. The General Model

Consider a price-setting, differentiated duopoly selling to an infinite sequence of heterogeneous buyers. In each period, a buyer demands at most one unit of the good from one of the two firms. We assume a sale always occurs and denote by x the premium a buyer is willing to pay for firm 2's product. The "preference parameter" x varies across buyers and is not observed by the firms. However, it is common knowledge that buyers' preference parameters are independently and identically distributed according to a differentiable cumulative distribution function $F(x)$. Let $f(x)$ denote the corresponding density function. We make several simplifying assumptions.

ASSUMPTION 1:   (a) $f(x) > 0$ *on the real line;*[5] (b) $f(x)$ *is differentiable;*[6] (c) $f(x)$ *is symmetric about zero;* (d) $H(z) \equiv F(x)/f(x)$ *is increasing.*

Assumption 1(d) has an interpretation in the context of a one–period, asymmetric–cost Bertrand model. Let c_1 be the cost of firm 1. If $P = p_2 - p_1$ is the price differential, then $F(P)$ is the probability that firm 1 makes a sale, and $p_1/H(P)$ is the price elasticity of expected demand for firm 1's product. The first-order condition for firm 1 is $p_1 - H(P) = c_1$. The assumption implies that, given p_2, firm 1's expected marginal revenue decreases as a lower p_1 increases expected sales.[7]

It will be useful to introduce some additional notation which also has an interpretation in the one-shot model. Let $C \equiv c_2 - c_1$ be the cost difference between firm 2 and firm 1. Subtracting firm 1's first-order condition from the corresponding expression for firm 2 yields $P + G(P) = C$, where $G(x) = H(x) - H(-x)$. This is an equilibrium condition determining the price difference as a function of the cost difference. Moreover, substituting firm 1's first-order condition back into its objective function, $(p_1 - c_1) \cdot F(P)$, yields an equilibrium expected profit $\Pi(P) \equiv H(P) \cdot F(P)$ in the one-shot game. These two functions, $G(\cdot)$ and $\Pi(\cdot)$, reappear later. We refer to $\Pi(\cdot)$ as the "one-shot profit function." Note that $G(x) = \Pi(x) - \Pi(-x)$, $\Pi(x)$ is increasing, and $\Pi'(0) = 1$.

The key assumption of our model is that a firm's unit cost is a decreasing function of cumulative past sales, $c(s)$. We further assume that learning is finite, in that a firm reaches the bottom of its learning curve upon making m sales.

ASSUMPTION 2:   (a) $c(s) > c(s+1)$ *for* $s < m$; (b) $c(s) = c(m)$ *for* $s \geq m$.

We maintain Assumptions 1 and 2 throughout.

Firms maximize expected discounted profits, and our solution concept is Markov perfect equilibrium (MPE). This is a subgame perfect equilibrium with the property that each firm's strategy depends only on the state of the game. The state of the game is defined by a pair (i, j), where i and j are the cumulative sales of firm 1 and firm 2 respectively. Since learning is bounded, state $(i, m + k)$ is equivalent to state (i, m) for $k > 0$. Therefore, a strategy for firm 1 is a mapping $p(i, j)$ that gives its price for each possible state of the game and has the property that $p(i, m + k) = p(i, m)$ for $k \geq 0$. A strategy for firm 2 is defined analogously, although we prove that a MPE must be symmetric.[8]

Given a strategy for each firm, we define recursively a value function $\nu(i, j)$, giving the value of the game for firm 1 in state (i, j). There is, of course, an analogous value function for firm 2, but we do not need to introduce notation for it explicitly. The following characterization of a MPE relates these value functions and the equilibrium strategies. It employs the following notation. First, $P(i, j)$ is the difference between firm 1 and firm 2's price, so firm 2's strategy is described by $p(i, j) - P(i, j)$, and a symmetric strategy satisfies $p(j, i) = p(i, j) - P(i, j)$. Second, $w(i, j) = \nu(i + 1, j) - \nu(i, j + 1)$ is firm 1's "prize" from winning a sale, and $W(i, j)$ is the difference between firm 1 and firm 2's prize. Third, $C(i, j) = c(i) - c(j)$ is the cost difference between the firms. Finally, δ is the discount factor, satisfying $0 < \delta < 1$.

THEOREM 2.1:   *A MPE has the following properties*:

$$p(i, j) - H(-P(i, j)) = c(i) - \delta w(i, j) \tag{2.1}$$

$$P(i,j) + G(P(i,j)) = C(i,j) - \delta W(i,j) \tag{2.2}$$

$$\nu(i,j) = \Pi(-P(i,j)) + \delta\nu(i,j+1) \tag{2.3}$$

$$\nu(i,m+1) = \nu(i,m) \tag{2.4}$$

THEOREM 2.2:   *There exists a unique and symmetric MPE.*

PROOFS: See Appendix A.

These equilibrium conditions have clear interpretations. Equation (2.1) is the first-order condition for the asymmetric cost one-shot game discussed before, except that the discounted "prize" from winning enters as a production subsidy. Accordingly, the difference in prices characterized by equation (2.2) equals the one-shot equilibrium price difference corresponding to these subsidized costs.

Equation (2.3) indicates that the value function can be decomposed into the sum of the one-shot profit corresponding to the equilibrium price difference and the discounted value of losing. This decomposition follows from the interpretation of the prize as a production subsidy, i.e., the value of winning is implicit in the one-shot profit function. The reader is cautioned that this profit function does not characterize short-run profit since it includes the prize from winning.

Our main point is that the learning curve creates implicit production subsidies. The significant complication arising in the dynamic model is that these subsidies are determined endogenously by the dynamic interaction of the firms. They depend on future possible paths of equilibrium prices. More specifically, equations (2.2), (2.3), and the boundary condition (2.4) determine the path of equilibrium price differences, and fully describe the evolution of market structure and the value functions of the firms. The implicit production subsidies are calculated by solving these equations.

3. Market Dominance

Once ahead, does a firm tend to stay ahead? Does this tendency increase with the length of the lead? Since $F(P(i,j))$ is the probability that firm j wins the next sale, these questions are equivalent to asking: Is $P(i, j)$ negative for $i > j$? Is $P(i, j)$ decreasing in i? We call a positive answer to the first question increasing dominance (ID) and a positive answer to the second increasing increasing dominance (IID). Note that IID implies ID because $P(i, i) = 0$ by symmetry (Theorem 2.2).

Lest these market dominance properties seem obvious, consider the following plausible intuition from Scherer and Ross (1990, p. 372):

"As the leading firm approaches the bottom of its learning curve, its incentive to constrain price in the hope of gaining future cost advantages weakens, and it will be tempted to price less aggressively and reap the profit fruits of its prior pricing restraint."

This intuition is incomplete. A firm at the very bottom of its learning curve maintains a strategic advantage as long as its rival has a higher cost. The desire to keep the rival from moving down its learning curve too quickly creates an incentive for even a mature leading firm to price aggressively.

The equilibrium characterization of the previous section indicates that market dominance properties depend on a "cost effect" and a "prize effect." The cost effect is easy to understand. As cost differences between firms widen so should price differences. The cost effect by itself suggests IID should hold, and indeed it does if the future is sufficiently unimportant.

THEOREM 3.1:   *For δ sufficiently close to zero, $P(i+1,j) < P(i,j)$ for $i < m$ and $j \leq m$.*

PROOF: Since $G(\cdot)$ is an increasing function by Assumption 1(d), the result follows from Assumption 2 and equation (2.2) as $\delta \to 0$.   *QED*

The prize effect is more interesting. It refers to the prize from winning that constitutes an implicit production subsidy. If the lagging firm has a sufficiently larger prize, then the prize effect could dominate the cost effect, and IID or even ID could fail.

An initial observation is that for $\delta > 0$ but sufficiently small, the prize effect reinforces the cost effect if the one-shot profit function is convex, as it is for many distribution functions, including normal or uniform distribution functions. To see this, observe that the prize difference, $W(i,j)$ equals the difference between the joint payoff if i wins and the joint payoff if j wins. For small δ, the joint payoff approximately equals the joint profit of a corresponding one-shot game, and the joint profit in the one-shot game increases as the cost gap widens if and only if $\Pi(\cdot)$ is convex. therefore, the prize effect widens price differences when the future is not too important and one-shot joint profits increase with the cost gap.[9]

This observation is interesting but not really consequential, because the cost effect always dominates when the future is discounted heavily. It is much more important to understand the prize effect when δ is large and the future weighs heavily. We begin by considering equilibrium pricing in the limit as δ goes to unity. The result is that firms always price as if at the bottom of their learning curves.

THEOREM 3.2:

$$\lim_{\delta \to 1} p(i,j) = c(m) + H(0) \tag{3.1}$$

PROOF: See Appendix B.

There is a clear explanation for this result. When δ equals unity, production is "timeless." Moreover, since there are an infinite number of buyers, each firm must reach the bottom of its learning curve eventually. Thus, in each period, the relevant marginal cost is $c(m)$ regardless of experience (cf. Spence (1981)), and each firm prices accordingly. It is precisely as if each firm plays repeatedly the one-shot Bertrand equilibrium with marginal cost $c(m)$.

Theorem 3.2 implies that price differences are negligible when the future is very important, i.e.

$$\lim_{\delta \to 1} P(i,j) = 0 \tag{3.2}$$

Therefore, each firm has an approximately equal chance of winning each sale and the market evolves accordingly.

Equations (2.1), (3.1), and (3.2) together imply that $w(i,j) \to C(i,m)$ as $\delta \to 1$. Therefore, $W(i,j) \to C(i,j)$. The cost effect and prize effect have opposite signs, but they exactly offset each other. A heuristic intuition is as follows. Firms get to the bottom of the learning curve eventually, but incur higher costs along the way. The difference between actual cost and cost at the bottom of the learning curve is a "learning cost." The sum of prospective learning costs for a firm with i previous sales is

$$\sum_{k=i}^{m-1} C(k,m)$$

Therefore, the difference in total prospective learning costs for a firm with cumulative sales $i + 1$ and a firm with cumulative sales i is simply $C(i,m)$. Since prices are approximately constant for δ close to unity, this is also approximately the difference in expected payoffs. That is $w(i,j) \to C(i,m)$ and $W(i,j) \to C(i,j)$.[10]

The observation that the prize effect exactly offsets the cost effect when the future matters as much as the present raises the following question. In the neighborhood of $\delta = 1$, does the cost effect or the prize effect dominate? If the cost effect dominates, then ID holds for δ less than but close to unity. We obtain a very sharp answer. Not only ID but IID holds in the neighborhood of $\delta = 1$.

THEOREM 3.3: *For δ less than but sufficiently close to unity, $P(i+1,j) < P(i,j)$ if $i < m$ and $j \leq m$.*

PROOF: Follows from Lemmas B.1 and B.2 in Appendix B.

Here is an intuitive explanation. If firms don't discount the future, then each prices as if cost is $c(m)$. In other words, each firm has a "subsidized cost" equal to $c(m)$. In the near term, both firms incur learning costs, and these are larger for the lagging firm. A firm that discounts the future a little bit is tempted to raise price slightly to gain a better margin of price over subsidized cost in the short run. Of course this reduces the probability of making the sale, but this disadvantage is offset somewhat by shifting learning costs into the future. This offset is greater for the lagging firm with the larger learning costs. Therefore, the lagging firm has a greater incentive to raise price, and this incentive increases with the size of the lag. In fact, as we prove in Appendix B,

$$\frac{dp(i,j)}{d\delta} \to -\sum_{k=i}^{m-1} C(k,m) \tag{3.3}$$

and

$$\frac{dP(i,j)}{d\delta} \to -\sum_{k=i}^{j-1} C(k,m) \qquad \text{for } i < j \tag{3.4}$$

As $\delta \to 1$, the mark-up of prices above $c(m) + H(0)$ is approximately proportional to prospective learning costs, and therefore the equilibrium price difference is approximately proportional to the difference in prospective learning costs. We conclude that IID holds for δ near unity. Another implication of (3.3) is that firm i's price is decreasing as it moves down its learning curve.

It remains to ask whether ID and IID hold for intermediate values of δ. To do so, we focus on the case of two-step learning, i.e. $m = 2$. Obviously, this also characterizes the final stages of learning for the general model with an arbitrary value of m, i.e. for $(i,j) \geq (m - 2, m - 2)$.

THEOREM 3.4: *If $m = 2$ and the one-shot profit function is convex, then ID holds. If, in addition, the learning curve is convex and either $\delta \leq 1/2$ or $c(m - 1)$ is not too large, then IID holds.*

PROOF: See Appendix C.

In the two-step learning model, ID means that $P(m - 1, m), P(m - 2, m)$, and $P(m - 2, m - 1)$ are all positive, and IID means that $P(m - 2, m) > P(m - 1, m)$ and $P(m - 2, m) > P(m - 2, m - 1)$. It is true that $P(m - 1, m) > 0$ and $P(m - 2, m) > 0$ hold even without the convexity assumptions. However, we use convexity of the learning curve to prove $P(m - 2, m) > P(m - 1, m)$, and convexity of the profit function to prove $P(m - 2, m - 1) > 0$. Finally, the additional restrictions on δ and $c(m - 1)$ ensure $P(m - 2, m) > P(m - 2, m - 1)$. Details and counterexamples are in Appendix C. Here we give some heuristic explanations.

The reason why $P(m - 1, m) > 0$ is instructive. It is explained by a simple fixed point argument shown in Figure 1. The "price locus" defined by $P + G(P) = C - \delta W$, describes how the equilibrium price difference (P) depends on the difference in subsidized costs ($C - \delta W$). However, the subsidized cost difference in state ($m - 1, m$) itself depends on the price differential because

$$W = -[\Pi(P) - \Pi(0)] + [\Pi(0) - \Pi(-P)]/(1 - \delta)$$

Thus the "subsidized-cost locus" graphs $C - \delta W$ as a function of P, $P(m - 1, m)$ and $W(m - 1, m)$ are determined jointly by the intersection of the two curves. The two curves have the general shapes illustrated and must intersect where $P(m - 1, m) > 0$.[11] However, $W(m - 1, m)$ could be either positive or negative depending on the size of δ.

The reason why $P(m - 2, m) > 0$ is similar, except that the subsidized-cost locus may be higher or lower. The reason for the shift is twofold: $C(m - 2, m)$ is different from $C(m - 1, m)$, and $W(m - 2, m)$ depends not only on $P(m - 2, m)$ but on $P(m - 1, m)$ also. If the locus shifts downwards, as it will if $C(m - 2, m - 1)$ is small but $P(m - 1, m)$ is large, then $P(m - 2, m) < P(m - 1, m)$ contradicting IID.[12] The convexity of the learning curve assures that $C(m - 2, m - 1)$ is not small enough for this failure of IID to happen.

A heuristic explanation for $P(m - 1, m) > P(m - 2, m)$ is as follows. If $c(m - 1)$ is large then the leading firm will have a large cost advantage in state ($m - 1, m$) and the price difference $P(m - 1, m)$ will be correspondingly large. The leading firm is not unhappy with this situation and so does not worry too much if the lagging firm wins in state ($m - 2, m$), particularly if $C(m - 2, m - 1)$ is small, in which case the lagging firm does not very much lower its cost by winning.

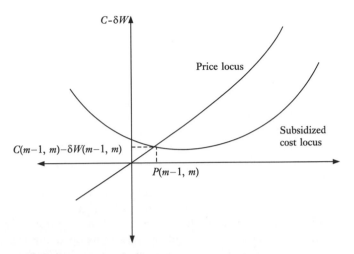

Figure 1   Equilibrium in state $(m - 1, m)$

The possibility of $P(m - 2, m) < P(m - 1, m)$ is fascinating because it implies the lagging firm is worse off by moving down its learning curve! To see this, observe that Theorem 2.1 implies

$$\nu(m - i, m) = \frac{\Pi(-P(m - i, m))}{1 - \delta}$$

Therefore $P(m - 2, m) < P(m - 1, m)$ translates directly to $\nu(m - 2, m) > \nu(m - 1, m)$.

It is also interesting that $P(m - 2, m - 1) < 0$ is possible if $\Pi(\cdot)$ is not convex. Details are in Appendix C, but the rough idea behind this failure of ID is as follows. The lagging firm prices aggressively to avoid state $(m - 2, m)$ which is highly unprofitable. This concern dominates the thinking of the lagging firm when (i) $C(m - 2, m - 1)$ is close to 0, so there is virtually no cost effect in state $(m - 2, m - 1)$, (ii) δ is small, so what happens beyond next period is irrelevant, and (iii) $\Pi(\cdot)$ is concave in the relevant range so the laggard loses more than the leader gains by moving to state $(m - 2, m)$ rather than $(m - 1, m - 1)$.[13] In these circumstances ID fails. Even if $\Pi(\cdot)$ is convex, so ID holds, IID may fail, i.e., $P(m - 2, m - 1) > P(m - 2, m)$ for related reasons.

We close this section by showing that ID implies learning is privately disadvantageous, in the sense that symmetric firms would be better off if no further learning were possible. All of the benefits of learning, and more, are competed away.

THEOREM 3.5: *If ID holds, then $\nu(i, i)$ is lower than it would be in an environment with no learning beyond (i, i), (i.e., $m = i$).*

PROOF: From equation (2.3),

$$\nu(i,i) = \Pi(0) + \sum_{j=i+1}^{\infty} \delta^{j-1} \Pi(-P(i,j)) < 0. \tag{3.5}$$

ID implies $\Pi(-P(i,j)) < \Pi(0)$ for $j > i$. Therefore $\nu(i,i) < \Pi(0)/(1-\delta)$ which equals the present value of profits in the absence of further learning.   *QED*

Anecdotal evidence supports the idea that a learning curve does indeed have a negative impact on industry profits. A first example is given by commercial aircraft construction, which is known to be subject to significant learning economies. Seitz and Steele (1985) state that out of 22 commercial aircraft developed, only three – the Boeing 707, 727, and the DC-8 – have been profitable. Returns on assets and on sales have been significantly below those for all manufacturing.

A second example comes from the semiconductor industry. "The chip business is a matter of yields, learning from experience and forward pricing. The greater the investment a manufacturer makes in a semiconductor plant, the more chips it can turn out. The higher is output, the lower its unit costs and the greater its operating experience. That translates, in turn, into higher yields and still lower unit costs" (*The Economist*, July 14, 1990). Competition for sales in the previous generation of memory chips (1-megabit DRAMs) was such that chip makers "almost bankrupted themselves." Now that a new generation of memory chips (4-megabit DRAMs) is overtaking the previous one, "Japan's giant chip makers are rushing into what looks like a suicidal expansion of 4-megabit chip production" (*The Economist*, October 13, 1990).

4. Predatory Pricing

Predation refers to actions that are unprofitable but for their possible contribution to a rival's exit (Ordover and Willig (1981)). By introducing an avoidable fixed cost into our model, we demonstrate how a learning curve can create equilibrium incentives for predatory pricing.

Specifically, we amend our model by assuming that firms incur a positive fixed cost each period they remain in the market. At the beginning of each period, firms decide simultaneously whether to remain or exit. Exiting, a firm gets a payoff of zero. Staying in, the firm pays a fixed cost in the amount $(1-\delta)A$. For expositional simplicity, we assume firms cannot re-enter after exiting.

If both firms stay in the market, then competition in that period proceeds as before, except that the possible future exit of a rival affects equilibrium pricing, as we shall demonstrate. If its rival exits, a firm with experience i gets an assumed monopoly payoff of $\nu^{\#}(i) - A$ for the subgame beginning at that date.[14] We assume that $\nu^{\#}(i) \geq \nu(i,j) + \nu(j,i)$ for all j; monopoly profit is greater than the sum of duopoly profits.

In what follows, we adopt the following notation. As in section 2, $\nu(i,j)$ denotes the equilibrium value function for the subgame beginning in state (i,j), assuming that $A = 0$. $\nu'(i,j)$ denotes the corresponding value function for the case $A > 0$, calculated before entry decisions are made. $P(\cdot)$ and $P'(\cdot)$ are distinguished similarly, as are $p(\cdot)$ and $p'(\cdot)$.

As our purpose here is to establish "possibility" results, we proceed by analyzing special cases and examples. We begin with the case of one-step learning, $m = 1$. In this case we know from Lemma C.1 in Appendix C and equation (2.3) that

$$\nu(1,0) > \nu(1,1) > \nu(0,0) > \nu(0,1)$$

If $\nu(0,1) = \Pi(-P(0,1))/(1-\delta) \geq A$, there obviously exists a MPE with no exit, but we show there might exist also a MPE with exit in state $(0, 1)$. Obviously, if $\nu(0, 1) < A$, exit must occur in state $(0, 1)$.

THEOREM 4.1: *If $m = 1$ and $(1 - \delta)A = \Pi(-P(0,1)) - \varepsilon$, then, for $|\varepsilon| > 0$ sufficiently small, there exists a MPE in which*:
   (a)   *both firms enter initially*;
   (b)   *the firm losing the first sale exits; and*
   (c) $p'(0,0) < p(0,0)$.

PROOF: See Appendix D.

Thus, if $\Pi(-P(0,1)) = (1 - \delta)A + \varepsilon$, where ε is a small positive number, there exist multiple equilibria, one involving predatory pricing and exit. The intuition behind the predation result is clear. The possibility of the rival's exit increases the "prize" from winning the first sale, inducing more aggressive pricing. On the other hand, if ε is a small negative number, it cannot be an equilibrium for both firms to remain in the market in state $(0, 1)$, and equilibrium necessarily involves predatory pricing in state $(0, 0)$ as the firms compete to survive.

In cases of multiple equilibria, the predatory one might be considered a "bootstrap" equilibrium. The leading firm sets a predatory price expecting that winning the next sale will induce exit, and this pricing behavior makes that expectation self-fulfilling. It is perhaps surprising that Markov perfection does not eliminate bootstrap equilibria of this sort.[15] Moreover, it is tempting to think that an appropriate forward induction argument would eliminate such equilibria, but that is not clear. Staying in rather than exiting might "signal" that the lagging firm expects to play the nonpredatory equilibrium, but a predatory response might in turn signal that the leader expects to play the predatory one. Which signal is more convincing?[16]

A possible policy drawback of the $m = 1$ predation result is that there is no distinction between predator and prey. Both firms are predating against each other in state $(0, 0)$. However, for more complicated learning curves, asymmetric market positions can emerge in which the lower cost firm predates. We show this for the case of two-step learning.

THEOREM 4.2: *Let $m = 2$; there exists parameters supporting an equilibrium with*
   (a)   *the lagging firm exiting in state $(0, 2)$*;
   (b) $P'(0,1) > P(0,1)$;
   (c) $p'(1,0) < p(1,0)$.

PROOF: See Appendix D.

These results provide a very satisfactory theory of predatory pricing, with the following features. First, an incumbent firm perceives that a lower price increases the probability that a rival will exit the market. Second, such exit is rational for the rival. Third, it was rational for the rival to have entered in the first place. Fourth, the possibility of the rival's exit leads the firm to price lower than it would were the rival committed not to exit. Fifth, such pricing increases the probability of exit.

Notice that prices below marginal cost are not necessarily predatory (cf. Areeda and Turner (1975)). Theorem 3.2 states that $p(i, j) \rightarrow c(m) + H(0)$ as $\delta \rightarrow 1$, and our assumptions certainly allow $c(i) > c(m) + H(0)$, in which case $p(i, j) < c(i)$ for δ sufficiently large. Therefore, below cost pricing can happen even when $A = 0$ precludes the possibility of exit. However, we next prove that once a firm reaches the bottom of its learning curve, there is no explanation for below marginal cost pricing.

THEOREM 4.3: $A = 0$ implies $p(m, i) > c(m)$.

PROOF: From equation (2.3), $w(m, i) = \Pi(P(i, m)) - (1 - \delta)\nu(m, i + 1)$. Therefore, from equation (2.1) and the definition of $H(\cdot)$,

$$
\begin{aligned}
p(m, i) &= c(m) + H(P(i, m)) - \delta \Pi(P(i, m)) + \delta(1 - \delta)\nu(m, i + 1) \\
&\geq c(m) + (1 - \delta)\Pi(i, m) + \delta(1 - \delta)\nu(m, i + 1) \quad > c(m) \qquad \textit{QED}
\end{aligned}
$$

The proof of Theorem 4.3 suggests that a mature incumbent might want to price below cost in order to induce exit. However, as the next theorem shows, this cannot be true for subgames along the equilibrium path.

THEOREM 4.4: *If along the equilibrium path both firms remain active in state (m, i), then $p(m, i) \geq c(m)$.*

PROOF: Suppose not, that is, $p(m, i) < c(m)$. Then,

$$
\begin{aligned}
\nu(m, i) &= [p(m, i) - c(m, i) + \delta\nu(m, i)]F(P(i, m)) + \delta[1 - F(P(i, m))]\nu(m, i + 1) \\
&= [1 - \delta F(P(i, m))]^{-1}\{p(m, i) - c(m, i))F(P(i, m)) \\
&\quad + [1 - F(P(i, m))]\delta\nu(m, i + 1)\} \quad < \nu(m, i + 1)
\end{aligned}
$$

since $\nu(m, i + 1) > 0 > p(m, i) - c(m, i)$.   *QED*

In other words, pricing below cost by a mature incumbent cannot occur on the equilibrium path even if $A > 0$. The reason is simple. If below cost pricing by the mature incumbent would drive the rival from the market, then the rival should have exited already, or never entered in the first place. However, we conjecture it is possible to explain equilibrium predatory pricing (in the sense of Areeda and Turner) by a mature incumbent by introducing declining demand into the model. Specifically, suppose that beyond a certain date, say t', buyers begin to arrive more slowly. This is captured by assuming that δ is lower after t'. Now suppose that the market is in state (i, m) at some date t prior to date t', and let $\nu(i, m, t)$ denote the value function for the lagging firm. Suppose that $\nu(i, m, t + 1) < \nu(i, m, t)$ since, other things being equal, the future looks less favorable as time goes on. The firm might stay in at date t, hoping to move down the learning curve, but exit at date $t + 1$ if it fails to do so. This gives the mature firm an incentive for predatory pricing at date t.

5. Normative Results

We have focused on positive economic issues, but our theory has normative implications too. Appendix E characterizes a social optimum, and proves several results. If the future matters sufficiently, i.e. $\delta \rightarrow 1$, equilibrium learning is too slow from society's standpoint, i.e., it would be better for the leading firm to learn more quickly. The rough intuition is that quicker learning better exploits "dynamic economies of scale." Moreover, for the case of two-step learning (i.e. $m = 2$), equilibrium learning is socially desirable even though it is privately disadvantageous.

It is also true that predatory pricing may be socially desirable. We have shown that, for specific parameter values, there may exist two equilibria, one where predation and exit occurs, and one where it does not. Which equilibrium is better socially? It is well known that free entry into an industry with scale economies may lead to excessive entry (Mankiw and Whinston (1986)). Therefore, it is not surprising that there may exist parameter values such that the predation equilibrium is socially better than the equilibrium with no predation. In fact, when the two equilibria co-exist, a comparison involves a tradeoff between several effects. The predation equilibrium features (i) less total production because of monopoly power; (ii) less product variety; (iii) lower production costs due to quicker learning; and (iv) lower fixed costs due to fewer firms in the market. It is not hard to construct examples where the last two effects dominate, making the predatory equilibrium better from society's standpoint (see Cabral and Riordan (1991)).

6. Conclusion

We modeled dynamic price competition with learning by doing for a duopoly facing a sequence of buyers with uncertain demands. We showed that market dominance can be increasingly self-reinforcing, that learning can be socially desirable but privately disadvantageous, and that equilibrium learning can be too slow from society's standpoint. We also developed a theory of predatory pricing arising from learning economies, and argued that predation might speed learning in a socially desirable way.

However, this agenda only scratches the surface. Learning economies give rise to many other interesting issues for strategic oligopoly interaction. For example, important issues surround the timing of production.[17] In our model, the timing of production was determined by the exogenous arrival of buyers. Certainly, this is very artificial. For example, in industries such as airframe manufacturing, where learning curves are known to matter (Wright (1936)), delivery dates are negotiated between buyers and sellers, and delivery lags are long. In general, the optimal timing of production trades off short-run scale economies and long-run learning economies. A very interesting issue is how strategic interaction affects this tradeoff.

There are also many policy issues surrounding learning economies. We addressed predatory pricing, but only briefly. Obviously, it would be desirable to have a much clearer delineation of when predatory pricing is likely to be harmful. Also, it would be interesting to address how enforcement rules against predatory conduct, such as the Areeda–Turner standard, affect dynamic oligopoly competition and the evolution of market structure. Still another area of policy application is the so-called infant industry argument for tariff protection in the presence of learning economies, discussed by Dasgupta and Stiglitz (1988) and Krugman (1984). Finally, oligopoly competition with learning economies might have implications for the optimal design of patent policy. The real advantage of patents may not be so much the temporary protection they afford, as the opportunity to move down the learning curve first.

Another issue for future research concerns the microeconomic foundations of the learning-by-doing hypothesis. This hypothesis might be interpreted to mean that process R&D is complementary with production, the simple learning curve being one extreme example. In this more general context, investments in cost reduction are endogenous, and firms' incentives to invest will depend on how much they produce and on their strategic positions. We conjecture (and can show in special cases) that firms will stop investing in process R&D at certain points. Thus, it seems possible that rival firms have different cost levels even in the long run, leading to a richer theory of long–run market structure.

Appendix A: Equilibrium

Proof of Theorem 2.1:   At (i, j) firm 1 solves the following maximization problem:

$$\max_p F(q - p)[p - c(i) + \delta\nu(i + 1, j)] + [1 - F(q - p)]\delta\nu(i, j + 1) \tag{A.1}$$

where q is the equilibrium price of firm 2. The first-order condition for firm 1 is

$$F(q - p) - f(q - p)[p - c(i) + \delta\nu(i + 1, j)] + f(q - p)\delta\nu(i, j + 1) = 0 \tag{A.2}$$

which simplifies to $p = c(i) + H(q - p) - \delta w(i, j)$. Substituting $p(i, j)$ and $P(i, j)$ for p and $(p - q)$ we obtain (2.1). Taking the difference between (2.1) and its symmetric counterpart for firm 2, and simplifying, we obtain (2.2). Furthermore, substituting $p(i, j)$, as given by (2.1), and $-P(i, j)$ for p and $(q - p)$ in the maximand of problem (A.1) and simplifying, we obtain (2.3). Finally, the boundary conditions (2.4) follow from the fact that (i, m) and $(i, m + 1)$ are equivalent states by Assumption 2.   QED

Proof of Theorem 2.2:   First, consider state (m, m). The boundary condition (2.4) implies $w(m, m) = 0$ and $W(m, m) = 0$. Since $C(m, m) = 0$ and $G(\cdot)$ is increasing, (2.2) implies $P(m, m) = 0$. Equations (2.3) and (2.4) then imply $\nu(m, m) = \Pi(0)/(1 - \delta)$, and equation (2.1) implies $p(m, m) = c(m) + H(0)$. This solution characterizes a unique and symmetric MPE for (m, m) subgames because Theorem 2.1 says (2.1)–(2.4) are necessary conditions, the firms are symmetric, and Assumption 1 implies the maximand of (A.1) has a unique interior maximum establishing sufficiency.

Next, consider state $(i, m), i < m$ and adopt the induction hypothesis that there exists a unique and symmetric MPE for the subgame beginning in state $(i + 1, m)$. By symmetry, there must also exist a unique and symmetric equilibrium for the subgame beginning in state $(m, i + 1)$. Using Theorem 2.1, firm 1's value function is

$$\nu(i, m) = \frac{\Pi(-P(i, m))}{1 - \delta}$$

and the corresponding value function for firm 2 is

$$\bar{\nu}(m,i) = \Pi(P(i,m)) + \delta\nu(m,i+1)$$

Therefore, under the induction hypothesis,

$$W(i,m) = \nu(i+1,m) + (1-\delta)\nu(m,i+1) - \frac{\Pi(-P(i,m))}{1-\delta} - \Pi(P(i,m)) \tag{A.3}$$

and, using equation (2.3) and $G(x) = \Pi(X) - \Pi(-x)$, equation (2.2) implies that $P(i,m)$ must solve

$$P + (1-\delta)\Pi(P) - \frac{\Pi(-P)}{1-\delta} = C(i,m) - \delta\nu(i+1,m) - \delta(1-\delta)\nu(m,i+1) \tag{A.4}$$

for P. The right-hand side is bounded and independent of P, while the left-hand side is continuously increasing, ranging between $-\infty$ and $+\infty$. It follows that equation (A.4) yields a unique solution for $P(i,m)$, given values of $\nu(i+1,m)$ and $\nu(m,i+1)$ that exist uniquely under the induction hypothesis. Given $P(i,m), p(i,m)$ is determined uniquely by (2.1), with

$$w(i,m) = \nu(i+1,m) - \frac{\Pi(-P(i,m))}{1-\delta} \tag{A.5}$$

as implied by (2.3) and (2.4). A parallel argument for state (m,i) establishes $P(m,i) = -P(i,m)$ and $P(m,i) = p(i,m) - P(i,m)$. Thus, under the induction hypothesis, (2.1)–(2.4) characterize necessary conditions for a unique MPE in state (i, m) and a symmetric MPE in state (m, i). Sufficiency follows from Assumption 1 as above. Finally, a similar, but even simpler, induction argument establishes a unique and symmetric MPE for other subgames.   *QED*

Appendix B: Market Dominance with High Discount Factors

LEMMA B.1:

$$\lim_{\delta\to 1} P(i,j) = 0 \tag{B.1}$$

PROOF: Define

$$S(i) \equiv \lim_{\delta\to 1} \frac{\Pi(0) - \Pi(-P(i,m))}{1-\delta} \tag{B.2}$$

From equation (2.3),

$$w(i,m) = \frac{\Pi(0) - \Pi(-P(i,m))}{1-\delta} - \frac{\Pi(0) - \Pi(-P(i+1,m))}{1-\delta} \tag{B.3}$$

and

$$w(m, i) = \Pi(P(i, m)) - (1 - \delta) \sum_{k=1}^{m-i-1} \delta^{k-1} \Pi(P(i + k, m)) - \delta^{m-i-1} \Pi(0) \qquad \text{(B.4)}$$

We prove by induction that $\lim_{\delta \to 1} P(i, j) = 0$ and

$$S(i) = \sum_{k=i}^{m} C(k, m) \qquad \text{(B.5)}$$

If our induction hypothesis holds for every $i' > i$, then (B.2)–(B.4) imply

$$\lim_{\delta \to 1} w(i, m) = S(i) - \sum_{k=i+1}^{m} C(k, m)$$

and

$$\lim_{\delta \to 1} w(m, i) = \lim_{\delta \to 1} \Pi(P(i, m)) - \Pi(0)$$

Substituting $W(i, m) = w(i, m) - w(m, i)$, and $G(P(i, m)) = \Pi(P(i, m)) - \Pi(-P(i, m))$ in (2.2), taking limits, and rearranging, we get

$$\lim_{\delta \to 1} [P(i, m) + \Pi(0) - \Pi(-P(i, m))] + S(i) = \sum_{k=i}^{m} C(k, m) \qquad \text{(B.6)}$$

It follows that $\lim_{\delta \to 1} P(i, m) = 0$ and that $S(i) = \sum_{k=i}^{m} C(k, m)$. In fact, if $\lim_{\delta \to 1} P(i, m) \neq 0$, then $S(i)$, as defined by (B.2) would be unbounded, contradicting (B.6).

Now if $\lim_{\delta \to 1} P(i', j') = 0$ for all $(i', j') > (i, j)$, equation (2.3) implies $\lim_{\delta \to 1} w(i, j) = S(i) - S(i + 1) = C(i, m)$. It follows from (2.2) that

$$\lim_{\delta \to 1} [P(i, j) + G(P(i, j))] = 0$$

Since $G(0) = 0$ and $G' > 0$, it must be that $P(i, j) \to 0$ $\qquad\qquad\qquad$ *QED*

PROOF OF THEOREM 3.2:   From equation (2.1), and Lemma B.1 we have

$$\lim_{\delta \to 1} p(i, j) = c(i) + H(0) - \lim_{\delta \to 1} w(i, j)$$

From the proof of Lemma B.1, we have $\lim_{\delta \to 1} w(i, j) = C(i, m)$. Substituting and simplifying yields the desired result. $\qquad\qquad\qquad$ *QED*

We next consider the monotonicity properties of $P(i, j)$ in the neighborhood of $\delta = 1$. In view of Lemma B.1, the next result implies that $P(i, j)$ is monotonic in its arguments for δ sufficiently close to one. Theorem 3.3 follows immediately.

LEMMA B.2:   For $i < j$,

$$\lim_{\delta \to 1} \frac{dP(i,j)}{d\delta} = -\sum_{k=i}^{j-1} C(k,m) \tag{B.7}$$

PROOF: Differentiating equation (2.2) with respect to δ, we get

$$\frac{dP(i,j)}{d\delta}[1 + G'(P(i,j))] + W(i,j) + \delta\frac{dW(i,j)}{d\delta} = 0 \tag{B.8}$$

The proof of Lemma B.1 establishes $\lim_{\delta \to 1} W(i,j) = C(i,j)$. Therefore, Lemma B.1, $G'(0) = 2$, and (B.8) imply

$$R(i,j) \equiv -\lim_{\delta \to 1} \frac{dP(i,j)}{d\delta} = \frac{1}{3}\left(C(i,j) + \lim_{\delta \to 1}\frac{dW(i,j)}{d\delta}\right) \tag{B.9}$$

Differentiating (B.4), we have

$$\frac{dw(m,i)}{d\delta} = \Pi'(P(i,m))\frac{dP(i,m)}{d\delta} + \sum_{k=i+1}^{m-1}\delta^{k-i-1}\Pi(P(k,m))$$

$$- (1-\delta)\sum_{k=i+1}^{m-1}\frac{d(\delta^{k-i-1}\Pi(P(k,m)))}{d\delta} - (m-i-1)\delta^{m-i-2}\Pi(0)$$

Therefore, Lemma B.1 and $\Pi'(0) = 1$ imply

$$\lim_{\delta \to 1}\frac{dw(m,i)}{d\delta} = -R(i,m) \tag{B.10}$$

and (B.9) implies $3R(i,m) = C(i,m) + \lim_{\delta \to 1} dw(i,m)/d\delta + R(i,m)$. Rearranging this last expression, using the fact that $S(i) = R(i,m)$ by L'Hôpital's rule applied to (B.2), and using (B.5),

$$\lim_{\delta \to 1}\frac{dw(i,m)}{d\delta} = 2R(i,m) - C(i,m)$$

$$= 2S(i) - C(i,m)$$

$$= S(i) + S(i+1) \tag{B.11}$$

Again using equation (2.3), calculation establishes that

$$\lim_{\delta \to 1}\frac{dw(i,j)}{d\delta} = \sum_{k=j}^{m-1}R(i+1,k) - (m-j)S(i+1) + \lim_{\delta \to 1}\frac{d\nu(i+1,m)}{d\delta}$$

$$- \sum_{k=j+1}^{m-1}R(i,k) + (m-j-1)S(i) - \lim_{\delta \to 1}\frac{d\nu(i,m)}{d\delta}$$

or, substituting (B.11) for

$$\lim_{\delta \to 1} \frac{d\nu(i+1,m)}{d\delta} - \lim_{\delta \to 1} \frac{d\nu(i,m)}{d\delta}$$

and rearranging,

$$\lim_{\delta \to 1} \frac{dw(i,j)}{d\delta} = \sum_{k=j}^{m-1} R(i+1,k) - \sum_{k=j+1}^{m-1} R(i,k) + (m-j)S(i) - (m-j-1)S(i+1) \qquad (B.12)$$

Using $W(i,j) = w(i,j) - w(j,i)$ and equations (B.10) and (B.12), (B.9) defines a linear recursive system in $R(i,j)$. Since $R(i,m) = S(i)$, the system has a unique solution. It can be easily checked that $R(i,j) = S(i) - S(j)$ solves the system. Therefore, for $i < j$,

$$\lim_{\delta \to 1} \frac{dP(i,j)}{d\delta} \equiv -R(i,j) = -[S(i) - S(j)] = -\sum_{k=i}^{j-1} C(k,m) \qquad QED$$

Lemma B.3:

$$\lim_{\delta \to 1} \frac{dp(i,j)}{d\delta} = -\sum_{k=i}^{m} C(k,m)$$

Proof: Using Lemma B.2 and equation (B.5) we can simplify (B.12) to get

$$\lim_{\delta \to 1} \frac{dw(i,j)}{d\delta} = R(i+1,j) + S(i) \qquad (B.13)$$

Differentiating equation (2.1) and taking limits, we get

$$\lim_{\delta \to 1} \frac{dp(i,j)}{d\delta} = -H'(0) \lim_{\delta \to 1} \frac{dP(i,j)}{d\delta} - \lim_{\delta \to 1} w(i,j) - \lim_{\delta \to 1} \frac{dw(i,j)}{d\delta}$$
$$= R(i,j) - C(i,m) - R(i+1,j) - S(i)$$
$$= -S(i)$$

which follows from $H'(0) = 1$, (B.13), and the fact that

$$\lim_{\delta \to 1} w(i,j) = C(i,m)$$

as was shown in the proof of Lemma B.1. QED

Appendix C: Two-step Learning

We begin by simplifying notation. Let $p \equiv P(m-1,m), q \equiv P(m-2,m)$, and $r \equiv P(m-2,m-1)$. In the $m=2$ case, ID means $(p,q,r) > 0$ and IID is equivalent to $q > p > 0$ and $q > r > 0$.

LEMMA C.1: $p > 0$.

PROOF: Define $X \equiv \Pi(p) - \Pi(0)$ and $x \equiv \Pi(-p) - \Pi(0)$. Notice that X is increasing and x is decreasing in p, both are zero when p is zero. Applying equation (2.3) we have $W(m-1, m) = -X - x/(1-\delta)$. Substituting into equation (2.2), and simplifying, we get

$$p + (1-\delta)X - x/(1-\delta) = C(m-1, m) \tag{C.1}$$

The left-hand side is an increasing function of p, equaling zero when $p = 0$. Since the right-hand side is positive, so must be p. $\qquad$ QED

LEMMA C.2: $q > 0$.

PROOF: Let $Y \equiv \Pi(q) - \Pi(0)$ and $y \equiv \Pi(-q) - \Pi(0)$. It can be shown from equations (2.2) and (2.3) that

$$q + (1-\delta)Y - y/(1-\delta) = C(m-2, m) - \delta[(1-\delta)X + x/(1-\delta)] \tag{C.2}$$

By an argument analogous to that in the previous proof, $q > 0$ if and only if the right-hand side is positive. But from equation (C.1) we know that

$$p = C(m-1, m) - (1-\delta)X + x/(1-\delta) > 0 \tag{C.3}$$

Therefore,

$$C(m-2, m) - \delta[(1-\delta)X + x/(1-\delta)] > p > 0 \tag{C.4}$$

and the proof is complete. $\qquad$ QED

LEMMA C.3: If $c(\cdot)$ is convex, then $q > p$.

PROOF: From equation (C.2), knowing that the left-hand side is increasing in q and that the right-hand side is not a function of q, we have the necessary and sufficient condition for $q > p$ that

$$p + (1-\delta)X - x/(1-\delta) < C(m-2, m) - \delta[(1-\delta)X + x/(1-\delta)] \tag{C.5}$$

which results from substituting p for q. Substituting $2C(m-1, m)$ for $C(m-2, m)$ and equation (C.1) for $C(m-1, m)$, and simplifying, inequality (C.5) becomes

$$p + (1-\delta)^2 X - (1+\delta)x/(1-\delta) > 0 \tag{C.6}$$

which is true, because the left-hand side is increasing in p and zero for $p = 0$, and $p > 0$. If $c(\cdot)$ is convex, then $C(m-2, m) > 2C(m-1, m)$. Therefore (C.6) implies (C.5). $\qquad$ QED

REMARK C.1: These proofs suggest counterexamples to Lemma C.3. Suppose that $C(m-2, m-1) = 0$, so that $C(m-2, m) = C(m-1, m)$. Comparing equations (C.1) and (C.2), we see that q is lower than p if and only if

$$(1 - \delta)X + x/(1 - \delta) > 0. \tag{C.7}$$

If we make $C(m - 1, m)$ very large, then, by equation (C.1), p will also be very large and so will X, whereas x is bounded below by $-\Pi(0)$. Therefore, given some δ, a sufficiently large $C(m - 1, m)$ will imply condition (C.7) and $q > p$.

LEMMA C.4: *If $\Pi(\cdot)$ is convex, then $r > 0$.*

PROOF: We consider two cases.
Case (i): $q > p$. Let $Z \equiv \Pi(r) - \Pi(0)$ and $z \equiv \Pi(-r) - \Pi(0)$. Calculation establishes

$$W(m - 2, m - 1) = -Y - \delta X - (y - 2\delta x)/(1 - \delta). \tag{C.8}$$

Therefore, equation (2.2) becomes

$$r + Z - z = C(m - 2, m - 1) + \delta Y + \delta^2 X + \delta(y - 2\delta x)/(1 - \delta) \tag{C.9}$$

Since $C(m - 2, m) = C(m - 2, m - 1) - C(m - 1, m)$, we can use (C.1) and (C.2) to substitute for $C(m - 2, m - 1)$ and get

$$r + Z - z = (q + Y - y) - (p + X - x) + 2\delta(X + x) \tag{C.10}$$

$r > 0$ if and only if the right-hand side is positive. Since $q > p$ by assumption $(q + Y - y) > (p + X - x)$. Furthermore, $X + x \geq 0$ if $\Pi(\cdot)$ is convex, and the right-hand side of (C.10) is positive.

Case (ii): $q \leq p$. If there exist parameter values such that $r \leq 0$, then r will also be nonpositive if we set $c(m - 2)$ equal to $c(m - 1)$ and keep other parameters unchanged. This can be seen from (C.10): since $c(m - 1)$ remains unchanged, so do the second and third terms on the right-hand side. Moreover, since $C(m - 2, m) = c(m - 2) - c(m)$ and $q + Y - y$ is increasing in q, the first term on the right-hand side becomes lower when we set $c(m - 2) = c(m - 1)$ as can be seen from equation (C.2). Finally, since $r + Z - z$ is increasing in r, the value of r remains negative.

We therefore assume $C(m - 2, m - 1) = 0$. From equation (2.2), $r > 0$ if and only if $W(m - 2, m - 1) > 0$. Expanding and rearranging (C.8) we get

$$\begin{aligned} W(m - 2, m - 1) = {} & [\Pi(q) + \Pi(-q) - 2\Pi(0)] + \delta[\Pi(p) + \Pi(-q) - 2\Pi(-p)] \\ & + \delta^2[\Pi(0) + \Pi(-q) - 2\Pi(-p)]/(1 - \delta) \end{aligned}$$

Convexity of $\Pi(\cdot)$ implies that the first term on the right-hand side is nonnegative. Monotonicity of $\Pi(\cdot)$ and the assumption that $q \leq p$ imply that the second term is nonnegative, and the third term is positive. *QED*

REMARK C.2: To construct a counterexample to Lemma C.4 let $C(m - 2, m - 1) = 0$. Then $P(m - 2, m - 1)$ has the same sign as $-W(m - 2, m - 1)$. From (C.8), $W(m - 2, m - 1) > 0$ if

$$-y - (1 - \delta)Y - \delta(1 - \delta)X + 2\delta x > 0 \tag{C.11}$$

As $\delta \to 0$, the left-hand side of (C.11) goes to $-y - Y$, which is positive if $\Pi(\cdot)$ is concave on the interval $[-q, q]$.

Notice that this counterexample is consistent with Theorem 3.1. There we are saying that for fixed $C(m - 2, m - 1) > 0$ we can make δ small enough so that $r > 0$. Here we are saying that, fixing $\delta > 0$ sufficiently small, we can make $C(m - 2, m - 1)$ small enough that $r < 0$.

Lemma C.5: $q > r$ *if and only if*

$$p + (1 - 2\delta)X - (1 + 2\delta)x > 0 \tag{C.12}$$

Proof: From equation (C.10) we have $q > r$ if and only if $-(p + X - x) + 2\delta(X + x) < 0$, which is equivalent to condition (C.12).   *QED*

Remark C.3:   Inequality   (C.12)   holds   if $\delta \leq \frac{1}{2}$.   This   follows   from $p > 0$ and $\Pi(p) - \Pi(0) > 0 > \Pi(-p) - \Pi(0)$.

Remark C.4:   Inequality (C.12) holds if $c(m - 1)$ is not too large. This follows from the facts that the derivative of the left-hand side of (C.12) evaluated at $p = 0$ equals 3, p is monotonically increasing in $c(m - 1)$, and p goes to zero as $c(m - 1)$ goes to zero.

Remark C.5:   It is possible to find counterexamples. For example, let $F(\cdot)$ be normal with a zero mean and variance σ^2. Choose $c(m)$ such that $P(m - 1, m) = 1$ solves equations (2.2)–(2.4) for state $(m - 1, m)$. Then, in condition (C.12), $p = 1$, and X and x are determined by σ^2. It can be shown numerically that this condition fails for σ^2 sufficiently small. Note that for these counterexamples $\Pi(\cdot)$ is convex and there is no restriction on the shape of the learning curve.

Proof of Theorem 3.4:   Follows from Lemmas C.1–C.5 and Remarks C.3–C.4.

Appendix D: Predatory Pricing

Proof of Theorem 4.1:   Adopt the equilibrium hypothesis that exit occurs only in state $(0, 1)$. Thus, $\nu'(0, 1) = 0$ and $\nu'(1, 1) = \nu(1, 1) - A$. Suppose the lagging firm were to deviate and stay in, and let q denote the rival's price. Under the hypothesis of equilibrium play in future periods, the deviant chooses p to maximize $[p - c(0) + \delta\nu'(1, 1)]F(q - p)$. The first-order condition is

$$p + H(p - q) = c(0) - \delta[\nu(1, 1) - A]$$

and the corresponding payoff (net of the entry cost) is $[\Pi(q - p) - (1 - \delta)A]$. On the other hand, the first-order condition for the rival is

$$q - H(p - q) = c(1) - \delta[\nu^{\#}(1) - \nu(1, 1)]$$

Thus, the equilibrium price difference, $P = p - q$, satisfies

$$\begin{aligned} P + G(P) &= C(0, 1) - \delta[\nu(1, 1) - A] + \delta[\nu^{\#}(1) - \nu(1, 1)] \\ &= C(0, 1) - \delta W(0, 1) + \delta A + \delta[\nu^{\#}(1) - \nu(1, 0) - \nu(0, 1)] \quad > C(0, 1) - \delta W(0, 1) \end{aligned}$$

the last inequality following from $\nu^{\#}(1) > \nu(1,0) + \nu(0,1)$. Since $P > P(0,1)$, the deviant's payoff from staying in is strictly less than $[\Pi(-P(0,1)) - (1 - \delta)A]$ by an amount independent of ε. Therefore, it is an equilibrium for the lagging firm to exit in state $(0, 1)$ if ε is sufficiently small.

Nevertheless, initial entry will be profitable if $\nu'(0,0) > 0$. By an analogue of equation (2.3), we have $\nu'(0,0) = \Pi(0) - (1 - \delta)A + \delta\nu'(0,1)$. Since $\nu'(0,1) = 0$ because of exit, it follows that initial entry occurs if $\Pi(0) > (1 - \delta)A$ which follows from $P(0,1) > 0$ (see Lemma C.1) if ε is sufficiently small.

It remains to show that exit in state $(0, 1)$ influences pricing in state $(0, 0)$. An analogue of equation (2.1) yields $p'(0,0) = c(0) + H(0) - \delta[\nu^{\#}(1) - A]$. Since $\nu^{\#}(1) > \nu(1,0)$ and $\nu(0,1)$ is approximately equal to A, $\nu^{\#}(1) - A > w(0,0)$, and we conclude that $p'(0,0) < p(0,0)$.   *QED*

Proof of Theorem 4.2:   Define P° and A° to satisfy

$$P^{\circ} + G(P^{\circ}) = C(0,2) - \delta[\nu(1,2) + \nu(2,1) - \nu^{\#}(2) - A^{\circ}]$$

and $A^{\circ} = \Pi(1 - P^{\circ})/(1 - \delta)$. If $A = A^{\circ} + \varepsilon$ for $\varepsilon > 0$, then $P'(0,2) \equiv P^{\circ}$. A° is the lowest value of A consistent with equilibrium exit in state $(0, 2)$. Moreover, for ε sufficiently small and δ sufficiently close to one, an evaluation of first-order conditions establishes that this is the only state in which exit occurs. By an analogue of equation (2.2),

$$\begin{aligned}
P'(0,1) + G(P'(0,1)) &= C(0,1) - \delta W'(0,1) \\
&= C(0,1) - \delta[\nu(1,1) - A] + \delta[\nu^{\#}(2) - \nu(1,1)] \\
&= C(0,1) - \delta W(0,1) + \delta A + \delta[\nu^{\#}(2) - \nu(2,0) - \nu(0,2)] \\
&> C(0,1) - \delta W(0,1)
\end{aligned}$$

Therefore, $P'(0,1) > P(0,1)$. By an analogue of equation (2.1), we have

$$\begin{aligned}
p'(1,0) &= c(0) + H(P'(0,1)) - \delta[\nu^{\#}(2) - \nu(1,1)] \\
&= c(0) + H(P'(0,1)) - \delta w(0,1) - \delta[\nu^{\#}(2) - \nu(2,0)] \\
&< c(0) + H(P(0,1)) - \delta w(0,1) \\
&= p(1,0)
\end{aligned}$$
                                    QED

Appendix E: Social Welfare

We define social welfare to be the sum of expected producer and consumer surpluses. We view the social planner as choosing a symmetric function $P*(i,j)$ such that, in state (i, j), the buyer receives firm 2's product if his preference parameter (x) exceeds $P*(i,j)$ and firm 1's product otherwise. Again, we assume that a transaction always takes place. In the following theorem, $\bar{y}$ is a buyer's expected value for firm 1's product.

Theorem E.1:   *The socially optimal solution has the following properties*:

$$P^*(i,j) = C(i,j) - \delta W^*(i,j) \tag{E.1}$$

$$U^*(i,j) = \bar{y} - c(j) + \delta U^*(i,j+1) + \Gamma(P^*(i,j)) \tag{E.2}$$

where $W^*(i,j) \equiv U^*(i+1,j) - U^*(i,j+1)$, and $\Gamma(x) \equiv \int_x^\infty [1 - F(a)]\,da$; and

$$U^*(i, m+1) = U^*(i, m) \tag{E.3}$$

PROOF: By Bellman's principle, $U^*(i,j)$ obeys the following equation:

$$U^*(i,j) = \bar{y} - c(j) + \delta U^*(i,j+1) + \max_P \int_P^\infty [x - C(i,j) + \delta W^*(i,j)]dF(x)$$

The first-order condition for optimality yields (E.1). Substituting this first-order condition back into the Bellman equation, and integrating by parts, yields (E.2). Finally, the boundary conditions (E.3) follow from the fact that (i, m) and $(i, m+1)$ are equivalent states.   *QED*

We next contrast equilibrium outcomes with those corresponding to maximized social welfare. We first note that there are potential social benefits from learning, contrary to the absence of private benefits.

THEOREM E.2: *The maximized social benefits from learning are greater than in a world with no learning beyond (i, i), $i < m$.*

PROOF: Trivial.

We next further characterize optimum values for $P^*(i,j)$.

LEMMA E.1: $\lim_{\delta \to 1} P^*(i,j) = 0$.

PROOF: Analogous to proof of Lemma A. 1.

LEMMA E.2:

$$\lim_{\delta \to 1} \frac{dP^*(i,j)}{d\delta} = 2 \lim_{\delta \to 1} \frac{dP(i,j)}{d\delta}$$

PROOF: From (E.2), we have

$$U^*(i,m) = \frac{\bar{y} - c(m) + \Gamma(P^*(i,m))}{1 - \delta}$$

Therefore,

$$W^*(i,m) = \frac{\Gamma(0) - \Gamma(P^*(i,m))}{1 - \delta} - \frac{\Gamma(0) - \Gamma(P^*(i+1,m))}{1 - \delta} \tag{E.4}$$

By Lemma E.1 and equation (E.1), we have $\lim_{\delta \to 1} W^*(i,j) = C(i,j)$. Therefore, (E.4) can be solved recursively to get

$$\lim_{\delta \to 1} \frac{\Gamma(0) - \Gamma(P^*(i,m))}{1 - \delta} = \sum_{k=i}^m C(k,m)$$

Finally, applying L'Hôpital's rule and $\Gamma(0) = -\frac{1}{2}$ and results in Appendix B we get

$$\lim_{\delta \to 1} \frac{dP^*(i,m)}{d\delta} = -2S(i) = 2 \lim_{\delta \to 1} \frac{dP(i,m)}{d\delta}$$

The remainder of the proof is similar to that of Lemma B.2.   *QED*

Lemmas B.1, E.1, and E.2 lead immediately to the following result.

Theorem E.3:   *For sufficiently large δ, the equilibrium probability of a sale by the leader is too low from society's point of view.*

Finally, we show that equilibrium two-step learning is socially advantageous if the learning curve is convex and IID holds. This contrasts withour previous conclusion that learning is privately disadvantageous if ID holds.

Theorem E.4:   *If m = 2, c(·) is convex and IID holds, then social welfare in equilibrium is greater than in a world without learning.*

Proof: The equilibrium in the world with learning involves a tradeoff with respect to the equilibrium in a world without learning. On the one hand, there is the positive effect of cost savings. On the other hand, there is the negative effect of price distortions. In state $(i,j), j \geq i$, expected cost savings are at least $F(P(i,j))C(i,j)$, the probability the low-cost firm makes a sale times the cost saving with respect to the high cost. (This is a lower bound of the cost savings because the highest cost ($c(0)$) can be higher than the high cost, that is, firm i's cost.) The loss due to price distortions is in turn given by

$$\int_0^{P(i,j)} x f(x) dx$$

An upper bound for this loss is given by $[F(P(i,j)) - \frac{1}{2}]P(i,j)$.

In all states (i, j) we have $C(i,j) = P(i,j) = 0$, so both bounds equal zero. Let us therefore consider the remaining states. From (C.4), we can see that $p = P(1,2) < C(1,2)$. As a result, $F(P(i,j))C(i,j) > (F(P(i,j)) - \frac{1}{2})P(i,j)$. A similar argument applies to showing $q = P(0, 2) < C(0,2)$ from (C. 5).

This leaves state (0, 1) to consider. By IID, $P(0,1) < P(0,2)$. By the argument presented above, $P(0,2) < C(0,2)$. By convexity of the learning curve, $C(0,2) < 2C(0,1)$. Together, these imply that $P(0,1) < 2C(0,1)$. Therefore, $F(P(0,2))C(0,2) - [F(P(0,2)) - \frac{1}{2}]P(0,2) > [1 - F(P(0,2))]C(0,2) > 0$.   *QED*

Notes

1   This idea formed the basis of the Boston Consulting Group's (1970, p. 54) advice to produce a lot early on.
2   Antecedents are Arrow (1962), who considered the learning curve hypothesis in a growth model, and Rosen (1972) who analyzed the implications of learning by doing for a competitive firm. See Mookherjee and Ray (1989) for a detailed literature review.
3   Mookherjee and Ray (1991) analyze a dynamic price-setting oligopoly with deterministic demand and learning by doing. They focus on "folk theorem" results, thus indicating the potential scope for cooperative behavior. In contrast, our restriction to Markov perfect

equilibria focuses on noncooperative strategic interaction. After completing our analysis, we learned of an article by Habermeier (1992) containing a model with a structure similar to our own. Habermeier analyzed the model numerically for special cases, focusing on the question of whether one firm will permanently dominate the market. This question does not arise in our model because of a technical assumption on demand. See note 5.

4   Independent work by Salant (1991) shows market dominance is self-reinforcing in a model with deterministic demand and stochastic learning. Budd, Harris, and Vickers (1993) analyze increasing dominance in a duopoly in which short-run profits are a function of a one-dimensional state variable that measures the extent to which one firm is "leading" the other. Their abstract model is more about R&D competition than learning curve competition, but it does have similarities: the market evolves uncertainly and the equilibrium concept is Markov perfection. They prove that if the future is discounted heavily, market evolution is governed by a "joint profit effect," i.e., increasing dominance obtains if greater asymmetry between firms increases joint profits. They also identify other effects that are of lower order importance when the future is discounted heavily but may be significant otherwise.

5   With a bounded support, it is possible that one firm will dominate the market permanently (Habermeier (1992)). Assumption 1(a) eliminates this possibility.

6   The assumption that $f(x)$ is differentiable matters for Lemmas B.2 and E.2.

7   More precisely, define for firm 1 the expected quantity $q = F(P)$, the inverse demand curve $\psi(q) \equiv p_2 - F^{-1}(q)$, and the revenue function $R(q) \equiv \psi(q).q$. Marginal revenue, $R'(q) = \psi(q) + \psi'(q) \cdot q$, is decreasing if $0 \geq 2 \cdot \psi'(q) + \psi''(q) \cdot q = -[1 + H'(P)]/f(P)$.

8   We allow prices to be negative. However, the equilibrium prices characterized by Theorem 2.1 shift by a if the learning curve is also shifted by a. We can therefore assure positive equilibrium prices by making a high enough.

9   This is similar to the joint profit effect identified by Budd, Harris, and Vickers (1993) when the future is discounted heavily.

10   We thank John Sutton for suggesting this intuition to us.

11   The price locus is upward sloping and intersects the origin. The subsidized cost locus has a positive intercept (assuming $C > 0$) and intersects the price locus once in the positive orthant.

12   To be precise the subsidized cost locus shifts up by an amount

$$C(m - 2, m - 1) - (1 - \delta)[\Pi(P(m - 1, m)) - \Pi(0)] - \delta[\Pi(-P(m - 1, m)) - \Pi(0)]/(1 - \delta)$$

With this modification the point of intersection between the price locus and the subsidized cost locus determines $P(m - 2, m)$.

13   Thus, in this case, the point profit effect, identified by Budd, Harris, and Vickers (1993), dominates.

14   With more structure on the model we could characterize $\nu^{\#}(i)$ explicitly, but we don't need to.

15   Maskin and Tirole (1988) demonstrate multiple Markov perfect equilibria with a similar character in a dynamic quantity setting model with no learning.

16   While formal forward induction concepts do not apply directly to our framework, we conjecture that a suitable adaptation of Van Damme's criterion would destroy both the accommodating equilibrium and the predatory one (see Fudenberg and Tirole (1992, Chapter 11)).

17   Majd and Pindyck (1989) analyze the optimal production plan of a price-taking firm with a learning curve, short-run decreasing returns to scale, and facing uncertain future prices. Fershtman and Spiegel (1983) compare optimal production under monopoly and competition. See also Spence (1981), Fudenberg and Tirole (1983), and Gulledge and Womer (1986) on optimal production plans for a monopolist.

References

Alchian, A. (1963): "Reliability of Progress Curves in Airframe Production," *Econometrica*, 31, 679–93.

Areeda, P. and D. Turner (1975): "Predatory Pricing and Related Practices under Section 2 of the Sherman Act," *Harvard Law Review*, 88, 697–733.

Argote, L., S. Beckman and D. Epple (1990): "The Persistence and Transfer of Learning in Industrial Settings," *Management Science*, 36, 140–54.

Arrow, K. J. (1962): "The Economic Implications of Learning by Doing," *Review of Economic Studies*, 29, 155–73.

Asher, H. (1956): *Cost-Quantity Relationships in the Airframe Industry*, Report 291. Santa Monica, Ca.: RAND Corporation.

Boston Consulting Group (1970): *Perspectives on Experience*. Boston: Boston Consulting Group.

Budd, C., C. Harris and J. Vickers (1993): "A Model of the Evolution of Duopoly: Does the Asymmetry Between Firms Tend to Increase or Decrease?" *Review of Economic Studies*, 60, 543–74.

Cabral, L. B. and M. H. Riordan (1991): "Learning to Compete and Vice Versa," ISP Discussion Paper # 17, Boston University.

Dasgupta, P. and J. Stiglitz (1988): "Learning-by-Doing, Market Structure and Industrial and Trade Policies," *Oxford Economic Papers*, 40, 246–68.

Dudley, L. (1972): "Learning and Productivity Changes in Metal Products," *American Economic Review*, 62, 662–9.

Fershtman, C. and U. Spiegel (1983): "Monopoly versus Competition: The Learning by Doing Case," *European Economic Review*, 23, 217–22.

Flaherty, M. T. (1980): "Industry Structure and Cost-Reducing Investment," *Econometrica*, 48, 1187–210.

Fudenberg, D. and J. Tirole (1983): "Learning-by-Doing and Market Performance," *Bell Journal of Economics*, 14, 522–30.

—— (1992): *Game Theory*. Cambridge, MA: The MIT Press.

Ghemawat, P. and A. M. Spence (1985): "Learning Curve Spillovers and Market Performance," *Quarterly Journal of Economics*, 100 (Supplement), 839–52.

Gilbert, R. J. and R. G. Harris (1981): "Investment Decisions with Economies of Scale and Learning," *American Economic Review*, Papers and Proceedings, 71, 172–7.

Gilbert, R. J. and D. M. G. Newbery (1982): "Preemptive Patenting and the Persistence of Monopoly," *American Economic Review*, 72, 514–26.

Gulledge, T. and N. Womer (1986): *The Economics of Made-to-Order Production*. Berlin: Springer-Verlag.

Habermeier, K. F. (1992): "The Learning Curve and Competition," *International Journal of Industrial Organization*, 10, 369–92.

Harris, C. and J. Vickers (1985): "Perfect Equilibrium in a Model of Race," *Review of Economic Studies*, 52, 193–209.

—— (1987): "Racing with Uncertainty," *Review of Economic Studies*, 54, 1–21.

Hirsch, W. (1952): "Manufacturing Progress Functions," *Review of Economics and Statistics*, 34, 143–55.

Joskow, P. L. and G. A. Rozanski (1979): "The Effects of Learning by Doing on Nuclear Power Plant Operating Reliability," *Review of Economics and Statistics*, 61, 161–8.

Krugman, P. R. (1984): "Import Protection as Export Promotion: International Competition in the Presence of Oligopolies and Economies of Scale," in *Monopolistic Competition and International Trade*, ed. by H. Kierzkowski. Oxford: Oxford University Press.

Lee, W. Y. (1975): "Oligopoly and Entry," *Journal of Economic Theory*, 11, 35–54.

Lieberman, M. (1984): "The Learning Curve and Pricing in the Chemical Processing Industries," *RAND Journal of Economics*, 15, 213–28.

Majd, S. and R. S. Pindyck (1989): "The Learning Curve and Optimal Production under Uncertainty," *RAND Journal of Economics*, 20, 331–43.

Mankiw, N. G. and M. D. Whinston (1986): "Free Entry and Social Inefficiency," *RAND Journal of Economics*, 17, 48–58.

Maskin, E. S. and J. Tirole (1988): "A Theory of Dynamic Oligopoly I: Overview and Quantity Competition with Large Fixed Costs," *Econometrica*, 56, 549–70.

Mookherjee, D. and D. Ray (1989): "Learning by Doing and Industrial Market Structure: An Overview," manuscript, Indian Statistical Institute, New Delhi.

—— (1991): "Collusive Market Structure under Learning-by-Doing and Increasing Returns," *Review of Economic Studies*, 58, 993–1009.

Newhouse, J. (1982): *The Sporty Game*. New York: Knopf.

Ordover, J. and G. Saloner (1989): "Predation, Monopolization and Antitrust," Chapter 9 in *Handbook of Industrial Organization*, Volume 1, ed. by Schmalensee and R. Willig. Amsterdam: North Holland.

Ordover, J. and R. Willig (1981): "An Economic Definition of Predation: Pricing and Product Innovation," *Yale Law Journal*, 91, 8–53.

Roberts, J. (1987): "Battles for Market Share," in *Advances in Economic Theory*, Papers Presented at the Fifth World Congress of the Econometric Society, ed. by T. F. Bewley. New York: Cambridge University Press.

Rosen, S. (1972): "Learning by Experience or Joint Production," *Quarterly Journal of Economics*, 86, 366–82.

Ross, D. R. (1986): "Learning to Dominate," *Journal of Industrial Economics*, 34, 337–53.

Salant, D. F. (1991): "Stochastic Innovation Duopoly (and Oligopoly) Races," GTE Technical Report, TR-0129-91-419.

Scherer, F. M. and D. Ross (1990): *Industrial Market Structure and Economic Performance*. Boston: Houghton-Mifflin.

Searle, A. D. and C. S. Goody (1945): "Productivity Increases in Selected Wartime Shipbuilding Programs," *Monthly Labor Review*, 6, 1132–42.

Seitz, F. and L. Steele (1985): *The Competitive Status of the U.S. Civil Aviation Manufacturing Industry*. Washington D.C.: National Academy Press.

Spence, M. A. (1981): "The Learning Curve and Competition," *Bell Journal of Economics*, 12, 49–70.

Stokey, N. (1986): "The Dynamics of Industrywide Learning," in *Equilibrium Analysis, Essays in Honor of Kenneth J. Arrow*, Volume 2, ed. by W. Heller et al. Cambridge: Cambridge University Press.

Vickers, J. (1986): "The Evolution of Industry Structure when there is a Sequence of Innovations," *Journal of Industrial Economics*, 35, 1–12.

Webbink, D. (1977): *The Semiconductor Industry*, Federal Trade Commission Staff Report. Washington: U.S. Government.

Wright, T. P. (1936): "Factors Affecting the Cost of Airplanes," *Journal of Aeronautical Sciences*, 3, 122–8.

Zimmerman, M. B. (1982): "Learning Effects and Commercialization of New Energy Technologies: The Care of Nuclear Power," *RAND Journal of Economics*, 13, 297–310.

CHAPTER NINETEEN

Preemption and Rent Equalization in the Adoption of New Technology

Drew Fudenberg and Jean Tirole

Source: Review of Economic Studies, 1985, 52, 383–401.

We study the adoption of a new technology to illustrate the effects of preemption in games of timing. We show that the threat of preemption equalizes rents in a duopoly, but that this result does not extend to the general oligopoly game. If the gain to preemption is sufficiently small, then the optimal symmetric outcome, which involves "late" adoption, is an equilibrium. This contrasts with Reinganum's result that in precommitment equilibria there must be "diffusion". We develop a new and richer formalism for modeling games of timing, which permits a continuous-time representation of the limit of discrete-time mixed–strategy equilibria.

1. Introduction

Research alone is not sufficient for technical progress: technological innovations yield no benefits until they are employed. Therefore social policy should consider the incentives for adopting innovations as well as incentives for their discovery. This paper analyses a market in which firms are deciding when to adopt a new technology. Adopting the innovation increases a firm's flow of profits, but adopting it sooner is more expensive than adopting it later. A monopolist would not adopt the innovation immediately, but would wait until the increase in flow profit just equalled the marginal cost of adopting sooner. The market is not monopolized, however, which has two related implications.

First, a part of each individual firm's return to adoption comes at the expense of its rivals, so the individual return exceeds the industry return. Thus we would expect the adoption times in non-cooperative equilibria to be sooner than would be optimal for the industry as a whole.

Second, if the information lags are short, so that firms can observe and respond to their rivals' actions, firms have an incentive for "preemptive adoption". By this we mean that firms will adopt sooner than they would choose to were their rivals' adoption dates fixed.

Firms adopt preemptively to prevent or delay adoption by their opponents. One might expect the threat of preemption to ensure that identical firms have the same equilibrium payoffs, because were one firm to adopt at time t and do better than a rival who adopts later, the rival would preempt the first firm by adopting just before t. We show that this intuition is correct in a duopoly, but that with more than two firms equilibrium payoffs need not be equal.

Two previous authors have studied the timing of the adoption of new technology. Scherer (1967) analysed the introduction of a product innovation in duopoly. He concluded that if the firms were required to precommit themselves to introduction times, then the equilibrium outcome would be for both firms to move simultaneously, at an earlier time than would maximize joint profits. Reinganum (1981a, b) analysed the adoption process using different specification of the payoffs, again requiring precommitment to adoption dates. She found that there must be a "diffusion", in that the firms adopt at different dates, even though the firms are ex-ante identical and there is no uncertainty.

When firms precommit themselves to adoption dates, preemption is ruled out by assumption. Precommitment strategies are equivalent to infinite information lags. To allow for preemption, we consider the alternative extreme case in which firms can respond immediately to their rivals' decisions; that is, adoption is perfectly observable and is instantaneous. Our model also covers the case of an adoption process that takes a fixed amount of time, if firms can observe their rivals' actions. The equilibrium concept we use is that of Perfect Equilibrium, which rules out empty threats, i.e. threats which would not be carried out.

In section 2 we briefly review Reinganum's model of technology diffusion. We show why in precommitment equilibria the early adopter does better than the later one. While there are as many equilibria as there are permutations of the firms, at any time, each firm always prefers an equilibrium in which it is the next to adopt.

In section 3 we consider the duopoly case (Reinganum (1981a)). We show that if firms cannot threaten to maintain their planned adoption times regardless of what happens before, then identical firms receive equal payoffs in equilibrium. The intuition is simple: Were one firm to plan on adopting first at a time, t, which gave it a higher payoff than the second adopter, the second firm could increase its payoff by preempting just before t. Faced with the preemption, the first firm could then do no better than to adopt when the second firm would have.

If the best response to early adoption is to adopt much later, the gain from preemption is high. The (unique) equilibrium times of adoption are then unequal. In this "diffusion" equilibrium, which prevails for example in a new market, both firms receive lower payoffs to quickly follow suit, several equilibria exist, and these equilibria are Pareto-comparable. In particular, the optimal symmetric adoption time is sustainable as an equilibrium. This time is later than all other equilibrium outcomes. Intuitively, adopting the innovation yields two types of benefits – it increases total industry profits and increases the adopter's share. Thus the industry's incentive to adopt is less than any individual competitor's, and so "late" adoption maximizes total profits. This outcome is enforced by the quick response to adoption, which provides a credible threat against the temptation of preemption.

Section 3 gives the economic intuition and the main results for the duopoly case. Traditional continuous-time strategy spaces are not adequate to capture and verify the intuitions of section 3. We therefore develop in section 4 a new and richer formalism for modelling games of timing which permits a continuous-time representation of the limit of discrete-time mixed-strategy equilibria. This formalism may be of independent interest to technically minded readers, since it can be used in more general games of timing. Those less technically minded may find section 4 to be too complicated. They should be reassured that all the economics of the problem are captured in section 3. Section 5 considers the model with more than two firms, and shows that rent equalization need not occur. Section 6 discusses some related work, and section 7 concludes.

2. The Model

There are n identical firms, indexed by $i = 1, \ldots, n$, in the industry. At time 0, a cost reducing innovation is announced. $\pi_0(m)$ is the net cash flow of firm i when m firm(s) have adopted the innovation, but firm i has not. $\pi_1(m)$ is firm i's net cash flow if m firm(s) including i have adopted. T_i is firm i's adoption date; and $c(t)$ is the present value of the cost of bringing the innovation on line by time t. Let T_{-i} denote the vector of dates of adoption by firm i's competitors. $V^i(T_i, T_{-i})$ is firm i's payoff. Suppose w.l.o.g. that firm i is the ith to adopt. Then:

$$V^i(T_i, T_{-1}) = \sum_{m=0}^{i-1} \int_{T_m}^{T_{m+1}} \pi_0(m) e^{-rt} dt + \sum_{m=i}^{n} \int_{T_m}^{T_{m+1}} \pi_1(m) e^{-rt} dt - c(T_i)$$

where $T_0 \equiv 0, T_{n+1} \equiv +\infty$, and r is the common interest rate.

We will make Reinganum's assumptions (with minor changes):

ASSUMPTION 1   (i) $\pi_1(1) - \pi_0(n-1) \leq - c'(0)$
                (ii) $\inf_t \{c(t)e^{rt}\} < [\pi_1(n) - \pi_0(n-1)]/r$
                (iii) $\forall t, (c(t)e^{rt})' < 0$, and $(c(t)e^{rt})'' > 0$

ASSUMPTION 2   (i) $\pi_1(1) - \pi_0(n-1) \leq - c'(0)$
                (ii) $\inf_t \{c(t)e^{rt}\} < [\pi_1(n) - \pi_0(n-1)]/r$
                (iii) $\forall t, (c(t)e^{rt})' < 0$, and $(c(t)e^{rt})'' > 0$

Assumption 1(ii) states that there are decreasing returns in the rank of adoption. The increase in profits due to adopting $(m - 1)$th exceeds that due to adopting mth. Thus from the revenue point of view firms have an incentive to adopt earlier than their competitors. Assumption 2(i) rules out immediate adoption, even for purposes of preemption. Adoption at date 0 gives the firm a cash flow not exceeding $\pi_1(1)$ whereas not adopting gives it a cash flow at least equal to $\pi_0(n - 1)$. Assumption 2(ii) requires that all firms adopt in finite time. It implies that for t sufficiently large it becomes a dominant strategy to adopt. Thus non-adoption is not an alternative. Assumption 2(iii) says that the "current cost", $e^{rt}c(t)$, is decreasing, but at a decreasing rate. Both conditions are satisfied by $c(t) = e^{-(r+\alpha)t}$, so that the current cost falls at rate α due to technical progress. The first part of the assumption is natural; the second ensures that the payoffs are quasiconcave. Reinganum makes somewhat stronger assumptions on c'' to obtain concavity.

Reinganum shows that for this model, there are adoption times $\mathcal{T}^* = (T_1^*, \ldots, T_n^*)$ that form a precommitment equilibrium, that every pure-strategy precommitment equilibrium is given by a permutation of $\mathcal{T}^*$, and that $T_i^* \neq T_j^*$ for $i \neq j$.

PROPOSITION 1.   *In a precommitment equilibrium the firms' equilibrium payoffs decline monotonically with the order of adoption.*

PROOF.   Let $\mathcal{T}^*$ be a precommitment equilibrium with $T_i^* < T_j^*$ for $i < j$. Then:

$$V^i(T_i^*, T_{-i}^*) \geqq V^i(T_1^*, \ldots, T_{i-1}^*, T_j^*, T_{i+1}^*, \ldots, T_j^*, \ldots, T_n^*)$$
$$= V^j(T_1^*, \ldots, T_{i-1}^*, T_j^*, T_{i+1}^*, \ldots, T_j^*, \ldots, T_n^*)$$
$$> V^j(T_j^*, T_{-j}^*)$$

where the first inequality follows from T_i^* being a best response, the equality from the symmetry of the payoff functions, and the second inequality from the monotonicity of V^j relative to the other firms' adoption times. ‖

It is easy to see that the adoption dates $(T_1^* < T_2^* < \ldots < T_n^*)$ are given by the following marginal conditions:

$$[\pi_1(m) - \pi_0(m - 1)]e^{-rT_m^*} + c'(T_m^*) = 0 \tag{1}$$

While precommitment equilibria in general fail to capture what is meant by "strategic behaviour", in this instance, they seem especially suspect. The firm which is able to precommit itself to adopt first does best, yet any firm can adopt first in equilibrium. The strategic interactions suppressed by precommitment would resurface in a competition to be the first to precommit.

3. Strategic Adoption in a Duopoly. The Heuristics and the Main Results

We now study the two-firm case in order to highlight some important features of strategic adoption. The general oligopoly case is considered in section 5.

The first thing to examine is what happens when one of the two firms has adopted at some time t. This continuation game is a simple one-player decision problem. The payoff of the remaining firm is the maximum over t' greater than or equal to t of $V(t', t)$. From the quasiconcavity of the objective function of the remaining firm, its optimal time of adoption is either T_2^*, or, if t exceeds T_2^*, t itself.

Having pinned down what happens in the continuation game, let:

$L(t) =$ (the leader's) payoff for the firm that succeeds in preempting the

'other firm at time t'

$$= \begin{cases} V(t, T_2^*) & \text{if } t < T_2^* \\ V(t, t) & \text{if } t \geqq T_2^* \end{cases}$$

$F(t) =$ (the follower's) payoff for the firm that is preempted at time t

$$= \begin{cases} V(T_2^*, t) & \text{if } t < T_2^* \\ V(t, t) & \text{if } t \geqq T_2^* \end{cases}$$

$M(t) =$ payoff of both firms if they adopt together at time t

$$= V(t, t).$$

The functions L, F and M are pictured in Figure 1. Let us check that we have drawn them correctly. First consider $t < T_2^*$. It is clear that $L(t) > M(t)$ since a firm's payoff increases with its rival's date of adoption. Second, $F(t) > M(t)$ since the best response to t is T_2^*. Next, using Assumption 2 (iii) we can show that $(L(t) - F(t))' = 0$ implies

$$(L(t) - F(t))'' = re^{-rt}(\pi_1(1) - \pi_0(1)) - c''(t) < 0$$

so $L - F$ is strictly quasi-concave.

We know that $L(0) < F(0)$ (from Assumption 2(i)); that $L(T_2^*) = F(T_2^*)$; and that $L(T_1^*) > F(T_1^*)$ (from Proposition 1). Thus there exists a unique $\tilde{T}_1$ in $(0, T_1^*)$ such that $L(\tilde{T}_1) = F(\tilde{T}_1)$.

Last, let $\hat{T}_2$ denote the optimal date for *simultaneous* adoption, i.e. $\hat{T}_2$ maximizes $M(t)$. Let us show that $\hat{T}_2$ is unique and exceeds T_2^*. First, $M(t)$ can be shown to be strictly quasi-concave. Second,

$$\left. \frac{\partial V(t, T_2^*)}{\partial t} \right|_{t=T_2^*} = 0 \Rightarrow M'(T_2^*) = \left. \frac{dV(t, t)}{dt} \right|_{t=T_2^*} = \left. \frac{\partial V(T_2^*, t)}{\partial t} \right|_{t=T_2^*} > 0$$

Therefore, $\hat{T}_2 > T_2^*$.

We will distinguish two cases:

CASE A. $L(T_1^*) > M(\hat{T}_2)$

CASE B. $L(T_1^*) \leqq M(\hat{T}_2)$.

Case A is pictured in Figure 1 and Case B in Figure 2.

Figures 1 and 2 suffice to give the economic intuition. The following reasoning is extremely loose and the reader is referred to section 4 for further analysis.

Consider first Case A. Neither firm can obtain more than $L(T_1^*)$. Therefore it is in each firm's interest to adopt at time T_1^* if the other firm does not adopt at exactly the same time. But if a firm knows that the other will adopt at time T_1^*, it wants to preempt at $(T_1^* - \varepsilon)$. Reasoning backwards, at any t between $\tilde{T}_1$ and T_1^*, firms want to preempt to avoid being preempted later on. Thus, as we show in section 4, there is adoption at time

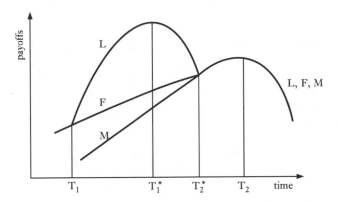

Figure 1   Case A

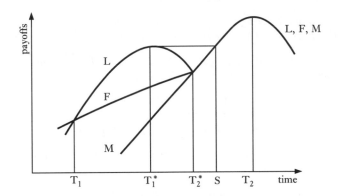

Figure 2   Case B

T_1 (and the follower adopts at time T_2^*). Before T_1 it is a dominant strategy not to adopt because the follower's payoff exceeds the leader's payoff and the joint-adoption payoff. We see that the equilibrium must involve *diffusion*, with adoption times T_1 and T_2^*.

Next consider Case B. Let S be defined by $S < \hat{T}_2$ and $L(T_1^*) = M(S)$. Note that past $\hat{T}_2$ it is a dominant strategy to adopt. We can first exhibit a class of equilibrium adoption times: choose $t \in [S, \hat{T}_2]$ and let the firms wait until t, and adopt in every subgame from t on. Clearly a firm cannot do better by preempting before t. Thus we have a continuum of joint-adoption equilibria indexed by the date of adoption $t \in [S, \hat{T}_2]$. These late adoption equilibria exhibit the dynamics predicted by Scherer (1980, p. 429), with "each industry member holding back initiating its R & D effort in the fear that rapid imitation by others will be encouraged, more than wiping out its innovative profits". Are there other equilibria? Imagine that firms adopt before S. Then the situation is as in Case A since a firm cannot obtain more than $L(T_1^*)$. By the same reasoning, equilibrium must involve diffusion (at dates T_1 and T_2^*). In section 4 we will prove the following proposition:

PROPOSITION 2.

(A) *If $L(T_1^*) > M(\hat{T}_2)$ there exists a unique equilibrium distribution over outcomes. With probability one-half, firm one adopts at T_1 and firm two adopts at T_2^*, and with probability one-half the roles of the firms are reversed.[1] Thus the equilibrium exhibits diffusion; and with probability one the adoption dates are T_1 and T_2^*.*

(B) *If $L(T_1^*) \leqq M(\hat{T}_2)$ two classes of equilibria exist. The first class is the (T_1, T_2^*) diffusion equilibrium. The second class is a continuum of joint-adoption outcomes indexed by the date of adoption $t \in [S, \hat{T}_2]$.*

Thus, depending on the parameters, there will be a unique equilibrium outcome (Case A) or multiple equilibrium outcomes (Case B). Note that in Case A the equilibrium is symmetric: each firm has an equal chance of adopting first. Despite this, there is zero probability of the firms' making a "mistake" and both adopting at T_1. In section 4 we will explain how the correlation involved here arises naturally in the continuous time limit of shorter and shorter time period. Before introducing the formal analysis we examine the properties of these equilibria. We have already "demonstrated":

PROPOSITION 3.   *In a Perfect Equilibrium the payoffs of the two firms are equated. The Perfect Equilibria are Pareto-comparable to the precommitment equilibria (from the firms' point of view).*

PROPOSITION 4.   *All joint-adoption equilibria, if they exist, Pareto-dominate the precommitment outcomes, which Pareto-dominate the diffusion equilibrium.*

PROOF.   The first assertion results from the fact that if $t \in [S, T_2^*]$, $M(t) \geqq L(T_1^*) > F(T_1^*)(L(T_1^*)$ and $F(T_1^*)$ are the firms' payoffs in precommitment equilibrium). To prove the second assertion notice that $L(T_1^*) > F(T_1^*) > F(T_1) = L(T_1)$. ‖

More interesting is the fact that when there are multiple equilibria, (Case B), all equilibria are Pareto-comparable.

PROPOSITION 5.   *Joint-adoption equilibria are Pareto-ranked by their date of adoption, later adoption being more efficient from the firms' point of view.*

PROOF.   This a consequence of the monotonicity of M up to $\hat{T}_2$. ‖

Thus in Case B the late joint-adoption equilibrium at $\hat{T}_2$ Pareto-dominates any other Perfect Equilibrium. As argued by Harsanyi (1964) and Fudenberg and Tirole (1983), if one equilibrium Pareto-dominates all others, it is the most reasonable outcome to expect. Consider for example the diffusion equilibrium in which firms adopt only to avoid preemption. This situation is comparable to that of two strangers attacking each other *solely* for self-defence (see Fudenberg and Tirole (1983) for another example). Such complete lack of trust is easily avoided by coordination on the Pareto-dominant equilibrium, which is the natural "focal point" of the game. The case against the equilibria with simultaneous adoption before $\hat{T}_2$ is even stronger. In such equilibria each firm adopts only because the other does. No preemption is involved, because after T_2^* there is immediate response to adoption, so coordination seems particularly easy. We stress that such coordination requires neither binding contracts (as the equilibrium is by its nature self-enforcing) nor explicit communication. We will call the joint-adoption equilibrium at $\hat{T}_2$ the Superior Perfect Equilibrium.

Last, we discuss the parameter values for which each case occurs. The joint-adoption equilibria require $M(\hat{T}_2) \geq L(T_1^*)$, or

$$D = \int_{T_1^*}^{T_2^*} (\pi_1(1) - \pi_0(0))e^{-rt}dt + \int_{T_2^*}^{\hat{T}_2} (\pi_1(2) - \pi_0(0))e^{-rt}dt - (c(T_1^*) - c(\hat{T}_2)) \lesseqgtr 0$$

Relatively large $\pi_1(1)$ correspond to markets with a large first-mover advantage: as $\pi_1(1)$ increases, T_1^* decreases and D goes up. In such markets the highly competitive diffusion equilibrium will prevail. In particular, we get the diffusion equilibrium in a new market, with $\pi_1(1)$ the monopoly profit and $\pi_0(0) = 0$. In this case the follower's payoff is unaffected by the time at which the leader adopts, so that the optimal joint adoption time $\hat{T}_2$ is the same as the optimal reaction time T_2^*. Thus we cannot have a joint-adoption equilibrium.

If the innovation is only advantageous when the follower has not yet adopted, so that $\pi_1(2)$ is near $\pi_0(0)$, and $(\pi_1(1) - \pi_0(0))$ is near $(\pi_1(2) - \pi_0(1))$, then the equilibrium is the (Superior) joint-adoption one. This will be the case, for example, if adopting first simply transfers profit to the adopter from the other firm, but the latter can regain an equal footing by following suit. Here the gain from preemption is low, as T_2^* is near T_1^*, while the joint optimum $\hat{T}_2$ is quite late, for the innovation has little joint value. Thus the firms can postpone adoption without explicit collusion because of the credible threat of quick response. In this case joint adoption at $\hat{T}_2$ is greatly preferable to the diffusion equilibrium.[2]

4. Strategic Adoption in a Duopoly: A Formal Analysis

4.1. The issues

To verify the intuitions of the last section, we must develop a new formalization of strategy spaces and payoffs for continuous-time games of timing, in which a player's only decision is to choose a (single) time to move. We shall see that the traditional formalization is not adequate, because it entails a "loss of information" in passing from discrete time with short periods to the continuous time limit. This loss of information prevents a continuous-time representation of the limits of discrete-time mixed-strategy equilibria. We therefore introduce a richer formalization which does allow a continuous-time representation of these limits.

The usual way to describe a player's strategy is to choose a function $G_i(t)$ which is non-decreasing, right-continuous and has range in $[0, 1]$ (see for example Pitchik (1982)). The interpretation of G_i is that the cumulative probability that player i has moved (adopted in our framework) by time t (conditionally on the other player(s) not having moved before) is $G_i(t)$. Then the player's payoff, for example, would be:

$$V^i(G_1, G_2) = \int_0^\infty [L(s)(1 - G_j(s))dG_i(s) + F(s)(1 - G_i(s))dG_j(s)]$$
$$+ \sum a_i(s)a_j(s)M(s) \tag{4.1}$$

where $a_i(s) = \lim_{\varepsilon \to 0}[G_i(s) - G_i(s - |\varepsilon|)]$ is the size of the jump in G_i at s.[3] This formalization allows mixed strategies, but it is not adequate for our purposes for two reasons. First, it does not specify what happens in all the possible subgames. For example, imagine that for some player i and for some t, $G_i(t) = 1$. Then the strategies do not specify what happens if players deviate and at time $(t + \varepsilon)(\varepsilon > 0)$ no one has yet moved. The Perfect Equilibrium concept, in order to rule out empty threats, requires that players optimize whatever the history (i.e. even for histories which are not reached on the equilibrium path). In particular strategies must be specified for every contingency. Of course the remedy to this problem is to "roll over" the cumulative distribution by defining $G_i^t(s)$ as the cumulative probability that player i moved by time $s \geq t$ conditional on no one moving before t and requiring that the family of functions G_i^t satisfy an intertemporal consistency condition (Bayes rule).

The second drawback of this formalization is that it is not quite the continuous-time analogue of discrete-time games of timing. To see this, consider the following game, dubbed the "grab-the-dollar game".[4]

Time is discrete: $t = 0, 1, 2, \ldots$ There are two players, with common discount factor $\delta < 1$. At each period t players can try to grab a dollar that lies between them. If at time t only one of the players tries, he gets δ^t and the other player gets zero. If both try, each loses δ^t. In both cases the dollar is gone. If nobody tries the dollar can still be grabbed in the following period. Mixed strategies are allowed.

In this game there is a unique symmetric equilibrium. At each period, if no player has tried to grab the dollar yet, each player tries to grab it with probability $\frac{1}{2}$. In this equilibrium both players have a zero payoff. If a player tries to grab the dollar at t, he wins and gets δ^t with probability $\frac{1}{2}$, and with probability $\frac{1}{2}$, there is a "mistake": both try at the same time and lose δ^t. The fact that there is a positive probability of mistake is an attractive feature of this equilibrium, because with information lags, coordination is difficult to achieve.

The formalism of (4.1) is inadequate to represent this equilibrium in continuous time. As the period length converges to zero, the probability that by any positive time a player has tried to grab the dollar converges to one, and so the strategies should be represented by a unit mass at time zero, that is, $G_i^0(s) = 1 \ \forall s \geq 0$. Using equation (4.1) the probability of mistake would also be equal to one; however, the limiting value of the probability of mistake is $\frac{1}{3}$. The problem is that many different strategies converge to a unit mass at time zero, including, for example, the strategies that specify "adopt with probability one in the first period". There has been a loss of information in passing to the continuous-time limit; the payoffs cannot be computed using the $G_t(\cdot)$ alone.

We will enlarge the strategy space to avoid this loss of information. In the grab-the-dollar game, if the probability that player i moves in each period is constant and equal to α_1, we would like the probability that player i wins to be $\{\alpha_i(1 - \alpha_j)/[\alpha_i + \alpha_j - \alpha_i\alpha_j]\}$ and the probability of a mistake to be $\{\alpha_i\alpha_j/[\alpha_i + \alpha_j - \alpha_i\alpha_j]\}$. We will do this by adding an extra function, $\alpha_i(t)$, to each player's strategy space, to represent the "intensity" with which players move at times "just after" $G_i(t)$ jumps to one. That is, $\alpha_i(t)$ will represent the "intensity" of an "interval of consecutive atoms". We will define the payoffs to equal the limits of the payoffs of the corresponding discrete-time games. The reader familiar with the idea of generalized curves in optimal control theory will notice the similarity between that construction and our own: both are devices meant to allow continuous-time models to more accurately represent discrete-time limits; and both are defined through their influence on payoffs.

In our adoption game, we will be particularly interested in what happens as the αs converge to zero with the length of the time-period. Notice that if each α_i is of order (Δt), then the probability of mistake is of order $(\Delta t)^2$. In the limit we have the Poisson-like result that there is zero probability of both moving simultaneously.[5]

Before proceeding, we note that the grab-the-dollar game has asymmetric equilibria. For example, "player one always grabs the dollar (if he has not yet done so), player two never grabs".[6] There are also equilibria in which players alternate grabbing, for example, "player one grabs at odd-numbered periods, player two grabs at even-numbered ones". These "alternating" equilibria have no continuous-time limit due to precisely the "chattering problem" to which generalized curves are a response. We have not attempted to extend our model to allow these chattering equilibria, because the (extreme!) coordination they require seems highly unreasonable.

Faced with the inadequacy of the usual continuous-time formulation, we chose to enlarge the strategy spaces. An alternative would have been to work directly with the discrete-time equilibria. We chose our approach because we view "continuous time" as a convenient mathematical construction intended to represent the notion of very short time periods. Thus we do not view our enlarged strategy spaces as more artificial than the usual ones. To the contrary, while the usual continuous-time strategy spaces are useful for some games, in games of preemption they are not correct.

We should point out that using continuous rather than discrete time makes a difference that is unrelated to randomization or to our enlarged strategy spaces. Continuous-time models have "more" pure-strategy equilibria than discrete-time models do. More precisely, the set of continuous-time (pure strategy) equilibria is not the set of limit points of discrete-time equilibria, but rather the set of limit points of discrete-time ε-equilibria with $\varepsilon \to 0$ along with the period length. (Fudenberg and Levine (1986). In an ε-equilibria each player's chosen strategy yields within ε of his optimal payoff.) For example, co-operation can be sustained in a finite-horizon continuous-time prisoner's dilemma, but not in a discrete-time one. Similarly, the joint adoption outcomes we described in section 3 are *not* discrete-time equilibria. To see this, let the time interval between periods be denoted Δ, and assume that the joint optimum $\hat{T}_2$ belongs to the time grid. Assume both firms waited until $\hat{T}_2$ to adopt. Then it is in the interest of any firm to adopt at $(\hat{T}_2 - \Delta)$ whatever its opponent play at that time, because adopting at $(\hat{T}_2 - \Delta)$ has no effect on one's opponent's date of adoption. By backwards induction it is clear that from T_1^* on, both firms adopt with probability one, so that only the diffusion equilibrium remains. This is an extreme implication of perfectness, reminiscent of the finitely repeated prisoner's dilemma. In both games a large gain from cooperation is destroyed by a small payoff to cheating in the last period.

One way to reconcile perfectness with cooperation in the discrete-time versions of these games is to allow players to ε-optimize, as we remarked above. Another way is to introduce a small amount of incomplete information, which has been shown to allow finite-horizon resolutions on the prisoner's dilemma (Kreps *et al.* (1982)) and the chain store paradox (Kreps and Wilson (1982a), Milgrom and Roberts (1982).) Assume that with probability $(1 - \eta)$, the payoffs are as before, but with probability η the firm is "incompetent". By this we mean that the firm has to observe the other firm's adoption for at least one period before adopting itself. Then we can show (see Fudenberg and Tirole (1984)) that for arbitrarily small $\eta > 0$, if $M(\hat{T}_2) > L(T_1^*)$ so that we are in case B, then in the limit of shorter time periods the adoption date converges to $\hat{T}_2$. The incomplete information not only restores joint adoption as *an* equilibrium but selects it as the *only* one. Of course, other kinds of incomplete information would yield other results. Fudenberg and Maskin (1986) have shown that any equilibrium outcome of an infinitely repeated game without discounting is an equilibrium outcome of a sufficiently long finitely repeated game. We conjecture that there is an analogous result relating continuous- and discrete-time equilibria. This might seem to weaken the case for joint adoption, but we think not. Our discussion of ε-optimization and incomplete information is not intended as the main argument for joint adoption. Rather, we find joint adoption plausible *a priori* and have argued against ruling them out on purely technical grounds.

4.2. Strategy spaces and payoff functions

We now introduce strategy spaces that take into account the two issues we have just discussed. We first define "simple" continuous time strategies that permit us to distinguish between "types" of atoms, and define payoffs and Nash equilibrium. We then straightforwardly extend these strategies to "closed-loop" strategies and define perfect equilibrium.

DEFINITION 1.   A simple strategy for player i in the game starting at t is a pair of real-valued functions $(G_i, \alpha_i) : [t, \infty) \times [t, \infty) \to [0, 1] \times [0, 1]$ satisfying:

   (a) G_i is non-decreasing and right-continuous.
   (b) $\alpha_i(t) > 0 \Rightarrow G_i(t) = 1$.
   (c) α_i is right-differentiable.
   (d)   If $\alpha_i(t) = 0$ and $t = \inf(s \geqq t | \alpha_i(s) > 0)$, then $\alpha_i(\cdot)$ has positive right derivative at t.[7]

Condition (a) ensures that G_i is a cumulative distribution function, $\alpha_i(t)$ will measure the "intensity" of atoms in the interval $[t, t + dt]$; thus condition (b) requires that if $\alpha_i(t)$ is positive then player i is sure to adopt by t. Conditions (c) and (d) are imposed for technical convenience.

To define the payoffs resulting to a pair of simple strategies, we need a bit more notation. Let

$$\tau_i(t) = \begin{cases} \infty & \text{if } \alpha_i(s) = 0 \; \forall s \geqq t \\ \inf(s \geqq t \mid \alpha_i(s) > 0) & \text{otherwise} \end{cases}$$

$\tau_i(t)$ is the time of the first "interval of atoms" in player i's strategy. Let $\tau(t) = \min(\tau_1(t), \tau_2(t))$. In the subgame starting at t, there is sure to be an adoption by time $\tau(t)$. Finally let $G_i^-(t)$ be the left-hand limit of $G_i(\cdot)$ at t, that is $G_i^-(t) = \lim_{\tau \to t^-} G_i(t)$.[8] The game begins at time $t \geqq 0$; so impose $G_i^-(t) = 0, i = 1, 2$. The payoffs are then

$$V^t(t, (G_1, \alpha_1), (G_2, \alpha_2))$$

$$= \left[\int_t^{\tau(t)^-} (L(s)(1 - G_j(s))dG_i(s) + F(s)(1 - G_i(s))dG_j(s)) + \sum_{s < \tau(t)} a_i(s)a_j(s)M(s) \right]$$

$$+ (1 - G_i^-(\tau(t)))(1 - G_j^-(\tau(t)))W^i(\tau(t), (G_i, \alpha_i), (G_j, \alpha_j))$$

where

$$W^t(\tau, (G_t, \alpha_i), (G_j, \alpha_j)) = \left[\frac{G_j(\tau) - G_j^-(\tau)}{1 - G_j^-(\tau)} \right] [(1 - \alpha_i(\tau))F(\tau) + \alpha_i(\tau)M(\tau)]$$

$$+ \left[\frac{1 - G_j(\tau)}{1 - G_j^-(\tau)} \right] L(\tau)$$

if $\tau_j(t) > \tau_i(t)$,

$$W^t(\tau, (G_t, \alpha_i), (G_j, \alpha_j)) = \left[\frac{G_i(\tau) - G_i^-(\tau)}{1 - G_i^-(\tau)} \right] [(1 - \alpha_j(\tau))L(\tau) + \alpha_j(\tau)M(\tau)]$$

$$+ \left[\frac{1 - G_i(\tau)}{1 - G_i^-(\tau)} \right] F(\tau)$$

if $\tau_i(t) > \tau_j(t)$, while if $\tau_1(t) = \tau_2(t)$,

$$W^t(t, (G_1, \alpha_1), (G_2, \alpha_2))$$

$$= \begin{cases} M(\tau) & \text{if } \alpha_i(\tau) = \alpha_j(\tau) = 1 \\ [(\alpha_i(\tau)(1 - \alpha_j(\tau))L(\tau)) + (\alpha_j(\tau)(1 - \alpha_i(\tau))F(\tau)) + (\alpha_i(\tau)\alpha_j(\tau)M(\tau))]/ & \\ (\alpha_i(\tau) + \alpha_j(\tau) - \alpha_i(\tau)\alpha_j(\tau)) & \text{if } 2 > \alpha_i(\tau) + \alpha_j(\tau) > 0 \\ \left[\dfrac{\alpha_i'(\tau)L(\tau) + \alpha_j'(\tau)F(\tau)}{\alpha_i'(\tau) + \alpha_j'(\tau)} \right] & \text{if } \alpha_i(\tau) = \alpha_j(\tau) = 0 \end{cases}$$

These payoffs are the same as those of equation (4.1) up to $\tau(t)$. With probability $(1 - G_i^-(\tau(t)))(1 - G_j^-(\tau(t)))$, none of the players has moved by $\tau(t)$. At least one of the cumulative distributions $G_i(\cdot)$ then jumps to one. If $\tau_j(t) > \tau_i(t) = \tau$, then the payoffs are computed as the limits of discrete time payoffs when firm i adopts with probability $\alpha_i(\tau)$ at each period and firm j adopts with probability $[(G_j(\tau) - G_j^-(\tau))/(1 - G_j^-(\tau))]$ at the first instant and with probability zero thereafter. This corresponds to a situation in which firm j plays an isolated jump (or a density) at τ, and firm i adopts "continuously" with intensity $\alpha_i(\tau)$ (we know that firm j does *not* have an interval of atoms at τ because $\tau_j(t) > \tau$). If $\tau_1(t) = \tau_2(t) = \tau$, the probabilities of getting L, F and M are computed from discrete-time limits with constant probabilities of moves $\alpha_i(\tau)$ and $\alpha_j(\tau)$. If $\alpha_i(\tau) = \alpha_j(\tau) = 0$, the payoffs are computed by a first-order Taylor expansion.[9]

DEFINITION 2.   A pair of simple strategies (G_1, α_1) and (G_2, α_2) is a Nash equilibrium of the game starting at time t (with neither firm having yet moved) if each player's strategy maximizes his payoff $V^1(t, \cdot, \cdot)$ holding the other player's strategy fixed.

DEFINITION 3.   A closed-loop strategy for players is a collection of simple strategies $(G_i^t(\cdot), \alpha_i^t(\cdot))_{t \geq 0}$ satisfying the intertemporal consistency conditions:
  (e) $G_i^t(t + \nu) = G_i^t(t + u) + (1 - G_i^t(t + \nu)) G_i^{t+u}(t + \nu)$; for $t \leq u \leq \nu$
  (f) $\alpha_i^t(t + \nu) = \alpha_i^{t+u}(t + \nu) = \alpha_i(t + \nu)$ for $t \leq u \leq \nu$.

The reason why we need a family of strategies (G_i^t) is, as we explained, that to test for perfectness we must define strategies even conditional on zero-probability events. Condition (e) ensures that the family of strategies is consistent between non-zero-probability events; that is, *if* time t is reached, and $G_i^t(\cdot)$ puts positive weight on times from $(t + u)$ on, then $G_i^t(s)$ should be consistent between t and $(t + u)$.[10] Condition (f) is a similar consistency condition.

DEFINITION 4.   A pair of closed-loop strategies $\{(G_1^t(\cdot), \alpha_1^t(\cdot))\}_{t \geq 0}$ and $\{(G_2^t(\cdot), \alpha_2^t(\cdot))\}_{t \geq 0}$ is a Perfect Equilibrium if for every t, the simple strategies $(G_1^t(\cdot), \alpha_1^t(\cdot))$, $(G_2^t(\cdot), \alpha_2^t(\cdot))$, are a Nash equilibrium.

4.3.   Proof of the existence of the equilibria of Proposition 2

Now that we have developed an adequate formalism we can prove Proposition 2. First let us prove the existence of the equilibria. Recall the two cases: If $L(T_1^*) > M(\hat{T}_2)$ the unique equilibrium outcome is diffusion at (T_1, T_2^*); if $L(T_1^*) \leq M(\hat{T}_2)$ then there is also a continuum of joint-adoption outcomes. We will exhibit strategies that support these two types of equilibria because the nature of the strategies is instructive. The proof that there are no other equilibrium outcomes is more technical; we have placed it in Appendix 1.
  We begin with the diffusion outcome:

LEMMA 1.   *The following symmetric strategies are a perfect equilibrium*:

$$G^t(s) = \begin{cases} 0 & s < T_1 \\ 1 & s \geq T_1 \end{cases}$$

$$\alpha(s) = \begin{cases} 0 & s < T_1 \\ \dfrac{L(s) - F(s)}{L(s) - M(s)} & T_1 \leq s < T_2^* \\ 1 & s \leq T_2^* \end{cases}$$

PROOF.   We will check that these strategies yield a Nash equilibrium starting at any $t \in [T_1, T_2^*]$. (Outside this interval it is obvious.) First consider a subgame starting at $t, T_1 < t \leq T_2^*$. If $G_i^t(t) = 0$ then firm i receives $F(t)$. If $G_i^t(t) = \lambda, 0 < \lambda \leq 1$, and firm i plays an isolated jump, firm i receives $\lambda[\alpha(t) M(t) + (1 - \alpha(t)) L(t)] + (1 - \lambda) F(t) = F(t)$. If $G_i^t(t) = 1$, and $\alpha_i(t) = a$, firm i receives

$$\frac{a[(1 - \alpha(t))L(t) + \alpha(t)M(t)] + (1 - a)\alpha(t)F(t)}{a + \alpha(t) - a\alpha(t)} = F(t).$$

Thus in each subgame in $[T_1, T_2^*)$, firms are indifferent between all possible choices, and we may specify whatever strategies we please. At $t = T_1$ the payoff to the given strategies is again $F(t)$ (here we use the formula for payoffs when $\alpha_i = \alpha_j = 0$), as is the payoff to all other choices. Finally we check that $\alpha'(T_1) > 0$ and that the strategies are intertemporally consistent. ‖

Notice that in equilibrium, one firm adopts at T_1 and the other at T_2^*. Even though the firms play mixed strategies at T_1, the probability of mistake is zero. This should seem intuitive, because the gain to preempting at T_1 is zero, and so neither firm would adopt at T_1 were there any possibility of mistake.

The coordination involved here may remind some readers of Aumann's (1974) notion of a correlated equilibrium. We should therefore stress that we have not introduced a jointly-observable coordinating device. The zero probability of mistake arises naturally in continuous time. In discrete time with short periods, the gain to preempting in the first period after T_1 is of order (dt), so in a mixed-strategy equilibrium each player must adopt with probability of order (dt) so that his opponent is willing to randomize. Then, as we remarked in section 4.1, the probability of mistake converges to zero with the period length.

LEMMA 2. *If $L(T_2^*) = M(S) \leqq M(\hat{T}_2)$, the following symmetric strategies are a perfect equilibrium for any $t_1 \in [S, \hat{T}_2]$:*

$$G^t(s) = \begin{cases} 0 & s < t_1 \\ 1 & s \geqq t_1 \end{cases}$$
$$\alpha(s) = \begin{cases} 0 & s < t_1 \\ 1 & s \geqq t_1 \end{cases}$$

PROOF. The given strategies yield each firm $M(t_1)$, while any deviation yields at most max $(L(T_1^*), F(s))$.‖

In this case each firm's credible threat to immediately adopt if the other does (at times after T_2^*) can enforce the Pareto-superior joint adoption equilibrium.

5. The Oligopoly Case

We now show that the possibility of preemption need not enforce rent equalization when there are more than two firms. For this purpose we need only consider the three-firm case. Equilibrium payoffs need not be equal with more than two firms for two basic reasons. First, the payoffs in the "continuation game" after one firm has already adopted need not be equal, because with two firms payoffs were only equated along the equilibrium *path*, and not in all subgames. With unequal continuation payoffs, different firms have different gains to moving first, and so the threat of preemption need not equate the equilibrium payoffs. Asymmetric continuation payoffs can arise in two ways: first, if multiple continuation equilibria exist, one can specify different continuations depending on the name of the preempting firm. This kind of asymmetry may in some subgames be dismissed by the requirement that the firms play the Superior Perfect Equilibrium in every continuation game, if one exists. Unfortunately, not all of the two-firm continuation games have a Superior Perfect Equilibrium. Some subgames contain equilibria which cannot be Pareto-ranked. (See Appendix 2 for an example.)

The second reason that equilibrium payoffs need not be equated with more than two firms is that the duopoly case is special in that the follower's response is continuous in the leader's move. This continuity disappears with more than two firms, even if the continuation outcome is symmetric and independent of the name of the first adopter. To see this, assume that we are in Case A, and let $\bar{T} > T_1^*$ be such that $L(\bar{T}) = M(\hat{T}_2)$, where L and M are the payoffs of the remaining two firms after one firm has adopted. Thus, $\bar{T}$ is the first date at which late joint adoption is a continuation equilibrium. Let us specify that if the first adoption, t, is before $\bar{T}$, the remaining two firms play the "diffusion" equilibrium, while for $t > \bar{T}$ the continuation outcome is joint adoption at $\hat{T}_2$. Then at $\bar{T}$, the payoff to preemption jumps up. If a firm adopts first at $\bar{T}$, the others wait until $\hat{T}_2$, while adopting first at $\bar{T} - \varepsilon$ prompts immediate adoption by one of the others.

Now even though the two-firm continuation equilibrium is symmetric, and superior when possible, there is scope for specifying asymmetric three-firm Perfect Equilibria. For example, "firm three adopts with probability one from $\bar{T}$ on and the other firms wait". Firm three makes more profit than its competitors. Nevertheless, firm one, say, cannot impose rent equalization by preempting firm three, since if it adopted at $(\bar{T} - \varepsilon)$ it would trigger immediate adoption by firms two and three. The discontinuity in the payoffs as a function of time gives scope for rents to be unequal.

6. Related Work

We have already mentioned the Reinganum and Scherer work on adoption with precommitment. Scherer himself realized that the precommitment assumption "is vulnerable to the criticism of myopia in ignoring subsequent rival reactions to one's own decision". This criticism was addressed in the work of Rao and Rutenberg (1979) on the timing of capacity expansion. They used a discrete-time sequential-move mode, and (implicitly) employed the perfect equilibrium solution concept. Because of their complicated specification of the payoffs (quite similar to that of Scherer) they were forced to use numerical techniques, and no general conclusions emerged. Gilbert and Harris (1984) analyzed preemptive capacity expansion in a continuous-time model. They concluded that with two or more identical firms, not only would payoffs be equalized but that all new plants would earn zero profits. The zero-profit equilibrium arises because, in contrast to the other models cited, each firm may build many plants, so that there is no opportunity cost to new investment.[11]

To avoid considering mixed strategies, Gilbert and Harris divide each time t into two "moments", t^- and t^+. Thus their game, like Rao and Rutenberg's, is one with sequential moves – firms are *unable* to move simultaneously. Our formalism makes this restriction unnecessary. We feel that this is an improvement because imperfect information and the accompanying possibility of "mistakes" are an important aspect of games of timing. While it is true that on the path of the diffusion equilibrium the probability of a mistake is zero, off the equilibrium path mistakes do occur. In contrast, with the Gilbert and Harris formalism in no subgame would both firms adopt before T_2^*.

7. Conclusion

While we have termed our model one of the adoption of new technology, the main insights extend to more general games of timing. For example, we have seen that the threat of preemption equalizes rents in a duopoly, but need not do so if there are more than two firms. The duopoly case is special because under reasonable conditions, the follower's response is continuous in the leader's move. This continuity disappears with more than two firms. The same phenomenon will naturally arise in other games of timing.

We have also seen that when the gain to preemption is sufficiently low, as for an innovation which simply captures a rival's market share, the optimal symmetric outcome is to be expected; while if moving first is very profitable, as in a new market, the equilibrium will involve early adoption and "diffusion". Again, such conclusions should emerge in more general settings.

One result which might not hold with a different payoff structure is the existence of a diffusion equilibrium Pareto-inferior to the equilibrium with precommitment. This may depend on the existence of precommitment equilibria with diffusion.

The two key assumptions underlying the preemption argument are that information lags are short and that the payoffs are common knowledge. We have already observed that relaxing the first assumption makes late adoption less plausible. Relaxing the assumption that the payoffs are common knowledge means that a firm is no longer sure that it will be preempted if it waits past T_1 to adopt. Because the rival's (distributional) strategy is now "smoothed out", the incentive to play aggressively is lessened. We conjecture that in this case the time of first adoption would be later than with complete information; this is an interesting topic for future research.

This paper considered only the case of identical firms. In our survey, Fudenberg and Tirole (1985), we extend the analysis to consider the case of an incumbent and an entrant, each of whom can adopt the new technology. We find that if the products are perfect substitutes and the flow profits are determined by Bertrand competition then, in equilibrium the incumbent adopts first at the time where the entrant is just indifferent between adopting first and adopting second. This strong result is the dynamic version of Gilbert and Newberry's work on the persistence of monopoly. It heavily relies on the absence of incomplete and imperfect information, and on the assumption of (zero-profit) Bertrand competition as discussed in the survey. If the incumbent either is unsure about the entrant's adoption cost (or more generally profit function) or observes the entrant's entry decision only with a lag, it may err and let the entrant adopt. Similarly, changing the nature of competition in the product market can reverse the persistence result.

Appendix 1. Proof of Proposition 2

In the text we exhibited equilibrium strategies. We now show that there are no other equilibrium outcomes. Let $\tau_i(t)$ denote firm i's first date of "intervals of atoms", in the subgame starting at time

t, i.e. $\tau_i(t) = \inf\{s \geq t | \alpha_i(s) > 0\}$, and let $\eta_i(t) = \inf\{s \geq t | G_i^s(s) > 0\}$. Note that if $\eta_i(0) < \tau_i(0)$, $\eta_i(0)$ is the first time of an isolated jump. And let $\tau(0) = \min\{\tau_1(0), \tau_2(0)\}$ and $\eta(0) = \min\{\eta_1(0), \eta_2(0)\}$.

Let us first assume that $\tau(0) \leq \eta(0)$.

LEMMA 2. $\tau(0) \leq \hat{T}_2$.

PROOF.   Imagine that $\tau(0) > \hat{T}_2$, and consider the subgame starting at $\hat{T}_2$ when none of the firms has adopted. Since there is no jump in G_i at $\hat{T}_2 (i = 1, 2)$, there is a positive probability of adoption strictly after $\hat{T}_2$. But it is a dominant strategy for both firms to adopt at $\hat{T}_2$ and thereafter (both $L(t)$ and $M(t)$ decrease). Therefore the firms would not be optimizing. (Note that the same lemma holds if $\tau(0) > \eta(0)$: then $\eta(0) \leq \hat{T}_2$.) ‖

LEMMA 3. $\forall i, G_i^0(T_1^-) = 0$.

PROOF.   Let us show that a firm does not want to adopt at $t < T_1$. If it did, its payoff would be either $M(t)$ or $L(t)$ depending on whether the other firm adopts or not. But each firm can guarantee itself at least $F(t)$ by waiting until T_2^*, say. Since $F(t) > \max\{M(t), L(t)\}$, a firm indeed does not want to adopt before T_1. Note that this lemma holds whether or not $\tau(0) \leq \eta(0)$. ‖

LEMMA 4.   Let $t \in [T_1, T_1^*)$. If $\tau(t) \leq T_1^*$, then $\tau(t) = t$

PROOF.   Assume that $t < \tau(t) \leq T_1^*$. Since neither firm's strategy contains an atom before $\tau(t)$, adopting at $(\tau(t) - \varepsilon)$ gives either firm a payoff $L(\tau(t) - \varepsilon)$. Thus, if $V^i(s)$ denotes firm i's valuation at time s, $\min\{V^1(\tau(t) - \varepsilon), V^2(\tau(t) - \varepsilon)\} \geq L(\tau(t) - \varepsilon)$ and $V^1(\tau(t) - \varepsilon) + V^2(\tau(t) - \varepsilon) \geq 2L(\tau(t) - \varepsilon)$. Now there is adoption with probability one at $\tau(t)$. Therefore, using the facts that F and L are increasing, and both exceed M, we have:

$$V^1(\tau(t) - \varepsilon) + V^2(\tau(t) - \varepsilon) \leq F(\tau(t)) + L(\tau(t))$$

Lastly $F(\tau(t)) < I(\tau(t))$ and therefore the last two inequalities are in contradiction for ε small enough. ‖

Let us now consider the two cases of Proposition 2.

(A) $L(T_1^*) > M(\hat{T}_2)$. Let us show that $\tau(0) \leq T_1^*$. Imagine that $\tau(0) > T_1^*$. Then in the subgame starting at T_1^* each firm can obtain payoff $L(T_1^*)$ since no firm has an atom at T_1^*. Since both firms cannot guarantee themselves a payoff $L(T_1^*), \tau(0)$ must be at most T_1^*. Thus from Lemma 4, $\tau(0) = T_1$: The only possibility is the diffusion outcome (T_1, T_2^*) unless there is a positive probability of mistake at T_1. But since $F(T_1) = L(T_1) > M(T_1)$, this probability must be zero (if $\tau_i(0) = T_1$, say, j would be better off not adopting at T_1 if there is a probability of mistake).

To complete our treatment of case (A) we must now show that Prob {firm one moves first} = Prop {firm two moves first} = $\frac{1}{2}$. From Lemma 4 and the right-continuity of the αs we know that firm one, say, has $\alpha_1(t) > 0$ in some open interval beginning at T_1. We claim that firm two also has $\alpha_2(t) > 0$ in some open interval beginning at T_1. If $\tau_2(T_1) > T_1$, then $G_2^{T_1}(T_1) = 0$, as adopting at T_1 is weakly dominated. As $G_2^{T_1}$ is right-continuous, for any $\delta > 0$, there exists $\varepsilon > 0$ such that $G_2^{T_1}(T_1 + \varepsilon) < \delta$. By waiting until $(T_1 + \varepsilon)$, firm one increases its profit $(L(T_1) = F(T_1))$ by at least $\{(L(T_1 + \varepsilon) - L(T_1))(1 - \delta)\}$ (since both F and L are increasing). So $\tau_2(T_1) = T_1$, which means that $\alpha_2(t) > 0$ in some open interval beginning at T_1. On some such interval we thus have $\alpha_1(t) > 0$ and $\alpha_2(t) > 0$. From the definition of payoffs, this implies that $\alpha_1(t) = \alpha_2(t) =$

$[L(t) - F(t)]/[L(t) - M(t)]$. So starting at t slightly bigger than T_1, the two firms have equal probabilities of adopting first. This also holds at T_1 as the αs are right continuous.

(B) $L(T_1^*) = M(S) \geqq M(\hat{T}_2)$. We know from Lemma 2 that if $\tau(0) \leqq T_1^*$, the equilibrium must be diffusion at (T_1, T_2^*). Let us assume that $T_1^* < \tau(0) < S$. Consider the subgame starting at T_1^*. Since there is no atom at T_1^*, both firms can guarantee themselves $L(T_1^*)$. Therefore

$$V^1(T_1^*) + V^2(T_1^*) \geqq 2L(T_1^*)$$

But since the game ends with probability one at $\tau(0) < S$, and $L \geqq M$ and $F \geqq M$,

$$V^1(T_1^*) + V^2(T_2^*) \leqq \max_{t\epsilon[T_1^*,\tau(0)]}\{L(t) + F(t)\} < 2L(T_1^*)$$

a contradiction. Next assume that $S < \tau(0) \leqq \hat{T}_2$. Let us assume that no firm ever wants to adopt between $\tau(0)$ and $\hat{T}_2$. Indeed since no firm adopts with probability one at any instant before $\tau(0)$ and M is increasing, it is in the interest of any firm to wait. Let $u \leqq T_2^*$ denote the supremum of the times such that at least one firm is willing to adopt at these times. There are two possible cases. Either for some ε and for some i, $G_i^{u-\varepsilon}(u) < 1$ or for all ε and all i, $G_i^{u-\varepsilon}(u) = 1$. Let us consider the former case. Then $\lim_{\varepsilon\to 0} G_i^{u-\varepsilon}(u) = 0$ since there is no atom before u. Thus i's probability of adoption between $(u - \varepsilon)$ and u converges to zero, and j's payoff to not adopting between $(u - \varepsilon)$ and $\tau(0)$ converges to $M(\tau(0)) > L(T_1^*) \geqq L(t) \forall t$. This contradicts the definition of u: close to u, firm j would not want to adopt. Next assume that for all ε, all i, $G_i^{u-\varepsilon}(u) = 1$. Then for any ε, the probability of adoption by time u is one. Therefore

$$V^1(u - \varepsilon) + V^2(u - \varepsilon) \leqq \max_{t\epsilon[u-\varepsilon,u]}\{L(t) + F(t)\} \tag{3}$$

But since there is no atom at $(u - \varepsilon)$, each firm can guarantee itself $L(u - \varepsilon)$ by adopting at $(u - \varepsilon)$ in the subgame starting at $(u - \varepsilon)$. Therefore:

$$V^1(u - \varepsilon) + V^2(u - \varepsilon) \geqq 2L(u - \varepsilon) \tag{4}$$

Clearly (3) and (4) are in contradiction for ε small if $u < T_2^*$. If $u = T_2^*$, the reader will check that the left-hand derivative of $(L + F)$ at T_2^* is $[(\pi_1(2) - \pi_0(1)) + (\pi_1(1) - \pi_0(0))]e^{rT_2} < 0$ from Assumption(ii). Therefore: $\max_{t\in[u-r,u]}\{L(t) + F(t)\} = L(u - \varepsilon) + F(u - \varepsilon) < 2L(u - \varepsilon)$, a contradiction. Therefore no firm adopts before $\tau(0)$. If $\tau(0) = S$, then the same reasoning holds except that a firm is indifferent between adopting at T_1^* and waiting until $\tau(0)$. Since $T_1^* < \tau(0)$, almost surely no firm adopts at T_1^*. Therefore almost surely the equilibrium involves joint adoption at S. Because of the "almost surely" statement we ignored the possible outcome (T_1^*, S) in the theorem.

Second, assume $\eta(0) < \tau(0)$.

LEMMA 5. *There are no isolated jumps in (T_1, T_1^*).*

PROOF. Imagine that $\eta_1(0) = \eta(0) < T_1^*$. Note that firm two does not adopt at time $\eta(0)$ if the subgame starting at $\eta(0)$ is reached: It can avoid a strictly positive probability of mistake by waiting a bit. There are two cases. Either there exists an interval $(\eta(0), \eta(0) + \varepsilon]$ in which firm two does not adopt, or for any $\varepsilon > 0$, firm two adopts with some probability in $(\eta(0), \eta(0) + \varepsilon]$. In the former case, firm one does not optimize when it adopts at $\eta(0)$: it could wait without fearing preemption, and adopt a bit later; it would do better because L increases. Therefore consider the latter case. Then $\forall \varepsilon > 0$,

$$V^2(\eta(0)) \leqq a_1 F(\eta(0)) + (1 - a_1) L(\eta(0) + \varepsilon)$$

where $a_1 > 0$ is the conditional jump in the distribution G_1 at time $\eta(0)$. By taking the limit when ε tends to zero:

$$V^2(\eta(0)) \leqq a_1 F(\eta(0)) + (1 - a_1) L(\eta(0))$$

Since firm two can guarantee itself $L(\eta(0) - \varepsilon')$ in any subgame starting at $(\eta(0) - \varepsilon')$, then firm two adopts with probability one before $\eta(0)$ (otherwise:

$$L(\eta(0) - \varepsilon') \leqq V^2(\eta(0) - \varepsilon') \leqq F(\eta(0)) + (1 - a_1) L(\eta(0))$$

a contradiction for ε' small). We are back to the proof of Lemma 4:

$$2L(\eta(0) - \varepsilon') \leqq V^1(\eta(0) - \varepsilon') + V^2(\eta(0) - \varepsilon') \leqq L(\eta(0)) + F(\eta(0))$$

a contradiction. We have already noticed that Lemma 3 always holds. Therefore $\eta(0) = T_1$. ‖

Lemma 6.   *There cannot exist an isolated jump in* $[T_1^*, T_2^*]$.

PROOF.   First assume that $T_1^* < \eta(0) \leqq T_2^*$. Let $\eta_1(0) = \eta(0)$, say. Since firm one is willing to adopt at $\eta(0)$ if it is not preempted before, its valuation at T_1^* is strictly less than $L(T_1^*)$. But it can guarantee itself $L(T_1^*)$ by adopting immediately in the subgame starting at T_1^*, a contradiction. Second, assume that $\eta(0) = T_1^*$. Firm two's valuation at T_1^* is at most:

$$V^2(T_1^*) \leqq a_1 F(T_1^*) + (1 - a_1) L(T_1^*)$$

if $L(T_1^*) > M(\hat{T}_2)$ (Case A). Since firm two can guarantee itself $L(T_1^* - \varepsilon)$ in the subgame starting at $(T_1^* - \varepsilon)$ and $L(T_1^* - \varepsilon) > V^2(T_1^*)$ for ε sufficiently small, it must be the case that firm two adopts with probability one before T_1^* in the subgame starting at $(T_1^* - \varepsilon)$. Again we are back to the proof of Lemma 4: Since the probability of adoption before T_1^* is one, one has:

$$2L(T_1^* - \varepsilon) \leqq V^1(T_1^* - \varepsilon) + V^2(T_1^* - \varepsilon) \leqq L(T_1^*) + F(T_1^*)$$

a contradiction.

Next consider Case B: $L(T_1^*) = M(S) \leqq M(\hat{T}_2)$. Let t denote the first time after T_1^* such that firm two is willing to adopt at t conditionally on none of the firms having adopted yet. We claim that $t > S$. If not

$$V^2(T_1^*) \leqq a_1 F(T_1^*) + (1 - a_1) L(T_1^*)$$

and the previous reasoning obtains. Let us therefore assume that firm two does not adopt in $[T_1^*, t)$ for $t > S$. Then firm one could do better than $L(T_1^*)$ in the subgame starting at T_1^*: it could wait until slightly after S to adopt without being preempted. Therefore in the subgame starting at T_1^* firm one does not optimize. ‖

Last, consider the case $\hat{T}_2 \geqq \eta(0) > T_2^*$. Let $\eta(0) = \eta_1(0)$, say. Notice that $G_1^{\eta(0)}(\eta(0)) = 1$. Since M is increasing before $\hat{T}_2$, firm two would not adopt in a neighborhood of $\eta(0)$. But this in turn implies that firm one itself should not adopt at $\eta(0)$. Similarly $G_2^{\eta(0)}(\eta(0)) = 1$: Both firms must adopt with probability one at $\eta(0)$. But for the rest of the proof of Proposition 2, it does not matter whether certain adoption by both firms at a given time corresponds to isolated or non-isolated jumps. This concludes the proof of Proposition 2. ‖

Appendix 2

This appendix shows that in some continuation games there is no Superior Perfect Equilibrium. Let $L, F,$ and M be the payoffs of the remaining two firms; let U satisfy $T_1^* < U < T_2^*$ and $L(U) > M(\hat{T}_2)$ (so we are in Case A).

There are several undominated equilibria at U: let $\bar{T} > U$ be such that $L(\bar{T}) = M(\hat{T}_2)$, and let one and two be the remaining firms.
Let

$$U \leqq \nu \leqq s < \bar{T} \quad \begin{cases} G_1^\nu(s) = 1 \\ \alpha_1(s) = 1 \end{cases} \quad \begin{cases} G_2^\nu(s) = 0 \\ \alpha_2(s) = 0 \end{cases}$$

and after $\bar{T}$ the equilibrium strategies correspond to late joint-adoption at $\hat{T}_2$ (see section 4). Then firm one makes more profit than firm two if firm three preempts at U. It can be checked that these strategies are indeed an equilibrium of the continuation game and that the outcome is undominated (firm one gets $L(U)$, which is the maximum it can get in the continuation game). Naturally, the strategies of firms one and two can be reversed, yielding a second undominated equilibrium.

Notes

1   The equal probability property is proved assuming that firms do not play weakly dominated strategies. Nothing else in the paper relies on this assumption.
2   Scherer (1967) points out that the precommitment equilibrium may involve adoption even when *never* adopting would maximize joint profits.
3   Pitchik used the equivalent formula

$$V^i = \int_0^\infty \left[\int_0^{t^-} F(s) dG_i(s) + L(t)(1 - G_j(t)) + a_j(t) M(t) \right] dG_i(s)$$

4   Richard Gilbert suggested this game as a stylized model of preemption. See Gilbert and Stiglitz (1979).
5   Strictly speaking, Poisson processes do not exhibit discontinuous cumulative distribution functions. However, consider two independent stationary Poisson processes each with intensity λ. For any λ there is no probability of mistake, and in the limit $\{\lambda \to \infty\}$ both processes

have an atom at time zero yet there is still zero probability of both events occurring simultaneously.

6   The "always grab" equilibria do not exist if $\delta > 1$.

7   This condition is not necessary. We make it to simplify the definition of the payoffs.

8   This limit exists for all t because $G_t(\cdot)$ is monotone.

9   More generally, we could recover the limiting probability distribution from the nth derivative of α_i at τ if the first $(n-1)$ were zero.

10 This is analogous to condition (5.3) of Kreps-Wilson (1982b).

11 While Gilbert–Harris do not examine the possibility of other equilibria in which new plants do earn a profit, they conjecture that this cannot occur.

References

Aumann, R. (1974): "Subjectivity and Correlation in Randomized Strategies", *Journal of Mathematical Economics*, 67–96.

Fudenberg, D. and Levine, D. (1986): "Limit Games and Limit Equilibria", *Journal of Economic Theory*, 38(2), April, 261–79.

Fudenberg, D. and Maskin, E. (1986): "Folk Theorems for Repeated Games with Discounting or with Incomplete Information", *Econometrica*, 54(3), May, 533–54.

Fudenberg, D. and Tirole, J. (1983): "Capital as a Commitment: Strategic Investment to Deter Mobility", *Journal of Economic Theory*, 31, 227–50.

Fudenberg, D. and Tirole, J. (1984): "Preemption and Rent Equalization in the Adoption of a New Technology" (Discussion Paper 28, CERAS).

Fudenberg, D. and Tirole, J. (1985): "Dynamic Models of Oligopoly", in Lesourne, J. and Sonnenschein. H. (eds) *Encyclopedia of Economics*, 52(3), July, 383–401.

Gilbert, R. and Harris, R. (1984): "Competition and Mergers with Lumpy Investments", *Rand Journal of Economics*, 15, 197–212.

Gilbert, R. and Stiglitz, J. (1979): "Entry, Equilibrium, and Welfare" (paper presented at the NBER Conference on Theoretical Industrial Organization, Montreal).

Harsanyi, J. (1964): "A General Solution for Finite Noncooperative Games, Based on Risk Dominance", in Dresher, M. et al. (eds) *Advances in Game Theory*, Annals of Mathematics, Study 52, Princeton, 627–50.

Kreps, D. and Wilson, R. (1982a): "Reputation and Imperfect Information", *Journal of Economic Theory*, 27, 253–79.

Kreps, D. and Wilson, R. (1982b): "Sequential Equilibria", *Econometrica*, 50, 863–94.

Kreps, D., Milgrom, P., Roberts, J. and Wilson, R. (1982): "Rational Cooperation in the Finitely-Repeated Prisoner's Dilemma", *Journal of Economic Theory*, 27, 245–52.

Milgrom, P. and Roberts, J. (1982), "Predation, Reputation and Entry Deterrence", *Journal of Economic Theory*, 27, 280–312.

Pitchik, C. (1982): "Equilibria of a Two-Person Non-Zerosum Noisy Game of Timing", *International Journal of Game Theory*, 10, 207–21.

Prescott, E. and Visscher, M. (1977), "Sequential Location Among Firms with Foresight", *Bell Journal of Economics*, 8, 378–93.

Rao, R. and Rutenberg, D. (1979): "Preempting an Alert Rival: Strategic Timing of the First Plant by an Analysis of Sophisticated Rivalry", *Bell Journal of Economics*, 10, 412–28.

Reinganum, J. (1981a), "On the Diffusion of New Technology: A Game-Theoretic Approach", *Review of Economic Studies*, 153, 395–406.

Reinganum, J. (1981b): "Market Structure and the Diffusion of New Technology", *Bell Journal of Economics*, 12(2), 618–24.

Scherer, F. M. (1967): "Research and Development Resource Allocation Under Rivalry", *Quarterly Journal of Economics*, 81, 359–94.

Scherer, F. M. (1980): *Industrial Market Structure and Economic Performance*, 2nd edn (Chicago: Rand MacNally).

Young, L. C. (1980): *Lectures on the Calculus of Variations and Optimal Control Theory* (New York: Chelsea Publishing Co.).

PART VII
Asymmetric Information

Introduction

One of the most important aspects of the game-theory "revolution" in IO has been the formal introduction of imperfect information, in particular asymmetric information. Prominent contributions in this area are the papers by Kreps and Wilson (1982) and Milgrom and Roberts (1982b). These papers are motivated by the so-called chain-store paradox, first proposed by Selten (1978). Consider a simple game where an entrant decides whether or not to enter a market that is initially monopolized. In case of entry, the incumbent decides whether or not to prey on the entrant. If entry costs are sunk, no amount of predation will lead the entrant to exit. A simple backwards induction argument implies that the *threat* of predation will not work either – at least not between rational players. The force of backwards induction works equally well when we consider a finite series of games of this sort played between a chain-store owner and a series of potential entrants.

This result is a paradox because one would have thought that the perspective of facing a large number of potential entrants would induce the incumbent to respond aggressively to entry, in the hope of creating a reputation for being a "tough" player. But how can we model the idea of reputation? Kreps and Wilson (1982) and Milgrom and Roberts (1982b) propose the following framework: with a small probability, an incumbent is of a type – the "crazy" type – that derives positive utility from fighting an entrant (even though this may imply negative profits). The entrants do not know the incumbent's type (the incumbent does). In this context, by fighting early entrants, a "normal" incumbent increases the entrant's posterior that the incumbent is of the "crazy" type. This "investment" in reputation is costly, since "normal" incumbents derive negative utility from predation. But it may pay off in the long run because it preempts entry: eventually, entrants will hold a posterior of the incumbent being "crazy" so high that no entry is the optimal strategy.

The papers by Kreps and Wilson (1982) and Milgrom and Roberts (1982a, b) were important for two reasons. First, they proposed a very reasonable solution to an important paradox in the IO theory of strategic entry and predation. Second, they set up a framework that has proved to be very useful in addressing a number of related issues (not only in IO but also in other areas of Economics, including Macroeconomics).

As mentioned in part 5, the Sylos-Labini model suffers from the criticism that firms usually cannot commit to prices. However, anecdotal evidence suggest that low prices are an important deterrent. As recently as a few months ago, the *Wall Street Journal Europe* pointed France Telecom as a successful case of an ex-monopolist reacting to potential competition. France Telecom lowered its telephone rates by so much that it discouraged most potential entrants, the argument goes. How can theory and empirical observation be reconciled?

Milgrom and Roberts (1982a) propose a solution based on asymmetric information. Suppose the entrant does not know the incumbent's cost, only the distribution of possible cost values. Before deciding whether to enter, the entrant observes the price set by the incumbent. In a signalling equilibrium, a lower-cost incumbents sets a lower price. If price is sufficiently low, then the entrant infers that the incumbent's cost is very low and decides not to enter. In other words, a low price effectively deters entry, even though there is no commitment to keep that price low upon entry.

Milgrom and Roberts (1982a) follow the framework of signalling equilibria first proposed by Spence (1971). Many other papers have applied Spence's ideas. Milgrom and Roberts' was one of the first applications in an IO context. Other important applications include Wolinsky (1983), a paper that derives conditions under which prices can signal product quality, and Khilstrom and Riordan (1984), who show that advertising can also be a signal of product quality. The latter follow the ideas first put forward by Nelson (1970, 1974), who argues that, in a model of repeat customers, introductory advertising may function as a signal of product quality. The idea is that a high-quality firm has a greater incentive to advertise because it has more to gain from attracting first customers (the reason being they will be come repeat customers).

It is apparent from this literature that there are various possible signalling equilibria. In particular, different actions (e.g., price, advertising level) may function as signal of the same private information (e.g., quality level). Which signal is best? Which signal should we expect to be used in equilibrium? Milgrom and Roberts (1986) propose an answer to this question in the context of the price-advertising-quality framework. The answer is, both advertising and price should be used as signals of product quality. Specifically, the most efficient signalling equilibrium is one where both strategic variables are used as a signal. This result is important not only for the particular application (which is, again, in the Nelson tradition), but also for the methodological contribution to modeling multi-dimensional signalling.

References

Khilstrom, Richard, E. and Michael H. Riordan (1984): "Advertising as a Signal," *Journal of Political Economy*, 92, 417–50.

Kreps, David M. and Robert Wilson (1982): "Reputation and Imperfect Information," *Journal of Economic Theory*, 27, 253–79.

Milgrom, Paul, R. and John Roberts (1982a): "Limit Pricing and Entry under Incomplete Information," *Econometrica*, 50, 443–60.

Milgrom, Paul R. and John Roberts (1982b): "Predation, Reputation and Entry Deterrence," *Journal of Economic Theory*, 27, 280–312.

Milgrom, Paul R. and John Roberts (1986): "Price and Advertising Signals of Product Quality," *Journal of Political Economy*, 94, 796–821.

Nelson, Phillip (1970): "Information and Consumer Behavior," *Journal of Political Economy*, 78, 311–29.

Nelson, Phillip (1974): "Advertising as Information," *Journal of Political Economy*, 81, 729–54.

Selten, Reinhard (1978): "The Chain-Store Paradox," *Theory and Decision*, 9, 127–59.

Spence, Michael, 1971, *Market Signaling*. Cambridge, Mass.: Harvard University Press.

Wolinsky, Asher (1983): "Prices as Signals of Product Quality," *Review of Economic Studies*, 50, 647–58.

CHAPTER TWENTY

Reputation and Imperfect Information

David M. Kreps and Robert Wilson

Source: *Journal of Economic Theory*, 1982, 27, 253–79.

A common observation in the informal literature of economics (and elsewhere) is that in multistage "games," players may seek early in the game to acquire a reputation for being "tough" or "benevolent" or something else. But this phenomenon is not observed in some formal game-theoretic analyses of finite games, such as Selten's finitely repeated chain-store game or in the finitely repeated prisoners' dilemma. We reexamine Selten's model, adding to it a "small" amount of imperfect (or incomplete) information about players' payoffs, and we find that this addition is sufficient to give rise to the "reputation effect" that one intuitively expects.

1. Introduction

The purpose of this paper is to present some game-theoretic models that illustrate the role of a firm's reputation. Allusions to reputational effects recur in the industrial organization literature on imperfect competition, but formal models and analyses have been lacking. Scherer [21], for example, points to

> the demonstration effect that sharp price cutting in one market can have on the behavior of actual or would-be rivals in other markets. If rivals come to fear from a multimarket seller's actions in Market A that entry or expansion in Markets B and C will be met by sharp price cuts or other rapacious responses, they may be deterred from taking agressive actions there. Then the conglomerate's expected benefit from predation in Market A will be supplemented by the discounted present value of the competition-inhibiting effects its example has in Markets B and C. (page 338)

The intuitive appeal of this line of reasoning has, however, been called the "chain-store paradox" by Selten [24], who demonstrates that it is not supported in a straightforward game-theoretic model. We shall elaborate Selten's argument later, but the crux is that, in a very simple environment, there is no means by which thoroughly rational strategies in one market could be influenced by behavior in a second, essentially independent market. What is lacking, apparently, is a plausible mechanism that connects behavior in otherwise independent markets.

We show that imperfect information is one such mechanism. Moreover, the effects of imperfect information can be quite dramatic. If rivals perceive the *slightest* chance that an incumbent firm might enjoy "rapacious responses," then the incumbent's optimal strategy is to employ such behavior against its rivals in all, except possibly the last few, in a long string of encounters. For the incumbent, the immediate cost of predation is a worthwhile investment to sustain or enhance its reputation, thereby deterring subsequent challenges.

The two models we present here are variants of the game studied by Selten [24]; several other variations are discussed in Kreps and Wilson [8]. The first model can be interpreted in the context envisioned by Scherer: A multimarket monopolist faces a succession of potential entrants (though in our model the analysis is unchanged if there is a single rival with repeated opportunities to enter). We treat this as a finitely repeated game with the added feature that the entrants are unsure about the monopolist's payoffs, and we show that there is a unique "sensible" equilibrium where, no matter how small the chance that the monopolist actually benefits from predation, the entrants nearly always avoid challenging the monopolist for fear of the predatory response. The second model enriches this formulation by allowing, in the case of a single entrant with multiple entry opportunities, that also the incumbent is uncertain about the entrant's payoffs. The equilibrium in this model is analogous to a price war: Since the entrant also has a reputation to protect, both firms may engage in battle. Each employs its aggressive tactic in a classic game of "chicken," persisting in its attempt to force the other to acquiesce before it would itself give up the fight, even if it is virtually certain (at the outset) that each side will thereby incur short-run losses.

After reviewing selten's model in section 2, we analyze these two models in sections 3 and 4, respectively. In section 5 we discuss our results and relate them to some of the relevant literature. In particular, this issue of the *Journal* includes a companion article by Milgrom and Roberts [13] that explores many of the issues studied here in models that are richer in institutional detail. Their paper is highly recommended to the reader.

2. The Chain-store Paradox

The models we analyze are variations on the chain-store game studied by Selten [24]. Consider a sequential game with two players called the *entrant* (or potential entrant) and the *monopolist*. The entrant moves first, electing either to *enter* or to *stay out*. Following entry, the monopolist chooses either to *acquiesce* or to *fight*. If the entrant stays out, the incumbent is not called upon to move. Payoffs to the players, depending on the moves selected, are given in Figure 1. We consider the case that $a > 1$ and $0 < b < 1$.

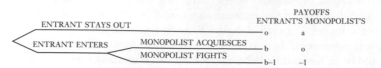

Figure 1   Selten's chain–store game.

How will this game be played? If the entrant enters, the monopolist chooses between the payoffs 0 if it acquiesces and −1 if it fights, so surely it will acquiesce. Anticipating this response, the entrant chooses between 0 if it stays out and b if it enters, and so it will enter. This is one Nash equilibrium of the game, but there is another: If the entrant were to anticipate that the monopolist would fight entry, then the entrant would want to stay out. Note that it costs the monopolist nothing to adopt the strategy "fight if entry" if no entry occurs. So this is a second Nash equilibrium. But this second equilibrium is not so plausible as the first. It depends on an expectation by the entrant of the monopolist's behavior that, faced with the *fait accompli* of entry, would be irrational behavior for the monopolist. In the parlance of game theory, the second equilibrium is *imperfect*. We suppose that the entrant adopts the "rational expectation" that the monopolist will acquiesce to entry, and we expect the first equilibrium to ensue.

Consider next the case that the game in Figure 1 is played a finite number of times. A single monopolist plays a succession of N different entrants, where the monopolist's total payoff is the sum of its payoffs in the N stage games. Allow the later entrants to observe the moves in all earlier stages of the game. Scherer's reasoning predicts that in this case the "reputation" effect might come to life: The monopolist, by fighting any early entry, might convince later opponents that it will fight, thus deterring later entries. Indeed, if this were the case, then also the early round opponents would not enter, not wishing to be abused for demonstration purposes. However, as Selten argues, this does not withstand scrutiny. In the last stage the monopolist will not fight because there are no later entrants to demonstrate for. So in the last stage, entry will surely occur. But then in the penultimate stage, the monopolist again has no reason to fight – it is costly in the short run and has no effect on the last stage. The next-to-last entrant, realizing this, will surely enter. This logic can be repeated, unraveling from the back: In each stage entry and acquiescence will occur. To be precise, this is the unique perfect Nash equilibrium of the game; cf. Selten [22, 23, 24]. Apparently, this model is inadequate to justify Scherer's prediction that reputational effects will play a role.

3. One-Sided Uncertainty

Our contention is that this inadequacy arises because the model does not capture a salient feature of realistic situations. (This contention was made first by Rosenthal [17], whose work we shall discuss in section 5.) In practical situations, the entrants cannot be *certain* about the payoffs to the monopolist. They may be unsure about the monopolist's costs, or they may be uncertain about nonpecuniary benefits that the monopolist reaps – this may be a monopolist who enjoys being tough. The latter might be more colorfully stated by saying that the monopolist plays tough "irrationally"; according to Scherer [21, p. 247], "...fear of irrational or avowedly rapacious action, then, rather than the expectation of rational pricing responses, may be what deters the potential new entrant from entering on a large scale." For whatever reason, the entrants may initially assess some positive probability p that the monopolist's payoffs are not as in Figure 1 but rather (in the simplest case) as in Figure 2, reflecting a short-term benefit from a fighting response. In this case, later entrants, observing earlier moves, will revise their assessment p on the basis of what they see. Perhaps in this case the reputation effect will come alive.

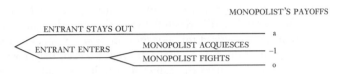

Figure 2 Payoffs for a tough monopolist

We model this formally as follows. There are $N + 1$ players, for N a positive integer. One of the players is the *monopolist*; the others are called *entrant N, entrant N − 1..., entrant 1. The monopolist plays the game in Figure 1 against each entrant in turn: First it plays against entrant N, then N − 1, etc. (We always index time backwards, and we refer to stage n as that part of the game that involves entrant n.) The payoffs for each entrant are given in Figure 1.*

The monopolist's payoffs are more complex: Its total payoff is the sum (undiscounted for now) of its payoffs in each stage, where the stage payoffs are either *all* as in Figure 1 or *all* as in Figure 2. The monopolist knows which payoff structure obtains. The entrants, on the other hand, initially assess probability δ that the monopolist's payoff structure is the second one. As the game progresses, each entrant (and the monopolist) observes all prior moves. Consequently, the history of moves prior to stage n may enable entrant n to revise this assessment if the history reveals some information about the relative likelihoods of the monopolist's two possible payoff structures.

This model conforms to Harsanyi's [7] formulation of a game with incomplete information. Alternatively, it is a game with imperfect information (among the entrants) and perfect recall, in which "nature" initially determines the monopolist's payoff structure, and nature's move is observed by the monopolist but not the entrants. In line with the first interpretation, we refer to the *weak monopolist* or the *strong monopolist*, meaning the monopolist if its payoffs are as in Figure 1 or Figure 2, respectively.

Since the players have perfect recall, there is no loss of generality in restricting attention to behavior strategies (Kuhn [10]). We wish to identify a Nash equilibrium of this game and, moreover, we wish the equilibrium identified to be *perfect*. That is, we wish to exclude equilibria that are based on expectations by one player of another's behavior that would not be rational for the latter to carry out if called upon to do so. Because our games have incomplete information, Selten's [22] concept of subgame perfection is inadequate. His concept of "trembling-hand" perfection (Selten [23]), on the other hand, is difficult to employ in games with strategy spaces as complex as those present here. So we use an analogous equilibrium concept called a *sequential equilibrium*. This is a refinement for extensive games of the usual Nash equilibrium that captures the spirit of Selten's perfectness criterion but that is much easier to apply. General definitions and properties of sequential equilibria are given in Kreps and Wilson [9], which we summarize here.

There are three basic parts to the definition of a sequential equilibrium: (a) Whenever a player must choose an action, that player has some probability assessment over the nodes in its information set, reflecting what that player believes has happened so far. (b) These assessments are consistent with the hypothesized equilibrium strategy. For example, they satisfy Bayes' rule whenever it applies. (c) Starting from *every* information set, the player whose turn it is to move is using a strategy that is optimal for the remainder of the game against the hypothesized future moves of its opponent (given by the strategies) and the assessment of past moves by other players and by "nature" (given by the assessment over nodes in the information set). The difference between this and the standard concept of a Nash equilibrium is that (c) is required for *every* information set, including those that will not be reached if the equilibrium strategies are followed. So each player will be willing to carry out its strategy at *every* point in the game, if ever it is called upon to do so. The properties are: Sequential equilibria exist for all finite extensive games. They are subgame perfect Nash equilibria. For a fixed extensive form and probabilities of nature's moves, as we vary the payoffs it is generic that all strict sequential equilibria are trembling-hand perfect, and the equilibrium path of each sequential equilibrium is an equilibrium path for some trembling-hand perfect equilibrium. Every trembling-hand perfect equilibrium is sequential.

In the context of the game analyzed here, the definition of sequential equilibrium specializes as follows. An equilibrium comprises a (behavior) strategy for each player *and*, for each stage $n = N, \ldots, 1$, a function p_n taking histories of moves up to stage n into numbers in $[0, 1]$ such that: (a) Starting from any point in the game where it is the monopolist's move, the monopolist's strategy is a best response to the entrants' strategies. (b) For each n, entrant n's strategy (contingent on a history h_n of prior play) is a best response to the monopolist's strategy *given that* the monopolist is strong with probability $p_n(h_n)$. (c) The game begins with $p_N = \delta$. (d) Each p_n is computed from p_{n-1} and the monopolist's strategy using Bayes' rule whenever possible. (We will not write (d) precisely – it will be transparent when we give the equilibrium below. That (d) implies "consistency of beliefs" in the sense of Kreps and Wilson [9] may not be apparent, but it does follow from the simple structure of the game being considered here.) The interpretation is that p_n gives the probability assessed by entrant n that the monopolist is strong as a function of how the game has been played up to stage n. Note that in (a) the monopolist's assessment over nodes in its information set is omitted, because all of its information sets are singletons.

We now give a sequential equilibrium for this game. This particular sequential equilibrium has the fortuitous property that, in terms of play from stage n on, p_n is a sufficient statistic for the history of play up to date n. That is, the choices of the players at stage n depend only on p_n and (for the monopolist) the move of entrant n; and p_n is a function of p_{n-1} and the moves at stage $n + 1$. We are lucky to be able to find a sequential equilibrium with this simple structure; it is not generally the case that one can find sequential equilibria for which the players' assessments are sufficient statistics for past play. (See remark (A) below.)

We begin by giving the functions p_n. Set $p_N = \delta$. For $n < N$, if the history of play up to stage n includes *any* instance that entry was met by acquiescence, set $p_n = 0$. If every entry so far has been met by fighting, and if k is the smallest index ($> n$) such that there was entry at stage k, then set $p_n = \max(b^{k-1}, \delta)$. If there has been no entry, set $p_n = \delta$.

This corresponds to the following recursive definition:

(a)   If there is no entry at stage $n + 1$, then $p_n = p_{n-1}$.
(b)   If there is entry at stage $n + 1$, this entry is fought, and $p_{n-1} > 0$, then
      $p_n = \max(b^n, p_{n+1})$.
(c)   If there is entry at stage $n + 1$ and either this entry is met by acquiescence or
      $p_{n+1} = 0$, then $p_n = 0$.

Now that we have described how p_n is computed at every node in the game tree, we can give the strategies of the players in terms of p_n.

Strategy of the monopolist

(a) If the monopolist is strong, it always fights entry.
(b) If the monopolist is weak and entry occurs at stage n, the monopolist's response depends on n and p_n: If $n = 1$, the monopolist acquiesces. If $n > 1$ and $p_n \geq b^{n-1}$, the monopolist fights. If $n > 1$ and $p_n < b^{n-1}$, the monopolist fights with probability $((1 - b^{n-1})p_\pi)/((1 - p_n)b^{n-1})$ and acquiesces with the complementary probability. (Note that when $p_n = 0$, the probability of fighting is zero, and when $p_n = b^{n-1}$, the probability of fighting is one.)

Strategies of the entrants

If $p_n > b^n$, entrant n stays out. If $p_n < b^n$, entrant n enters. If $p_n = b^n$, entrant n randomizes, staying out with probability $1/a$.

PROPOSITION 1.   *The strategies and beliefs given above constitute a sequential equilibrium.*

PROOF.   We only sketch the proof, leaving details to the reader. In the context of this game, there are two things to verify: First, the beliefs of the entrants must be consistent with the strategy of the monopolist, in the sense that Bayes' rule holds whenever it applies. Second, starting from any information set in the game, no player has the incentive (in terms of the payoff for the remainder of the game) to change its selection of move at that information set. For entrants, this verification is made using the beliefs given above. (Once this is verified, the Bellman optimality principle together with the fact that beliefs are Bayesian consistent ensures that no player can unilaterally change its strategy and benefit starting from any point in the game tree.)

The verification of Bayesian consistency is easy. If no entry takes place at stage n, nothing is learned about the monopolist, and we have $p_{n-1} = p_n$ in such instances. If $p_n \geq b^{n-1}$, then the monopolist is supposed to fight entry. If $p_n = 0$, then the monopolist is supposed to acquiesce. So in these cases, Bayes' rule implies that $p_{n-1} = p_n$ (as long as the monopolist follows its strategy). In each case, this is what we have. Finally, for $p_n \in (0, b^{n-1})$, there are positive probabilities that the monopolist will acquiesce and that it will fight entry. It only acquiesces if it is weak, and, indeed, in this case we have $p_{n-1} = 0$. If it fights, Bayes' rule requires that

$$p_{n-1} = \text{Prob(monopolist strong}|\text{monopolist fights)}$$
$$= \text{Prob(monopolist strong and fights)}/\text{Prob (fights)}$$
$$= \frac{\text{Prob (fights}|\text{strong)} \cdot \text{Prob (strong)}}{\text{Prob (fights}|\text{strong)} \cdot \text{Prob (strong)} + \text{Prob (fights}|\text{weak)}] \cdot P(\text{weak})}$$
$$= \frac{1 \cdot p_n}{1 \cdot p_n + [((1 - b^{n-1})p_n)/((1 - p_n)b^{n-1})][1 - p_n]} = b^{n-1}$$

which is what we have posited. Thus beliefs and strategies are Bayesian consistent.

Note that there are two instances in which Bayes' rule does not apply: $p_n \geq b^{n-1}$ and the monopolist acquiesces to entry; $p_n = 0$ and the monopolist fights. In each case we set $p_{n-1} = 0$. In words, we assume that any acquiescence is viewed by the entrants as "proof" that the monopolist is weak, and the entrants are unshakeable in this conviction once it is formed. This assignment of beliefs off the equilibrium path is *somewhat* arbitrary – there are other assessments that work as well. But this assignment is not wholly capricious – there are assessments that would not give an equilibrium. (This will be discussed more fully below.)

(Repeating an earlier contention, this set of assessments is consistent in the sense of Kreps and Wilson [9]. A direct proof is not difficult.)

Verification that the entrants are playing optimally is straightforward. If $p_n \geq b^{n-1}$, entrant n expects entry to be fought, and so it stays out. If $p_n \in (b^n, b^{n-1})$, acquiescence will occur with positive probability, but with probability less than $1 - b$. Again it is better to stay out. If $p_n = b^n$, acquiescence follows entry with probability $1 - b$, and the entrant is indifferent. If $p_n < b^n$, the probability of acquiescence exceeds $1 - b$, and the entrant enters.

To see that the strong monopolist is playing optimally, note that if the entrants follow the strategy above, acquiescence at any point results in more future entries than does fighting. In the short run fighting is better for the strong monopolist, and in the long run fewer entries are better, so the strong monopolist will always fight.

Finally, for the weak monopolist, one can verify inductively that given that these strategies are followed from stage n to stage 1, the expected payoff to the weak monopolist from stages n to 1 is given by the following function of p_n:

$$\begin{aligned} \nu_n(p_n) &= a(t - k(p_n) + 1) + 1 && \text{if } b^n < p_n = b^{k(p_n)-1} \\ &= a(t - k(p_n) + 1) && \text{if } b^n < p_n < b^{k(p_n)-1} \\ &= 1 && \text{if } p_n = b^n \\ &= 0 && \text{if } p_n < b^n \end{aligned}$$

where $k(p) = \inf\{n : b^n < p\}$ for $p > 0$, and $k(0) = \infty$. Now suppose that entry occurs at stage n. By acquiescing, the monopolist receives zero both in this stage and in the rest of the game (since p_{n-1} will be set equal to zero). By fighting, the monopolist receives -1 in this stage and future expected payoffs of 0 if $p_n = 0$, 1 if $p_n \in (0, b^{n-1}]$, and more than 1 if $p_n > b^{n-1}$. Thus the weak monopolist is happy to follow the strategy given above. ■

It is easiest to understand the nature of this equilibrium by tracing through the play of the game for "typical" values of δ and b, say $\delta = \frac{1}{10}$ and $b = \frac{1}{2}$. Note that in this case, $k(\delta) = 4$. Refer to Figure 3. At stage N (presumed to be greater than 4) the game begins with $p_N = \delta$. At this stage, the monopolist would fight entry regardless of its payoffs, so entry is forestalled. The game evolves along arrow (a) to the point $p_{N-1} = p_N = \delta$. Note that *if* there is entry, the monopolist is willing *ex post* to fight – to acquiesce moves the game along arrow (b) to $p_{N-1} = 0$, from which point the monopolist nets zero. Fighting costs 1 immediately, but acquiescing costs much more in the future. (Note that all that is necessary is that acquiescence cost at least one – as long as acquiescence resulted in

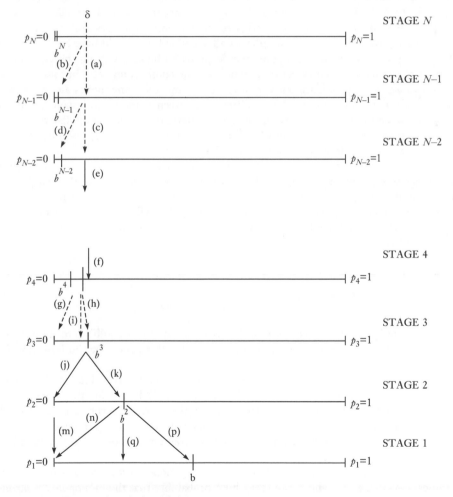

Figure 3   Temporal evolution of the game

$p_{N-1} \leq \frac{1}{16}$ this would be so in this case. So here is one place where the non-Bayesian reassessments need not be *precisely* as specified above to have an equilibrium. But note that $p_{N-1} \leq \frac{1}{16}$ is necessary – otherwise the weak monopolist would rather acquiesce than fight at this stage.) The game continues in this fashion (arrows (c), (e), and (f)) until date 4 $(= k(\delta))$. At this date the monopolist might acquiesce if it is weak and if it is challenged – the strategy of the weak monopolist is chosen so that following entry, acquiescence leads to $p_3 = 0$ (arrow (g)) and fighting leads to $p_3 = b^3$ (arrow (h)). But this does *not* give entrant 4 enough incentive to enter – the game actually evolves along arrow (i) to $p_3 = \delta$. At date 3 the weak monopolist again will randomize if challenged (so that arrows (j) and (k) give the posteriors), and now there is high enough probability of acquiescence for entrant 3 to enter. If the monopolist acquiesces, the game moves along arrow (j) to $p_2 = 0$. At this point the monopolist is known to be weak, and entrants 2 and 1 both enter with the monopolist acquiescing each time. The monopolist thereafter is supposed to acquiesce; if it fights instead at, say, stage 2, entrant 1 disregards this and continues to believe that the monopolist is weak. That is, $p_1 = 0$ if either the monopolist acquiesces *or* if it fights. (Note that we could have $p_1 \leq \frac{1}{2}$ if the monopolist fights, and still we would have an equilibrium. But if $p_t > \frac{1}{2}$, then the weak monopolist would prefer to fight, upsetting the equilibrium. Again there is some freedom in defining beliefs off the equilibrium path, but not complete freedom.) Back at stage 3, if the monopolist fights entry, the game moves along arrow (k) to $p_2 = \frac{1}{4}$. At this point entrant 2 is indifferent between entering and staying out, and chooses between the two randomly. If entrant 2 enters, the weak monopolist randomizes between acquiescence (arrow (n)) and fighting (arrow (p)). If entrant 2 stays out, the game moves along arrow (q) to $p_1 = \frac{1}{4}$ (and entrant 1 surely enters).

The remarkable fact about this equilibrium is that even for very small δ, the "reputation" effect soon predominates. Even if the entrants assess a one-in-one-thousand chance that the monopolist would prefer (in the short run) to fight, if there are more than ten stages to go the entrant stays out because the monopolist will *surely* fight to preserve its reputation. Note the "discontinuity" that this causes as the number of stages in the game goes to infinity:

$$\lim_{N \to \infty} \nu_N(\delta)/N = a \quad \text{if } \delta > 0$$
$$= 0 \quad \text{if } \delta = 0$$

The obvious question at this point is: To what extent is this equilibrium unique? It is not the case that it is the unique Nash equilibrium for this game, for the following four reasons.

(a) There are other Nash equilibria that are not sequential equilibria. (That is, that are not, roughly speaking, perfect.) For example, it is a Nash equilibrium for the monopolist to fight any entry (regardless of its payoffs), and for the entrants never to enter. But this behavior is not "ex post rational" for the weak monopolist in stage 1. In general, we wish to allow only sequential equilibria, and we confine attention to those for the remainder of this discussion.

(b) There are sequential equilibria where the strong monopolist acquiesces to entry. For example, if $N = 2$, $b = \frac{1}{2}$, and $\delta = \frac{2}{3}$ (very high probability that the monopolist is strong), it is a sequential equilibrium for entrant 2 to enter, the monopolist to acquiesce to this entry regardless of its payoffs, and for entrant 1 to adopt the strategy: Stay out if the monopolist acquiesces in stage 2; enter if the monopolist fights in stage 2. (In stage 1, the monopolist responds with its ex post dominant action.) This is sequential because it is supported by the following beliefs of entrant 1:

Prob (monopolist strong | acquiescence in stage 2) $= p_2 = \frac{2}{3}$

Prob (monopolist strong | fight in stage 2) $= \frac{1}{4}$

For the given strategies, the first of these reassessments follows from Bayes' rule, and the second is "legitimate" because Bayes' rule does not apply: There is zero prior probability that the monopolist will fight in stage 2.

Although this is a sequential equilibrium, we contend that it is not very sensible. The flaw is in the beliefs of entrant 1 – if there is fighting in stage 2, entrant 1 revises *downward* the probability that the monopolist is strong. Intuitively it seems at least as likely that the strong monopolist would defect and fight as that the weak monopolist would do so. Thus it seems intuitive that entrant 1 will assess

Prob (strong|fight) $\leq$ Prob (strong|acquiesce)

But if we insist on this condition holding, then the equilibrium given immediately above is excluded.

Putting this formally, we will call the beliefs $\{p_n\}$ of the entrants *plausible* if given two histories h_n and h'_n of play up to stage n, if h_n and h'_n are the same except that some plays of "fight" in h_n are "acquiesce" in h'_n, then $p_n(h_n) \geq p_n(h'_n)$. We wish to allow only sequential equilibria that are supported by plausible beliefs. Note that this is not true of the equilibrium immediately above, but it is true of the equilibrium Proposition 1.

(c) In the sequential equilibrium given in this section, there is some freedom in describing what happens off the equilibrium path. For example, we have said that if $p_n = 0$ and the monopolist fights entry, then the entrants set $p_{n-1} = 0$. Thus once $p_n = 0$ in our equilibrium, every subsequent entrant enters. But we would also have an equilibrium if we set $p_{n-1} = b^{n-1}$ after such a defection from the equilibrium, and then entrant $n - 1$ would randomize between entering and staying out. Note well, this concerns the behavior of entrant $n - 1$ only off the equilibrium path, but in terms of strategies it is a different equilibrium. We cannot hope to have uniqueness off the equilibrium path.

(d) Finally, there is a bit of freedom in defining equilibria along the equilibrium path when $\delta = b^n$ for some $n \leq N$: The behavior of entrant n in this case need not conform to the strategy above – any randomization will work.

Except for these four problems, we do get uniqueness:

PROPOSITION 2. *If $\delta \neq b^n$ for $n \leq N$, then every sequential equilibrium with plausible beliefs has on-the-equilibrium-path strategies as described previously. Thus every sequential equilibrium with plausible beliefs has the value functions given above.*

The proof is by induction and is left to the reader. We simply note that in carrying out the induction one establishes the following:

(a)   The value function of the strong monopolist (in equilibrium) will be a nondecreasing function of p_n, and the strong monopolist will therefore fight any entry.

(b)   The value function of the weak monopolist will be a nondecreasing function of p_n and will be given by the formula in the proof of Proposition 1 for $\delta \neq b^n, m \leq n$.

(c)   If there is entry at stage n and if the monopolist fights this entry, then entrant $n-1$ must stay out with probability exactly $1/a$.

By going through this proof, the reader will see the intuition behind this equilibrium, which we will try to summarize here. As long as beliefs are plausible, the strong monopolist will always fight entry. Thus any acquiescence is conclusive proof that the monopolist is weak. Moreover, such evidence once given must result in zero payoff for the monopolist – the argument of Selten that we have given in section 1 applies (with minor modifications). If entrant n is to enter, then it must be that there is probability $1 - b$ (at least) that the monopolist will acquiesce, which requires that the weak monopolist is randomizing or simply acquiescing. This also requires that $p_n \leq b$, and, from Bayes' rule, that *if* this entry is met by fighting, then $p_{n-1} \geq p_n/b$. Thus if we begin with $\delta > b^m$, there can be *at most* m entrants who have a positive probability of entering. As N gets large, then, the value to either monopolist must asymptote to aN, and, for $N > 2m$, the weak monopolist would always wish to fight entry. (In fact, in the equilibrium in turns our that this is true for $N \geq m$.)

We close this section by listing several extensions and embellishments of the basic model.

(A) We have dealt above with the case $a > 1$. If $0 < a \leq 1$, then the same basic structure for the equilibrium emerges, in that for sufficiently large n, entrants do not enter because the monopolist will fight with probability one. The play near the end of the game is more complicated however. In particular, one cannot obtain an equilibrium where entrant n's strategy depends only on p_n – it depends instead on p_n and the history of play in the last j rounds, where j is the smallest integer such that $ja > 1$.

(B) If the monopolist discounts its payoffs by a factor ρ per period, the following results. If $\rho > 1/a$, then the equilibrium is *precisely* as above except that the randomizing probabilities of the entrants must change. If $\rho \leq 1/(a+1)$, then the equilibrium is quite different – the weak monopolist acquiesces at the first entry, so entrants enter if $p_n < b$ and stay out if $p_n > b$. For ρ such that $1/(a+1) < \rho \leq 1/a$, the basic character of the equilibrium is just as in the case of $\rho > 1/a$ – for large enough n entrants stay out because the monopolist will fight any entry. But the equilibrium is complicated for small n, resembling the equilibrium in the undiscounted case where $a < 1$.

(C) Suppose that instead of the sequential game depicted in Fig. 1, each stage consists of a two-by-two simultaneous move game, Table 1, where the payoffs with probability $1 - \delta$ are shown in (a) and the payoffs with probability δ are shown in (b). (We assume $0 < b < 1$ and $a > 1$.) Otherwise the structure of the game is the same: One of these two bimatrices is chosen at the outset, according to the probabilities given. One monopolist plays against N entrants in sequence. The monopolist knows which bimatrix was chosen; the entrants do not.

For $\delta = 0$, the argument of Selten is easy adapted to show that the *unique* equilibrium (perfect or not) has row 2, column 1 played in each stage. This is because row 2 is strongly dominant in the stage game. But for $\delta > 0$ we get an equilibrium almost identical to the

Table 1

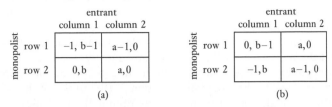

(a)   (b)

one discussed above: For stages n such that $b^n < \delta$, the monopolist plays row 1 regardless of which bimatrix was selected, and the entrant responds with column 2. (The play of the game is a bit different near the end of the game.) So we see that a little incomplete information can not only make an imperfect equilibrium perfect (more accurately, sequential) – it can also make as part of a sequential equilibrium the play of an action that with very high probability is *strongly dominated* in the stage game.

(D) Paul Milgrom has pointed out to us that similar equilibria can be found even when every player in the game knows the payoffs of the monopolist, as long as this knowledge is not *common knowledge*. That is suppose all the entrants know the monopolist's payoffs, but they are not certain whether their fellow entrants have this information. Then (with the proper precise specification) they fear that the weak monopolist will fight (for large n), in order to maintain its reputation among the other entrants. This being so, the entrant will not enter. And the monopolist, even if it knows that all the entrants know that it is weak, may be willing to fight entry early on, in order to help "convince" subsequent entrants that it (the monopolist) is not sure that the entrants know this. (Precise arguments of this form are found in Milgrom and Roberts [13].) Selten's argument requires that it is common knowledge that the monopolist is weak. In real-life contexts this is a very strong assumption, and weakening it ever so slightly (more slightly than we have done above) can give life to the "reputation" effect.

(E) We have dealt exclusively with the case of a single monopolist playing against N different entrants. Another interesting case is where a single monopolist plays N times against a single entrant. For the game we have analyzed in this section, this turns out to have no effect on the equilibrium. (We leave this to the reader to verify.) But as we shall see in the next section, this is due (at least in part) to the fact that there is no uncertainty about the payoffs of the entrants.

4. Two-Sided Uncertainty

In this section we consider what happens when the monopolist is unsure about the payoffs of the entrants. The most interesting formulation of this problem is where a single monopolist plays the stage game of Figure 1 a total of N times against a single opponent. The payoff to each player is the sum of the player's payoffs in each stage. The monopolist's payoffs are as in Figure 1 or Figure 2, with probabilities $1 - \delta$ and δ, respectively. The entrant's payoffs are as in Figure 1, for some b such that $0 < b < 1$ with probability $1 - \gamma$ and for some other $b > 1$ with probability γ. Each player knows its own payoffs at the start of the game, and each is unsure of the payoffs of its opponent. The payoffs are statistically independent.

Continuing the terminology of section 3, we shall refer to the weak entrant as the entrant if its payoffs satisfy $0 < b < 1$, and the strong entrant if its payoffs satisfy $b > 1$.

Note that the strong entrant does better to enter than to stay out in any stage, even if the monopolist is sure to fight. Because it seems plausible that entry will not decrease the probability that the monopolist will acquiesce subsequently, we look for equilibria where the strong entrant always enters. Thus any failure to enter brands the entrant as weak, at which point we are back to the situation of section 3. (Recall that it did not matter there whether there was a single entrant or N entrants.) Similarly, we look for an equilibrium where the strong monopolist always fights. Thus any failure to fight brands the monopolist as weak, following which the entrant always enters and the monopolist always acquiesces. We search, then, for an equilibrium of the following sort: The strong entrant always enters. The strong monopolist always fights. The weak entrant chooses a strategy that is a mixture of "stopping rules": A stopping rule gives the date at which the entrant will "give in" and not enter if the monopolist has not acquiesced yet. (The entrant may later re-enter, as we will then follow the equilibrium of section 3.) The weak monopolist will also mix among stopping rules: A stopping rule for the monopolist gives the date at which the monopolist will first acquiesce if the entrant has not retreated first. If one side or the other gives in, we move to either the situation of section 3 or to where entry-acquiescence follows until the game ends.

Giving a complete specification of the equilibrium that is obtained is extraordinarily tedious, because it is based on some very involved recursions. Still, we can give a rough description of what happens. At any stage n the previous play of the game is summarized into two statistics: p_n, the probability assessed by the entrant that the monopolist is strong; q_n, the probability assessed by the monopolist that the entrant is strong. (The game begins with $p_N = \delta$ and $q_N = \gamma$.) Thus the "state space" of the game at stage n is the unit square, as depicted in Figure 4. The edge $q_n = 0$ is the subject of section 3. The edge $p_n = 0$ can be analyzed using the argument of Selten with the conclusion: The entrant always enters, and the weak monopolist always acquiesces.

The square is divided into two regions by a curve, as shown. If (p_n, q_n) lies in region I, say at the point x, then the entrant enters regardless of its payoffs, and the weak monopolist randomizes. If the weak monopolist acquiesces, the game evolves to the point y (actually, to this point in the *next* square – the square for stage $n - 1$). If it fights, or if it is strong and hence fights, the entrant uses Bayes' rule to compute p_{n-1}, landing at the point z on the curve, and just *beyond* the curve in region II of the next square. If (p_n, q_n) lies in region II, say at x', then the weak entrant randomizes. If it stays out, the equilibrium of section 3 ensues – and the next stage begins a the point y'. If it enters (or if it is strong and therefore enters), the monopolist recomputes the probability that it is strong, landing at the point x'' along the curve. Then the monopolist randomizes (if weak), and the game evolves to y'' or to z''. Both z and z'' are in region II of the next square, so the next round begins with randomization by the weak entrant, and so on.

Except for the very start of the game, when $p_N = \delta$ and $q_n = \gamma$, most of the play takes place along the curve. (Actually, the curve shifts slightly as n changes.) So we see an initial jump to the curve (or to one of the two edges), followed by a slow climb up the curve with ever present the chance that a jump to one of the edges will occur. With probability one, a weak player will eventually give in, so we either jump to an edge eventually or, if both players are strong, we reach the point $p_0 = q_0 = 1$. This is a game of "chicken," where

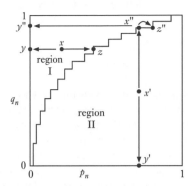

Figure 4   State space of the game at stage n

once begun, each side (if weak) randomizes between a small probability of giving in and a large probability of daring the other side for one more round. The relative size of these probabilities is required by the conditions of an equilibrium: Daring once more costs something this round, but giving in is costly for the rest of the game. So it must be that daring once more does not give either player a substantial chance of *immediate* gain; the opponent must be about to "dare" once again with large probability.

While it is tedious to give the exact equilibrium in the discrete time formulation, it is relatively simple to do so in a continuous time version of the game. So we shall now develop that continuous-time version. (We should forewarn the reader: We will be somewhat sloppy in what follows. But everything we say can be made exact.)

To begin, consider the game of section 3 played against a single entrant over the time period N to 0. Instead of playing at times $N, N-1, \ldots, 1$, for the stakes (per stage) given in section 3, we imagine that an integer K is given, and that the game is played "more frequently, for reduced stakes," with play at times $N, (KN-1)/K, (KN-2)/K, \ldots, 1/K$, for stakes $1/K$ times the stakes given. It is the *number* of times that the monopolist has left to demonstrate its "toughness" that is decisive in section 3, so we find that if $k(\delta) = n$, the entrant stays out (and the monopolist would surely fight) at all times $t > n/K$. As K goes to infinity, we see that the entrant stays out until "the very last instant" of time.

With this limiting result as motivation, we now consider the "continuous-time" version of the above game, played over a time interval T to 0. At each time $t \in [T, 0]$, the entrant chooses whether to enter or to stay out, and the monopolist chooses whether to fight entry or to acquiesce. A realization of the entrant's strategy is formalized as a (measurable) function $e : [T, 0] \to \{0, 1\}$, where $e(t) = 1$ means that the entrant is entering at date t. A realization of the monopolist's strategy is formalized as a function $f : [\mathrm{T}, 0] \to \{0, 1\}$, where $f(t) = 1$ means that the monopolist is fighting at date t. (We have a "closed-loop" game, so pure strategies would be a pair of functions $\mathbf{e}$ and $\mathbf{f}$ where $\mathbf{e}(t)$ is $F((\mathbf{e}(s), \mathbf{f}(s)), s < t)$-measurable, and $\mathbf{f}(t)$ is $F(\mathbf{f}(s), s < t; \mathbf{e}(s), s \le t)$-measurable. We shall not try to be more precise about this here; instead we trust the reader's ability to see how to formalize what follows.) Given realizations e and f, payoffs to each side are determined by measuring the lengths of times during which there is not entry $(e(t) = 0)$, during which entry is fought

$(e(t) = 1, f(t) = 1)$, and during which there is acquiescence to entry $(e(t) = 1, f(t) = 0)$, and assigning payoffs accordingly. For example, if λ denotes Lebesgue measure, then the weak monopolist's payoff is

$$\lambda\{e(t) = 0\} \cdot a - \lambda\{e(t) = 1, f(t) = 1\}$$

In this game, an equilibrium calls for the entrant to stay out as long as the monopolist does not acquiesce and to always enter after any acquiescence is observed; for the strong monopolist to fight any entry; and for the weak monopolist to fight as long as it has not acquiesced yet and to acquiesce forever after an acquiescence. The reader can easily verify that this is an equilibrium. Moreover, if by some "mistake" the entrant entered before time 0, the weak monopolist would want to fight: By acquiescing it saves an "instantaneous" one unit, but then it invites entry for the remainder of the game – a substantial loss that outweighs the instantaneous savings.

(The reader is entitled to be somewhat skeptical about this. By moving to a continuous-time formulation, we have obtained some of the features of the supergame (infinitely repeated) formulation. For example, the equilibrium above is "perfect" even if $\delta = 0$, just as in the supergame with $\delta = 0$. But in the case $\delta = 0$, this equilibrium is not the limit of discrete-but-more-rapid equilibrium play. What justifies this particular equilibrium in the case $\delta > 0$ is that it is the limit of discrete equilibria. We shall return to this point after we discuss the case of two-sided uncertainty.)

Now consider the continuous-time game where there is uncertainty on both sides. The formulation is as above, but now there is uncertainty (at the outset) about the entrant's payoffs as a function of the realizations of e and f. We are looking for an equilibrium with the following characteristics: (1) The strong monopolist always fights. (2) The strong entrant always enters. (3) By virtue of (1), if the monopolist ever declines to fight an entry, it is revealed as weak. Thereafter, the entrant always enters and the weak monopolist always acquiesces. (4) By virtue of (2), if the entrant ever fails to enter it is revealed as weak. Assuming that the monopolist has not previously been revealed as weak, the game proceeds as above, with the weak entrant staying out until the end and the monopolist always ready to fight.

Just as in the discrete time formulation, an equilibrium with these features can be recast as an equilibrium in "stopping rules" for the weak entrant and monopolist – each choosing the date at which it will "give in" if its opponent has not given in yet. If the entrant gives in first (at date t), then regime (4) above takes effect, with the weak monopolist obtaining at for the rest of the game, and the weak entrant receiving 0. If the monopolist gives in first at t, regime (3) ensues, with the weak entrant receiving bt and the weak monopolist receiving 0. Until one side or the other gives in, the weak monopolist receives -1 per unit of time, and the weak entrant receives $b - 1$ per unit of time. The equilibrium condition is that each player's stopping time should be optimal given the probability distribution of the other's, and given the assumption that the other player, if strong, will never give in. This game is very similar to the "war of attrition" game; cf. Riley [16] and Milgrom and Weber [14]. It is formally equivalent to a two-person competitive auction, where the stopping times are reinterpreted as bids. This observation will be especially useful later when we discuss the connection between this continuous-time formulation and the discrete-time formulation of the game. (We are indebted to Paul Milgrom for acquainting us with the "war of attrition" and for pointing out the relevance of his work with Weber.)

It is easiest and most illustrative to present the equilibrium using a diagram similar to Figure 4. In Figure 5 we have the "state space" of this game – the unit square, interpreted exactly as in Figure 4. The bottom boundary is where the entrant is known to be weak. Along this boundary (excluding the left-hand endpoint) the weak monopolist's payoff function (at date t) is $v_t(p, 0) = at$ and the weak entrant's is $u_t(p, 0) = 0$. The left-hand boundary is where the monopolist is known to be weak – here (including the bottom endpoint) $v_t(0, q) = 0$ and $u_t(0, q) = bt$.

The nature of the equilibrium is just as in the discrete case: The state space is divided into two regions by a curve $f(p, q) = 0$ that passes through the points $(0, 0)$ and $(1, 1)$. If the initial data of the game place us in region I, then the game begins with the entrant entering for sure and the monopolist (if weak) randomizing between fighting and immediate capitulation. This randomization is such that if the monopolist does fight at time T, the entrant revises its assessment that the monopolist is strong so as to go to the curve $f(p, q) = 0$. From region II it is the (weak) entrant that randomizes between immediate capitulation and entry – if it does enter, the monopolist revises its assessment that the entrant is strong up to a point where the curve $f(p, q)$ is reached. Thereafter, the weak monopolist and weak entrant randomize "continuously" between keeping up the fight and capitulating – this is done in a fashion so that as long as they continue to fight, the Bayesian reassessments of each side that the other is strong causes (p_t, q_t) to slide up along the curve toward $(1, 1)$. (Of course, if one side or the other capitulates, transition is made to the appropriate boundary.) There is a time $T^0 > 0$ such that by this time, one side or the other (if weak) has given in with probability one – if both sides are strong, at this time the point $(1, 1)$ has been reached, and we remain there until time $t = 0$.

The difference between this equilibrium and the one for the discrete time game (and the reason that this one is so much easier to compute) is that the curve $f(p, q) = 0$ does not change with t in the continuous-time case. This is so because in the continuous-time version of the game, a game of duration $T/2$ is strategically equivalent to a game

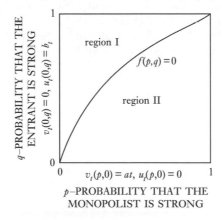

Figure 5   State space of the continuous-time game

of duration T, so long as the priors (δ, γ) are the same. All that changes is that everything takes place twice as rapidly – we could as well think of the game taking place at the same speed but for half the stakes. The values are half as large, but nothing else changes.

We now present a heuristic derivation of the equilibrium, assuming that it has the form outlined above. Note first that along the curve the value functions for each side must be identically zero. This is so because (by hypothesis) both sides are randomizing continuously, and one outcome of these randomizations transfers them to points (the lower boundary for the entrant and the left-hand boundary for the monopolist) where the value function is zero. Let $\pi_t(p_t, q_t)$ and $p_t(p_t, q_t)$ be the hazard rate functions associated with the weak monopolist's and entrant's randomizations at time t with posteriors p_t and q_t lying along the curve. That is, in the time interval $(t, t - h)$ there is (up to terms of order $o(h)$) probability $(1 - p_t)\pi_t(p_t, q_t)h$ that the monopolist will give in, and $(1 - q_t)\rho_t(p_t, q_t)h$ that the entrant will give in. Assuming sufficient continuity, if the value functions are to be constant (and zero) along the curve, it is necessary that the expected change in value to the weak monopolist be zero. Up to terms of order $O(h)$, this is

$$-h + [(1 - q_t)\rho_t(p_t, q_t)h][at] = O(h)$$

That is, the weak monopolist's immediate cost $-h$ of keeping up the bluff should be offset by the small chance $(1 - q_t)\rho_t(p_t, q_t)h$ that the entrant will give in multiplied by the large gain at that will accrue in this event. The analogous argument for the entrant gives

$$(b - 1)h + (1 - p_t)\pi_t(p_t, q_t)hbt = O(h)$$

Dividing by h and passing to the limit, we get

$$\rho_t(p_t, q_t) = 1/(at(1 - q_t)) \quad \text{and} \quad \pi_t(p_t, q_t) = (1 - b)/(bt(1 - p_t))$$

Consider next the evolution of the posteriors p_t and q_t. The probability table that the monopolist would construct at date t for the joint probability distribution that the entrant is weak or not and will give in or not in the interval $(t, t - h)$ is given in Table 2 (up to terms of order $O(h)$). Thus the conditional probability that the entrant is strong, conditional on not giving in over the interval $(t, t - h)$, is

$$q_{t-h} = q_t/[1 - (1 - q_t)\rho_t(p_t, q_t)h]$$

Thus, ignoring terms of order $O(h)$,

$$(q_t - q_{t-h})/h = q_t(1 - q_t)\rho_t(p_t, q_t)$$

Passing to the limit, this gives $\dot{q}_t = (q_t - q_t^2)\rho_t(p_t, q_t) = q_t/(at)$. Similarly $\dot{p}_t = p_t(1 - b)/(bt)$. Thus along the curve we must have

$$dq_t/dp_t = (q_t b)/((1 - b)ap_t)$$

Table 2

	weak	strong	
give in	$(1 - q_t)\rho_t\,(p_t,q_t)h$	0	$(1 - q_t)\rho_t\,(p_t,q_t)h$
not	$(1 - q_t)(1 - \rho_t\,(p_t,q_t)h)$	q_t	$1 - (1 - q_t)\rho_t\,(p_t,q_t)h$
	$(1 - q_t)$	q_t	

This is independent of t, and it is easily integrated to give $q_t = k(p_t)^c$ where k is a constant of integration and $c = b/((1 - b)a)$. To ensure that $(1, 1)$ is on the curve, we must have $k = 1$. Therefore the curve is given by

$$f(p, q) \equiv q^{(1-b)/b} - p^{1/a} = 0$$

(Note well the normalization of k so that $(1, 1)$ is on the curve. This will be important later on.)

We can solve similarly for q_t and p_t. Integrating $\dot{q}_t = q_t/(at)$ yields $q_t = k't^{-1/a}$. Analogously, $p_t = k''t^{-(1-b)/b}$. The constants k' and k'' are determined by the initial conditions. Suppose, for example, that we initially have a prior (δ, γ) that lies in region II. Then the initial randomization is by the weak entrant and yields posterior $q_T = \delta^c$ if the entrant does enter. Solving for k' yields $k' = \delta^c T^{1/a}$. Solving for k'' yields $k'' = \delta T^{(1-b)/b}$. Thus

$$p_t = \delta(T/t)^{(1-b)/b} \quad \text{and} \quad q_t = \delta^c(T/t)^{1/a}$$

Note that these yield $p_t = 1$ and $q_t = 1$ for $t = T\delta^{ac} = T\delta^{b/(1-b)}$. (Of course, both p_t and q_t hit one simultaneously as the curve has been normalized to pass through $(1, 1)$.) The point to note here is that in this equilibrium, the posterior $(1, 1)$ will be reached at a time T^0 strictly between T and 0 (unless $\delta = 0$ or 1) so long as neither player gives in previously. But of course, the posterior $(1, 1)$ can only be reached if with probability one both of the weak players would have given in. So, according to this equilibrium, if the two players are both strong, they will learn this before the game terminates. Put another way, the date T^0 previously referred to is $\delta^{b/(1-b)}T$ (for (δ, γ) in region II). The formulae change somewhat for (δ, γ) in region I, but the qualitative conclusions are the same.

Does this heuristic derivation hold up? That is, do we really have an equilibrium? There are two things to worry about. First, in several places the heuristic arguments that we give depend somewhat on sufficient regularity of the functions π_t and ρ_t. The reader can make these arguments rigorous for the functions that we derived. Second (and more substantially), the necessary conditions that were developed for π_t and ρ_t were necessary for the value functions to be *constant* along the curve. To have an equilibrium we require somewhat more: The value functions must be identically *zero* along this curve. This is where the normalization of the curve comes in: At the point $(1, 1)$, the value functions are clearly zero for each weak player, as each is certain that the other is strong. Put another way, suppose (once the curve is reached) that one side or the other is weak and decides *not* to randomize but simply to wait out its opponent. The conditions that gave us π_t and ρ_t

ensure that the change in expected value is zero as this goes on. (For the technically minded, apply Dynkin's formula to the appropriate generalized Poisson process.) And at date $T0$, if nothing has happened the player that is waiting *knows* that its opponent is strong – it should immediately give in for a value of zero. Thus the value all along the curve is zero. This, with a little careful argument, suffices to show that we really do have an equilibrium.

Two final comments about this equilibrium seem in order. First, the value functions to each (weak) player are easily computed. In region II, they are $u_T(\delta, \gamma) = 0$ and $\nu_T(\delta, \gamma) = [(\delta^c - \gamma)/\delta^c]aT$; in region I, they are $u_T(\delta, \gamma) = [(\gamma^{1/c} - \delta)/\gamma^{1/c}]bT$ and $\nu_T(\delta, \gamma) = 0$. That is, they are simple linear interpolates of the value of zero along the curve and the values along the bottom boundary in region II and the left-hand boundary in region I.

Second, we noted earlier that the continuous-time formulation can introduce equilibria that are not limits of the equilibria for discrete-time models. We should like to know that the continuous-time equilibrium just presented is indeed the limit of the discrete-time equilibrium with which we began this section. We have not checked all the details, but we are quite sure that this is so. To see this, recall that the discrete time game can be posed as an optimal stopping problem where the entrant is limited to stopping at, say, discrete times $T, (TK - 1)/K, \ldots, 1/K$ and the monopolist is limited to stopping at times (say) $T - 1/(2K), (TK - 3/2)/K \ldots, 1/(2K))$. The continuous-time problem is one where stopping at any time $t \in [T, 0]$ is possible. It is easy to move from the discrete-to-continuous-time versions of the problem when there is one-sided uncertainty, so we know that we have convergence of the value of "stopping" at particular times. As K goes to infinity, the sets of available strategies also converge, and the methods of Milgrom and Weber [14] apply to show convergence of the equilibria of the discrete games to the continuous-time version. (Indeed, Paul Milgrom has shown us how, by viewing the continuous-time game as a game in distributional strategies, it is simple to derive the equilibrium given above.)

Before concluding this section, we also note that this gives just one sort of formulation of the problem with two-sided uncertainty. We might consider what happens when a single monopolist plays against a succession of different entrants (each of whom plays the game once), where the monopolist is uncertain of the entrants' payoffs. In such a game we would have to specify the way in which the entrants' payoffs are related – they might all be identical (perfectly correlated, from the point of view of the monopolist), or they might be independently and identically distributed, or something between these two extremes. Both of these extreme cases are analyzed in detail in Kreps and Wilson [8]. The case of identical entrants gives the most interesting comparison with the model analyzed above: With identical entrants who only play the game once, the first entrant nearly always "tells the truth" by refusing to enter if weak, and the weak monopolist will with substantial probability fight the first few entries, just to keep the weak entrants "honest." What this illustrates is that the game of "chicken" that we see above requires *both* two-sided uncertainty *and* that each side has a stake in maintaining its reputation. When it is only one side that will participate in many stages, the other has little motivation to dissemble and will not fight too hard to attain/maintain its reputation. (Another interesting formulation of the problem is where there is a population of entrants and a population of monopolists, and in each round there is a random assignment of one monopolist to one entrant, in the manner of Rosenthal [18] and Rosenthal and Landau [19]. We have done no analysis of this formulation.)

5. Discussion

We have presented these simple examples to illustrate formally the power of "reputation" in finitely repeated games. That reputation is powerful in reality is very well appreciated: In the context of Industrial Organization, recall the quotation from Scherer in section 1. Consider the importance of reputation in contract and labor negotiations; in a firm's employment practices; in a firm's "good name" for its product; in the maintenance of a cartel (or in the prisoners' dilemma game); in international diplomacy. To each of these contexts, our analytical structure can be applied to yield the conclusions: If the situation is repeated, so that it is worthwhile to maintain or acquire a reputation, and if there is some uncertainty about the motivations of one or more of the players, then that uncertainty can substantially affect the play of the game. There need not be much uncertainty for this to happen. The power of the reputation effect depends on the nature of one's opponents; notably on whether they also seek to acquire a reputation.

Phenomena that bear the interpretation of "reputation" are not entirely new to the literature of formal game theory. They are implicit in much of the literature on super-games, where the stage game is repeated infinitely often, or where there is always high enough probability of at least one more repetition (Rubinstein [20] is a representative citation). Indeed, Dybvig and Spatt [6] make explicit use of the reputation interpretation in a super-game context. What is new in this paper (and in Milgrom and Roberts [13]) is the observation that with a very little imperfect information, these effects come alive in finitely repeated games. Comparing the two approaches is difficult, but it is worth noting that in the models reported here, the problem of multiplicity of equilibria that plagues the super-game literature is substantially alleviated. Also, we believe that we have interesting models of the sorts of "wars" that might go on between players to see which equilibrium will ensue. But we are far from ready to make a very informed comparison of the two approaches – at this point, we can only claim that this seems to be an interesting alternative way to produce reputation effects.

A point made briefly in section 3 is worth repeating here. To keep matters simple, we posited the simplest type of uncertainty: Players are uncertain about the payoffs of their fellows. But it does nearly as well if there is no uncertainty about players' payoffs, but there is uncertainty about whether this is so. In the parlance of game theory, for these effects to disappear, payoffs must be common knowledge. (Milgrom and Roberts [13] present formal models to back up this contention.) This is a very strong assumption for any real-life application.

The reader may object that in order to obtain the reputation effect, we have loaded the deck. That is, we have a model where reputation is easily shattered, making it all the more valuable; there are at most two types of each player; and each player has only two possible actions. To the first of these criticisms we plead guilty: The power of reputation seems to be positively related to its fragility. As for the second, the models of Milgrom and Roberts [13] have continua of types of monopolists, so this does not seem crucial to our conclusions. And to the third, we do admit that this has made it easy for us to get a "pooling equilibrium" (to borrow a term from the insurance literature), where one type successfully mimics another. The analysis of Milgrom and Roberts [12] shows that with a continuum of actions, one can also get screening equilibria in these sorts of models. But this is not necessary: Crawford and Sobel [3] investigate a class of models with a continua of actions where some pooling is necessary in any equilibrium. The assumption of only two actions makes things easier for us, but we doubt that it is crucial.

What is evident from our simple examples is that a very little uncertainty "destabilizes" game-theoretic analysis in games with a fairly large number of stages. The reader may suspect that something more is true: By cleverly choosing the nature of that small uncertainty (precisely – its support), one can get out of a game-theoretic analysis whatever one wishes. We have no formal proposition of this sort to present at this time, but we certainly share these suspicions. If this is so, then the game-theoretic analysis of this type of game comes down eventually to how one picks the initial incomplete information. And nothing in the *theory* of games will help one to do this.

This reinforces a point made by Rosenthal [17]. Rosenthal investigates the original chain-store game and makes the point with which we began: The paradoxical result in Selten's analysis is due to the complete and perfect information formulation that Selten uses. In a more realistic formulation of the game, the intuitive outcome will be predicted by the game-theoretic analysis. Rosenthal does not provide this analysis, despairing of the analyst's ability to solve an adequate formulation. Instead, he suggests an analysis using the paradigm of Decision Analysis, where one tries to assess *directly* how the entrants will respond to early round fighting by the monopolist. Such an analysis can certainly lead to the intuitive outcome, as shown by Macgregor [11]. But, as Rosenthal notes, the weakness in this approach is the *ad hoc* assessment of entrants' behavior. We have carried out a game-theoretic analysis of *one* very simple incomplete information formulation. We therefore have avoided *ad hoc* assumptions about the entrant's behavior. But we have made *ad hoc* assumptions about their information, and we have found that small changes in those assumptions greatly influence the play of the game. So at some level, analysis of this sort of situation may require *ad hoc* assumptions.

We have presented models in this paper that demonstrate the reputation effect as simply and as powerfully as possible. In order to do this, we have not tried to model realistic settings from Industrial Organization or some other economic context. (Milgrom and Roberts [13] rectify this deficiency: They concentrate somewhat more on the application of these ideas.) To illustrate how these ideas might be applied, we close with two examples.

The first concerns the problem of entry deterrence, especially the papers of Spence [26] and Dixit [4, 5]. These papers take the basic framework of Bain [1] and Sylos-Labini [27] and ask: What can the monopolist do prior to the entrant's decision point to make predation optimal in the short run? (The answers they give include such things as expanded capacity, sales networks, etc.) The relevance of this question is that the *threat* of predation is only credible if predation is *ex post* the optimal response, so the monopolist must make it so in order to forestall entry. What our model suggests (and what can be demonstrated formally) is that in repeated play situations, the actions taken by the monopolist need not make predation actually ex post optimal – what they must do is to make predation *possible* and, perhaps, increase the probability assessed by the entrants that it is *ex post* optimal. If deterrence is the objective, the appearance and not the reality of *ex post* optimal predation may be what is important.

The second context is that of a monopolist producer of a durable capital good where, for whatever reason, the monopolist is unable to maintain a rental market but must sell outright his product. In a multiperiod setting, where the monopolist is assumed to be sequentially optimizing, this can severely diminish the monopolist's market power. (See Bulow [2] and Stokey [25].) Supposing the monopolist produces subject to a capacity constraint, the monopolist is often *better off* with a tighter constraint. This is because the constraint prevents the monopolist from "over-producing." Then, if that constraint is the matter of private information for the monopolist, a monopolist with a loose constraint can successfully (in an equilibrium) masquerade as having a more stringent constraint, thereby recouping some of his lost market power. In essence, as the number of periods goes to infinity (as one comes closer to a continuous-time formulation), the monopolist can successfully attain the reputation of a "low capacity" producer even if his capacity is (with probability approaching one) high. Moorthy [15] presents an example along these lines.

References

1 Bain, J. S. (1956): "Barriers to New Competition," Harvard University Press, Cambridge, Mass.

2 Bulow, J. (1982): "Durable Goods Monopolists," *Journal of Political Economy*, 90(2), April, 314–22.

3 Crawford, V. and Sobel, J. (1981): "Stategic Information Transmission," University of California at San Diego, mimeo.

4 Dixit, A. (1979): "A Model of Duopoly Suggesting a Theory of Entry Barriers," *Bell Journal of Economics* 10, 20–32.

5 Dixit, A. (1980): "The Role of Investment in Entry-Deterence," *Economic Journal* 90, 95–106.

6 Dybvig, P. and Spatt, C. (1980): "Does it Pay to Maintain a Reputation?" Financial Center Memorandum No. 32, Princeton University.

7 Harsanyi, J. (1967–1968): "Games with Incomplete Information Played by Bayesian Players, Parts I, II, and III," *Management Science* 14, 159–82, 320–34, 486–502.

8 Kreps, D. and Wilson, R. (1981): "On the Chain-Store Paradox and Predation: Reputation for Toughness," Stanford University Graduate School of Business Research Paper No. 551.

9 Kreps, D. and Wilson, R. (1982): "Sequential Equilibria," *Econometrica*, 50.

10 Kuhn, H. (1953): "Extensive Games and the Problem of Information," in H. Kuhn and A. Tucker (eds), *Contributions to the Theory of Games*, Vol. 2, 193–216, Princeton University Press, Princeton, N.J.

11 Macgregor, M. (1979): "A resolution of the Chain-store Paradox," University of California at Berkeley, mimeo.

12 Milgrom, P. and Roberts, J. (1982): "Limit Pricing and Entry under Incomplete Information: An Equilibrium Analysis," *Econometrica*, 50, 443–60.

13 Milgrom, P. and Roberts, J. (1982): "Predation, Reputation, and Entry Deterrence," *Journal of Economic Theory*, 27, 280–312.

14 Milgrom, P. and Weber, R. (1980): "Distributional Strategies for Games with Incomplete Information." Northwestern University Graduate School of Management, mimeo.

15 Moorthy, S. (1980): "The Pablo Picasso Problem," Stanford University Graduate School of Business, mimeo.

16 Riley, S. (1980): "Strong Evolutionary Equilibria and the War of Attrition," *Journal of Theoretical Biology*, 82.

17 Rosenthal, R. W. (1981): "Games of Perfect Information, Predatory Pricing and the Chain-store Paradox," *Journal of Economic Theory*, 25, 92–100.

18 Rosenthal, R. W. (1979): "Sequences of Games with Varying Opponents," *Econometrica*, 47, 1353–66.

19 Rosenthal, R. W. and Landau, H. J. (1979): "A Game-Theoretic Analysis of Bargaining with Reputations," Bell Telephone Laboratories, mimeo.

20 Rubinstein, A. (1979): "Strong Perfect Equilibrium in Supergames," *International Journal of Game Theory*, 9, 1–12.

21 Scherer, F. (1980): *Industrial Market Structure and Economic Performance*, 2nd edn, Rand McNally College Publishing Company, Chicago.

22 Selten, R. (1965): "Spieltheoretische behandlung eines oligopolmodells mit nachfragetragheit," *Z. Staatswissenschaft*, 121.

23 Selten, R. (1975): "Reexamination of the Perfectness Concept for Equilibrium Points in Extensive Games," *International Journal of Game Theory*, 4, 25–55.

24 Selten, R. (1978): "The Chain-Store Paradox," *Theory and Decision*, 9, 127–59.

25 Stokey, N. (1979): "Self-fulfilling Expectations, Rational Expectations, and Durable Goods Pricing," Northwestern University, mimeo.

26 Spence, A. M. (1977): "Entry, Capacity, Investment and Oligopolistic Pricing," *Bell Journal of Economics*, 8, 534–44.

27 Sylos-Labini, P. (1962): *Oligopoly and Technical Progress*, trans. E. Henderson, Harvard University Press, Cambridge, Mass.

CHAPTER TWENTY-ONE

Limit Pricing and Entry under Incomplete Information: An Equilibrium Analysis

PAUL MILGROM AND JOHN ROBERTS

Source: *Econometrica*, 1982, 50, 443–60.

Limit pricing involves charging prices below the monopoly price to make new entry appear unattractive. If the entrant is a rational decision maker with complete information, pre-entry prices will not influence its entry decision, so the established firm has no incentive to practice limit pricing. However, if the established firm has private, payoff relevant information (e.g., about costs), then prices can signal that information, so limit pricing can arise in equilibrium. The probability that entry actually occurs in such an equilibrium, however, can be lower, the same, or even higher than in a regime of complete information (where no limit pricing would occur).

1. Introduction

The basic idea of limit pricing is that an established firm may be able to influence, through its current pricing policy alone,[1] other firms' perceptions of the profitability of entering the firm's markets, and that the firm may thus set its prices below their short-run maximizing levels in order to deter entry. As such, limit pricing has constituted a major theme in the industrial organization literature for at least the last thirty years, and during the past decade in particular it has been the subject of a number of papers employing formal models of maximizing behavior.[2] For the most part, these latter analyses have concentrated on the decision problem of the established firm, taking as given the limit-pricing assumption that a lower pre-entry price will deter or restrict entry. In this context, the typical conclusion is that an optimal price-output policy in the face of threatened entry will involve prices which are below the short-run monopoly level, but still above the level that would prevail after entry. This conclusion had led to some debate as to the appropriate public policy regarding such limit pricing, since there appears to be a tradeoff between the benefits to society of lower pre-entry prices and the costs arising from entry being limited or deterred.

In this paper we present a re-examination of the limit pricing problem. Our model differs from most of the existing literature in that we treat both the established firm and potential entrant as rational, maximizing economic agents. This naturally leads to a game-theoretic, equilibrium formulation. However, once one adopts this approach, it is not immediately obvious why limit pricing should emerge at all.

This point has been made explicitly by J. Friedman [3] in one of the few existing game-theoretic treatments of pricing in the face of potential entry of which we are aware. Friedman notes that, under the usual sort of assumptions on demand, the profits which would accrue should entry occur are completely independent of the pre-entry price. Since in Friedman's model both the established firm and the entrant are completely informed as to demand and cost conditions, these post-entry profits are fully known when the entry decision is made. Then the inescapable logic of (perfect) equilibrium (Selten [19]) requires that the entry decision be independent of the pre-entry price. This means that any attempt at limit pricing would serve only to squander pre-entry profits and so there would be no limit pricing.

Friedman's argument will be generally valid in any complete-information, game-theoretic model in which the established firm's pre-entry actions do not influence post-entry costs and demand. In such a model, then, the intuitive idea underlying the traditional concept of limit pricing – that potential entrants would read the pre-entry price as a signal concerning the price and market shares they can expect to prevail after entry – finds no formal justification. In contrast, a formalization of this intuition is the very heart of our model.

Specifically, we consider situations in which neither the established firm nor the potential entrant is perfectly informed as to some characteristic of the other which is relevant to the post-entry profits of both. The central example of such a characteristic, and the one on which we initially concentrate, is the other firm's unit costs. In such a situation, the pre-entry price may become a signal regarding the established firm's costs, which in turn are a determinant of the post-entry price and profits for the entrant. Thus the relationship assumed in the earlier literature emerges endogenously in equilibrium in our model: a lower price (by signaling lower costs) tends to discourage entry. Thus, too, limit-pricing behavior arises in equilibrium, with the established firm attempting to influence the entry decision by charging a pre-entry price which is below the simple monopoly level.

The entrant, meanwhile, will seek to infer the established firm's costs (and thus the profitability of entry) from observation of the pre-entry price. In making this inference, of course, it will have to employ some conjecture regarding the established firm's pricing policy, i.e., the relationship between the established firm's cost and the price it charges. In Nash equilibrium, this conjecture must be correct. Indeed the very definition of equilibrium in this context involves rational expectations by each firm about the other's behavior. Thus, the entrant will allow for limit pricing in making its inferences and its entry decision.

Thus, in equilibrium, the established firm practices limit pricing, but the entrant is not fooled by this strategy. Consequently, the probability that entry actually occurs in equilibrium need not be any lower than it would be in a world of full information, where limit pricing would not arise. Indeed, the probability of entry in the limit pricing equilibrium may even be higher than with complete information, even though the pre-entry price is lower. In particular, this means that the alleged tradeoff for society between lower prices and delayed or deterred entry may never arise.

In the next section, we illustrate these claims in the context of a simple model with linear demand and constant unit costs. In this model we compute equilibria for two specific examples. One of these involves only two possible levels of costs for the entrants and for the established firm: the other involves a continuum of possibilities on each side. In section 3 we consider a more general model. The final section contains our conclusions.

2. Two Examples

Consider the market for a homogeneous good in which there is an established firm, denoted firm 1, and a potential entrant, firm 2. Initially, each firm knows its own unit cost, $c_i, i = 1, 2$, but it does not know the other firm's cost level. Firm 1 is a monopolist, and it must pick a quantity Q to produce (or a price to charge) as a monopolist, given its knowledge of c_1 and its beliefs about c_2. Firm 2 will observe this choice and then (knowing c_2 but not c_1) must either enter the market or decide to stay out. If it enters, it incurs an entry cost of K, each firm learns the other's cost, and then the two firms operate as Cournot duopolists. If it does not enter, firm 1 will henceforth enjoy its monopoly profits without further fear of entry.

We summarize the notation and profit formulae with linear demand and constant unit costs in Table 1. To simplify the payoff formulae, we normalize the post-entry profits of the established firm to be zero if entry occurs, so it receives only its first period profit as its payoff in this event. If entry does not occur, its payoff is its first period profit plus the discounted value of a reward to deterring entry. This reward is equal to the excess of its monopoly profit over its profit as a Cournot duopolist.

The extensive form game corresponding to this set-up is one of incomplete information, since the players do not know the numerical values of the payoffs corresponding to any pair of decisions they make. Attempting to analyze such a game directly would easily lead one into a morass of infinite regress. The approach we adopt instead is that proposed by Harsanyi [6], which involves replacing this *incomplete* information game by a game of *complete* but *imperfect* information.[3] One then treats the Nash equilibria of this second game as the equilibria of the original game.

The imperfect information game involves another player, "Nature," which is indifferent over all possible outcomes. Nature moves first and selects c_1 and c_2 according to the probability distributions, H_i, giving the players' beliefs. Then player i is informed about c_i but not about c_j, and for each realization of c_1 and c_2 the game tree unfolds as above.

Table 1

Present value to i of \$1 accruing after entry	δ_i
Unit production cost of firm i	c_i
Fixed cost of entry for firm 2	K
Inverse demand	$P = a - bQ$
Simple monopoly output	$m(c_1) = (a - c_1)/2b$
First period profit for firm 1	$\Pi_1^0(Q, c_1) = (a - bQ - c_1)Q$
Monopoly profit for firm 1	$\Pi_1^M(c_1) = (a - c_1)^2/4b$
Cournot profit for firm i	$\Pi_i^C(c_1, c_2) = (a - 2c_i + c_j)^2/9b$
Reward to firm 1 from deterring entry	$R(c_1, c_2) = \Pi_1^M(c_1) - \Pi_1^C(c_1, c_2)$
Payoff to 1 if entry occurs	$\Pi_1^0(Q, c_1)$
Payoff to 1 if no entry	$\Pi_1^0(Q, c_1) + \delta_1 R(c_1, c_2)$
Payoff to 2 if entry	$\delta_2 \Pi_2^C(c_1, c_2) - K$
Payoff to 2 if no entry	0
Range of possible c_i values	$[\underline{c}_i, \bar{c}_i]$
Probability distribution function for c_i (j's beliefs about c_i)	H_i

In any extensive form game, a player's strategy is a specification of the action it will take in any information set, i.e., the player's actions at any point can depend only on what it knows at that point. Here, the information sets for firm 1 are defined by the realized values of c_1 (given by "Nature's move") and those for firm 2 by a realization of c_2 and a choice of Q by firm 1. Thus, a (pure) strategy for 1 is a map s from its possible cost levels into the possible choices of Q and a (pure) strategy for 2 is a map t from $\mathbb{R}^2$ into $\{0, 1\}$ giving its decision for each possible pair (c_2, Q), where we interpret 1 as "enter" and 0 as "stay out."

A pair of strategies constitutes an equilibrium if each maximizes the expected payoff of the player using it, given that the other is using its specified strategy. This is the standard Nash equilibrium notion. However, to accentuate the rational expectations character of Nash equilibrium, it is helpful to use the following, equivalent definition. An equilibrium consists of a pair of strategies (s^*, t^*) and a pair of conjectures $(\bar{s}, \bar{t})$ such that (i) firm 1's pricing policy s^* is a best response to its conjectures $\bar{t}$ about firm 2's entry rule, (ii) the strategy t^* is a best response for firm 2 to its conjecture $\bar{s}$, and (iii) the actual and conjectured strategies coincide. We formalize these conditions as follows: (i) for any $c_1 \in [\underline{c}_1, \bar{c}_1]$ and any $s : [\underline{c}_1, \bar{c}_1] \to \mathbb{R}_+$,

$$\Pi^0(s*(c_1), c_1) + \delta_1 \int_{\underline{c}_2}^{\bar{c}_2} R(c_1, c_2)[1 - \bar{t}(c_2, s^*(c_1))]dH_2(c_2)$$

$$\geqq \Pi^0(s(c_1), c_1) + \delta_1 \int_{\underline{c}_2}^{\bar{c}_2} R(c_1, c_2)[1 - \bar{t}(c_2, s(c_1))]dH_2(c_2)$$

(ii) for any $c_2 \in [\underline{c}_2, \bar{c}_2]$ and any $t : [\underline{c}_2, \bar{c}_2] \times \mathbb{R}_+ \to \{0, 1\}$,

$$\int_{\underline{c}_1}^{\bar{c}_1} \left[\delta_2 \Pi_2^C(c_1, c_2) - K\right] t^*(c_2, \bar{s}(c_1)) dH_1(c_1)$$

$$\geq \int_{\underline{c}_1}^{\bar{c}_1} \left[\delta_2 \Pi_2^C(c_1, c_2) - K\right] t(c_2, \bar{s}(c_1)) dH_1(c_1)$$

(iii) $(s^*, t^*) \overset{\bullet}{=} (\bar{s}, \bar{t})$.

Given this framework, we first study a parameterized family of examples where the H_i are two-point distributions and, for specific values of the parameters, compute equilibria. Later in this section we will allow for a continuum of possible cost levels ("types") for the two firms.

Thus, suppose that the demand curve is $P = 10 - Q$, that $K = 7$, that $\underline{c}_1 = 0.5, \underline{c}_2 = 1.5, \bar{c}_1 = \bar{c}_2 = 2.0$, that $\delta_1 = \delta_2 = 1$, and that the costs are independently distributed with $H_2(c_2 = \bar{c}_2) = p = 1 - H_2(c_2 = \underline{c}_2)$ and $H_1(c_1 = \bar{c}_1) = q = 1 - H_1(c_1 = \underline{c}_1)$.

With these specifications, the payoffs are as follows:

$$R(\underline{c}_1, \underline{c}_2) = 10.31 \qquad\qquad \Pi_2^C(\underline{c}_1, \underline{c}_2) - K = -0.75$$

$$R(\underline{c}_1, \bar{c}_2) = 9.12 \qquad\qquad \Pi_2^C(\underline{c}_1, \bar{c}^2) - K = -2.31$$

$$R(\bar{c}_1, \underline{c}_2) = 9.75 \qquad\qquad \Pi_2^C(\bar{c}_1, \underline{c}_2) - K = 2.00$$

$$R(\bar{c}_1, \bar{c}_2) = 8.89 \qquad\qquad \Pi_2^C(\bar{c}_1, \bar{c}_2) - K = 0.11$$

$$m(\underline{c}_1) = 4.75 \qquad\qquad \Pi_1^M(\underline{c}_1) = 22.56$$

$$m(\bar{c}_1) = 4.00 \qquad\qquad \Pi_1^M(\bar{c}_1) = 16.00$$

Note that if 1's costs were known to be $\underline{c}_1$, neither type of potential entrant would want to enter, while if c_1 were known to be $\bar{c}_1$, both would want to enter. Thus, the probability of entry, if the entrant were to be directly informed of the realized value of c_1, is simply q, the probability that $c_1 = \bar{c}_1$. Of course, if firm 2 were so informed, there would be no point to limit pricing and Q would simply be set at the short-run profit-maximizing level of $m(c_1)$.

Note, too, that if firm 2 were unable to observe Q and were uninformed about c_1, then it would want to enter if its expected profits were positive, i.e., if $q\Pi_2^C(\bar{c}_1, c_2) + (1-q)\Pi_2^C(\underline{c}_1, c_2) - K \geq 0$. If $0.954 > q > 0.273$, then this inequality holds for $\underline{c}_2$ and not for $\bar{c}_2$, so the low cost entrant would come in and the high cost entrant would not. (For $q < 0.273$, neither would want to enter, and for $q > 0.954$, both would want to enter.)

In fact, if 2 is not directly informed about c_1 but can observe Q, it will attempt to make inferences about the actual value of c_1 from its observation of Q, using its conjectures about 1's behavior. Note that in equilibrium, the only values of Q which could be observed are $s^*(\underline{c}_1)$ and $s^*(\bar{c}_1)$. Now in this set-up there are only two possibilities: either $s^*(\underline{c}_1) = s^*(\bar{c}_1)$, or else the two values differ. An equilibrium with the first of these properties is called *pooling*, while in the other situation the equilibrium is *separating*. Thus, in pooling equilibrium, observing Q gives no information, while the observation of Q in a separating equilibrium allows the value of c_1 to be inferred exactly.

Thus, in a separating equilibrium (s^*, t^*), entry will occur if $s^*(\bar{c}_1)$ is observed and will not if $s^*(\underline{c}_1)$ is observed: *entry takes place in exactly the same circumstances as if the entrant had been informed about the value of c_1*, i.e., with prior probability q. Moreover, this will be true in any separating equilibrium of any model of this type: in any separating equilibrium, observing the equilibrium choice of the established firm allows a precise and accurate inference to be made about the firm's characteristic. Thus, in such an equilibrium, *limit pricing will not limit entry* relative to the complete information case (in which there would be no limit pricing because the possibility of influencing the entrant's decision does not arise).

In a pooling equilibrium, the entrant can infer nothing from observing Q and so enters if its expected profit is positive. Thus, as noted above, if $q \in (0.273, 0.954)$, only the low cost entrant will come in. Thus, in a pooling equilibrium, the probability of entry is $(1 - p)$, while in a separating equilibrium the probability of entry is q.

We now will show that, in this example, so long as p is not too small, there are both pooling and separating equilibria, that all equilibria involve limit pricing, and that the probability of entry in a pooling equilibrium may equal, exceed or fall short of that in a separating equilibrium (or, equivalently, under complete information).

First, we show that the following strategies constitute a separating equilibrium:

$$s^*(\underline{c}_1) = 7.2, \quad s^*(\bar{c}_1) = m(\bar{c}_1) = 4.0$$

$$t^*(c_2, Q) = \begin{cases} 1 & \text{if } Q < 7.2 \\ 0 & \text{otherwise} \end{cases}$$

Note that since $s^*(\underline{c}_1) > m(\underline{c}_1), s^*$ is a limit pricing strategy. Notice too that from our earlier discussion, t^* is clearly a best response to s^*. Thus, we need to check that s^* is optimal, given t^*. First, note that unless the high cost established firm produces at least 7.2, it cannot deter any entry. But, this level is high enough that it is not worthwhile for $\bar{c}_1$ to produce it, even though in so doing it would eliminate all entry. To see this, note that producing $Q = s^*(\underline{c}_1)$ yields the payoff

$$\Pi_1^0(\bar{c}_1, s^*(\underline{c}_1)) + pR(\bar{c}_1, \bar{c}_2) + (1 - p)R(\bar{c}_1, \underline{c}_2) = 15.51 - 0.86p$$

while producing $m(\bar{c}_1)$ yields $\Pi_1^0(\bar{c}_1, m(\bar{c}_1)) = 16$, which exceeds $15.51–0.86p$ for all $p \geqq 0$. Finally, note that the low cost firm has no reason to produce more than $s^*(\underline{c}_1)$. If it produces less, it is sure to face entry, and thus its best choice in this range would be

$m(\underline{c}_1)$. But $s^*(\underline{c}_1)$ yields an expected payoff of $26.87-1.19p$, which for all $p \leqq 1$ strictly exceeds the payoff $\Pi_1^M(\underline{c}_1) = 22.56$ from producing $m(\underline{c}_1)$. Thus, $s^*(\underline{c}_1)$ is also optimal.

We now demonstrate the existence of a pooling equilibrium given by

$$s^*(\underline{c}_1) = s^*(\bar{c}_1) = m(\underline{c}_1) = 4.75$$
$$t^*(\underline{c}_2, Q) = 1$$
$$t^*(\bar{c}_2, Q) = \begin{cases} 0 & \text{if } Q \geqq 4.75 \\ 1 & \text{otherwise} \end{cases}$$

Note again that our earlier discussion indicates that t^* is a best response to s^*, given $q \in (0.273, 0.954)$. Further, it is evident that s^* is optimal if $c_1 = \underline{c}_1$, since any increase in Q would not deter entry, and any decrease in output would both increase entry and reduce first period profits. Finally, if the established firm has $c_1 = \bar{c}_1$, it similarly has no incentive to increase output, while cutting output could at best yield the monopoly first period return, but would induce certain entry. This gives a payoff of 16.00, which is, for $p > 0.063$, less than its current return of $\Pi_1^0(\bar{c}_1, 4.75) + pR(\bar{c}_1, \bar{c}_2) = 15.44 + 8.89p$. Thus, if $p > 0.063$, this is also an equilibrium, and since $s^*(\bar{c}_1) > m(\bar{c}_1)$, it, too, involves limit pricing.

To summarize, our pooling equilibrium required that the probability p of the entrant having high costs exceed 0.063 and that q lie in (0.273, 0.954), while our separating equilibrium existed for all p and q. In a separating equilibrium, the probability of entry is q, which is just the probability that the established firm is of the high cost type, while in our pooling equilibrium, the probability of entry is $1 - p$, the probability of the entrant having low costs.[4] Clearly, we may have $1 - p$ greater than, less than, or equal to q and still meet the requirements for existence of both equilibria. *Limit pricing equilibria may involve less, the same, or more entry than occurs in the full information (no limit pricing) case.*

It is, of course, true in either type of equilibrium that if the limit-pricing firm were to charge a higher price than is called for by the equilibrium strategy, then it would face a greater threat of entry. This is because the entrant would interpret this high price as meaning that the firm's costs were higher than they in fact are, and thus entry would appear more attractive. (Note that the entrant's inferences will be correct only if firm 1 adheres to its equilibrium strategy.) Indeed, it is this balancing of foregone first period profits against the reward to deterring entry which characterizes the equilibrium and it is this threat of increased entry which leads the established firm to maintain its expanded output. Thus, in this sense, limit pricing does limit entry.

A useful way to think about these results is to consider limit pricing as the outcome of competition between the types of the established firm, with high cost types attempting to mimic low cost ones and low cost firms attempting to distinguish themselves from the high cost ones. Then whether a pooling or a separating equilibrium is established is a matter of whether it is the high or low cost type which is successful. This competition could, of course, be purely a conjectural one in the mind of the entrant, but it might also be more concrete. Specifically, one can imagine that there are a number of currently monopolized markets, all of which are identical except that a percentage p have high cost incumbents and the rest have low cost incumbents. There is also a limited supply of venture capital, which is available to an entrant whose costs are unknown a priori. Then the competition between types of established firms becomes real, with each established firm attempting to make entry into its market appear unattractive.[5]

The active role assigned to the entrant in this model and the corresponding significance of the beliefs and conjectures embodied in the entrant's strategy lead to the existence of a multiplicity of equilibria, both in this example and more generally. Our example actually has a continuum of both separating and pooling equilibria, where each class of equilibria is parameterized by the critical level of Q such that observation of a lower output than this level induces increased entry. In general, there is a large class of entrant's strategies t such that t and the best response to it constitute an equilibrium: many possible conjectures by the entrant as to the outcome of the competition among established firms are consistent with rational expectations. Thus, there is no unique limit price in these models.[6]

One way to attempt to narrow the set of equilibria is to place restrictions on the possible strategies for the entrant. For example, one could require that, conditional on observing *any* Q, the entrant assign probabilities to Q having been the choice of each type of established firm. Then one would require that, for each Q, $t^*(c_2, Q)$ be a best response, given these conjectures. This is the essence of the concept of sequential equilibrium due to David Kreps and Robert Wilson [10], and it is clearly in the spirit of the perfectness criterion for equilibria (Selten [19]).[7] However, as is easily verified, our equilibria already satisfy this condition, and still we have the unwanted multiplicity. Thus one might consider further restrictions on the entrant's conjectures. In particular, one might hypothesize that the entrant will not conjecture that the competition between types of established firm will be unnecessarily wasteful. This results in considering only those equilibria (s^*, t^*) for which there is no other equilibrium where the payoffs to the various types of established firms weakly dominate those under (s^*, t^*). The two particular equilibria we have identified here meet this condition. Other separating equilibria all involve $s^*(\bar{c}_1) = m(\bar{c}_1)$ and $s^*(\underline{c}_1) > 7.2$,[8] other pooling equilibria must involve lower payoffs for the low cost established firm,[9] and neither equilibrium dominates the other.

Although there are no equilibria in this example where $s^* \equiv m$, the monopoly output, this strategy could arise in equilibrium with other specifications of the parameters. This would happen if the profit to a high cost firm in producing its monopoly output and then facing certain entry exceeded its profits from producing the monopoly output of the low cost firm and then avoiding all entry. However, if there are a continuum of types (cost levels) possible for the established firm and the H_i are atomless, this cannot happen: at most only a set of firms of measure zero could produce their monopoly outputs in equilibrium.

Both to establish this claim and to explore more completely the nature of the limit pricing problem in a framework with less discontinuity, we now examine a specification of the model with a continuum of possible cost levels. Thus, suppose that the distribution of c_j is given by a continuous density function $h_j(c_j)$ which is positive on $[\underline{c}_j, \bar{c}_j]$. We will initially concentrate on separating equilibria.

Assume that 2 conjectures that 1 will play some strategy $\bar{s}$. Then, for any Q in the range of $\bar{s}$, the entrant's best response is to act as if $c_1 \in \bar{s}^{-1}(Q)$, and to enter if and only if the expected value of $\delta_2 \Pi_2^C(c_1, c_2) - K$, conditional on $c_1 \in \bar{s}^{-1}(Q)$, is positive. If $\bar{s}$ is monotone decreasing, then $\bar{s}^{-1}(Q)$ is a singleton and so 2 should enter if and only if

$c_2 \leq \gamma(\bar{s}^{-1}(Q))$, where $\gamma(c_1) \equiv (a + c_1 - 3\sqrt{bK})/2$ is the highest level of c_2 permitting successful entry against a firm with costs c_1. Thus, for $Q \in$ range $\bar{s}$, 2's best response satisfies

$$t(c_2, Q) = \begin{cases} 1 & \text{if } c_2 \leq \bar{g}(Q) \\ 0 & \text{otherwise} \end{cases}$$

where $\bar{g} = \gamma \circ \bar{s}^{-1}$.

Now, suppose that 1's conjecture is that t is of this general form, so that 2 will be deterred from entering if c_2 exceeds some value $g(Q)$. Then 1's expected payoff is

$$G(c_1, Q) = \Pi_1^0(c_1, Q) + \delta_1 \int_{g(Q)}^{\bar{c}_2} R(c_1, c_2) h_2(c_2) dc_2$$

Maximizing with respect to Q yields

$$0 = \frac{\partial \Pi_1^0}{\partial Q} - \delta_1 R(c_1, g(Q)) h_2(g(Q)) g'(Q)$$

But, in equilibrium, the conjectures must be correct (i.e., $\bar{s} = s^*, g = \gamma \circ s^{*-1}$), so we have that $s^*(c_1)$ must satisfy

$$0 = \frac{\partial \Pi_1^0(c_1, s^*(c_1))}{\partial Q} - \frac{\delta_1 R(c_1, \gamma(c_1)) h_2(\gamma(c_1)) \gamma'(c_1)}{ds^*(c_1)/dc_1} \tag{1}$$

Note that, so long as $R(c_1, \gamma(c_1)), h_2(\gamma(c_1))$, and $\gamma'(c_1)$ are positive and $ds^*/dc_1 < \infty$ (i.e., s^* is differentiable at c_1), then this first-order condition implies that $\partial \Pi_1^0/\partial Q < 0$. Thus, the simple monopoly solution $m(c_1)$, which is defined by $\partial \Pi_1^0/\partial Q = 0$, cannot arise in equilibrium. If the entrant were to conjecture $\bar{s} = m$ and respond optimally, then by increasing output slightly from $m(c_1)$ to, say, $m(c_1) + \varepsilon = \bar{s}(c_1')$, the established firm can eliminate the threat of entry from firms in the interval $(\gamma(c_1'), \gamma(c_1)]$. This increase in output has a first-order effect on Π_1^0 of zero, since $\partial \Pi_1^0/\partial Q = 0$ at $m(c_1)$, but a non-negligible first-order effect on the expected value of the reward to deterring entry. Thus, in any model of this type, so long as: (i) it is more profitable to be a monopolist than to share the market, (ii) beliefs are given by a positive density, and (iii) higher costs for the established firm encourage entry, essentially all established firms must be limit pricing in a separating equilibrium.

Of course, in such an equilibrium, s^* is invertible and so there is the same entry as if c_1 were known directly.

Now, to obtain an explicit solution for a particular specification, suppose that $\underline{c}_i = 0$ and that h_2 has, for $c_2 \geq \gamma(0)$, the particular form

$$h_2(c_2) = 8b\rho/[4(a - c_2)\sqrt{bK} - 7bK]$$

where the parameter ρ reflects the probability of there being a viable potential competitor. Also, assume that $\bar{c}_i < a/2$, which ensures that the usual first-order conditions define a Cournot equilibrium after entry. As well, assume that $a \geqq 7\sqrt{bK}/2$, which both ensures that h_2 is a density for any choice of $\bar{c}_2 < a/2$ and also implies that $\gamma(0) > 0$, so that even low cost established firms are threatened by entry. Finally, assume that $\gamma(\bar{c}_1) < \bar{c}_2$, so that $h_2(\gamma(\bar{c}_1)) \neq 0$.

Then, substituting for $R(c_1, \gamma(c_1)) = [2(a - c_1)\sqrt{bK} - bK]/4b$ and h_1 and rearranging terms yields

$$\frac{ds^*}{dc} = \frac{\delta_1 \rho}{[a - c_1 - 2bs^*(c_1)]}$$

This differential equation was derived on the assumption that s^* was monotone decreasing on $[\underline{c}_1, \bar{c}_1]$. The solutions meeting this condition and satisfying the non-negativity condition for expected profits form a non-intersecting family parameterized by a boundary condition, which we may take to be the value of $s^*(\bar{c}_1)$. Since each member of this family with the appropriate specification of t^* can constitute an equilibrium,[10] the multiplicity of equilibria in the earlier example carries over.

As suggested earlier, it seems reasonable to concentrate on solutions which are Pareto efficient. There is a unique such solution among the separating equilibria. In it, the highest cost firm, which will stand revealed as a weakling in any case, does not limit price. Alternatively, we can also eliminate the multiplicity by imposing the condition that an entrant whose costs exceed $\gamma(\bar{c}_1)$ will never enter, no matter what value of Q is observed, since such an entrant could never expect to recoup the entry cost K. Under either of these specifications, the boundary condition becomes $s^*(\bar{c}_1) = m(\bar{c}_1) = (a - \bar{c}_1)/2b$. The corresponding solution of the differential equation is then given implicitly by

$$0 = m(c_1) - s^*(c_1) + \delta_1 \rho - \delta_1 \rho \exp\left[\frac{m(\bar{c}_1) - s^*(c_1)}{\delta_1 \rho}\right]$$

Now, let t^* be specified by $t(c_2, Q) = 1$ iff $c_2 \leqq \gamma(s^{*-1}(Q))$ for Q in the range of s^* and, say, by $t(c_2, Q) = t(c_2, s^*(\underline{c}_1))$ for $Q > s^*(\underline{c}_1)$ and $t(c_2, Q) = t(c_2, s^*(\bar{c}_1))$ for $Q < m(\bar{c}_1)$. For s^* and t^* to be an equilibrium it is clearly sufficient that $G(c_1, Q)$ be pseudo-concave in Q for each c_1, so that the first-order condition (1) guarantees an optimum. For this, it is in turn sufficient (see [11]) that

$$\frac{ds^*(z)}{dz} \leqq \inf_{c \in [0, \bar{c}_1]} \frac{\delta_1 \gamma'(z)[R(c_1, \gamma(z)) - R(z, \gamma(z))]h_1(\gamma(z))}{(z - c)}$$

$$= \inf_{c_1} \frac{\delta_1(1/2)[(z - c_1)(24\sqrt{bK} - 6a - z + 7c_1)/36b]}{(z - c_1)} \left(\frac{8b\rho}{2(a - z)\sqrt{bK} - bK}\right)$$

$$= \frac{\delta_1 \rho[24\sqrt{bK} - 6a - z]}{9[2(a - z)\sqrt{bK} - bK]}$$

Since $ds^*/dz = -1/[2b(1 - \exp[(m(\bar{c}_1) - s(z))/\delta_1\rho])]$ is strictly decreasing and bounded above by $-1/(2b)$, if the right-hand side of the inequality were always positive, i.e., $6a + \sup z < 24\sqrt{bK}$, we would then be assured that (s^*, t^*) is an equilibrium. Thus, since $\bar{c}_1 = \sup z < a/2, a < 48\sqrt{bK}/13$ provides a sufficient condition.

It is straightforward to obtain comparative statics results for this example. Let $A \equiv [m(\bar{c}_1) - s(c_1)]/(\delta_1\rho) \leqq 0$. Then

$$\partial s^*/\partial\rho = \delta_1\frac{[1 + (A - 1)\exp A]}{1 - \exp A} > 0$$

$$\partial s^*/\partial\delta_1 = \rho\frac{[1 + (A - 1)\exp A]}{1 - \exp A} > 0$$

and

$$\partial s^*/\partial\bar{c}_1 = \frac{\exp A}{2b(1 - \exp A)} > 0$$

The intuition behind the first two results is clear. Regarding the third, the idea is that the possibility of there being higher cost firms leads the current $\bar{c}_1$ firm to limit price in order to distinguish itself, and then all lower cost firms must further increase their outputs.

Since the particular h function that we chose to permit computation resulted in $R(c_1, \gamma(c_1))h(\gamma(c_1))$ being constant, comparative statics with respect to a and b reveal the effects of changes in first period demand only. Note too that changes in these parameters affect both m and s^*, so interest centers on the effects on $s^* - m$. These are obtained by $\partial s^*/\partial a = 1/2b = \partial m/\partial a$, and $\partial s^*/\partial b < -(a - c_1)/2b^2 = \partial m/\partial b$: increases in a do not affect the amount of limit pricing, while increases in b reduce the amount of limit pricing by increasing the marginal cost of this activity (as measured by c_1 less the marginal revenue at $s^*(c_1)$) while leaving the marginal return (in the second period) unaffected.

Since the density function we used depends on K, comparative statics with respect to K cannot legitimately be interpreted in the natural way as indicating the effect of changing entry barriers.[11] To allow such an analysis, suppose instead that the established firm's beliefs are given by a density function which is independent of K. In this case, if $K = 0$, then $R(c_1, \gamma(c_1))h(\gamma(c_1)) \equiv 0$, and no limit pricing will occur. It is only the fact of positive K that causes the marginal entrant to enter with a strictly positive level of output. With no cost of entry, a marginal entrant comes in with an output which is essentially zero, and there is no return to deterring such entry. Similarly, if K is very large (Bain's blockaded entry case), no possible level of $\underline{c}_2$ will permit positive profits, the threat of entry disappears, and again no limit pricing will occur. In the particular example we calculated, K was such that $\gamma(\underline{c}_1) > \underline{c}_2$, so even low cost established firms were threatened and practiced limit pricing. A fourth possibility comes when K is high enough that $\gamma(\underline{c}_1) < \underline{c}_2$, so that there is a set $[\underline{c}_1, c_1^*)$ of firms against which no potential entrant would want to enter. An interesting aspect of our model is that even firms in this range may practice limit pricing. The essential cause of this is that, if $m(c_1') \leqq s(c_1'')$ for some $c_1' < c_1^* < c_1''$, then by producing $m(c_1')$, the low cost firm becomes identified with higher cost firms which are subject to entry. These latter firms may be expected to be limit pricing, so $s^*(c_1'') > m(c_1'')$, and thus $m(c_1') = s^*(c_1')$ is possible. By increasing output to (slightly more than) $s^*(c_1^*)$, which, to a first approximation, does not reduce the value of Π^0, the low cost firm can eliminate the threat of entry and thus increase second period expected returns.

Finally, we should mention that although we have concentrated on separating equilibria, other equilibria are possible in the continuum of types framework. A result of Milgrom and Weber [13] indicates that we need not concern ourselves with mixed strategy equilibria in games of this type. However, pure pooling equilibria are conceptually possible, as are equilibria where s^* is a decreasing step function.[12] In any pooling equilibrium, all types of the established firm are better off producing the equilibrium output Q^* than they are changing their output and facing the different probability of entry this different value of Q implies. For example, if entry is relatively unlikely when $Q = Q^*$ (perhaps because low values of c_1 are very likely a priori), and any deviation from Q^* brings certain entry, then if the $\bar{c}_1$ type is willing to produce Q^*, a pooling equilibrium will be maintained. In general, the form of the entrant's conjectures (as embodied in its strategy) which is necessary to support a pooling equilibria is typically discontinuous in Q, and the same sort of discontinuities underlie step-function equilibria.

It is clear that the extended example we have been discussing involves a number of special features, such as the linearity of demand and cost, and the assumption that post-entry competition yields the full information Cournot outcome. However, these assumptions serve mainly to simplify arguments and facilitate computation; they do not drive the results. Indeed, so long as the entrant's post-entry profits decrease in c_2 and increase in c_1 while the established firm strictly prefers to be a monopolist than to share the market ($R(c_1, c_2) > 0$), our principal conclusions remain: if pre-entry price can be a signal for post-entry profits, even if it does not directly influence profitability, then limit pricing will emerge in equilibrium, but entry need not be deterred relative to the complete information case. Moreover, as we shall argue in the next section, even if we allow for much more general uncertainty and for post-entry profits being dependent on pre-entry actions, a similar conclusion is valid.

3. Entry Deterrence and Rational Expectations

In this section we consider a fairly general two-period model of entry deterrence and entry under incomplete information. While we do not provide a complete analysis of this model, we do indicate some of the implications of equilibrium for the firms' behavior.

Rather than setting up a general formal model from scratch, let us re-interpret the model in section 2 with some modifications. In particular, we now view c_1 and c_2 as belonging to some arbitrary measurable spaces, and we will view Q as an action belonging to some other arbitrary space. Suppose further that 2 observes only some variable q which is correlated with Q, and suppose, too, that the payoffs depend not only on c_1, c_2 and the action y taken by the entrant (which may also now belong to some arbitrary space), but also on Q and possibly on a random variable θ, the realization of which is not revealed until the firms make their choices. Finally, let all the random variables have some arbitrary joint distribution.

This framework is obviously very general. In particular, it allows for capital investment which affects marginal costs, advertising and other means of achieving brand loyalty, general forms of demand and cost functions, varying scales and forms of entry, imperfect observability of actions, uncertainty as to how the post-entry game will be played, and arbitrary dependencies among all the random elements of the model.

As before, it is useful to analyze equilibrium via strategies, s^* and t^*, and conjectures, $\bar{s}$ and $\bar{t}$. (These may be taken to be either pure or mixed strategies.) Thus, firm 1 conjectures that 2's strategy is t, for each value of c_1 it will select an action $Q = s(c_1)$ to maximize the expected value of its perceived payoff, conditional on c_1. Unless expected second-period payoffs are insensitive to Q, both through any direct effect on second-period profits and also through the effect on 2's conjectured action, the solution for the established firm's maximization problem will not be the same as the solution to the problem of maximizing the expected value of first-period profits. Thus, we would generally expect that the threat of entry will alter behavior: some generalized form of limit pricing will be a characteristic of equilibrium.

In making its decision, the entrant will seek to maximize its expected payoff conditional on its private information c_2 and its (imperfect) observation of Q, given its conjecture $\bar{s}$. Should it happen that the observation of the signal q in equilibrium permits a precise inference via $\bar{s}$ about c_1, then entry will of course occur in precisely the same circumstances as if c_1 had been directly announced. In this case, the only effect of the generalized limit pricing on entry will be through the direct effect of Q on 2's post-entry profits (as, for example, when the choice of Q affects demand or cost). If this effect is zero, then, as in the example in section 2, limit pricing will still occur, but it need not deter entry relative to the complete information case.

However, the unrestricted dimensionalities allowed for c_1 and Q suggest that an invertible strategy s^* is unlikely. Moreover, so long as the random noise term relating q and Q is neither perfectly correlated with c_1 nor degenerate, then even if s^* is an invertible function of Q one would not expect a noisy observation of Q via q to permit a precise inference of the value of c_1. Thus one must expect that such exact inferences will be impossible in equilibrium, and that residual uncertainty will remain concerning c_1 when the entry decision is made. In this case, the entrant must base its entry decision y on the expected value of its profits, as a function of Q, y and the exogenous uncertainty θ, conditional on the values of c_2 and q, and given its conjecture $\bar{s}$ about 1's behavior. With some abuse of notation, let us write this as

$$E(\Pi_2(c_1, c_2, \bar{s}(c_1), y, \theta) | q(\bar{s}(c_1), \theta), c_2) \tag{2}$$

Then the question is that of whether the established firm can, through its choice of Q, cause the entrant in equilibrium to lower its estimate of the profitability of entry.

Consider what 2's estimate of its prospects are a priori, knowing c_2 but before observing q. This is just the expectation of expression (2), conditional on c_2. Then, in equilibrium, where $\bar{s} = s^*$, so that 2's conjecture is correct, this a priori estimate is

$$E(E[\Pi_2(c_1, c_2, s^*(c_1), y, \theta) | q(s^*(c_1), \theta), c_2] | c_2) \tag{3}$$

But, by a standard result in probability theory, expression (3) is equal to $E(\Pi_2(c_1, c_2, s^*(c_1), y, \theta)|c_2)$. But this, in turn, is simply what firm 2 would estimate its profits to be if it were to receive no information.

In this sense, then, the observation of the established firm's actions cannot, in equilibrium, systematically bias the entrant's expectations. If without any information it would have estimated its expected profits at $\overline{\Pi}$ then the fact that it will receive the signal cannot lead it to expect to receive less than $\overline{\Pi}$. Put a different way, if there are some values of c_1 and c_2 such that observing $s^*(c_1)$ (directly or indirectly) causes an entrant with characteristics c_2 to underestimate the profitability of entry, then there is an offsetting set of values for c_1 and c_2 where observing $s^*(c_1)$ causes the entrant to overestimate its prospects.

4. Summary and Conclusions

In his original analysis of limit pricing, Bain [1, p. 453] argued that although "current price...need play no direct role [in the entry decision], since the anticipated industry price *after entry* and the entrant's anticipated market share are the strategic considerations," the potential entrant may "regard this price as an indicator" of post-entry profitability. Given this, Bain developed his theory of limit pricing, from which a large literature has emerged. A weakness of this literature has been the failure to model both the established firm and the entrant as strategic agents. However, if one models the situation described by Bain as a game of complete information, no limit pricing can emerge in equilibrium [3].

In this paper we model the problem considered by Bain of entry deterrence and entry as a game of incomplete information. In this game, Bain's arguments are valid: although pre-entry actions by the established firm may not influence post-entry profitability, they may become signals for some unobservable determinants of profits. Limit pricing, or, more generally, deviations from short-run maximizing behavior, then emerge in equilibrium, just as earlier analyses had found. However, an unsuspected feature also emerges. Since the entrant will, in equilibrium, recognize the incentives for limit pricing, its expectations of the profitability of entry will not be consistently biased by the established firm's behavior. Then, depending on the particular equilibrium that is established and the parameters of the model, the probability of entry may fall short of, equal, or even exceed what it would be if there were complete information and thus no limit pricing.

One conclusion of this analysis is for the appropriate public policy towards limit pricing. If pre-entry price does not influence post-entry demand and if the two-period modeling used here is appropriate, then limit pricing should not be discouraged, since it means lower prices and cannot, overall, limit entry. More generally, the admittedly incomplete analysis in section 3 might suggest a stronger statement regarding strategic moves taken by established firms to deter entry. To the extent that these actions are not objectionable per se, but rather are of potential concern only because of signaling effects which it is feared may deter entry, then they are in fact benign. The question is whether either of these suggestions would stand up under a full examination of a richer model. In particular, it would seem that embedding the opportunity for limit pricing in a multi-period model where predation is possible and where reputations are a factor would be an important extension of the present analysis. This is a problem we hope to address in future work.

Notes

1 Although some recent treatments of entry deterrence incorporate other strategic variables, the standard, traditional approach is to treat the choice of the pre-entry price as the firm's only decision and to assume no dependence of post-entry profits on this choice.

2 The idea behind limit pricing can be traced back through the work of J. Bain [1] and J. M. Clark [2] at least to a paper by N. Kaldor [7]. The recent formal investigations begin with D. Gaskins [5], M. I. Kamien and N. L. Schwartz [8], and G. Pyatt [16]. See F. M. Scherer [18] and S. Salop [17] for further references.

3 An extensive form game has imperfect information if some player at some point must make a move without having been fully informed about all the previous moves made by the other players.

4 If $q < 0.273$, then there is a pooling equilibrium against which the probability of entry is zero. If $q > 0.954$, then entry would be certain if a pooling equilibrium were established. But then each type of established firm would find that its monopoly output represents a profitable deviation. Thus, there could be no such equilibrium.

5 See E. Gal-or [4] for a more explicit model along these lines. Also see D. Kreps and R. Wilson [9] and P. Milgrom and J. Roberts [12] for multi-market models of entry deterrence through predation.

6 There is a second source of non-uniqueness which involves the specification of $t^*(c_2, Q)$ for values of Q outside the range of s^*. Since such values of Q are observed with probability zero, the maximization of expected return places no constraint on t^* at these points. Then, even within the constraint that s^* be a best response to the entrant's strategy, there are typically many strategies t^* which constitute equilibria with s^*. However, all such t^* for a given s^* give the same evolution of the play of the game (the same Q values being chosen and the same entry decisions being made). Thus, this non-uniqueness is less crucial.

7 This correspondence is not coincidence, as Kreps and Wilson [10] have shown: every perfect equilibrium is sequential.

8 Note, in particular, that $s^* = m$ is not an equilibrium strategy, since the $\bar{c}_1$ firm would be willing to produce $m(\underline{c}_1)$ to eliminate all entry.

9 While it might seem that any other pooling equilibrium would have $s^*(c_1) > m(\underline{c}_1)$, this need not be the case. However, if the entrant's conjectures regarding the value of c_1, given Q, are continuous in Q, pooling equilibria with higher than monopoly prices disappear. If, in addition, the probability assigned to $c_1 = \underline{c}_1$ rises sufficiently rapidly in Q, then only separating equilibria can exist. These continuity and monotonicity conditions are similar in spirit to Myerson's properness criterion [14].

10 So long as the first-order condition (1) actually gives a maximum.

11 The possibility of normalizing 2's payoff means that lowering δ_2 corresponds to raising K.

12 The possible equilibria are characterized in [11].

References

1 Bain, J. (1949): "A Note on Pricing in Monopoly and Oligopoly," *American Economic Review*, 39, 448–64.

2 Clark, J. M. (1940): "Toward a Concept of Workable Competition," *American Economic Review*, 30, 241–56.

3 Friedman, J. (1979): "On Entry Preventing Behavior," in *Applied Game Theory*, ed. by S. J. Brams, A. Schotter and G. Schwodiauer. Wurzburg, Vienna: Physica-Verlag, 236–53.

4 Gal-or, E. (1980): "Limit Price Entry Prevention and its Impact on Potential Investors – A Game-Theoretic Approach," Ph.D. dissertation, Northwestern University.

5 Gaskins, D. (1971): "Dynamic Limit Pricing: Optimal Pricing Under Threat of Entry," *Journal of Economic Theory*, 2, 306–22.

6 Harsanfyi, J. C. (1967/1968): "Games with Incomplete Information Played by 'Bayesian' Players." Parts I, II and III, *Management Science*, 14, 159–82, 320–4, and 486–502.

7 Kaldor, N. (1935): "Market Imperfection and Excess Capacity," *Economica*, 2, 33–50.

8 Kamien, M. I. and N. Schwartz: (1971): "Limit Pricing and Uncertain Entry," *Econometrica*, 39, 441–54.

9 Kreps, D. and R. Wilson: (1980): "On the Chain-Store Paradox and Predation: Reputation for Toughness," Discussion Paper 551, Graduate School of Business, Stanford University.

10 —— (1980): "Sequential Equilibria," Discussion Paper 584, Graduate School of Business. Stanford University.

11 Milgrom, P., and J. Roberts (1980): "Equilibrium Limit Pricing Doesn't Limit Entry," Discussion Paper 399R. Center for Mathematical Studies in Economics and Management Science, Northwestern University.

12 —— (1980): "Predation, Reputation, and Entry Deterrence," Discussion Paper 427, Center for Mathematical Studies in Economics and Management Science, Northwestern University.

13 Milgrom, P., and R. Weber (1980): "Distributional Strategies for Games with Incomplete Information," Discussion Paper 428. Center for Mathematical Studies in Economics and Management Science, Northwestern University.

14 Myerson, R. (1978): "Refinements of the Nash Equilibrium Concept," *International Journal of Game Theory*, 7, 73–80.

15 Ortega-Reichert, A. (1968): "Models for Competitive Bidding Under Uncertainty," Ph.D. dissertation, Stanford University.

16 Pyatt, G. (1971): "Profit Maximization and the Threat of New Entry," *Economic Journal*, 81, 242–55.

17 Salop, S. C. (1979): "Strategic Entry Deterrence," *American Economic Review*, 69, 335–8.

18 Scherer, F. M. (1979): *Industrial Market Structure and Economic Performance*. 2nd edn. Chicago: Rand McNally and Company.

19 Selten, R. (1975): "Reexamination of the Perfectness Concept for Equilibrium Points in Extensive Games," *International Journal of Game Theory*, 4, 25–55.

CHAPTER TWENTY-TWO

Price and Advertising Signals of Product Quality

PAUL MILGROM AND JOHN ROBERTS

Source: *Journal of Political Economy*, 1986, 94, 796–821.

We present a signaling model, based on ideas of Phillip Nelson, in which both the introductory price and the level of directly "uninformative" advertising or other dissipative marketing expenditures are choice variables and may be used as signals for the initially unobservable quality of a newly introduced experience good. Repeat purchases play a crucial role in our model. A second focus of the paper is on illustrating an approach to refining the set of equilibria in signaling games with multiple potential signals.

Although we economists have included advertising and other selling expenses in various of our models at least since the 1930s, it is only within the last decade or so that we have begun to offer explanations of why advertising might affect customers' choices and thus of why firms might choose to advertise.

The most successfully developed of these models involve firms' using advertising to inform potential customers about the existence, characteristics, and prices of the commodities they offer. This work has obvious relevance to the huge volume of advertising that is directly informative on these dimensions. Most newspaper advertisements (including especially want ads) would seem to be of this sort.

However, a nontrivial amount of advertising (especially on television) has little or no obvious informational content. A relatively recent example is the ad that was shown when Diet Coca-Cola was introduced: a large concert hall full of people, a long chorus line kicking, a remarkable number of (high-priced) celebrities over whom the camera pans, and a simple announcement that Diet Coke is the reason for this assemblage. Another example from the same period is the advertising campaign for the 1984 Ford Ranger truck, which featured these trucks being thrown out of airplanes (followed by a half dozen sky divers) or driven off high cliffs. These ads carry little or no direct information other than that the product in question exists. But if that is the message being sent, these ads seem an inordinately expensive way to transmit the information. Indeed, the clearest message they carry is, "We are spending an astronomical amount of money on this ad campaign."

In a series of provocative articles, Nelson (1970, 1974, 1978) has suggested that the latter is, in fact, the primary message of such ads and, moreover, that this is a useful, positive message to prospective customers. Nelson differentiated between products on a "search good" versus "experience good" basis. With the former, the relevant character-istics of the product are evident on inspection, and, because there is little gain to misrepresentation, ads for them can be directly informative. With the latter, crucial aspects of the product's quality are impossible to verify except through use of the product. Thus, unless the product is given away, one must buy without really knowing what one is getting. In such a circumstance, a seller's claims to be offering high quality are unverifiable before purchase. In the absence of strong and sure penalties for misrepresentation, such claims can be freely copied. They are consequently meaningless, and consumers will rationally ignore them. As a result, ads for such a product cannot credibly convey much direct information about the product. Yet it remains in the interests of consumers to identify high-quality goods and of the producers of these "best buys" to make themselves known.

Nelson's crucial insight was that the mere fact that a particular brand of an experience good was advertised could be a signal to customers that the brand was of high quality. It is clear that if high-quality brands advertise more and if advertising expenditures are observable (even if not perfectly so), then rational, informed consumers will respond positively to advertising, even if the ads cannot and do not have much direct informational content. What then is needed to complete the explanation is a reason why advertising should be differentially advantageous for high-quality sellers so that they will be willing to advertise at levels that low-quality sellers will not mimic.

The factor on which Nelson focused to provide this linkage was repeat purchases. He argued that, because a high-quality product is more likely to attract repeat purchases, an initial sale is, *ceteris paribus*, more valuable to a high-quality producer, and such a firm would be willing to expend more – on advertising or whatever – to attract an initial sale. This relationship would then provide the basis for the correlation of quality with the net benefits of signaling that is needed in the standard Spence-type analysis to obtain a separating equilibrium.

Nelson's approach is very insightful and appealing, but it is not worked out in terms of a formal model. Moreover, further consideration reveals what proves to be a major gap in his analysis. Specifically, Nelson did not explicitly treat the pricing decision and the determination of the resultant markup. Yet these are crucial questions.

On the pricing side, if the firm is able to select the price it will charge (subject to whatever competitive pressures may exist), might it not prefer to stimulate sales through its pricing rather than via uninformative ads? Or, if advertising does convince customers of a product's high quality, might not the firm want to alter its price in response to the increased demand? But note that, if such possibilities result in prices that vary system-atically with quality, then Nelson's explanation of advertising is undercut. Customers can now infer quality from price and so have no need to look to advertising for a hint as to what quality might be. In this circumstance, why should firms waste money on ads?

But even if the role of prices as possible signals is put aside, their determination remains crucial. This is because the value of an initial sale depends not just on the volume of resulting repeat sales but also on the markups received. Nelson's *ceteris paribus* assumption apparently means that markups are taken to be the same on high- and low-quality products, and some version of this assumption is clearly indispensable. For if markups were sufficiently greater on low-quality goods (as they would be if prices were the same but production costs were steeply increasing in quality), then the value of an initial sale would be negatively correlated with quality. If customers then responded positively to ads, it would be the low-quality firms that would do the advertising, while if customers understood the incentives facing firms, neither type of firm would advertise.

It thus becomes important to attempt to formulate Nelson's basic ideas in a complete, formal model incorporating both the pricing and advertising decisions. In fact, a number of authors since Nelson have investigated the relationship between quality and the use of the noninformative or image advertising on which he focused, and some have been explicitly interested in formalizing his ideas. However, the issues of both prices and quantities being choice variables that could be signals and of repeat sales being a key phenomenon have not, to our knowledge, been satisfactorily incorporated into a formal analysis.[1]

In this paper we offer a modeling based on the repeat sales mechanism in which both price and advertising are decision variables that may potentially be used as signals of quality.[2] We show that in equilibrium both may simultaneously be used as signals, with the chosen levels of both prices and advertising differing between high- and low-quality firms (and, moreover, differing for the high-quality firms from the levels that would be chosen in the absence of the informational asymmetry about quality). This means, in particular, that customers could in fact infer product quality from observing either price or advertising volume. However, if a high-quality firm were to cut back on either dimension – price or advertising – of its signaling and move the relevant variable toward its full-information optimal level, then a low-quality firm would be willing to mimic, the signal would no longer be credible, and customers would ignore it. Meanwhile, in such an equilibrium the firm uses both variables to signal (rather than just one) since this achieves the desired differentiation at minimal cost. A corollary of this result is that an effective ban on purely dissipative signals (such as advertising is here) may lead to a Pareto-worsening in the allocation of resources.

Three points are worth noting here. First, while we will consistently refer to advertising, the analysis clearly applies to any observable expenditure that does not directly provide information or otherwise improve demand or costs. A shop in a high-rent location or highly visible corporate social responsibility activities are obvious examples. Second, the analysis is strictly applicable only to new products whose quality is not generally known. Thus it says little about advertising for established brands. Third, we emphasize that quality in this analysis is not treated as a choice variable but rather as exogenously given. The problem is not the moral hazard one that the firm may have incentives to cheat by cutting quality. Indeed, we do not even assume that lower quality is necessarily cheaper to produce. It is thus probably best to think of our model as one in which the firm's R&D effort has generated a product of some particular given quality that the firm must decide how to introduce.

While the primary purpose of this paper is to study the role of pricing and advertising for newly introduced experience goods, it may also offer some methodological contribution through providing the analysis of multiple variables being used simultaneously to signal for a single unobservable variable and through illustrating a method of obtaining a "small" set of equilibria and even uniqueness in signaling situations modeled as games.

The second of these actually underlies the first. Models based on games of incomplete information, and signaling models in particular, have typically suffered from an embarrassing plethora of (Nash) equilibria. Not only are there often both pooling and separating equilibria (as well as partial-pooling ones), but also there are typically a horde of each of these types. The source of this multiplicity is the indeterminacy of the inferences that individuals draw "off the equilibrium path," that is, when they see a level of the signal that they can tell ought not to have arisen in equilibrium. Bayes's rule gives no guidance in such situations, and the usual equilibrium notions are unspecific about how such inferences should be made. Yet the beliefs that are formed off the putative equilibrium path and the actions that they generate determine what individuals can accomplish by deviating from the prescribed strategies. They are thus crucial determinants of what will, in fact, be equilibrium behavior. The assumption of equilibrium thus places relatively few restrictions on behavior, and, consequently, many different behavior patterns can be supported in equilibrium.

A long and growing list of authors have addressed the problem of paring down the set of Nash equilibria in signaling models by restricting the allowable beliefs.[3] The approach we use here is first to work only with sequential equilibria, a refinement of the Nash concept developed by Kreps and Wilson (1982). This both forces us to be explicit about the out-of-equilibrium beliefs and restricts them somewhat. More significantly, we also require that the equilibria be immune to sequential elimination of dominated strategies (Moulin 1979; Pearce 1982)[4] and that they meet a further "intuitive criterion" proposed by Kreps (1984).[5] Both of these conditions serve to restrict beliefs further and in economically reasonable ways. Moreover, Kreps (1984) has shown that they are implied by the concept of strategic stability proposed by Kohlberg and Mertens (1984) for general normal form games.[6]

The use of sequential equilibrium eliminates separating Nash equilibria in which low-quality firms, even though revealed as low-quality, deviate from their full-information optimal price or spend money on ads because customers would otherwise buy even less than the full-information amount. Sequential elimination of dominated strategies then requires that the set of price–advertising pairs taken as indicating high quality be as large as possible, in that if it were any larger it would include choices that would be mimicked by a low-quality firm. It thereby rules out separating equilibria with excessive, inefficient amounts of signaling by the high-quality firm since such sequential equilibria are supported only by the belief that a low-quality producer played a dominated strategy. Finally, application of the Kreps (1984) criterion eliminates any equilibria involving pooling on a price–advertising pair at which an appropriate generalization of Spence's signaling condition is met.[7] Thus the only candidates for equilibrium that meet all our requirements involve the low-quality firm's picking its full-information optimum and the high-quality firm's doing just enough signaling to distinguish itself.

In this context, the equilibrium choices of prices and advertising are given by the solution of a constrained optimization problem for the high-quality producer. The same conditions on profit functions can be used to show that the solution to the problem is unique and that, if the full-information prices of the two types of producers are not too dissimilar, then the solution involves positive levels of advertising as well as price signaling. Of course, this use of both signals is natural given that they are the choice variables in an optimization problem and that the conditions on the profit functions ensure an interior solution.[8]

1. Price and Advertising Signals: A Diagrammatic Exposition

Most of the key ideas underlying our analysis of multidimensional price and advertising signals for quality can be developed graphically. We do so here under assumptions on the existence and shapes of the function relating the firm's equilibrium profits to its initial price and advertising choices and to its actual and perceived quality. In the next section we will present a detailed analysis of a fully specified model.

Consider a firm that has just developed a new product of which it is the sole producer.[9] The product may be of either high quality (*H*) or low quality (*L*). The firm knows the actual, realized quality, but the potential customers do not, and there is no credible direct way by which the firm can provide this information before customers make their initial purchase decisions. The firm's immediate decision variables are the price, *P*, at which it will introduce the product and the amount, *A*, that it will spend on introductory advertising over and above whatever level is optimally used to inform potential customers of the good's existence, its price, and its verifiable characteristics. These two variables are shown on the axes of figures 1–6 below.

Customers, after observing *P* and *A*, make their initial purchase decisions and, through direct use of the product or communication with users, then gain information about product quality. The firm then sets its second-period, post-introductory price and carries out any additional advertising it wishes. Customers observe these choices and make their decisions as to whether to buy again in light of the current prices and the information now available. If there are additional post-introductory periods, this latter pattern is repeated in each.

A full specification of this sequence of possible actions, of the information available at each point, and of the resultant payoffs would yield a game of incomplete information in extensive form. A sequential equilibrium would then involve strategies for each player (firm or customer) giving the choice to be made at each decision point as a function of the information then available,[10] as well as beliefs for the customers at each point about the firm's true quality. The beliefs would have to be consistent with the information structure of the problem and, to the extent possible, with the hypothesis that the given strategies were being played, and starting from any decision point the strategies would have to be best responses to one another, given the beliefs. (For full details, see Kreps and Wilson [1982].)

In fact, our interest focuses not on the whole play of the game, as given by the full equilibrium strategies, but rather only on the initial equilibrium choices of *P* and *A* by the firm and on the resulting customer beliefs. To study these, it will be enough to assume that each such choice (*P*, *A*) induces a unique equilibrium pattern of customer beliefs – represented by the probability $\rho(P, A)$ that is assigned to the firm's producing high quality – and that together these induce a uniquely defined expected present value for the firm's profits throughout the game.

Let $\Pi(P, q, p) - A$ denote the function giving the expected present value of the profits to a firm of true quality $q(q = L \text{ or } H)$ that sets an introductory price of P, spends A on introductory advertising, and is believed with probability $\rho = \rho(P, A)$ to be producing quality H. Note that advertising here has no direct impact on demand or gross profits. Its only possible influence is through prepurchase perceptions of quality. It is thus a purely dissipative signal.

In the present context, it is natural to think that initial sales will be increasing in the perceived quality, as modeled by ρ, and that repeat sales will increase in actual quality, q. These conditions hold in the example in the next section, but it may be possible to concoct examples in which they do not hold but the following lines of analysis would apply. In any case, we do not assume that Π increases in actual quality because costs might also depend on q, but we will assume that profits are increasing in ρ.

Of special interest will be situations in which ρ is zero or one, that is, where customers believe they know the true quality. In such cases, it will be convenient to define $\pi(P, q, L) = \Pi(P, q, 0)$ and $\pi(P, q, H) = \Pi(P, q, 1)$. Thus $\pi(P, q, Q)$ denotes the gross profits of a firm of actual quality ("type") q that is initially perceived to be of type Q and sets price P.

If actual quality were known by potential customers before purchase, then $\pi(P, q, q) - A$ would be the relevant profit function net of advertising expenditure for a firm known to be producing quality q. Clearly, the optimal advertising budget in these circumstances is $A = 0$. Denote the optimal value of P for a firm known to be of type q as P_q^q, that is, P_q^q is P_H^H or P_L^L. We call these the "full-information prices."

Under the actual information conditions that initially obtain with experience goods, q and Q may differ. In this context, define P_Q^q as the maximizer of $\pi(P, q, Q)$. We can now give a first answer to the question whether there exists a separating sequential equilibrium of the signaling game, that is, a sequential equilibrium at which the customers can distinguish high- and low-quality firms by the different price–advertising choices they make.

PROPOSITION 1.   There exists a separating sequential equilibrium if and only if for some $(P, A) \geq 0$

$$\pi(P, H, H) - \pi(P_L^H, H, L) \geq A \geq \pi(P, L, H) - \pi(P_L^L, L, L) \tag{1}$$

At any separating sequential equilibrium, the high-quality firm chooses a (P, A) satisfying (1), the low-quality firm chooses $(P_L^L, 0)$, and customers' beliefs are given by $\rho(P, A) = 1$ for the point chosen by the high-quality firm, $\rho(P_L^L, 0) = 0$, and, for all other (P', A'), $\rho(P', A')$ sufficiently small (e.g., zero) that neither player wishes to deviate to (P', A').

The inequalities (1) assert that a high-quality firm would rather choose (P, A) and be perceived as high-quality than be perceived as low-quality and optimize accordingly, while the low-quality firm has the reverse preference. Whatever choice (P_L, A_L) is made by the L, in separating sequential equilibrium this choice must yield $\rho(P_L, A_L) = 0$, and the best such choice is $(P_L^L, 0)$.

The situation in which a separating equilibrium exists is depicted in figure 1. Note that points *under* a given isoprofit curve correspond to *higher* levels of profit. Thus the

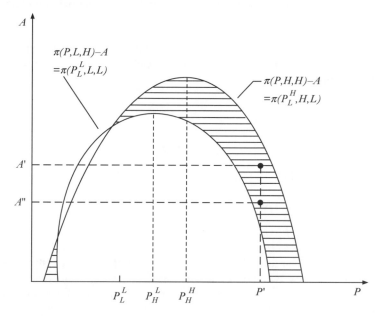

Figure 1   Existence of separating equilibrium

inequalities hold over the indicated region, and each point in the region corresponds to at least one separating sequential equilibrium.

From this we see that there are typically many separating sequential equilibria. However, most of these equilibria involve customer beliefs that are arguably implausible. For example, the point (P', A') corresponds to an equilibrium only because customers believe that a firm choosing (P', A'') is likely to be a low-quality producer, even though such a choice is dominated for an L. The best that can happen if an L chooses (P', A'') is that it is taken for an H, but this is worse than the worst that can happen when $(P_L^L, 0)$ is chosen, namely, that the firm is taken for an L. If customers believe that firms do not make dominated choices, then $\rho(P', A'')$ must be one, and the equilibrium where H chooses (P', A') is overturned.

More generally, we shall want to limit our attention to equilibria that remain equilibria even after dominated strategies are removed sequentially from the game.[11] Immunity to sequential elimination of dominated strategies means not only that such strategies are never played (though they could be in Nash or sequential equilibrium) but, more significantly, that the "off-the-equilibrium path" beliefs assign zero probability to such strategies whenever possible. In particular, if a (P, A) pair would necessarily represent play of a dominated strategy for one type of firm but not for the other, beliefs following observation of such a choice must ascribe zero weight to the type for which the strategy is dominated. This economically natural condition does not follow from sequentiality, let alone from the Nash assumption. Its absence could result in signaling at very high levels only because lesser amounts are interpreted as (perhaps) indicating that the firm is an L, even though adopting such a choice would be dominated for an L.

Henceforth, we shall reserve the term "equilibrium" for sequential equilibria with this immunity property.

PROPOSITION 2.   There exists a separating equilibrium if and only if there is some (P, A) such that (1) holds. At any separating equilibrium, the choice (P_H, A_H) of the high-quality firm must be a solution to

$$\max_{P,A} \pi(P, H, H) - A \tag{2}$$

subject to $\pi(P, L, H) - A \leq \pi(P_L^L, L, L)$ and $P, A \geq 0$

If the solution (P^*, A^*) to (2) is such that $A^* > 0$, then P^* solves

$$\max_{P} \pi(P, H, H) - \pi(P, L, H) \tag{3}$$

subject to $\pi(P, L, H) - \pi(P_L^L, L, L) > 0$.

With elimination of dominated strategies, $\rho(P, A) = 1$ at a separating equilibrium precisely for those points lying on or above the curve $A(P)$ defined by the isoprofit curve $\pi(P, L, H) - A = \pi(P_L^L, L, L)$ when this yields $A \geq 0$, and $A(P) = 0$ otherwise. It must be one for such points for the reasons given above. It cannot be one for points below the $A(P)$ curve, for then an L would make such a choice, be taken as an H, and overturn the equilibrium. The choice that an H makes at a separating equilibrium must yield $\rho = 1$, and since it is free to make any such choice, the first part of the proposition follows. Intuitively, the Lagrange multiplier of the constraint in (2) measures the marginal benefit of advertising. When $A^* > 0$, it must equal the marginal cost, which is unity. Using this observation, the second characterization in the proposition can be derived from the first. Finally, the set of points satisfying (1) is closed and so, if nonempty, contains points satisfying the constraints in (2). This gives the existence result. Of course, whenever there is a unique solution to (2), there is only one separating equilibrium in the game.

Let us now examine some specific cases to see when equilibria involving advertising are most likely to arise. For simplicity, we shall henceforth assume that $\pi(P, L, H)$ is strictly concave in P and that $A(P)$ is positive on an interval $(\underline{P}, \bar{P})$ with $\underline{P} > 0$.

Suppose first that $P_H^H \notin (\underline{P}, \bar{P})$; this is the case in which the "natural," full-information price differential is enough to render mimicry unprofitable. Figure 2 illustrates one such case, in which $P_H^H > \bar{P}$. This may occur, for example, when a new high-quality product is very expensive to produce and is aimed at a limited market. A low-quality, low-cost, mass-market producer may be unwilling to limit itself to the small "upscale" market, despite its high margins per unit, so that pricing at P_H^H is enough alone to signal high quality. The case in which $P_H^H < \underline{P}$ has a similar interpretation: When the new high-quality product is very cheap to produce and is aimed at a mass market, the introducing firm may set a low initial price or give away free samples in launching the product. It thereby establishes a large base for repeat sales, which would not be worthwhile if its quality were low. In either case, no costly signaling and, in particular, no advertising are practiced.

Thus a necessary condition for advertising to occur at equilibrium is $P_H^H \in (\underline{P}, \bar{P})$ or, equivalently,

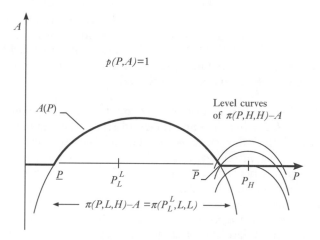

Figure 2 Condition (4) fails; equilibrium at the full- information price

$$\pi(P_H^H, L, H) > \pi(P_L^L, L, L) \tag{4}$$

This condition says that an L would willingly set its price at P_H^H if by so doing it could change its perceived quality from L to H.

Condition (4) leads to signaling but is not by itself sufficient to ensure that the solution to problem (2) involves a positive level of advertising. If advertising is to occur at equilibrium, the solution to problem (2) must occur at a tangency (P^T, A^T) between the isoprofit curves of $\pi(P, L, H) - A$ and $\pi(P, H, H) - A$ with $P^T \in (\underline{P}, \bar{P})$ and $A > 0$. (Note that the isoprofit curves of each type of firm q are vertically parallel with slope equal to $\partial \pi[P, q, H]/\partial P$.) As a necessary condition for an equilibrium with advertising, we thus require that there exist a price P^T at which the isoprofit curves for the two types of firms (both perceived as being high-quality) are tangent and which satisfies

$$\pi(P^T, L, H) > \pi(P_L^L, L, L) \tag{5}$$

Condition (5) is equivalent to requiring that $P^T \in (\underline{P}, \bar{P})$ so that $A(P^T) > 0$.

Note, however, that even if P^T exists the second-order conditions may fail. This leads us to consider the curvature properties of the objective function in (3):

$$\pi(P, H, H) - \pi(P, L, H) \text{ is pseudoconcave in } P \tag{6}$$

$$\pi(P, H, H) - \pi(P, L, H) \text{ is strictly pseudoconvex in } P \tag{7}$$

Condition (6) implies that a tangency point is in fact a maximum for problem (3), while (7) means that such a point is actually a minimum.

Proposition 3.   Assume that there exists some (P, A) for which (1) holds so that a separating equilibrium exists. If conditions (4)–(6) hold,[12] then there is a separating equilibrium with positive advertising. If the condition in (6) is replaced by strict pseudo-concavity, there is a unique separating equilibrium. If either (4) or (5) fails or if (7) holds, then all separating equilibria have zero advertising.

Think of the H's problem as one of selecting P and A optimally while imposing enough costs on an L making the same choice to render such mimicry unprofitable. If condition (4) holds, then this choice must deviate from the unconstrained optimum at $(P_H^H, 0)$ and so must involve costs for the H. Solving the problem then involves considering the relative effects on each type of firm of changing P and A. Changes in A always affect the profits of either type equally, but the effects of changes in P are more subtle. Condition (6) can be interpreted as saying that movements of P toward P^T involve less cost (or confer more benefits) for an H than for an L, while under (7) movements away from P^T are always cheaper for an H than an L. Suppose now that conditions (5) and (6) hold. Then the costs of price adjustment are equalized for the two types at P^T and further adjustments in P are more costly for the H than for the L, but the necessary differentiation has not been achieved. The H then prefers to distinguish itself by increasing advertising rather than adjusting price further. On the other hand, if (5) fails, then price adjustments (toward P^T) are cheaper for the H than for the L over the entire relevant range and no advertising is employed (figure 3), while if (7) holds, then the H's problem is again solved at a boundary point of the interval $[\underline{P}, \bar{P}]$ (see figure 4).

Figures 5 and 6 illustrate possible cases with positive advertising. We see that price might be raised or lowered from P_H^H for signaling purposes, depending on whether P_H^H exceeds or falls short of P_H^L. If these values agree (and so also equal P^T), then all signaling is via advertising.

In summary, the solution to the optimization problem and, under (1), the choice of the H in separating equilibrium is $(P_H^H, 0)$ if $P_H^H \notin (\underline{P}, \bar{P})$, is $(\underline{P}, 0)$ or $(\bar{P}, 0)$ if P_H^H is "too close" to $\underline{P}$ or $\bar{P}$ (i.e., [5] fails) or if condition (7) holds, and is (P^T, A^T) if (4)–(6) hold. The questions that remain are whether the conditions of (1) are met, so that the separating equilibrium exists, and whether there are other, nonseparating equilibria.

In fact, there may be pooling equilibria in this game, that is, equilibria in which both the H and the L select the same point (P, A) with positive probability. Indeed, when there is no point (P, A) satisfying (1), separating equilibria will not exist, and any equilibrium will involve pooling. Nevertheless, one may argue on various grounds that pooling equilibria are implausible for this model, at least when separating equilibria exist. For one thing, they make much more severe informational demands on the customers than do separating equilibria. To play their separating equilibrium strategies, customers need know only $A(P)$, which determines the set of things a low-quality producer would be willing to do to be thought high-quality and thus what choices credibly signal high quality. The customers need not know the profit function of the H, nor need they agree on the probability that a given producer is an H, as they must to play their parts in a pooling equilibrium.

A recent game-theoretic development, due to Kreps (1984), provides an additional way to criticize the pooling equilibrium, though it does rely on the customers' being very well

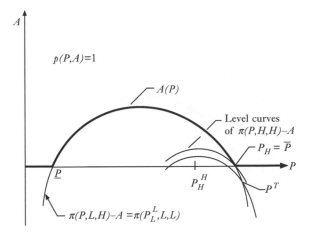

Figure 3 Condition (5) fails; equilibrium at $(\bar{P}, 0)$

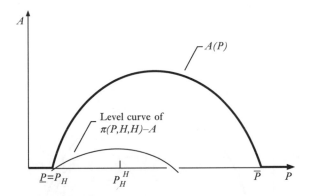

Figure 4 Condition (7) holds; equilibrium at $(\underline{P}, 0)$

informed. The idea is this: Fix some pooling equilibrium whose "stability" is to be checked. Suppose that the high-quality firm would strictly prefer to spurn its equilibrium choice and choose some point (P, A) that is not currently being chosen if by so doing it would be thought high-quality. Suppose, too, that a low-quality firm would rather adhere to the equilibrium price and advertising levels and be thought to be high-quality with the given equilibrium probability than play (P, A), no matter what inferences the customers might draw from the observation of (P, A). Then, according to the Kreps criterion, if (P, A) were played, the customers should infer that it is a move by a high-quality firm. The reasoning is that a low-quality firm could never benefit from such a move and thus would not even experiment with it, but a high-quality firm just might. However, if customers formed their beliefs this way, then an H could profitably separate itself, and the pooling equilibrium would not survive.

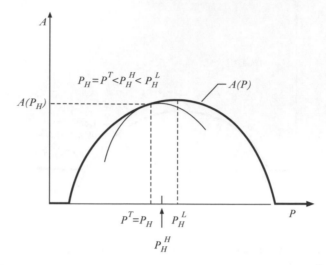

Figure 5 Equilibrium with positive advertising and lowered price $(P_H < P_H^H)$

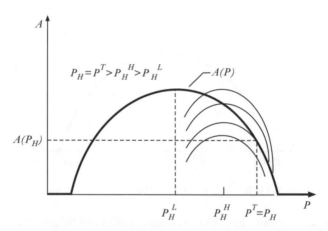

Figure 6 Equilibrium with positive advertising and raised price $(P_H > P_H^H)$

Kreps has applied this criterion to a game-theoretic version of Spence's (1973) labor market signaling model. He found that the criterion rules out all pooling equilibria. This finding relies only on the now-familiar single-crossing property of indifference curves that holds in Spence's model. This property reflects the hypothesis that the cost of signaling by acquiring education is inversely related to a worker's ability. The corresponding condition in our model would be that an H always be more willing to signal than an L in return for a given change in its perceived quality. What signaling means in our multidimensional, nonmonotonic context is, however, complicated. Intuitively, the appropriate condition is that there exist some feasible direction in price–advertising space such that it takes a smaller increase in perceived quality to compensate a high–quality firm than a low–quality firm for a move in that direction. To express this as a condition on marginal rates of substitution, we assume that $\Pi(P, q, \rho)$ is continuously differentiable with $\partial\Pi/\partial\rho > 0$. Then the appropriate condition is: For any P and ρ, one or more of the following three inequalities holds:

$$\left(\frac{\partial\pi^H}{\partial P}\right)\left(\frac{\partial\pi^H}{\partial P} - \frac{\partial\pi^L}{\partial P}\right) > 0 \tag{8a}$$

or

$$\frac{\partial\pi^H}{\partial\rho} - \frac{\partial\pi^L}{\partial\rho} > 0 \tag{8b}$$

or

$$\left(\frac{\partial\pi^L}{\partial P}\right)\left(\frac{\partial\pi^L/\partial P}{\partial\pi^L/\partial\rho} - \frac{\partial\pi^H/\partial P}{\partial\pi^H/\partial\rho}\right) > 0 \tag{8c}$$

where all derivatives are evaluated at (P, ρ), and $\pi^q(P, \rho) \equiv \Pi(P, q, \rho)$.

These inequalities state that at any point (P, A, ρ) it is possible to find a direction of change that involves increasing ρ and not decreasing A and that makes the H better off and the L worse off. Inequality (8b) states that there is some small increase in ρ and A alone that does this, while (8c) requires that there exist some increase in ρ and small change in P (which will be costly for an L) that has the desired effect. The first factor in (8c) is positive when it is costly for an L to increase its price and negative when it is costly for an L to reduce it. Finally, inequality (8a) requires that there be some small change in P (which will be profitable for an H) and increase in A that makes an H strictly better off and an L strictly worse off. Certainly, an H would be delighted to make such a change to enhance its perceived quality very slightly, while an L would not.

Two important implications follow from condition (8).

PROPOSITION 4. Assume that (8) holds. Then a separating equilibrium exists and satisfies the Kreps criterion. Moreover, no pooling equilibrium satisfies the Kreps criterion.

PROOF. It is immediate from the definitions that any separating equilibrium satisfies the Kreps condition. Thus, for the first part of the proposition, it suffices to prove that such an equilibrium exists. One does this by showing that there exists a path $\{(P(t), A(t), \rho(t)); 0 \le t < 1\}$ beginning at $(P_L^H, 0, 0)$ and ending with $\rho(1) = 1$, where the profits of an H increase along the path and the profits of an L do not. Then, since $\pi(P_L^H, L, L) \le \pi(P_L^L, L, L)$, the point $(P(1), A(1))$ satisfies inequality (1), and proposition 2 applies. (Note that, for this argument, the inequalities in [8] can be weak.)

A similar construction is used to prove that there cannot be a pooling equilibrium satisfying the Kreps condition. Suppose there were an equilibrium at which both an H and an L play some (P', A') and are thought high-quality with probability ρ'. If there is a path starting at (P', A', ρ') and ending at some point $(P, A, 1)$ along which the profits of an H increase and those of an L decrease (weakly), then (P, A) overturns the equilibrium according to the Kreps condition. Thus we can prove both parts of the proposition simultaneously by proving that there is such a path starting from any (P', A', ρ').

Fix (P', A', ρ') and let $\bar{\rho}$ be the supremum of $\rho(1)$ over all paths $\{(P(t), A(t), \rho(t))\}$. Suppose $\bar{\rho}$ is actually attained by a path ending at the point $(P, A, \bar{\rho})$ and that $\bar{\rho} < 1$. Then, whichever of (8a)–(8c) holds, there exists a direction $\Delta = (\Delta_P, \Delta_A, \Delta_\rho)$ such that $\Delta_p > 0, \Delta_A \geq 0$, and $\Pi(P + \epsilon\Delta_P, q, \bar{\rho} + \epsilon\Delta_\rho) - (A + \epsilon\Delta_A)$ is increasing in ϵ when $q = H$ and decreasing when $q = L$. Then the path attaining $\bar{\rho}$ can be extended, contradicting the hypothesis that $\bar{\rho}$ is the supremum over all paths. We omit the purely technical argument that the supremum $\bar{\rho}$ is actually attained by some path.   QED

Thus, under conditions (4), (5), (6), and (8), we have a unique equilibrium satisfying the Kreps criterion. In it, advertising signals quality, even though this advertising carries no direct information and, in effect, corresponds to a public burning of money. It is used, however, because signaling is worthwhile for the high-quality firm and doing so with both price and advertising is cheaper than with price changes alone. Indeed, suppose that advertising of this sort were banned. Then the firm might well continue to signal but to do so through price alone. In this case, price might rise to $\bar{P}$, which represents a Pareto-worsening: profits fall for an H and are unchanged for an L, while customers end up with the same information as before but pay higher prices.

Because the conditions we have stated here are on an endogenous construct, the Π function, it is not immediately obvious to what extent they can be met in a fully specified model in which repeat sales are explicit. We present such a model in the next section. In it, (4)–(6) hold, but the strict inequality in (8) holds only almost everywhere. We also obtain some comparative statics results that suggest how a firm introducing a new, high-quality product would select its price and advertising levels as its costs varied.

2. Analysis of an Explicit Example

We consider the following specialization of the setup described in the previous section. Quality is operationalized as the probability that a randomly selected customer will find the product satisfactory. Potential customers know only that the product is of one of two possible quality levels, L or H, $1 \geq H > L > 0$, and each initially assigns strictly positive prior probability to each possibility.

The set of potential customers corresponds to an interval $[0, R]$ with a uniform distribution[13] and total mass R. We also assume that the probability of the good's being satisfactory to consumer r is independent of r and that customers have no use for more than one unit of the good per period. A customer with valuation r who buys in a particular period at price P receives utility in that period of $r - P$ if the good turns out to be satisfactory and of $-P$ if it does not. A customer who does not buy receives zero. For simplicity, we assume that customers who do not purchase in the first round can never purchase the good. We also assume that an individual can learn whether the good is satisfactory for him or her from only a single purchase. Both of these assumptions can be relaxed.

The costs of production for a firm producing x units of quality q are $C_q x$.[14] Although one might expect that $C_H > C_L$, we do not assume this (see below). Thus, if the firm sets price P and advertising level A in some period and produces and sells x units of quality q, its profit in that period is $(P - C_q)x - A$.

Both the firm and customers maximize the expected present value of their payoffs up to a common (finite or infinite) horizon, T, using a common discount factor $\delta \in (0, 1)$. Let $\Delta = \sum_1^T \delta^t$.

To analyze the game that results from this setup, we assume that each decision maker acts in a sequentially rational fashion, following a strategy from each point forward that maximizes his or her expected payoff given his or her current information and beliefs and the conjectured behavior of the others. We further require that these beliefs be formed in a manner consistent (whenever possible) with the initial beliefs and the hypothesis that the observed history of play has been generated by the specified strategies, and that the conjectured behavior be consistent with the actual choices. Thus we are employing a refinement of the Nash equilibrium concept in the spirit of the game-theoretic criteria of perfectness (Selten 1975) or sequentiality (Kreps and Wilson 1982). Moreover, we require that the equilibrium be unaffected by sequentially eliminating dominated strategies from the normal form of the game. (We will impose our final restriction, the Kreps criterion, later.)

With a continuum of customers, as long as individual purchases are not observable, it is clearly a dominant strategy for each to act as a price taker in any period. Given this, it can easily be shown that, once we eliminate dominated strategies, the equilibrium demand facing the firm with true quality q at a price p in any postentry period is $q(R - p)$ if p exceeds the valuation r^* of the marginal customer in the first period and $q(R - r^*)$ otherwise, because only a fraction q of the initial $R - r^*$ purchasers will be satisfied with the good and willing to consider repeat purchases. Thus post-introductory advertising has no value and will not be used. Moreover, post-introductory prices will always weakly exceed r^* in any equilibrium, and so the marginal customer in the initial period will obtain no surplus on repeat sales. Consequently, he or she will make an initial purchase at price P only if it is expected to be worthwhile on its own. If ρ is the probability assigned to the true quality being H, the marginal customer is then defined by $\rho H r^* + (1 - \rho)L r^* = P$. Defining the expected quality $Q(\rho) = \rho H + (1 - \rho)L$, we then have $r^* = P/Q(\rho)$. The individual uncertainty about whether the good will prove satisfactory lowers the willingness to pay below the valuation placed on a unit known to be satisfactory. Thus first-period demand at price P with advertising A is $R - [P/Q(\rho)]$, where $\rho = \rho(P, A)$. These relationships are shown in figure 7.

Given these demand relations, the firm that initially charged P and had perceived quality $Q(\rho)$ will charge a constant price in all post-entry periods of $p = \max[P/Q(\rho), m(q)]$, where $m(q) = (R + C_q)/2$ would be the simple monopoly price if the good were sure to be satisfactory. Note that the introductory price P is lower than p as long as $Q(\rho) \neq 1$; that is, introductory discounts are used as long as the good is not perceived as surely satisfactory.

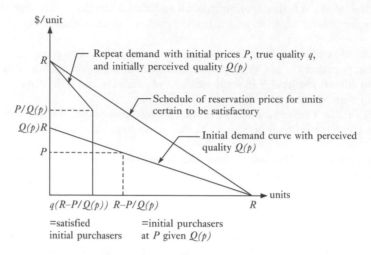

Figure 7   Demand relationships in the example

The profits $\Pi(P, q, \rho)$ of a firm of type q charging an introductory price P and regarded as being a high-quality producer with probability ρ thus are

$$\left[R - \frac{P}{Q(\rho)}\right](P - C_q) + \Delta q\left\{R - \max\left[\frac{P}{Q(\rho)}, m(q)\right]\right\}\left\{\max\left[\frac{P}{Q(\rho)}, m(q)\right] - C_q\right\}$$

When $\rho = 0$ (respectively 1) $Q(\rho)$ is L (respectively H), and, defining $\pi(P, q, H) = \Pi(P, q, 1)$ and $\pi(P, q, L) = \Pi(P, q, 0)$, we have an exact correspondence with the notation in the previous section.

Using these profit functions, one can routinely check the various conditions assumed in the previous section. First, although (8) does not hold as stated, a variant in which the inequalities are weak is satisfied. As examination of the argument given in support of proposition 4 reveals, this is sufficient to establish the existence of a separating equilibrium in the example.

To examine this equilibrium we must check the other conditions. One easily sees that condition (6) holds if $C_H \geq C_L$. In fact, $\pi(P, H, H) - \pi(P, L, H)$ is strictly concave for $C_H > C_L$, while for $C_H = C_L$ this function is constant for $P < Hm(H)$ and then decreases. When $C_L > C_H$, either (4) fails because $P_H^H < \underline{P}$ or (7) holds because $\partial\pi(P, H, H)/\partial P < \partial\pi(P, L, H)/\partial P$ for all $P \geq \underline{P}$. Moreover, in this latter case we have $\pi(\underline{P}, H, H) > \pi(\bar{P}, H, H)$. For $C_L < C_H < C_L[(H + \Delta H)/(1 + \Delta H)] \times [(1 + \Delta L)/(H + \Delta L)]$ we have $\underline{P} < P^T < P_H^H$, where

$$P^T(\rho) = Q(\rho)\left[\frac{R}{2} + \frac{(1 + \Delta H)C_H - (1 + \Delta L)C_L}{2\Delta(H - L)}\right]$$

is the price at which $\Delta\Pi(P, H, \rho)/\partial P = \partial\Pi(P, L, \rho)/\partial P$ and where $P^T = P^T(1)$.[15] For higher values of C_H, P^T exceeds P_H^H. However, as long as C_H does not exceed C_L by too great an amount, (5) holds and so $P^T < \bar{P}$. Finally, (4) holds for values of C_H lying in an open interval containing C_L.

From this, we see that except when $C_H = C_L$ there is a unique separating equilibrium. For $C_H < C_L$, the equilibrium involves a price $P_H \leq \underline{P}$ and no advertising. Here $P_H = P_H^H < \underline{P}$ if (4) fails, and $P_H = \underline{P} \leq P_H^H$ if (4) holds. At $C_H = C_L$, there is an interval $[\underline{P}, Hm(H)]$ of prices P_H and corresponding advertising levles $A(P_H)$ that constitute equilibrium choices for the H. Note that $A(P_H)$ is positive over this interval except at $P_H = \underline{P}$. For $C_H - C_L$ positive but not too large, the unique solution is at $P_H = P^T$ with $A(P^T) > 0$. In this range, the equilibrium level of advertising first increases, then decreases with the cost and the price. Finally, once C_H is sufficiently large that (5) fails, the solution again involves $A = 0$, but with $P_H \geq \bar{P}$. If (5) fails but (4) still holds, the solution is $P_H = \bar{P}$; if (4) fails as well, the solution is $P_H = P_H^H > \bar{P}$. These relationships are shown in figure 8.

The intuition behind these results is simple. Assume that some signaling activity is necessary, that is, $P_H^H \in (\underline{P}, \bar{P})$. With $C_H < C_L$, the H unambiguously finds price reductions cheaper than does the L: not only is producing to meet the higher initial quantity demanded less expensive for the H, but also a greater fraction of the initial customer base

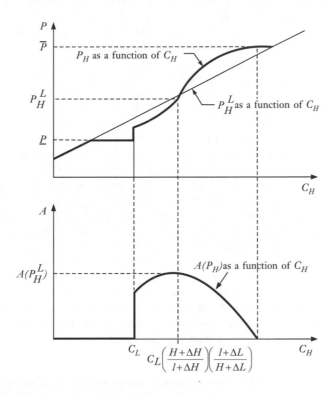

Figure 8   Equilibrium values of A and P_H as C_H varies

will make repeat purchases that are more profitable for the H as well. Thus the producer of a new, high-quality good that represents a technological breakthrough yielding very low relative costs of production will introduce its product at very low prices, perhaps giving free samples, but will not use advertising as a signal of its quality. When C_H exceeds C_L, the relative effects of price changes on the two types of firm (given that each is perceived as an H) is more complicated. Increasing price and reducing quantity is less costly in terms of profits in the introductory period for the H since it receives a smaller markup at any price. However, the effect on the profits from repeat sales of raising the introductory price might be larger or smaller for the H than for the L. For $P > Hm(H)$, the effect is negative for both, but which is the more negative depends on the relative size of two effects. Raising price costs the H less "per customer" lost, since it receives a lower markup, but the H's larger fraction of repeat purchasing means it loses customers at a greater rate than does the L when P is increased. Unless $P_H^H = P_H^L = P^T$, the overall effects will differ between the two firms at P_H^H, and the H will find a price change to be a cost-effective way to signal. Whether advertising is also used then depends on whether the costs of price increases are equalized for the two types before P is reached. If they are, advertising results; if not, only price signaling occurs.

While there is generically a unique separating equilibrium in this model (i.e., except when $C_H = C_L$), there will also be a very large set of pooling equilibria. For example, if $\bar{\rho}$ is the common prior assigned to H, then any point (P^*, A^*) with $\Pi(P^*, H, \bar{\rho}) - A^* \geq \max \pi(P, H, H) - A(P)$ and $\Pi(P^*, L, \bar{\rho}) - A^* \geq \pi(P_L^L, L, L)$ can give a pooling equilibrium. These points alone can constitute an open set.

The issue then is whether any of these pooling equilibria survive application of the Kreps criterion. In fact, as the failure of (8) to hold everywhere might suggest, some do. In particular, if there exists a separating equilibrium in which the H has a positive level of advertising, then there also exist pooling equilibria. These are of two forms. First, there may be a family of pure strategy equilibria in which both types choose the same price and advertising level with probability one. The members of this family all involve a common price $P^T(\bar{\rho})$, where $\bar{\rho}$ is the common prior assigned to the firm being an H. The equilibria in this class are indexed by the level of advertising, which must not exceed $A(\bar{\rho}) = \Pi(P^T(\bar{\rho}), H, \bar{\rho}) - [\Pi(P^T, H, 1) - A(P^T)] = \Pi(P^T(\bar{\rho}), L, \bar{\rho}) - \Pi(P_L^L, L, 0)$. These equilibria always include one in which no advertising is used. Their existence depends on $\bar{\rho}$'s being sufficiently high that $A(\bar{\rho}) \geq 0$, that is, on its being sufficiently likely a priori that the firm is high-quality. There will also be a second family of pooling equilibria involving mixed strategies. In these, each type randomizes between its separating equilibrium choice, $(P_L^L, 0)$ or $(P^T, A(P^T))$, and points of the form $(P^T(\rho), A(\rho))$, where $P^T(\cdot)$ and $A(\cdot)$ are as above and ρ is the posterior probability that the firm is an H given that the commonly chosen point is observed. These two classes of pooling equilibria survive application of the Kreps criterion because prices of the form $P^T(\rho), \rho \in [0, 1]$, are precisely and uniquely those at which (8) fails, so that one cannot find a move in (P, A, ρ) space that benefits the H and not the L. Since (8) holds except at prices $P^T(\rho)$, all other pooling equilibria are eliminated.

3. Conclusion

We have constructed a model to formalize Nelson's insight that apparently uniformative advertising for an experience good could be a signal for product quality. In doing so, we have also treated the pricing decision of the firm and allowed for the possibility that price itself might be a signal. Our analysis has confirmed and extended Nelson's fundamental point: advertising may signal quality, but price signalling will also typically occur, and the extent to which each is used depends in a rather complicated way, inter alia, on the difference in costs across qualities.

Interestingly, while our analysis confirms Nelson's fundamental point concerning the role of advertising, its inclusion of the pricing decision upsets the intuition that a high-quality producer will have a higher marginal benefit from attracting an initial sale and that this would provide the basis for the high-quality firm's being willing to advertise more. As noted earlier, all the requisite signaling takes place through the price unless choice of the price P^T does not, by itself, achieve the necessary differentiation. Only in this case is advertising used as a signal. But the present value to a firm perceived to be high-quality of an additional sale achieved through pricing is $(L - H)\partial\pi(P, q, H)/\partial P$, and at P^T this is independent of the firm's actual quality!

The essential difficulty is that the notion of the "marginal benefit to attracting another initial sale" is not well defined: in particular, it depends on who the marginal customer is, that is, on the price being charged and on the beliefs that customers hold. Moreover, once one allows that price might be a choice variable, then ambiguity remains even after the price and beliefs are specified because there are several ways one might generate the sale. If one imagines somehow obtaining an extra sale without changing perceived quality or price, then, at price P^T and perceived quality H, the marginal profit for a firm of type q from an extra sale in the example is $\{P^T[(1 + \Delta q)/H] - C_q(1 + \Delta q)\}$, and this expression is greater for $q = H$ than for $q = L$. If the additional sales are generated through extra advertising, however, then the marginal benefit is greater for the low quality producer as long as price does not exceed $P^T(\rho)$ and, in particular, if $P \leq P^T = P^T(1)$. If price is the means used to increase sales, then the net marginal benefits from an additional sale are a negative constant, $(L - H)$, times $\partial\pi/\partial P$. If $C_H > C_L$, then, in separating equilibrium with signaling, this marginal benefit is always at least as large for the low-quality producer because the solution always involves $P^H \leq P^T$.

Notes

1   Kihlstrom and Riordan (1984) present an interesting model of advertising as a signal. In their model, however, firms do not choose prices. Instead, a firm's advertising alone determines whether customers believe it to be high- or low-quality, and once this assignment to one or the other submarket is made, prices are determined via a standard supply and demand model. In equilibrium, prices in fact end up being correlated with quality but are not used to infer quality. Schmalensee (1978) offers a model in which consumers follow a rule of thumb. In it, low-quality producers may do the advertising because markups are negatively correlated with quality and customers do not recognize the negative advertising–quality relationship. Johnsen (1976) directly attempts to formalize Nelson's argument but does not obtain existence of equilibrium

when both prices and ad budgets are choice variables. (We are grateful to Ed Prescott for this reference.)

2   Klein and Leffler (1981) offer an alternative, complementary explanation for introductory advertising. In their formulation, unlike ours, quality is a choice variable, and the problem is to motivate firms not to cheat by cutting quality. The incentive to maintain quality comes through positive markups and repeat sales, which are lost once cheating is discovered. However, these profits must be reconciled with free entry. This is achieved by requiring new firms to sink resources on ads in an amount equal to expected operating profits before they can attract any business (see also Shapiro 1983).

3   Among the relevant references are papers in which the arguments rely on economic intuition related to the specific context of signaling (e.g., Riley 1975; Milgrom and Roberts 1982; Engers and Schwartz 1984), others involving systematic, game-theoretic approaches of more general applicability (e.g., Selten 1975; Kreps and Wilson 1982; Kohlberg and Mertens 1984; Banks and Sobel 1985; Cho 1985; Cho and Kreps 1985), and a few in which both lines are pursued (e.g., Kreps 1984).

4   A strategy is dominated if there is another strategy that yields the player at least as high payoffs against every specification of strategies for the other players and strictly more against some strategies. Note that eliminating the dominated strategies for one player may result in previously undominated strategies for another now being dominated.

5   The essence of this criterion is that at equilibrium there ought not to exist actions that are not being taken but that, if believed to signal high quality, would be advantageous for the high-quality firm to take but not for the low-quality firm. Such acts should be interpreted as, in fact, signaling high quality, and their existence would then upset the equilibrium.

6   Kreps (1984) uses the same methods as we do to obtain uniqueness in a Spence-type univariate model of job market signaling. The relationship between the economic and game-theoretic arguments for eliminating various outcomes is made very clear in this highly recommended paper.

7   This condition involves certain strict inequalities on derivatives of the profit functions. In section 2 we develop an example in which these conditions hold only almost everywhere. As a result, in the example there is generically a unique separating equilibrium, but there may also be equilibria with pooling on the small set of points at which the conditions fail.

8   See Johnsen (1976), Grossman (1981), Hughes (1983), Kohlleppel (1983a, 1983b), Quinzii and Rochet (1984), Holmström and Weiss (1985), and Wilson (1985) for other models explicitly using multiple signals. The Wilson paper is of particular interest here since it extends our analysis to a continuum of qualities and any finite number of signaling variables.

9   The assumption of monopoly seems natural in this context, at least in comparison with the perfectly competitive alternative. Treating the intermediate case of oligopoly would involve significant additional problems.

10   For the firm, this information includes its actual quality, so a strategy for the firm may specify different actions depending on what its actual quality is. Given this, it will be convenient to use terminology that might suggest that both high- and low-quality producers actually exist, even though there is only one firm and its actual quality is either definitely H or definitely L.

11   The discussion here will involve only simple elimination of dominated strategies for the firm because we are working with a reduced-form profit function. In general, the appropriate notion is sequential elimination of dominated strategies in the full game.

12   Note that (s) and (6) together actually imply (4).

13   The uniform distribution gives rise to a linear demand, which, in turn, facilitates computation. However, our basic results hold as long as the distribution of reservation prices gives rise to a demand curve showing decreasing marginal revenue.

14   We ignore any fixed costs because their inclusion would have no effect on the solution.

15 Note that $\partial\Pi(P,H,\rho)/\partial P \gtreqqless \partial\Pi(P,L,\rho)/\partial P$ and $\partial\Pi(P,H,\rho)/\partial\rho \gtreqqless \partial\Pi(P,\pi,\rho)/\partial\rho$ as $P \gtreqqless P^T(\rho)$.

References

Banks, Jeffrey and Sobel, Joel (1985): "Equilibrium Selection in Signalling Games," discussion paper no. 85–9. La Jolla: Univ. California, San Diego, Dept. Economics.

Cho, In-Koo (1985): "A Refinement of the Sequential Equilibrium Concept," mimeo. Stanford, Calif.: Stanford Univ., Grad. School Bus.

Cho, In-Koo and Kreps, David M. (1985): "More on Signalling Games and Stable Equilibria," mimeo. Stanford, Calif.: Stanford Univ., Grad. School Bus.

Engers, Maxim and Schwartz, Marius (1984): "Signalling Equilibrium Based on Sensible Beliefs: Limit Pricing under Incomplete Information," discussion paper no. 84–4. Washington: Dept. Justice, Antitrust Div., Econ. Policy Office.

Grossman, Sanford J. (1981): "The Informational Role of Warranties and Private Disclosure about Product Quality," *Journal of Law and Economics*, 24, December, 461–83.

Holmström, Bengt R. and Weiss, Laurence (1985): "Managerial Incentives, Investment, and Aggregate Implications: Scale Effects," *Review Economic Studies*, 52, July, 403–25.

Hughes, Patricia (1983): "Signaling by Direct Disclosure under Asymmetric Information," mimeo. Vancouver: Univ. British Columbia.

Johnsen, Thore (1976): "Advertising, Market Equilibrium and Information," Ph.D. dissertation, Carnegie-Mellon Univ.

Kihlstrom, Richard E. and Riordan, Michael H. (1984): "Advertising as a Signal," *Journal of Political Economy*, 92, June, 427–50.

Klein, Benjamin and Leffler, Keith B. (1981): "The Role of Market Forces in Assuring Contractual Performance," *Journal of Political Economy* 89, August, 615–41.

Kohlberg, Elon and Mertens, Jean-François (1984): "On the Strategic Stability of Equilibria," working paper no. 1-785-012. Boston: Harvard Univ., Grad. School Bus. Admin.

Kohlleppel, Laurenz (1983*a*): "Multidimensional Market Signalling," discussion paper no. 125. Bonn: Univ. Bonn, Inst. Gesellschafts-und Wirtschaftswissenschaften.

—— (1983*b*)): "Properties of Sorting Equilibria," discussion paper no. 133. Bonn: Univ. Bonn, Inst. Gesellschafts-und Wirtschaftswissenschaften.

Kreps, David M. (1984): "Signalling Games and Stable Equilibria," research paper no. 758. Stanford, Calif.: Stanford Univ., Grad. School Bus.

Kreps, David M. and Wilson, Robert (1982): "Sequential Equilibria," *Econometrica*, 50, July, 863–94.

Milgrom, Paul and Roberts, John (1982): "Limit Pricing and Entry under Incomplete Information: An Equilibrium Analysis," *Econometrica*, 50, March, 443–59.

Moulin, Hervé (1979): "Dominance Solvable Voting Schemes," *Econometrica*, 47, November, 1137–51.

Nelson, Phillip (1970): "Information and Consumer Behavior," *Journal of Political Economy*, 78, March/April, 311–29.

—— (1974): "Advertising as Information," *Journal of Political Economy*, 81, July/August, 729–54.

—— (1978): "Advertising as Information Once More," In *Issues in Advertising: The Economics of Persuasion*, edited by David G. Tuerck. Washington: American Enterprise Inst.

Pearce, David (1982): "Ex Ante Equilibrium: Strategic Behavior and the Problem of Perfection," research memo no. 301. Princeton, N.J.: Princeton Univ., Dept. Economics.

Quinzii, Martine and Rochet, Jean-Charles (1984): "Multidimensional Signaling," technical report no. 453. Stanford, Calif.: Stanford Univ., Inst. Math. Studies Soc. Science.

Riley, John G. (1975): "Competitive Signalling," *Journal of Economic Theory*, 10, April, 174–86.

Schmalensee, Richard (1978): "A Model of Advertising and Product Quality," *Journal of Political Economy*, 86, June, 485–503.

Selten, Reinhard (1975): "Reexamination of the Perfectness Concept for Equilibrium Points in Extensive Games," *International Journal Game Theory*, 4(1), 25–55.

Shapiro, Carl (1983): "Premiums for High Quality Products as Returns to Reputations," *Quarterly Journal of Economics*, 98, November, 659–79.

Spence, Michael (1973): "Job Market Signaling," *Quarterly Journal of Economics*, 87, August, 355–74.

Wilson, Robert (1985): "Multi-dimensional Signalling." *Economics Letters*, 19(1), 17–21.

Index